Nuclear Weapons and the Future of Humanity

The Fundamental Questions

Edited by
Avner Cohen
and
Steven Lee

ROWMAN & ALLANHELD
PUBLISHERS

ROWMAN & ALLANHELD

Published in the United States of America in 1986
by Rowman & Allanheld, Publishers
(a division of Littlefield, Adams & Company)
81 Adams Drive, Totowa, New Jersey 07512

Library of Congress Cataloging in Publication Data
Main entry under title:

Nuclear weapons and the future of humanity.

  (Philosophy and society series)
  Includes bibliographies and indexes.
  1. Nuclear weapons—Moral and ethical aspects—
Addresses, essays, lectures. 2. Nuclear warfare—
Moral and ethical aspects—Addresses, essays, lectures.
3. Antinuclear movement—Addresses, essays, lectures.
4. World politics—1975-1985—Addresses, essays,
lectures. I. Cohen, Avner, 1951-   II. Lee,
Steven. III. Series.
U264.N82   1986   172′.24   84-18362
ISBN 0-8476-7257-3
ISBN 0-8476-7258-1 (pbk.)

    86 87 / 10 9 8 7 6 5 4 3 2 1

Printed in the United States of America

CONTENTS

TABLES

PREFACE AND ACKNOWLEDGMENTS

Four horsemen herald apocalypse at the close of the 20th century: the population explosion, environmental deterioration, resource depletion and, above all, the prospect of catastrophic thermonuclear war. All these contemporary nightmares are man-made, by-products of a highly sophisticated civilization at its limits. The last horseman's visage is the most frightening of all: nuclear war poses the virtually unintelligible threat—the sudden end of civilized life.

To say that the threat of nuclear holocaust is our preeminent problem is not to deny the importance of the other apocalyptic threats, nor to ignore the significance of the acute social and economic injustices that plague humanity, nor to claim that the nuclear threat can be reduced or removed without seriously addressing some or all of these other problems. It is simply to affirm that in our time no threat is more ominous. In a sense, the very threat of nuclear war transcends politics and culture, for it would bring an end to both. What is at stake is sensed clearly in contemporary culture: witness the dramatic way in which the issue has come recently to dominate the public consciousness.

This collection of essays addresses the profound and complex issues—what we call the fundamental questions—raised by the nuclear predicament. Effective action to remove or reduce the nuclear threat requires an understanding of these issues. This book originated in our deep concern, as citizens and as teachers, about these issues. As citizens we realized that the public debate focuses almost exclusively on specific political proposals (e.g., the call for a nuclear freeze, or a pledge of no-first-use) or weapons systems (e.g., the debates over the MX or cruise missile), without considering in depth the basic *presuppositions* involved in our thinking about the nuclear predicament. As teachers and scholars we have noticed a dearth of scholarly treatment of the presuppositional issues. This volume is a discussion of these fundamental questions concerning our thinking about nuclear weapons, and concerning culture, rationality, human nature, morality, and political and social philosophy in the nuclear age. Further, we believe that the fundamental questions cannot adequately be addressed piecemeal, but must be considered together. To this end, we have sought to provide a group of essays that is comprehensive of the fundamental aspects of the nuclear predicament.

This presuppositional and comprehensive orientation, we believe, distinguishes this volume from many others that have been published in this area. In its basic structure and organization and in the depth of its discussions, this anthology is designed to carry the nuclear discussion beyond what is found in much of the popular writing in this area. At the same time, special efforts have been made to avoid the sense of "scientific" technicality and narrowness too often characteristic of academic works in the fields of international relations or strategic studies. These works are often by their very nature and disciplinary ideology restricted in scope (for example, by exclusion of value issues), and so largely preclude discussion of the fundamental questions. We seek to avoid both superficiality and narrowness—to provide a careful and systematic treatment of the fundamental questions concerning nuclear weapons.

Since fundamental questions are in some sense always philosophical questions, most of the essays in this volume are philosophical. Until recently, however, academic philosophers have had little to offer on these matters. (Notable exceptions are Bertrand Russell, Karl Jaspers, and Arne Naess—the latter a contributor to the volume—all of whom, a generation ago, wrote books on the nuclear threat and its impact on humanity.)* In the English-speaking world, philosophers for many years took a rather narrow view of their own discipline, not seeing it as their business to address questions of war and peace or to meddle with matters of public policy in general. But for a variety of reasons, some of them internal to philosophy as a discipline and others having much to do with the present rise of nuclear consciousness, this picture has changed dramatically. As the volume shows, many philosophers nowadays are deeply involved in addressing fundamental questions raised by nuclear weapons.

Yet it is our strong conviction that fundamental or presuppositional questions of this kind cannot be seriously addressed in separation from the concrete information on the issues or in isolation from a variety of theoretical perspectives. As a result, we planned this collection to have a strong interdisciplinary component, with contributors from fields such as political science, economics, history of ideas, medicine, physics, and biology.

We should keep in mind that the Cold War years of the mid-1960s witnessed a period of concern with nuclear weapons similar to our own. During that period of intellectual and public ferment over nuclear weapons, discussion of the fundamental questions was restricted primarily to non-philosophers. Many of the points being raised by those currently addressing these issues were raised twenty years ago. Indeed, some of the pieces written then sound surprisingly fresh and relevant to the present situation. The work of the 1960s should not be forgotten; rather, it should be built upon. We should recognize, however, that the situation of the 1980s is in some important ways different from that of the 1960s. The essays in this volume reflect today's concerns.

To provide a comprehensive account of the nuclear predicament and to develop the issues in a progressive fashion, the volume is divided into five parts. An introductory essay outlines the unifying theme of the fundamental questions—the transcendent nature of the nuclear threat and the resulting discontinuity between the reality of the nuclear predicament and our modes of thinking and acting upon it. Part I serves as the "factual basis" for the entire volume by providing basic information about nuclear weapons and nuclear strategies, including discussions of the history of the nuclear arms race, some potential causes of nuclear war, and the effects of a full-scale war. Part II discusses the historical and cultural aspects of living with the nuclear threat. The essays here ask us to reflect on the ways in which the pres-

---

*Bertrand Russell, *Common Sense and Nuclear Warfare* (London: Allen and Unwin, 1959); Karl Jaspers, *The Future of Mankind* (Chicago: University of Chicago Press, 1961); Arne Naess, *Gandhi and the Nuclear Age* (Totowa, N.J.: Bedminster, 1965).

ence of man-made apocalyptic potential transcends history, culture, and morality. Part III examines the odd, at times paradoxical, nature of nuclear thinking. A variety of issues are considered, including the nature of nuclear deterrence strategy, assessments of the risk of nuclear war, and the rationality of the use of nuclear weapons. The theme of Part IV is the extent to which nuclear weapons fail to fit our traditional understanding of the morality of military matters. Some of the specific issues are the influence of morality on political decisions about nuclear weapons, the morality of the use of nuclear weapons, the morality of nuclear deterrence, and the implications of these issues on our actions in confronting the nuclear threat. The final part considers the ways in which our traditional modes of political thinking may need to be altered given the existence of nuclear weapons. Among the fundamental changes these essays argue for are the substitution of a world government for the system of sovereign states, a growing international public consciousness of the nuclear threat, the adoption of a policy of unilateral disarmament, and a change in the relation between state and society through a revitalized democracy or a social revolution within nuclear states.

As the above discussion indicates, this book contains relatively little about the specific nuclear issues that dominate the media. A glance through the index will reveal only a few references to such topics as the MX missile, the deployment of medium-range missiles in Western Europe, or the proposal for a nuclear freeze. These are *not* the fundamental issues, though they are not unimportant. Indeed, the likelihood of there being a nuclear war in the near future is sure to be affected by how they are decided. The relation of this volume to these issues is that of theory to practice: one must understand the fundamental questions in order to be able to make effective decisions about the practical issues. It is a mistake to argue that time spent on the fundamental issues and away from direct political activity is time wasted. To evaluate adequately the correctness of practical measures, an understanding of the presuppositions is required.

The fundamental questions have, of course, been recognized since the dawn of the nuclear age. But they have not always been given the careful attention they deserve. There are, moreover, two reasons why further examination of the fundamental questions is especially important at this time. First, since the combined nuclear arsenals of the United States and the Soviet Union are now larger than they have ever been, both in terms of the number of strategic warheads and in the total equivalent megatonnage of those warheads,* it is more likely now than ever before that a general nuclear war would result in the destruction of civilization, and perhaps the extinction of our species. The potential of nuclear war to lead to these ends is the most important aspect of the fundamental questions nuclear weapons raise. Second, the growing emphasis on counterforce targeting and war-fighting capability in current U.S. nuclear weapons policy in effect denies the important differences between nuclear and nonnuclear weapons implicit in the destructive potential of nuclear war, and so may increase significantly the risk that the weapons will be used. The recognition of these differences is central to an understanding of the fundamental questions.

---

*Ground Zero, *Nuclear War—What's in It for You?* (New York: Pocket Books, 1982), Appendix C.

Any project of this scope accumulates many debts. To Hobart and William Smith Colleges, where most of this joint effort has taken place, we owe special, warm thanks: for providing leave to one of us to help in the completion of the project at its crucial moments, for supplying funds to cover the large mailing, telephone, and photocopying expenses, for generously providing secretarial time, and for the general encouragement we received. To the Ford Foundation, and especially to Dr. Enid Schoettle of its International Affairs Programs, we are grateful for providing two grants enabling us to meet twice to complete the editorial labors so difficult at an overseas distance.

Of course, we would like to thank all the authors of this volume for tolerating our active editorial policy, particularly our requests, sometimes made under severe time constraints, for revisions in their draft papers. We owe particular thanks to our friend and contributor Stephen Toulmin, who gave time and advice in the first stages of the project. We are grateful to our friend Mark Glouberman, who read all the earlier versions of our introductory essay and provided us with a great many comments and suggestions. Also, we appreciate heartily the advice, suggestions and encouragement from our friends Scott Brophy, Cherry Rahn, Miriam Shuchman, and Gretta. We cannot here mention individually all the others who were of help to us in this project, but we thank them nonetheless.

A different kind of thanks is due to Jonathan Schell, whose *The Fate of the Earth* helped to trigger a large public interest in many of the fundamental questions taken up in this book.

Of special value toward the end of the project have been Janet Johnston and Carol Rosenthal. It is a pleasure to thank Linda Alexander, Mary Watkins, Ann Rago, and Marie Schwartz for their efforts in transforming manuscript into typescript.

Finally we would like to thank our families and close friends—Cherry, Amanda, Charlotte, Lilah (Steven's), Adina, Tuvia, and Vered (Avner's)—who for over two years tolerated the eccentricities to which work on this project has driven us.

A.C. and S.L.
Geneva, NY
October 1985

Nuclear Weapons
and the
Future of Humanity

1
THE NUCLEAR PREDICAMENT

Avner Cohen
Steven Lee

The unleashed power of the atom has changed everything save our modes of thinking, and we thus drift toward unparalleled catastrophe.

Albert Einstein[1]

THE SINGULARITY OF THE NUCLEAR PREDICAMENT: NOTES ON DISCONTINUITY

The more we reflect on nuclear holocaust and the greater our efforts to understand its nature, the more we realize the enormous difficulties in imagining such an eventuality. We do not know what it would be like, how it should be conceived, to what it could be compared. Since a nuclear holocaust has no precedent in either scope or scale within the history of human civilization, it is a possibility that surpasses the limits of mundane human experience and human imagination. But it not only would be unprecedented in its destructiveness, it could be terminal. Given the present size of the nuclear arsenals, nuclear war has the potential to bring every thing human to an end. Nuclear holocaust could be the human event to end all human events.

We think of human events as taking place within the ever-continuing stream of human history. The awareness of a future to be filled, of the completion of present acts by future acts, is an essential characteristic of human consciousness. To say that a certain human eventuality would be unprecedented is to make an historical judgment and thus to assume an historical future. But the real potential of nuclear holocaust to destroy human civilization threatens an end to history itself. Thus, the very making of historical judgments about nuclear holocaust becomes paradoxical. With the absence of the human narrator and a cultural context, there would be no narrative. In this sense nuclear holocaust would be transcendent: it would take place at some point in historical time, yet it could put an end to history itself.

The difficulty of making judgments about a nuclear holocaust in human terms gives this eventuality some of the character of a Kantian *Ding-an-sich*. A nuclear holocaust may be likened to a singularity. In mathematics, a singularity is a point at which the value of a function becomes infinite or undefined. The physical and biological destructiveness of a nuclear holocaust, especially the prospects for a "nuclear winter,"[2] would cause total collapse of the human universe, of the physical, biological, cultural, and social environments that make human life possible. Human existence as we understand it would then become an "undefined value." The human universe of language, meaning, and significance would be lost. Any persons who physically survived the holocaust would encounter radical difficulties in understanding the postwar landscape. The entire human landscape, our primary point of reference for understanding, would be absent.

The singular nature of nuclear holocaust may be seen in both experiential and institutional terms. War as an experience can be grasped only against our ordinary universe of experience. The ordinary world of experience is a necessary background for making sense of other experiences; it constitutes the "given," the framework by which everything else can be described, evaluated, and judged. For example, a striking aspect of our ordinary experience of war is that no matter how intense, war is not omnipresent; it does not take place everywhere. Combat can always be separated from non-combat, the rear from the front, the hell of the battlefield from the world beyond. Phenomenologically, war presupposes a fairly intact world beyond the battlefield. This contrast would disappear in a nuclear holocaust; the hell would be all-encompassing.

War as an institution makes sense only in reference to the constellation of political and social institutions in which it occurs. Wars are always linked to *political* objectives and are initiated to promote certain national interests. Nations go to war to save, or preserve, or promote their forms of life, not to lose them. The success of war is measured largely in terms of the achievement of those objectives. It makes no sense to talk of victory if both sides lose the very political and social institutions in whose interests the conflict is initiated. But such a loss would probably be the outcome of a nuclear war, even a "limited" one.

The potential of nuclear holocaust to nullify everything human is obscured by our labeling such an event as "war." We use this familiar concept because it is the only one available, even while its use carries implications based on our historical experience of war, much of which would not apply in the case of a nuclear war. We think of war as limited in place and time, as a contest in which one side or the other can achieve its political objectives. But a nuclear war may have none of these qualities. The use of the concept *war* (as well as other traditional concepts pertaining to military matters) in relation to the nuclear predicament tends to obscure the latter's unique and singular nature.

There is a *discontinuity* or a *failure of fit* between the reality of the nuclear predicament and our modes of thinking about it. Discontinuity occurs whenever old modes of thinking no longer suit a new reality, but becomes problematic when the "gap" between the old modes of thinking and reality results in our taking inappropriate action. Because we act in the world based on how we conceive it, a discontinuity between the two can lead us to act in ineffective or unintentionally self-defeating ways. The action may fail to promote or may actually undercut the purpose it was supposed to achieve. In this respect, the discontinuity between the nuclear reality and our conceptualization of it is highly problematic.

The first task, then, is to reveal the unique and singular nature of the nuclear threat, and the resulting discontinuity between the reality of this threat and our conceptual resources for understanding it. We must critically examine the presuppositions of our thinking about the nuclear predicament and seek to understand the relations among the phenomena of war, morality, politics, and civilization in the nuclear age. This is the fundamental task; it should precede choice of a course of action.

We are in the nuclear predicament largely because nuclear weapons policy decisions have been based on a prenuclear understanding of political and military reality, which has blocked us from seeing clearly the uniqueness of nuclear weapons. We need to appreciate Einstein's insight that our modes of thinking must change. In this essay we seek to substantiate Einstein's call for conceptual and political revision by discussing how the nuclear reality is at variance with our traditional modes of thinking. In the next section we examine the discontinuity between our traditional political or prudential thinking about military matters and the nuclear reality. In the third section we consider the discontinuity between our traditional ways of thinking about the morality of military practice and the nuclear reality. Based on an understanding of these prudential and moral discontinuities, we offer in the last section some preliminary thoughts on the problem of our extrication from the nuclear predicament.

CIVILIZATION, WAR, POLITICS, AND THE NUCLEAR PREDICAMENT

War as an Institution of Organized Violence

War is a *distinct* species of violence. In contrast to other forms of violence (brutality, vendetta, riots, raiding, and the like), war is reconciled with the purposes of organized society. (The only other form of violence having this character is, of course, that used by police forces.) We think of war as the activity of armed violence performed *for* a political community *by* its military organization. Both these societal elements are indispensable to our notion of war, and distinguish it as a species of violence from others. Accordingly, we define war as large-scale armed conflict between *political* communities.

Obviously, war is by far the most highly organized, best planned and most systematic form of violence; or, as von Clausewitz put it, "War is an act of violence pushed to its utmost bounds."[3] Even the most primitive wars, such as organized armed conflicts between members of relatively small, stateless societies, require a considerable amount of planning and preparation, cooperation and coordination. This is even more true for modern wars.

The institutional nature of war is also evident in its normative dimension. Acts of war as such are neither deviant nor criminal; they are, above all, *socially approved* activities of mass violence. They carry the mark of the political authority. Indeed, societies view military service (particularly at times of war) as a citizen's highest civic duty. Since war is waged on behalf of a political community, violence on the battlefield receives its *legitimacy* from the community. Unlike other forms of violence, the institution of war has always been associated with rich, value-laden, culturally significant vocabularies of approval as well as condemnation. Throughout the ages, warring cultures have developed special spheres of moral discourse—normative codes of rights and wrongs—for times of war.[4] Many moral restrictions on the conduct of war have been canonized into international law and especially into the conventions governing the conduct of war.

An examination of the way the ordinary language of war functions reveals the same special character of war as a unique species of violence. We refer to and judge martial violence quite differently than we do other forms of violence. Most nonmartial forms of violence are viewed as illegitimate, i.e., as criminal, whereas most violence in war is viewed as legitimate. Indeed, the very fact that not all martial violence is regarded as legitimate and morally permissible demonstrates once more this institutional character of war. We draw a clear distinction between war crimes and other activities of war.

War and Civilization

In essence, the phenomenon of war is indigenous to civilization. Further, war is a socially approved institution of organized violence whose evolution has gone hand in hand with that of civilization. Warfare as a human practice became more sophisticated as civilization advanced, particularly as the institutions of politics became more centralized. In this way, the phenomenon of war is parasitic on civilization. To put it differently, war is fundamentally a creation, a by-product, of civilization; it is possible only within conflict situations peculiar to civilized societies. To clarify further this claim about the intrinsic links between war and civilization and its implications for the question of nuclear war, it is worth looking at the genesis of war as a distinct socio-cultural institution.

In human social evolution, warfare is a quite recent, distinct form of organized violence whose origin can be traced to the rise of civilization, particularly to the "invention" of politics itself. According to Susan Mansfield, for at least 200,000 years human hunters possessed the technical capacity to create shock weapons such as axes and clubs, and for about 25,000 years had as well the capacity to kill other humans with relative ease and safety (by bow and arrow or spear); yet it appears that "the species did not deliberately make weapons in order to wage war during these long, early years of human evolution."[5] Furthermore, while artifacts from those early times tell us a great deal about daily human practices, they give no indication that humans were engaged in battles against other humans. In fact, no weapons specifically designed to be used against other humans have been found that can be dated before the emergence of Neolithic man—the founder of agriculture—in approximately 10,000 B.C. This, of course, is not to deny that early humans sporadically fought and killed other humans with hunting tools; early *homo* was aggressive and often highly violent. Yet it appears that the species was not in general occupied with warfare during these early periods of human evolution; war as a *social institution*, a species of organized violence, was not yet a part of the human behavioral repertoire.[6]

When did the institution of war emerge, and in what circumstances did it evolve? Its prototypes appeared during the crucial stages of the so-called transition to civilization. As far as archeological and anthropological evidence can tell us—and one must remember that all claims here are speculative and highly interpretative, the evidence being circumstantial and indirect—the first signs associated with war can be found in the later Neolithic period. The first identifiable weapons are found in communal sites used by societies with a mixed economy of hunting and agriculture. The first clearly fortified settlements, perhaps the most distinctive signs of warlike activity, appeared sometime after the rise of the first agricultural settlements, still long before the occurrence of social changes associated with the urban revolution.

In some respects Neolithic man is genuinely entitled to be called the "inventor" of warfare. His combats were definitely rule-governed group activities; they exhibited basic patterns of warfare skills; they involved genuine weapons; and they were awarded a great deal of time and resources.[7] Nevertheless, for the purpose of analysis, these elements are not sufficient to constitute "primitive" warfare as warfare in the full contemporary sense.[8] The absence of a professional and centralized military organization, of a unified hierarchical command, enforced discipline, and sustained logistical support, distinguishes "primitive" from "civilized" warfare.[9] Thus Harry Turney-High, in his classic study of primitive warfare, asserts that non-literate man is essentially a warrior, not yet a soldier: he engages in battles but does not wage war.[10] The Neolithic warrior, Turney-High concludes (p. 23), has not yet reached the "military horizon" of "adequate teamwork, organization and command working." But the difference here is more than a merely military issue; it is clearly related to the political-social differences between Neolithic and civilized societies.

In essence, what distinguishes primitive warfare from civilized warfare is the absence of highly developed political-coercive institutions. Primitive combats appear politically insignificant; they cannot be considered armed conflicts among *political* communities. They involve no strategic objectives (in our sense) beyond winning the fighting itself, that is to say, beyond inflicting the greatest possible damage and pain (usually death) on the opponent. The warfare itself is accompanied by ritualistic practices in which much attention was given to the rites of death.[11] Actually, for all that we know of Neolithic warfare, no interest was shown in taking over the opponent's territory.

There is a striking correlation between the military efficiency of a community and the level of its political centralization. In primitive societies, like Neolithic ones, which have very loose formal political structures, the warrior obviously has little in the way of a coercive system to impose upon the vanquished. In the absence of politics as an institution, primitive warfare does not function as a coercive instrument of political imposition.[12] Although the institution of warfare existed, there was no war answering von Clausewitz's definition: "simply the continuation of policy with the admixture of other means."[13] Thus, *a fortiori,* primitive war cannot function as an instrument of imposing the conditions of peace, as Clausewitz frequently requires of a genuine war. The fact is that tribal warriors fight for objectives quite different from those that activate civilized states; and whatever their objectives may be, they are not political in our sense.[14] As often noted, the most common cause of primitive engagements is *revenge,* the objective being simply to inflict death on the other group in order to avenge a previous death.[15]

We are now ready to reconsider our earlier claim about the strong conceptual and historical links between war, politics and civilization. War, along with politics, is a relatively new human "invention" made possible by the transition to civilization. The marriage between politics and war, as Kenneth Boulding points out, is not accidental; it is a matter of necessary historical development. Both are by-products of the emergence of the new form of human organization, *civilization,* and particularly the rise of the city-state as a social entity.[16] In this respect, the urban revolution (very much like its predecessor, the agricultural revolution) should be viewed as one of the unique thresholds in human history where a single, distinguishable development has great and lasting consequences for human consciousness and practice in general, well beyond its immediate impact—the institutions of war and politics.[17]

With the rise of the city-state and the first realization of the idea of a sovereign political community, around 4,000–3,000 B.C. in Mesopotamia and Egypt, we find the first evidence for the institution of war. It appeared as an essential feature of intercity politics.[18] In Mesopotamia, the cradle of civilization, cities were walled almost from their very beginning. As formal political authority depends on coercive means, we date the emergence of the regular army as a new social organization to this period.[19] It is perhaps the very appearance of the regular army as the political instrument designed to protect the sovereignty of a political community that constitutes the substantial difference between primitive warfare and "civilized" warfare.

Sovereign States, Deterrence, and War

Beyond the particular details of the urban revolution as an historical occurrence, certain fundamental relationships exist between politics, coercion, deterrence, and war. To begin with, there is the essential link between politics and power; politics is *about* power. Since no formal political authority can be maintained without coercive means—coercion being the primary manifestation of power—the very idea of the sovereign state is necessarily linked to both internal and external coercive systems. A coercive institution of law enforcement for securing domestic order and a coercive military institution for securing the community from external threats are two sides of the same coin. Both are essential aspects of the political regime founded on sovereign states; both are intrinsic elements of the pursuit of power. And most significant, each of these coercive systems is built upon *threats*.

Ever since the appearance of sovereign states, international politics has centered on the question of the distribution of power. The Hobbesian picture of the "state of nature" is often taken to reflect the distinctive power-oriented and lawless features of international politics. Sovereign states pursue their national interests in the most selfish manner. And yet, despite the absence of ultimate law-giving and law-enforcing authorities standing above sovereign states, the international arena is not in a state of constant instability—a war of all against all. In fact, if the international order is likened to a state of nature, it is not of the Hobbesian sort. On the contrary, it is the very Hobbesian intuition that what prevails in the international realm is not law or morality, but power alone, and particularly the *threat* to use force, that explains the relative stability of most world-orders. The maintenance of political order through threats is precisely what the notion of world-order presupposes. In principle, the possibility of war is ever-present in the international system, but in actuality we find more periods of stability and order than periods of disruption. In politics, a *credible* threat of war normally replaces the actual fighting.

Deterrence is one of the most fundamental species of threat system. As a general mechanism to control social behavior, its roots can be traced to basic, biologically programmed postures of animal behavior.[20] In essence, deterrence is a way of convincing an adversary *not* to act in a certain way by threatening the infliction of harm should the adversary so act. Considered in its purity, deterrence is a threat distinguished by its negative form. While an ultimatum, for example, is a threat designed to coerce an adversary to act in a certain way, or undo something already done, deterrence is the use of threats to prevent an act from being committed in the first place. Within the human realm, we find traces of deterrence postures in a variety of social interactions, from the practice of religious beliefs and child rearing to the working of law enforcement and international politics.

In the sphere of international politics, deterrence keeps political conflicts contained within the boundaries of threats.[21] If the threats are successful, they are neither executed nor tested, they simply deter. As such, deterrence is a *constitutive* element in any political arrangement of world-order among sovereign states (e.g., *pax romana,* balance of power). It defines the power boundaries among the participants in a given world-order, and determines the harm a state risks in defying those boundaries. Viewed in this way, deterrence is more than just an isolated threat of retaliation; it is a *system* composed of threats, commitments, strategic postures, and the like that constitutes the entire defense policy of a nation. Viewed from the level of the entire international system, deterrence is the ever-present regulatory mechanism of order and stability among sovereign states. The *holistic* nature of deterrence invests political threats and commitments with significance above and beyond the immediate situation in which they arise.[22] What is at stake is often the entire posture of national security, for a response to one threat may affect the way in which other threats are perceived. In this broad sense, deterrence is the by-product of the ever-prevailing condition of the regime of sovereign states, a condition expressed in the old adage that peace can be achieved only through preparing for war (*si vis pacem, para bellum*).[23] In the Hobbesian context of insecurity, hostility, and mutual suspicion that typifies relationships among antagonistic and competitive powers, deterrence is the most prudent response to the ever-present threat of aggression. Deterrence is, therefore, essential for world politics.[24]

Of course, the actual use of force can also help deter an adversary's future aggression. This makes clearer our earlier point about the difference between "primitive" and "civilized" wars, which now may be cast in terms of the distinction between *revenge* and *deterrence* as motivations for fighting. While revenge is primarily of psychological significance, the significance of deterrence is primarily political. Deterrence is future-oriented: its sole function is to manipulate future behavior and maintain political order. Revenge, on the other hand, is concerned with the satisfaction of the offended for an act already committed, and with the reestablishment of a disrupted balance. That revenge may have some deterrent value is, of course, undeniable, but deterrence is extraneous to its primary design and motivation. Whereas in primitive warfare fighting is an end in itself, in "civilized" wars fighting is instrumental to the political purpose of imposing a state's political will on the enemy and deterring future challenges to that will. But war is a costly instrument. While the fighting itself serves a significant role in Neolithic man's ritualistic life, within the state system military threats are preferable to war.

What is it that makes a deterrence system successful? The immediate answer is, of course, *credibility.* To be effective, deterrent threats must be credible in the eyes of the threatened; the threatener must be perceived as having the *capability* and the *will* to carry out the threats, if need arises.[25] But how, in general, is deterrence credibility achieved?

A comparison between the mechanisms of legal punishment and military deterrence may shed some light on the complexities of the latter. As mentioned earlier, the emergence of politics involved the creation of both internal and external coercive systems, each relying on a form of deterrence. Legal punishment is the deterrence system designed to maintain internal order, while armed forces are the instruments of deterrence for maintaining national security. Both legal and political systems use the threat of inflicting harm to prevent certain undesired behavior. But the nature of deterrence credibility is significantly different in the case of military deterrence. For one, the relation between order and coercive power is different in the two cases. Legal punishment is an exercise of legitimate authority, something more than the ability to deploy coercive power. Military deterrence, however, has little to do with legitimate authority; it is simply a *political* instrument, and its function is merely pragmatic: to maintain order and stability in the environment of international politics where authority is lacking. There is little that is legitimate or illegitimate about the particular distributions of power in political world-orders; no "higher" laws govern the making of such political systems. World-orders simply reflect *perceptions* of power and interests among sovereign political entities. Thus, the credibility of military deterrence, unlike that of legal-punishment deterrence, is not generally supported by the aura of authority.

Another difference concerns the means of achieving credibility. Legal-punishment deterrence achieves credibility primarily through *actual* infliction of punishment. Carrying out the threat against the relatively few actual law-breakers allows the general threat more effectively to constrain the behavior of the many potential law-breakers. Paradoxically, the long-term success of the threat of legal punishment is significantly enhanced by its occasional failure. Violations of the law, as long as their number remains within bounds, do not undermine the credibility of the legal system, because it is the carrying out the threat of punishment against the violators that guarantees that the threat will generally be credible. Military deterrence systems, however, cannot as readily rely on occasional cases of carrying out the threat to enhance the threat's overall credibility. Carrying out the threat means, of course, a military action and, as we argued above, such action does have deterrent value. But the social and economic costs of military action are much higher than the social and economic costs of arresting and punishing lawbreakers, so the execution of a military threat is a much more costly means of enhancing credibility than the execution of a threat of legal punishment. In addition, going to war incurs the risk that one's side will lose, in which case the military deterrent system will have completely failed. Carrying out the threat of legal punishment incurs no such risk. In the case of a nuclear war this would be the inevitable result for both sides.

Additional problems with military deterrence arise from *intrinsic uncertainties* facing any attempt to maintain the stability of world-orders over time. These uncertainties are due to the very nature of political power: its amorphousness and temporal mutability. Political systems are fundamentally dynamic entities in which geopolitical changes and, in particular, fluctuations in the strategic balance of power (through arms races) are inevitable. In general, since the supremacy of power (through mechanisms of military deterrence) is the ultimate foundation of international politics, no world-order arrangement can be entirely stable or final.

Significant implications about the mechanism and limits of military deterrence follow from this point. While threats of legal punishment are explicit and relatively invariant, the threats involved in military deterrence are often ambiguous, mostly implicit, and subject to interpretation. Since deterrent postures are ways of signalling a certain message—they are essentially communicative acts—the way they are understood is necessarily interpretative in nature. The notorious "hermeneutic circle," typical of any interpretative act, is present here as well. There is no neutral, objective raw material to be the foundational starting point of the entire interpretative process. The meaning assigned to any isolated deterrent threat depends on the entire interpretative framework in which that threat is placed. In this case it is the interpretation of the opponent's entire foreign and defense policy (i.e., intentions, policies, interests, commitments, military moves on the ground). As such, not only is military deterrence always liable to misinterpretations and miscalculations in ways that may lead to its failure, but systematic biases of all kinds are, in fact, inevitable.[26]

Another important epistemic feature of deterrent threats has to do with the inherent uncertainties about their scope of application. In international politics, boundaries of threats are hard to determine in detail prior to the occurrence of a crisis in which the threats are actually challenged. Consider, for example, NATO's official threat, known as the policy of extended deterrence, to use tactical nuclear weapons in the event of a Soviet conventional-weapons attack on Western Europe. During the three decades of this policy, the scope of the threat has never been spelled out in the detail needed to cover all the relevant hypothetical situations. Nowadays, many contend that this policy is devoid of any military and political credibility.[27] The point is that the history of international relations supplies many cases of resort to force from miscalculation due to insufficient credibilty of deterrence postures. The lesson is obvious: if we continue to rely on the mechanism of deterrence, war cannot be excluded.

The Paradox of Nuclear Deterrence

Humanity has reached an unprecedented stage in its history—a point at which the delicate and dialectical relationship between civilization and war has been pushed to its limits. War, which emerged and developed together with the institution of politics, now threatens the very existence of politics.

The institution of war is a *political* instrument; it is the resort to force to advance political purposes and to settle political conflicts between sovereign communities. But nuclear war has little to do with politics as such, for no political conflict could be settled by nuclear means; it would simply be *dissolved*. If the classical political objective of war was the achievement of a "better peace" for the winner,[28] this objective has evaporated in the nuclear age. For the survivors of nuclear holocaust, "the political, cultural, and ideological distinctions that separate the West from the Soviet Union would be seen, in comparison with the literally inconceivable contrasts between *any* pre-atomic and *any* post-atomic societies, as almost insignificant."[29] At stake in a postnuclear war world would not be which political system would survive, but whether any would. In the past, world-order breakdown might lead to the fall of a particular political system, but it never threatened the very possibility of politics, culture, and civilization. We are now in a radically new human predicament—a predicament in which the means to human apocalypse are at our disposal.

When we acknowledge that use of nuclear weapons in a political conflict would be completely pointless, the fundamental question becomes: what is the rationale for their existence? If nuclear weapons are in fact utterly unusable, what political role remains for them?

This has been the most fundamental question of the nuclear era from its very outset, and the question is even more important now that the nuclear arsenals contain more than 50,000 warheads (with a total explosive power of over a million Hiroshima bombs). As early as 1946, in a pioneering treatise on the relationships between nuclear weapons and politics, Bernard Brodie responded to this question and challenged the basic notions of military strategy in light of the nuclear reality: "Thus far the chief purpose of our military establishment has been to win wars.

From now on its chief purpose must be to avert them. It can have almost no other useful purpose."[30] Nuclear deterrence is supposed to do precisely this job: avert nuclear war. Deterrence is what gives nuclear weapons a legitimate political purpose within the contemporary international environment. But though the idea of nuclear deterrence has become the cornerstone of arrangements of global security since the end of World War II, the rationality of the policy has often been questioned; and at times nuclear deterrence has even seemed paradoxical.

As an idea, nuclear deterrence may be regarded as an attempt to reconcile two principles, each of which by itself appears to be an indispensable and self-evident truth:

1. *The Principle of Classical Deterrence:* Threatening retaliation with nuclear weapons is the *only* regulatory mechanism available in international politics to prevent great-power war.
2. *The Principle of Singularity of Nuclear Weapons:* Nuclear weapons are *sui generis* in the sense that using them as weapons (i.e., firing them at an opponent) makes the notions of war and victory inapplicable; their use in war cannot politically be justified, because such use would defeat any political purpose.

The Principle of Nuclear Deterrence is a conjuction of these two principles:

3. *The Principle of Nuclear Deterrence:* Threatening to do what would serve no political purpose is the only way to avoid nuclear war; nuclear deterrence is both *indispensable* and *sui generis*.

According to this principle, the *only* proper role for nuclear weapons is deterrence, that is, to ensure that they will never be used in actuality. What constitutes the singular nature of nuclear deterrence is the capacity in the two largest nuclear arsenals for mutual destruction, and the expectation that any nuclear exchange would immediately involve or very likely escalate quickly to use this capacity. Its use in retaliation would be a form of apocalyptic retribution, a kind of cosmic revenge, and this makes nuclear deterrence radically distinct from all past forms of military deterrence. Nuclear weapons have the peculiarity that the *whole* purpose in planning for their use is the prevention of their use. The sole purpose of the threat of a massive, nuclear retaliatory strike is to ensure that the other side never "forgets" their *sui generis* nature, never contemplates the possibility of a successful nuclear first strike, since any such attack would be tantamount to suicide.

The policy of nuclear deterrence has often been put forward as the explanation for the fact that there have been no wars between the great powers since World War II. Of course, while conflicts between the superpowers have not miraculously disappeared, patterns of international conduct have changed in such a way that conflicts are handled now with extra caution to avoid situations with a potential for direct confrontation.[31] Nevertheless, to acknowledge that conflict management in global politics has radically changed in the nuclear age is one thing, but to say that nuclear deterrence is the best guarantee for future global stability and security is another. The former does not imply the latter. The alleged success of nuclear deterrence in the past does not guarantee its future success.[32] In fact now, more than ever before, doubts are being raised about nuclear deterrence. The reason is that the Principle of

Nuclear Deterrence cannot serve as a coherent basis for long-term policy. The difficulty with the principle is shown by the following problems:

1. *The Usability Problem:* The more deterrentlike we make nuclear deterrence, that is, the more "usable" we make the weapons for the sake of the threat's credibility, the more likely it is that the weapons will be used.[33]
2. *The Credibility Problem:* The more we consider nuclear weapons as *sui generis*, that is, as unusable, the more incredible the threat to use them becomes, and the more likely the threat will fail.[34]

The first is a problem for the Principle of Classical Deterrence, and the second is a problem for the Principle of Singularity.

Consider the former. The starting point of all deterrence thinking, as pointed out in the last section, is that the institution of war is a concomitant phenomenon of international politics; within the regime of sovereign states the possibility of war cannot be excluded. Credible deterrence depends on demonstrating a *genuine* readiness and resoluteness to carry out the threat and to go to war. In a word, *credibility* of the deterrent threat requires the *usability* of the weapons. Otherwise the threat would be ineffective. But the more usable we make the weapons and the more we treat them as mundane, the more likely they are to be used. One reason is this: since threatening with usable weapons is more credible, it generates in either side a real incentive for a preemptive attack at times of crisis. In general, the more nuclear deterrence becomes deterrent like (i.e., credible), the more likely it is to have all the other weaknesses and uncertainties that characterize non-nuclear military deterrence systems. Further, as emphasized earlier, no deterrence system can ever guarantee its future success, since governments (like individuals) can always err and act imprudently, even irrationally (e.g., through miscalculation of the other's intentions). But with the nuclear arsenals of today we cannot afford to err even once.

Let us move now to the second problem. According to the Principle of Singularity, best manifested in the existing capacity for mutual destruction, the uniqueness of modern nuclear weapons lies in the fact that their use as weapons can serve no political purpose. But once we recognize nuclear weapons as unique, the threat of retaliation becomes incredible. There are two cases to consider. First, the threat of nuclear retaliation against a conventional attack or a limited nuclear attack is not credible, because nuclear retaliation in such circumstances (even limited nuclear retaliation) could bring a full-scale nuclear response whether immediately or after several escalatory stages. If complete destruction is likely, the threat of such retaliation cannot be made believable. The capacity for "escalation dominance" is only a chimerical advantage given the capacity for assured destruction possessed by each side.

The second case concerns the threat of nuclear retaliation against a full-scale nuclear first strike. If the *raison d'etre* of the threat of a retaliatory strike is to prevent a first strike from being launched, what political or military reason would remain to launch a second strike once a first strike had already been made? As Jonathan Schell puts it, "the logic of deterrence strategy is dissolved by the very event—the first strike—that it is meant to prevent. Once the action begins, the whole doctrine is self-canceling."[35] Given that retaliation in response to a full-scale first strike could serve no purpose, the threat of such retaliation is not credible.

The source of the incredibility is different in the two cases. In the first, the threat is not credible because it is a threat to do something that would lead to one's own destruction. In the second, the threat is not credible because it is a threat to do something after one has already been destroyed. But the ultimate source of the incredibility is the same in each case: the *sui generis* destructive potential of existing nuclear arsenals. The incredibility problem in the second case has been frequently discussed in strategic writings since the critique of the policy of Massive Retaliation in the 1950s. But what is not always recognized is that the attempt to solve this problem by adopting a nuclear strategy of counterforce is vitiated by the incredibility problem in the first case.

What the usability and the credibility problems show is that when the Principles of Classical Deterrence and of Singularity are combined into the Principle of Nuclear Deterrence, paradox results. If nuclear deterrence increasingly resembles traditional forms of military deterrence, nuclear war is rendered more likely; but if nuclear deterrence becomes less like traditional forms of military deterrence, in respect for the *sui generis* character of nuclear weapons, nuclear war is still made more likely. There is a fundamental incompatibility between traditional forms of military deterrence and the singular nature of nuclear weapons. The classical forms of military deterrence depend on war: on its possibility to make the threat credible, and on its actuality to achieve the political goals should the threat fail. The utter destructiveness of nuclear war makes it unable to play either role. Understanding this incompatibility is crucial for comprehending the nuclear predicament: politics as traditionally understood is incompatible with the nuclear reality. The two do not hang together.

It is useful here to recognize the implications for nuclear deterrence of our earlier comparison between legal-punishment deterrence and military deterrence. Legal-punishment deterrence not only can tolerate occasional failures, but actually relies on the execution of the threat in such cases to strengthen, through enhanced credibility, the deterrent system as a whole. But due to the much greater costs involved in executing the threat, military deterrence is much less able to tolerate failures obliging the execution of the threat. More important, nuclear deterrence cannot tolerate even a single failure. Thus nuclear deterrence, first, is inherently much riskier than other forms of deterrence since a single failure is a failure of the policy as a whole; and second, it is unable to rely on a primary mechanism for deterrence credibility, the execution of the threat in isolated cases.

We have seen that nuclear war, given the present size and configuration of nuclear arsenals, can serve no political purpose. The dialectical relationship between war and civilization has come full circle: nuclear war would be a form of primitive warfare for which the motivation would be backward-looking revenge, rather than forward-looking deterrence. But what we see now is that if nuclear war can serve no purpose, neither can the threat of nuclear war; for the effectiveness of the threat depends on whether execution of the threat is a real political option. We can rely neither on nuclear war nor on the threat of nuclear retaliation as a policy to achieve political goals, such as national security.

This illustrates Einstein's warning (quoted at the beginning of this essay) about the fundamental discontinuity between the nuclear reality and the way in which we think of this reality. If we admit (as we should) the uniqueness involved in the eventuality of nuclear holocaust, we can no longer retain our old political intuitions about deterrence and war; while if we decide to continue thinking of the nuclear reality in traditional political-military terms, we fail to recognize the singular nature of nuclear weapons. In essence, the Principle of Nuclear Deterrence is incoherent, for it attempts to preserve *both* our prenuclear intuitions about politics and war and our postnuclear understanding.

The Present Predicament: Rethinking the Unthinkable

The paradox involved in the Principle of Nuclear Deterrence cannot be dismissed as the product of abstract reasoning applied in an area foreign to it, the nonabstract realm of concrete military affairs. In fact, if a general lesson is drawn from a study of the four decades of nuclear strategic thought, it is that strategic theory has failed to make the reality of nuclear weapons politically relevant. The fundamental dilemma of nuclear strategic thought has always been, to use Herman Kahn's phrase, how to think the unthinkable: the problem of finding an appropriate sense in the language of strategy for a weapon that appears to defy that language's powers of expression. Much of the history of recent strategic thought can be seen as a dialectical movement from thinking of nuclear weapons as "usable" for military purposes (massive retaliation and flexible response), to realizing the *sui generis* nature of nuclear war that renders the bomb utterly "unusable" (as in the doctrine of Mutual Assured Destruction, or MAD), and finally to the present paradoxical synthesis— countervailing strategy—that combines a capacity for assured destruction with a counterforce capability for "nuclear war fighting."[36] A brief historical examination of this dialectic will reveal the enormous danger of the present predicament.

Perhaps the philosophically most significant lesson to be drawn from the early phases of Western nuclear thought, roughly the period from 1945 to 1965, is that the fundamental question was not whether nuclear weapons should be used (i.e., whether they could serve legitimate political purposes) but how they should be used (i.e., what kind of nuclear strategy would render their use politically most effective). Indeed, until the advent of MAD, it was presupposed by American nuclear strategy that nuclear weapons could serve the range of political purposes that weapons had traditionally served. An assumption of strategic thinking prior to 1965 was that the use of nuclear weapons was part of the calculus of global strategic considerations. After all, it was the United States that used nuclear weapons first, a use motivated in part by global considerations separate from its war with Japan.[37]

Another moral can be drawn from the first two decades of the nuclear age. The drive for military superiority, characteristic of arms races in general, also characterized the nuclear arms race during this period. During those years the United States had an overwhelming nuclear advantage over the Soviet Union, starting with its exclusive monopoly before 1949. It continued to maintain its monopoly on strategic means of delivery until 1956, and until 1966 or 1967 its margin of nuclear superiority over the Soviets was sufficient to allow it to contemplate the option of a first strike. This edge had a remarkable impact on the manner in which the United States conducted its foreign and defense policy.[38] During this period, on at least five occasions the United States threatened (explicitly or implicitly) to use nuclear weapons to promote and protect its specific interests around the globe. Further, nuclear deterrence included the notion of *extended deterrence,* the commitment by the United States to use nuclear weapons to counter Soviet aggression against NATO countries and other vital American interests abroad. Indeed, the current NATO threat to resort to nuclear power in the event of Soviet invasion of Western Europe, a threat regarded by many today as devoid of credibility, is a strategic residue of the time when the U. S. still had a significant superiority in nuclear weapons.[39]

The MAD strategy, advocated by McNamara and U.S. doctrine between 1965 to 1974, constituted a dramatic change in the fundamentals of nuclear thinking.[40] The theoretical core of MAD is a total rejection of military superiority as an adequate ideal for the nuclear age. The rationale for such a conceptual shift was the recognition that the nuclear arms race had reached a unique point, beyond which the use of nuclear weapons could no longer play a meaningful role in global politics. Yet nuclear weapons could not be disinvented. The only remedy was to create a global arrangement to ensure the nonuse of nuclear weapons. The only role remaining for nuclear weapons was to prevent their ever being used. This meant that *parity* and *stability* had to replace *superiority* and *usability* as the primary concepts in deterrence thinking.

For the new global arrangement required by MAD thinking, two conditions of deterrence stability are vital: (a) mutual vulnerability of the entire societal infrastructure of the adversaries, and (b) mutual invulnerability of both sides' second-strike (retaliatory) nuclear forces. These measures are to guarantee that the temptation to resort to a nuclear first strike does not arise, even in times of crisis. The invulnerability of retaliatory forces accounts for the deterrence stability of MAD: no side can be denied its capability to inflict unendurable destruction on the other's societal infrastructure. Yet this capability must not be perceived as a first-strike (counterforce) capability. MAD thinking thus requires a clear distinction between war-initiating or war-fighting (first-strike) capabilities and war-deterring (second-strike) capabilities; the former are forbidden, the latter are necessary. Once this distinction is lost or ignored, the vital element of deterrence stability breaks down.

Obviously, MAD is not a unilateral nuclear strategy. It must be mutually accepted as a component within a wider framework for global security cooperation. Deterrence stability can be achieved only through an atmosphere of cooperation, not of excessive competition. Above all, MAD thinking requires that both sides abandon attempts to achieve superiority and instead accept parity, preferably by public agreement. This point is significant, for it shows that in at least two respects MAD thinking is at odds with the traditional logic of deterrence: (a) under a genuine MAD regime, nuclear deterrence is divorced from other aspects of international politics; (b) under a genuine MAD regime, there are ultimate limits to the arms race since, in principle, the nuclear arms race must end once the armament levels assure mutual destruction.

As we know only too well, neither of these requirements has been fulfilled. The doctrine was never matched by any significant mutual restraint in the arms race. Just as the Soviet Union never adopted the American notion of limited nuclear war (inherent in the Flexible Response Doctrine), it did not accept the MAD reasoning.[41] The Soviet Union viewed the very logic of MAD as militarily unrealistic and politically incredible. The Soviets ridiculed the claim implicit in MAD that strategic nuclear weapons were "unusable". Aware of the credibility problem in MAD thinking, the Soviets insisted that *all* weapons are "usable."

Moreover, despite the hopes of its advocates, MAD never served as a basis for negotiating comprehensive arms reductions. Although some specific agreements were achieved, their overall success (compared to expectations) was limited. Again we see the similarity between the nuclear arms race and nonnuclear arms races.

Nuclear arms negotiations were viewed as an intrinsic component of the arms race itself, as a means of seeking unilateral strategic advantage, not as a means of imposing external restraint upon the arms race. In fact, the method of negotiations through "bargaining chips" only accelerated the nuclear arms race, rather than reducing its pace and stabilizing it.[42]

With no genuine agreement about mutual strategic restraint, the nuclear arms race in the last decade has gone unchecked. While the rhetoric of assured destruction is still used in public, none of MAD's original stabilizing requirements is in place. These requirements were totally eroded and undermined by a combination of technological and political developments. As always, technological "progress" in the arms race undermined the requirements of restraint. Above all, the advent of new weapons-delivery technology (e.g., MIRV and improvements in ballistic guidance systems) shed serious doubts on the invulnerability of strategic retaliatory forces.[43] Deployment of *countervalue* systems, so essential for MAD thinking, has been superseded by deployment of *counterforce* systems based on the new delivery technology. Due to such developments, the possibility of a limited nuclear first strike against the opponent's nuclear forces has become the nightmare of all strategic planners (e.g., the notorious "window of vulnerability"). After all, if nuclear war must be fought, a first strike against the enemy's ICBMs should be the most effective mode of action. The new generation of ICBSs, like the American MX, has the potential not only to cause such fear, but to create "nuclear temptations."[44] As often happens, one type of nightmare generates another, in this case the "launch on warning" procedure by which vulnerable ICBMs could be launched before they would be struck by incoming warheads.

As is typical in an arms race situation, changes in weaponry are matched by changes in strategic thought. By the early 1970s (officially 1974) MAD was replaced by a new nuclear strategy, the Nixon-Schlesinger strategy of Selective Options. This was essentially an updated version of Kennedy's Flexible Response, a switch to a counterforce strategy. In its theoretical foundations the new doctrine constituted a return to the fundamental ideas of traditional military deterrence thinking: superiority, usability, and credibility. It emphasized the essential link between deterrent postures and international politics, and between political credibility and military usability. Its whole justification was to make nuclear deterrence again politically relevant. Obviously, this emphasis on usability eroded the distinction between *deterring* and *war-fighting* capabilities; from the new perspective the two are seen as coextensive and largely overlapping in theory and in practice.

The present phase of the nuclear arms race brings the dialectical movement full circle. Once again we face the dilemma of the nuclear age—how can one fight a nuclear war? Once again a new generation of strategic planners emerges, insisting on thinking the unthinkable and attempting to incorporate the reality of nuclear weapons into traditional modes of military thinking.[45] Naturally, most of these efforts have centered around the concept of limited nuclear war (LNW).[46] Versions of this idea have risen and fallen time and again during the history of nuclear thinking, but their fundamental motivation was always the same: to "humanize" nuclear war, that is, to make it more warlike, less apocalyptic. After all, if LNW is a feasible strategic option, then nuclear policy becomes more political and less paradoxical.

We cannot fully discuss here the complex issue of LNW, but some brief comments are necessary. The fundamental problem is *not* whether LNW is possible, but whether we have any basis for predicting its likelihood, so that is could be discussed as part of *rational* strategic planning. To put it bluntly, attempting to fight a LNW would be a total gamble in circumstances of complete uncertainty, since no one really knows whether or how such war could be controlled or terminated. We know virtually nothing about how individual decisionmakers would react after the first nuclear blast, or how the entire chain of command and its communication system would function. Accordingly, no one can, with any assurance, plan a limited response in advance. All we know is that even a few small warheads would kill millions even if their use were strictly part of counterforce strategy. As McGeorge Bundy put the matter, "Of course, no one can prove that any first use of nuclear weapons will lead to a general conflagration; but what is decisive is that no one can come close to proving it will not."[47] Discussion of LNW is pretending knowledge where there is none, and worse, attempting to make the pretense believable.

To sum up, what is worrisome, even ominous, about the present phase of the nuclear arms race is that it is conducted in double-talk. Current (Western) strategy incorporates elements of both assured destruction and war fighting into one rhetoric. Although both sides speak of parity, each suspects that the other intends superiority. Although both sides publicly deny any leanings toward a first-strike capacity or any belief in the possibility of victory, the weapons and strategies they develop are clearly perceived as first-strike oriented.

What makes the present situation so ominous is not only the existence of geopolitical conflicts between the superpowers, but the unique situational logic of the nuclear predicament that conjures up apocalyptic nightmares and preemptive temptations. Given the fact that we live in an aging world-order, a global order which while founded more than 40 years ago has to cope with new problems, this situational logic may well be tested in a real-world conflict situation. While we all know our political world-order cannot last indefinitely, and its death could be the death of all world-order, we seem unable to abandon it or replace it by another. The nuclear predicament is the result of the dialectical relationship between human technology, pushed to new heights by the human mind, and our traditional political understanding. Once the technology is pushed this far, it transcends politics and becomes alienated from the context in which it was created. Nuclear weapons no longer have the qualities of genuine weapons, yet we continue to conceive our situation in outdated Hobbesian terms, i.e., in terms of sovereign states.

THE MORAL PROBLEM OF NUCLEAR WEAPONS

One important way in which nuclear weapons are discontinuous with currrent ways of thinking about military matters concerns our traditional notions of limits in war, especially moral limits. The business of morality in war is the imposition of limits. To understand the moral problems posed by nuclear weapons, we must understand how nuclear weapons fail to fit our traditional ways of thinking about these moral limits. The failure of fit is revealed in the claim that nuclear weapons make self-defense morally problematic. Let us set the discussion of moral limits in context by considering the broader question of the relation between the use of nuclear weapons and the idea of limits in general on war. The basic truth here seems to be that traditional notions of limits in war, moral and otherwise, cannot be applied in the case of nuclear war.

Limits in War

What kinds of limits apply to the amount of destruction one side can cause the other in war? A useful distinction may be drawn between limits that are other-imposed and limits that are self-imposed.

Other-imposed limits arise from such factors as the amount of manpower available for combat, the degree of public support for the war effort, the financial and natural resources available, the state of weapons technology, and the extent of the enemy's defensive capabilities. These place an upper limit on the amount of destruction that each side in a war is capable of inflicting. None is under the direct or immediate control of military decisionmakers. Some can be indirectly influenced by the decisionmakers; for example, leaders can sponsor research and development programs to advance weapons technology, or can engage in propagandistic efforts to increase public support for the war. But in any given historical situation, the degree to which these factors can be influenced by the military decisionmakers is usually relatively small.

But military leaders may choose not to reach this upper limit; they may restrict their own actions beyond the limits imposed by outside factors. Self-imposed limits fall into two general categories: the prudential and the moral. Prudential limits concern the self-interest of the nation at war. A nation at war will sometimes regard the use of all of the violence it can command as not in its self-interest. Military leaders may be capable of more violence than they believe is necessary to win, and the nation may have little to gain and much to lose by using the excess. Moral limits, in contrast, arise not from a concern merely for self-interest, but from a concern that takes account of the interests of all persons, friend and foe alike.

The destruction wrought by the use of nuclear weapons fails to fit these kinds of limits. Not only do nuclear weapons effectively render meaningless all other-imposed limits, they also cannot be used in a way that observes self-imposed limits. While nuclear weapons make effectively limitless the amount of destruction of which a nation is capable, their nature is such that they cannot be used in ways respectful of traditional notions of prudential and moral limits on violence. We tend to think of war in terms of these sorts of limits on destructive violence, so the failure of nuclear weapons to fit these categories illustrates again the discontinuity between our usual conception of war and the reality of war with nuclear weapons.

Consider the various sorts of other-imposed limits that generally apply. The amount of military manpower available is virtually irrelevant as a source of limitation, since a nuclear war, at least a strategic one, is fought without troops. A nuclear war would be so brief that there would be no time for public reaction to influence its course. The brevity of a nuclear war also means that in the midst of the war the extent of available financial and natural resources would impose no limits. Nor is nuclear war a traditional war of attrition, for there would be no opportunity to mobilize resources to produce more armaments.[48] Even in the nuclear age, the state of weapons technology limits the available potential for destruction: one can envision weapons technologies more destructive than present ones. But present weapons technology is at the point where it no longer places any *effective* limits on destruction. The destructive potential in existing nuclear arsenals is so great as to be virtually limitless from the human perspective; no increment in destructive power would made an effective difference.

Finally, there is the factor of the enemy's defensive capabilities. Because there is no existing defense against a nuclear warhead carried by a ballistic missile, nor a reliable one likely in the foreseeable future, none of the enemy's military capabilities can directly limit the amount of destruction done by a nuclearly armed opponent. (There is serious question not only of when but of whether ballistic missile defense under the Strategic Defense Initiative or "Star Wars" program could be reliably implemented.) Of course, if one side practices a policy of nuclear deterrence, that is, if it possesses the capability to retaliate with nuclear weapons if attacked and threatens such retaliation, it may succeed in deterring the other side from an initial nuclear attack. But deterrence works by influencing the decisions of the opponent's military leaders, not by physically interrupting an attack once underway. Physical interruption is, of course, how defense capabilities traditionally have functioned. For this reason, an opponent's capacity for nuclear retaliation should not be regarded as a defensive capability or an other-imposed limiting factor on the nuclear destruction of which a nation is capable. Rather, it is part of the background determining a self-imposed or chosen limitation, specifically a prudential one. As nuclear weapons turn defense into deterrence, a nation loses the ability directly to control the amount of destruction visited upon it. So given present nuclear arsenals, none of the other-imposed factors can serve effectively to limit the destruction of a nuclear war.

Because there are no longer any effective other-imposed limits, the self-imposed limits become all-important. Destruction, if it is to be limited, must be limited by choice. Yet nuclear weapons, we will argue, take warfare beyond traditional self-imposed limits. If nuclear weapons are used at all, they cannot be used in a manner respecting prudential or moral limits.

For a number of reasons, the use of nuclear weapons would invariably violate prudential limits on destructive violence in war. The most important reason, as mentioned above, is the existence of policies of nuclear deterrence. Given that each major nuclear power has an arsenal of deliverable nuclear warheads largely invulnerable to a nuclear strike by the other, any use of nuclear weapons runs the grave risk of initiating nuclear retaliation. This is, of course, the point of the policy of nuclear deterrence: to make nuclear attack contrary to the prudential interests of one's opponent. But even in the absence of an opposing retaliatory capacity, there are reasons why the use of nuclear weapons would be contrary to a nation's self-interest. First, nuclear weapons are unlike other weapons in that their use on a large scale involves harm to the user. Nuclear radiation is so widespread an effect that it would invariably harm a nation firing nuclear weapons. In addition, as recent studies concerning the so-called "nuclear winter" have shown, if either great power fired even a fraction of its nuclear weapons, a sun-blocking layer of smoke would probably be created causing severe damage over the entire Northern Hemisphere.[49] Second, the use of nuclear weapons against an opponent would defeat many of the prudential objectives that standardly motivate nations at war. For example, the economic exploitation of an opponent would be rendered difficult or impossible by nuclear devastation.

Traditional Moral Limits in War

Before taking up the question of whether the use of nuclear weapons in war necessarily violates moral limits, some discussion is in order about the general problem of drawing moral limits on destructive violence in war. The idea of morally limiting war is the idea of distinguishing between the actions of war that are morally permissible and those that are not. The project of placing moral limits on war falls between two extremes: the pacifist position that would morally disallow any action of war; and the position, known as realism, that no moral limits are applicable in war. For the pacifist, no violence against persons is justifiable, so war is not something in which to find moral limits, but rather something to be ruled out completely. In contrast, the supporter of moral limits on war recognizes as justifiable *some* violence against persons, paradigmatically defensive violence.

The realist, on the other hand, regards no actions of war as being morally unacceptable. Moral limits are, in one way or another, irrelevant or inapplicable in the context of war.[50] The only self-imposed limits on war recognized by the realist are prudential. It would be a mistake to identify realism with prudentialism, however, for these positions, as usually understood, differ in some respects. Realism is characterized in opposition to morality, as a form of amoralism. But prudence does not so directly rule out moral considerations; the prudent person often recognizes that observing at least some moral limits has prudential value. In any case, our interest here is not to consider arguments for or against pacifism or realism, but merely to fix the two poles between which those seeking to impose moral limits on war are located.

One form of moral limitation on war is in terms of *conventional* moral rules. A set of conventional moral rules, or a positive morality, is a set of norms common to the members of a social group and recognized as of special importance by them.[51] Conventional moral rules are integral, limiting parts of human institutions and social practices; they are traditional, in the sense that they develop and grow within the institutional or practical tradition of which they are a part.

The institution or practice of war has its own set of conventional moral rules.[52] The central tradition of conventional moral rules limiting war that has developed in the West over the past several centuries is the *just-war tradition.* "The just war tradition represents the coalescence of the major effort Western culture has made to regulate and restrain violence."[53] The sources of the development of this tradition are diverse. In addition to the accepted rules of war that have been embodied in international law, major contributions to the tradition have been made by Christian theologians and military professionals. Despite such diversity, there is considerable consensus on the major points.[54]

The just-war tradition distinguishes between two levels of moral judgment of war: moral judgments about whether a nation should go to war (referred to as judgments of *jus ad bellum)* and moral judgments about how a war, once initiated or joined, should be conducted (judgments of *jus in bello*). This is a difference between morality *of* war and morality *in* war. A number of conditions must be satisfied if a war is to be morally permissible at the level of *jus ad bellum,* the most important being that the war be defensive rather than aggressive. But more important here is a discussion of *jus in bello,* since our concern is whether a war, aggressive or defensive, may be conducted through the use of nuclear weapons.[55]

The two main conditions for determining *jus in bello* are the principles of *discrimination* and *proportionality.* The principle of discrimination (or noncombatant immunity) is that violence in war is to be directed only against those in the opponent's military service and others, such as munition workers, directly involved in its war effort. Noncombatants, who do not directly participate in the war effort, are morally immune from attack. Military violence should be used in a way that discriminates between these two groups. The principle of proportionality is that the amount of violence used in a military action be no more than directly proportional to the end the violence seeks to achieve. The kinds of ends in question here are two: the proximate end of the particular military action in question, such as winning a certain battle, and the ultimate end of the entire war.[56]

A useful way to illustrate the limitations imposed by these two principles is the example of what is morally justifiable for individual self-defense. One is justified in using violence in self-defense only against the attacker; violence may not be used against others not involved in the attack, no matter what relation they may have to the attacker. This feature of justified self-defense corresponds to the principle of discrimination; in the case of war, the attackers are paradigmatically those in the military service of the attacker. Further, one is not justified in doing more harm in self-defense than is threatened by the attacker.[57] (This feature corresponds to the principle of proportionality.) The example of self-defense reveals an important characteristic of the two principles. While there is often considerable room for disagreement about how much harm a defender is justified in inflicting, there is much less room for disagreement concerning the identity of the persons against whom self-defensive violence may be justifiably used. This holds as well in the case of the two principles limiting wartime violence. While the principle of proportionality tends to be flexible and elastic in its application, the principle of discrimination is much more rigid in its application.[58] The proscription of violence upon noncombatants is the most restrictive feature of the limitations on war set by the just-war tradition, and so the principle of discrimination counts as the most important feature of this tradition.

The principle of discrimination, however, includes a restrictive qualification on the idea that noncombatants are always immune from attack. This qualification has taken various forms within the just-war tradition, but one characteristic form is in terms of the doctrine of double-effect. On this doctrine, it often makes an important moral difference whether a harmful effect of an action is intended (that is, intended as an end of the action or as a means to the end) or is merely foreseen. Some actions with harmful effects (specifically, those where the harmful effects are outweighed by good effects) will be morally permissible if the harmful effects are merely foreseen, but not intended. The principle of discrimination, qualified by the doctrine of double-effect, morally disallows all actions that intend harm to noncombatants; but if an action does merely foreseen harm to noncombatants, the principle will often permit it. (For a military action with merely foreseen harmful effects to be permissible, it must satisfy the principle of proportionality.) Thus, the just-war tradition characteristically places great emphasis on the rightfulness of intention: intention to harm noncombatants makes violence against them completely impermissible.

If the principle of discrimination did not include such a restriction, the limitations placed on war by the just-war tradition would be much more severe, since few military actions pose no risk of harm to noncombatants. The just-war tradition is a tradition of limited war, but not too limited. This allows the tradition to fulfill an important *political* function. With the qualified principle of discrimination, the just-war tradition can often in good conscience recommend restrictions on military actions that do not go too far beyond the restrictions recommended on prudential grounds.[59] This makes it much more likely that the tradition's restrictions will be heeded by decisionmakers. Were the restrictions too severe, they would invariably be ignored, and the tradition would risk political irrelevance, that is, risk its prescriptions being completely unheeded by military decisionmakers.

But there is danger for the tradition in the other direction as well. The tradition can become politically more relevant, that is, be given greater heed by decisionmakers, by more strongly qualifying the principle of discrimination. But to do this would compromise the tradition's moral authority by moving it away from its basic concern to provide protection for noncombatants. The tradition has in the past sought to maintain both its moral authority and its political relevance. But a tension exists here: efforts to better secure either of these tend to weaken the hold on the other. Modern developments in war have raised the level of this tension. Two pervasive features of contemporary nonnuclear war raise special concern for the principle of discrimination: the tendency toward total war, involving the large-scale targeting of civilian areas through aerial bombing; and the attempts to suppress militarily guerilla resistance movements. In both kinds of military activities many noncombatants are killed, and many of these deaths are surely intended. If these activities are condemned to the extent apparently required by the principle of discrimination, the just-war tradition seriously risks political irrelevance. But if these activities are tolerated by the tradition, its moral authority is placed in jeopardy. [60]

In any case, the just-war tradition represents the traditional way in which we think about the moral limitation of war. The question remains: can nuclear weapons be used in conformity with these limits? What are the implications of the just-war tradition for the use of nuclear weapons in war? Before answering, we will take a brief look at what moral theories have to say about the limitation of war.

Moral Theories and War

One way to set moral limits on human activity other than by appealing to conventional moral rules consists of considering the requirements set by a moral theory. A moral theory provides a comprehensive and systematic principle or set of principles that determine requirements on human action and that are based in one way or another on considerations of reason. The requirements set by moral theories often coincide with those set by conventional moral rules—but not always, for their bases differ. Conventional moral rules derive their authority from the tradition of which they are a part, while the requirements of moral theories are justified on rational grounds. Of the moral theories that have been propounded, most are either consequentialist or deontological in form.

A consequentialist theory determines the moral status of an action exclusively in terms of the value or disvalue of the action's consequences. An action is morally correct if and only if it brings about a balance of value over disvalue greater than that of any other action (including doing nothing) that the agent could have performed. [61] Different consequentialist theories characterize value in different ways, with the most popular form, utilitarianism, identifying it with pleasure, happiness, or preference realization. On any consequentialist theory, the use of violence brings about immediate disvalue in the harm and suffering it directly causes. The main condition of limitation on military action set by a consequentialist theory is, then, that the action is permitted only if its short-term and long-term consequences are of sufficient value to counterbalance the disvalue of the violence it directly involves.

Deontological theory sets moral limits much differently. An action is morally permitted if and only if it is permitted by a certain set of moral rules; the action's consequences have no direct bearing. Different deontological theories view this set of rules as determined in different ways, but all the theories agree that it is in general morally permissible to use violence against a person only if that person has taken some action, such as attacking another, that justifies the violence. If the person has not taken such action, he or she is morally innocent and normally cannot justifiably be subject to violence by another. Thus deontological theory, like the just-war tradition, insists on the distinction between combatants and noncombatants. Combatants through their actions endanger at least the military personnel of the opponent. Noncombatants, who do not, are in this sense morally innocent, and so it is immoral to use military violence against them.[62] Thus, one of the main limitations that deontological theory imposes on violence in war is that it is not to be directed at noncombatants.

Should the just-war tradition itself be seen as a moral theory alongside consequentialist and deontological theories? It is better not to regard it as a moral theory.[63] The just-war tradition is not a comprehensive account of how one ought to act, for it is limited to military actions. And, being a tradition, it does not adequately exemplify the systematic and rationally grounded character of moral theories, although a number of important moral thinkers in the tradition have worked at systematizing just-war thinking and giving it rational grounding. But it is foremost a tradition, remaining closely tied to the conventional moral rules of war that constitute its prescriptions.

The principles of the just-war tradition, however, have close connections with both deontological and consequentialist theories. We have already pointed out how the just-war tradition recognizes, with deontological theory, the importance of the distinction between combatants and noncombatants. The principle of discrimination within the just-war tradition represents a chief concern of deontological theory. Likewise, the principle of proportionality takes into account the consequences of military actions, and so expresses a concern peculiar to consequentialist theory.[64] The two basic principles of *jus in bello* thus consider factors of central moral relevance in both deontological and consequentialist theories. In this sense, the just-war tradition sets limitations on violence in war from both deontological and consequentialist perspectives.

Just War and Nuclear War

What are the implications of the just-war tradition for the use of nuclear weapons in war?[65] The use of nuclear weapons in war violates both the principle of proportionality and the principle of discrimination. Consider proportionality first. The use of nuclear weapons in war would involve so many deaths, both locally and globally, that no military goal their use could achieve, whether short term or long term, would be proportional to the harm done. Even a small number of nuclear weapons directed at isolated military targets would, because of wind-borne radiation, lead to so many deaths that the harm would still be disproportionally large in comparison with any possible military gain. Even more important, given the current international distribution of nuclear weapons, the use of even a single one would very likely lead to escalation, making the *expected* harm from the use of a few weapons far greater than the actual harm those weapons alone could cause. Thus any use of nuclear weapons in war violates the principle of proportionality.

Showing that the use of nuclear weapons cannot satisfy the principle of proportionality is sufficient by itself to show that the just-war tradition rules out their use, for according to the just-war tradition wartime violence is justified only if *both* principles are satisfied. But it is also important to consider the implications of the principle of discrimination for the use of nuclear weapons.

The fact that most of the fatalities in a nuclear war would be noncombatants seems to indicate that the use of nuclear weapons in war would violate the principle of discrimination. But some would argue that, in the light of the doctrine of double-effect, some uses of nuclear weapons in war would not run afoul of the principle of discrimination, in those uses where the resulting noncombatant deaths are not intended.[66] If the warheads are aimed at cities, the noncombatant deaths are intended and the principle is violated. But if the warheads are aimed at isolated military targets, noncombatant deaths, although foreseen, would not be intended. This argument in terms of the doctrine of double-effect is appropriate in the case of nonnuclear weapons, but it does not work when applied to the use of nuclear weapons.

Nonnuclear weapons are discriminate weapons, that is, they can be used in a manner that discriminates between combatants and noncombatants in terms of the harm caused.[67] But nuclear weapons are *inherently indiscriminate*: they cannot be used in a way that discriminates between combatants and noncombatants. This is due not only to the geographically widespread effects peculiar to nuclear weapons, especially radiation, but also to the global effects, such as the "nuclear winter." When a nonnuclear explosive is used against an isolated military target, the only certain deaths are combatants. When a nuclear explosive is used, the deaths of both combatants and noncombatants are assured. This is a crucial moral difference between nuclear and nonnuclear weapons.[68]

The inherent indiscriminateness of nuclear weapons has important implications for the way in which the principle of discrimination applies to their use. The principle of discrimination is meant to apply to weapons that *can* be used discriminately—for example, against military rather than civilian targets. A clear implication of the principle of discrimination, when understood in this way, is that an inherently indiscriminate weapon cannot be used at all. It is, then, futile to apply the distinction between intended and merely foreseen effects to try to find some use for nuclear weapons that does not violate the principle of discrimination. *A weapon that is inherently indiscriminate cannot be used with a discriminate intention*—the weapon will not serve that role. The distinction is lost between harm to noncombatants that is intended and harm that is merely foreseen.

Such an interpretation of the principle of discrimination may seem to go beyond the confines of the just-war tradition, but this does not mean that it lacks historical warrant from the tradition. In being inherently indiscriminate, nuclear weapons are unlike the weapons the just-war tradition has had to consider. But it is certainly appropriate to draw out the implications of the tradition for the new military reality. Since the principle of discrimination is meant to allow only the discriminate use of weapons, we may infer that it does not allow any use of weapons that are inherently indiscriminate. If the principle of discrimination means anything, it must be understood to rule out *any* use of nuclear weapons. This is a token of the moral peculiarity of nuclear weapons.

The use of nuclear weapons thus transgresses the traditional moral limits set on destruction in war, just as it goes beyond prudential limits. The only way to respect these limits is not to use nuclear weapons at all. The just-war tradition implies *nuclear pacifism*, the position that any use of nuclear weapons in war is morally impermissible. In the case of nuclear war, the just-war tradition ceases to be a doctrine allowing limited war and instead joins hands with pacifism in rejecting war altogether. The tradition thus no longer maintains, as far as nuclear war is concerned, a position between realism and pacifism; and in losing this intermediate position it may seem to risk political irrelevance. But the position rejecting the moral possibility of nuclear war would be treated as politically irrelevant only by those decisionmakers who believe that a nuclear war is prudentially possible. For those decisionmakers who believe that nuclear weapons could never be used in war, that the sole purpose of the weapons is deterrence, this position may be acceptable (although these decisionmakers could not *profess* its acceptability, for this would undercut the credibility of the deterrent).

The Morality of Nuclear Deterrence

To understand fully the discontinuity between the nuclear reality and our traditional ways of thinking about the morality of military activity, we must consider the implications of the just-war tradition not merely for the use of nuclear weapons in war, but also for their use to threaten, that is, for the policy of nuclear deterrence. The concept and logic of deterrence have already been discussed. Our present concern is with the morality of nuclear deterrence, and specifically with what our moral tradition has to say about deterrence.

It may seem odd to apply the just-war tradition to nuclear deterrence, since this policy involves no overt violence. But it is a military policy; although it is designed to avoid war, it might actually make war more likely, and it would certainly make a war more destructive. In addition, because nuclear deterrence involves a threat to innocent persons, it is a form of hostage-holding; and the holding of hostages is a form of violence, broadly understood, even if the threat is never carried out. So it is not inappropriate to apply the principles of the just-war tradition to nuclear deterrence policy.

When these principles are applied, the result is that nuclear deterrence fails to satisfy the principle of discrimination, although it may satisfy the principle of proportionality. If nuclear deterrence policy works well, that is, if it is more successful than any alternative policy in deterring an attack with nuclear weapons, then clearly the value of the objective achieved, the avoidance of war, is far greater than the harmful effects of the policy. The principle of proportionality would obviously be satisfied. How well does the policy work?[69] Many people believe that deterrence has kept the two superpowers from both nuclear and conventional war over the past 40 years, and that it will continue to do so. But the fact that no war has occurred in this time is not by itself convincing evidence that nuclear deterrence will make war much less likely in the future. First, the absence of war may be due to factors other than deterrence policy, or it may be due to a factor working in conjunction with deterrence policy that may not be operative in the future.[70] Second, the nature of deterrence policy has been changing, moving toward a much greater emphasis on counterforce capability, so that even if the old form of deterrence policy has worked well, this does not necessarily indicate that the new form will be as effective. Whether nuclear deterrence satisfies the principle of proportionality remains an open question.

The relevant feature of nuclear deterrence policy from the perspective of the principle of discrimination is that it involves an intention to kill noncombatants. Because most of those who would die in a nuclear retaliatory attack are noncombatants, the intention to retaliate involved in nuclear deterrence is an intention to kill noncombatants. The principle of discrimination disallows intentions to harm noncombatants. The just-war tradition accepts what has been called the wrongful intentions principle: it is wrong to intend an action that is wrong.[71] So adopting a military policy involving the intention to kill noncombatants is morally impermissible. Thus nuclear deterrence policy fails to satisfy the principle of discrimination.

Several criticisms of this argument are possible.[72] First, the intention to harm noncombatants is a *conditional* intention; that is, it would be carried out only if the nation were attacked first. But the conditional nature of the intention is morally relevant only if it were certain that the condition would never be fulfilled, which is not the case. Second, the threat to retaliate may be only a bluff, and so involve no intention at all to fire nuclear weapons.[73] But it seems that deterrence policy must always in fact be more than bluff; otherwise the all-important credibility of the policy would be likely weakened.

Third, it would be argued that the intention involved in deterrence may be an intention that only military targets be attacked, in which case the deaths of noncombatants would not be intended, but merely foreseen. But even if deterrence policy has only such an intention, the inherently indiscriminate nature of nuclear weapons, shows that intending to attack only military targets with such weapons is not sufficient to satisfy the principle of discrimination. In addition, there is good reason to think that deterrence does not, and probably could not, involve only an intention to attack military targets.[74] The threat to cities is thought to be necessary, at least as a last resort, to guarantee so much destruction that the opponent will not be tempted to risk attack.

Because nuclear deterrence policy fails to satisfy the principle of discrimination, the just-war tradition must regard the policy as morally impermissible.[75] Deterrence involves morally misusing innocent noncombatants to achieve a military objective. Deterrence is a policy of holding hostage the civilian population of one's opponent, and hostages are morally misused even if the threat against them is never carried out; for they are, in any event, put at significant risk of harm, since the threat *may* be carried out. Deterrence is an example, on a massive scale, of treating persons as means rather than ends.

The just-war tradition, then, implies a nuclear pacifism that is even stronger than the version discussed above. The just-war tradition stands opposed not merely to the use of nuclear weapons in war, but to their use for deterrence as well. Thus, the mere possession of nuclear weapons for deterrence puts a nation in transgression of traditional moral limits on military activity. There is no longer any moral ground between realism and pacifism, as far as nuclear weapons are concerned. The just-war tradition can no longer perform its traditional role of delineating an area of legitimate military activity, for in the case of nuclear weapons no such area exists.

This shows the basic discontinuity between the reality of nuclear weapons and our traditional ways of conceiving the morality of military matters. Part of this traditional conception is that military activity is sometimes morally possible, at least in self-defense. But when the traditional principles are applied to nuclear weapons, the result is the opposite: military activity is not allowed, and even the defensive stance of deterrence becomes morally problematic. So our traditional conception of the morality of military affairs fails to fit the present military reality. Perhaps Michael Walzer had something like this point in mind: "Nuclear weapons explode the theory of just-war. They are the first of mankind's technological innovations that are simply not encompassable within the familiar moral world."[76]

The claim has been made that the just-war tradition is irrelevant in the nuclear age. We have seen the sense in which this is true. It is not that the just-war tradition fails to yield moral prescriptions regarding nuclear weapons, for it yields the prescriptions of nuclear pacifism. Rather, the pacifistic prescriptions it does yield, are of a fundamentally different sort than the limited-war prescriptions yielded by it in the prenuclear age. It is not that the moral prescriptions of the just-war tradition are no longer clear; it is that they are clearly no longer prescriptions for war, nor even for deterrence. Does the just-war tradition continue to provide moral guidance in the nuclear age? The answer is "yes" if the range of possibilities includes abandoning a military policy based on nuclear weapons. The answer is "no" if it is taken for granted that military policy will be based on nuclear weapons so the question becomes only how nuclear weapons should be used.

The kind of irrelevance that the just-war tradition has in the nuclear age is *political* irrelevance. The political function of sanctioning limited military activity traditionally fulfilled by the just-war tradition, which gave the tradition what political relevance it had, is now lost, especially in the light of the tradition's implications for the policy of nuclear deterrence. The unilateral abandonment of deterrence policy seems prudentially impossible, politically completely infeasible. The just-war tradition's prescribing such abandonment makes the tradition politically irrelevant, a stance which no political leader would take seriously. Advocating the unilateral abandonment of deterrence is seen as the height of political irresponsibility.

The inherent indiscriminateness of nuclear weapons is their moral peculiarity, and it results in the discontinuity between the nuclear reality and our traditional way of thinking about the morality of military matters and in the political irrelevance of the just-war tradition. The central requirement of our moral tradition that warfare be directed only at combatants presupposes the use of discriminate weapons. What we should not relinquish from our moral tradition is the primary relevance of the difference between combatant and noncombatants. Nuclear weapons are morally impossible because they make this difference impossible to observe. The only way to impose traditional moral limits on contemporary military activity is not to use nuclear weapons, either to attack or to deter an opponent. But the unilateral abandonment of nuclear deterrence remains a politically impossible prescription.

The Moral Problem

The contemporary political irrelevance of the just-war tradition indicates the problem that nuclear weapons pose for the moral tradition: a radical split between the moral and the prudential. The moral point of view is distinct from the prudential point of view, and their prescriptions often differ.[77] But this natural tension between the two is not regarded as a sharp separation. Morality frequently requires some sacrifice of self-interest, but not an overwhelming sacrifice; morality is practical, not utopian. This feature of morality was in the past characteristic of the just-war tradition: in playing the political role of allowing limited war it did not require an unacceptable sacrifice of national self-interest, and so maintained political relevance. The political relevance of the just-war tradition began to diminish in the 20th century as civilian slaughter became characteristic of warfare, culminating in the invention and use of inherently indiscriminate nuclear weapons. But the sharp break between the just-war tradition and national self-interest has come over the policy of nuclear deterrence; here the requirements appear to diverge completely. In this way, deterrence policy has led to a radical break between prudence and morality.

The problem for our moral tradition, then, is to repair the break nuclear weapons have wrought between morality and prudence. Three general responses to this problem are possible, which we label *realism, just-war revisionism,* and *modified prudentialism.*

1. The *realist* would treat the break between morality and national self-interest as another indication that morality itself must be rejected. If the moral tradition appears to make nuclear weapons policy impossible, this simply shows that the need for a nuclear weapons policy makes morality impossible. Whether or not morality applies to domestic politics, the arena of international politics is a realm in which moral considerations do not apply. The split between morality and prudence regarding nuclear weapons policy simply brings their point into clearer focus. The politically necessary in the international arena is frequently morally impossible, and so it would be foolish to allow oneself to be bound by moral considerations. If this has not been clear to some before, the sharpness of the opposition between morality and prudence in the case of nuclear weapons should make it finally obvious. This realist response obviously does not seek to mend the break between morality and prudence, but instead to recognize the break as an old and permanent feature of international relations.

2. *Just-war revisionism* seeks to repair the break between morality and prudence by recognizing that the moral tradition must change with technological advances. A policy as politically irresponsible as the unilateral abandonment of deterrence must be morally irresponsible as well. Because nuclear weapons have thrown our concerns about military security into sharp conflict with our traditional moral concerns, the moral concerns must be altered. The just-war tradition must be altered so that priority is given to the principle of proportionality; greater moral concern must be given to consequences than to the principle of discrimination. We can no longer afford the luxury of the principle of discrimination as a necessary condition for moral permissibility. It seems that consideration of consequences would bring the moral prescription regarding nuclear weapons policy much more into line with the prudential prescription. Most of those who argue for the moral justifiability of nuclear deterrence do so by giving greater weight to the consequences.[78] The break is repaired by revising the moral tradition.

3. The third response, *modified prudentialism,* seeks to mend the break from the other direction by determining whether the prudential prescription regarding nuclear weapons policy might be more in line with the moral tradition than first appearances suggest. What is morally responsible may be politically responsible after all. The argument is that some policies alternative to nuclear deterrence are more likely to avoid nuclear war, so deterrence policy is not in our prudential interest. This involves, of course, a negative answer to the question raised earlier: does nuclear deterrence work well?[79] That deterrence works well is supported by the traditional assumption that the greater one's military strength, the greater one's military security. But if nuclear weapons have falsified this assumption, continued acceptance of the assumption creates a situation in which military behavior appar-

ently in the national interest is, in fact, imprudent and self-defeating. When present military reality is properly appreciated, national self-interest is seen to be in much closer agreement with the just-war tradition. The break between prudence and morality is repaired by a modified understanding of the requirements of prudence. The just-war tradition is once again seen to be politically relevant.

The moral problem for our moral tradition raised by nuclear weapons is serious and largely unprecedented, reflective of the moral peculiarity of these weapons. It not only concerns policies of war, but also policies of deterrence. Our response to this problem will involve one of the three approaches just presented. Realism simply rejects the problem; so if we seek a solution, we must adopt one of the other two approaches: we must either argue for revising our moral tradition, or argue that our prudential understanding of the nuclear reality is in need of modification. Whichever response we select, our choice will have *political* implications.

PROLOGUE TO POLITICS

Nuclear weapons are a political problem, and will require a political solution. The purpose of moral discussion is to serve as a guide to action. The three responses discussed above to the moral problem inherent in the nuclear predicament may be used to set forth and analyze the political and policy alternatives we face. Realism would support a continuation of the present regime of technological innovation and an increasing strategic emphasis on counterforce capability. Just-war revisionism would support a continuing reliance on nuclear deterrence, although probably not of the sort emphasized under the present regime. Modified prudentialism would support the radical political step of abandoning nuclear deterrence policy.

These three general political alternatives differ from one another in large part due to the different assumptions made about where national self-interest lies. To understand the prudential issues involved, we need to consider the earlier discussion of the relation between war and civilization. War and military deterrence, which have developed in the service of political power, now threaten to destroy politics along with everything else. Military power for deterrence has in the past served the self-interest of nations by helping to preserve a favorable world-order; when deterrence failed, war was initiated to serve the same purpose. But nuclear war can no longer serve such prudential, political purposes, and it is doubtful that deterrence can continue to do so either. This creates a prudential and political discontinuity between our way of thinking about military matters and the military reality. Our thinking that war and deterrence can be of prudential value, that nuclear weapons can safely inhabit the familiar political world, fails to fit the nuclear reality. In truth, nuclear weapons are highly antithetical to traditional political assumptions.

Realism accepts the apparent political irrelevance of our moral tradition as striking evidence for its claim that morality has no role to play in decisions regarding military matters. Moral scruples should not keep us from using nuclear weapons in the way that weapons have traditionally been used. Nuclear weapons are simply another kind of weapon for the old activity of international coercion and for the maintenance of world-order; they are part of the familiar political world. Since nuclear weapons are not to be treated differently, nations should do with them what they have always done with arms: seek to improve them and to produce more of them to achieve or maintain military superiority; and plan to fight a war with them in which one's side will prevail, should deterrence fail. In this way realism would support the present regime in its emphasis on greater development of strategic counterforce capability.

Whatever one may think of this position from a moral perspective, it flies in the face of the prudential discontinuity between our traditional political thinking and the nuclear reality. The singular nature of nuclear weapons means that they cannot be used for the same prudential purposes as can other weapons. A nuclear war would destroy whatever political goal it was fought to achieve, and there is good reason to think that nuclear deterrence, especially of the counterforce variety practiced under the present regime, also would not achieve, at least in the long term, its traditional political purpose. Realism, in this form, is the height of imprudence. Nuclear weapons have forced a split between prudence and realism. Realists, concerned to fend off the attacks of moralists, have failed to appreciate that the traditional confluence of realism and prudentialism has been undermined. In this sense the realists are, ironically, the last of the dogmatists.

Just-war revisionism, like realism, accepts the need for nuclear deterrence. But unlike realism, it views deterrence in moral terms, and as a result its specific policy prescriptions differ from those of realism in several important respects. First, since just-war revisionism has a moral concern with a policy's consequences for all humans, it would not sanction a nuclear war even if one's side could prevail by destroying an opponent's nuclear forces in a first strike. The just-war revisionist thus would not see nuclear war a real option, as the realist might.

Second, this moral concern with a policy's consequences for all humans would lead proponents of this position to advocate the type of nuclear deterrence that is least risky in terms of these sorts of consequences, although it might be more costly in terms of the factors of special concern to the realist, such as national prestige and diplomatic weight. It is reasonable to assume that the least risky form of nuclear deterrence threatens nuclear attack only in retaliation against a nuclear attack, and is based on invulnerable warheads aimed only at an opponent's economic targets, rather than its nuclear forces. Thus, a type of "minimum deterrence" is likely to be recommended, rather than the realist's kind of counterforce-emphasis deterrence.[80]

A third point of policy difference concerns the long-term desirability of nuclear deterrence policy. The realist sees deterrence as a necessary feature of international relations, a policy to be maintained indefinitely. But the just-war revisionist, viewing nuclear deterrence in moral terms, would want this policy ended as soon as possible. Although the policy is morally desirable to the extent that it works to avoid war, it fails to satisfy the principle of discrimination. Because of this flaw, it is important that other ways of avoiding war be found as soon as possible so that nuclear deterrence can be abandoned. Michael Walzer argues that the state of Supreme Emergency, which he claims justifies nuclear deterrence, cannot be regarded as a permanent state, and that we must make every effort to move beyond it so deterrence need no longer be practiced.[81] Similarly, the U.S. Catholic bishops, in their pastoral letter, argued that the moral acceptability of nuclear deterrence is strictly conditional on deterrence being taken as the first stage in a process of nuclear disarmament.

Despite these differences between the two positions, just-war revisionism may, because of its acceptance of deterrence, be subject to the same criticism as realism: in assuming that deterrence avoids war, it fails to understand the discontinuity between our traditional assumptions about prudent political behavior and the military reality created by nuclear weapons. If deterrence with nuclear weapons cannot ultimately work in the way that military deterrence has traditionally worked, it cannot achieve the traditional political ends of deterrence, and it becomes imprudent. But just-war revisionism would at least be less subject to this criticism than realism, since the more extreme form of realist deterrence policy is more imprudent than the more moderate form likely to be prescribed by just-war revisionism. Further, just-war revisionism may not be subject to the prudential criticism at all, depending on how seriously proponents of this view take the need to abandon nuclear deterrence policy as quickly as possible.

If there is a prudential discontinuity between our traditional political thinking and present reality created by nuclear weapons, it follows that we must fundamentally alter our political thinking. Given the destructive power of nuclear weapons, our very survival depends on it. We must, to use Jonathan Schell's apt phrase, "reinvent politics."[82] We must fundamentally alter our political thinking so as to make possible the avoidance of nuclear war without nuclear deterrence, since nuclear deterrence itself cannot succeed indefinitely. Just-war revisionism's commitment to abandon deterrence as quickly as possible, if taken seriously, would require just such a fundamental change in political thinking. Its support for deterrence would then be genuinely provisional and temporary, a means of buying time until the necessary change in political thinking could be effected. On the other hand, if just-war revisionism does not take seriously the need to abandon deterrence, then it is indeed subject to the same criticism as realism.

The third position, modified prudentialism, gives no support to nuclear deterrence policy, and thus explicitly recognizes the need for fundamental change in our political thinking required by the prudential discontinuity. What kinds of alternative political possibilities might serve this requirement for change?

The traditional sorts of political policies that are no longer prudential in the age of nuclear weapons are the policies of sovereign nation-states. Of course, sovereignty creates the entities that practice war and deterrence. The protection and promotion of sovereignty seem to require threat systems, which inevitably break down and lead to war. The obvious implication of such an analysis has been recognized by many throughout the nuclear age, from Einstein to Jonathan Schell: the prudential need for the abolition of national sovereignty through the creation of a world government.[83] Indeed, this presumably is the kind of change in our thinking Einstein was alluding to in our opening quotation.

Yet, there may be ways other than the abolition of national sovereignty to change fundamentally our political thinking that would involve means of avoiding war without deterrence. A number of possibilities have been envisioned.[84] A growing transnational awareness of the nuclear danger among the peoples of the world might cause them to demand that their governments negotiate multilateral disarmament treaties leading to abolition of nuclear weapons. The fundamental change in political thinking in this case would consist in the realization of the idea that people from several nations could work together on a common problem in a way that bypasses the traditional allegiance of citizen to state. Another possibility is that some form of state organization might come into being through social revolution that would be free from the need states have traditionally had to seek to maintain a favorable world order through domination and deterrence. A change in political thinking involved in a social revolution might break the historical connection between sovereignty and the deterrence-war system. Finally, a unilateral decision by one side to disarm might lead to the avoidance of nuclear war without that side having substantially to surrender its sovereignty. The change in political thinking here is the recognition that it may be possible to maintain sovereignty through conventional arms or nonviolent resistance without reliance on a nuclear threat system.

Each possibility would require fundamental changes in our political thinking, a "reinvention" of politics. But the human species has gone through profound changes in its social organization before, such as at the birth of civilization and the "invention" of politics itself. If politics could be "invented" in response to a basic change in human circumstances, it is possible for it to be "reinvented" to meet another basic change.

The general direction in which we must move is the same whether we seek to overcome the prudential discontinuity or the moral discontinuity created by nuclear weapons. We must change our way of political thinking to assure our survival. Whether or not we should sanction nuclear deterrence as an interim measure, we must move quickly to a political arrangement in which nuclear war is avoided without nuclear deterrence. If the discontinuities remain and we continue to behave politically as prenuclear experience has taught us to behave, we will behave not only immorally, but imprudently, and in a massive way, by seriously risking nuclear oblivion. Nuclear weapons, by radically increasing the apparent gap between morality and prudence, may force us to question the realist assumption that they are disparate. Realism in the nuclear age results simply from a failure to recognize that the advent of nuclear weapons has changed not only what we ought morally to do, but what we ought prudentially to do.[85]

NOTES

1. Otto Nathan and Heinz Norden, eds., *Einstein on Peace* (New York: Schocken, 1968), p. 376.
2. See Carl Sagan, "Nuclear War and Climatic Catastrophe," *Foreign Affairs* 62, no. 2 (1983): 257–92. See also Paul and Anne Ehrlich's essay, Chap. 3.
3. Karl von Clausewitz, *War, Politics, and Power* (1832), trans. Edward M. Collins (Chicago: H. Regnery Co., 1962), p. 62.
4. From this naturalistic perspective it appears that the just-war tradition is not *the* moral discourse on war; rather, it is merely the dominant Western version of moral discourse on war. Seen in this way, war as a human institution, as a rule-governed activity, is a culturally taught practice constrained by morally significant restrictions arising from within the culture itself.
5. Susan Mansfield, *The Gestalt of War* (New York: Dial Press, 1982), p. 21.
6. This historical claim about the absence of the institution of war prior to the Neolithic period is highly correlated to the anthropological evidence on "precivilized" contemporary societies. Keith Otterbein, in his quantitative cross-cultural study of primitive warfare, *The Evolution of War* (New Haven, CT.: HRAF Press, 1970), argues in favor of viewing the institution of war in evolutionary terms. See also David Fabbro, "Peaceful Societies," *Journal of Peace Research* 15 (1978): 67–83. All of Fabbro's peaceful societies can be described as precivilized societies.
7. Mansfield, *Gestalt of War*, pp. 21–23.
8. This is a methodological difficulty that many contemporary anthropologists face in dealing with the notion of "primitive warfare." Although primitive war-

fare contains some elements essential for warfare as a distinct institution of violence, it also differs significantly in strategy, objectives and organization from genuine "civilized" (i.e., political) war. Against this difficulty one can read Otterbein's evolutionary thesis viewing "primitive" and "civilized" wars as on a continuum (i.e., assuming the existence of some political structure as a given for any human organization). See also Mansfield, *Gestalt of War*, pp. 23–24.

9. For a quantitative cross-cultural analysis see Otterbein, *Evolution of War*, pp. 17–81; see also Harry H. Turney-High, *Primitive War: Its Practice and Concepts* (Columbia: The University of South Carolina Press, 1949).

10. Turney-High writes (p. 21): "The bulk of nonliterate mankind failed to establish certain simple rules and strategy. This is what kept nonliterate man a warrior instead of a soldier, despite the fact that he ordinarily valued war and the warrior far more than does civilized man."

11. The role of death ritual in primitive war is well explored by Mansfield, *Gestalt of War*, pp. 20–40.

12. Indeed, this point about the high correlation between the evolution of the institutions of war and politics is the main thesis in Otterbein's evolutionary account of primitive warfare. He argues for two evolutionary and interrelated theses: (1) "As a political community evolves in terms of increasing centralization, the more evolved the manner of waging war"; (2) "The more evolved the manner of waging war, the more likely that the political communities of a cultural unit will be militarily successful" (Otterbein, *Evolution of War*, pp. 105–6).

13. Karl von Clausewitz, *On War*, ed. and trans. Michael Howard and Peter Paret (Princeton: Princeton University Press, 1976), p. 69.

14. On this issue see Elman R. Service, "War and Our Contemporary Ancestors," in Morton Fried et al., eds., *War: The Anthropology of Armed Conflict and Aggression* (Garden City: Natural History Press, 1968), pp. 160–61.

15. For an interesting speculation on the psycho-historical roots of revenge in Neolithic societies see Mansfield, *Gestalt of War,* pp. 41–54.

16. This claim is forcefully presented with reference to world history by Kenneth E. Boulding in his *The Meaning of the Twentieth Century* (New York: Harper & Row, 1964), pp. 75–103.

17. Of course, a very similar claim can be made about the nuclear predicament. Einstein's words at the head of this essay say just this. See also Berel Lang's essay, Chap. 5.

18. Boulding explicates the links among civilization, politics, and war by appealing to the economic forces behind the rise of the city. Two factors, he insists, were crucial for the emergence of the city-state as a new social-political entity: an economic surplus and a system of coercion. These factors are mutually connected. The city as a new type of human organization becomes a viable option only for societies that have already reached a certain level of surplus (required to maintain a large nonagricultural population); while it is only through a system of coercion that it becomes possible to manage (i.e., collect, expropriate, regulate) such a "common wealth" for urban life. Boulding, *Twentieth Century*, pp. 79–83.

19. Regular army constitutes the linkage between economic surplus and coercion: economic surplus is vital to fund and maintain regular forces, while the latter is

the necessary instrument to enforce the political (i.e., coercive) system. Ibid, p. 79.

20. See Kosta Tsipis, "The Arms Race as Posturing," in David Carlton and Carlo Schaerf, eds., *The Dynamics of the Arms Race* (London: Croom Helm, 1975), p. 81.
21. For a good discussion of various definitions of deterrence in the context of international politics see Patrick M. Morgan, *Deterrence: A Conceptual Analysis*, 2nd ed. (Beverly Hills: Sage Publications, 1983), especially chaps. 1 and 2.
22. See Franklin B. Weinstein, "The Concept of Commitment in International Relations," *Journal of Conflict Resolution* 13, no. 1 (1969): 39–56.
23. This neo-Clausewitzian idea was developed by a number of contemporary theoreticians. See Michael Howard, "Military Power and International Relations," in John Garnett, ed., *Theories of Peace and Security: A Reader in Contemporary Strategic Thought* (New York: Macmillian, 1970), pp. 41–49; Raymond Aron, *Peace and War*, trans. Richard Howard and Annette Barker Fox (New York: Praeger, 1968).
24. Patrick Morgan, *Deterrence*, Chap. two, distinguishes between two types of deterrence: deterrence in the broad sense as developed here ("general deterrence") and a special form of deterrent posture ("pure deterrence"). While general deterrence is the ever-present regulatory mechanism of war-avoidance and stability in the international arena, pure deterrence is an explicit threat, an infrequent occurrence. The former is a matter of long-term capabilities and interests; the latter is a matter of particular aggressive intentions. The context of pure deterrence typifies situations of actual crisis, when the option of resorting to military force is a very real one and not just hypothetical. For the purpose of our analysis, pure deterrence can be seen as a limiting case of deterrence in general. In fact, once war-avoidance is seen as the general principle of all deterrence forms, we can reformulate Morgan's distinction by appealing to our distinction between *military-system stability* and *geo-political stability* (see introduction to section I of this volume). What Morgan considers as the chief weakness of general deterrence—fuzziness, vagueness, and amorphousness— appears to us as crucial for understanding the kind of uncertainties involved in military deterrence under the regime of sovereign states.
25. In the case of a *mutual* deterrence system we must also add the requirement of system-stability; that is, deterrent threats to be effective must not prompt destabilizing countereffects as a response to the threats themselves.
26. See, for example, Robert Jervis, *Perceptions and Misperceptions in International Politics* (Princeton: Princeton University Press, 1976); idem, "Hypotheses on Misperceptions," *World Politics* 20 (1968): 454–79.
27. NATO's nuclear policy is now more controversial than ever. For a criticism of this policy, see McGeorge Bundy, George F. Kennan, Robert S. McNamara, and Gerard Smith, "Nuclear Weapons and the Atlantic Alliance," *Foreign Affairs* 60, no. 4 (1982): 753–68; see also George W. Ball, "The Cosmic Bluff," *The New York Review of Books*, 21 July 1983.
28. "The object of war is to attain a better peace . . . Hence it is essential to conduct war with constant regard to the peace you desire . . . Victory in the true sense implies that the state of peace, and of one's people, is better after the war

than before." B.H. Liddel Hart, *Strategy* (New York: The New American Library, 1974), pp. 353–74.

29. Michael Howard, "On Fighting a Nuclear War," *International Security* 5, no. 4 (1981): 14.

30. Bernard Brodie, ed., *The Absolute Weapon* (New York: Harcourt, Brace, 1946), p. 76.

31. For this claim see Michael Mandelbaum, *The Nuclear Question* (New York: Cambridge University Press, 1979), especially p. 279; also Stephen Kaplan, *Diplomacy of Power* (Washington, D.C.: Brookings Institution, 1981), especially pp. 667–77.

32. Often a justification for the policy of nuclear deterrence is given in the form of a semi-inductive argument in which the evidence for its success is the fact that so far no military confrontation between the superpowers has occurred. For two fundamental reasons, we believe this argument to be faulty. First, no connection has been demonstrated between the fact that war was avoided and the policy of nuclear deterrence. As Morgan points out (chap. 8, this volume), since our understanding of nuclear deterrence is very slight, we are not clear about the relationships between international politics and nuclear deterrence. In fact, some people may argue that it is in spite of this policy of nuclear deterrence that no nuclear war has taken place so far. Second, even if we see inductive evidence of the link between war avoidance and nuclear deterrence, this does not have much bearing on the future, for stability, an essential feature of successful nuclear deterrence, may be lacking in the future.

33. This problem is known in the literature as the usability paradox. See the Harvard Nuclear Study Group, *Living with Nuclear Weapons* (New York: Bantam, 1983), p. 34.

34. This problem is known in the literature as the Mutual Assured Deterrence (MAD) paradox. See John Holdren's essay, Chap. 2, and Schell, *Fate of the Earth*, pp. 200–203.

35. Schell, p. 202.

36. In the introduction to his excellent historical study *The Evolution of Nuclear Strategy* (New York: St. Martin Press, 1981), Lawrence Freedman writes, "the use of the word 'evolution' is somewhat misleading for it suggests progress along a learning curve. . . . I believe it to be false. What is impressive is the cyclical character of the debates." Without disputing anything in Freedman's reconstruction of the nuclear history that stands behind this judgment, we prefer to understand this cyclical movement in a semi-Hegelian dialectical fashion. Referring to the history in terms of dialectical movement highlights the sense of contradiction involved in the present historical stage—having elements of both MAD and counterforce in one policy—without losing the circular aspect of the history at large. Also see Aaron Friedberg, "A History of the U.S. Strategic doctrines—1945 to 1980," in Amos Perlmutter and John Gooch, eds., *Strategy and the Social Science* (London: Frank Cass, 1981), pp. 37–71; see also John Holdren's essay, Chap. 2, this volume.

37. On the controversy over the decision to drop the bomb on Hiroshima and Nagasaki, the literature is vast. See, for example, Gregg Herken, *The Winning Weapon* (New York: Random House, 1981); Daniel Yergin, *Shattered Peace: The Origins of the Cold War and the National Security State* (London: Handre Deutsch, 1977); L. Giovannitti and F. Freed, *The Decision to Drop the Bomb*

(London: Methuen & Co., 1967); and the recent exchange between Joseph Alsop and David Joravsky, "Was the Hiroshima Bomb Necessary?" *The New York Review of Books*, 23 October 1980, pp. 37–42.

38. See Freedman, *The Evolution of Nuclear Strategy*, especially pp. 45–91.
39. On this issue see note 27.
40. On the history of MAD, see Freedman, *Evolution*, pp. 225–54.
41. See David Holloway, *The Soviet Union and the Arms Race* (New Haven: Yale University Press, 1983).
42. See Herbert F. York, "Bilateral Negotiations and the Arms Race," *Scientific American* 249, no. 4 (October 1983): 149–60, and Holdren, Chap. 2, this volume.
43. Freedman, *Evolution*, pp. 351–54; see also Ted Greenwood, *Making the MIRV: A Study in Defense Decision Making* (Cambridge: Ballinger, 1975).
44. See Theodore Draper, "Nuclear Temptations," *The New York Review of Books*, 19 January 1984, pp. 42–50.
45. The paradigm for this approach is Colin S. Gray and Keith Payne, "Victory is Possible," *Foreign Policy* 59 (1980): 14–27; also Colin S. Gray, "Nuclear Strategy: The Case for a Theory of Victory," *International Security* 4, no. 1 (1979): 54–87.
46. For a good discussion and an historical survey of the concept of limited nuclear war see Ian Clark, *Limited Nuclear War* (Princeton: Princeton University Press, 1982).
47. McGeorge Bundy, "A Matter of Survival," *The New York Review of Books*, 17 March 1983, p. 3.
48. It is, of course, true that both public support and the resource base, though irrelevant to the course of the war once it has started, do place limits on the arms build-up occurring prior to the war. Yet, the history of the nuclear arms race has shown that these factors have not been strong enough to place effective limits on the amount of destructive power that has accumulated, at least in the case of the great powers.
49. Sagan, "Nuclear War and Climatic Catastrophe."
50. For a valuable discussion of realism, see Richard Wasserstrom, "On the Morality of War: A Preliminary Inquiry," in Wasserstrom, ed., *War and Morality* (Belmont, Calif: Wadsworth, 1970), pp. 78–85.
51. On the nature and criteria of the existence of social or conventional moral rules, see H.L.A. Hart, *The Concept of Law* (Oxford University Press, 1961), especially chap. 5.
52. For a discussion of the conventional rules of war, see Richard Wasserstrom, "The Laws of War," *The Monist* 56 (1972): 1–19.
53. James T. Johnson, *Just War Tradition and the Restraint of War* (Princeton University Press, 1981), p. 41.
54. Ibid., pp. xxi-xxii.
55. For a thorough discussion of *jus ad bellum* and *jus in bello* in just-war theory, see William O'Brien, *The Conduct of Just and Limited War* (New York: Praeger, 1981).
56. Ibid., pp. 38–40.
57. This is rejected as a moral feature of self-defense by Jan Narveson; see his "Pacifism: A Philosophical Analysis" in Wasserstrom, ed., *War and Morality*, pp. 74–75.

58. O'Brien, *Just and Limited War*, p. 42.
59. On the political function of the just-war tradition, see the essays by Jean Bethke Elshtain and Stephen Toulmin, Chaps. 13 and 19.
60. On these points, see the essay by Joseph Margolis, Chap. 7.
61. In cases where all the actions an agent can perform in some situation will bring about more disvalue than value, the morally correct action, according to a consequentialist theory, will be the one that brings about the least disvalue. This qualification, especially relevant to the morality of war, should be understood as part of the account.
62. It is a notorious problem that not all noncombatants may be morally innocent, since some may indirectly contribute greatly to the war effort. (Correspondingly, many combatants may be morally innocent if, for example, they are made to fight against their will.) This problem, however, is irrelevant where nuclear weapons are concerned: because of the number of deaths involved in their use, many persons would die who are morally innocent on anyone's account (young children, for example). On this point see John Ford, "The Morality of Obliteration Bombing," in Wasserstrom, *War and Morality*, pp. 15–41.
63. Johnson, *Just War Tradition*, pp. xii, 19.
64. But the principle of proportionality is not a purely consequentialist moral principle, one reason being that the value pursued in consequentialist moral theories requires a consideration of the interests of all persons, whereas the value the principle of proportionality weighs against the disvalue of the violence is in terms of the interests of the attacking nation only. Neither is the principle of proportionality merely prudential, for the disvalue of the violence is in terms of the interests of others, that is, those being attacked.
65. For an important discussion of the application of the just-war tradition to the use of nuclear weapons, see the U.S. Catholic bishops' pastoral letter, "The Challenge of Peace," *Origins* 13, no. 1 (19 May 1983).
66. This position is argued for by Paul Ramsey. See his *The Just War: Force and Political Responsibility* (New York: Scribner's, 1968).
67. Biological and chemical weapons may be exceptions to this claim.
68. Another crucial moral difference between nuclear weapons and nonnuclear weapons is the capacity nuclear arsenals may possess to destroy the human species. Such destruction would destroy everything of moral value that would accrue to future generations. A further morally relevant difference is the effect that nuclear war, in contrast with nonnuclear war, would have on species of nonhuman animals.
69. The question of how well deterrence policy works is discussed in the essays of Jefferson McMahan, Arne Naess, and Russell Hardin, Chaps. 10, 17, and 23. See also Douglas Lackey, "Missiles and Morals: A Utilitarian Look at Nuclear Deterrence," *Philosophy and Public Affairs* 11 (1982): 189–231.
70. On this point see the essay by Patrick Morgan, Chap. 8.
71. The wrongful intentions principle is discussed by Gregory Kavka, "Some Paradoxes of Deterrence," *Journal of Philosophy* 75 (1978): 285–302.
72. Some of these criticisms and others are discussed by Douglas Lackey, Chap. 16.
73. John Hare argues in Chap. 9 that the threat to retaliate is a bluff. He finds strong reasons nevertheless to regard nuclear deterrence as morally unacceptable.

74. On this point see Douglas Lackey's essay, Chap. 16, and also the discussion of Paul Ramsey's position in Michael Walzer's *Just and Unjust Wars* (New York: Basic, 1977), pp. 278–83.

75. This view is not universally shared. It is rejected, for example, by Paul Ramsey and by the Catholic bishops in their pastoral letter. But we would argue that attempts to salvage the political relevance of the just-war tradition by interpreting it to permit nuclear deterrence surrender the tradition's moral authority, turning it into (to use Jean Elshtain's phrase) a form of "modified realism."

76. Walzer, *Just and Unjust Wars*, p. 282.

77. The problem of the relation between morality and prudence is complex and difficult, and nothing we say here will shed much light on the general theoretical issue. We shall simply assume that there is some opposition between them, ignoring the arguments that ultimately they are, in one way or another, completely co-extensional.

78. See Kavka, "Some Paradoxes," the Catholic bishops' pastoral letter, Walzer, *Just and Unjust Wars*, and Russell Hardin's essay, Chap. 10. See also Terry Nardin's essay, Chap. 15, for a critique of Walzer in defense of the moral tradition.

79. The argument against nuclear deterrence on prudential grounds is similar to the argument against it on consequentialist moral grounds. See the references in note 69 above.

80. Paradoxically, counterforce deterrence is often recommended on the moral grounds that it is in conformity with the principle of discrimination whereas minimum, countercity deterrence is not. We have argued against this view in the previous section. In any case, the riskiness factor is more important for just-war revisionism, since, in sanctioning deterrence at all, it has already given greater moral weight to the consequences than to the principle of discrimination.

81. Walzer, *Just and Unjust Wars*, p. 283.

82. Schell, *Fate of the Earth*, p. 226.

83. See Einstein, note 1, and Schell, ibid.

84. The three possibilities mentioned below are discussed in Chapters 22-25.

85. We would like to acknowledge all the other authors in this volume, whose papers were fresh in our minds as we wrote this essay, and whose ideas certainly contributed to our arguments in many more ways than the few we have specifically acknowledged in earlier footnotes. In addition, we thank the following people for their comments and criticisms on earlier drafts of this essay: Scott Brophy, Larry Campbell, Robert S. Cohen, Haim Gans, Mark Glouberman, Richard Rorty, Miriam Shuchman, and Gary Stahl.

PART I

THE PRESENT THREAT:
NUCLEAR ARMS AND NUCLEAR WAR

In the U.S. and Western Europe, it is now commonly assumed and often asserted that the risk of nuclear war has reached unprecedented peaks. The threat of nuclear war, it is claimed, is more real and concrete than ever before. This basic conviction has given rise to a new consciousness. Born of a concern that ten years ago was only remotely felt by most of us, the project of preventing nuclear war has become the dominant moral-existential commitment of our time. No longer can political questions concerning nuclear weapons be considered only as a matter of international politics; today these questions have implications for the survival of human civilization, perhaps even of the species.

Are these concerns justified? Is the risk of nuclear war now greater than in the past? This section seeks to answer these questions. Its task is twofold. First, it will provide a factual basis for succeeding essays, furnishing the basic information about nuclear-weapons policies and the potential causes and long-term effects of nuclear war. Second, based on this information, this section will justify and explain the claim that the risk of nuclear war is now greater than before.

When assessing the likelihood of the outbreak of war, *two* distinguishable (though interrelated) factors must be considered: (a) the geo-political situation, which has a greater or lesser potential to undergo crises that could spark a war; and (b) the military-strategic system, within which geo-political crises are interpreted, evaluated and responded to. War is never a by-product of a geo-political crisis alone. A geo-political crisis leads to war only if the military-strategic system has propensities to become destabilized under those circumstances. These two factors lead to two different dimensions for assessing the risks of nuclear war: (A) the stability of the present world-order in terms of the likelihood of geo-political crises arising (*geo-political stability*); and (B) the stability of the present military-strategic system in terms of the likelihood of a failure of nuclear deterrence under crisis situations (*military-system stability*).

The authors in Chapters 2 and 3 examine the risk of nuclear war from these two perspectives. John Holdren looks at the nuclear threat from the "inside," from the perspective of military-system stability. In presenting the main trends and features of the nuclear arms race from 1945 to the present, he shows how technological innovations, strategic doctrines, political pressures, and national perceptions have closely interacted in each phase of the race, and how they have led us to the present predicament. In outlining this history, Holdren sets out the reasons why the current phase of the nuclear arms race is, indeed, more alarming than before.

On the technology side, the introduction of MIRV (Multiple Independently targetable Re-entry Vehicle) technology, along with increased accuracy of ballistic guidance-systems, has led to a tremendous rise in the size and quality of both superpowers' nuclear arsenals. These changes in weapon systems marked also a return to counterforce strategy—viewing nuclear weapons as genuine "war-fighting" instruments to be used against the opponent's military forces. The upshot of all those developments, as Holdren details, has been the destabilization of the entire strategic system: a fundamental shift from an emphasis on a retaliatory or second-strike posture to a war-fighting or first-strike posture. During peacetime, such a strategic posture may increase tensions and suspicions between the superpowers, while at times of crisis it encourages temptations of preemptive attacks.

In Chapter 3, Paul and Anne Ehrlich assess the risk of nuclear conflict from the "outside," from the perspective of the geo-political stability of the present world-order. Looking at the present international world-order in terms of a single *holistic* ecosystem, the Ehrlichs call our attention to a variety of environmental problems that constitute a serious and growing threat to the stability of the human ecosystem. From this ecological perspective, various aspects of the current Population-Resources-Energy (P-R-E) crises are analyzed to show how they could lead to a heightening of international tensions that increase the risk of nuclear war. Their prediction is unequivocal and gloomy: "If current population-resource-environment trends are allowed to continue, a nuclear holocaust seems nearly certain within the lifetimes of today's children."

The other side of the linkage between nuclear war and environmental problems is that nuclear war would have catastrophic consequences on our ecosystem. Until very recently, studies about the effects of nuclear war were mostly limited to consideration of immediate and local affects (e.g., blast, fire, radiation), while the issue of the global and long-term ecological consequences were neglected. The Ehrlichs have been actively engaged in a series of comprehensive studies on the subject (the "nuclear winter" studies), and the second part of their paper presents some of those new findings. Even making allowance for the uncertainties, a shocking picture of the post-nuclear-war world emerges. With existing arsenals, the Ehrlichs conclude, nuclear war could bring about the end of civilization in the Northern Hemisphere, not excluding the possibility of the extinction of *Homo sapiens* as a biological species.

2
THE DYNAMICS OF
THE NUCLEAR ARMS RACE:
HISTORY, STATUS, PROSPECTS

John P. Holdren

INTRODUCTION

The simplest explanation of the nuclear arms race is that it has been the product of the inventiveness and the myopia of weapons designers on both sides, reinforced by the entrenched economic and political power of the weapons manufacturers. The designers have been allowed to let their imaginations run free, so the argument goes, and they have been ably supported by the manufacturers who advocated building and deploying whatever weapons the imaginations of the designers could conceive. Lord Solly Zuckerman, former chief scientific advisor to the government of the United Kingdom, has described the role of the nuclear weaponeers this way:

> The men in the nuclear weapons laboratories of both sides have succeeded in creating a world with an irrational foundation, on which a new set of political realities has in turn had to be built. They have become the alchemists of our times, working in secret ways that cannot be divulged, casting spells which embrace us all. They may never have been in battle, they may never have experienced the devastation of war; but they know how to devise the means of destruction. And the more destructive power there is, so one must assume they imagine, the greater the chance of military success.[1]

The simplicity of this "mad scientist" picture of the nuclear arms race is appealing, and it unquestionably contains a good deal of truth. But Lord Zuckerman would be the first to agree that it is not the whole story. The weapons makers alone did not cause the arms race. It has also been driven by the theories of military strategists (not always concocted in response to possibilities provided by the weaponeers), by the very real competition for global influence between two incompatible ideologies, by the dreams and fears of generals, and by the beliefs of bureaucrats and politicians; and it has depended on the consent of the public. In short, the nuclear arms race can only be explained as the interaction and coevolution of weapons technologies, military doctrines, international power struggles, domestic political pressures, and perceptions (by decisionmakers and the public) on both sides.

I attempt to trace the intricate dynamics of the nuclear arms race through its four-decade history for two compelling reasons. First, the best way to comprehend completely the nature and the dangers of our present predicament is to understand how we got into it. Second, this background is an essential prerequisite for thinking intelligently about ways to get out. The remainder of this chapter, then, is divided into three parts: a history of the nuclear arms race, emphasizing the interactions of technologies, doctrines, politics, and perceptions; a description of the key features of the present predicament, including the characteristics of nuclear and conventional military forces and the implications of these characteristics for the probability of nuclear war; and a discussion of the problems and prospects of nuclear arms control and disarmament.[2]

HISTORY

Underlying Phenomena

Four phrases provide the key to understanding the history of the nuclear arms race: the military industrial complex, the action-reaction syndrome, worst-case analysis, and the fallacy of the last move.

The military-industrial complex includes not only the designers and manufacturers of weapons, whose influence on the arms race has been documented by Zuckerman and many others,[3] but also: (a) the armed forces, whose branches compete with one another—as well as with their counterparts on the opposing side—in upgrading their arsenals; (b) the governmental defense bureaucracies, which maintain and expand their influence by guarding jealously the weapons programs under their jurisdiction and by campaigning tirelessly for new ones; and (c) the defense-oriented legislators on the Western side who stay in office with the help of the steady flow of money they steer into military facilities and defense industries in their districts.[4]

The action-reaction syndrome means simply that each time one side develops a new weapon or refinement, or takes a major geo-political initiative, the other side feels obliged to emulate or counter it. The reaction may be in kind (for example, one side deploys a particular type of missile because its adversary is doing so); it may be a specific countermeasure (for example, deployment or more air defenses by one side to counter more bombers on the other); or it may be a general increase in weapons development and deployment in response to a broadly threatening move by the adversary (such as the 1950 U.S. military buildup in reaction to the Communist invasion of South Korea).[5]

Worst-case analysis means that each side tends to assume the worst about both the military capabilities and the intentions of the other side, and tries to develop its own capability to cope with this "worst case," preferably with a further margin of safety for the sake of prudence. The U.S. government argues that, given its responsibilities not only for the defense of the nation but for the defense of democracy, to do any less would be irresponsible. The government of the Soviet Union, of course, makes the same argument, substituting "communism" for "democracy." But both sides cannot simultaneously enjoy the "margin of safety" in military capability vis-à-vis the other that each desires. (The impossibility arises from the dual-purpose capabilities—offensive or defensive—of many categories of weapons. If it were possible for each side to possess strictly defensive weapons in excess of what would be required to neutralize the offensive forces of the other side, the problem of worst-case assessments on both sides would be much less troublesome.)

The fallacy of the last move is the supposition by either side that one more weapons system (or any other strengthening of military force) would provide the margin of safety—or other advantage—it seeks. It is a fallacy because, although each side would like to have the advantage of the last move, neither will concede that advantage to the other; thus there is never a "last move," only "action-reaction."

These four phenomena, embedded as they are in a context of continuous East-West competition for geo-political advantage, amount to a prescription for an unending arms race. Their effects have been compounded, moreover, by what a psychoanalyst of nations might call Russia's "invasion complex" and the United States's "Pearl Harbor complex." The Russians, who have been invaded four times in this century, have an almost pathological preoccupation with ensuring that it never happens again. Americans, who were surprised at Pearl Harbor, are unusally obsessed with the possibility of "bolt from the blue" sneak attacks. These fears have contributed to the size and character of the respective military buildups on both sides, and continue to do so.

The Rhetoric of Fear

Throughout the history of the nuclear arms race, leaders on both sides have used rhetoric about nuclear forces—and about intentions relating to their use—for two main purposes: as intimidation aimed at reducing the adversary's inclination to counter or initiate attempts to alter the geo-political status quo, and to frighten their own society into bearing the economic burdens of high military spending. A prominent example of rhetoric to intimidate was the much-publicized 1954 speech by U.S. Secretary of State John Foster Dulles, in which he expressed the U.S. policy to deter Communist aggression by depending "primarily upon a great capacity to retaliate, instantly, by means and at places of our own choosing."[6] Corresponding examples on the other side were Soviet Communist Party Chairman Nikita Khrushchev's premature boast in 1960 that "the Soviet Union is now the world's strongest military power,"[7] his gloating at about the same time about imminent Soviet superiority in intercontinental ballistic missiles, and his celebrated threat to "bury" the West. It is difficult to imagine that such rhetoric, notwithstanding its intention merely to intimidate, did not in fact simply heighten the resolve of the adversary to strengthen his own forces.

The arms race that these factors have helped to produce has been (and continues to be) extremely expensive—consistently claiming from 5 to 7 percent of the Gross National Product of the United States and perhaps twice this percentage of the substantially smaller GNP of the Soviet Union.[8] These costs have posed something of a problem for political and military leaders, who, to varying degrees, need the consent of the people to proceed. The bill for the arms race must, one way or another, be paid out of national wealth and/or consumption, and people pay most willingly for armaments when they are frightened. Thus arises the second rationale for a rhetoric of fear. Of course, the rhetoric motivated in this way is heard by one's adversaries as well as by the intended audience at home, and thus it, too, undoubtedly has served at times to heat up the arms race as well as to finance it.

It is instructive to look, on the U.S. side, at the remarkable uniformity of arms race rhetoric in this second category over the past 30 years:

— In 1952, Dwight D. Eisenhower ran for president on the "bomber gap," asserting that the previous administration had permitted the Soviet Union to develop a dangerous lead in intercontinental bombers. After his election, Eisenhower told the American people that sacrifice would be necessary to support the expenditures needed to close this threatening gap. (When the facts became known some years later, it turned out that the "gap" had been in favor of the U.S. The Soviet Union had no operational intercontinental bombers at all until 1956.)
— In 1960, John F. Kennedy ran for president on the "missile gap," depicting (with the assistance of the ill-considered rhetoric of Nikita Krushchev, mentioned above) a growing risk of Soviet superiority that would soon become critical. In office, he avowed that sacrifice would be needed to close the gap. (Later, it turned out that, again, the gap had been in the United States's favor.)
— In 1980, Ronald Reagan ran for president proclaiming a "window of vulnerability": our nuclear deterrent was in growing jeopardy because of the purported vulnerability of our land-based intercontinental ballistic missiles to a first strike by increasingly accurate Soviet ICBMs. In office, he declared that the Soviets enjoyed a "margin of nuclear superiority," and he called on the American people to ante up for massive increases in military spending to close the gap.

Of course, that the rhetoric about Soviet superiority was wrong in the 1950s and 1960s does not prove that it is wrong in the 1980s, but certainly there is some cause for skepticism. The present state of the East-West military balance will be explored later in this chapter, but first it's appropriate to look more closely at the history of who had what and when.

Who Started It?

The unpleasant truth is that, in the action-reaction pattern of technological developments in the nuclear arms race, it has usually been the United States that acted—by introducing a new class of weapons—and the Soviets who reacted. This pattern is displayed in Table 2.1.[9] In some of these cases—for example, the tests of practical hydrogen bombs and of intercontinental ballistic missiles —the close succession of the "firsts" on the two sides suggests that what occurred was likely the outcome of a close race to a common goal rather than the action-reaction syndrome. On the other hand, it was probably each side's conviction that the other would pursue the development in any case that furthered the research in these instances.

As Table 2.1 indicates, the United States actually had a monopoly on nuclear weapons from 1945 to 1949 and a monopoly on the capacity to deliver them in quantity against the adversary's homeland until 1956. Because it enjoyed the use of airbases in Europe and elsewhere around the periphery of the Soviet Union, the United States had the capability to launch bombing attacks on that country using even the medium-range B-29 and B-50 aircraft that were its only nuclear-capable

Table 2.1 Milestones in the Nuclear Arms Race

Milestone	Year of achievement USA	USSR
Test of atomic (fission) bomb	1945	1949[a]
Deployment of intercontinental bomber	1948	1956
Deployment of jet bomber	1951	1954
Test of practical hydrogen (fusion) bomb[b]	1954	1955[c]
Deployment of tactical nuclear weapons in Europe	1954	1957
Deployment of nuclear artillery	1954	1980
Strategic reconnaissance for targeting	1955	1962
Test of intercontinental ballistic missile	1958	1957
Deployment of ICBM	1959	1960
Deployment of sub-launched ballistic missiles	1960	1964[d]
Deployment of solid-fuel ICBM	1963	1968
Deployment of swing-wing, supersonic bomber	1967	1974
Test of multiple independent re-entry vehicles	1968	1973
Deployment of MIRV	1970	1975

[a] Fission bombs were subsequently tested successfully by the United Kingdom (1952), France (1960), China (1964), and India (1974).

[b] The first nuclear test in which fusion reactions contributed to the yield was conducted by the U.S. in May 1951, a feat not matched by the Soviets until August 1953. The first demonstration of the principle that permits fusion explosions of essentially unlimited power was a U.S. test conducted 1 November 1952. None of these early devices was a deliverable weapon, however.

[c] Fusion bombs were subsequently tested successfully by the United Kingdom (1957), China (1967), and France (1968).

[d] The early Soviet missile subs, unlike their U.S. counterparts, could not launch their missiles while submerged. The first "modern" Soviet missile sub (nuclear-powered, capable of firing while submerged) was deployed only in 1968.

bombers between 1945 and 1948. The Soviets had no forward bases from which to strike the United States, and they had neither intercontinental bombers nor in-flight refuelling capability for medium-range bombers until the advent of the long-range TU-20 "Bear" and MYA-4 "Bison" bombers in 1956/57.[10]

Of course, the nuclear arms race has been a race in numbers of weapons as well. Some of the key features of this quantitative arms race from 1950 to 1980 are shown in Tables 2.2 and 2.3. Not included in these tables are the "tactical" or "battle-field" nuclear weapons, such as short-range nuclear-capable missiles and aircraft, nuclear artillery, and nuclear mines. Tables 2.2 and 2.3 show that although the Soviet Union posed a growing nuclear threat to Europe from the early 1950s onward, its intercontinental strategic nuclear forces were much smaller than those of the United States well into the 1960s. (The validity of this statement would not be altered if the Soviet sub-launched missiles assumed to be targeted on Europe and Asia were considered available for the intercontinental mission.) The few hundred nuclear weapons theoretically deliverable against the United States by the Soviet

Union as early as 1960 did represent a force to be taken seriously, however, since that number of bombs could virtually obliterate every major city in the country, along with much of its industrial capacity. The notion of meaningful Soviet "inferiority" at this time rested in part on the idea that the bombers carrying the vast majority of the Soviet weapons would have great difficulty penetrating U.S. air defenses.

The essence of the asymmetry in the U.S. and Soviet strategic nuclear capabilities through the mid-1960s had to do with the credibility of striking first. Until 1966 or 1967, the U.S. intercontinental forces were so superior in every category—numbers and quality of bombers, of land-based missiles, and of missile submarines—that it was possible to contemplate a first strike directed against the much smaller Soviet forces, using only a fraction of the U.S. arsenal, in which a large part of the Soviet retaliatory capacity would be destroyed before it could be used. The Soviet leaders would then face the choice of capitulating or launching a relatively weak retaliatory blow, with the latter course sure to result in their country's complete destruction by the sizable remaining forces of the U.S. At the same time, no such "attractive" first-strike option was open to the Soviet Union, because its forces were insufficient to destroy a suitably large fraction of the U.S. forces in an initial blow. This asymmetry—that the United States could and the Soviet Union could not credibly threaten to resort to the first use of intercontinental nuclear weapons against its adversary's homeland—gave meaning to the term "nuclear dominance."

Uses and Consequences of U.S. Dominance

During the approximately two decades of overwhelming U.S. nuclear advantage from 1945 until the mid-1960s, the United States left little doubt that it considered the use—and the threat of use—of its nuclear might in support of its interests to be acceptable. It is not widely appreciated, however, that the U.S. use of nuclear weapons against Japan at the end of World War II may well have been intended as much to impress and intimidate the Soviet Union as to bring the war with Japan to a prompt conclusion.[11] And still less is the general public aware of the number of occasions in the postwar period on which the United States threatened, explicitly or implicitly, to use nuclear weapons in support of its interests. For example:

— In June 1948, at the outset of the Berlin blockade, President Truman dispatched two groups of B-29 bombers to England in a transparent show of nuclear muscle. It became known much later that no nuclear bombs actually accompanied these aircraft, but the impression at the time—presumably shared by the Soviets—was the opposite.[12]

— In November 1950, President Truman in a press conference warned that the U.S. might use nuclear weapons against the Chinese communists in Korea.[13]

— In February and July 1953, the new Eisenhower administration threatened secretly to use nuclear weapons against China, as a means of forcing a settlement in Korea.[14]

— In 1954, the use of U.S. tactical nuclear weapons to relieve the French in the siege of Dienbienphu in Indo-China was seriously considered, and some reports hold that three weapons actually were offered to the French. Around the same

Table 2.2   Intercontinental Strategic Nuclear Forces, 1950-80

	1950	1955	1960	1965	1970	1975	1980
Intercontinental bombers[a]							
United States	520	1309	1735	807	501	489	428
Soviet Union	0	0	145	195	195	189	156
Intercontinental land-based missiles[b]							
United States	0	0	42	854	1054	1054	1052
Soviet Union	0	0	4	224	1220	1267	1018
Intercontinental sea-based missiles[c]							
United States	0	0	32	496	616	616	536
Soviet Union	0	0	0	15	41	196	522
Intercontinental warhead delivery capability[d]							
United States	500?	2310	4362	4002	3689	7725	9200
Soviet Union	0	0	294	629	1651	1875	6156

[a] Includes bombers capable of reaching the respective homelands on round-trip missions, allowing for basing and in-flight refueling capabilities, and estimated to be assigned to such missions.

[b] Includes missiles of intercontinental range estimated to be assigned to missions against the respective homelands. Excluded are 290 (1975) to 380 (1980) Soviet SS-11 and SS-19 variable-range ballistic missiles assigned to targets in Europe and Asia. (See Table 2.3.)

[c] Includes submarine-launched ballistic missiles estimated to be assigned to missions against the respective homelands. Excluded are 40 US Polaris/Poseidon missiles assigned to the Supreme Allied Commander for Europe from 1965 on, and 36 (1960) to 445 (1980) Soviet sub-launched ballistic missiles assigned to regional missions. (See Table 2.3.)

[d] Includes bombs and warheads deliverable by the above-listed vehicles at their rated payloads. The delivery capability exceeded the actual number of weapons on hand until at least 1955.

Source: Largely adapted from Robert P. Berman and John C. Baker, *Soviet Strategic Forces: Requirements and Responses* (The Brookings Institution, 1982), Tables 3.1 and 3.2; supplemented by Stockholm International Peace Research Institute, *The Arms Race and Arms Control* (Cambridge, MA: Oelgeschlager, Gunn, & Hain, 1982); International Institute for Strategic Studies, *The Military Balance, 1982-83* (London, 1982); and David Alan Rosenberg, "U.S. Nuclear Stockpile, 1945 to 1950," *Bulletin of the Atomic Scientists* (May 1982): 25-30.

time, Secretary of State John Foster Dulles warned the Chinese that intervention on their part would produce "grave consequences," hinting that these might include the use of nuclear weapons against China itself.[15]

— In 1958, President Eisenhower directed the armed forces to prepare to use nuclear weapons against an anticipated Iraqi move into the Kuwaiti oilfields.[16]

From the time the North Atlantic Treaty was ratified in 1949, moreover, it has been the explicit U.S. commitment to the NATO alliance that this country would resort to the first use of nuclear weapons if that were deemed necessary to repel a Soviet invasion of Western Europe.[17] This position was based initially on the widely shared assessment that the Soviets enjoyed massive conventional military superiority (measured in quantities of soldiers, artillery, and tanks) in Europe, and on the perception of NATO leaders that the U.S. and European publics would not tolerate the levels of economic sacrifice and military mobilization needed to match the Soviet conventional forces. (Some new analyses, based in part on recently declassified documents from the early post-World War II period, suggest that the Soviet conventional forces were by no means as formidable at the time as the official NATO position indicated.[18] As discussed further below, there is reason to think that the capabilities of Soviet conventional forces vis-à-vis those of NATO are still being exaggerated in the collective and individual statements of NATO governments today.)

In any case, the official rationale at the end of the 1940s for embracing a U.S. nuclear deterrrent against a Soviet conventional attack was that this was our only "affordable" option. Using the specter of unmatchable Soviet conventional power as the justification for building up enormous nuclear forces had the attraction of being readily salable to the public, an asset unlikely to have been shared by some of the other rationales that probably were in the heads of U.S. decisionmakers at the time.[19] Whatever the rationales, this posture of nuclear deterrence of conventional threats depended for its credibility on the strategic nuclear superiority that gave the U.S. "escalation dominance": if NATO resorted to nuclear weapons to blunt a Soviet conventional attack and the Soviets responded in kind, the U.S. could always threaten to escalate to the use of intercontinental nuclear forces.

It is not my intention to pass judgment on whether the U.S. use of nuclear weapons at the end of World War II and its subsequent threats to use nuclear weapons were justifiable. I wish simply to use this history to make two points. First, the idea that nuclear bombs are actually usable as military weapons and as instruments of coercion in international affairs is an invention of the Western powers—the United States and its postwar allies. The Soviets have subsequently done their share of nuclear saber-rattling but, contrary to the impression sometimes conveyed by the authorities in Washington, D.C., we did it first.

Second, for much of the history of the nuclear arms race, the Soviets have perceived themselves (with reason) as engaged in a desperate struggle to catch up. They did not like having their freedom of action constrained by U.S. nuclear dominance, any more than we would have liked the reverse. This circumstance exacerbated what many authorities consider a historical Russian inferiority complex, which seems to have led the Soviets to deploy almost indiscriminately whatever weapons they have been able to develop, and to react to U.S. advances by building larger and more numerous versions of the same thing—albeit, in most cases, five years or so later.

Two Soviet Buildups

Throughout the 1950s, the Soviets were so far behind the United States in long-range nuclear weaponry that they may have entertained little hope of closing the gap; perhaps they simply decided that the massive effort necessary to do so was not worth the trouble. As Table 2.3 reveals, they instead poured much of their effort during this period into medium-range nuclear weaponry—less sophisticated and less expensive than the intercontinental variety—with which they could threaten America's European allies. In this sense, their strategic deterrent against an attack on their homeland by the intercontinental forces of the United States was to hold Europe "hostage."

Some people would have argued that the massive conventional forces of the Warsaw Pact were sufficient in themselves to accomplish the desired hostage holding—and indeed this is all the Soviets had in the period of U.S. nuclear monopoly until 1949. But the Soviets recognized that backing up the Red Army with nuclear weapons targeted on Europe would be essential to maintain the credibility of their threat in the face of nuclear-armed NATO adversaries. As Table 2.3 indicates, the Soviet capability to deliver medium-range nuclear weapons against Europe surpassed NATO's capability to respond in kind (leaving aside the enormous intercontinental forces of the U.S.) between 1955 and 1960.

In a prime example of the overbuilding mentioned above, the Soviets continued to expand their medium-range nuclear forces through the 1960s and 1970s, reaching levels well in excess of any imaginable need. Perhaps they were continuing to try to compensate for inferiority at the intercontinental level. Just as likely, the same technological momentum, bureaucratic inertia, and military empire-building known to operate in the West made it difficult for them to stop. (Additionally, these and other Soviet force levels were and are inflated by a Soviet reluctance to decommission weapons when they are obsolete or no longer needed. The Soviet medium-range bomber totals for 1970 through the present, for example, are dominated by 580 1954-vintage TU-16 "Badgers," whose U.S. counterpart was retired from service in 1966.)

At the beginning of the 1960s, the Soviet leadership evidently decided to rectify the imbalance in intercontinental nuclear forces by deploying some of their abundance of medium-range nuclear missiles in Cuba where they could easily cover the major targets in the United States. (Perhaps the Soviets regarded their planned deployments in Cuba as a straightforward counter to the medium-range U.S. Thor and Jupiter missiles being deployed on their own periphery in Turkey, Italy, and England.) In any case, the Soviets apparently underestimated the U.S. reaction to this move. In 1962, President Kennedy used this country's conventional military superiority in the region and the explicit threat of nuclear war to force the Soviets to back down and remove the missiles.

In a clever piece of statesmanship, Kennedy gave Khrushchev a way to save face at home: in "exchange" for the Soviets' removal of their missiles from Cuba, Kennedy promised to remove the Thors and Jupiters from Europe and Turkey. (It had already been decided that these were provocative, vulnerable, and unnecessary since their targets could be covered as effectively by U.S. sub-launched missiles and the new Minuteman ICBM.) Kennedy also promised to refrain from invading Cuba, a concession Khrushchev later insisted in his memoirs had been his main aim in threatening the deployments in the first place.[20] This last claim notwithstanding, most of the evidence indicates that the Soviets were frustrated and humiliated by the Cuban missile affair. Khrushchev lasted only two more years in power, and his successors initiated a massive buildup of Soviet intercontinental nuclear forces clearly intended to end the U.S. dominance that had contributed to their humiliation in 1962.

This new Soviet buildup, which became apparent starting in 1965, initially emphasized land-based intercontinental ballistic missiles. Between 1966 and 1975 the Soviets introduced six new types of ICBMs, including their first solid-fueled ICBM (the SS-13) and one giant model (the SS-18) with twice the payload of the largest ICBM the United States had ever deployed.[21] (Having failed to duplicate U.S. feats of miniaturization of both warheads and guidance systems, the Soviets needed much larger payloads to deliver the same explosive yield.) On a parallel track somewhat behind the ICBM program, the Soviets also introduced four new submarine-launched ballistic missiles (SLBMs) between 1968 and 1978. Another followed in 1981/82. No corresponding effort was made to upgrade the Soviet intercontinental bomber force; for a variety of reasons (psychological and historical/institutional, as well as technological) the Soviets value missiles far more highly than bombers for intercontinental missions.[22]

The result of this buildup is evident in Table 2.2. The number of Soviet land-based ICBMs assigned to intercontinental roles nearly quintupled between 1965 and 1975, a period in which the number of U.S. ICBMs grew by 23 percent. Indeed, the number of Soviet ICBMs passed the corresponding U.S. figure before 1970. And if one counts as "intercontinental" those Soviet missiles that have this capability but are now believed to be assigned shorter-range, regional missions (as was done, for example, throughout the two phases of the Strategic Arms Limitation Talks between the two superpowers), the Soviet numerical advantage in land-based ICBMs by 1975 was about 1.5 to 1.

With respect to numbers of submarine-launched ballistic missiles, the Soviets passed the United States in 1975, if one counts all the SLBMs on both sides. If one excludes from the category of "intercontinental" sea-based missiles those parts of the submarine forces on both sides believed to be assigned regional roles, the Soviet Union caught up in numbers of intercontinental SLBMs only around 1980.

Was the United States Standing Still?

One cannot dispute the reality of the two Soviet nuclear buildups —of regional and intercontinental forces—just described. But it is a serious distortion to suggest, as the Reagan administration has done repeatedly, that U.S. nuclear capabilities were standing still during the 15 years between 1965 and 1980, when most of the Soviet expansion took place. It is true that the numbers of U.S. intercontinental missiles, land-based and sub-launched, increased during this period by less than 25 percent, while the size of the U.S. intercontinental bomber force fell by almost half. But the number of nuclear bombs and warheads deliverable against the Soviet Union—a far more meaningful index of destructive capacity than missiles and bombers—increased during this period from 4,000 to more than 9,000 (see Table 2.2). By this measure, the Soviet Union had not caught up with the United States in intercontinental nuclear forces even by 1980 (nor have they today), and this remains true even if regionally assigned but intercontinentally capable forces are counted in the intercontinental category.

In addition to the quantitative increase of more than 5,000 U.S. intercontinental nuclear bombs and warheads during the 1965— 80 period when the Reagan adminis-

Table 2.3 Regional Strategic Nuclear Forces, 1950-80

	1950	1955	1960	1965	1970	1975	1980
Medium-range bombers[a]							
United States	45	147	130	192	192	164	164
European NATO	70	178	276	226	190	148	115
China	0	0	0	12	18	60	90
Soviet Union	n.a.	1296	1296	880	724	660	655
Medium- and intermediate-range land-based missiles[b]							
United States	0	0	105	0	0	0	0
European NATO	0	0	0	0	0	18	18
China	0	0	0	0	0	80	122
Soviet Union	0	0	200	705	897	918	960
Regional sea-based missiles[c]							
United States	0	0	0	40	40	40	40
European NATO	0	0	0	0	48	112	128
Soviet Union	0	0	36	105	365	569	445
Regional warhead delivery capability[d]							
United States	n.a.	282	235	196	298	632	628
European NATO	n.a.	300	337	330	324	364	342
China	0	0	0	12	18	140	212
Soviet Union	n.a.	324	986	2057	2227	2395	3425

[a] Includes forward-based US and NATO bombers with combat radius over 1500 kilometers, Soviet bombers with this combat radius, and US and NATO carrier-based bombers.

[b] Includes land-based missiles with ranges between 1000 and 6000 kilometers plus Soviet variable-range missiles sometimes counted with intercontinental forces but assigned to regional missions. See Table 2.2, note b.

[c] Includes US and Soviet sub-launched missiles sometimes counted with intercontinental forces but assigned regional missions.

[d] See Table 2.2, note d.

Note: Table does not include "battlefield" and "tactical" nuclear weapons.

Source: See Table 2.2.

tration has said our nuclear arsenal was stagnating, there were also many qualitative improvements in U.S. strategic forces:

— Minuteman II (1966) and Minuteman III (1970) ICBMs—new missiles in configuration and capability, with little in common with Minuteman I other than name.
— Two new types of submarine-launched ballistic missiles— the Poseidon C-3 (1970) and the Trident C-4 (1979). A new class of missile submarines had been introduced in 1964, and another was added in 1981.
— The FB-111 supersonic strategic bomber (1970). With aerial refueling or the use of "forward" bases, it can strike the Soviet Union and return. The older and slower but longer-range B-52 bombers were upgraded extensively with

advanced electronics, structural strengthening to permit low-altitude penetration of air defenses, and other improvements. To further increase the bombers' capability to penetrate air defenses, they were provided (starting in 1972) with more than 1,000 nuclear-armed, air-launched, supersonic ground-attack missiles.

One particular qualitative change introduced by the United States in this period had an impact on the arms race larger than that of all the other developments combined. It was the Multiple Independently targetable Reentry Vehicle (MIRV), which made it possible to strike three, ten, or even fifteen separate targets with warheads dispersed from a single ballistic missile. This U.S. invention was responsible for the huge increase in deliverable warheads in our strategic nuclear arsenal between 1970 and 1978, a period in which the number of U.S. "delivery vehicles" (land-based missiles, sub-launched missiles, and bombers) actually decreased.

First tested by the United States in 1968 (see Table 2.1), MIRV was promoted as a relatively inexpensive solution to two problems: the rapid increase in the number of U.S.S.R. targets to be destroyed in a nuclear war, and Soviet development of an antiballistic missile (ABM) system. The increase in targets was largely in the form of dispersed Soviet ICBM silos, each of which would have to be allocated two or more U.S. warheads to provide a high probablility of destruction. Widespread deployment of a Soviet ABM system might likewise require additional U.S. warheads, to saturate and thus overwhelm the defense. The extra warheads needed for these purposes could be delivered far more cheaply by MIRV, it was argued, than by providing each warhead with its own individual missile.

Evidently disturbed by the MIRV technology's potential and by the U.S. lead in it, the Soviets indicated some interest in reaching an agreement to forbid or greatly constrain it as part of the SALT I negotiations. They were joined in this desire by a number of U.S. analysts, who saw in MIRV the specter of an unbounded arms race once the Soviets duplicated the technology—as they surely would. But the Nixon administration, led on this point by Secretary of State Henry Kissinger, was unwilling to negotiate away such a promising U.S. advantage. U.S. deployment of MIRV (on Minuteman III) began in 1970, and the SALT I agreement of 1972 was concluded with no restraints whatever on this technology.[23]

As predicted by everyone not held in sway by the fallacy of the last move, the Soviets then developed their own MIRV technology, testing it in 1973 and commencing deployment in 1975. What surprised most observers, however, was how rapidly and extensively they then proceeded to implement it. While the U.S. Minuteman III ICBM carried three warheads, the Soviets put four on one of their smaller ICBMs and six to eight on their larger ones. By 1980, the Soviet land-based intercontinental missile force mounted about 5,000 warheads, more than twice the number on U.S. land-based ICBMs. Perhaps this should be termed the "action-overreaction" syndrome.

Coupled with improvements in warhead accuracy—another technological refinement pioneered by the United States and subsequently mimicked by the Soviets—the massive multiplication of Soviet land-based warheads called into question the theretofore taken-for-granted invulnerability of U.S. land-based ICBMs against preemptive attack. Thus arose the much-discussed "window of vulnerability." Rarely (if ever) in history has technological innovation in weaponry backfired so resoundingly to the disadvantage of the inventors. To understand fully the dimensions of the predicament into which the advent of highly accurate, MIRVed missiles has

plunged the superpowers and the rest of the world, it is necessary to digress somewhat into the history of the doctrines developed to rationalize the functions of
nuclear weapons.[24]

The Evolution of Nuclear Doctrine: Early Thinking

During the brief U.S. monopoly on nuclear weapons (1945-49), there was much
discussion among the national political and military leaders concerning the effect of
U.S. possession of the bomb on the likelihood and outcome of future conflicts—
especially conflicts with the Soviet Union. No coherent strategy for the use of
nuclear weapons emerged from these discussions, however, other than a conviction
that the United States must be prepared to use "the bomb" against the Soviet Union
to defend Western Europe. (It was widely supposed, from about 1947 onward, that
the Soviets were eagerly awaiting an opportunity to march on Western Europe with
the massive Red Army.)

Just *how* nuclear weapons would be used in this contingency, and how effective
they would be, were more difficult questions. The popular impression in the United
States was that our exclusive possession of the atomic bomb assured early victory in
any hostilities, even without mobilizing a large army; professional military and
civilian analysts were much less sure. One thing some of the professionals knew,
but the public did not, was that the U.S. stockpile of usable nuclear weapons in the
late 1940s was very small (about 50 in mid-1948). Moreover, until about this time,
the professionals believed that producing the fissionable materials for a much larger
stockpile would be extremely expensive, and they were unsure how many of these
precious weapons could reach Soviet targets aboard the propeller-driven B-29s and
B-50s then serving as our nuclear bomber force.[25]

Several events in the period from mid-1948 to 1951 combined to alter drastically
the previous state of uncertainty in official U.S. thinking about the role of nuclear
weapons.

1. Improvements in fissionable-material production and fission-bomb design
removed the economic barrier to production of a much larger stockpile, while the
emerging possibility of thermonuclear (hydrogen fusion) bombs promised eventually to remove all limits to the destructive power that could be affordably deployed.

2. The introduction in 1948 of the truly intercontinental B-36 heavy bomber,
and in 1951 of the faster- and higher-flying B-47 medium bomber, substantially
removed earlier doubts about U.S. ability to deliver nuclear bombs against the
Soviet homeland in quantity.

3. The Soviet explosion of its own atomic bomb, in August 1949, ended the
U.S. monopoly and thus seemed to leave only one option for maintaining a decisive
U.S. advantage—namely, racing to retain its sizable lead in quantity and quality of
nuclear weaponry.

4. Finally, the combination of the Berlin Blockade (1948), the triumph of the
Communist revolution in China (1949), and the invasion of Korea (1950) fed Western fears of a monolithic and aggressive world communism, removing any chance
that the United States would relinquish the nuclear advantage that seemed its greatest asset against such a threat.

The Doctrine of Massive Retaliation

These factors resulted in the buildup of U.S. nuclear forces through the 1950s and the enunciation, early in the Eisenhower administration, of the doctrine of *massive retaliation*. This doctrine was not quite as simplistic as most of its public interpretations. It did rely on massive retaliation with nuclear weapons against the Soviet homeland as a deterrent against any Soviet use of nuclear weapons against the United States and as the response of last resort in the event of imminent success of a Soviet attempt to overrun Western Europe. It did not envision massive nuclear retaliation as the appropriate response to any and all Soviet and Chinese infringements of U.S. interests. It was intended to back up continuing reliance on local defense by conventional forces of the United States and its allies, and to permit the use, in regional conflicts, of the growing U.S. arsenal of "tactical" nuclear weapons without fear of this provoking a Soviet nuclear attack on the United States itself. (The use of tactical nuclear weapons for traditional military purposes on the battlefield— as distinguished from strategic nuclear bombing of the adversary's population centers and industrial base— was increasingly promoted by Western political and military leaders throughout the 1950s as a way to avoid the excessive economic burdens of a strictly conventional defense.)

It was widely recognized, even in the early 1950s, that the massive-retaliation doctrine would inevitably be undermined by eventual Soviet acquisition of the capability to impose intolerable nuclear devastation on the United States. (This recognition was heightened by the Soviet test of a practical fusion bomb in late 1955, less than two years after the United States had attained this goal.) If the threat of massive retaliation cannot be carried out without the destruction of one's own society, is it a credible threat? Eisenhower's secretary of state, John Foster Dulles, argued that tough talk and the skillful use of ambiguity ("brinkmanship") could continue to convince the Soviet Union that U.S. leaders had the nerve to carry out their threat and thus maintain deterrence, even after the Soviets had the capacity to respond in kind. When, in the period from 1956 to 1959, the advent of a long-range Soviet bomber force and the first few Soviet ICBMs brought this capacity into being, the critics of Dulles's position voiced growing doubts.

In the early 1950s, little thought had been given to the possibility that retaliatory capacity, once in place, could be neutralized by actions taken by the other side. There seemed little prospect of completely successful defense against a concerted bomber attack, but radar would provide sufficient warning to allow one's retaliatory force to be dispatched before it could be destroyed. Helped along by the advent of the ICBMs and the imminent deployment of sub-launched ballistic missiles, this thinking began to change in the late 1950s.[26] It became possible to imagine that, under some circumstances, the side striking first might destroy enough of its adversary's retaliatory capacity to come out "ahead" in the exchange. As noted earlier, this idea extended the lease on life of the notion of significant U.S. nuclear superiority: as long as we had nuclear forces enough larger than those of the Soviets to contemplate striking first, the idea of a massive attack on the Soviet Union as our response of last resort would retain some deterrent value. Of course, this idea of the "counterforce" use of nuclear weapons to deprive the other side of its retaliatory capacity stimulated the eventual acquisition of nuclear arsenals on both sides much larger than would have been needed, for retaliation against cities, if the nuclear forces on both sides were themselves safe from attack.

Despite the debilitating effects of growing Soviet intercontinental nuclear capability on the U.S. doctrine of massive retaliation in the form enunciated in the early years of the Eisenhower administration, massive retaliation held official sway as the centerpiece of American nuclear strategy until Eisenhower left office at the beginning of 1961. Until that time, U.S. war planning called for launching everything we had, at the outset of a nuclear war with the Soviet Union, in a massive attack on that country, its Eastern European satellites, and China.

The Doctrine of Flexible Response

President Kennedy and Secretary of Defense Robert McNamara had been much impressed with the growing objections to reliance on massive retaliation, and they moved quickly to institute their own approach—the doctrine of flexible response. The essence of this approach was that the United States should have a range of weapons—from conventional, to "small" nuclear, to large nuclear —on which it could draw to tailor an appropriate response to any contingency. So the "national command authorities" (the president, secretary of defense, joint chiefs of staff, and so on) could have the degree of flexibility that this range of weapons and options was intended to provide, substantial improvements in the systems for "command, control, communication, and intelligence" (C^3I in arms-race jargon) during a conflict would be required; this necessity was part of the doctrine, and efforts were initiated at once to accomplish the needed improvements.

Two other essential (and interrelated) ingredients in the doctrine of flexible response were damage limitation and city avoidance. Damage limitation meant striking early at the military forces—particularly nuclear forces—of the adversary to reduce the damage those forces could do to one's own side. City avoidance meant not striking early at the adversary's population centers —while holding in reserve sufficient forces to do so later as a last resort—to give the opponent every possible incentive to refrain from striking one's own cities. The ideas of "limiting" a nuclear war and of "prevailing" in such a war by destroying more of an adversary's forces than he can destroy of one's own were no longer new by this time, having been explored earlier by theorists in defense think-tanks and elsewhere; but this was their first appearance as the cornerstones of national nuclear doctrine.

In its initial incarnation in the Kennedy/Johnson administrations (which with respect to nuclear strategy and doctrine might more appropriately be called the McNamara administration), the doctrine of flexible response was rather short-lived. Its downfall can be attributed to three factors. First was the logical implausibility of city avoidance, given the close proximity of many military targets to cities and the low accuracy and high explosive power of the then-available nuclear weapons. The second factor was the practical difficulty of damage limitation, given the diminishing vulnerability of Soviet nuclear forces under the anticipated trends: increasingly dispersed and numerous ICBMs in hardened silos, and increasing numbers of submarine-launched ballistic missiles hidden at sea. But the crowning defect of the doctrine of flexible response, perhaps not entirely unrelated to the first two, was the failure of the Soviet Union to accept it. (Whatever the other defects of the idea of limited nuclear war, it requires bilateral restraint.)

Prior to the death of Stalin in 1953, Soviet military doctrine had held that neither striking first nor the advent of nuclear weapons was of much importance.[27] (This view was doubtless influenced by the circumstance that, at the time, the Soviet Union had neither a sizable stockpile of nuclear weapons nor a means of delivering them against its principal adversary, the United States.) After Stalin's death, the official Soviet view evolved rapidly, in stride with the growing nuclear arsenals on both sides. By 1958, Soviet doctrine held that a surprise attack (in either direction) using nuclear weapons could be decisive, and that the future belonged to ICBMs.

The Soviet strategists of this and later periods apparently did not deduce from these propositions that nuclear war was inevitable or desirable. Rather, they held that their country must develop a combination of military forces and posture to deter any potential adversary from mounting a nuclear attack on the Soviet Union. This meant that the Soviet Union should be prepared to respond to any nuclear attack with a massive nuclear retaliatory blow. Indeed, as had been the case on the U.S. side, Soviet analysts gave considerable attention to the circumstances in which nuclear "preemption" — striking first with nuclear forces in the conviction that the adversary is about to do so—would be a prudent course. The Soviets ridiculed Mr. McNamara's ideas about flexible response and limited nuclear war in public statements as well as in military writings. Presumably seeing in these propositions a U.S. attempt to turn its continuing superiority in nuclear forces into a usable advantage in time of conflict, the Soviets were having none of it: they insisted that any use of nuclear weapons by the superpowers against one another would inevitably become a full-scale nuclear war, resulting in overwhelming destruction.

The Doctrine of Assured Destruction

As a result of the Soviets' growing nuclear capabilities, their uncooperative attitude toward flexible response, and the other defects of that doctrine, it had by 1965 been superseded as the cornerstone of U.S. strategy by the doctrine of *assured destruction* (more widely known today by the acronym MAD, for Mutual Assured Destruction).[28] The key idea in MAD is that a state of stable, mutual deterrence will obtain if each side has the capacity to inflict unendurable destruction on the other society, and if neither can deprive the other of this capability, even with the most devastating sneak attack.

One interesting aspect of the assured-destruction doctrine is that, in contrast to "flexible response" and other counterforce approaches, it offers a way to decide how much is enough and thus avert an endless, escalating arms race. Under MAD, as soon as a side has sufficient, invulnerable nuclear forces to destroy enough of the other's society that the loss would unquestionably be considered intolerable, the side with this sufficiency can stop building nuclear weapons and invest its resources in something else. Secretary McNamara and the analysts he brought to the Department of Defense concluded that the ability to destroy a fifth to a third of the Soviet Union's population and a half to three quarters of its industrial capacity would be sufficient, and that this level of destruction would be assured by the weapons already in the U.S. arsenal by the mid-1960s. To the dismay of those military leaders, civilian strategists, weapons makers, and politicians committed to a continuing buildup of nuclear forces to maintain a lead over the Soviet Union, McNamara used these arguments to beat down most of their proposals for more and better strategic weaponry.

Perhaps the most remarkable implication of the MAD doctrine is that stability depends on the vulnerability of the population and industrial capacity of each side and on the invulnerability of each side's nuclear weapons. If the weapons were vulnerable, then either side could expect to gain by firing first—a source of instability. If the population and industry of one side or the other were not vulnerable, then that side would have nothing to lose by firing on its adversary. (Morality is presumed not to enter this calculus!)

Aware of this logic and renowned as a logical individual, Secretary McNamara further horrified the advocates of U.S. nuclear superiority by taking the position, in the mid-1960s, that the United States should not seek to deny the Soviet Union the "assured destruction" capability against us that it sought. That is, we should try neither to obtain the capacity to wipe out Soviet nuclear forces in a first strike, nor to find ways to protect our population against a Soviet nuclear attack—given only that the Soviets would similarly refrain from threatening our weapons or defending its population. Alas, there were strong indications that such Soviet restraint would not be forthcoming simply because Mr. McNamara said it made sense. This situation strengthened the hand of the many military leaders and weapons technologists in the United States to whom McNamara's position was anathema, and he reluctantly concluded that the mutual restraint required for stability would have to be formally agreed upon through negotiations. The ensuing 15-plus years of negotiations (described in some detail below) have been less than completely successful.

Beyond the need for mutual restraint to maintain stability (and the associated risk that the stable balance will be shattered by a breakthrough in population defense or counterforce capability by one side or the other), the doctrine of mutual assured destruction has some further liabilities:

1. The basis for the mutual restraint needed for stability tends to be undermined by the insistence of each side that it is not the one that needs to be deterred. Thus, Soviet leaders argue that the United States should know that the Soviet Union would never strike the U.S. homeland with nuclear weapons unless we struck theirs first. This being the case, is stability harmed if the Soviet Union deploys some strictly defensive measures (for example, civil defense, anti-ballistic missiles)? U.S. leaders (after Kennedy/Johnson/McNamara) have been known to make the mirror image of this argument.

2. It is morally repugnant to base one's security on holding hostage hundreds of millions of innocent individuals with the threat of incineration or lingering death if deterrence fails.

3. A threat that amounts to retaliation by suicide is at best credible only as a deterrent against the ultimate provocation by the adversary, namely, a massive nuclear attack on one's homeland. But by thus reducing the credible deterrent functions of nuclear weapons to a single one—discouraging a massive nuclear attack— the MAD doctrine deprives national leaders of cherished flexibility to employ nuclear deterrence against lesser threats. Most important in this connection is the greatly reduced credibility, under the MAD doctrine and corresponding nuclear-force postures, of the proposition that U.S. nuclear forces can deter the Soviets from a conventional attack on Western Europe, or stop them if they try.

4. MAD's usefulness as a deterrent even against the ultimate threat is at least questionable, for at the level of mutual assured destruction the very notion of deterrence becomes a paradox. The problem is usually stated this way: in order to deter, it must be credible that a threatened action actually will be carried out if deterrence fails; but at this level, if deterrence failed there would be no sense in carrying out

the threatened action. If the Soviet Union had just launched an attack that assured the destruction of the United States, what would it avail the U.S. president to carry out his threat to destroy the Soviet Union, too? The way out of this paradox, it is generally argued, is that deterrence is preserved by the impossibility of the potential attacker's knowing in advance whether the leader on the other side will respond "rationally." Nevertheless, the MAD doctrine remains susceptible to the criticism that it offers no helpful guidance to national leaders when guidance about what to do is most needed—namely, when deterrence seems about to fail.

Finally, MAD shares some shortcomings with virtually all other deterrent approaches, notably the chance of technological accidents and the perhaps inaccurate assumption that the leaders on both sides are sane (and preferably cautious). The former is a particularly troublesome possibility if the deterrent forces on either side (or both) are not really invulnerable: the most straightforward compensation for this defect is to be prepared to "launch on warning" of incoming enemy bombers or warheads; but that posture makes errors in detection, failures of communication, and computer malfunctions potentially catastrophic. Soviet leaders showed strong interest in launch on warning to remedy their perceived vulnerability to preemptive attack in the mid-to-late 1960s, and the United States has consistently refused to rule out adopting this posture (on the grounds that eliminating the possibility would simplify Soviet planning for a preemptive attack).[29]

Selective Options and Nuclear War Fighting

As had been the fate of earlier nuclear doctrines, MAD was undermined by a combination of its inherent shortcomings (real and perceived) and the march of technological "progress" in nuclear weaponry. The Nixon administration, coming into office in early 1969, was deeply troubled by the lack of options available to the national leadership under the MAD doctrine, and it spent its first term looking for alternatives. The U.S. development of Multiple Independently targetable Reentry Vehicles (MIRV), coupled with sizable improvements in warhead accuracy, seemed to make it possible to find the desired escape from MAD in a revitalized version of flexible response, which came to be called *selective options*.

The new doctrine was approved by President Nixon early in his second term and made public by Secretary of Defense James Schlesinger in January 1974. (Some called it the "Schlesinger doctrine.") It called for diverse nuclear forces (by implication much larger than those needed for MAD) capable of coping with a wide range of contingencies. The possible uses of nuclear weapons under this doctrine included isolated "warning" shots to demonstrate national "resolve" in a crisis (long a preoccupation of Nixon and Kissinger), selective assistance to conventional forces in combat, and damage limitation at impending "higher levels of violence" by means of preemptive destruction of the adversary's nuclear forces.

According to the doctrine, such uses of nuclear weapons could have two distinct although interrelated purposes. First, as a sort of extension of pre-hostilities diplomacy, they could influence the Soviets' motivation, persuading them to terminate the hostilities before things got worse. Second, they could serve militarily to achieve "escalation dominance,"[30] meaning the ability to attain distinct military superiority at some level of the "escalation ladder" (thus forcing a rational adversary to concede when—or, better, before—that level is reached).

As with the flexible-response doctrine from which it was derived, selective options emphasized counterforce uses of nuclear weapons and avoidance of striking at cities. This idea was now more credible because improved warhead accuracy and lower yields made possible by this improvement had encouraged the notion that military targets could be destroyed with minimum "collateral damage" to civilians.

Two other changes in the status of the nuclear forces on the two sides were thought to offer hope that selective options could succeed as strategic doctrine where the substantially similar flexible response had failed. First, both sides now possessed invulnerable second-strike forces—numerous submarine-launched missiles that could not be found and destroyed at sea, and more ICBMs in hardened silos than the adversary had warheads of sufficient accuracy and power to destroy— which reduced the chance of automatic escalation of nuclear fighting by alleviating the *use them or lose them* syndrome. Second, the Soviets themselves were starting to deploy nuclear weapons suitable for a "controlled counterforce" role, giving reason to think that their previous reluctance to contemplate less-than-total nuclear war might be diminishing.

In fact, however, the Soviets continued to display their old reluctance to limit nuclear war along the lines of the U.S. doctrines of flexible response and selective options. They had come to think that it might be possible to contain the use of nuclear weapons to a "theater" of battle, notably Europe; but their own doctrine's stress on the need to strike early and powerfully in pursuit of decisive victory left no room for ideas such as city-avoidance or limitation of collateral damage, much less selective nuclear shots to encourage a diplomatic settlement.[31] If nuclear weapons were used at all in a European conflict, the Soviets would use theirs without restraint: so their public pronouncements suggested and their military literature made clear. There was, similarly, no indication that nuclear strikes against the Soviet homeland—whether originating from the United States or Europe, and whether limited or not—would be responded to with any less than the full use of Soviet intercontinental nuclear forces against the United States.

This position on the Soviet side, which has not changed to this day, could hardly be a clearer prescription for the escalation of *any* use of nuclear weapons by NATO or the Soviet Union into an unlimited nuclear war between the superpowers. That is what critics (on both sides) of "limited nuclear war" had been saying all along. But this did not discourage the Nixon administration, or its successors, from concluding that the United States must be prepared to fight a prolonged but limited nuclear war. The Soviets, after all, might be bluffing about the nature of their responses to limited use of nuclear weapons by others. They might be deterred from carrying out the threat of all-out use of their nuclear weapons, moreover, as long as the United States maintained a secure "assured destruction" capability in the form of invulnerable and powerful strategic nuclear forces held in reserve through the course of the limited nuclear war fighting. Accordingly, the means to maintain and to be able to control this "assured destruction" reserve were given high priority even in the midst of efforts to expand limited-war-fighting capabilities.

The idea that the Soviets might not really believe in nuclear deterrence a la "mutual assured destruction," but were in fact seeking their own capability to win a nuclear war—perhaps even to win an unlimited one—was strongly reinforced by the Soviets' continuing buildup of intercontinental nuclear forces beyond the point (say, 1970) when their "assured destruction" capability could no longer be doubted. While this continuation might be explained by Soviet determination to attain real parity after their humiliation in 1962, or even by simple momentum in their own military-industrial complex, pessimists could easily attribute to it a more malevolent motivation—especially in the light of the Soviets' growing counterforce capability (after 1975) in the form of land-based ICBMs with increasingly numerous and accurate MIRVed warheads. The gloom was compounded by the nature and number of continuing Soviet deployments of nuclear weapons in Europe in the late 1970s: a steady increase in the numbers of the supersonic Backfire medium-range bomber, and the 1977 introduction and subsequent buildup of the formidable SS-20 intermediate-range ballistic missile (with solid fuel, mobile launchers, and three rather accurate MIRV warheads per missile).

It will be recalled that MIRV was an American invention, as were the improved guidance systems that made possible the high-confidence destruction of "hard" targets, such as missile silos and command bunkers, specially reinforced to withstand the effects of "near miss" nuclear explosions. Once the Soviet Union also possessed these technologies—and was making up for its lag in acquiring them by deploying them at a great rate—their unsettling consequences had to be faced.

The heart of the matter was the *exchange ratio*: the number of missiles an attacker must expend to destroy one of the adversary's missiles in its silo. As long as each missile carried only one warhead, an attacker would have to expend at least one to destroy one, always assuming that the enemy had not been so foolish as to emplace its missiles close together. In practice, the exchange ratio would be less favorable to the attacker than one for one, because of less-than-perfect reliability and accuracy in the attacking missiles. In this situation, neither side has an incentive to launch a first strike against the adversary's missiles: since the attacking side must expend more than one missile to destroy one, the result of the attack would be to worsen the balance of forces from the attacker's viewpoint.

This stable situation is turned upside down as soon as the missiles are equipped with MIRV. Even if two warheads of a certain accuracy must be expended to be sure of destroying one of the adversary's missiles in its silo, a single MIRVed missile with ten warheads of this accuracy can eliminate five missiles on the other side. All else being equal, the more warheads on a missile, the better the exchange ratio it provides in a first strike—and the more tempting the target it makes for a MIRV-armed adversary pondering his own first strike. The result is called *crisis instability*: in a crisis that seems to have the potential to degenerate into nuclear war, the likelihood of that actually happening must be higher if a significant advantage accrues to the side that shoots first.

This sort of thinking led to growing concern in the Nixon and Ford administrations about the vulnerability of U.S. land-based ICBMs to a preemptive attack by increasingly MIRVed Soviet ICBMs. It was argued that, since the most advanced U.S. ICBM (Minuteman III) carried only three warheads, while the greater payload of the much-larger Soviet ICBMs would permit them to carry two to four times as many, a serious asymmetry was developing. (U.S. sub-launched ballistic missiles carried as many as 14 warheads each, but their combination of accuracy and power was not sufficient to threaten well-hardened targets such as Soviet ICBM silos.) In the early 1970s, therefore, the U.S. defense community began to search in earnest for a "response" to the threat to our land-based ICBMs. Two criteria were paramount: the U.S. response should reduce the vulnerability of our ICBMs to preemptive attack, and it should increase our capacity to mount a preemptive attack on the Soviet land-based ICBMs. Tit for tat; action-reaction. The search for a way to achieve these aims was to span the administrations of Richard Nixon, Gerald Ford, Jimmy Carter, and Ronald Reagan. Its culmination in early 1983, with the plan to emplace 100 ten-warhead, MX missiles in Minuteman silos, will be discussed later.

In the meantime, U.S. doctrine on the use of nuclear weapons continued to be an uneasy mixture of nuclear war fighting and assured destruction. President Carter took office at the beginning of 1977, troubled about nuclear weapons and skeptical of the possibility of limiting a nuclear war. That skepticism was shared by his secretary of defense, Harold Brown, a physicist and former director of the Livermore weapons laboratory, who was the most technically knowledgeable individual to hold that office since the nuclear arms race began. But the hope that the Carter administration might prudently retreat from notions of nuclear war-fighting was soon demolished by a combination of worst-case analysis, foreign policy setbacks, and partisan politics. The worst-case analysis went as follows: the increased MIRV-ing and accuracy of Soviet warheads was providing the Soviet Union with a growing "controlled counterforce" capability, suitable for fighting a limited nuclear war; even though we doubted that such a war could actually be limited— and we thought they doubted it, too—we could not be sure that the Soviets would not try to use their capability; if they did, we should have the ability to respond in kind—that is, with limited, counterforce use of nuclear weapons—rather than being forced to choose between defeat or the total destruction of both societies.

The conviction that we must match (or even better) any nuclear war fighting capability that the Soviets happen to possess was cast in concrete for the Carter administration by the setbacks in Afghanistan, Iran, and Poland, and by increasingly strident Republican accusations that the administration's policies were leaving this country impotent to deal with external threats. The result, in the end, was that the Carter administration outdid itself in rationalizing, codifying, and refining the nuclear-war-fighting notions of its predecessors. The culmination of this process was President Carter's approval in July 1980 (four months before the election) of Presidential Directive 59. As explained by Defense Secretary Brown, its rationale was the need for "extended deterrence":

> But deterrence must restrain a far wider range of threats than just massive attacks on U.S. cities. We seek to deter any adversary from any course of action that could lead to general nuclear war. Our strategic forces must also deter nuclear attacks on smaller sets of targets in the U.S. military forces, and be a wall against nuclear coercion of, or an attack on, our friends and allies. And strategic forces, in conjunction with theater nuclear forces, must contribute to deterrence of conventional aggression as well.[32]

Presidential Directive 59 did more than formally reaffirm the dangerous notion that nuclear weapons can do more than deter the use of nuclear weapons by others. It enunciated its own version of nuclear-war-fighting doctrine, the "countervailing strategy," the key element of which was to attack the ability of the Soviet leadership "to maintain control after a war starts."[33] This meant targeting the Soviet leaders in their offices and command bunkers, along with communications and reconnaissance capabilities. The idea, of course, was to dissuade the Soviets from thinking that they could achieve their objectives in a limited nuclear war with the United States. But the effect of carrying out the strategy, if deterrence failed, would be to virtually guarantee that any nuclear war would become an unlimited one—no leaders or control mechanisms would be left to stop it.

With this refinement in the theory of how to fight a nuclear war, it was only left to the Republican administration taking office a few months later to figure out how to win one, a task President Reagan and his associates tackled with considerable enthusiasm. [34]

THE ARMS RACE IN THE EIGHTIES

Restoring Parity or Pursuing Superiority?

By mid-1983, two and a half years into the Reagan administration, U.S. defense spending was nearly 40 percent greater than in the last Carter budget, and further increases are being sought. [35] President Reagan has claimed that the Soviets enjoy "a definite margin of superiority" in strategic nuclear weaponry, [36] and the official NATO view is that the Warsaw Pact is superior in the European theater both in long-range nuclear weaponry and in conventional forces. NATO continues to take the position that deterring a Soviet attack on Western Europe requires a credible NATO threat to resort to the use of nuclear weapons if necessary to stop such an attack, and that maintaining the credibility of this threat now requires substantial "modernization" of NATO's theater nuclear forces.

Among the U.S. and other NATO programs that have been set in motion to remedy the perceived deficiencies in our nuclear posture are the following:

— The United States plans to deploy 100 new MX land-based ICBMs in Minuteman silos, starting in December 1986, and 100 new B-1B intercontinental bombers, also starting in 1986. Each MX will have ten MIRV warheads; each B-1B will carry perhaps 30 air-launched cruise missiles.
— Throughout the 1980s, the United States will deploy new Trident missile submarines at a rate of more than one a year. Each Trident sub initially will carry 24 Trident I missiles, each armed with eight MIRV warheads. Starting in 1989, these missiles are scheduled to be replaced with the Trident II, whose more powerful and more accurate warheads (up to 14 per missile) will give it a formidable first-strike potential against hard targets.
— The United States started in December 1982 to refit its B-52 intercontinental bombers to carry 12 air-launched cruise missiles each. This number will soon be increased to 20, and by 1990 at least 150 B-52s will be so equipped. In mid-1984, deployment of nuclear-armed, sea-launched cruise missiles on surface ships and attack submarines will begin, the total number of such missiles to reach as many as 4,000 by 1990.
— In the late 1980s, the United Kingdom will deploy the first of four of its own Trident submarines, to replace the four Polaris submarines now serving as the mainstay of the British strategic nuclear forces. Like the Polaris submarines, the new ones will carry 16 missiles each, but instead of the present three warheads per missile (not independently targetable), the Trident II missiles (to be purchased from the United States) will carry eight to 14 MIRV warheads each. France, which now deploys five ballistic-missile submarines carrying a total of 80 single-warhead missiles, will by 1990 have expanded and modernized this

force to comprise seven submarines carrying 112 missiles and nearly 600 warheads.
— Starting in December 1983, the United States began to deploy 108 medium-range Pershing II ballistic missiles in West Germany and 464 ground-launched cruise missiles divided among West Germany, England, Italy, and (perhaps) Belgium and the Netherlands. Each missile carries a single nuclear warhead.

Western critics of the official U.S./NATO perceptions and programs argue that the U.S. buildup is aimed not at restoring parity, but at achieving superiority (which, after all, was an explicit goal in the Republican platform on which Ronald Reagan ran successfully for President in 1980). They argue further that NATO's threat to use nuclear weapons if necessary to repel a Warsaw Pact attack *cannot* be made credible, not least because nuclear war fighting in Europe would destroy that which was to be defended. And they claim that the projected new U.S. and NATO deployments, as well as pursuing the undesirable and the unattainable at an unbearable monetary cost, will increase the chance of nuclear war and reduce the chance of controlling the arms race.[37]

The position of the Soviets is that an overall balance of military capabilities—nuclear and conventional—exists now between NATO and the Warsaw Pact, and that the Soviet Union will do whatever is necessary to prevent the West from reestablishing its earlier superiority. In particular, the Soviets threaten to respond to any further U.S./NATO nuclear deployments with their own additional deployments. They have also called on NATO to join them in their pledge of "no first use" of nuclear weapons, which they formalized before the United Nations in 1982—an invitation NATO remains disinclined to accept.[38]

To examine these positions critically requires looking first at the balance of nuclear and conventional military forces as it stood in the early 1980s.

The Military Balance: Intercontinental Forces

Table 2.4 shows the intercontinental nuclear forces of the United States and the Soviet Union as they stood at the end of 1982.[39] Unlike Tables 2.2 and 2.3, Table 2.4 considers to be "intercontinental" all Soviet land-based and submarine-based ballistic missiles that have intercontinental capability, regardless of the regional (European, Asian) missions to which several hundred of these missiles are thought to be assigned. This convention follows the counting rules agreed to by both sides during the SALT negotiations that extended from 1967 to 1980. The U.S. FB-111A and Soviet Backfire medium-range bombers were not counted in SALT and are not included in Table 2.4, although under some circumstances both could undertake intercontinental missions. (They are considered later in Table 2.5.)

As Table 2.4 indicates, there are substantial differences in composition between the U.S. and Soviet intercontinental forces. Most important, the Soviets have more than 70 percent of their warheads and more than 75 percent of their megatonnage in land-based ICBMs, while the U.S. forces are much more evenly distributed among land-based ICBMs, submarine-based missiles, and intercontinental bombers. The Soviet Union has somewhat more total megatonnage, but the United States has a greater total number of bombs and warheads.

Characteristics beyond those shown in the table are also important. For example, while the Soviet submarine force seems superior to that of the U.S. in number of

Table 2.4   U.S. and Soviet Intercontinental Nuclear Forces, 1982

	USA	USSR
Intercontinental ballistic missiles (land-based)		
Missiles[a]	1,052	1,398[b]
Warheads	2,152	5,230
Equivalent megatonnage[c]	1,400	4,600
Submarine-launched ballistic missiles		
Missiles[a]	544[d]	950[e]
Warheads	4,960	1,770
Equivalent megatonnage	800	1,100
Intercontinental bombers		
Aircraft	319[f]	150
Bombs/warheads	2,464[g]	300
Equivalent megatonnage	1,700[g]	300
Totals		
Delivery vehicles	1,915	2,498
Bombs/warheads	9,600	7,300
Equivalent megatonnage	3,900	6,000

[a] Includes only missiles emplaced in silos, in submarine launch tubes, or on other launchers—not reloads or spares.

[b] Includes 260 SS-11 and 120 SS-19 variable-range missiles capable of intercontinental missions and counted under SALT but apparently assigned regional missions.

[c] Equivalent megatonnage (EMT) accounts for the reduction in efficiency of producing blast damage as warheads increase in size. (Blast damage scales with the 2/3 power of explosive yield.) The EMT of a given set of warheads is the number of 1-megaton warheads that would produce the same blast damage.

[d] Forty to fifty of these missiles (400 warheads) are assigned to the commander of NATO forces in Europe and should therefore be considered to be assigned regional roles, but they are counted under SALT.

[e] These 950 missiles are on nuclear submarines and are counted under SALT. About 400 of these missiles, plus another 50 on diesel submarines and not counted under SALT, are believed to be assigned regional rather than intercontinental roles.

[f] Includes 288 active aircraft (75 B-52Ds, 123 B-52Gs, 90 B-52Hs) and 31 active reserve (3 B-52Ds, 22 B-52Gs, 6 B-52Hs), but not 28 B-52Gs assigned to conventional roles and 223 B-52s (various models) in storage (which, however, are counted under SALT).

[g] Assumes 78 B-52Ds with four 1-megaton bombs each, 14 B-52Gs with twelve 200-kiloton cruise missiles and four 1-megaton bombs each, and another 131 B-52Gs and 96 B-52Hs with four 1-megaton bombs each and 1020 200-kiloton short-range attack missiles among them (4-6 per aircraft).

Source: Stockholm International Peace Research Institute, *World Armaments and Disarmament: The 1982 SIPRI Yearbook* (Cambridge, MA: Oelgeschlager, Gunn, and Hain, 1982); and International Institute for Strategic Studies, *The Military Balance 1982-83* (London: IISS, 1982).

missiles and megatonnage, it actually is much inferior in real capability. The Soviet Union manages to keep only 15 to 25 percent of its missile submarines at sea (as opposed to vulnerable in port) at any given time, while the United States keeps 50 to 75 percent at sea. Those Soviet submarines that are at sea, moreover, are much more vulnerable to detection and destruction than are the U.S. missile subs: the Soviet subs are noisier, U.S. detection technology is better, and geography forces Soviet subs to pass through a few easily monitored straits on their way to the open ocean.

The U.S. intercontinental bomber force is not only quantitatively superior to that of the Soviets by every index, it is qualitatively superior as well: the U.S. aircraft are, on the whole, more modern and more capable, and the supersonic ground-attack missiles and air-launched cruise missiles that many carry greatly increase their firepower and ability to penetrate air defenses. About a third of the U.S. bombers are on alert at any given time, capable of taking off on short notice to avoid being destroyed on the ground by a surprise attack. None of the Soviet bombers is kept on everyday alert. On the other hand, the Soviet Union maintains much more extensive defenses against bombers than does the United States. By no means would all of the bombs and warheads carried on U.S. bombers get through.

The key message of Table 2.4, however, is that both sides possess intercontinental nuclear forces far in excess of the amount needed to destroy the other as a functioning society. In the 1960s, Robert McNamara's Pentagon analysts concluded that 200 deliverable megatons would suffice for the "assured destruction" of the Soviet Union. The widely advertised figure of 400 megatons included a twofold margin of safety to account for imperfect reliability and penetration. In 1982, the U.S. intercontinental nuclear forces amounted to 20 times the 200-megaton assured destruction level, and the corresponding Soviet forces amounted to 30 times that level. Even if a Soviet first strike *could* succeed in destroying all the U.S. ICBMs, all the bombers, and all submarines in port—which is implausible in the extreme— the U.S. submarines safely at sea would retain about two-and-a-half times the deliverable megatonnage that McNamara's analysis found sufficient to destroy the Soviet Union.

Regional Nuclear Forces

Table 2.5 shows the regional nuclear forces—those of less than intercontinental range—in the arsenals of NATO, the Warsaw Treaty Organization, and the People's Republic of China.[40] The table follows the convention of the Stockholm International Peace Research Institute in classifying regional forces as long range over 1,000 kilometers, medium range from 200 to 1,000 kilometers, and short range as less than 200 kilometers. The short-range systems often are referred to as "battlefield" nuclear weapons.

The figures shown in the table represent total inventories of regional-range, nuclear-capable missiles and aircraft possessed by the countries indicated, no matter where deployed. (The single exception is the short-range category, which applies only to systems deployed in Europe; the global data for these systems are fragmentary.) Except for the "total stockpile" figures, the numbers of bombs and warheads shown are the theoretical "single-launch" delivery capabilities, assuming that each missile launcher and aircraft is used once. Ignoring reload missiles and

Table 2.5 Regional Nuclear Forces, 1982

	NATO	WTO	CHINA
Long-range regional land-based missiles[a]			
Missiles[b]	18	581	114
Warheads	18	1,247	114
Regional submarine-launched ballistic missiles[c]			
Missiles	144	49	3
Warheads	144-272[d]	49	3
Long-range regional nuclear-capable aircraft[a,e]			
Aircraft	1,339[f]	1,410[g]	120[h]
Bombs/warheads	2,826	3,100	240
Medium-range regional nuclear-capable missiles[i]			
Missiles/warheads	180	1,006-1,216[j]	?
Medium-range regional nuclear-capable aircraft[e]			
Aircraft	3,568[k]	2,286[l]	1,100?[m]
Bombs/warheads	4,298	2,286	1,100
Short-range regional nuclear-capable missiles and artillery[n]			
Missiles	229	1,076[o]	?
Artillery pieces	2,137	168	?
Total stockpile of nuclear weapons for regional forces			
Bombs/warheads/mines	18,000?	15,000?	500??

[a] Long-range regional forces are those with range (or, in the case of aircraft, unre-fueled combat radius) exceeding 1,000 kilometers.

[b] Includes missiles on launchers, not reloads or spares. Excludes intercontinental-range missiles counted under SALT (and listed in Table 2.4) but assigned to regional roles. Chinese total includes four T-4 ICBMs presumed targeted on Soviet Union.

[c] Excludes missiles counted under SALT (and listed in Table 2.4) but assigned to regional roles.

[d] The 64 British Polaris A-3 missiles carry three warheads each, but these are often counted as one because they are not independently targetable (they fall in a triangular pattern around the aim point). For purposes of penetrating the modest anti-Ballistic Missile system deployed around Moscow, however, the three warheads per missile are just as valuable as if they were MIRVed.

[e] Includes aircraft on carriers and assigned to naval aviation as well as in air forces. Not all aircraft considered nuclear-capable are assigned to nuclear roles. Accordingly, nuclear bomb/warhead figures denote theoretical capabilities, not real inventories.

ᶠ Included are U.S. FB-111A, F-111D/E/F, and A-6E; U.K. Buccaneer; French Mirage IVA; and NATO F-16, Jaguar, and Tornado. Assumed nuclear weapon loads per aircraft: FB-111A, four; F-111D/E/F/, three; A-6E, F-16, and Buccaneer, two; all others one.

ᵍ Included are Tu-22M Backfire, Tu-16 Badger, Tu-22 Blinder, and Su-24 Fencer. Backfire assumed to carry three nuclear weapons; all others assumed to carry two.

ʰ Chinese bombers are denoted B-6 but are identical to Soviet T-16 Badger. They are assumed here to carry two nuclear weapons each.

ⁱ Medium-range regional forces are those with range (or, in the case of aircraft, unrefueled combat radius) between 200 and 1,000 kilometers.

ʲ Both figures assume that half the Soviet inventory of Scud missiles are the longer-range Scud-B. The lower figure excludes 210 SS-22s, SS-23s, and SS-C-1b missiles counted by Western authorities but not admitted by the Soviets. Both figures include 568 dual-capable, sea-launched cruise missiles thought to be intended mainly for antiship roles; most analyses of "European theater" nuclear forces have excluded these missiles.

ᵏ Included are U.K. Sea Harrier, French Mirage IIIE and Super Etendard, and NATO F-4E, A-7, and F-104G (but excluding Canadian, Danish, and Norwegian aircraft, which are unlikely to have nuclear roles). Aircraft configured as fighter-interceptors, for reconnaissance, and for electronic countermeasures are not counted. The A-7 are assumed to carry two nuclear weapons each; all others are assumed to carry one.

ˡ Included are Soviet and other WTO MiG-21, MiG-23/27, Su-7, Su-17, and Su-25 configured for ground-attack roles. Aircraft configured as fighter-interceptors, for reconnaissance, and for electronic countermeasures are not counted.

ᵐ This figure is based on 580 B-5 light bombers and some 500 F-4 and A-5 ground-attack fighters. How many of the latter actually are nuclear-capable is not certain.

ⁿ These forces have ranges less than 200 kilometers. Most are dual-capable (conventional or nuclear). Figures under this heading are for European theater only.

ᵒ Includes 154 short-range, nuclear capable, sea-launched cruise missiles assigned to antiship roles and often excluded from analyses of theater nuclear forces.

Source: See Table 2.4.

bombs for some systems tends to understate potential destructive capacity, but to assume that all nuclear-capable systems actually are assigned nuclear roles would tend to overstate it.

As the welter of detail in Table 2.5 suggests, it is possible to promote diverse impressions about the balance of regional nuclear forces simply by selecting different categories of forces for attention. The Reagan administration has chosen to focus on long-range regional land-based missiles and their warheads, indices in which the Warsaw Treaty Organization has an enormous advantage. (The administration chooses also to omit China from its comparisons, and to count only weapons in and around Europe—as if that were the only area where a collision of U.S. and Soviet interests could erupt into war, and as if the enormous additional regional-range nuclear forces maintained in the United States could not be brought to bear where needed.)

If one looks at the whole spectrum of regional nuclear forces, however, it is hard to see much basis for the view that NATO is meaningfully inferior to the Warsaw Treaty Organization. The WTO has an overall edge in missiles, but NATO remains superior overall in nuclear-capable aircraft and in total number of nuclear bombs and warheads. The total size and diversity of the regional nuclear arsenals on both sides, in fact, are so great as to render academic any asymmetries in individual categories. Use of any substantial part of these arsenals in a regional conflict would utterly devastate the region being fought over. And if, nevertheless, some analysts wish to insist that gaps in certain categories of regional nuclear weaponry represent real liabilities, they should be reassured by the adaptability of the enormous stocks of intercontinental nuclear weapons to fill regional roles.

Conventional Forces

It is sometimes asserted that the United States has no choice but to try to maintain nuclear superiority over the Soviet Union, to offset the inability or unwillingness of this country and its NATO allies to match the conventional military power of the Warsaw Pact. Is the Warsaw Pact actually so much more powerful than the West in conventional forces? Is there indeed no prospect of countering conventional offensive power with conventional defensive capability, rather than with nuclear threats?

Table 2.6 displays some indicators of conventional military power and underlying economic strength for NATO, the Warsaw Treaty Organization, and China. These figures differ from those publicized by the Reagan administration in several important respects.[41] First, the Reagan administration comparisons omit China, although the Soviet Union continues to deploy about one-fourth of its military forces opposite the Chinese border. Second, the Reagan figures omit Spain, which joined the NATO alliance in May 1982, and France, which has been a member since the inception of the alliance in 1949. (France withdrew its military forces from integrated NATO control in 1966, but remains committed—as a full member of the alliance itself—to consider an attack on any member to be an attack on herself. The Soviet Union cannot and does not count on France to stand aside in the event of a Warsaw Pact attack on, say, West Germany.)

The figures in Table 2.6 do not support the notion of overwhelming Warsaw Pact superiority. NATO has more than one and a half times the population, more than three times the economic power, and more active military personnel than the War-

Table 2.6 Indices of Conventional Military and Economic Power, 1982

	NATO	WTO	CHINA
Population (millions)[a]	625	381	1,000
Gross National Product[b] (billions US$)	6,035	1,718	500
Military spending[c] (billions US$)	290	220	40
Military personnel (millions)			
Active	5.3	4.8	4
Reserve	6.2	7.1	12
Combat aircraft[d]			
Planes	11,300	10,600	6,100
Helicopters	9,900	2,500	350
Major warships[e]			
Surface	435	295	34
Submarines	277	362	103
Main battle tanks	28,000	63,000	10,500
Major anti-tank guns and anti-tank missile launchers	40,000+	36,000+	8,000+
Artillery, mortars, and multiple rocket launchers	26,100	38,700	29,200

[a] Population figures are from *1982 World Population Data Sheet* (Washington, DC; Population Reference Bureau, 1982).

[b] NATO and WTO GNP figures are based on 1980 data from *World Development Report 1982* (Washington, DC; World Bank, 1982), extrapolated to 1982 using the 1981 and 1982 growth rates supplied therein for industrial market and nonmarket economies. Figures for Chinese GNP vary from 300 to 600 billion U.S. dollars.

[c] NATO and WTO military spending figures are based on 1981 data from *The Military Balance 1982-83* (London: International Institute for Strategic Studies, 1982), extrapolated to 1982 using recent growth rates supplied therein (except for the U.S. contribution, for which official Department of Defense figures were used). The Chinese figure is a very rough estimate based on military spending at 7 to 8 percent of GNP.

[d] Planes and helicopters designed and configured to carry and use such weapons as guns, bombs, rockets, depth charges, and torpedoes. Transport, reconnaissance, and electronic-countermeasure aircraft are not included. These figures include the nuclear-capable aircraft listed in Tables 2.4 and 2.5.

[e] Includes armed submarines and armed surface ships from aircraft carriers down to (and including) frigates. Minesweepers, patrol boats, and transport ships are not included.

Source: Except as noted above, source is the same as in Table 2.4.

saw Treaty Organization; and NATO spends more on defense. NATO also has more major surface warships, more combat helicopters, and about the same number of combat airplanes. WTO advantages over NATO in reserve military personnel, submarines, and artillery-type weapons are reversed when Chinese forces are brought into the balance. Only in heavy tanks does the Warsaw Pact have a numerical advantage over all its potential adversaries combined, and this advantage is offset by NATO superiority in major antitank weapons. (When smaller antitank missiles carried by individual soldiers are counted, moreover, NATO has more than five antitank weapons for every Soviet tank.)

Of course, aggregate numbers of the sort shown in Table 2.6 do not tell the whole story about relative military power. It is necessary to consider the quality of the forces as well as their quantity, meaning not only the technological characteristics of the weapons, but also the capabilities of communication systems and supply lines, the level of training and morale of the troops, the ability and initiative of the officers, the speed of mobilization of reserves, the likely cohesion of the alliances under various circumstances, and more. While consideration of these factors reveals both assets and liabilities from NATO's viewpoint, the former probably outweigh the latter.[42] Soviet weaponry, for example, while superior to that of the Chinese, is on the whole still inferior technologically to that of NATO. Perhaps most important, the reliability of the troops from such Warsaw Pact members as Poland and Czechoslavakia, under the circumstance of a WTO invasion of the West, must remain a major question mark for the Soviets.

A more pessimistic assessment of the NATO/Warsaw Pact balance can be constructed by focusing exclusively on the forces arrayed opposite the "Central European Front," namely, the boundary between the Federal Republic of Germany, on the western side, and the German Democratic Republic and Czechoslovakia, on the eastern side. It is generally supposed that a major war in Europe, if it comes at all, would start here. Leaving aside the question of the reliability of their allies, the Soviets could muster an initial local superiority of men and conventional weaponry amounting to a factor of 1.2 to 1.5 in this region. These ratios are far from the factor of 2.5 to 3 preponderance of offense over defense generally thought to be necessary to give the offense a high probability of decisive victory.[43]

Nuclear "Defense" of Europe

Although, as the foregoing analysis suggests, the prospects for a conventional defense of Europe are by no means as dismal as is often alleged, many Europeans remain extremely nervous about the threat on their eastern borders. With today's weapons, even a conventional war in Europe could devastate the continent. This circumstance increases the attractiveness—to some Europeans—of deterring all conflict in Europe with the threat that any such conflict is likely to escalate into global nuclear war.

Toward the end of the 1970s, Europeans of this persuasion were made increasingly uneasy by a combination of developments that seemed to undermine the credibility of the threat of escalation on which they believed their security depended. One such development was the Soviet upgrading of their intermediate-range nuclear forces targeted on Europe, greatly increasing their counterforce/nuclear war fighting capabilities in that theater. Another was the US-USSR stalemate at the level of war fighting capabilities in that theater. Another was the US-USSR stalemate at the level of intercontinental nuclear forces, making it seem less likely that the United States would use these forces to offset Soviet theater advantages or to escalate to intercontinental strikes against the Soviet Union itself in retaliation for a Warsaw Pact attack on Western Europe.

These European concerns about the credibility of the U.S. commitment to the nuclear defense of Europe were shared by many policymakers in the United States. The eventual result was the so-called "two-track" decision certified by NATO leaders in Brussels in December 1979.[44] The approach agreed upon was intended not only to reinforce the "linkage" of U.S. stragegic forces to the defense of Europe, but also to strengthen U.S. strategic nuclear capabilities against the Soviet Union in a manner not constrained by the agreement on intercontinental forces being sought in the SALT II negotiations.

The first "track" consisted of the commitment, mentioned above, to begin deploying in Western Europe, in December 1983, 108 Pershing II ballistic missiles and 464 ground-launched cruise missiles. All these nuclear-armed missiles could reach targets not only in the European theater but in the Soviet Union itself. With the Pershing's high accuracy and short flight-time, it would augment the "time-urgent, counterforce" capabilities now residing largely in the U.S. land-based ICBM force. And by placing in the path of a Warsaw Pact invasion of Western Europe a weapon that is manifestly part of U.S. strategic forces, the Pershing II deployment ostensibly would tighten the link between those forces and the defense of Europe. (It has sometimes been suggested, for the benefit of U.S. audiences, that the purpose of the new deployments is to make it possible for this country to participate more effectively in a nuclear war in Europe *without* resorting to intercontinental weapons, with the attendant dangers of escalation to a global war. It cannot be emphasized enough that the official rationale is the opposite: to convince the Soviets, for deterrence's sake, that a nuclear war could not be confined to Europe.)[45]

The cruise missiles, also highly accurate but lacking the Pershing's short flight-time, would take over some of the nuclear missions of NATO's dual-capable aircraft. Not only would the cruise missiles be better able to penetrate Warsaw Pact air defenses than would the aircraft, but they could also free some of the latter for conventional roles and thus strengthen NATO's conventional posture.

The proposed NATO deployments have serious drawbacks, however. First, the Pershing II's "prompt counterforce" capability is synonymous with first-strike potential. That missile's combination of high accuracy and short flight-time is in fact unprecedented; the SS-20, for example, is as fast but only a tenth as accurate. The Soviets claim they fear especially the Pershing's ability to destroy with almost no warning not only their hardened missile silos, but also the command bunkers in which their leaders would take shelter in time of conflict. (This capability fits disconcertingly well with the "countervailing strategy" announced in 1980 in Presidential Directive 59.) Just as NATO argued that the SS-20s were a qualitatively new threat requiring a NATO response, so the Soviets now argue that the Pershings will require a response on their part. One possibility that has been mentioned is putting the Soviet nuclear forces within range of Pershing II on a launch-on-warning footing, which of course would aggravate the hair-trigger nature of the nuclear standoff and increase the chance of nuclear war by mistake.

The ground-launched cruise missiles that NATO proposes to deploy do not have the crisis-instability characteristics of the Pershings (and SS-20s), but their deployment could trigger arms-race instability by opening up a new arena of competition that would be especially difficult to bring under control. Because cruise missiles are very small, highly mobile, and usable with both conventional and nuclear warheads, each side could find it difficult to be sure of how many nuclear-armed cruise missiles were in the other side's arsenal. This difficulty not only would complicate arms-control agreements; it would also surely aggravate the worst-case assessment syndrome that has combined with the action-reaction phenomenon to drive much of the arms race to date. But the United States has perhaps a five-year lead in cruise-missile technology (as it once did with MIRVs) and is reluctant to give up this "advantage."

The second track of the December 1979 NATO decision was designed to allay fears about the liabilities of the first: it proposed bilateral U.S.–Soviet negotiations to limit intermediate-range nuclear weaponry in Europe, which, if completely successful, would remove the "necessity" to deploy the Pershings and cruise missiles. These negotiations took place (off and on) in Geneva starting in 1980 and ending with the Soviet walkout in November 1983. The Soviets had made several significant concessions in the course of the negotiations, but it became apparent that the Reagan administration wanted the new deployments worse than it wanted any conceivable agreement.

ICBM Vulnerability and the MX

The other major nuclear arms race issue of the 1980s has proven to be the theoretical vulnerability of land-based ICBMs, brought about (as discussed above) by the combination of MIRVing and increased accuracy of the ICBM warheads on both sides. That U.S. ICBMs eventually would become vulnerable to a Soviet first strike was recognized even in the 1960s, and the search for a solution began in the Nixon administration.

For a time, it was thought that ICBM fields could be defended with antiballistic missiles (ABMs), but this idea was abandoned officially soon after the signing of the ABM treaty in 1972. (Under that treaty each side initially was permitted two ABM sites—a figure reduced by subsequent agreement to one site each—but the United States did not exercise this option for long.) Thereafter, the search for a solution focused on a new missile, the MX, which was to have two characteristics: its basing mode was to make it invulnerable to attack, and it was to restore "parity" by threatening Soviet missiles as they were threatening ours.[46]

In fact, however, it is highly questionable whether the U.S. ICBMs were or are vulnerable in any meaningful sense. Under carefully controlled conditions and over well-tried trajectories, individual Soviet ICBMs have demonstrated accuracy sufficient (given the explosive yield of the warheads) to produce an 80-percent probability of destroying a Minuteman silo for each warhead delivered. It is exceedingly unlikely, however, that this performance could be matched in a perfectly coordinated launch of hundreds of operational missiles over previously untried over-the-pole trajectories.[47]

Even if the Soviets thought they had solved the technical problem just described, it is far from clear what they could hope to accomplish militarily or politically by carrying out this feat. First, they could never be sure that the United States would not launch its ICBMs upon receiving satellite and radar warning of the incoming Soviet missiles. Second, even if the United States, by failing to launch on warning, permitted its ICBMs to be destroyed in their silos, we would still possess intercontinental bomber forces and submarine-launched ballistic missiles sufficient to destroy the Soviet Union several times over. (The bombers could not all be destroyed in the same attack that gets the ICBMs, because many would take off upon warning of the Soviet launches, and the submarines at sea cannot be targeted at all.)

The hand-wringers about ICBM vulnerability have claimed that a Soviet first strike against U.S. Minutemen would give the Soviets "escalation dominance": by using only a fraction of their land-based ICBMs to destroy all of ours, the Soviets would have deprived us of our most effective nuclear-war-fighting weapons (an evaluation based on the speed, accuracy, and flexibility/control of ICBMs), while retaining some of their own; since our only recourse would be to threaten the destruction of Soviet cities using our bombers and subs—a prescription for mutual suicide, given the remaining Soviet forces—we would be out of credible options.

The hand-wringers' argument is wrong on two crucial counts. First, the hypothesized destruction of the U.S. land-based ICBMs would produce at least 10 to 20 million "collateral" deaths among the American public. The Soviet leaders must realize that this level of destruction would cause automatic massive U.S. retaliation with the bombers and subs, leading to the total devastation of both societies. Second, it is not true that the U.S. bombers and submarine-launched missiles would provide no options beyond countercity retaliation. The sub-launched missiles have sufficient accuracy and power to destroy nearly all military targets in the Soviet Union, and the bombers—with their combination of gravity bombs, supersonic ground-attack missiles, and air-launched cruise missiles—could destroy even the most hardened missile silos and command bunkers.

It is ironic, given all the uproar about ICBM vulnerability in the United States, that the Soviet Union is in fact more vulnerable than we are. ("The window of vulnerability", as Nobel Laureate Hans Bethe has said, "is on the other side of the house.") On paper, a first strike using the 550 U.S. Minuteman III MIRVed missiles (1650 warheads, all more accurate than any the Soviets now possess) could destroy more than 90 percent of the modern MIRVed Soviet ICBMs (150 SS-17s, 308 SS-18s, 310 SS-19s). The Soviets would be left mainly with inaccurate, "city-buster" SS-11s and SS-13s, while the United States retained 450 highly accurate Minuteman IIs. Since, moreover, the Soviets have far more of their nuclear power concentrated in their land-based ICBMs than does the United States, such a preemptive attack would be a much bigger blow to their nuclear-war-fighting capability than a Soviet preemptive attack would be to ours.

In April 1983, the President's Commission on Strategic Forces (the "Scowcroft Commission") conceded three key points to critics of the contention that the U.S. needs the MX:[48] first, that the survivability of U.S. bombers and submarines makes the theoretical vulnerability of our land-based ICBMs militarily unimportant; second, that no basing mode has yet been identified for the MX that would make it *less* vulnerable than the Minutemen; and, third, that MIRVed, accurate, land-based ICBMs, by offering a favorable "exchange ratio" to the side that fires first, do decrease the security of both sides by increasing the chance of nuclear war. Having thus disposed entirely of the original rationale for the MX, and having explained further why its deployment would exacerbate existing dangers, the commission

Table 2.7 Major Nuclear Arms Control Agreements

Partial Test Ban Treaty (signed 8/63, in force 10/63; parties US, USSR, UK). Prohibits nuclear explosions in the atmosphere, in space, under water, and under any circumstances producing radioactive fallout outside the country conducting the test.

Outer Space Treaty (signed 1/67, in force 10/67; 76 parties, including US, USSR, UK). Prohibits stationing in earth orbit or elsewhere in space any nuclear weapons or other weapons of mass destruction.

Treaty of Tlatelolco (signed 2/67, in force 4/68; parties include 23 Latin American countries, but not in force for Brazil, Argentina, or Chile). Prohibits acquisition, storage, deployment, testing, and use of nuclear weapons by all Latin American countries. Under a Protocol to the treaty, countries outside Latin America possessing nuclear weapons agree not to use or threaten to use nuclear weapons against parties to the treaty.

Non-Proliferation Treaty (signed 7/68, in force 3/70; 115 parties including the US, USSR, and UK but not France or China). Prohibits countries possessing nuclear weapons or nuclear-weapons technology from transferring these to others; prohibits others from receiving these. Obligates countries without nuclear weapons to subject their peaceful nuclear energy facilities to International Atomic Energy Agency safeguards against diversion for nuclear explosives. Entitles countries without nuclear weapons to peaceful nuclear technology and assistance from countries with such weapons. Obligates countries with weapons to pursue negotiation toward (a) cessation of the nuclear arms race and (b) nuclear disarmament.

Sea-Bed Treaty (signed 2/71, in force 5/72; 66 parties, including US, USSR, UK). Prohibits emplacing nuclear weapons or other weapons of mass destruction on or under the sea bed and ocean floor outside the 12-mile territorial limit.

SALT I ABM Treaty (signed 5/72, in force 10/72; parties US, USSR). Permits each country to deploy ABM systems protecting at most two areas: the national capital and one ICBM complex. (A protocol signed 7/74 and in force 5/76 reduced the allowance to one area per country.) Each system must not exceed 100 launchers and 100 missiles.

SALT I Interim Agreement (signed 5/72, in force 10/72; parties US, USSR). Establishes five-year freeze on aggregate number of fixed land-based ICBM launchers and ballistic-missile launchers on modern submarines. Limits US to 710 ballistic-missile launchers on submarines and 44 modern ballistic-missile subs and USSR to 950 ballistic-missile launchers on submarines and 62 modern ballistic-missile subs. When the agreement expired in 10/77, both the US and the USSR formally stated their intention to refrain from any action incompatible with its provisions.

Threshold Test Ban Treaty (signed 7/74, not yet ratified but being observed; parties US, USSR). Prohibits underground nuclear weapons tests exceeding a yield of 150 kilotons. Underground explosions for peaceful purposes are covered by a separate agreement.

Peaceful Nuclear Explosions Treaty (signed 5/76, not yet ratified but being observed; parties US, USSR). Prohibits individual underground nuclear explosions for peaceful purposes exceeding 150 kilotons yield and group explosions for peaceful purposes exceeding an aggregate yield of 1,500 kilotons.

SALT II Treaty (signed 6/79, not ratified but being observed; parties US, USSR). Establishes an initial ceiling on both parties of 2,400 aggregate ICBM launchers, submarine ballistic-missile launchers, heavy bombers, and air-to-surface ballistic missiles with range over 600 kilometers, falling to 2,250 at the end of 1981. Imposes sublimits of: 1320 MIRVed launchers (ICBMs, SLBMs, air-to-surface ballistic missiles, and cruise-missile-equipped bombers); 1200 MIRVed ballistic-missile launchers; and 820 MIRVed ICBM launchers. Establishes freezes on number of warheads on current ICBMs and ceilings for number of warheads on other MIRVed delivery vehicles. Allows each side one new type of ICBM with a maximum of 10 warheads. To remain in force until the end of 1985.

Source: Characteristics summarized from Stockholm International Peace Research Institute, *World Armaments and Disarmament: The 1982 SIPRI Yearbook* (Cambridge, MA: Oelgeschlager, Gunn, and Hain, 1982).

then (astonishingly) recommended that the United States proceed to deploy 100 MX missiles, carrying 1,000 warheads, in existing Minuteman silos. Their rationale appears to have been that the Soviet Union must not be permitted to have even the appearance of a capability that the United States lacks (associated, in this case, with land-based ICBMs carrying more than three warheads) and that the Soviets will not get serious about negotiating limits on such weapons until the United States demonstrates its "resolve" by deploying its own.

 The Reagan administration immediately embraced the Scow croft report as an endorsement of its policies on strategic forces —as indeed the report was tailored to be—and is pushing ahead with the MX. Unless Congress comes to its senses, therefore, we will shortly see the United States demonstrate its resolve by deploying yet another expensive, unnecessary, and destabilizing weapon—sug gesting that three and a half decades of increasingly dangerous action and reaction in the nuclear arms race have taught us nothing at all.

PROBLEMS AND PROSPECTS OF ARMS CONTROL

It is often said that arms control efforts to date have not so much controlled the nuclear arms race as managed it, and the history of the size and character of nuclear arsenals tends to support that view. Not surprisingly, both sides have often approached negotiations as one more means for seeking unilateral advantage: both have sought controls mainly on weapons systems in which the other was thought to have an advantage, while seeking to exempt from limitation those systems in which it was ahead. Agreed-upon numerical limits have tended to codify the inventories already achieved, or soon expected, rather than requiring reductions; and build-ups have proceeded apace *during* the process of negotiation, diminishing month by month the value of any agreement that might eventually be reached. The idea of acquiring bargaining chips, to be used in future negotiations or even in ongoing ones, has actually accelerated the arms race in some instances. Once acquired, of course, these chips almost never are given up. And when negotiated agreements have managed to close off certain avenues of the arms race, the result usually has been simply to divert the efforts of the weaponeers into the other channels still available.[49]

Major Agreements

The major agreements in the history of nuclear arms control are summarized in Table 2.7. Within this group, those that come closest to being exceptions to the foregoing generally gloomy view of arms control are those that have limited the testing of nuclear weapons. These prohibitions on testing, albeit far from comprehensive, almost certainly have slowed the development of new forms and applications of nuclear weapons. Particularly useful has been the inability of both sides to test, in the atmosphere, the "fratricide" effect of two warheads arriving almost simultaneously at the same target. The lack of such tests is a major and benign uncertainty reducing the confidence of both sides in their ability to destroy the land-based ICBMs of the other side in a first strike.

 In the same vein, it is a great misfortune that the trilateral (US-USSR-UK) negotiations toward a comprehensive test ban (CTB), which began in 1977, fell apart in

1980 after solving most of the substantive problems associated with verifying such a ban.[50] There is little doubt that a major factor in the collapse of these negotiations was the intense lobbying of the U.S. weapons laboratories and the Joint Chiefs of Staff, who argued that continued testing would produce dramatic breakthroughs in ballistic missile defense and other applications of nuclear weapons.

The most important outcome of the first round of Strategic Arms Limitation Talks (SALT I) was the ABM treaty, without which the continuing attempts of both countries to develop defenses against ballistic missiles would surely have stimulated a runaway offensive arms race. Notwithstanding the logic of the treaty, however, it probably was approved only because both sides became convinced that ABM technology was not yet good enough to be very useful. President Reagan's March 1983 resurrection of official enthusiasm for ballistic missile defense may bode ill for the long-term viability of this very useful treaty.[51]

The SALT I Interim Agreement and the SALT II Treaty are the best imaginable examples of "arms-control" agreements codifying not merely the status quo, but also any pending weapons developments in which either side was very interested at the time. As noted above, the United States successfully resisted Soviet attempts to limit MIRVs in the SALT I negotiations, when the U.S. had a significant lead in this technology, and our side similarly resisted Soviet attempts to limit cruise missiles in SALT II. The Soviets, for their part, successfully negotiated limits on MIRved ICBMs generous enough not to imperil their ambitious programs in this dimension of nuclear weaponry. At the same time, it is hard to dispute that SALT I and SALT II were better than no agreement at all, and it is to be hoped that both sides will continue to observe those limits until something better is negotiated.

Prospects for Future Agreements

Hopes for early progress in nuclear arms control rest on three sets of negotiations presently underway. One, the negotiations in Geneva on European/intermediate-range nuclear forces, has already been discussed above. The second is the Strategic Arms Reduction Talks (START), also in Geneva, which began in 1982. The third relevant set of talks is that on Multilateral Balanced Force Reductions (MBFR), which has been going on in Vienna since 1973. (This last set of talks deals with conventional forces in Europe, not nuclear forces; but for reasons made clear above it is unlikely that any long-term agreeement on nuclear forces in Europe will succeed unless a satisfactory conventional balance can be maintained, as well.)

At the moment, there is little sign of progress in any of these three sets of negotiations. They are all entangled, as such negotiations always have been, in endless disputes over the categories of weapons to be included, the indices by which the capabilities of these weapons will be measured and balanced off against one another, and the procedures with which each side will verify the compliance of the other in any agreement reached. Each side may also have other reasons for delay: the Soviets may hope Mr. Reagan will be replaced, in the 1984 election, by a more tractable leader, and the Americans may think the Soviets will become more reasonable once the United States has more of its pending bargaining chips on the table. All this, of course, is a recipe for continuation of the nuclear arms race while our leaders dither.

What could be done? There has been no shortage of promising proposals. Here is an abbreviated selection.

1. An *interim freeze* on all testing, production, and deployment of nuclear weapons and long-range nuclear delivery vehicles —comprehensively defined and quickly agreed upon for a period of, say, five years—could provide a starting point, circumventing the perennial problem of continuing buildups while negotiations proceed.[52] While verification of such an agreement could not be perfect, such violations as might escape detection could hardly be large enough to upset the existing balance of nuclear power in the space of five years. Indeed, the risks associated with the possibility of violations would be minuscule in comparison to the costs and risks associated with the further deployments of intercontinental and theater nuclear weapons that are now pending.

2. *Subsequent negotiations on substantial reductions* in the nuclear arsenals on both sides should be focused on eliminating the most destabilizing weapons—those combining high counterforce capability with vulnerability to preemption by the other side.[53] These negotiations should also be consolidated into a single forum, eliminating the often-artificial distinctions between, for example, "theater" and "strategic" weapons. This approach would terminate the otherwise endless set of disputes over the boundaries of categories of weapons, and it would permit balancing off the inevitable asymmetries within different categories in the larger context of a robust global balance.

3. The United States and its NATO allies should *abandon the doctrine of extended deterrence*—trying to deter nonnuclear attacks with the threat of initiating nuclear war—and with it our posture of first use of nuclear weapons if necessary in Europe.[54] A conventional war being lost in Europe could not be salvaged with nuclear weapons, and the deterrent value of the threat of escalation is outweighed by the dangers associated with trying to make the threat credible. Almost certainly the existing NATO conventional forces are adequate to deter any Soviet inclination to invade Western Europe, and if careful reexamination suggests otherwise, then the necessary improvements in conventional forces should be considered inexpensive insurance against useless escalation into nuclear war.

4. The United States and the Soviet Union should seek an *immediate moratoriam on the further militarization of space,* restricting the uses of satellites to reconnaissance and communication and abandoning efforts at antisatellite weapons and space-based missile defense.[55] The alternative is a further arms race in space, which at best will be staggeringly expensive but fruitless, and at worst will substantially increase the chance of nuclear war.

The foregoing may appear an ambitious agenda, the more so because of the modest accomplishments of the past three and a half decades of attempts at nuclear arms control. It is hard to imagine, however, given the nature of the threat, that any less will suffice. The most important prerequisite is a new awareness on the part of the leaders on both sides that no risks associated with arms control can compare with the dangers of continuation along the present path. There is, after all, only one function of nuclear weapons in this world that can withstand analysis, and that is to discourage their use by others who have them. For that purpose, both sides already have far more than enough.[56]

NOTES

1. Lord Solly Zuckerman, *Nuclear Illusion and Reality* (New York: Viking Press, 1982), pp. 105-6.
2. Probably the best introductory book covering this set of topics is Bruce Russett, *The Prisoners of Insecurity: Nuclear Deterrence, the Arms Race, and Arms Control* (San Francisco: W.H. Freeman, 1983). A more detailed book, indispensable for the serious student of the arms race, is Lawrence Freedman, *The Evolution of Nuclear Strategy* (New York: St. Martin's Press, 1981).
3. See, for example, Herbert F. York, *Race to Oblivion: A Participant's View of the Arms Race* (New York: Simon and Schuster, 1970); idem, *The Advisors: Oppenheimer, Teller, and the Superbomb* (San Francisco: W.H. Freeman, 1976); Jacques S. Gansler, *The Defense Industry* (Cambridge: M.I.T. Press, 1980).
4. Adam Yarmolinsky, *The Military Establishment* (New York: Harper & Row, 1971); Sam Sarkesian, ed., *The Military-Industrial Complex: A Reassessment* (Beverly Hills: Sage Publications, 1972); Richard J. Barnet, *Roots of War* (New York: Atheneum, 1972).
5. More detailed treatments of the action-reaction syndrome are provided by George W. Rathjens, "The Dynamics of the Arms Race," *Scientific American,* April 1969, reprinted in Herbert F. York, ed., *Arms Control: Readings from Scientific American* (San Francisco: W.H. Freeman, 1973); and Jeremy J. Stone, "When and How to Use 'SALT,' " *Foreign Affairs* 48, no. 2 (January 1970): 262-73.
6. Quoted in Freedman, *Evolution of Nuclear Strategy,* p. 85.
7. Ibid., p. 265.
8. Ruth Leger Sivard, *World Military and Social Expenditures 1982* (Leesburg, VA: World Priorities, 1982).
9. Good references on this history include the Russett and Freedman books cited in note 2, plus Herbert F. York, ed., *Arms Control: Readings from Scientific American* (cited in note 5); and Philip Morrison, "The Spiral of Peril: A Narrative of the Arms Race," *Bulletin of the Atomic Scientists* (January 1983): 10-17.
10. In principle, the Soviets' medium-range piston-engine TU-4 "Bull" bomber (a B-29 imitation that entered service in 1948) and their TU-16 "Badger" jet-engine medium bomber (which entered service in 1954) could have bombed parts of the continental United States on one-way "suicide" missions. In reality, there is no sign that the TU-4 was ever assigned any nuclear role. See Robert P. Berman and John C. Baker, *Soviet Strategic Forces: Requirements and Responses* (Washington, D.C.: The Brookings Institution, 1982), p. 42.
11. See, e.g., Gregg Herken, *The Winning Weapon: The Atomic Bomb in the Cold War, 1945-50* (New York: Random House, 1981).
12. Ibid.; David Alan Rosenberg, "U.S. Nuclear Stockpile, 1945 to 1950," *Bulletin of the Atomic Scientists* (May 1982): 25-30.
13. Dan Ellsberg, "Introduction", in *Protest and Survive,* E.P. Thompson and Dan Smith, eds. (New York: Monthly Review Press, 1981); Freedman, *Evolution of Nuclear Strategy,* p. 72.
14. Ellsberg, "Introduction"; Freedman, *Evolution,* pp. 84-85.
15. Ellsberg, "Introduction"; Freedman, *Evolution,* p. 89.

16. Ellsberg, "Introduction."

17. McGeorge Bundy, George F. Kennan, Robert S. McNamara, and Gerard Smith, "Nuclear Weapons and the Atlantic Alliance," *Foreign Affairs* 60, no. 4 (Spring 1982): 753-68.

18. Matthew A. Evangelista, "Stalin's Postwar Army Re-appraised," *International Security* 7, no. 3 (Winter 1982/83): 110-38; David Alan Rosenberg, "The Origins of Overkill: Nuclear Weapons and American Strategy, 1945-60," *International Security* 7, no. 4 (Spring 1983): 3-71.

19. Such possible rationales include the maintenance and exploitation of the global supremacy inherent in substantial superiority in nuclear weaponry and the preservation of a unique role —and hence unique influence—for the United States as the protector of its European allies. See Herken, *The Winning Weapon,* and the references cited in note 18.

20. Nikita Khrushchev, *Khrushchev Remembers* (London: Andre Deutsch, 1974).

21. A seventh type, the mobile, solid-fueled SS-X-16, was prohibited by the SALT I treaty and was never deployed. The SS-13 experienced difficulties with its propulsion and guidance systems, and only 60 were deployed. On this and subsequent details of Soviet nuclear forces, the key references are Berman and Baker, *Soviet Strategic Forces*; Stockholm International Peace Research Institute, *The Arms Race*; and International Institute for Strategic Studies, *The Military Balance*.

22. Berman and Baker, *Soviet Strategic Forces*, pp. 45-48.

23. The best account of the MIRV debate and decision is Ted Greenwood, *Making the MIRV: A Study in Defense Decision Making* (Cambridge, MA: Ballinger, 1975).

24. I have relied heavily, in my summary of the history of strategic doctrine, on the superb and definitive account by Lawrence Freedman, *Evolution of Nuclear Strategy.* See also Henry S. Rowen, "The Evolution of Strategic Nuclear Doctrine," in *Strategic Thought in the Nuclear Age,* ed. Lawrence Martin (Baltimore: Johns Hopkins University Press, 1981), pp. 131-56; and Desmond Ball, "U.S. Strategic Forces: How Would They Be Used?" *International Security* 7, no. 3 (Winter 1982/83): 31-60.

25. Herken, *The Winning Weapon*; Rosenberg, "U.S. Nuclear Stockpile."

26. The earliest ICBMs required hours of preparation to fire and were vulnerable to being destroyed on their launching pads, but once launched they reached their targets in half an hour. Thus, they offered an advantage to the side that managed to launch a surprise first strike. With their even shorter flight-time, sub-launched missiles fired from just offshore might catch most of the adversary's bombers on the ground.

27. Stalin's dogma, which could not be challenged while he was alive, was that the key factors in determining the outcome of any war were "the stability of the rear, the morale of the army, the quantity and quality of the divisions, the armaments of the army, and the organizational ability of the army commanders." See Freedman, *Evolution of Nuclear Strategy,* p. 58. See also Berman and Baker, *Soviet Strategic Forces,* chap. 2.

28. This MAD acronym was coined in the early 1970s by one of the doctrine's critics, from the combination of "mutual deterrence" and "assured destruction." As Lawrence Freedman points out in his definitive survey of the history of nuclear strategy, however, the mutual-assured-destruction doctrine is no

crazier than any of the other doctrines that have held sway in this field—and less crazy than some. In any case, the acronym has stuck.

29. Freedman, *Evolution of Nuclear Strategy,* pp. 287-88.
30. This concept seems to have been invented by Herman Kahn during the nuclear war theorizing at the Rand Corporation in the late 1950s and early 1960s, in which James Schlesinger was a participant.
31. Freedman, *Evolution,* p. 381.
32. Cited in Russett, *Prisoners of Insecurity,* p. 153.
33. Cited in Freedman, *Evolution,* p. 393.
34. A concise and illuminating treatment of the similarities and differences of nuclear strategy under Nixon/Ford, Carter, and Reagan is provided by Robert C. Gray, "The Reagan Nuclear Strategy," *Arms Control Today* 13, no. 2 (March 1983). The rhetoric of the early Reagan administration on nuclear strategy and nuclear war fighting is explored in Robert Scheer, *With Enough Shovels: Reagan, Bush, and Nuclear War* (New York: Random House, 1982). A degree of moderation in the rhetoric—although not in the adherence to the concept of nuclear war fighting—is evident in the exchange between Theodore Draper and Secretary of Defense Caspar Weinberger published in *The New York Review of Books,* 18 August 1983.
35. Caspar W. Weinberger, *Report of the Secretary of Defense to the Congress on the FY 1984 Budget, FY 1985 Authorization Request and FY 1984-88 Defense Program* (Washington, D.C.: U.S.G.P.O., 1983).
36. April 1982 news conference, quoted in Russett, *Prisoners of Insecurity,* p. 13.
37. See, for example, "Preparing for Nuclear War: President Reagan's Program," *Defense Monitor* 10, no. 8 (Washington, D.C.: Center for Defense Information, 1982); Daniel Ford, Henry Kendall, and Steven Nadis, *Beyond the Freeze: The Road to Nuclear Sanity* (Cambridge, MA: Beacon Press, 1982); and E.P. Thompson and Dan Smith, eds., *Protest and Survive* (New York: Monthly Review Press, 1981).
38. *Whence the Threat to Peace?* (Moscow: Military Publishing House, 1982); Marshal of the U.S.S.R. Dmitri Ustinov, "The Soviet Union's Military Superiority," *Defense Science 2001+* 2, no. 2 (1983): 46-47; "Yuri Andropov's Speech at Kremlin Dinner," *Press Bulletin of the Permanent Mission of the Soviet Union* 79 (527) (May 1983).
39. A definitive new reference on the U.S. nuclear arsenal is Thomas B. Cochran, William M. Arkin, and Milton M. Hoenig, *Nuclear Weapons Databook. Vol. I. U.S. Nuclear Forces and Capabilities* (Cambridge, MA: Ballinger, 1983).
40. The members of NATO are Belgium, Canada, Denmark, the Federal Republic of Germany, France, Greece, Italy, Luxembourg, the Netherlands, Norway, Portugal, Spain, Turkey, the United Kingdom, and the United States. The members of the Warsaw Treaty Organization (WTO) are Bulgaria, Czechoslovakia, the German Democratic Republic, Hungary, Poland, Romania, and the Soviet Union.
41. U.S. Department of Defense, *Soviet Military Power* (Washington, D.C.: U.S.G.P.O., March 1983); and nationally televised speech by President Reagan, 23 March 1983, printed in full in *The New York Times,* 24 March 1983.
42. Many of the relevant characteristics are discussed in Stockholm International Peace Research Institute, *World Armaments and Disarmament: The 1982*

SIPRI Yearbook (Cambridge, MA: Oelgeschlager, Gunn, and Hain, 1982); and International Institute for Strategic Studies, *The Military Balance 1982–83* (London: IISS, 1982). See also The Boston Study Group, *The Price of Defense* (New York: Times Books, 1979); C. Bertram, ed., *New Conventional Weapons and East-West Security* (London: IISS, 1979); Benjamin S. Lambeth, "Uncertainties for the Soviet War Planner," *International Security* 7, no. 3 (Winter 1982/83): 139-66; and Andrew Cockburn, *The Threat: Inside the Soviet Military Machine* (New York: Random House, 1983).

43. Admiral John Marshall Lee, Study Director, *No First Use* (Cambridge, MA: Union of Concerned Scientists, 1983). See also John J. Mearsheimer, "Why the Soviets Can't Win Quickly in Central Europe," *International Security* 7, no. 1 (Summer 1982): 3-39.

44. Good discussions of the background for the two-track decision are provided by David C. Elliot, "Decision at Brussels: The Politics of Nuclear Forces," Discussion Paper no. 87, California Seminar on International Security and Foreign Policy, Santa Monica, August 1981; and Raymond L. Garthoff, "The NATO Decision on Theater Nuclear Forces," *Political Science Quarterly 98*, no. 2 (Summer 1983): 197-214. See also Raymond L. Garthoff, "The Soviet SS-20 Decision," *Survival* 25, no. 3 (May/June 1983): 110-19.

45. The official rationale is plainly stated in Richard Burt, "NATO and Nuclear Deterrence," in *Nuclear Weapons in Europe*, The Arms Control Association (Lexington, MA: Lexington Books, 1983), pp. 109-19.

46. A good supplement to the following discussion of the MX is Herbert Scoville, *MX: Prescription for Disaster* (Cambridge: M.I.T. Press, 1981). For more detail on alternative basing modes and other technical issues, see Office of Technology Assessment, Congress of the United States, *MX Missile Basing* (Washington, D.C.: U.S.G.P.O., 1981).

47. If the launches were not coordinated so that the warheads all landed simultaneously, the Minutemen not destroyed in the first wave could be launched in retaliation before the warheads assigned to them arrived. A detailed treatment of the difficulties inherent in carrying out a coordinated strike against missile silos is provided by Matthew Bunn and Kosta Tsipis, "The Uncertainties of a Preemptive Nuclear Attack," *Scientific American* 249, no. 5 (November 1983): 38-47.

48. General Brent Scowcroft, chairman, *Report of the President's Commission on Strategic Forces* (Washington, D.C.: U.S.G.P.O., April 1983).

49. A more detailed account of the obstacles in arms-control negotiations is given in Herbert F. York, "Bilateral Negotiations and the Arms Race," *Scientific American* 249, no. 4 (October 1983): 149-60.

50. Herbert York and G. Allen Greb, "The Comprehensive Nuclear Test Ban," Discussion Paper no. 84, Santa Monica, June 1979; G. Allen Greb and Warren Heckrotte, "The Long History: The Test Ban Debate," *Bulletin of the Atomic Scientists* 39, no. 7 (August/September 1983): 36-42.

51. Christopher Paine, "The ABM Treaty: Looking for Loopholes," *Bulletin of the Atomic Scientists* 39, no. 7 (August/September 1983): 13-16.

52. The most comprehensive treatments of the freeze concept to date are Federation of American Scientists, *Seeds of Promise: The First Real Hearings on the Nuclear Arms Freeze* (Andover, MA: Brick House, 1983); and Center for Science and International Affairs, *The Nuclear Weapons Freeze and Arms*

Control, Proceedings of a Symposium at the American Academy of Arts and Sciences, 13–15 January 1983.

53. A variety of detailed proposals for reductions are collected in Philip J. Farley, Betty G. Lull, Gerard C. Smith, Herbert Scoville, Jr., and Michael Krepon, *Nuclear Arms Control Options for the 1980s* (Washington, D.C.: The Arms Control Association, 1982); and Burns H. Weston, Thomas A. Hawbaker, and Christopher R. Rossi, eds., *Toward Nuclear Disarmament and Global Security* (Boulder, CO: Westview Press, 1984).

54. In addition to the references listed in notes 17 and 43, see Robert S. McNamara, "The Military Role of Nuclear Weapons," *Foreign Affairs* 62, no. 1 (Fall 1983): 59-80; and Herbert F. York, "Beginning Nuclear Disarmament at the Bottom," *Survival* 25, no. 5 (September/October 1983): 227-31.

55. See, for example, "Militarizing the Last Frontier: The Space Weapons Race," *The Defense Monitor* 12, no. 5 (Center for Defense Information, 1983); and Richard L. Garwin and Carl Sagan, "Ban Space Weapons," *Bulletin of the Atomic Scientists* 39, no. 9 (November 1983): 2.

56. For useful comments on various drafts of this chapter, I thank Avner Cohen, Anne Ehrlich, Paul Ehrlich, Peter Gleick, Allen Greb, Ernst Haas, John Harte, Steven Lee, Christopher Paine, Rob Socolow, and Jeremy Stone. The chapter was completed in fall of 1983 and has not been updated to reflect subsequent developments.

3
ECOLOGY OF NUCLEAR WAR: POPULATION, RESOURCES, ENVIRONMENT

Paul R. Ehrlich
Anne H. Ehrlich

For almost four decades, the threat of nuclear war has darkened the human future. During the same period, the expanding human population, the depletion of nonrenewable resources, increasing environmental degradation, and the widening rich-poor gap have also made the prognosis for civilization less than bright. Unfortunately, these twin threats—nuclear war and the deepening population-resource-environment predicament—are not independent of one another.

As populations expand, their resource needs and environmental impacts increase accordingly, and competition among nations for the limited pool of available global resources inevitably intensifies. Environmental deterioration affects not only the health and well-being of human beings directly, it undermines the productivity of agricultural and natural ecosystems on which they depend; when it is imposed by one group of people on another, conflict can arise. International tensions are further exacerbated by the huge differences in wealth, power and access to resources that exist between the less-developed and the industrialized nations. In the first part of this essay, we briefly describe the global population-resource-environment predicament and consider ways in which heightening international tensions arising from it might increase the chances of war.

While this global predicament has developed, with its underlying sources of conflict, war itself has become increasingly deadly. A nuclear war of any significant size, besides killing and maiming hundreds of millions of human beings immediately, would be the ultimate environmental catastrophe. In the second part of this chapter, therefore, we look at the devastating ecological consequences of a nuclear war and their impacts on the plight and the prospects of the human survivors.

THE HUMAN PREDICAMENT

Contrary to economic mythology (e.g., Simon 1980), Earth's resources are finite, and so is its carrying capacity for *Homo sapiens*. Although humanity in the past has successfully augmented that carrying capacity through technological advances, and doubtless can further augment it in the future, the process clearly has limits.

Indeed, there is reason to believe those limits are either being approached now or have even been passed (Ehrlich, Ehrlich, and Holdren 1977; Ehrlich and Mooney 1983).

Population Growth

The basic elements of the situation consist of the interrelationships among the human population and its resource base and environment. The global population now numbers about 4.9 billion people, having increased since 1940 by more than the population grew in the preceding several million years of human history. The current growth rate is about 1.8 percent per annum (Population Reference Bureau 1983), which, if it held steady, would double the population in about 40 years.

Concealed within these aggregated figures is enormous regional disparity. It is not too great an oversimplification to say that the world is divided into two broad population classes: those living in the rich, industrialized nations (overdeveloped countries, or ODCs), and those living in relatively poor, largely agricultural nations (less-developed countries, or LDCs). The great bulk of the world's resources, including food, is controlled by the approximately one-fourth of the world's population living in industrialized countries. In the poor countries, large fractions of the populations live in poverty and have, at best, barely enough to eat. Indeed, 15 to 20 million people—mostly infants and small children—die prematurely each year, largely because of undernourishment and poverty.

In general, rates of population growth in the ODCs are low, or, in a few cases, even negative. The average rate of natural increase in the populations of Europe, for example, is around 0.6 percent; that of North America, 0.7 percent; and of the USSR and Japan, 0.8 percent. These growth rates, if held constant, would yield doubling times of over 100 years; but the rates of population growth in these regions are generally declining.

The situation in the less-developed countries contrasts sharply, as many of them have population growth rates in the vicinity of 3 percent per annum or even more, with doubling times of 25 years or less. Birth rates—and hence population growth rates—have declined somewhat in many LDCs in the last decade. But some of the poorest and fastest-growing countries have not yet shown any sign of decline. Table 3.1 gives 1983 population data in LDCs.

Consider what it means for a nation's population to double in 25 years or less. If the standard of living is to be maintained, supplies of essentially every good and service must be duplicated. Where there is one home today, there must be two in 25 years. For every physician and hospital today, there must be two in 25 years; the capacity of manufacturing plants, road and railway systems, communications networks, and so on, must be doubled. And perhaps most important, food supplies must be doubled, either by increased agricultural production or increased imports, or both.

This list only scratches the surface, but the message is clear. Such duplication of facilities, production, and services in a mere quarter of a century would be extremely difficult for a developed nation like the United States to accomplish. And the United States has the advantages of plenty of capital, a fully developed industrial base, excellent transportation and communication systems, a single language, a high level of education, and a relatively honest and efficient government. The average less-developed country has none of these.

Table 3.1   Representative Growth Rates and Doubling Times of Populations in Less-Developed Countries

Country	Population (millions)	Growth rate (%)	Doubling time (years)
Egypt	46	3.1	22
Nigeria	84	3.3	21
Kenya	19	4.1	17
Ethiopia	31	2.5	27
Congo	2	2.6	26
Jordan	4	3.6	19
India	730	2.1	33
Bangladesh	97	3.1	22
Malaysia	15	2.4	29
China	1023	1.5	46
Mexico	76	2.6	27
Brazil	131	2.3	30
Colombia	28	2.0	35
Peru	19	2.6	26

Note: All data for 1983.

Source: Population Reference Bureau, 1983.

Indeed, rapid population growth is a major factor contributing to the poverty of those nations. First, it is an obstacle to saving—to putting aside capital to be used in raising the standard of living. Resources in LDCs must be constantly plowed back into trying to provide subsistance for ever-increasing numbers of people. Population growth, therefore, seriously hinders efforts to "develop" poor countries and to improve their standards of living.

To make the situation even more difficult, poverty itself seems to be a major contributor to large family size and thus to population growth. People in richer, more-industrialized nations have much smaller families; today in most ODCs, the average family has two children or less, whereas in most LDCs they range between three and eight. To a considerable degree, then, poor nations are caught in a vicious spiral in which rapid population growth helps to perpetuate the conditions that generate continued population growth.

This does not mean that it is an unbreakable spiral, although the classic "know-nothing" solution of simply industrializing all the poor countries is clearly not the answer. Not only does industrialization in itself seem to have little effect on family size; it is both extraordinarily unlikely to occur, and would be extraordinarily undesirable if it did. To understand this, one need only consider the problems of a poor country that is attempting to industrialize in a world where highly efficient nations, such as Japan, Germany, and the United States, have already saturated many, if not most, markets and could easily supply any new ones.

The gap in affluence between the overdeveloped and less-developed nations has been a global fact of life since World War II, and for the most part it has steadily widened. Only a handful of countries (mostly in southern Europe) have managed to cross the line from poor to relatively rich; significantly, those few nations have also succeeded in reducing their population growth rates to levels comparable to those of the ODCs.

Meanwhile, the widening gap between the two major groups of nations has become an increasing source of tensions and conflict at the international level. Frustrated aspirations of people in poor countries, where unemployment rates are commonly high, have led directly to rising rates of migration both within countries (from countryside to city) and between countries (from poorer to richer). Examples of the latter are the flows of people from Mexico to the United States; from Turkey, North Africa, and southern Asia to Europe; from Ghana to Nigeria; from poor southern African nations to South Africa; from the Middle East to Kuwait and Saudi Arabia, and so forth. A celebrated case in the 1960s, in which population pressures were acknowledged to be an important factor, was that of migration from El Salvador to Honduras, which led to forcible expulsion of the immigrants and a war. The potential for such migrations to engender serious international conflict is obvious.

Even more ominous, these frustrations appear to be an important driving force behind the contemporary rise of terrorist activities. These activities are sometimes associated with revolutionary movements, which may spread to neighboring countries and often embroil major powers in their struggles. Prominent examples are the PLO in the Middle East, the Iranian revolution, and the current conflicts in Central America. It is not too difficult to imagine how detonation of a nuclear weapon by a terrorist, revolutionary, or extremist national group (such as the Khaddafi regime in Libya), properly timed and placed, could trigger a nuclear holocaust. Both sources of trouble—large-scale migrations and terrorism—can be expected to intensify as populations continue to grow and the poor nations find it increasingly difficult to accommodate additional people.

As well as the tensions generated by rapid growth, the world population situation is made even grimmer by what is known as the momentum of population growth. The details need not concern us here but, because of the youthful age composition of rapidly growing populations, it normally takes about one lifespan (60 to 70 years) for a population to stop growing once the average family size has dropped to replacement level—slightly more than two children per married couple. In practical terms, this means that should the average family size in India, for example, drop from more than five today to just over two children by A.D. 2010 and stay there (and if death rates did not rise dramatically because of famines or other catastrophes), the Indian population, about 730 million in 1983, would continue growing until nearly the end of the next century, reaching around 2 billion.

That is why numbers such as 8-12 billion (two or more times today's population size) are projected by most demographers as the probable range of the "peak" world population size (United Nations 1982). And those numbers are predicated on rather rapid worldwide declines in birth rates. Even if population control quickly takes hold everywhere, the global population is "committed" to the lower peak of 8 billion—unless it is overtaken by some megacatastrophe that kills human beings by the billions. A nuclear war could be just such an event, although hardly a recommended method of population control.

The Resource Base

From the population figures, one might conclude that the "population explosion" is a problem mainly of the poorer nations. But that assumption would be incorrect.

Table 3.2   Comparative Energy Consumption, Selected Countries

Country	Per capita energy consumption (kg coal equiv.)	Country	Per capita energy consumption (kg coal equiv.)
Egypt	496	India	191
Nigeria	144	Bangladesh	46
Ethiopia	29	Malaysia	838
Congo	87	China	602
Kenya	109	Mexico	1770
Jordan	632	Brazil	761
United Kingdom	4942	Colombia	769
USSR	5595	Peru	619

Source: UN 1979/80 Statistical Yearbook.

Not only numbers of people count in generating overpopulation; the calculations must include the behavior of those populations. The important question is, what is the impact of the population on its resource base and on local and global environments?

One can think of that impact as being roughly the product of population size, multiplied by the level of affluence of the average individual in the population, in turn multiplied by a measure of the efficiency of the technologies used to produce each unit of affluence (Ehrlich and Holdren 1971). When one considers the impacts of populations on their resources and environments, an entirely different picture emerges.

Perhaps the best measure of overall impact, easily found in government statistical records, is energy consumption. Energy use is intimately tied to virtually all human activities that involve consumption of nonrenewable resources and lead to environmental deterioration. It takes energy to manufacture and operate motor vehicles, jet planes, railroads, ships, air conditioners, and electric toothbrushes; to build dams, shopping centers, and freeways; to synthesize plastics, pesticides, and fertilizers; to run high-yielding farms; to turn forests into woodchips; and so forth.

An average citizen of the United States, for example, used more than 10,400 kilograms of coal equivalent in energy in 1980. Corresponding figures for per capita energy use in some other nations are shown in Table 3.2.

In a sense, therefore, the birth of each American baby is likely to have more than 50 times the impact on the planet as the birth of a baby in India and nearly 360 times the impact of a baby in Ethiopia! From the standpoint of impacts on global resources and environment, population growth in rich nations is a much more serious threat than population growth in the poor nations. Although India's population is more than three times as large and growing three times as fast as that of the United States, the growth of the U.S. population still has about five times as much impact.

One need not examine statistics in detail to see why. Americans fly in jet planes, drive automobiles, eat food produced by energy-intensive agriculture, use energy extremely wastefully, produce and distribute numerous toxic synthetic chemicals, use and throw away mountains of nonbiodegradable plastics, and so on. The average Indian does none of these things. Here, too, is another reason that to industrialize all the developing nations would be extremely undesirable: consider what would happen to the global environment if 4.9 billion people escalated their ecological impacts to the American level!

This does not mean that population growth in India and other poor countries is without serious consequences. While the global impact of individuals in industrial countries may be relatively large, resource constraints and environmental deterioration can be severe in regions with large, rapidly expanding populations, even if the people are very poor. Poverty, indeed, is often an obstacle to environmental protection as well as to economic development.

Overpopulation occurs when the population of an organism is so large that some individuals lack adequate access to resources, or the carrying capacity of its environment is being degraded, or the population suffers social problems arising from its density. By any of these standards, Earth is already overpopulated with *Homo sapiens.*

Because the *behavior* of the individuals as well as their *numbers* is an important factor in generating overpopulation, the degree of overpopulation created by 4.9 billion human beings could be considerably reduced if each person, on the average, were less affluent, or if the technologies for creating the average level of affluence were more benign, or if people were more tolerant of one another. It is questionable, however, whether any combination of affluence, technology, and social change could reduce the impact of 4.9 billion people so that Earth would no longer be overpopulated.

What is worse, of course, is that the degree of overpopulation will increase dramatically as the human population continues to grow. The increase will not be linear—that is, increasing the human population by 50 percent will not simply increase by 50 percent the total impact that human beings have on their resources and environment. Each person added to the human population in the future seems almost certain to create a disproportionate burden on the global resource base.

There are several reasons for this. One is that the cheap and easy ways of supporting the population on a short-term basis are being rapidly exhausted. Civilization is in the final stages of squandering a one-time bonanza of fossil fuels. Most of the high-grade, easily accessible reserves of these and other mineral resources have been or are now being exploited. In the future, therefore, people must be supported on lower-grade, relatively inaccessible, and more difficult to mobilize resources on the average; hence each unit of affluence will tend to require more energy use than those supplied in the past. And as population growth increases the number of people among whom the depleted resources must be distributed, the rate of depletion will accelerate, and the costs of obtaining each unit will tend to rise still faster.

Reflecting this situation, production costs for many important minerals have been rising in real terms for the past decade—petroleum being only the most prominent example (Ehrlich, Ehrlich, and Holdren 1977; Petersen and Maxwell 1979; Cook 1976 and 1982). Much of the rise in the price of oil, of course, has been due to the near-monopoly of exportable production by the OPEC nations and their manipulations of the world market. Nevertheless, part of the intent of the high prices was to dampen the rising rates of consumption—much of it extremely wasteful—of what was recognized as a nonrenewable resource.

The rising prices, particularly of oil and products derived from it, have seriously hampered development efforts in LDCs and contributed to economic troubles virtually worldwide. Because of these disruptive effects and the vulnerability of the majority of the world's nations to supply interruptions, oil has become an acknowledged source of potential international conflict (Choucri 1982). In the mid-1970s, for instance, a spate of articles appeared in the United States seriously proposing a military takeover of the Mideast oilfields to prevent another oil embargo. The Soviet invasion of Afghanistan aroused so much alarm in the U.S. government because of Afghanistan's proximity to the oil-rich Persian Gulf region and because the Soviets are expected to become oil importers by the 1990s. Any number of strategically important minerals, major sources of which may be controlled by one or a few nations, also are potential sources of conflict.

As the depletion of exploitable reserves of nonrenewable resources progresses, increases in either population or in consumption per person would spell increases in the rate of consumption of most resources. Both are likely to occur. If history is any guide, tensions arising from competition among nations for ever-scarcer resources will escalate. Furthermore, progressively lower-grade resources will have to be tapped, thereby generating immensely greater environmental costs as well.

Renewable Resources and Environmental Costs

The mounting environmental costs of supporting an already huge and still-growing human population have received increasing attention in recent years. Just as accessible mineral resources have been depleted, the capacity of many environmental systems to absorb abuse has also been largely consumed or exhausted, and many others are threatened. The economic costs of measuring, monitoring, and abating air and water pollution (or of failing to abate them) are most familiar to the public, but these problems are less intractable than other, more subtle, relatively irreversible threats to the human support system.

Population pressures are rising on land itself and on the supposedly renewable—but nonetheless limited—resources that land provides: soils, freshwater, forests, and so forth (Brown 1981; Eckholm 1982; Holdgate, Kassas, and White 1982). Demand is rising on suitable pieces of land for competing uses: to grow crops, graze livestock, or produce forests; to be used for mineral extraction, transportation facilities, urban development; or for recreation and preservation of natural ecological systems.

In many regions, shortages of freshwater are being felt, as dependable sources are subjected to increasing competitive pressure for crops, industry, or domestic urban use. Conflicting claims on water sources between cities, counties, and states have become more and more frequent in recent decades. Even tension between nations is possible: for instance, the dispute between Mexico and the United States over rights to Colorado River water, and that between Israel and Jordan over the Jordan River. In arid regions, where demand for water can be expected to rise even faster than the population grows, such altercations may well become commonplace. And even where water supplies are more than adequate, maintaining their quality is a growing problem.

Forests around the world are fast shrinking or being converted to tree farms in response to demand for timber, pulp, and fuel, or for other amenities (Eckholm

1982; Council on Environmental Quality 1980). Much of the forest loss in poor countries is because of exploitation by developed countries, whose own forests have already been depleted or converted to fast-growing, but inferior quality, wood. Some developing countries have begun to see that they are losing a priceless, sometimes irreplaceable, resource with little compensation.

The continuing loss or conversion of the world's forests—especially in the tropics—represents a devastating depletion of Earth's biological diversity, with possibly severe effects in the long term on the ability of natural ecosystems to continue delivering their indispensible services in support of human life (Ehrlich and Ehrlich 1981). Local results would include destabilized climate and increased floods, droughts, and soil erosion, leading to reduced agricultural production and/or increased need for irrigation and fertilizers, to less-dependable water supplies, and numerous other problems.

To the extent that tropical forests influence climate on a global scale, nations far removed from the site of massive deforestation have a stake in the results. It is not impossible, for instance, that wholesale removal of the forest of the Amazon Basin could have climatic repercussions on the North American Midwest—the world's breadbasket.

Pressures on oceanic and freshwater systems have led to a slowing of the increase in world fisheries yields and to severe depletion of many of the most desirable fish stocks. Armed hostilities have occurred between fishing nations exploiting a shared stock. Among countries that have caused tension in coastal U.S. fishing waters are the Soviet Union and Japan. Recent trends, such as bilateral fisheries management treaties and the Law of the Sea Treaty (which has yet to be signed by the United States), have helped to reduce the frequency and intensity of these disputes. Nonetheless, opportunities still exist for conflict wherever nations compete for a shared, limited resource; and any small conflict holds the potential for escalation to a full-scale war. Devastating wars in the past have been triggered by more trivial matters than fishing rights.

The Food System

One politically sensitive area in which disproportionate environmental costs have already visibly occurred is the production of food. Since most of the world's high-quality arable land is already under cultivation, global population growth and increases in demand related to growing affluence in the rich countries have led to intensified agricultural production on existing cropland—a trend that has built-in biological limits. It also carries important environmental consequences through the intensive use of farm chemicals and the pollution problems they often create.

The other alternative is extension of agriculture to more and more marginal land, which usually is already being exploited as forest or rangeland. Such land, to be made productive, must be subjected to larger and larger "inputs": labor to clear vegetation and rocks, irrigation to supplement inadequate rainfall, fertilizers to enhance soil fertility, and so forth. All these requirements increase the demand for nonrenewable resources, especially for petroleum to run irrigation pumps, to manufacture and transport fertilizers and pesticides, and to transport food to markets.

Simultaneously, some of Earth's best farmland is continually being taken out of production. Cities classically have developed in rich agricultural areas; as they expand, millions of hectares of farmland disappear forever each year under houses, highways, shopping centers, airports, reservoirs, and the like. Even more land around the world is lost to food production because of various forms of degradation: soil erosion and nutrient depletion; salinization and waterlogging from faulty irrigation systems; and spreading desertification. These problems result from poor land management or from overintensive land use (overgrazing or overcultivation). Thus, in a period when rapid, substantial, and sustainable increases in food production are urgently needed, much of the cropland (and range land) base on which food must be grown is undergoing deterioration that undermines and jeopardizes future productivity.

In poor countries, poverty and population pressures are usually the underlying causes of deterioration of cropland and rangeland. The reduction in agricultural productivity that sooner or later follows is a particularly serious matter for developing countries. Most of them are already importing food to meet the needs of their growing populations; many also depend on the exportation of agricultural products to earn foreign exchange for needed imports. An increased need to import food, fertilizers, and fuel would add to the already enormous financial burdens of heavily indebted LDCs—and to international tensions between rich and poor nations. Nor are rich nations immune to any of these essentially preventable (but extremely difficult, time-consuming, and costly-to-reverse) problems. Economic pressures on farmers to produce more crops this year with little concern for productivity 20 or more years in the future are generating similar abuses of the land.

An important consequence of regional differences in population growth and in agricultural productivity in the last 45 years has been a dramatic shift in the patterns of world trade in grains—the staples on which people largely depend, directly or indirectly. Before 1940, all major regions of the world, with the exception of Europe, were net exporters of food. Today most major regions of the world, excepting North America and Australia, are food importers. The prairies of North America are the main feeding bastion of humanity, where large, dependable surpluses of food can be grown. By 1980, more than 100 nations in some degree relied on its bounty to feed their populations.

The world's growing dependence on a tiny handful of suppliers is even starker in the case of food and feed grains than for petroleum. The United States has already capitalized on this dependency by using food as a political "weapon," principally and most overtly against the Soviet Union, which has become increasingly dependent on imports to maintain its dietary standards (Brown 1982; Johnson 1983). The most overt use of the weapon was the brief embargo on grain shipments to the USSR in 1980-81, following the Soviet invasion of Afghanistan. Despite the obvious dangers of the situation, that the United States is now part of the Soviet "breadbasket" may be a positive factor. The short-sightedness of launching a nuclear strike on a major source of one's food might somewhat restrain the aggressiveness of Russian policy-makers.

On the other hand, Soviet military planners might conclude that a nuclear war (which they expect to "win") would reduce the Soviet population and Soviet demand sufficiently that the loss of North American food would not be significant. More plausibly, they might conclude that after "winning" they could extort even more food from North America. (It seems unlikely that the Soviet military have any more realistic view of the agricultural and environmental consequences of such a war than do the American military.) They might believe a "limited" war might spare most of the agricultural capacity of the United States. It is even conceivable that American manipulations of the global grain market might so enrage the Russians as to goad them into starting a war.

The American relationship with the Soviet Union is not the only food-related peril. The growing dependency of most of the world on a few food-exporting nations almost certainly will be an increasingly destabilizing force in the world's political situation (Brown 1981). Among the countries dependent on imports for more than half their grain supplies are Japan and several Middle Eastern nations. China, a nuclear power, has also become an important grain importer, and India has been one intermittently for decades.

In the early 1980s, the European Community emerged as a significant exporter of food, backed by protectionist price subsidies and aggressive marketing policies. The effect was to intensify fluctuations in world grain prices and supplies, which were mostly absorbed by the United States (U.S.D.A. 1983; O'Brien 1983). Fairly high grain reserves in 1983, partly because of recession and reduced demand, elicited dire predictions of a trade war. The unquestioned need for increased food supplies in poor countries is not equivalent to economic demand; the destitute and hungry millions have essentially no purchasing power.

In addition to the political power held by suppliers of any scarce resource, the flow of food exports is vulnerable to disruption from the vagaries of weather, depredations of pests, and crop diseases, any of which could cause a massive crop failure. A decline of even a few percent in the world grain harvest—particularly if the failure occurred in North America—could wreak havoc in the world grain market and cause food prices to skyrocket. The poorest people in the poorest nations would suffer most, but a significantly reduced amount of food available for the export market would surely lead to fierce competition—if not conflict— over what remained.

Other Environmental Problems

Two other serious and intractable environmental threats are caused mainly by industrial activities—the burning of fossil fuels—but they too may have adverse consequences for food production. The first is acid precipitation, caused by air pollutants from factories, power plants, and automobiles. The most obvious results are the disappearance of much of the aquatic life from lakes and streams in severely affected regions, such as eastern North America and Scandinavia. Yet acid rain occurs over wide areas of the globe and, if unchecked, is likely to cause even more widespread damage. The more subtle effects of acid precipitation on forests, soils, and possibly crops are just beginning to be learned.

Acid rain, and the air pollution that generates it, has already caused political friction between some industrial nations: Canada and the United States; Norway and Sweden versus France, Germany, and the United Kingdom. As the natural buffering capacities of soils and rock are exceeded in wider areas, the damaging effects of acid precipitation on forests, fisheries, and agriculture will become more and more apparent. Acid rain carried by wind across national boundaries may increasingly be a source of international conflict. Among areas at possible risk, although not yet noticeably damaged, are the Rocky Mountains of North America, southern Europe, and Japan.

The second, even more difficult problem is the buildup of carbon dioxide in the Earth's atmosphere, an unavoidable result of fossil fuel combustion, especially of coal. Since coal is the most abundant (albeit the most polluting) fossil fuel, its increased use in the future is very likely. The precise results of the carbon dioxide buildup are unpredictable in detail, but the consensus among scientists is that it will cause a gradual rise in the average global temperature, which in turn may lead to significant changes in climate in most regions. Any change in climate is a threat to agricultural production, simply because farmers and crop systems need time to adapt to a significant shift. Other possible long-term consequences may include melting of polar ice caps and a rise in sea level, inundating many low-lying cities and farmland areas.

This problem and the responsibility for causing it—since every society contributes to it—may be sufficiently diffuse to prevent its becoming a specific source of conflict. Still, reductions in food production caused by carbon dioxide-induced climate changes would surely heighten international tensions. Moreover, the conspicuously higher consumption of petroleum by the United States in the mid-1970s, when an "oil shortage" was a global problem, did engender resentment among more frugal users. This resentment was defused when the United States established effective oil conservation measures and significantly reduced its per capita consumption—and its share of world consumption—by the early 1980's. Similarly, to the extent that the United States and other heavily industrialized countries are perceived in the world community as being disproportionate contributors to the atmospheric CO_2 buildup, especially by nations not benefiting from that industrial activity, they may be blamed for any adverse consequences.

Growing Interdependence:
A Stabilizing or Destabilizing Trend?

Throughout the industrial era, trade has generally tended to expand between nations as well as between regions within countries. In part this has been a natural outgrowth of improved methods of transport, which made possible the rapid movement of goods over long distances. Increasing affluence, especially in rich countries, also helped create markets for exotic goods. But the trend is also a result of populations outgrowing local resource bases and drawing on the surplus resources and products of other regions in exchange for their own.

A small, sparse population in a given area can be relatively self-sufficient. But no area—or country, even the largest—is well enough endowed with all resources to provide for a large population. The USSR and China, both very large in territory, are probably the nations most nearly self-sufficient today; yet each is a major importer of food. And China's huge population is supported at a very low level of resource consumption per person.

The United States, although endowed with enormous natural wealth, is increasingly dependent on imports to sustain its large population's affluent lifestyle. Most of the world's nations are smaller and less blessed with a variety of resources; those they have in abundance must be traded for others they lack. A few nations lacking in resources, such as Japan, the Netherlands, Hong Kong, and Singapore, prosper by providing a service: they turn imported resources into exportable manufactured goods.

This growing interdependence of nations is not necessarily a bad situation. Indeed, the exchange of resources and commodities between regions and nations allows the support of many more people and/or greater average affluence in all the regions involved in the trade network. As in so many other situations, diversity is the key to security and stability. If a nation imports each needed resource from a variety of suppliers, a cut-off from any one, or even two or three, is not a serious threat. Similarly, exporting to numerous buyers helps to stabilize markets, especially in food commodities, of which supplies (hence demand and prices) can fluctuate severely.

Dangers arise when one nation or a united group of nations can control supplies of an essential commodity. OPEC's leverage in the oil market is one obvious example; the United States's grain-exporting capacity is another. The opportunities for disrupting the world trade system, the world monetary system, and political balances of power by withholding supplies have already been demonstrated to an increasingly jittery world. This situation is transparently destabilizing and contains the seeds of global conflict.

As the human population continues to grow, the international trade network can be expected to continue rising in importance—unless it is inhibited by protectionist economic policies, as has been a recent trend, or disrupted by politically inspired trade blackmail. The result of inhibiting the growth of trade would be a restriction of everyone's access to distant resources and thus, in essence, a reduction in global carrying capacity.

People in rich countries would experience, if not an actual decline in their standards of living, at least little improvement. The implications for poor countries are even more serious: restricted access to markets for their exports, higher prices for imports of essential resources and commodities, and possible bankruptcy. As the rich-poor gap became a chasm, the bitterness and resentment it nurtured could lead to thoughts of military revenge. Some developing countries (China, India, and probably South Africa) already possess nuclear weapons; others undoubtedly could obtain or develop them fairly easily.

It should be clear that, to support the inevitably expanding human population for the next several decades, expansion and diversification of world trade should be fostered. Protectionist policies should be discouraged; they not only inhibit and distort trade patterns, they also can destabilize markets. Even more important, policies that favor some countries over others—especially those that put LDCs at a severe disadvantage—should be abandoned. And the sooner the international community can find a way to outlaw the withholding of exportable essential commodities for purely political reasons, the more secure the world will be.

THE ENVIRONMENTAL CONSEQUENCES OF NUCLEAR WAR

All the problems described thus far must be viewed in a context of the continued spread of nuclear weapons. By early in the next century, it seems likely that most nations and even some subnational groups (terrorists, organized crime) will possess atomic bombs (Ehrlich, Ehrlich, and Holdren 1977; Holdren 1983). In such a world, squabbles over territory, resources, or environmental degradation would be unaffordable, and the perils of slipping into a full-scale nuclear war simply too great. Indeed, if current population-resource-environment trends are allowed to continue, a nuclear holocaust seems nearly certain within the lifetimes of today's children. What would be the impact of a nuclear war on human resources and environments?

One thing can be said with certainty—a full-scale nuclear war would be a catastrophe beyond precedent in human history. A standard scenario (Ambio Advisors 1982) depicts the equivalent of approximately half a million Hiroshima-size nuclear weapons detonated in the Northern Hemisphere. A much smaller number would be exploded in the Southern Hemisphere, primarily in Australia and South Africa.

The environmental consequences of such a war cannot be foretold in detail. First, they would depend on the distribution and sizes of the weapons detonated and on the proportion exploded on the surface rather than high enough so their fireballs did not touch the ground. The results would also depend heavily on the season of the year in which the war occurred. Beyond those uncertainties, fundamental gaps in knowledge of how natural ecosystems work make detailed predictions impossible, even if the exact pattern and timing of the nuclear explosions were known. Still, more than enough is known to paint a general picture of the ecological consequences of a large-scale nuclear war (Ehrlich 1983).

In addition to the almost unimaginably horrible immediate effects of blast, fire, and radiation on the targeted human population, the surrounding environment would be devastated, especially by gigantic fire-storms. In a full-scale war, as much as four-fifths of the territory of the United States might be set ablaze (Federation of American Scientists 1981). Huge areas of agricultural and other land would be exposed to massive erosion of irreplaceable topsoil by both water and wind following the burn-off of vegetation. The dust bowl days on the Great Plains and the mudslides following chaparral fires in California are only small hints of the scale of this problem.

Irreversible pollution of much groundwater would be caused by seepage from millions of ruptured chemical storage tanks. Chemical run-off and the destruction of sewage systems would flood surface waters with pollutants. This pollution, combined with the silt from eroding farms and rangelands, would exterminate much of the life in streams. Onshore oceanic waters would also suffer heavily from siltation and a flush of chemical pollutants. Such an assault on the swamp and estuarine nurseries of many commercially important fisheries could result in a sharp reduction of oceanic fish production.

But these horrendous consequences would almost certainly be trivial in comparison with those resulting from atmospheric perturbations (Turco et al. 1983). The sky over the entire Northern Hemisphere could be darkened for weeks or months by a combination of smoke and soot from the enormous fires, debris injected into the atmosphere by weapons detonations themselves, and fugitive dust from burned-over areas. Ninety-nine percent or more of the incoming sunlight might be excluded. Beneath the spreading clouds of smoke and dust, temperatures in interior continental areas would plummet within weeks to well below freezing, regardless of the season. Only islands and coastal areas, moderated by the oceans, could experience less extreme cooling.

The consequences of this prolonged darkness and cold both for any surviving people and for ecosystems not destroyed outright by blast or fire would be grim beyond measure. Most surface water sources would soon be frozen over, making water extremely difficult to obtain for surviving people, livestock, and wildlife. To the degree that the atmospheric darkening occurred within the growing season, photosynthesis—the source of energy that powers all significant ecosystems, including agricultural ones—would be drastically curtailed (if not halted altogether) in plants not killed by freezing temperatures or the direct effects of the war. The cold weather, severe reduction or elimination of photosynthesis, on top of the widespread burning of croplands and the heavily eroded soil, would make farming virtually impossible.

Photosynthesis would also be virtually halted in natural communities (such as forests), thus contributing to the collapse of any ecosystems that had survived fire, blast, and freezing. As a result, surviving human beings would lose the indispensable services that ecosystems normally provide to society (Ehrlich 1983; Ehrlich et al. 1983). Those services include maintenance of the quality of the atmosphere, amelioration of the climate, provision of fresh water, generation and maintenance of soils, disposal of wastes, recycling of nutrients essential to agriculture, control of the vast majority of potential pests of crops and vectors of disease, provision of food from the sea, and the maintenance of a vast "genetic library" from which humanity has already withdrawn the very basis of civilization. Without these services in abundance, industrialized society cannot persist (Ehrlich and Ehrlich 1981).

The screening out of sunlight and the low temperatures could only be the most dramatic atmospheric impact of a full-scale nuclear war in the Northern Hemisphere. A hemispheric smog could be generated, so severe and so pervasive that the air in the cleanest areas would resemble a smoggy day in Los Angeles. Not only would this pose a serious health risk for any survivors—especially the wounded and the elderly—but it would add to the stress on surviving crops and ecosystems. Plants are expecially sensitive to pollutants such as ozone and PAN (peroxyacetyl nitrate), which would be present in the smog at tens to hundreds of times normal levels.

The detonations of a full-scale nuclear war could also result in severe depletion (perhaps 50 percent) of the stratospheric ozone layer, greatly increasing the admission of ultraviolet radiation to the surface. While they persisted, the smoke and dust clouds would screen out the UV-B, but the recovery of the ozone layer would occur more slowly. Thus, when the clouds had finally dissipated, surviving plants and animals would be exposed to a new assault—high levels of damaging ultraviolet light. Other than its induction of skin cancers in human beings and its capacity to cause genetic damage, not much is known about the effects of UV-B on different organisms, except that plants grown under low levels of light are more sensitive to it.

The multiplicity of assaults would cause a general decline in ecosystems not destroyed outright by direct effects of the war. Stresses from reduced light, low temperatures, climatic change, smog, UV-B, and radiation would eliminate many species and lead to upsurges of the small, hardy organisms that often are vectors of disease or competitors with *Homo sapiens* for food. Flies, roaches, mosquitoes, coyotes, and weeds would have a much better chance of survival than deer, songbirds, oak trees, and soybeans. Recovery of ecosystems would be extremely slow at best, and the regenerated systems might be almost unrecognizable. Recovery of agriculture in some form would be faster, but could still take several years.

The problems to be faced by the scattered, hungry, injured, radiation-sick survivors of the war itself, who would be struggling to stay alive in cold and darkness, trying to cope with poisonous smog, in most cases without heat or power, and in many cases without adequate shelter or access to water, food, medicines, and other supplies, can only be imagined. In the Northern Hemisphere, the disruption of natural services provided by ecosystems alone would make any sort of reestablishment of civilization extremely difficult or even impossible. At the least, decades to centuries would be required.

The situation in the Southern Hemisphere is more difficult to predict. Mixing times of the atmosphere between the Northern and Southern Hemispheres are now measured in years, so one might expect that much of the tropospheric pollution would settle out of the atmosphere before it reached the Southern Hemisphere. There is some reason to suspect, however, that the soot and dust in the Northern Hemisphere might cause atmospheric changes that would speed the movement of debris and radioactivity to the south. In the worst case, the entire surface of the planet might be shrouded in darkness and cooled to below-freezing temperatures for many weeks. In this case, the long-term survival of any human groups—as well as many other large animal species—might be questionable.

Even if the Southern Hemisphere escaped the atmospheric effects, it would not remain unscathed. Radiation and air pollution levels would rise both from detonations in the Southern Hemisphere itself and from the transfer of radiation and pollutants from the Northern Hemisphere. In addition, scenarios can be constructed under which one of the outcomes of the war might be long-term global climatic changes that had serious consequences for Southern Hemisphere populations. The most certain consequences of the war for the South would be economic and psychological. Less-developed nations of the tropics and farther south depend on the North for a wide variety of goods, particularly food and high-tech items. An immediate and serious loss for many poor countries would be fertilizers; LDCs as a group still import more than half of what they use from developed countries. But most critical would be the abrupt cut-off of grain and oil imports.

Over a billion people in the northern temperate regions could be directly affected by the war; the few remaining survivors would be in desperate straits, in no condition to help people elsewhere. This does not include another billion in China, which is largely temperate but might escape the full impact of the war. Inhabitants of China and the subtropical and tropical regions adjacent to the warring regions, which include some of the world's most densely populated areas (such as India, Bangladesh, Southeast Asia, and Mexico) could suffer many of the ecological effects—especially those attending the loss of sunlight—if not the direct impacts. Their situation would not be much better than than of their northern neighbors, and survival of more than a relatively small number of people is problematical.

The psychological, social, and political consequences for people in the Southern Hemisphere of the disappearance of much of the human population can only be imagined. The hemisphere south of the equator contains a minority of the human population, well under a half-billion people, who would suddenly find themselves in a changed physical world, cut off from all communication and trade with the North. Most Southern Hemisphere nations are not noted for their political or social stability. Some of those that are relatively self-sufficient and stable (e.g., Australia) are likely to have been direct victims of the conflict. It would doubtless be a very long time before southerners, if they escaped total devastation, became sufficiently organized and unafraid of lingering radiation to attempt recolonization of the Northern Hemisphere.

The results of the war, however, might not be universally deleterious for the South. For example, the raping of the resources of poor countries by northern industrial nations would cease. About the only thing that can be said with assurance is that, desperate as the situation in the Southern Hemisphere might be after a full-scale nuclear war, survivors there would be living in a paradise compared with survivors in the Northern Hemisphere. While the extinction of *Homo sapiens* is not a likely consequence of an all-out nuclear war, the end of civilization in the industrialized world of the North is a virtual certainty.

REFERENCES

Ambio Advisors. 1982. "Reference Scenario: How a Nuclear War Might Be Fought." *Ambio* 11:94-99.

Brown, L.R. 1981. *Building a Sustainable Society.* New York: W.W. Norton & Co.

_____. 1982. "U.S. and Soviet Agriculture: The Shifting Balance of Power." *Worldwatch Paper 51.* Washington, DC: Worldwatch Institute.

Choucri, Nazli. 1982. "Power and Politics in World Oil" *Technology Review* 85(7):24.

Cook, E. 1976. "Limits to Exploitation of Nonrenewable Resources." *Science* 191 (20 February): 677–82.

_____. 1982. "The Consumer as Creator: A Criticism of Faith in Limitless Ingenuity." *Energy Exploration and Exploitation* 1, no. 3: 189–201.

Council on Environmental Quality and U.S. Department of State. 1980. *The Global 2000 Report to the President,* Vol. 2. Washington, DC: U.S.G.P.O.

Eckholm, E.P. 1982. *Down to Earth.* New York: W.W. Norton & Co.

Ehrlich, P.R. 1984. "When Light Is Put Away: Ecological Effects of Nuclear War." In *The Counterfeit Ark,* ed. J. Leaning and L. Keyes. Boston: Ballinger.

Ehrlich, P.R., and A.H. Ehrlich. 1981. *Extinction: The Causes and Consequences of the Disappearance of Species.* New York: Random House.

Ehrlich, P.R., A.H. Ehrlich, and J.P. Holdren. 1977. *Ecoscience: Population, Resources, Environment.* San Francisco: W.H. Freeman & Co.

Ehrlich, P.R., and J.P. Holdren. 1971. "Impact of Population Growth." *Science* 171 (26 March): 1212–17.

Ehrlich, P.R., and H.A. Mooney. 1983. "Extinction, Substitution, and Ecosystem Services." *BioScience* 33, no. 4: 248–54.

Erlich, P.R., et al. 1983. "Long-Term Biological Consequences of Nuclear War." *Science* 222 (23 December): 1293–1300.

Federation of American Scientists (FAS). 1981. "One Bomb—One City." *F.A.S. Public Interest Report* 34 (2): 3.

Holdgate, M.W., M. Kassas, and G.F. White, eds. 1982. *The World Environment: A Report by the United Nations Environment Programme.* Dublin: Tycooly International Publishing Ltd.

Holdren, J.P. 1983. "Nuclear Power and Nuclear Weapons: The Connection Is Dangerous." *Bulletin of the Atomic Scientists* (January).

Johnson, D.G. 1983. "Agriculture—Management and Performance." *Bulletin of the Atomic Scientists* (February): 16–22.

O'Brien, P.M. 1983. "The Functioning of the World Market and Its Impact on the World Food Outlook." Paper presented at the January meeting of the Global Foresight Committee, Washington, DC.

Petersen, U., and R.S. Maxwell. 1979. "Historical Mineral Production and Price Trends." *Mining Engineering* 31, no. 1 (January): 25–34.

Population Reference Bureau. 1983. *1983 World Population Data Sheet.* Washington, DC.

Simon, Julian. 1980. "Resources, Population, Environment: An Oversupply of False Bad News." *Science* 208 (27 June): 1431–37.

Turco, R.P., O.B. Toon, T.P. Ackerman, J.B. Pollack, and Carl Sagan. 1983. "Nuclear Winter: Global Consequences of Multiple Nuclear Explosions." *Science* 222 (23 December): 1283–92.

United Nations. 1981. *1979/80 Statistical Yearbook.* New York.

United Nations, Department of International and Social Affairs. 1982. *World Population Prospects as Assessed in 1980.* New York.

U.S. Department of Agriculture. 1983. *Outlook and Situation* (WAS-31). Washington, DC.

Manuscript submitted June 1983 and not substantially revised since then.

PART II

APOCALYPSE REVISITED:
THE CULTURE OF NUCLEAR THREATS

We live in a world in which omnicide has become a real possibility, a world with stockpiles of devastation material sufficient to put an end to all civilized life, possibly even to extinguish the human species; and the stockpiles are constantly growing. Our civilization not only has the potential to destroy itself, but puts its entire safety at the mercy of its doomsday fears. Indeed, those fears have been designated as the rationale for a global policy of security—the policy of nuclear deterrence— that is said to ensure world peace and order. The span between civilization and its annhilation lies only in the *willingness* to push the button.

By and large, it can be argued (as Berel Lang does in Chap. 5) that the nuclear bomb is one of the unique causal factors in human history whose actual and symbolic consequences affect human consciousness far beyond its immediate historical context. Nuclear weapons redefine the human condition itself. Yet we have been insufficiently attentive to the existential and moral meaning of the nuclear threat overshadowing civilization. Perhaps our failure to acknowledge the threat of omnicide amounts to a denial of our new human predicament. We have regarded nuclear explosives only as politically and militarily significant, and have not seen them as matters of the most pressing human concern. As in other aspects of modern life, we have left the actual engagement with the issue almost entirely to the "experts"; and the experts, with their assumption of value neutrality and their euphemistic vocabulary, have produced "rational" strategic theories of how to manage and win nuclear wars, independently of the meaning of such a catastrophe in human terms. The next three chapters deal with the existential, cultural, and historical aspects of living under the threat of man-made apocalypse.

Gary Stahl argues in Chapter 4 that our present nuclear predicament radically redefines and reshapes the basic facts of the human condition. This is so, he claims, because of the essential role of the future in shaping the meaning of human life. In a way, the future is ever-present in the present; no moral meaning for human acts is possible without the assurance of a future. From a moral point of view, all acts are "exemplary"—they constitute an invitation to put the moral universe together in a certain way. From this perspective, the policy of nuclear deterrence raises questions about the very possibility of a moral universe. The threat of omnicide means not only the potential physical end of humanity, but an already actual distortion of our present moral world. Our "credible" threats of omnicide threaten one of our most human features—being a *future-projecting* animal.

Berel Lang in Chapter 5 provides a moral and cultural analysis of the nuclear predicament. His starting point is the unique conjunction of the reality of *genocide* and the imminence of *omnicide* at a single historical moment. Lang's essay attempts to account for the historical and conceptual link between these two extraordinary phenomena, and considers their implications for the redefinition of culture and the history of morality. The core of the link lies in the very concept and practice of technology. Both the actuality of genocide and the prospect of omnicide depend on the existence of a certain level of technology. Technology enormously increases the scope of moral choice. The link between genocide and omnicide, however, is more than just a matter of similar technological origins; in fact, the threat of nuclear omnicide entails the phenomenon of genocide. The utter arbitrariness involved in the annihilation of an entire population entails, perhaps, the most distinctive feature of omnicide.

In Chapter 6 Richard Popkin explores historically the apocalyptic vision in the 17th century in relation to the apocalyptic vision in the nuclear age. During the 17th and 18th centuries the apocalyptic interest was closely linked to the rise of the "New Science." Some of the greatest scientists of the time were actively engaged in "Millenarian Science"—an attempt to explain scriptural history and apocalyptic prophecies in scientific and realistic terms. Within the traditional millenarian perspective, the End of the World is viewed as a *desirable* step in the spiritual progress of humanity and the cosmos —what Popkin calls *Triumphant Apocalypse*. But from the secular perspective, apocalyptic triumph is a vain hope; history is no longer seen as a vehicle of some extra-human meaning. The vision of nuclear holocaust is seen as the *Catastrophic Apocalypse*, the final end of humanity. Archaic sentiments do not, however, fade away as easily as post-Enlightenment thinkers had hoped. Millenarianism, although outside today's "official" intellectual agenda, is still deeply incorporated into mainstream fundamentalist Christianity in America. Since we now have the capacity to bring on apocalypse through human agency, any movement of political significance adhering to the doctrine of the Triumphant Apocalypse could be a source of danger.

4
REMEMBERING THE FUTURE

Gary Stahl

The question that the peril of extinction puts before the living . . . is: Who would miss human life if they extinguished it? To which the only honest answer is: Nobody. That being so, we have to admit that extinction is no loss, since there cannot be a loss when there is no loser: and we are thus driven to seek the meaning of extinction in the mere anticipation of it by the living, whose lives this anticipation corrupts and degrades.
Jonathan Schell, *The Fate of the Earth*

As the meaning of the past is not completed until the present, so the meaning claimed by our present acts waits on the future for its completion. Just as there is a sense in which one can change the past by making it lead to this present, so the shape of the future can either distort or complete our present attempts to give significance to our lives and acts. In this way the threatened nuclear self-destruction of mankind redefines the shape of the moral world in which we live.

It is a commonplace that we can make quite different futures out of the same incident: an injury suffered while driving drunk can precipitate a major change in character and commitment or become an excuse for endless whining about the capriciousness of fate. Or a cowardly suicide can give a twisted shape to the promising events of an earlier life. Thus the meaning of a person's act is not self-contained, but is matter to be shaped and given form as it is incorporated into character and expressed in later actions.

The other side of this proposition is that our present acts are in part an invitation to make the future in a certain way; the intended future shapes the present within which we now act. In this sense all actions are "exemplary": they have their roots in the narrative within which agents have built up a distinctly human world and defined themselves within it; but as acts which carry on this eternally incomplete

Background research for the essay was sponsored by a grant from the Council on Research and Creative Work at the University of Colorado. I would like to thank the editors of this volume for unusually detailed and helpful criticism.

task, they are exemplary for the ways in which this world can continue to be reaffirmed or redirected. Thus, for example, there is an aspect of a moral action that may become the possible basis of a rule that others, or the agent himself, may freely choose to follow. The exemplary force is the claim that if this implicit rule is followed, the moral world articulated by actions will be sustained and advanced.[1]

The present policy of nuclear deterrence is taken as a particular act, the proposal of a rule of action that is the principled denial of the possibility of a moral world: our acts of beginning omnicide thus—as exemplar—invite other actions to follow a principle that contradicts the possibility of sustaining and advancing that world of moral space and time without which man as agent cannot exist. Thus omnicide is not only the threat of future disaster, but the presence of a distortion already begun: as we "remember" *that* possible future, we degrade this actual present.

Put another way, if man ends in this threatened mutual suicide, then history will have an end that redefines all its beginnings and strivings. If our present is the past of *that* future, it has a different significance than we thought. It will not have this significance *for* anyone, for there will *be* no one in whose past it could be incorporated and completed; such completion as it has must lie in our anticipatory remembrance *now*.

Another aspect of this "remembering the future" serves not to give a meaning—however corrupt—but to deny meaning. For one of the ways in which our present acts take on provisional meaning is in our imaginative grasp of the futures they invite. To some extent we, or others after us, may go on to actualize or deny these invited futures. But the self-destruction of mankind that we prepare is the nonexistence of all futures, thus the inhibition of the provisional meaning of the present: provisional meaning becomes empty gesture.

Neither this inhibition, nor the distortion mentioned above, is a *psychological* reaction to the threat of annihilation; they are ways in which the world of action is redefined by our preparations for omnicide. Thus they call for epistemological arguments, not psychological evidence. (That the human niche within which we come to be has been reshaped *does* have fundamental psychological consequences, but they are not my focus here.)

PRESUPPOSITIONS

In working out this argument, I assume, first, that there is a possibility that a full-scale nuclear exchange would destroy the world of man; even if there were physical survivors, their lives would not in any distinctive sense be "human." (A less catastrophic prediction is considered below.) Second, I assume that some form of naturalism is the most adequate stance to take. This means simply that consciousness emerges in the evolutionary process through accident and will perish without significance. There is no external context of meaning—neither a God with a plan nor a structure of moral law—within which history takes place and is given meaning. Whatever meaning there is to man and his works is *within* the world of space and time he articulates through his actions. (It would be inappropriate to characterize history itself as "insignificant," as if it lacked something it might have had; in the absence of consciousness or purpose "for whom" it could be either significant or insignificant, it can best be called "nonsignificant.")

The roots of this argument are in the inescapable incompleteness of man and his world. This can be described from two perspectives: first, there is the openness of evolutionary process without purpose or fixed end. The contingent emergence of the distinctively human level of consciousness is a *continuing* process, subject to revision by accident as well as deliberate action (including omnicide). Second, there is the openness of the developmental proces within which an individual makes a world and is made a self. For self is an achievement, not a given: the newborn lacks both the conscious self of agency and a world into which such agency could act. Genetically encoded needs and patterns interact with the threats and invitations of the environment, but the building of a self-conscious agent who defines, and is defined by, the world into which he acts is a gradual and always unfinished process.

In this process, the kinds and dimensions of self are co-emergent and co-determinant with the institutions they make and are made by.[2] So at one level of generality we can talk about the activities that shape the structures within which "the good, the true, and the beautiful" can be defined and pursued. But the variety of intersecting and intertwining structures is most sharply caught in Ernst Cassirer's descriptions of symbolic forms as forms of self-knowledge and self-development.[3]

The drive of the argument is best displayed by emphasizing the moral, and this only in some aspects. My concern is with the unavoidable instability and incompleteness of any world individuals have built up within which they can treat each other (and themselves) as *persons*, and not as mere objects to be manipulated and used. This perilous balance reflects the fact that the world of institutions is a form of action imposed on the pre-moral energies of biological and psychological organisms. Here the moral is a supervenient dimension, a characteristic way of doing things so as to respect and further the distinctly human dignity that is created and defined by these actions of mutual respect. It is no small matter to determine just what actions further and which threaten this respect, or how one could tell the difference, or just what is meant by "respect" or by "persons": indeed, to do so is the main job of the philosophical discipline of normative ethics. But however these matters are resolved, the forms of moral institutions, however defined, bring partial order and meaning to the whole substrate of capacities and activities that are material to be shaped. Man may be *at most* an ethical being, but he is *at least* all his biology and inheritance make him. Just as there are no moral actions without the biological substrate, there are no distinctly moral actions that are nothing but biological.

HUMAN ACTION AS EXEMPLARY

Since the imposition of moral (or aesthetic or cognitive) order on the indifferent energies of an evolving organism is always incomplete and partial, each act is incomplete and partial. In the absence of some nonnaturalistic framework to establish and guarantee an unchanging world of moral institutions with a shape and claim independent of the act, it falls to the act to *make actual* and sustain and develop appropriate moral institutions. By "moral institutions" I mean any potentially shared habit that affects persons insofar as they are distinctly human.[4] This is the perfectly ordinary sense in which we speak of promise-keeping or "the family" as moral institutions precisely insofar as there are expected ways in which individuals treat each other as moral persons, and not simply in accordance with biological necessity or perceived self-interest.

Since any particular act contains a principle that can be followed repeatedly, each act is a potential institution. Each act is generalizable: to say that something is the right thing to do in a specific set of circumstances is to say that it would be the right thing to do in any circumstances that are the same in relevant respects. Thus, each act offers itself as exemplar of a principle to be followed in future similar circumstances. The tentative and incomplete structure of the moral world is reaffirmed and redirected through acts that say something will or will not do as a way of putting together a distinctly human world. The act is both an affirmation or reshaping of the past and an invitation to the future to affirm and continue—to institutionalize—this act by doing the same thing in relevantly similar circumstances.

This is easiest to see in acts that dramatically confront the moral contingency of the world, that reassert the past in the face of peril or challenge it in the name of the future. But the most ordinary and habitual act also has this element. To continue to do as one has done, as the world of institutions would command us to do, is to say "this will do."[5] It is to make oneself even more firmly the kind of person who habitually acts in this way, whose moral character is expressed in just *this* kind of action. It is to take this kind of action in this kind of circumstances and hold it up as an exemplar to be followed by oneself and others. It is to incorporate the act's meaning into the narrative structure of individual life and of history.

Just *how* this invitation is taken up may be a matter of routine, so much so that the exemplary character of the act in relation to the maintaining of moral institutions is passed over completely. Indeed, the usual view is that the moral meaning of the act rests completely in its relation to some *previously* existent rule, at best external in the mind of God, at least (relatively) secure in the bosom of the state—not as dependent on acts for on-going ratification.

But where we are dealing with a living tradition, we are quite aware that the narrative is unfinished, a challenge to which the answer is uncertain: what the future free acts of ourselves and others will make of it is unknown. Later we will (perhaps) know more; history will make things clearer. It is important to emphasize that what is incomplete here is the *meaning*, not merely the knowledge of it. Without the responses it has yet to call forth, the meaning of the act is underdetermined, not yet fully actual.

This sense in which we are ignorant of what is not yet actual must be distinguished, at least in degree, from that in which the present act is thought of as a cause related to the future as effect. Here a chain of events is set in motion, and the end is not yet known. The relevant meaning of the act is essentially complete, but our knowledge is unfinished. "The die is cast," but we must wait to see just how. This is also the sort of attitude we take toward the past in all the ways we say "You can't change the past," "What's done's done," "No use crying over spilt milk." The implication is that while our knowledge can grow and change, the meaning we come to know has as much fixity as an evolving and contingent world permits it.

This way of looking at things is important and unavoidable. The consequences of an act *are* often less clear to its actors and contemporaries than to history; it *does* take time to see the end of what we have started. But if it is right to see the space and time of moral institutions as a continual and imperiled creation, then this way of looking at things is, however necessary, not sufficient. Acts surely have causes, and are causes, and there are familiar and appropriate senses in which our ignorance about effects is related to time, as well as to whatever contingencies the world is subject to. But if actions have any meaning as moral, they must have reasons as well as causes. We must be free to complete the challenge of the past in ways that we think make moral sense, not just in ways that are the eddies and effects of what has gone before.

These choices, and the responsibility for becoming what one has chosen, set the minimal condition under which anyone can be *either* moral or immoral. This means recognizing that certain kinds of considerations count in decisions: having promised to do some thing is a reason for doing it, even if it is not in one's self-interest; seeing that a contemplated action would threaten someone's human dignity is a reason not to do it (it may not be a conclusive reason, for sometimes one must choose the lesser of evils). We can and do ignore such considerations; the evil man may consciously act against them. But someone for whom they could not be considerations could not act in the moral realm at all. His behavior (I would not call it "action") would be *non*moral.

Where these sorts of things *are* reasons for someone, then the fact that they are is one of the causes of his acting the way he does. Anyone who wants to predict the actions of a moral agent must know at least this about him, that as a moral agent he is someone for whom considerations involving the dignity of persons "have weight."[6] They have this weight because he has chosen to make them his reasons; that they *are* reasons is one of the causes of his action.

It may be that this distinction cannot be defended. Certainly the tradition of determinism is long and vigorous. If this is so, then all this talk about the moral (or aesthetic, or cognitive) implications of omnicide is empty foolishness. I cannot here argue that it is not; I assume it is not. And if it is not, then we must insist on the distinction between our ignorance of the meaning of an act because its exemplary meaning has not yet been fully answered by the free choice it calls for, and our ignorance of the consequences of events that are basically complete in meaning but as yet not fully known in effect.

DETERRENCE, OMNICIDE, AND MAD

To say that the moral meaning of the act is incomplete is not to say that it has not begun, or that we cannot see the provisional meaning of the institution it calls forth. This is the sense in which the beginning act of omnicide is poisonous. As an act at the shifting point of the present, it is the power to accept or reject the invitation of the past, and to offer itself as an exemplar to the future. As such, it rejects those acts of the past that affirmed the dignity of man; it invites us to organize the future on a principle that holds the existence of man hostage to the sovereign interests of nation states, and ultimately rejects the dignity of human existence as a matter of principle.

To make this clear, I must be more specific about the principle embodied in these preparations for omnicide. For the defenders of the strategy of nuclear deterrence insist that preparations for mutual annihilation simply reaffirm the established principles that, in affairs between nations, weakness invites aggression, and that the strength and willingness to wage and win a war is the best assurance of peace. The threat to destroy mankind is necessary to preserve it: the aim is peace, not war, and the invitation to the future is to preserve peace by making war unthinkable and self-destructive.

These are the announced intentions of the deterrence strategists, and I assume that most of them are made in good faith: they do not *intend* to make an act that is an exemplar embodying a principle that denies human dignity. But their intentions do not determine how the acts of omnicide function to redefine the space and time of moral action. Though there would *be* no acts without intention, the intention of the actor(s) does not fully determine meaning.

In the first place, many actions come to embody principles that were not explicitly in mind at the outset. Often we muddle into something, blundering along in habit and half-formed notions, and only later, if at all, realize what we were doing (that thought follows on actions is a well-established principle). Indeed, some situations, such as divorces and bereavements, almost exclude the possibility that living through them includes being clear about intentions. (Often one learns what one has done only by seeing, perhaps in a novel, how someone else has acted; only then can one step back enough to be objective.)

Even where our actions have been explicit in intention, we can come to see we were mistaken in what we took these intentions to have been. More complicated instances involve the fact that the intention, like the act that fulfills it, comes to be articulated only over time: what we set out to do is modified in the doing. And we may come, by imperceptible steps, to do something we did not foresee.

I believe something like this happened to deterrence strategy. The road from rational deterrence to MAD is paved with good intentions (in what follows I take the basic thinking of MAD as paradigmatic of deterrence theory).[7] But what has emerged, whether intended or not, as the defining principle of MAD is this: if deterrence fails, and one nation destroys another, the attacked nation must be (this is what a "credible deterrent" means) capable of striking back and willing to do so ("from its grave") to destroy the attacker. Note, however, that even if the motives that set this doctrine in motion were utilitarian and rational, the final act would have no possible utilitarian justification: there is no possible end to which the final strike could be a means.

This point is one of the reasons for insisting on the term "omnicide" rather than "war." For "war," as von Clausewitz says, is "a continuation of politics by other means," and no possible goal, political or otherwise, can be achieved by ending the human race. The final act of destruction must be done "on principle," not for some end of self-interest. For there would be no one whose interest could be served.

What is striking about this principled act is that it is the corruption of Kant's categorical imperative: "Act in such a way that you always treat humanity, whether in your own person or in the person of another, never simply as a means, but always at the same time as an end." For Kant the essence of the moral lies in respecting human dignity quite apart from self-interest. That is why the imperative commands categorically—that is, unconditionally—and not merely on the condition that some interest be served. Kant says that once one has eliminated all self-interest from the motive to act, no other motive remains but respect for the moral law as embodied in human dignity. MAD says that once one has eliminated all self-interest from the motive to make the final strike, no other motive remains but the gratuitous degradation and destruction of all human agents. So what we have in MAD is principled evil: destruction of human dignity for its own sake, "on principle," and not as a condition of some further good.[8]

Supporters of nuclear deterrence will deny that this is their intent: they maintain that *respect* for human dignity, especially the dignity correlative with political freedom, makes it necessary to threaten destruction in order to preserve freedom. There is much here that needs reply: (a) the ideological arrogance that sees human freedom or dignity as the exclusive property of any one political sovereignty (whether its language is 18th century abstractions or 19th century pseudo-science is irrelevant); (b) the difficulty common to us all of being clear about our motives, especially where denial can cooperate to support a course that favors our power, wealth, or status; (c) the simple fact that our leaders consistently lie to us (if they are deceiving themselves as well, it is even more dangerous); and (d) the fact that people can be held responsible for deliberate acts even if such acts were not deliberately willed in the consciousness that they were wrong. If we were making moral judgments about the integrity of persons, we would have to meet all these issues. But none of them is essential to the issue of how the on-going act of omnicide redefines the moral world of action.

Even if we grant the pure heart of every general and politician and war-game computer, it would not change the exemplary power of an international commitment to a policy that, under circumstances of either aggression or accident, would destroy mankind for no conceivable end. (I rule out religious notions of Armageddon; but see Popkin, Chapter 6, this volume.) If the meaning of an act were neatly contained in some instantaneous moment of intention, the case might be different; one might argue that the meaning of the act was set, whatever the future made of it, whatever acts it called forth to shape moral space and time. But I have argued that this does not apply even to *single* acts of a single consciousness, let alone to the extended emergence of omnicide as a principle guiding many minds over extended time. Quite apart from all considerations of mistaken and evolving intentions in agents, the act's unavoidable incompleteness as exemplar ensures that moral meaning *cannot* be exhaustively set by original intention. Only the free acts that accept or reject its invitation can do this.

In all of this we are talking of "an" act, like omnicide, that is begun in the preparations of thousands and affirmed—through votes or taxes or the refusal to rebel—in the compliance of millions; we are talking about an act that shapes international relations, national budgets, and the decisions of the young on whether to bring children into the world. So to talk about "accepting or rejecting its invitation" to see the world in its way, to institutionalize the principle it articulates and exemplifies, is quite inadequate. For it is an invitation we cannot turn down. We *do* live as targets of institutionalized terror, although we have gone beyond "mere" terrorism as the use of indiscriminate violence for political ends: MAD threatens gratuitous death that eliminates all ends. As citizens of a nation-state we *do* hold the world hostage to the quirks of our political system as it "representatively" pursues our ideological view of the world. The world we make bears the shape of terror and, as we are shaped by this world, we bear its imprint.

This is not rhetoric, but the inevitable consequence of the fact that self and world make up an "open system" in which what we do shapes the world in ways that elicit and demand from us further actions that shape ourselves. In evolutionary terms: our actions help define the niche that defines the relevant conditions for survival, moral as well as physical. MAD has defined a niche in which all human dignity and survival is degraded as a matter of principle.

This is true even if deterrence theory works. Since an act is completed by the future, imagine a future in which the terror of MAD has kept the fingers from the buttons long enough for mutual terror to seem no longer imperative. We can hope and imagine that mortal antagonisms would die out as a result of increasing economic interdependence, or in the perception of common interests in the face of ecological disaster, or in the blurring of national differences under the pressures of a triumphant technology. Would this not prove that MAD was sane?

I think not. An avoidance of death (I cannot call that "peace") through mutual terror is already a redefinition of the conditions of life. An end achieved by that means is itself reshaped. As John Dewey always insisted, we must look not at isolated ends abstracted from possible means, but at the complex of means-ends: racial integration achieved by violent suppression has a different value as an end than integration reached through mutual cooperation; the avoidance of destruction through threatened terror creates a different sphere for action than the continuation of life through cooperation.

But suppose one pretends not only that there will be a future time in which we see that MAD has averted destruction, but that MAD was the *only* way of averting destruction. Even in this most improbable of scenarios, it is worth pointing out that what ends up being preserved by our MADness is different than what we set out to preserve. And if it were true that we can continue to live only at the price of institutionalized terror, then that says something about the meaning of our history that has had this future. It partially completes the past in a way that makes it impossible to think of MAD as simply a new way of preserving old values. It is the admission that the dignity of man cannot be sustained, that the possibility of biological survival makes it necessary to threaten to end history; for it seeks survival as an end in an act that embodies a principle degrading and denying all ends. This is indeed a contradiction. But how else can one describe the retaliatory strike from the grave, a strike with no goal, demanded as a matter of principle, commanded categorically? So even if the MADmen are right about deterrence, they are wrong in seeing it as a new means to old ends, a continuation of history with the same meaning.

Let us look at one further change in assumptions: suppose we dismiss the notion that a full-scale nuclear exchange would be omnicide. Suppose "only" Russia, Europe, and North America would be destroyed. My argument that MAD must be a gratuitious degradation of human dignity would no longer necessarily hold. For if some population were expected to survive, one could argue that it would be "rational" for superpower A—already doomed—to destroy superpower B so that this third group would escape the domination of B and possibly carry on the values of A. This would be arrogant beyond belief, but it would not be self-contradictory. Yet it would still denigrate and distort the world of action. We would still live with the increasingly matter-of-fact acceptance of a matrix of action defined by mutual terror. The exemplary acts of the past that moved toward the construction of a world of human dignity would now be seen as inescapably flawed and incapable of completion.

CONCLUSION

Neither ignorance nor numbness will help us here. The more it is commonplace that the survival of the highest values can be hoped for only by preparing for the death of the innocent, the more insidious is the redefinition. Now the denial of human dignity is no longer a threat to be met, but the condition of life. It is as hard to exaggerate as it is to specify the impact of the restructuring of the space and time within which we achieve such humanity as we can. In art and science as well as morals, action is at best an inconclusive and incomplete response that makes determinate some of the ways in which the world presents itself as determinable. But invitations not made cannot be answered; possibilities not considered cannot be acted on.

We do not live in some existentialist fantasy where past and present are infinitely pliable and all alternatives equally plausible: we live in a world where we answer the exemplary call of the past, which defines the need and realm of action. The artist may reject or modify the insistent ways the world has been seen, but he begins *there*. And the style of science, the world as seen through the lens of paradigms, is equally a response to matters lit by the concerns of the past—or a failure to see what lies hidden in the darkness of the unimaginable. As we grow comfortable with the notion that we are targets from birth and potential destroyers through our deaths, we accept a diminished sense of ourselves and others. The distinctively human is no longer that big a deal. The small insult and degradation is of less moment, the shoddy less a surprise. What the arts celebrate is less distinctive, as is the sense of wonder and high judgmental responsibility without which the tasks of knowing are simply the "jangling of the ganglia" in response to stimuli.

That these high human things can still go on in the face of MADness is both true and a matter of wonder. But they are less likely, and they themselves carry a provisional meaning, a hopeful power, that is less compelling against the deadening weight of our diminished world. It is their bad luck to come to be in a world less able to see and respond to their exemplary power. Given the incompleteness of the momentary act and the need of the future to bring it to fruition, this does not mean that such acts are simply unappreciated. They are less than they might have been, as are we.[9]

If the MADmen are right, there is no alternative to this world of degraded dignity: we are (in Camus's phrase) both "victims and executioners." Whether they are right or not, we now live in a distorted world that makes alternatives harder to see. Fortunately, they are not right, as the other contributors to this volume have seen, and make clear.

NOTES

1. The classic text for the notion of the "exemplary" is, of course, Kant's *Critique of Judgment*. For an attempt—more detailed than is possible here—to look at the implications of this concept for ethics, see my "Completing the Past," forth coming in *The Philosopher in the Community: Essays in Honor of Bertram Morris*, ed. Lang, Sacksteder, and Stahl (Lanham, Md.: The University Press of America, 1984).
2. See Gary Stahl, "Locating the Noumenal Self," *Kant-Studien* 71, no. 1 (1981).
3. Ernst Cassirer, *Philosophie der Symbolischen Formen*. Part I (1923), Part II (1925), and Part III (1929) (Berlin: B. Cassirer, 1923-29).
4. George Herbert Mead, "Evolution Becomes a General Idea," in *Mead on Social Psychology*, ed. Strauss (Chicago: University of Chicago Press, 1956), p.34.
5. See John Dewey, *Quest for Certainty* (New York: Minton Blach, 1981).
6. Stephen Toulmin, "Reasons and Causes," in *Explanation in the Behavioral Sciences*, ed. Robert Borger and Frank Cioffi (Cambridge: Cambridge University Press, 1970).
7. For a careful examination of the relation of MAD to other deterrence policies, see John Holdren, Chapter 2, this volume.

8. For an analysis of genocide as principled evil, see Berel Lang, "The Uniqueness of Genocide" in *The Philosopher in the Community.* See also his essay in this volume, Chapter 5.
9. This situation is neatly caught in Alasdair MacIntyre's description of "modernity" as characterized by the "obliteration of any genuine distinction between manipulative and non-manipulative social relation." He takes the characters of the Manager, the Rich Aesthete, and the Therapist as paradigmatic; I add the overlooming figure of the Deterrence Theorist. See Alasdair MacIntyre, *After Virtue* (Notre Dame: University of Notre Dame Press, 1981).

5
GENOCIDE AND OMNICIDE: TECHNOLOGY AT THE LIMITS

Berel Lang

Are we not always living the life that we imagine we are?
Thoreau, *Journals*

It may seem at first glance that genocide and omnicide have no special causal or conceptual relation to each other aside from the terrible prospect that they in common mark out of gratuitous death—murder—on a large scale. Omnicide, recently shaped as a concept and pressed on our consciousness by the specter of nuclear war, threatens the extinction of mankind, perhaps of all life; genocide, fearsome with its elevation of annihilation to an impersonal and arbitrary principle that considers individual persons only as the members of a *genos* or group, seems nonetheless to be cut to a lesser scale, an occurrence that mankind has already, in fact, survived at least once and may even have learned from. That the 20th century is now faced with the continuing prospect of both these practices could, even with a clear recognition of their enormity, be viewed as no more than an unfortunate coincidence, further complicating an already complex historical period, but not bearing in any fundamental way on the cultural structures or the ethical norms of that or subsequent times.

If the history of past responses to extreme situations is a guide, moreover, the occurrence of these two phenomena might be expected to make little difference, even on ideological or theoretical reflection. So, for example, they would be unlikely to affect the belief in theodicy shared by traditional religions with modern science, according to which history is rational, progressive, in the long run working for the good; on these accounts, all problematic events, whether as slight as a traffic accident or as large as a holocaust, will eventually be explained and justified. For the skeptic, too, the conjunction of genocide and omnicide might serve as no more than confirmation of what he already had assumed: the constant failing—the unhappy consciousness—of man, only reinforced now by the irony that as man has increasingly gained control over nature through his technological ingenuity, he has found himself increasingly victimized by that same power, the slave once again asserting itself as master.

But the fact remains that such appeals to abstract theory refuse to take history seriously: we quickly recognize, from what they do not say as well as from what they do, that no historical occurrence or set of events would be admitted by them as counterevidence to their conclusions (in this sense, there *is* no difference between a traffic accident and a holocaust). And although metaphysical "first principles" may underlie even the most rudimentary attempts to identify the relationship between historical and moral analysis, surely we do better to begin from the immediacy of such analysis than from the abstractions to which it may eventually drive us. A person living in 1984 will hardly, whether by ignorance or by denial, escape the consequences of living in a social and conceptual space that, for the first time in history (so I shall claim) includes these two extraordinary moral phenomena—the realities and imminence of genocide and omnicide.

The complexities of historical causality make it unlikely that we shall ever fully understand why those phenomena have obtruded themselves as or when they have and what the connection between them is. It is not evident, to be sure, that even *with* such an understanding, we could be certain that genocide would not recur or that omnicide would not reach its conclusion; the most optimistic of predictions must yet admit a significant probability that these will impinge sharply, even decisively, on man's future no matter *what* he does, individually or collectively. Nor can there be much comfort in the remote possibility—since accidents do happen—that the dangers thus posed may be averted even if man does nothing to evade them, if he moves into the future as heedlessly as he has into the present. But between these alternatives of historical determinism and random chance, there is a point on which understanding and practice converge, where historical criticism may make a difference; toward that point the comments here are directed.

THE RELATION BETWEEN GENOCIDE AND OMNICIDE

I shall address two principal issues in the relation between genocide and omnicide. The first is the question of how we can account for the recent appearance within a period of some 25 years—almost simultaneously and yet both for the first time—of the threats, and more than the threats, the *realities*, of genocide and omnicide.[1] The second is the question of what the implications are of the occurrence (is it too strong to say the invention?) of these phenomena *beyond* their most immediate and obvious consequences if realized: what happens to the culture, for example, for which they appear even as real *possibilities*?

These questions are themselves open to question. The first depends on a presupposition that must itself be argued, that genocide and omnicide are indeed phenomena of the 20th century—in effect, that they are *new* social facts and that it is in part because of the way in which they *are* novel that they bear so forcibly on the culture of which they are part. To be sure, even if precedents *were* found for them, this would not necessarily alter the likely significance of their present role; but the claim for their common and recent origin is pertinent in a number of ways, epitomized in one inference from them for the existence of a "negative" history of ethics—that the imagination and practice of evil-doing, like those more commonly claimed for good, may *also* reveal a history of progress. And again: there are few points in human history of which the assertion can be made that at those points a specific, large, and readily distinguishable causal factor appeared *for the first time*, one which would act symbolically as well as practically, in prospect as well as in fact, and thus affect—beyond its immediate historical consequences—human consciousness and social practice in general.[2]

It is impossible to detail here in full the evidence for genocide and omnicide as recent historical developments, but the outline of that evidence can be made clear. Admittedly, Rafael Lemkin, who coined the term "genocide," alleged a number of precedents to 20th-century instances, as in Rome's destruction of Carthage and in Titus's (again, Rome's) attack on the Jews.[3] But as his own initial conception of the term was modified (for example, in the formulation of the U.N. Convention on Genocide),[4] so too, it seems, do those earlier alleged precedents need to be qualified in comparison to the Nazi genocide against the Jews that appears as its first full instance—in effect, as a standard or paradigm against which other putative instances must be measured. The purpose of the Nazi genocide was physical and not only cultural or religious or ideological annihilation: the *genos*, itself defined in (*purportedly*) biological terms, was to be destroyed. Thus, it was not the group in association with a geographical area or in respect to a negotiable property (possessions, affiliations) that was threatened with extermination, but the group as such, wherever its members might be, with no option of conversion or substitution (e.g., paying a ransom). It can be shown that no other of the many alleged instances of genocide, in the harsh examples that range from Carthage to the Turkish massacre of the Armenians (1915-17), answers exactly to these criteria. (The Armenians, for example, were sometimes given the option of conversion to Islam, and the Turks did not threaten them beyond the boundaries of Turkey itself.) Certainly, there has been no instance of genocide as systematically and consistently elaborated by its perpetrators as the Nazi genocide against the Jews.

The analogous assertion of historical innovation in the prospect of omnicide is in one sense much simpler to demonstrate, in another sense more difficult. It is simpler in the sense that only with the technological achievement represented by the development of the atomic and hydrogen bombs, readily assignable in terms of chronology to World War II and its aftermath, does omnicide become part of social reality; from this limited point of view, there is no question of historical precedent. On the other hand, the latter thesis is complicated on *other* grounds, since although it might be argued plausibly, that before the 20th century even the idea of genocide had not occurred—surely not, in any event, as a serious practical option—there have been recurrent instances of apocalyptic thinking, one promised element of which was the end of mankind or perhaps of history as such. Noah's ark sailed against the background of this prospect in biblical thinking, and the Stoic doctrine of periodic conflagrations provided another version of an anticipated end.[5] Premonitions such as these, moreover, were also often tied to human action, the cataclysms held then to be consequences (if only in the form of divine judgments) of human conduct; they were, in other words, within man's control.

Notwithstanding these and other parallels (one might speak even of an *impulse* for apocalyptic thinking, which may also underlie them), a significant difference between the historical predictions of apocalypse and the current apprehension of omnicide seems evident. It may be possible to describe or to explain the development of nuclear weapons in more abstract terms (theological or metaphysical), but, at least ostensibly, that development took place in a secular and instrumental context, at the instigation of governments and through the actions of individuals who are now (themselves or their successors) also in a position to decide when or how those weapons will be used. If we ask who is in a position now to trigger a nuclear conflict that might well result in omnicide—meaning a threat to civil and biological existence as we know it—a reply could, with little exaggeration, refer to almost every country on earth; even a response limited to nations that have, or are in a postion to have, their own nuclear weapons would include some three-fourths of the world's population. The point here is that whatever the precedents for the *idea* of omnicide, never before has the capacity for initiating such an act been so generalized or widespread; never before has the capacity—and the knowledge of its existence—lain so immediately and readily within man's own power, not only that of nations or other large corporate entities, but of relatively small groups of people, even of individuals; never before has the option of taking action that would be, literally, limitless in its consequences for human existence been so evidently a possible social "choice." So far as *any* geo-political decisions are within the purview of governments and their citizenry, this one evidently is too. This is, furthermore, more than only a matter of capacity or potentiality. The planning for nuclear war entails acceptance of the possibility that such a war may result in omnicide—and that the acceptance of this latter possibility, together with other features of such planning, even where the ostensive end is deterrence, amount to an intention for omnicide. This set of conditions supports the claim that as a culture we experience the prospect of omnicide for the first time. Never has the possibility rested so evidently in human—all-too-human—hands. Never have those hands used that possibility as an instrument for shaping—willing—the future.

TECHNOLOGY, PUBLIC POLICY, AND MORAL HISTORY

Even if the claims that genocide and omnicide (for the one, the fact; for the other, the prospect) are innovations of the 20th century were true, this would not in itself establish a relationship between them or between them and, except in the most general way, anything else in their then-common background. But I mean in addition, to make the latter assertions as well: that the two phenomena are in fact interrelated, and that it is more than accidental that they appeared when and as they did. They occur, in other words, within a single framework of causal implication.

It will be evident that no account of such relationships can expect to identify necessary and sufficient conditons for them; few historians would suppose this as a meaningful ideal for accounts of even much less complex phenomena. I mean, then, to outline a plausible historical and conceptual connection between them, to call attention both to the present social context as it is affected by that connection and to the latter's origins. The basic features of this connection are themselves exemplified in the concept and practice of technology; for it can be shown that it is in large measure under the influence of that source that genocide and omnicide have assumed their present shapes. Their dependence on technology is at once conceptual and material.

One point of contact between technology and the threat of omnicide is so obvious as to be vacuous: the willingness to risk the destruction of mankind by a nuclear holocaust has presupposed the technological and scientific achievements required for the development of nuclear weapons. This banality has even more general and significant implications, as it calls attention to the role of technology as a factor in setting the stage for and then in shaping morally significant—nontechnological—decisions, and even before that in the design and realization of morally significant ends. The history of ethical values, it should come as no surprise, is closely related to the history of the *possibility* of action. (It is a commentary on the institutional bias of philosophy that writers on ethics have paid too little attention to this connection to provide even a likely model of this relation: the social history of ethics is usually left to the anthropologists and their studies of "primitive" ethical systems.) Two aspects in particular of this connection are worth noting here—the first, an additional instance of the way in which technology may provide a basis for change or innovation in moral history; the second, where technology itself, both as a concept and as an institutional structure, discloses a morally significant character.

With respect to the former aspect: just as technology plays an obvious role in establishing the possibility of the threat of omnicide, it also figures in the background of the Nazi genocide, and indeed of the concept of genocide as such. It is perhaps too strong to claim that without the technological means then available, what we now see as the gradual evolution in Nazi thinking toward the "Final Solution," culminating in the administrative formulation of that concept at the Wannsee meeting in January 1942, would have been inhibited or even averted. But there is no question that both the idea and the detail of technological accomplishment were important factors in the development of that conception and in in its implementation. The deathcamps located in Eastern Europe that were the principal instruments of the Nazi genocide depended for their work of extermination on a system of transportation and communication without which the very conception of a "final" and centralized solution for the Jews of Europe—that could provide, for example, a common registry and destination for the Jews of Holland, Greece, or Hungary with those of Poland or Russia—would have been a practical irrelevance, a brutal fantasy. That the means used for the extermination itself were initially makeshift and (in terms of their uses) inefficient pales beside the enormity of the purpose to which those means were directed, and also, in the end, to the very efficient means of murder that were eventually contrived.

The bureaucratic and mechanized administration of the "Final Solution" that enabled a figure as close to the center of its work as Adolf Eichmann to claim that he himself had not "taken part" in the killings, indeed that he had "nothing against the Jews," is itself a remarkable technological and social development. (This development includes the unusual changes in language-use itself that have been shown to be correlated with technological development; those changes also played an important part in the Nazi genocide.)[6] At issue here is action that is more than only social and *a fortiori* more than individual; thus we can understand Eichmann's statements (and his history) as indicative of *personal* moral blindness or "thoughtlessness" (Hannah Arendt's term)[7] only if we are also willing to say that such personal moral incapacity emerged and acted somehow independent of the bureaucratic apparatus, and this seems clearly incorrect. Bureaucracy itself, we know, has both a social history and a social personality—each tied closely to the history and character of technology.[8] The "organic" conception of the state, which is presupposed by fascism and according to which each of its parts (or citizens) is a means only of *realizing* the whole, provides a natural home for the development of a bureaucracy that works best when questions about purpose are detached from the individual act or agent.

Finally, too, the idiom of germs and disease, which was a central theme in the Nazi justification for the genocide against the Jews, required to support the claim that the Jews were not human beings at all and thus did not have to be treated as human beings, was obviously much more than just a rhetorical figure. It presupposed a conception of disease and of medical science that special technological developments had made possible and that, before the late 19th century, could have been viewed even by its advocates as no more than an ominously useful fiction.

There is ample evidence that even these several and in some ways quite separate strands of technological development did not come together easily. The balance of evidence suggests that Hitler himself had not seriously intended the idea of genocide before the early years of World War II—that is, had not seen it as a genuine option.[9] There undoubtedly are a variety of reasons, moreover, both for this delay *and* for the occurrence of the intention when it did arise. But it seems evident nonetheless that the technological feasiblity of realizing that intention, of making it plausible both as idea and as practice, was a significant factor in its history; surely it is difficult even to imagine its occurrrence in the absence of the features cited.

The limits of the claim I have been making so far should be recalled: it is not that genocide and omnicide are linked *necessarily* to the history of technology, much less to specific moments in that history. There is no *a priori* reason why some group or person in A.D. 942 should not have conceived a threat of genocide (and acted on it) of exactly the same sort that was to be made and acted on a thousand years later. But in point of fact this did not happen, and certain quite specific technological advances preceded the occurrence of genocide and the threat of omnicide when they did arise: *prima facie*, this connection is more than an accidental convergence.

The latter claim, it might be objected, is still not restricted enough. For even supposing that the historical line traced were creditable, does it imply anything more than (circularly) that a nuclear war will be fought with nuclear weapons (in the same way that an army equipped with spears will fight with them), or that an industrialized nation may turn its technological resources to devising means of extermination as it might also turn those resources (even at the same time) to improving medical care? But, again, the argument presented is not that genocide and omnicide have followed necessarily from the advances of technology, only that there is a material and conceptual connection between the two historical lines. The objection cited, it will be noted, is itself a version of the more general view that inventions of any kind (from bombs, one supposes, to the wheel) are value-neutral, that the user, not the maker or the process of making, is accountable for the consequences that use of the object may lead to. This general thesis, however, is itself specious, assuming a radical indeterminacy in the nature of an object's function or use that is in one sense self-contradictory (not everything is possible, either at any moment of history or for every object; we recall here Napoleon's quip that "you can do anything with a bayonet except sit on it"). It furthermore suggests a version of the fact-value distinction, with the implied premise in that distinction of hard and autonomous facts—the artifacts that are value-neutral—that is also problematic.

Reference to the fact-value distinction has a special pertinence in this context since it introduces a second, more important aspect of technology that bears on the phenomena of genocide and omnicide; namely, its own ideational or structural character and the way in which that character is then conceptually implicated in those phenomena. The issues here are complex, and the concept and practice of technology are undoubtedly open to alternate descriptions. But the evidence and precedents for the one adduced here are substantial; these center on the fact-value distinction and on the related distinction between means and ends—for both of which it can be shown that technological practice provides seriously defective accounts. Those accounts (and a number of allied ones) are intrinsic to the practice of technology. They are also significant features of the setting in which the presence of genocide and omnicide makes itself known, where we find the "aestheticization of politics" that Walter Benjamin identified with fascism, but which, placed against a background of which fascism is only one part, turns out to have an even longer reach.

The argument here is of necessity compressed and sketchy. If one starts with the conception of technology or "technique" suggested by Jacques Ellul in his classic work on *The Technological Society*,[10] we find, first, that technique acts to "mechanize" the world, conceiving its own role as that of a problem-solver and thus acting to reduce the parts of the world—events, objects, eventually people—to discrete and enumerable units that are then reconnected by a single "final cause" or principle that is itself more like a means, namely, efficiency. Because technique is effective only as the "facts" of a situation—its problematic—are defined *for* it, not in the determination of purpose or justification, it soon moves from being something external to man, used by him for his purposes, into "his very substance" (p. 6). The process thus obscures and in any event separates the role of purpose or ends from the mechanism of technology and even from the concerns of its user. The issue of means or process comes to be the central preoccupation of technology, and this in turn ensures that the issue of values is virtually excluded as nonrational or emotive; the single feature at all comparable to value that is acknowledged appears in the relation between the machine and its product—that is, in the ideal of efficiency. The effect of this conglomerate method as a "framing" device is to deny all external or contextual questions, to emphasize the mechanistic features of duplicability, interchangeability, *im*personality—shaping not only the solutions to all problems, but also the problems themselves in this image. The method and devices useful for devising solutions thus come to acquire the status of ends; the question of why is reduced insistently to how; the status of the individual is equated with that of a part related only mechanically to a more inclusive whole.

At work here is a tacit purpose, in Max Frisch's words, "to so arrange the world that we don't have to experience it": for experience, too, is now subordinated to a dominant form, to the remoteness effected by "aestheticization," and to a goal which, if it is accessible at all, will be openly nonrational, even arbitrary, except as it conforms to the will of force or efficiency. The pattern thus defined is exactly that of the conceptual framework in which the practices of genocide and omnicide are found. In the latter, too, the domination of a formal purpose appears that initiates judgment—and then the extermination—of a group with no consideration of anything the individual members of that group have been or done; here, too, the claim that an end as wanton as the destruction of mankind might be warranted by an (alleged) threat to one group of people *because* the mechanism for such total destruction exists. The process of action becomes so dominant in these cases, so intricate, so much a matter of problem-"solving," that the relation of the means to the ostensive end—and then the character of the end itself—is obscured. It is predictable, even inevitable, that individual persons are reduced to means exclusively, parts of the mechanism, and thus expendable as the work of the mechanism itself seems to require it.

The phenomena of both genocide and omnicide, then, whether viewed as ideals—and we need to remind ourselves constantly that they *have been* viewed as ideals, explicitly or covertly—or if only as useful means, see the act of problem-solving as detachable from the issue of what the status or origin of the problem is, what it is about (much less from the more-general question about the nature of problem as such). The phrase "the Final Solution," must echo in the mind of anyone at all aware of the amorphous shape of history; for even beyond the perverse irony that infects that phrase, we must also recognize its literal core—that for it, as a preface to genocide and again for omnicide (which would be, after all, a still more final solution), it is the way that *problems* are first conceived, individually and in kind, with the premise that all questions translate into problems and that for every problem there *is* a solution, that conduces also to the substance of the particular and grotesque character of a "final" solution. On the face of it, a claim that humanity may be destroyed in order to save humanity would seem an evident absurdity. To understand how such a claim could be accepted as the basis for a strategy of international purpose suggests an unusual pattern of conceptualization and practice—and just such a pattern, it seems, is fixed in the technological frame work. The latter framework is usually directed to lesser issues and "problems," but it is naturally— *natively*—unable to distinguish between the orders or substance of problems as such; thus, no problems—and no solutions—would be, *could* be, ruled out by it.

Again, it is not my contention that the conceptualization and practical development of technology define necessary or sufficient conditions for the phenomena of genocide and omnicide. In a period of history where such complex factors as nationalism, totalitarianism, industrialization, class-structure are all in motion, any single line of explanation will by that fact be known to provide at most only an opening on the whole, one that is limited by the formulation of the question from which it starts. But there can be no doubt about the reality of the objects of that question, in genocide and omnicide. And if we ask then why the latter appeared when and as they did in recent history, asking here for a *moral* history that includes but also perforce goes beyond the ostensively material conditions, characteristic features of technology turn out also to be features of *their* structures. Formally, such a finding of recurrence (more modestly, of analogy) may be less than an historical account might hope for; it surely does not preclude the relevance of other factors (although it may be related to them as well: I should argue that the configuration outlined also bears, for example, on the apparently independent questions of why the Nazi genocide should have taken root in Germany, and why, when it did, it should have taken the Jews as its object); nor does it imply that the technological ideal itself does not have a history requiring explanation. But these qualifications do not affect the claim made so far for one element in the common background, causally tied to them, of the phenomena of genocide and omnicide.

THE CULTURE OF NUCLEAR THREATS

The question still remains whether genocide and omnicide are related to each other other than by elements of a common origin and chronology. Here it seems to me important to note features of a more direct connection *between* them. The main one is the fact that the threat of omnicide *presupposes* the phenomenon of genocide; that is, that omnicide itself implies genocide, is possible only by taking genocide for granted. I mean by this claim something more than the vacuous logical relation that to risk the death of everyone is also to risk the death of the "kinds" of which individuals are members as well as of the single kind to which the individuals taken together belong. The point I would stress is more substantive, namely, that the threat of omnicide as it is now evident is based on the willingness of those who pose the threat to destroy a group (usually a nation) with no distinction made or even possible between combatants and noncombatants, between adults and children, etc., and with no limits on the numbers or extent of extermination. It may be objected that this is not an inevitable feature of the threat of nuclear war; it is possible to plan a more limited "action," and it is even possible that such limitations might work in practice. But the actual planning of nuclear deterrence is invariably of a different order than this. The idea of a nuclear strike (first or counter-) is to prevent a response in kind, indeed, *any* significant response, and the most obvious way to assure this is by preparation that, if implemented, would result in the virtual annihilation of a populace. Certainly no safeguards, not even any professions of safeguards, are offered by the nuclear planners against such an outcome. (And this says nothing, of course, about the distinct possibility of a global chain-reaction that might be triggered by severe, even "limited" nuclear explosions.) The logic of this planning suggests that if a single bomb could be built that would *by itself* destroy an entire populace, this too would be readily sought (*many* of them, of course) as part of the arsenal of preparedness. Genocide has, in fact, been so much taken for granted as a feature of nuclear war that it has not, to my knowledge, even been mentioned as one of its presuppositions.

Undoubtedly, one reason for such avoidance is the common place assumption that nuclear war is like any other war, only larger in scale; because wars of the past have characteristically pursued the conquest, not the annihilation, of an enemy, this is also the ostensive purpose of nuclear war: any other outcome becomes an exceptional or chance occurrence. In *any* war, it could be argued along the same lines, and certainly in recent, nonnuclear conflicts, attacks have occurred which, notwithstanding the generally limited goals of those wars, have blurred any distinction between combatants and non-combatants; in this sense, again, nuclear war might seem no different in principle from nonnuclear war. But the response to this objection is no less obvious: that in none of these other instances, devastating as they have been, has it been imaginable that an attack would, either by itself or in conjunction with the response it evoked, result in the virtual destruction of a people, thus, that this destruction might follow necessarily—not as the result of an independent decision—from a first, purportedly limited decision. It may well be that had such a possibility been an option in the past, it would in fact have been chosen; but I am not asserting that individual or corporate agents in the past were more morally enlightened than their successors, only that the choices available to the latter have changed radically, that the prospect of genocide as well as that of omnicide is now *entailed* in the willed consideration of nuclear war.

I do not wish here to discuss whether such a decision could ever be justified, although it seems to me obvious that it could not be. That question is related to the distinction between "just" and "unjust wars," as well as to the question of the general justification of value assigned to human life, and both those issues involve reference to a wide (but not incomprehensible) range of principles and facts. The more limited claim made here is that genocide, newly recognized and condemned as an unusually heinous crime, is implicit also in the threat of omnicide by way of nuclear war (that is, by those who prepare it). Genocide is one outcome (perhaps the only one) in fact that could *prevent* the omnicide they are otherwise prepared to risk, since the total destruction of an enemy nation might well be the only way of preventing the escalation and general conflagration that would almost certainly follow if enough of the enemy survived to mount a response (that would in turn evoke a further response, and so on).

This relation of implication, it should be noted, moves in the other direction as well, albeit less dramatically; for there is also a clear sense in which genocide lays the ground for, if it does not strictly imply, omnicide. This is not only a psychological point, although it is also that. Elias Canetti, in *Crowds and Power,* has suggested that monetary inflation in the Weimar Republic had something to do with the later Nazi genocide, as it accustomed people to thinking in otherwise unimaginable numbers. It is a much shorter step from conceiving the destruction of a kind (in genocide) to an enlargement in the notion of "kind" that omnicide involves.

Such a suggestion that concepts may have a life-history independent of judgments that are passed on them does not mean that someone who recognizes the phenomenon of genocide must himself somehow be contaminated by the idea, but only that concepts often manage to escape their original or primary contexts. But more than this, since, again, the process of transference is not only psychological. Genocide, notwithstanding the ostensively general rationale that prefaces its determination of an object, includes in that determination an intrinsically arbitrary feature; that is, the rationale itself is always underdetermined. To treat an individual person only as an instance of a group and thus as fully "defined" by that membership is in effect to deny the status of that individual. This, for example, is what the concept of collective guilt does when it ascribes the real (let us assume) guilt of a few members of a group to the group as a whole. Genocide passes just such a judgment of collective guilt (more neutrally, of identification); omnicide does so on a still larger scale, as it wills the sacrifice of the entire group of groups; there are here, in effect, no prohibitions. The willingness to threaten universal destruction may not mean that this judgment has been explicitly made (the wonder is, in fact, that people are willing to make such threats even in the absence of that judgment—that is, even without the semblance of a justification for the mass extermination of omnicide). But either the planners of nuclear warfare do not take account of such a possibility at all—in which case they are seriously irresponsible even in their own terms, as planners—or this judgment is accepted as a presupposition—in which case they are (at best) morally blind.

The willingness to risk omnicide is invariably accompanied by justification based on one or both of two grounds: that threats of nuclear attack are necessary to avoid the necessity of actualizing them and/or that certain principles justify even the risk that the threats might have to be actualized—thus, that the principles would justify the worst consequences of omnicide if those should occur. And here, too, there is a formal resemblance to the justifications provided for genocide, and not only because of their (common) questionable logic. For one thing, the justifications are both put in terms of *defense* against an enemy who is an actual or potential initiator: consideration that the means even of defense may be open to question; that the construction of an arsenal—even if genuinely for defense—may by its own momentum alter its ostensive purpose; that there are consequences to be taken account of in killing as such (and particularly in nuclear war) that are quite independent of any claims (even if warranted, certainly if unwarranted) of self-defense—all these are simply ignored, subordinated to an unquestioned end that in fact seems to be contradicted by them. The Mutually Assured Destruction (MAD) doctrine, moreover, tends to ignore or to deny its own intentions, on the grounds that they are only hypothetical—that is, that a counterstrike would be initiated only if someone else launched a first strike. But the history of warfare shows clearly that preemptive strikes are easily conflated with supposed counterstrikes; and more than this, a hypothetical intention is an intention nonetheless. To be sure, intentions are not the only elements that matter in moral judgment, and there is undoubtedly a distinction to be drawn between intentions that appear as part of an action and those that are attached to hypothetical or contrary-to-fact actions (what so-and-so would choose to do or have chosen to do if such-and-such were to happen or had happened). But there is no question that the latter are indeed intentions.

It might be argued that the discussion so far ignores an obvious and large difference between genocide and omnicide, namely, that the former is directed by an agent against someone else, whereas the latter will by definition include the agent himself. Do the adherents of the MAD doctrine "intend" suicide by it? And are they then only deceiving themselves and/or others by stressing the notion of deterrence? Or are they perhaps higher minded because they are willing to sacrifice themselves? But although intentions are functions of actions that include evidence of what the agent had "in mind," they are not *restricted* to that evidence. I have tried to show in the discussion of technology why a MAD proponent would be unlikely to anticipate or even to care very much about this suicidal intention, why he would think that *he* would escape its consequences. The MAD doctrine in practice turns out not to be simply a means for deterrence; it is invoked as a justification for being *ahead* of likely enemies or opponents—and what motivates this is not unreasonably seen as an expectation that the MAD proponent himself will survive a nuclear holocaust, if only the technology is right. Technology has room for obsolescence, but it has no place for mortality. Thus the will for omnicide comes cloaked with an illusion very much like that of genocide—that its agents have a transhistorical sanction.

It is conceivable, of course, that someone who is not suicidal in any conventional sense and who also recognizes the qualitatively different scale of nuclear war—a latter-day Samson—might be willing to destroy himself and everyone else in the name of an ostensive principle or set of principles. It is even possible that an absolute moral judgment might at some point be passed to the effect that it would indeed be *better* that mankind should cease to exist, that mankind collectively *deserves* the fate of omnicide; or, less dramatically, that whether mankind exists or not, given the infinitesimal place that that existence occupies in cosmic space and time, makes virtually no difference, one way or the other. But none of these is a judgment that men, individually or as a group offering judgment on other people as well as on themselves, are now or ever likely to be in a just position to make. Justice, we have learned— requires wisdom as well as power. We might well grant that certain principles are so important as to warrant self-sacrifice; but as it becomes increasingly doubtful that we can justify the sacrifice of others who may have no knowledge of the principle for which they are sacrificed, or who may know it and reject it, so too the decision to sacrifice *everybody* (or even to risk this) seems unwarranted by any principle that is not also accompanied by an extraordinary egoism (not a principle at all) on the part of the person or group choosing to act in that way. It could be maintained only by someone who felt that the individual—most evidently, *other* individuals—had no right or even possibility of self-determination; and we have seen how this is the basis for the putative justification, in another context, of genocide as well.

Last: if we ask (as I have been) what it is that makes the willing of genocide and omnicide possible, one feature remains to be noted that has been involved only indirectly so far but that is so basic that it has even then dominated the view. The "final cause" that shapes genocide and omnicide in common is not distinctive because it involves the act of killing. Virtually all societies of which we have knowledge have provided an institutionalized sanction for varieties of killing, whether through capital punishment, through provision for waging war or, more tacitly, through significant imbalances in the distribution of economic means that then turn into verdicts on life and death for some members of the society. It might be argued, moreover, that the numbers of (actual or potential) victims in each of these categories are large, and that at a certain point it does not matter how or under what circumstances those victims fall. To this extent, it might be objected, the differences between genocide and omnicide, on the one hand, and the other institutionalized forms of killing, on the other, are incidental. (Certainly pacifists might be inclined to argue along this line, although the objection would not necessarily be exclusively theirs.)

But it is nonetheless important to recognize that in genocide and omnicide we encounter the distinctive notion of *generic* killing, in which the category of the *genos* is raised to a principle—and *this* is a significant difference from other instances even of premeditated killing, as it is always arguable (although not necessarily correct) that some practical end *might* be served by the act. In genocide, the contention that an instrumental purpose is intended (as in the Nazi claim that annihilation of the Jews was identical to the cure for a disease) is quickly undermined as we see the contradictory impulse which *defines* the *genos* quite independent of any practical consequence (and sometimes openly opposed to it: the Nazis pursued the extermination of the Jews even when they were aware that this purpose of "self-defense" was interfering with the ability of Germany to carry on the war it was engaged in). A similar claim can be made for the threat of omnicide where, again, the pretense that it might serve a practical purpose—an ostensive end—is still more quickly discredited. In both phenomena, then, there figures a willingness, finally an intention,[11] to raise killing to the level of a principle, the end of which turns out to be the principle itself: as the notion of a kind insofar as it applies *at all* to human beings—a particular group or humankind as a whole—seems disconnected, substantively, even logically, from the act of killing even so far as that act might be defended on instrumental grounds if it were directed against individuals; so when it is built into the act, as in generic killing, we recognize a demonic purpose, one we suspect to have inverted the distinction between good and evil altogether. If there is even a *psychological* justification here, it is the justification of myth—a reversion to the cult of sacrifice or, more simply, to the search for a scapegoat.

OMNICIDE AND THE REDEFINITION OF CULTURE

Little has been said so far about the second question mentioned in the opening lines of this essay, concerning the consequences of genocide and omnicide (even as possibilities) for the social reality of the culture in which they appear. The issues here are complex, not least because the concept of culture has become problematic, often being invoked honorifically (as shorthand for "*high* culture") or, at the other extreme, sociologically—for *any* set of social norms and practices no matter how restricted the set. Whether one can speak of a world-culture as now challenged by the phenomena of genocide and omnicide, or even of a "western" culture as most immediately confronted by that challenge, are also questions that are perhaps unanswerable except by stipulating a definition of culture. In any event, they require more systematic attention than can be accorded them here. But at least two social and symbolic implications do follow from the complex of features outlined; these bear on the technological background to genocide and omnicide and then to the impulse for violation (in which violence is the most extreme but also the most open manifestation) that complex of factors supports.

The first of these implications is that genocide and omnicide are social phenomena in the broadest sense of that term; they are not merely geo-political or psychological or military eruptions that are then shut off (and so isolable) from the life of the society in general. This is due not only or principally to the extent of their immediate consequences, large as these must be. Enough has been written about the "mass" society and "technological man" to make the point obvious that consequences of those phenomena are evident in virtually every area of social existence: in legal and political institutions that seem increasingly to be detached from any sense of purpose or final cause; in social relations, where the notion of a "universal man"—the technological ideal—threatens the possibility of community; in the arts, where we find that their objects (when any are admitted at all) turn out to be the arts themselves (painting as "about" painting, writing as "about" writing, etc.). There are many problems, no doubt, in speaking of "the spirit of an age," but the evidence is compelling of links among these cultural developments (at least in advanced countries) and between them and the technological ideal I claim to be the background for genocide and omnicide. In them all the mechanism and method become the focus of concern, and this means that if the purpose of the means is not entirely ignored, it is shaped to serve that means, rather than the other way round. It may be too much to claim (as it would be too much for any historical phenomenon) that genocide and omnicide are inevitable outcomes or accompaniments of the technological ideal. But they are unquestionably consistent with that ideal; in the ways I have suggested, they epitomize it.

Admittedly, it is easy—perhaps inevitable—to romanticize or (more neutrally) to exaggerate selected features of past history and thus to contrast it invidiously with the present; it is also easy, perhaps for the same reasons, to mistake the proportions or causal features of the present. Moreover, we know about culture, T.S. Eliot suggests, that it is "the one thing we cannot deliberately aim at."[12] The consciousness we have of the present culture is in this sense at least as much a symptom of it as an agent capable of working on it. But the realities of genocide and omnicide are unmistakable and too large to be unmotivated or gratuitous. We might assume, then, even *without* other evidence, that they do not stand by themselves; there is ample evidence, so I have argued, of a pattern of which they are part.

It may seem that the second implication I have referred to—the impulse for violation—is even at odds with the first one, that technology presupposes perhaps a *too-strong* conception of normalcy, of homogeneity. But the sense of normalcy there is the result of a conflation of norms and the differences among them—a conflation that first denies them any serious role, and then enlarges that denial into a rejection of the concept of purpose or value altogether. What finally emerges is the threat of violation not to any particular norm or set of them, but to all norms, and thus even to the possibility of the concept itself. Much anthropological evidence has testified to the role played by normative distinctions (as between the sacred and the profane, the permissible and the impermissible) in the structure of all societies. The inference is often drawn from this evidence that the pattern of division as it gives a shape to social existence is the object of such rules, rather than any particular content— and this interpretation underscores the possibility that I take to be realized in the context of genocide and omnicide, that the pattern of social structure itself is finally the victim of their violence. So far as culture impinges on social reality at all, it does this by way of a network of norms (again, the particular ones hardly matter) that have authority for members of the culture. Such norms may be set to any possible level or object ("Where there is dirt," Mary Douglas writes, "there is system.")[13] The arbitrariness, the indifference to the issues of context or reason, the denial of persons and individuality, the mechanization of the social process, all of which are constant themes internal to the concepts and *a fortiori* to the practices of genocide and omnicide, consistently challenge the standing of such norms as such, and thus also, we may predict, the possibility of culture in even a minimal sense. Even the concepts of truth and falsity need to be understood culturally as instances of such norms; as Phillip Rieff writes, "Sociologically, a truth is whatever militates against the human capacity to express everything."[14] The closing phrase of that statement is especially significant, it seems to me, and fully exemplified in the many attempts to understand *why* the Nazi genocide against the Jews occurred. Those attempts, serious and reflective as they often have been, seem yet consistently to fall short of the events they are intended to account for—and the reason for that may lie in this: that as they look for reasons and causes within a structure where the lines of what is permissible, either in reason or in practice, are clearly marked, the actions they try to understand were intended precisely to challenge the possibility of any such lines, to see how far the human will could extend when unfettered. To the extent that this is relevant to understanding the phenomenon of genocide (and by extension, omnicide), it also threatens what otherwise serves as the foundation for culture as such, at least in the large array of cultures to which we have had access.

From a slightly different direction that converges on the same point, George Steiner notes the improbability that "one can devise a model of culture without a utopian core":[15] culture, it seems, requires at least the illusion of potential value—more generally, the contrast defined by the very assertion that there *are* norms. But in the presence of the menace of genocide and omnicide, mere survival becomes the "utopian core," or at least the only possible candidate for such a core, and it is arguable whether that can serve as a basis for culture, or indeed for anything more than the kind of struggle that those two phenomena themselves embody. No doubt many cultures have "sublimated" adversity and hardship into social dreams of a utopian future; but those dreams have been at some level compatible with the reality that fostered them, and it is difficult to foresee what transmutations would be possible for a collective experience shaped by the threats of genocide and omnicide. When Dostoyevsky predicted that "If God is dead, then everything is permitted," he had, with all his prescience, only a dim anticipation of the practices that man might yet devise as a means of assuring that the distinction between what is permitted and what is not permitted should simply be discarded.

It is true that I have not taken account of the human—and cultural—capacity to block out, to forget, or to ignore, and thus perhaps to act "*as if*" genocide and omnicide were no more than remote or accidental possibilities. But for one thing, thinking (even forgetting) requires something to think *with*, and the constitution of that is not entirely within the control of the thinker. And second, we might—we *ought*—not choose to forget that genocide and omnicide, whatever else they are, are also, even first, products of the human imagination. One danger in forgetting this is that we may as a consequence be led to think that we need concern ourselves with nothing else; and since the threatened end would radically transform the world, we must anticipate it, prevent it, with *our own* transformation. If we do not change everything, in other words, we change nothing (since the change we are trying to prevent would *also* change everything—into nothing). This has always been the impulse of apocalyptic thinking, and it is the impulse that has led many of the antinuclear protests and recent discussions of genocide (of the Nazi genocide or others) to lose sight of the immediate injustices and brutality in social practice that are themselves almost certainly elements in shaping just the feared future realizations of genocide and omnicide. One way to avoid thinking seriously of the end, in other words, is by thinking exclusively of the end. A second, no less urgent, danger in forgetting or denying the human origins of genocide and omnicide would be in concluding that the world in which we find them is the only possible world. It is hardly a sacrifice of the "facts" of nature and of history that the 20th century has celebrated to agree with Thoreau that "we always live the life we are imagining we are"—and then it should also be possible to work, as he did, at imagining a different one.

NOTES

1. I refer to the "phenomena" of genocide and omnicide in a way that may seem to ignore the fact that genocide has "occurred" in the 20th century, where omnicide may seem only to be threatened or possible. But these modalities are not so easily distinguished. Genocide as defined in the U.N. Convention does not presuppose completion of the act of extermination, but only the evident intent to complete that act. Gary Stahl argues in (Chapter 4) that the process of omnicide has already begun; the point I emphasize is that the will to risk ominicide as the consequence of actions taken in itself raises the question of intentions and thus of moral judgment on the "act" of omnicide.
2. The question of what analogous examples there might be is difficult, in part because such examples come from various directions and also vary in scope (so, for example, the Enlightenment concept of equality as it worked its way into the American and French revolutions). Such comparisons become more plausible as genocide and omnicide are seen in relation to the concept and practice of technology.
3. See Rafael Lemkin, *Axis Rule in Occupied Europe* (Washington, DC: Carnegie Endowment for International Peace, 1944). For more recent analyses of the concept of genocide, see Uriel Tal, "On the Study of the Holocaust and Genocide," *Yad Vashem Studies* 13 (Jerusalem, 1979), pp. 7-52; and Berel Lang, "The Concept of Genocide," *Philosophical Forum* (Spring 1984).
4. See Nehemiah Robinson, *The Genocide Convention* (New York: Institute of Jewish Affairs, 1960).
5. For other examples, see Richard H. Popkin, Chapter 6, this volume.
6. See, e.g., George Steiner, *Language and Silence* (New York: Atheneum, 1967); Nachman Blumenthal, "On the Nazi Vocabulary," *Yad Vashem Studies* I (Jerusalem, 1957). More generally, see H. D. Lasswell, Nathan Leties, et al., *Language of Politics* (Cambridge: M.I.T. Press, 1965); and George Orwell, "Politics and the English Language," in his *Collected Essays* (New York: Harcourt, Brace, 1965).

7. Hannah Arendt, *Eichmann in Jerusalem*, rev. ed. (New York: Viking, 1973).

8. See, e.g., Hannah Arendt, *The Origins of Totalitarianism* (New York: Meridian Books, 1958), chap. 7: "Race and Bureaucracy"; Alvin W. Gouldner, *Patterns of Industrial Bureaucracy* (Glencoe, IL: Free Press, 1954); Henry Jacoby, *The Bureaucratization of the World*, trans. E. Kanes (Berkeley: University of California Press, 1973).

9. See on this point, Yehuda Bauer, *The Jewish Emergence from Powerlessness* (Toronto: University of Toronto Press, 1979).

10. Jacques Ellul, *The Technological Society*, trans. J. Wilkinson (New York: Vintage, 1964). Cf. also for a related account from a different direction, Herbert Marcuse, *One Dimensional Man* (Boston: Beacon Press, 1964).

11. I return to the notion of omnicide as *intended* since the possible qualifications on that usage do not seem to me compelling. Suppose that the nuclear holocaust that must be admitted as at least possible *does* occur. At that point, the argument (from whatever side and by whoever is left to make it) that the nuclear arsenals had been *intended* to prevent such an outcome would be challenged *at least* by a charge of negligence (for some events, the very fact that they occur is sufficient evidence of this). And although negligence may be understood as involving an agent who did *not* intend the consequences of his action, an alternate description is that what he *did* intend can be judged culpable. In genocide, intention and culpability are more evident (although even then, because of their corporate status, complex) but not essentially different.

12. T.S. Eliot, *Notes Towards the Definition of Culture* (New York: Harcourt, Brace, 1949), p. 17.

13. Mary Douglas, *Purity and Danger* (London: Routledge and Kegan Paul, 1966), p. 35.

14. Philip Rieff, "The Impossible Culture." *Salmagundi* (1982-83).

15. George Steiner, *In Bluebeard's Castle* (New Haven: Yale University Press, 1971), p. 71.

6
THE TRIUMPHANT APOCALYPSE AND THE CATASTROPHIC APOCALYPSE

Richard H. Popkin

*But the day of the Lord will come as a thief in the night; in
which the heavens shall pass away with a great noise, and the
elements shall melt with fervent heat, the earth also and the
works that are therein shall be burned up.*

*Looking for and hasting unto the coming of the day of God,
wherein the heavens being on fire shall be dissolved and the
elements shall melt with fervent heat?*

*Nevertheless we, according to his promise, look for new
heavens and a new earth, wherein dwelleth righteousness.*

Second Peter 3:10-13

This biblical text has been coupled with the dramatic vision in The Revelation of
Saint John the Divine of what will transpire at the end of days —the overthrow of
the Antichrist, the chaining up of Satan, the Reign of Jesus Christ on Earth for a
thousand years, the battles of Gog and Magog, the Day of Judgment (chap. 20)—
after which John proclaimed "And I saw a new heaven and a new earth: for the first
heaven and the first earth were passed away; and there was no more sea. And I John
saw the holy city, new Jerusalem, coming down from God out of heaven, prepared
as a bride adorned for her husband." Further God shall wipe away men's tears "and
there shall be no more death, neither sorrow, nor crying, neither shall there be any
more pain: for the former things are passed away." (chap. 21, verses 1-4)

These passages provide the basis for a view of the triumphant Apocalypse, a
transformation of the world which will bring about a wonderful and glorious state.
For many centuries, their official reading was that they described in allegorical
form what had already happened when Jesus became incarnate and established His
Church on earth. (St. Augustine provided the metaphysical theological basis for
such a reading.) To think otherwise would indicate that the ongoing world, guided
by the Church established by Jesus, was to be overthrown. Millenialism, the view

that Jesus would return to earth and rule on earth for a thousand years according to the scenario laid down in Revelation, was declared a heresy. The rebellious behavior of the various groups in the Middle Ages who pursued the millenium showed the danger of the view.[1]

During the Reformation millenarianism became a more influential force. Millenarians saw their challenge to Roman authority as part of the predictions in Second Peter, Revelation, and Daniel (especially concerning the overthrow of the four monarchies). With the success of the Reformation in England and Holland and parts of Germany, Protestant theologians started claiming not only that they were reforming and purifying Christianity by getting back to its real message; they were also fulfilling part of the prophesies. The Church of Rome, they proclaimed, was the Antichrist. In breaking its power, the Protestants were starting to play their roles in preparing for an actual historical millenium about to commence in Europe.[2] The very pious and very learned theologian of Cambridge, Joseph Mede, believed he had found the key to the Book of Revelation, in relating its scenario to the Thirty Years War, the struggles against the Turks, the trials of the English and French Protestants, the development of world trade, the increase of knowledge, etc. Mede also set forth a calculus for determining when the various pre-millenial events would occur.[3] (The Scottish mathematician, John Napier, offered a similar calculus.)[4] Mede was the teacher of John Milton, Henry More, and Isaac Barrow (the teacher of Isaac Newton). His views became all-important during the Puritan Revolution, when his books and letters were widely read as explanations of what was then happening, and as plans of what was to come. The English Puritans under Cromwell proclaimed that they were ushering in the millenium, while various leaders were announcing such delightful pre-millenial events, as the conversion of the Jews, would take place in 1656, the battle of Armaggedon a few years later, and the Second Coming by the late 17th century.[5]

Along with these happy expectations came a desire to understand all of the aspects of what was to transpire. Many of the prevailing millenarian intellectual groups were convinced that, as Daniel had predicted, knowledge would increase as the end of history approached. They were also convinced that nature as well as history was guided by God's providential plan, and that the careers of both were outlined in Scripture, and could be understood, at least dimly, by our God-given reason. A crucial part of the transformation that was to come was the achievement of universal knowledge. The closer mankind got to the end, the more they would know. Schemes, such as those of Bacon and Comenius were designed as ways of aiding and abetting this increase in knowledge.

What was to be known was both natural and divine. God as the Author of Nature had provided scientific means for understanding the created world. God as the Author of Scripture had provided other means for grasping the revealed world. For most millenarian scientists in the 17th and 18th centuries the new physics was God's design for the created world, which began circa 4004 B.C. and would last until the millenium, and the Apocalypse, when conditions set forth mainly in the Book of Revelation would supersede those of the normal natural world of the interim between Creation and the onset of the Millenium (in Jewish theology, a period of 6,000 years).

From early in the 17th century, millenarian scientists had been in the forefront of developing and advancing the new science, and applying it towards explaining Scriptural history. The physics of the creation of the world was dealt with by Henry

More in terms of the new science as a way of showing the accuracy of the account in Genesis. Part of More's *Antidote to Atheism* was to show the harmony of science and Scripture. Comenius' plan for universal knowledge involved a sort of Baconian science guided by Scripture and Divine Light.[6]

The three critical issues for the religious scientists were: (1) how to explain the mechanics of creation; (2) the hydraulics of the Flood;[7] and (3) the astrophysics of the Apocalypse. More felt he had solved the first; many people worked on the second. The third had, perhaps, greater interest, since it was what was to come. And, if a series of historical events in the 17th century, such as the Thirty Years War, the Puritan Revolution, etc. were the prelude to the Millenium, it was time to work out the physics of history's revealed finale. The pre-Millenial scenario of Revelation 19-20 seems to be taking place. This would be followed by a happy thousand year reign of Jesus. Then the traumatic end of history as we know it would occur with the Day of Judgement as graphically described in Revelation 20:11-15, to be followed by the end of nature as we know it, by a great conflagration.

SOME SEVENTEENTH CENTURY VIEWS ON THE APOCALYPSE

This cataclysmic end was examined calmly by leading scientists and theologians, seeking to understand what exactly would occur. They accepted that *a*, or *the*, Holocaust would take place as part of the Divine Plan, and that this total destruction of the world as we know it would be a triumphant event, to be desired by all good and true believers. The normal course of nature would cease, and God, through special Providence, would bring about the totally new state of affairs—the new heaven and the new earth. When we think of the funereal, dire predictions today describing such a calamity, it is heart-rending to look at a couple of seventeenth century versions of what was expected to transpire as the necessary and unavoidable, but much to be desired, end of history.

Thomas Burnet (1635-1715) produced the most detailed account in his *Telluris Theoria Sacra* (1680), and its English version, *The Sacred Theory of the Earth* (1684), followed by six later editions.[8] The book, on the title-page of the second edition, says it contains "an Account of the *Original of the Earth*, and of all the General Changes which it hath already undergone, Or Is To Undergo Till the Consummation of all Things."[9] Books I and II deal with the Deluge and Paradise, and are dedicated to the King.[10] Books III and IV are "Concerning the Burning of the World, and Concerning the New Heavens and New Earth" and are dedicated to the Queen. In the dedication, Burnet apologized for presenting Her Majesty with "a World laid in ashes" but assured her that according to the divine Promises that after the present earth is destroyed there will be a new earth that is "Paradisiacal."[11]

In the Preface to the Reader, Burnet stated that the third part of his book dealt with "a Subject own'd by all, and out of dispute: *The Conflagration of the World.*" The only questions at issue were "the bounds and limits of the Conflagration, the Causes and the Manner of it." Burnet claimed his only novelty was that he followed St. Peter's "Philosophy" in supposing "that the burning of the Earth will be a true liquefaction or dissolution of it, as to the exterior Region." So, Burnet set out "to propose an intelligible way, whereby the Earth may be consum'd by Fire."[12] (Given the state of scientific knowledge at the time, it was somewhat difficult to explain how, with all of the water on earth, the world could be set on fire, and how solid matter could be burned up.) Burnet devoted one hundred seventy pages to accounting for the conflagration that was to come. Although certainly not depressed or upset by this, he did say, "For to see a World perishing in Flames, Rocks melting, the Earth trembling, and an Host of Angels in the clouds, one must be very much a Stoick, to be a cold and unconcerned Spectator of all this."[13]

Burnet, in orderly fashion, developed his explanation. He rejected the possibility that the sun might draw nearer the earth, and cause the fire, or that a central fire would come from within the earth. When the conflagration comes, "there will be a sort of liquefaction and dissolution."[14] Its natural causes will include volcanoes, burning coals, lakes of pitch and brimstone and "oily liquoeirs dispenst in several parts of the Earth."[15] All growing things will become fuel to this vast fire. There will be fiery events in the atmosphere, lightning, meteors. "At the Conflagration, God will rain down Fire from Heaven, as he did once upon Sodom; and at the same time the subterraneous store-houses of Fire will be broken open, . . . And these two meeting and mingling together, will involve all the Heaven and Earth in flames."[16] As Burnet developed the details about how all of this might happen, he offered both natural causes, and miraculous ones to bring about the total destruction of the world, the result of Divine Providence acting both naturally and supernaturally. In much the way Jonathan Schell has recently described what will happen in a nuclear war, Burnet described the way the world would be consumed, bit by bit, until it is reduced to "a Fiery Chaos." Burnet explained that it was only fitting that the fire should begin at the seat of the Antichrist, namely Rome, and spread from there throughout Italy, and throughout the world.[17] After offering all sorts of details about what would happen, Burnet finally made a comment that indicated there was something sad about this future. "I am apt to think that Providence hath so contriv'd the period of their (the stars') motion, that there will be an unusual concourse of them at that time, within the view of the Earth, to be a prelude to this last and most Tragical Scene of the Sublunary World."[18] But before the reader became worried or maudlin, Burnet assured him or her, that according to Scripture the world would not become "eternal rubbish, without any hopes of restoration."[19] Instead, from the ashes of this world will arise a New Earth. And so the reader can turn from this most "Tragical Scene," bid farewell to the present world, and turn for enjoyment to what is to come. The next chapter deals with the Coming of the Savior "descending in the Head of an Army of Angels, and a Burning World under his feet."[20] Burnet brought out various passages in Scripture to indicate how marvelous the world would then be forever and ever.

The third book of Burnet's *Sacred History of the Earth* ends with a sobering conclusion that, again, reminds us of what we hear today. "If the Conflagration of the World be a reality, as, both by Scripture and Antiquity, we are assur'd it is: If we be fully perswaded and convinc'd of this: Tis a thing of that nature, that we cannot keep it long in our thoughts, without making some moral reflections upon it. 'Tis both great in its self, and of universal concern to all Mankind."[21] Most of the authors in this volume would certainly agree. What follows underscores the difference between the Triumphant Apocalypse and the Catastrophic one. Burnet made the immediate human concern the following, "Who can look upon such an Object, A World in Flames, without thinking with himself, Whether shall I be in the midst of these flames, or no? What is my security that I shall not fall under this fiery vengeance, which is the wrath of an angry God?"[22] Survival is possible in Burnet's picture of the Apocalypse, not by physical endurance, but by spiritual action. The remainder of his conclusion is an attempt to make people realize that their survival is possible only if they are or become true and believing Christians. The last book of Burnet's opus is a joyous account of the New Heaven and New Earth in which the true believers will live.

Another scientist-theologian of the time, John Ray, 1627- 1705, presented his version of what had and would happen. Ray, a fellow of the Royal Society, and a leading expert on plants and animals (he had written a history of fish), presented the world with *Three physico-theological discourses, concerning I. The primitive chaos and the creation of the world. II. The general deluge, its causes and effects. III. The dissolution of the world and future conflagration.* The work ran through several editions and was reprinted throughout the 18th century.[23]

A different and still more "scientific" version of the Triumphant Apocalypse was developed in the writings of William Whiston (1667-1752). Burnet had written before the great theory of modern physics of Isaac Newton had been presented to the world (in *Principia mathematica* of 1687). As a result Burnet's account was full of questionable scientific claims, plus some unneeded supernatural ones. Whiston, enthused by Newton's system of the world, used it in his *A New Theory of the Earth* to show how the Mosaic creation and the great Conflagration could be accounted for on strictly Newtonian principles.[24] At the outset Whiston made clear he was not opposing Scripture with science. Scripture told the true history of the world from its commencement onward; the world God created operated on Newtonian principles. *"The Mosaick Creation is not a Nice and Philosophical account of the Origin of All Things: but an Historical and True Representation of the formation of our single Earth out of a confused chaos, and of the successive and visible changes thereof each day, till it became the habitation of Mankind."*[25] This world as described in Scripture is clearly accountable in a natural way; Whiston worked out the physics of the universe around us, and its development including the universal deluge recorded in the Bible. He then declared that "Since the Deluge there neither has been, nor will be, any great and general Changes in the state of the World, till that time when a Period is to be put to the present Course of Nature."[26] That period will be when the world is consumed in fire as described in 2 Peter 3: 7-12. "But this is so fully attested by the unanimous consent of Sacred and Prophane Authority, that I shall omit other particular Quotations."[27] The physics of what will happen to the earth in the millenium are presented. There will no longer be any sea. There will be no succession of day and night, just perpetual day. And at the conclusion of the millenium, the Final Judgement and Consummation of all things, "The Earth will desert its present Seat and Station in the World, and be no longer found among the Planetary Chorus."[28]

In tracing the physical history of the earth from Creation through the developments in the biblical account, Whiston offered Newtonian explanations of all that occurred, and all that presently exists in the world. The same natural processes that have gone on since the Flood will continue until an end of the present natural world occurs.[29] The only other natural causes that produce any great and general changes in the sublunary world are bodies that can approach the Earth, namely comets. Then, Whiston cheerily asserted, the next approach of the comet (Halley's comet?) "will, in all probability, bring the present State of Things to a Conclusion, and *Burn* the World."[30] The world is safe enough until the Conflagration.

Whiston ended his work with conjecture about how the world will end in terms of the actions of comets. A comet coming close to the Earth could retard its annual motion so that it approached nearer to the sun, which "wou'd scorch and burn, dissolve and destroy it in the prodigious degree" and turn the Earth from being a Planet into a comet.[31] This could explain the Conflagration, but would eliminate the possibility of a future world. So, Whiston offered a less drastic comet theory, namely, that the comet dried out the atmosphere and emptied the seas and oceans. This could have heated the earth to cause a general conflagration, as well as earthquakes, tidal waves, etc. There would be changes in the physical world up to the conclusion of the millenium, the Final Judgement and the Consummation of all things. Then "the Earth will desert its present Seat and Station in the World" and will no longer be a planet.[32]

Whiston, like Burnet, saw nothing particularly sad about his picture of this Triumphant Apocalypse, since the faithful would be saved. Newton was so pleased to see the Divine Drama explained in terms of Newtonian physics that he had Whiston appointed as his successor as Lucasian Professor of Mathematics at Cambridge. Until fired for proclaiming his anti-Trinitarian heresies, Whiston poured out scientific-theological works about what was to happen. He gave the Boyle lectures on the Accomplishment of Scriptural Prophecies, showing that reasonable scientific persons should expect that those prophecies not yet fulfilled will be, since so many have already been fulfilled. He went around predicting in coffee houses when the world would come to an end, and revised his predictions whenever another earthquake was reported. (Fortunately, he died before the Lisbon Earthquake.) The impending Apocalypse would be benign, in fact, glorious, for true believers.[33]

Newton himself apparently shared many of Whiston's radical religious views, but kept them to themselves. As Whiston became a public heretic, Newton cast him aside. Only posthumously, a sanitized version of Newton's *Observations of Daniel and Revelation* appeared.[34] And, until this day, Newton's vast writings on prophecy, the millenium and the Apocalypse have not been edited and published; nevertheless, what is so far known clearly shows he was a firm believer in the Triumphant Apocalypse.[35]

VIEWS ABOUT THE APOCALYPSE IN THE EIGHTEENTH AND NINETEENTH CENTURIES

Newtonian physics provided a way of construing the world without Providence. Newton and some of his disciples saw the physical world described by Newtonian physics as the explanation of what has happened, is happening, and will happen between God's Creation of the World, and His transformation of it in the Apocalypse. However, for some Enlightenment thinkers who scorned the claims of Scriptural history, the new physics revealed a world that just went on and on according to fixed laws, with no end or purpose. Similarly, some proposed, was the case with human history. Pierre Bayle, Voltaire, David Hume and Edmund Gibbon, the so-called philosophical historians, rejected prophetic history.

Bayle, especially in the articles on Old Testament biblical figures, in the *Historical and Critical Dictionary*, portrayed their careers as being the result of the same nasty *human* motivations as those encountered at any time or place in human history. The *comédie humaine* as set forth by Bayle neither progressed nor deteriorated, and it certainly exhibited no Providential direction or goal. In fact, as he declared, history is nothing but the lies, misfortunes and catastrophies of the human race. Voltaire followed Bayle with a similar non-Providential picture of what has been going on. But whereas Bayle showed the biblical heroes as just ordinary

immoral and dishonest people, Voltaire went on to insist on the virulent malevo-
lence and stupidity of the ancient Hebrews, and the horrendous viciousness of the
Christians. The history of the people in Scripture and their heirs in the Jewish and
Christian worlds was the history of a monumental blight that had poisoned the
human scene for two thousand years, but that might be overcome by the benign
secularism and rationalism of the Enlightenment. Hume, as a philosopher and as an
historian, saw man, at all times, functioning as a natural being, with no guidance
beyond natural propensities and forces. Religion was one of the unfortunate out-
growths of human ignorance and inability to cope with the world. Hume wrote *The
Natural History of Religion* showing how it developed in terms of human factors.
The Bible for Hume was a primitive document, written by a rude and ignorant people, that present day reasonable men could hardly give any credence to. Prophecy
was not really possible, since knowledge of the future was unattainable. "All the
philosophy, therefore, in the world, and all the religion, which is nothing but a
species of philosophy, will never be able to carry us beyond the usual course of
experience, or give us measures of conduct and behaviour different from those
which are furnished by reflections on common life. No new fact can ever be
inferred from the religious hypothesis, no event foreseen or foretold."[36] Gibbon,
the last of the triumvirate of "philosophical historians" applied this way of analyzing human history to one case study, how Christianity grew and overthrew the
Roman Empire. Unlike St. Augustine, who saw this as one of the clearest evidences
of Divine Providence, it was for Gibbon a sad, sad picture of the follies and foibles
of mankind. Some of the few good or noble aspects of human behavior were
crushed by avarice, nastiness, intolerance, corruption, etc.[37]

Bayle, Hume, Voltaire and Gibbon saw human history as really getting nowhere,
and having no ultimate goal. The escape from alleged Providential history would at
least allow reasonable people to see the human situation for what it really is. Man
and nature would presumable go on indefinitely. The best one could expect was a bit
of enlightenment and understanding, and more restrained moral (and not religious)
behavior. For the philosophical historians, there was not going to be any Apocalypse of any kind, just a dreary procession of human, self-interested developments.
The less pessimistic Enlightenment thinkers, those who believed in the genuine and
indefinite perfectability of mankind, also saw no real Apocalypse. The Jeffersons,
the Condorcets, foresaw human reason and good will emancipating people from
their former religious shackles, and gradually solving various human problems
through education and science.

As both the pessimistic and optimistic Enlightenment thinkers cast the Judeo-
Christian tradition aside, and rejected its scenario from Creation to Apocalypse,
there were still people who persisted in looking for the Triumphant Apocalypse.
Among the leading scientists of the 18th century, two, David Hartley and Joseph
Priestley, still linked their scientific understanding of the world with their millenarian expectations. Hartley (1707-1757) applied Newtonian science to human mental
life, and developed a mechanistic theory of psychology. In his *Observations on Man*
of 1749, Hartley devoted the first book to scientific psychology, and the second
(which is rarely read) to religious matters. Proposition 85, Book II, states, "*It is not
probable, that there will be any pure or complete Happiness, before the Destruction
of this World by Fire.*"[38] Hartley explained that the pre-Millenial events seemed to
be imminent, including the Restoration of the Jews and the universal establishment
of Christianity. Then, as St. Peter has told us, "The Earth must be burnt up, before

we are to expect *a new Heaven and a new Earth, wherein dwelleth Righteousness.*"[39] Hartley happily looked forward to this triumphant state in the reasonably near future.

Joseph Priestley (1733-1804), the great chemist and theoretician of electricity, united his materialistic, scientific views together with active Millenarian concerns, based on reading the Providential signs to the current events of the time. He believed that God had so designed the world that it was about to be transformed from its normal natural ways, to the dynamic end of nature and history foretold in Scripture. By 1787 Priestley was so convinced the moment for the Conversion of the Jews had arrived that he published a *Letter to the Jews* informing them of the good news. The French Revolution increased Priestley's conviction that the Millenial prophecies were about to be fulfilled. Priestley became an enthusiastic supporter of the Revolution, and, like Tom Paine, was elected to the Revolutionary Assembly. Because of his pro-French views, he had to flee from England to America, where Benjamin Franklin got him a post at the University of Pennsylvania. As Priestley surveyed the world from the other side of the Atlantic, he announced that the great Millenial events were beginning, the Pope had been captured by the French army, and kings of the earth were being overthrown. Within fifty years he expected the deliverance of the Jews, the fall of the Turkish Empire and the Second Coming of Christ.[40]

Hartley and Priestley were the two most important scientific figures expecting the Triumphant Apocalypse. There is a huge literature by theologians, interested intellectuals and fervent believers, interpreting the events of the American and French Revolutions, and the Napoleonic Wars, as culminating events leading up to the Millenium. Some saw Napoleon as the Antichrist, whose downfall would soon be followed by the Triumphant Apocalypse. Others voiced suspicions that Napoleon might be the Jewish Messiah. Napoleon issued a coin in 1806, after his series of military victories culminating at Austerlitz, in which he, the Emperor, is shown handing a new set of tablets of the law to a kneeling Moses.[41]

This kind of millenial interpretation of events went on through the next decades, each revolution presaging some new development. The French revolution of 1830, the Polish revolution of 1831, the revolutions of 1848, the U.S. Civil War, etc., all have had their interpreters, who saw them as the penultimate events before the millenium with all the good things that were to follow. Some in England and American figured out the Millenium would begin in 1843. William Miller in 1841 gave lectures in the United States about *Evidences from Scripture and History of the Second Coming of Christ about the year 1843.*[42] The incredible missionary, Joseph Wolff, who was constantly travelling through the Middle East and trying to convert Jews, saw the final signs of the imminent great events. He came to America in 1837 and told Congress that the millenium would begin in 1846.[43] (John Quincy Adams, who heard him, commented, however, that the date seemed a bit too soon.)[44] Millenial groups like the Mormons and the Seventh Day Adventists arose and flourished as believers prepared for the Triumphant Apocalypse.

Although there has been no let-up in millenial interest and expectation through the nineteenth and twentieth centuries, it has had little support from scientific people, or from established church groups. The millenialists are mainly to be found among fundamentalists and evangelical groups. The scientific community has, in the main, moved to various sorts of agnostic, or vaguely deistic views about what directing force or forces there may be.

This position was put quite solemnly in Bertrand Russell's essay, "A Free Man's Worship." The world is seen as a determined state of affairs, governed by scientific laws. There is no purpose or goal being achieved as these laws lead to the gradual cooling of our planet, and the termination of human existence millions and millions of years in the future. Realizing that no Apocalypse lies ahead, Russell foresaw the "free man" as one who can wrestle with present problems of starvation, illness, poverty, etc., without expecting any permanent paradise.[45]

The humanistic, democratic socialism that Russell coupled with his overall pessimism about the nature and destiny of man was severely jolted by the tremendous man-made destruction of human beings in World War I, in Stalinist Russia and in Nazi Germany. Although apocalyptic slogans were used to create enthusiasm in these wars—the war to end all wars, the creation of the workers' paradise, the thousand year Reich—each of these developments showed how man-made power could be used to subject and destroy human life. Because each was limited geographically, no matter how horrible and destructive, they did not reach the proportions of the Apolcalypse described in Scripture. (That is not to say, that if Hitler or Stalin had been more successful militarily, and had conquered England, or China, that the results would not have been more horrendous, and closer to the destruction of the whole human race, instead of just groups of humans.)

THE CATASTROPHIC APOCALYPSE

Only at the end of World War II did the possibility of total, rather than mass, destruction of mankind, become a realistic possibility. As various scientists realized the import of the new armaments unleashed on Hiroshima and Nagaski, and philosophers like Russell, Albert Schweitzer, and Karl Jaspers conceived of the magnitude of the total danger from man-made destruction, the notion of the Catastrophic Apocalypse began to make its appearance. The world might really end with a bang and not a whimper. It might not peter out over millions of meaningless years. It might not, as Russell earlier had contended, end in a long serious struggle to find human meaning and accomplishment in a universe without values or goals. It might not be, as Albert Camus contended at the end of World War II, a totally absurd situation in which men either made their own values, and risked the consequences of their ultimately meaningless acts, or abandoned the scene by individual self-destruction, suicide.[46] Instead, one had to face the realization that human history, world history could and might end in the destruction of everything human by nuclear war. At any moment, the nuclear military powers, a constantly growing group of political societies, could unleash their awesome destructive power, and terminate the old heaven and the old earth.

Various mournful writers, including some of those appearing in this volume, have cried out about the impending Catastrophic Apocalypse, describing it in quite strikingly similar terms to the Millenialists' picture, except for the new technological features involving radioactivity. Jonathan Schell has graphically portrayed "the tremendous scene of devastation, suffering and death" that would occur in a nuclear holocaust.[47] In the first part of his *The Fate of the Earth*, called "A Republic in Insects and Grass," he details, in much the way Thomas Burnet did two centuries ago, the way the human world and the physical world can now be destroyed. The first crucial difference in these strikingly similar accounts is that Burnet's picture of the Apocalypse is through "acts of God," while Schell's unfortunately is through acts of man. As he concludes the terrifying first part, Schell makes crystal clear that we have now arrived at a new stage of human history because of the existence of so many man-made megatons of nuclear explosive power—"the zone of the risk of extinction."[48] The vicissitudes of human existence up to now always involved the risk of some people's annihilation, so many, many people's annihilation in the great slaughter of warfare, conquest, famine, and natural disasters. But these have been within the frame of life. Now we are faced with the genuine possibility of extinction. This would not just be "the defeat of some purpose but an abyss in which all human purposes would be drowned for all time. We have no right to place the possibility of this limitless, eternal defeat on the same footing as risks that we run in the ordinary conduct of our affairs in our particular transient moment of history." And, as he ends this part, Schell eloquently states the result of the catastrophic Apocalypse. "In trying to describe possible consequences of a nuclear holocaust, I have mentioned the limitless complexity of its effects on human society and on the ecosphere—a complexity that sometimes seems to be as great as that of life itself. But if these effects should lead to human extinction, then all the complexity will give way to the utmost simplicity—the simplicity of nothingness. We—the human race—shall cease to be."[49]

Robert Jay Lifton described the Apocalypse facing us as a set of absurdities including one, that "organizations of human beings . . . stand poised to destroy virtually all of human civilization—destroy humankind—in the name of destroying one another."[50] The second absurdity is "the knowledge on the one hand that we, each of us, could be consumed in a moment together with everyone and everything we have touch or loved, and on the other, our tendency to go about business as usual—continue with our routines—as though no such threat existed."[51] The first absurdity is part of what distinguishes the notion of the Triumphant Apocalypse from the Catastrophic one: the Catastrophic Apocalypse would occur through direct human agency, whereas the Triumphant Apocalypse would occur directly through God's agency. It is interesting to note that the second absurdity was just as apparent amongst the true believers of the 17th century as it is among the doom-sayers of the present era. For example, John Dury, one of the most important Millenial activists in the mid-17th century, was bombarding Parliament with pleas for needed reforms before the Millenium. He was negotiating all over Protestant Europe to bring the evangelical churches together before Jesus returned. He also, in 1650, wrote the preface to a work presenting the key to the Book of Revelation in which he calmly told the reader that by 1655 Rome would be destroyed, the Turkish Empire would crumble, the Jews would convert, and the Millenium was just around the corner. *At the very same time*, Dury was putting the ransacked library of Charles I in order in St. James' Palace, and was asking Parliament for funds to build shelves in the royal chapel, so that he could get the books and manuscripts off the floor, and in reasonable order. When I realized that Dury's preface to Von Franckenberg's *Clavis Apocalyptica* was written at the very same time as he was attending to the practical needs of his function as librarian, it boggled my mind. How could somebody who believed that this world would last only five more years really care about putting up shelves and putting the king's books in order?[52] Then when I read Lifton's statement of that second absurdity, I realized that all of us who take seriously the possibility of nuclear holocaust, and who also go about our daily business, are behaving mentally and physically like Dury three centuries ago. We may firmly believe the best or the worst will soon occur, but in the interim we are human, all too human.

Of course, the most striking difference between the vision of the Triumphant Apocalypse and that of the Catastrophic one, is that in the former, after all the horrendous destruction, there will be a new heaven and a new earth in which the "saved" human beings will go on, and in the latter there will be no human events, no matter what kind of heaven and earth may survive. The descriptions of kinds of destruction differ only technologically.

THE TRIUMPHANT APOCALYPSE IN THE NUCLEAR AGE

Those who are pointing out the terrible nature of the Catastrophic Apocalypse are presenting a terrible warning about our possible future. There are, however, present day proponents of the Triumphant Apocalypse whose 'glad tidings' also should be listened to, since they may influence our future, or present another way in which it may be doomed to destruction.

Present-day millenialists have brought the picture of Triumphant Apocalypse up to date, in terms of nuclear warfare, and in terms of the Providential role of the human organizations that will fight the battle of Armageddon. While many agnostic scientists and philosophers concerned themselves with the destructive picture of no human future, and no meaning or value in human history, others, still believing that human history is a Divine Drama, saw, once again, that the scenario in the books of Daniel and Revelation had come to life and could be identified with actual on-going historical developments. Many mid-twentieth century millenarians saw new signs that the Triumphant Apocalypse was near at hand when the tiny state of Israel was declared. The ingathering of the Jews, their return to their ancient homeland, were critical pre-millenial events that had been forecast. This showed that God was still active in history, and that the pre-Millenial events were occuring. "Israel is God's time-piece" a religious advertisement in the *New York Times* proclaimed. Most fundamentalist groups (with the exception of the Seventh Day Adventists) have been Zionistic over the last two centuries. The return of the Jews to Palestine was an expected and desired pre-Millenial event. Various fundamentalist proclamations during the 19th and 20th centuries in England and America, called for the Restoration of Israel, and the establishment of a Jewish state (to be followed hopefully by the conversion of the Jews).

The role of Christian Zionists in bringing about the Jewish state has not been fully appreciated, though it had been noted that many Christians have actively aided and abetted Jewish Zionism and Jewish settlement in Palestine.[53] When the Jewish State was proclaimed in 1948, these Christian Zionists believed that a new state in Providential history had arrived. There has been an outpouring of books and pamphlets relating the existence and development of the Jewish state to prophecies in Scripture.[54] The stormy history of the Jewish state, culminating in the "liberation" of the holy sites in Jerusalem in the Six Day War, led some of the fundamentalist commentators to see that Israel was playing the crucial role in the end of human history. And the fact that Israel's enemies, the surrounding Arab states, were supplied and aided militarily by the godless Soviet Union, made the whole drama clear. The battle of Armageddon (which is, of course, in Israel proper) will be fought between Israel and Russia, and will be the nuclear war that will destroy the present world.

Let me outline just two versions of the view, to show how the probability of the nuclear holocaust has been united with the vision of the Triumphant Apocalypse to make the headlong rush to destruction, centered on Israel versus Russia, a cheering prospect, instead of the dire and desolate one offered by Schell, Lifton, Falk and many others. These two versions had great success as popular explanations of what is going on, and going to occur.

Salem Kirban's *Guide to Survival* was first published in 1968, and was in its eleventh printing five years later, having sold over 250,000 copies by then.[55] On the cover, besides the title, is the stark statement—"HOW THE WORLD WILL END". Sometime in the near future several *Million* people will suddenly *Disappear* from this earth 'in the twinkling of an eye.' When this happens—and if you still remain—then Read This Book, for it will be your *Guide to Survival.*"[56] In the preface, Kirban stressed that events now occuring all over the world "have an alarming parallel with the prophetic Scriptures in Daniel and Relevation regarding The Last Days."[57] We are told in no uncertain terms "The world is rapidly coming to an end. It is on an irreversible course."[58] All sorts of developments like growth of drug addiction, rock music, pornography, labor troubles, nuclear armament, church secularization, air pollution, population explosion, are offered as signs that the world is nearing its end. The points raised by many of the authors in this volume about the dangers of the nuclear arms race, and other military developments, are also stressed by Kirban, as indications of our precarious state at present. All of this then is portrayed as part of God's plan as revealed in biblical prophecies. The international developments are placed in the prophetic plan, the most important being the emergence of the state of Israel, and the role of Russia in trying to destroy Israel. This conflict will lead to mass destruction through nuclear warfare, as well as the destruction of nature through God's miraculous actions. Oceans will turn to blood, the earth will be scorched, and the rivers dried up.[59]

All of these man-made and Divine tribulations are to bring about the turning of the people of Israel to Christ, to separate those to be saved from those who will not be, to destroy Satan's power, and to punish unbelievers. The disastrous events will get even worse when Russia invades Israel. This will be the final battle. And, wonderfully, just at the climactic moment, when all is almost lost at the battle of Armageddon (which takes place in northern Israel), Christ will appear and destroy the power of the Antichrist (Russia). "With the Battle of Armageddon coming to an end, this brings to a close the great 7 year Tribulation Period, and heralds the time when Christ will return to earth *with* his believers (those who are born again or saved)."[60] The Triumphant Apocalypse has occurred and ushered in the millenium. Kirban's book ends with a supremely happy picture of what is in store for the true believers after the Nuclear Holocaust. The choice is left to the reader as to whether he or she will become a true believer, or will suffer obliteration in the final tribulations.[61]

A more widely known version of this new form of the Triumphant Acpocalypse view is that in Hal Lindsey's *The Late Great Planet Earth*, which first appeared in 1970.[62] The birth of the state of Israel is portrayed as the necessary pre-condition for the prophecized seven year period of tribulations that will be climaxed by the visible return of Jesus Christ. Lindsey pointed out that Bible students were unable to figure out the prophetic messages of World Wars I and II, but when David Ben-Gurion read the Israeli Declaration of Independence on May 14, 1948, this was a paramount prophetic sign, setting the stage for the end of history.[63] Israel is the fuse of Armageddon.[64] Once the Jews had been restored as a nation, then the rest of the prophecies in Revelation would be fulfilled. Lindsey appealed back to Increase

Mather's claims about the role of a restored Jewish state in his book, *The Mystery of Israel's Salvation* of 1669.[65] Three stages of the development of the Jewish state have to occur—first, that the Jewish nation be reborn in Palestine; second, that the Jews take possession of the holy sites in Jerusalem; and, third, that the Temple be rebuilt on its historic site. The first was accomplished in 1948, the second in 1967, and the third is yet to occur, but will happen at the critical moment.[66]

Since the rebirth of the Jewish state is a vital part of the prophetic scheme, we can see the rest of it unfolding by interpreting present developments in terms of biblical prophecies. Russia is a Gog, the enemy of Israel. Moshe Dayan is quoted as saying the next war will not be with the Arabs, but with Russia. Russia is the Northern Confederacy "destined to plunge the world into its final great war which Christ will return to end."[67] Russia will arm and equip all sorts of allies, and then they will attack Israel together. They will be defeated, and Christ will return to prevent the annihilation of mankind.[68]

Chapter 12 of Lindsey's book deals with World War III. It begins with quotations from Albert Einstein, J. Robert Oppenheimer, John F. Kennedy and Pope Paul VI, about what a catastrophe another war would be. This is followed by a quotation from Jesus, dated A.D. 33, "you will be hearing of wars and rumors of wars—then there will be a great tribulation, such as has not occurred since the beginning of the world until now, nor ever shall. And unless those days had been cut short, no life would have been saved."[69] The events leading up to World War III are described, with charts showing how Russia and its allies will attack Israel from land and sea. This will lead to a nuclear exchange, with all the horrors that have been predicted by scientists.

Lindsey's description of what will happen at Armageddon is not much different from Jonathan Schell's forecast, except for "A Bright Spot in the Gloom."[70] This bright spot is first "the greatest period of Jewish conversion to their true Messiah will begin." Then the Russians will be miraculously destroyed, and "As the battle of Armageddon reaches its awful climax and it appears that all life will be destroyed on earth—in this very moment Jesus Christ will return and save man from self-extinction."[71] Thus, instead of a world of grass and insects, there will be a Triumphant Apocalypse for those who will be saved. (Lindsey reports that an oil company has found a gigantic seismic fault running east and west through the center of the Mount of Olives in Jerusalem.[72]) The earth will split at this point. The believing Jewish remnant will run into this crack in the earth, and will escape the terrible devastation God will pour out on the godless armies attacking Israel. This devastation is described in Zachariah 14:12 "Their flesh shall consume away while they stand upon their feet, and their eyes shall consume away in their holes, and their tongue shall consume away their mouth." As Lindsey points out, this is what has been described as happening to people in a thermonuclear blast.[73] All of the unbelievers, the godless will be destroyed, and Jesus will rule over the happy believers. After Judgement Day Christ will form a new heaven and a new earth out of atomic materials, where glorified persons without sin will live. There will be only "righteousness, peace, security, harmony and joy."[74] Such will be the Triumphant Apocalypse of the nuclear age.

Lindsey's sequel, *There's a New World Coming*,[75] first published in 1973 (just after the Yom Kippur War), contains a verse by verse explication of the Book of Revelation in terms of contemporary events, and those to come in the impending Apocalypse. The United States as well as the rest of the world will be levelled.[76]

"Apparently the devastation will be so tremendous that not only will all cities be destroyed, but the land itself will be ripped apart. The coastlines and continents will be changed and all the mountains will be shifted in elevation."[77] In case the reader becomes depressed by this picture that "may sound like the end of global life," he or she is told that things will change when Jesus returns to earth, halts the destruction, and brings about a new world.[78] The carnage of men and beasts will be a needless tragedy, since if people had had the right beliefs, this would not have to happen.

But, Lindsey goes on, since the earth will be ravaged, Jesus will have to restore it. The restoration will be the highest state of development of the animal, vegetable and mineral worlds. "The sky will be bluer, the grass will be greener, the flowers will smell sweeter, the air will be cleaner, and man will be happier than he ever dreamed possible."[79] What more could be hoped for following the Triumphant Apocalypse!

The new heaven and the new earth are made possible by the disintegration of the old ones. We could not understand what was being forecast in 2 Peter 3:7 until we knew about nuclear energy. Now we know about the vast explosive forces that can be released in a nuclear explosion. "Just think what will happen to this old ball of *terra firma* when God releases all the atoms in our earth and its surrounding universe!"[80] Lindsey then quotes the text of second Peter, "But the day of the Lord will come as a thief in the night, in which the heavens shall pass away with a great noise, and the elements shall be disintegrated with intense heat; the earth also, and all its works, shall be burned up."

After portraying how wonderful everything will be after the Triumphant Apocalypse, in the New Jerusalem, Lindsey points out that some readers may take this to be a wild fairytale. Others, who realize what is going on, and "what's in store for them in eternity is so thrilling that they can hardly wait to get there!"[81] If there are doubters about this scenario, Lindsey states, "To the skeptic who says that Christ is not coming soon, I would ask him to put the book of Revelation in one hand, and the daily newspaper in the other, and then sincerely ask God to show him where we are on His prophetic time-clock."[82] We are almost at the end, for which to Lindsey is the most joyful possible news.

DANGERS IN THE NEW TRIUMPHANT APOCALYPSE

This reading of the nuclear holocaust as glad tidings, differs, of course, from the catastrophic reading, on the basis of some belief in God's involvement in history, so that no matter how terrible the nuclear catastrophe, God's intervention will make survival for some believing remnant possible, and will make this survival not a return to primitive, brutal conditions, but a step forward into earthly paradise. The conviction that the nuclear destruction is bound up with the scenario in Daniel and Revelation, and is integrally related to events now occurring in the Middle East, allows its believers to accept all the terrible forecasts about World War III with hope and cheer. For those who have lost belief in God acting in history, and specifically in God acting in history according to what is prophesied in the Old and New Testaments, there remains only a cold, cruel, empty, meaningless world to follow all of the destruction.

A post-Enlightenment reading of the situation—catastrophe without hope—may be both more realistic and less dangerous than this new version of the Triumphant

Apocalypse. It is more realistic in that it accepts the layers and layers of scepticism about the Bible as a source of special Truth, and recognizes the folly of the centuries and centuries of attempts to identify human historical events and developments with the cryptic passages written in ancient Israel. It is less dangerous in that it does not and will not encourage persons and governments to act as if prophetic history were going on. In Cromwell's day, in Napoleon's day, casting events in Biblical terms may have caused some mayhem, even great destruction, but it could not cause total destruction, because of the technical limitations of the means of warfare. We are now in a period when people seeing themselves as the agents of God can literally blow up the world.

Those who see present events as leading to a Triumphant Apocalypse are in some ways scarier than the military types, stolidly preparing in the United States and in the U.S.S.R. for a possible nuclear confrontation. The military and political leaders of the super-powers still seem to act within the bounds of prudential calculations about the destructive abilities of their weapons and those of their opponents. If they did not, World War III would have already occurred. Instead we have torturous, involuted negotiations taking place, all sorts of propaganda moves, vast investments of mental and material substance devising more lethal offensive and defensive weapons. All of these may seem crazy if looked at from some independent moral vantage point. But nonetheless, this has gone on now for over thirty-five years without catastrophe. Given how easy it would be for World War III to begin by accident, and how close we came to its beginning at the time of the Cuban Missile Crisis, there is some indication that those in control function within a realm of rational calculation and prudential decisions.

Perhaps the real Dr. Strangeloves of our time are those who happily envision world wide conflict starting out of the troubles between Israel and its neighbors as developments leading to the Triumphant Apocalypse. Because of their religious convictions about the outcome, they are willing to encourage the most militant and risky policies on the part of the present Israeli government, even to the point of the use of nuclear weapons, if need be, by Israel. They are also willing to encourage a policy of support of Israeli militancy by the United States so that Israel will be in the forefront in a confrontation between the two great nuclear powers, America and Russia. Militant anti-Communism joined to the reading of the Book of Revelation as an account of present and near future developments in the Middle East may be the most dangerous recipe now available for total destruction of human existence.

In Israel itself many people have noticed how supportive various Christians have been of the rebuilding of a Jewish state. Christian Zionism has been important from the first inkling of Jewish interest and concern about returning to the Promised Land in the early nineteenth century. Some Christians have linked the development of a Jewish national homeland with the antecedent events to the Second Coming. During World War II, the British commander in Palestine, General Orde Wingate, suddenly cabled Winston Churchill to send all available equipment to Palestine, *because* the battle of Armageddon was about to begin. Churchill instead transferred the millenialist Gen. Wingate to the Burmese front, where he died. Wingate, however, had trained the secret Jewish army, and his leading military disciple was General Moshe Dayan.[83]

From the time of Ben-Gurion's proclamation of the Jewish state in 1948, various Christian millenialists have not only gleefully set forth their scenario of the forthcoming Triumphant Apocalypse, they have encouraged Israeli leaders to be firm and militant. After the wars of 1967 and 1973 this apocalyptic military advice and support has been more and more forthcoming, especially from American fundamentalist millenarians. With the emergence of the Reverend Jerry Falwell, and the Southern Baptist leaders as a national political force—the Moral Majority—an alliance was developed between former Prime Minister Menachem Begin, his hard-line supporters, and these millenarian Christians. I doubt that either side bothers to listen to the various reasons of the other for supporting the same extreme military policies. It seemed enough for Begin that important American Protestant religious leaders support his attack on the Baghdad nuclear reactor, the invasion of Lebanon, the bombing of Beirut, the potential annexation of the West Bank, and can influence important American leaders. It seems to be enough for American millenarians that Israel keep up its aggressive belligerency, preparatory to the Triumphant Apocalypse.

The present Christian millenarians are not an insignificant group, especially in the present American scene. James Watt, an ex-cabinet minister in the Reagan administration, openly holds their views. Many other leaders, elected and appointed, are strongly supported by the Moral Majority, and use their influence to push some of its agenda. The recently overthrown president of Guatemala belongs to a California based evangelical group. Another California millenarian group helps finance the militant Christians in southern Lebanon. The political force of American millenarians is just beginning to be felt in many areas of the society, including education, social policy and foreign policy. These people were largely ignored politically during the first two centuries of America's history, though they have been involved and active from Colonial times onward. Recent developments in America and Israel seem to have galvanized the evangelical groups to become a political force, capable of exerting a fair amount of pressure on local, state and federal governments. President Reagan and some of his advisers, as well as some of the ardent non-religious anti-Communists, are, perhaps, too comfortable with this alliance, and have accepted the fundamentalist programmes on many issues, as indicated by Reagan's statements since his renomination.

HOW WILL IT END?

This odd alliance of Christian fundamentalist Millenarians and hard-core Jewish nationalists might seem bizarre.[84] But when this strange union is helping to develop the capability of starting World War III with a Nuclear Holocaust, it becomes extremely dangerous as well. And, in this case, neither the nationalistic, fanatical followers of Menachem Begin, nor the preachers happily anticipating the Triumphant Apocalypse seem to be restrained by the prudential considerations of the leaders of the Pentagon and the Kremlin. The latter probably only want to fight with all their destructive resources if they are fairly sure they will win. The former "know" they will win because of their reading of the texts about Providential History, and hence will probably not be restrained by normal considerations. As indicated above, these millenarians accept the gloomiest scenarios of Jonathan Schell and others. They accept them cheerfully, because they "know" there will be a saving remnant, and have firm belief that they will be part of it. This assurance may lead them to take much greater risks than the military leaders of the superpowers. An unwavering belief in the Triumphant Apocalypse, coupled with the power of the Israeli military machine, may be what actually brings about the Catastrophic Apocalypse, unless Scripture, as read by the millenarians, is true. But, if it is, even on their most benign reading, it won't help many of us, or the world we live in.

NOTES

1. On this, see Norman Cohn, *The Pursuit of the Millenium* (New York, 1961); Ernest Lee Tuveson, *Millenium and Utopia* (Gloucester, Mass. 1972); and Margaret Reeves, *The Influence of Prophecy in the Late Middle Ages, A Study in Joachimism* (Oxford, 1969).
2. See Katherine R. Firth, *The Apocalyptic Tradition in Reformation 1530–1645* (Oxford, 1979); and Leroy E. Froom, *The Prophetic Faith of our Fathers*, Vol. II (Washington, 1948).
3. On Joseph Mede, see John Worthington, "The Life of the Reverend and Most Learned Joseph Mede," in Mede, *Works* (London, 1664); Peter Toon, editor, *Puritans, the Millenium and the Future of Israel: Puritan Eschatology* (Cambridge and London, 1970); and Firth, op. cit., chap. vii.
4. John Napier, *Plaine Discovery of the Whole Revelation of Saint John* (Edinburgh, 1593).
5. Christopher Hill, *Antichrist in Seventeenth Century England* (London 1971); and Clark Library Lecture on "Till the Conversion of the Jews" (forthcoming). See also Toon, op. cit.
6. Charles Webster, *The Great Instauration* (London 1975), pp. 47ff; R. H. Popkin, "The Third Force in 17th Century Philosophy: Scepticism, Science and Millenarianism," *Nouvelles de la Republique des Lettres*, III (1983), pp. 35–63. See also Johann Amos Comenius, *Natural Philosophie Reformed by Divine Light* (London, 1651); and Henry More, *Antidote Against Atheism* (London, 1655).
7. Don Cameron Allen, *The Legend of Noah* (Urbana, Illinois 1963).
8. The second edition of 1691 has been reproduced as Thomas Burnet, *The Sacred Theory of the Earth*, with an introduction by Basil Willey (Carbondale, Illinois, 1965). It is this edition that will be referred to below.
9. Burnet, op. cit., title page, p. 11.
10. Burnet, op.cit., "To the King's most Excellent Majesty," pp. 13–14.
11. Ibid., "To the Queen's most Excellent Majesty," pp. 231–32.
12. Ibid., "Preface to the Reader," p. 233.
13. Ibid.
14. Ibid., Book III, chap. vii, p. 271.
15. Ibid., p. 272.
16. Ibid., p. 277.
17. Ibid., Book III, Chap. x, "*Concerning the beginning and progress of the Conflagration, what part of the Earth will first be Burnt. The Manner of the future destruction of Rome. The last state and consummation of the general Fire.*"
18. Ibid., Book III, chap. xi, p. 298.
19. Ibid., p. 299.
20. Ibid., end of chap. xi, and beginning of chap. xii, p. 299.
21. Ibid., Book III, "Conclusion" p. 306.
22. Ibid.
23. On John Ray, see the article on him by Charles Webster in the *Dictionary of Scientific Biography*, Vol. XI, pp. 313–18.

24. On Whiston, see the forthcoming study on him by James E. Force.
25. William Whiston, *A New Theory of the Earth, From its Original, to the Consummation of all Things, Wherein the Creation of the World in Six Days, the Universal Deluge, and, the General Conflagration, As laid down in the Holy Scripture, Are shown to be perfectly agreeable to Reason and Philosophy* (London, 1696). This work has been reprinted by the Arno Press (New York, 1978), p. 3.
26. Ibid., p. 208.
27. Ibid., p. 209.
28. Ibid., pp. 214–215. The quotation is on p. 215.
29. Ibid., p. 367.
30. Ibid.
31. Ibid., p. 368.
32. Ibid., p. 378.
33. On Whiston's career, see Force's forthcoming work.
34. Isaac Newton, *Observations upon the Prophecies Daniel, and the Apocalypse of St. John* (London, 1733).
35. A few papers were published in H. McLachlan, *Sir Isaac Newton's Theological Manuscripts* (Liverpool, 1950), and "Fragments from a Treatise on Revelation" appear in Appendix A of Frank Manuel, *The Religion of Isaac Newton* (Oxford, 1979). Professors B. J. Dobbs, R. S. Westfall, and myself have taken on the project of organizing the publication of Newton's theological and alchemic writings.
36. David Hume, *An Enquiry Concerning Human Understanding*, Selby-Bigge edition (Oxford, 1966), p. 146.
37. On Bayle, Voltaire, Hume and Gibbon as philosophical historians, see R. H. Popkin, "Bible Criticism and Social Science," *Boston Studies in the Philosophy of Science* XIV, pp. 350–60; "Scepticism and the Study of History," in W. Yourgrau, *Physics, Logic and History* (New York, 1970), pp. 209–19; my introductory essay, pp. ix–xxxi in *David Hume, Philosophical Historian*, edited by D. F. Norton and R. H. Popkin (Indianapolis, 1966); and R. H. Popkin, "Hume: Philosophical versus Prophetic Historian," *Southwestern Journal of Philosophy* VII (1976), pp. 83–95.
38. David Hartley, *Observations on Man* (London, 1749), Part Two, p. 380.
39. Ibid.
40. See Joseph Priestley, *Memoirs of Dr. Joseph Priestley to the Year 1795, written by Himself, with a Continuation to the time of his decease by his son, Joseph Priestley*, ed. T. Cooper (London, 1806); and the account of Priestley's Millenarianism in Clarke Garrett, *Respectable Folly* (Baltimore, 1975), chap. 6. Priestley's *Letter to the Jews* was answered by the English Jew, David Levi. I deal with their controversy in an article, "Predicting, Foretelling and Divining from Nostradamus to Hume," *History of European Ideas*, forthcoming.
41. Some of the background of this is discussed in my paper "La Peyrère the Abbé Grégoire and the Jewish Question in the Eighteenth Century," *Studies in Eighteenth-Century Culture*, Vol. IV (1975), pp. 209–22.
42. William Miller, *Evidences from Scripture and History of the Second Coming of Christ about the year 1843* (Troy, New York, 1841). In Froom, *The Prophetic Faith of our Fathers*, Vol. III, many 19th century millenarian theories are described.

43. Wolff's career is described in Froom, op. cit., Vol. III, pp. 461–81; and in H. P. Palmer, *Joseph Wolff, His Romantic Life and Travels* (London, 1935).
44. Cf. John Quincy Adams, *Memoirs*, edited by Charles Francis Adams (Philadelphia, 1874), Vol. X, p. 7.
45. Bertrand Russell, "A Free Man's Worship," chapter iii in *Mysticism and Logic and other Essays* (London, 1921).
46. Albert Camus, *Le Mythe de Sisyphe* (Paris, 1942).
47. Jonathan Schell, *The Fate of the Earth* (New York, 1982), p. 7.
48. Ibid., p. 95.
49. Ibid., pp. 95–96.
50. Robert Jay Lifton and Richard Falk, *Indefensible Weapons, The Political and Psychological Case Against Nuclearism* (New York, 1982), p. 4.
51. Ibid., pp. 4–5.
52. On Dury, see J. Minton Batten, *John Dury, Advocate of Christian Reunion* (Chicago, 1944); and R. H. Popkin, introduction to the reprint edition of Dury's *The Reformed Librarie-Keeper*, Augustan Reprint series (Los Angeles, 1984).
53. In Naham Sokolow's *The History of Zionism* (London, 1919), many Christian aiders and supporters of Zionism are discussed. See also Mayir Vereté, "The Restoration of the Jews in English Protestant Thought, 1790–1840," *Middle Eastern Studies*, VIII (1972), pp. 3–50. I am working on a study on the Christian roots of Zionism.
54. For example, David L. Cooper, *Messiah: His Final Call to Israel* (Los Angeles, 1962); Joseph H. Hunting, *Israel. A Modern Miracle* (Murrunbee, Australia, 1969); Wilbur M. Smith, *Israeli/Arab Conflict* (Glendale, Calif., 1967); S. Maxwell Coder, *Israel's Destiny* (Chicago, 1978); Charles L. Feinberg, *Israel. At the Center of History and Revelation* (Portland, Oregon, 1980).
55. Salem Kirban, *Guide to Survival* (Huntington, Pennsylvania, 1973). The dates of the eleven editions are listed on p. 3.
56. Ibid., cover page to the eleventh edition.
57. Ibid., p. 12.
58. Ibid., p. 21.
59. Ibid., chps. i–xi.
60. Ibid., p. 256.
61. Ibid., pp. 271–72.
62. Hal Lindsey, with C. C. Carlson, *The Late Great Planet Earth* (Grand Rapids, Michigan, 1970).
63. Ibid., p. 43.
64. Ibid., p. 44.
65. Ibid., p. 50.
66. Ibid., pp. 50–52.
67. Ibid., p. 59.
68. Ibid., p. 71.
69. Ibid., p. 146.
70. Ibid., p. 167.
71. Ibid., pp. 168–69.
72. Ibid., p. 174.
73. Ibid., p. 175.

74. Ibid., p. 179.
75. Hal Lindsey, *There's A New World Coming, A Prophetic Odyssey* (Santa Ana, Calif., 1973). It was in its sixth printing of 100,000 copies per printing by January 1974.
76. Ibid., pp. 226–27.
77. Ibid., p. 227.
78. Ibid.
79. Ibid., pp. 270–71.
80. Ibid., p. 287.
81. Ibid., p. 297.
82. Ibid., p. 306.
83. Concerning General Orde Wingate see Christopher Sykes, *Orde Wingate, A Biography* (Cleveland, 1959). Wingate came from a family that was engaged in millenarian activity.
84. A most bizarre episode is reported in the Jerusalem Post, International editions, March 20–26 and March 27–April 2, 1983. It is reported that the First Congress on Inquiries into the Origin of Life and Evolution, organized by a group of Orthodox scientists from Ben Gurion University, and sponsored by the Israeli Ministry of Education, was held at the campus of Hebrew University. The speakers included both Jewish intellectuals from Israel, but also Dr. Duane Gish of the Creation Research Center in San Diego, a leading Fundamentalist fighter in the U.S. against the Darwinist theory of evolution. The conference apparently agreed that the theory of evolution was just "speculation," "secular dogma" or "myth." It will be interesting to see how much of the Fundamentalist program in the U.S. will be supported by Jewish nationalists in America and Israel, and how far the Fundamentalist churches will go in adjusting their program to accept Israel for what it is, rather than what they expect it to be at the time of the Second Coming.

PART III

CONCEIVING THE INCONCEIVABLE: THE ODDITY OF NUCLEAR THINKING

We encounter the *transcendent* nature of the nuclear predicament by reflection on our modes of prudential thinking. All attempts to comprehend the reality of nuclear warfare face a *unique* difficulty: our prenuclear intuitions appear inadequate to make sense of the reality of nuclear war; the utter irrationality of nuclear war explodes everything with it, including the prudential thinking that has made such war possible. Because of this essential tension, nuclear discussions are notorious for reaching conceptual impasses and paradoxes. One example of this tension is the way we are pulled between the view that the nuclear situation is *unique*, and the view that it is largely *continuous* with prenuclear military reality. Indeed, the primary dilemma of nuclear strategy has always been how to think about nuclear weapons in the context of our political and military intuitions and practices. The chapters in this part are concerned with various aspects of nuclear thinking.

In Chapter 7 Joseph Margolis explores the conceptual entanglements of nuclear war. The very phenomenon of war, he claims, makes no sense under individualistic assumptions. If war makes sense at all, it does so because war is a *corporate* human activity; its rationality lies in individuals adhering to collective interests. There must be a threshold level of violence, Margolis continues, at which no collective goals whatsoever would be worth pursuing. For this reason there is no prudentially oriented policy capable of justifying absolute (nuclear) war. Global nuclear war is, then, utterly irrational. But what of the rationality or morality of limited nuclear war, or of risking nuclear war on the hope that it would remain limited? Margolis concludes with some reflections on these questions.

In Chapter 8, Patrick Morgan questions the theoretical basis of deterrence thinking. Going beyond the common criticisms about deterrence credibility, Morgan argues that we lack any genuine sense of what nuclear deterrence is, how it really works and affects politics, under what political circumstances it is likely to fail, and above all, how to assess its overall worth. The historical record is just not sufficient to reveal whether the absence of great-power war in the last four decades is due to deterrence *per se*, or whether deterrence seems to work only because the international system is currently in a configuration favoring stability. The lesson of these uncertainties about deterrence, Morgan concludes, is that we must not rely on nuclear deterrence alone and must develop other political mechanisms for avoiding war.

John Hare also examines deterrence thinking from the perspective of politics. He rejects the common view that deterrent threats are "conditional intentions," and urges us to consider instead the idea that deterrence may work by "bluff." He argues that bluffs not only are frequent phenomena in politics, but are actually a constitutive feature of political practice. This means that the current moral discourse about nuclear deterrence that concentrates on the question of the moral status of conditional intentions is misguided. It follows that the moral verdict on deterrence cannot be based on deontological considerations alone; the moral evaluation of deterrence is highly tied to the question of its risk.

Russell Hardin's chapter takes up the question of assessing the risk of deterrence. The idea of risk is indispensable for any comparison between policies, yet its measurement is elusive. One problem is its subjective quality. What decisionmakers think the strategic situation to be determines in large part what it is. From the perspective of game theory—the theoretical framework Hardin uses—one sees not only that there is no objective way to determine what "game" best represents our strategic situation, but that there would be no way to know when we have moved from one game to another. Risk assessment is essentially an interpretive business, especially in the area of nuclear weapons policy where the counterfactuals are so far beyond our experience. Yet we have no alternative but to consider the risks, Hardin argues, since they are our primary basis for moral and prudential evaluation. He concludes that while minimum deterrence is almost certainly less risky than present policy, we lack sufficient information to determine whether unilateral disarmament is more or less risky than either minimum deterrence or present policy.

Richard Watson's essay is, perhaps, the most pessimistic voice in the entire collection. Yet, for moral reasons, Watson is quite reluctant to accept the full implications of his pessimism as the final verdict on our condition. This essential ambivalence makes his argument highly dialectical. For Watson the long-term probability of nuclear war is extremely high. His pessimism, the result of an essentially naturalistic approach, regards the eventuality of nuclear war as a form of "species rationality," a kind of solution to future ecological pressures. Nevertheless, pessimism about the human career is one thing, while endorsing the implications of such pessimism for political activity is another. Only self-conscious individuals, Watson insists, are genuinely moral agents, and individualism is the only place where any hope may lie.

7
THE PECULIARITIES OF NUCLEAR THINKING

Joseph Margolis

THE DIFFICULTIES FOR CONVENTIONAL VIEWS
OF NUCLEAR WAR

Nuclear thinking has its own peculiar career. The prospect of the creeping inevitability of destroying the order and life of our planet is on everyone's mind. We take all
nuclear preparations that sustain or increase that risk to fix the modern paradigm of
utter political irrationality. And yet it is surely difficult, within the space of that
charge, to deny the clear continuity of every feature of such preparation with whatever may fairly be supposed to characterize human prudence and political reasonableness. How could behavior be utterly irrational if the entire race is drawn to it?
And how could it be rational if it threatens in the most radical way whatever reason
favors protecting? To accept the paradox is to accept the need for a clinical examination of nuclear thinking itself—held free, for an interval at least, from the perceived
need to be committed regarding the morality of actual and imminent policies. Total
nuclear disarmament could hardly be judged irrational, but it seems most unlikely;
and nonnuclear armament embodies the conventional view of political reason, but
in a way that now seem impossible to separate completely from the nuclear in the
context of political prudence. Here is the still center of the great debate.

All speculation about nuclear war rests on the supposed distinction between such
war and what, euphemistically, we term "conventional" warfare. The intended
demarcation, of course, is that between a military and a civilian population,
between combatants and noncombatants. No doubt the distinction is still meaningful, but it is entirely inoperable in *every* case of recent nonnuclear war—for
instance, Afghanistan, Beirut, El Salvador, or Vietnam. Those states that are militarily most advanced cannot even use their nonnuclear weapons in a way consistent
with the conventional distinction and the anticipated objectives of modern warfare;
and neither they nor their third- and fourth-world clients are really able or disposed
to maintain a strict distinction. Current technology and the complexities of mobilizing whole populations—whether at an advanced or primitive level—are entirely
against it.

There is no simple demarcation between the two that can stand. For instance,
speaking brutally, there is no generally recognized sense in which the use or plan-

ned use of *very* restricted nuclear weapons—perhaps an extremely small neutron bomb with a maximum yield of well below 500 rads[1]—may be taken, formally, to convert a "conventional" military confrontation into a "nuclear" one—*in that sense in which the demarcation flags a fundamental change in the viability of moral or prudential justification for particular encounters actual or intended.* So construed, it is obvious that we can be nickeled and dimed to death by the continuing attempts to perfect field and tactical weapons. Also, what hangs on the distinction is quite different from predicting the likelihood of military self-restraint (in particular, nuclear restraint) under imaginable circumstances. It is equally obvious that the demarcation rests on a presumption that we can distinguish between just and unjust wars *in conventional terms.* But that which was more or less canonical within early modern warfare is now either completely outmoded by military technology and the real conditions for mobilizing peoples at war or so radically altered by those factors that little, if anything, of older assurances can be given about testing intuitions regarding the use of small nuclear weapons within an enlarged conception of conventional warfare.

One Christian militiaman, for example, who acknowledged before cameras his own participation in the Beirut massacre, declared without hesitation his intention to "stay the course" if possible, observing that, in Lebanon, a Palestinian child of eight might well be—had already proved to be—as effective a bomber as a man in uniform. Admitting the horror of all that implies (the penalty of the most modest technology in crowded, civilian-populated streets), who can deny its ubiquity and what it entails? Nevertheless, many who condemn the serious tolerance of the use of any nuclear weapons on the grounds of the just-war concept unaccountably ignore the import of current nonnuclear technology and ideological saliencies. This is surely at least one essential defect of the so-called "second draft" (1982) of the National Conference of Catholic Bishops' pastoral letter on war and peace, that so many have waited to receive.[2]

The question remains: if the current race for *non*nuclear weapons is headlong even among technologically backward countries, if such weapons cannot effectively discriminate between combatant and noncombatant, if aggressive and retaliatory strikes typical of the use of such weaponry cannot really be restricted to moderate estimates of military restraint, if the ideological demands of waging modern warfare threaten to erase or radically alter the distinction between combatant and noncombatant, if the moral and juridical tradition is disposed to accommodate such adjustments within the range of nonnuclear hostilities, then what could possibly serve as a further, reasoned principle for claiming that the bare use of very limited, determinately targeted nuclear weapons (perhaps even less destructive than "conventional" weapons) could by itself convert an "admissible" war into a nuclear one: where, by that charge, one signifies that a *sui generis* condemnation is at once in order—a condemnation that does not apply in the other case?

This is not to say that nuclear war and nuclear warfare are not *sui generis* in some important sense. It is only to say that convincingly condemning them must be systematically linked to the acknowledged grounds on which so-called conventional wars are similarly assessed. If, for instance, a reasonable division between combatants and noncombatants (however drawn) is essential to the distinction between just and unjust war and impossible to maintain in the context of contemporary nonnuclear wars, then the condemnation of nuclear warfare will prove trivial and otiose. On the other hand, if it were possible to construe contemporary wars as potentially just or at least as defensible, without insuring a (sharp) demarcation between combatant and noncombatant, then it would no longer be an easy matter to condemn restricted nuclear weapons within the scope of thus "adjusted" conventional war; *nor*, for that matter, would such an adjustment automatically clarify the sense in which other, more extreme possibilities of nuclear warfare could be fairly vindicated or condemned. The developing evidence seems to confirm that the firepower of selected nuclear weapons can be made to compare favorably with those used or contemplated in nonnuclear war; that the division between combatant and noncombatant cannot be effectively maintained in either nonnuclear or nuclear war, and the ideology of contemporary war increasingly tolerates its erasure; and that the risk of all-out nuclear war cannot be shown to be controllable within the usual range of nonnuclear war any more effectively than within the range of wars in which small nuclear weapons are introduced—if the capacity for all-out war is also present and military devastation otherwise imminent. Both individually and collectively, these developments undermine the argument for the allegedly *sui generis* nature of nuclear war and nuclear weaponry.

In our own time, Michael Walzer has pressed as strenuously as any the conceptual linkage between distinguishing between just and unjust wars and between combatants and noncombatants. Viewing war in a sanguine way as "a rule-governed activity,"[3] Walzer straightforwardly affirms that a certain set of rules of war (justifiably and casuistically variable) tend

> to set certain classes of people outside the permissible range of warfare, so that killing any of their members is not a legitimate act of war but a crime. Though their details vary from place to place, these rules point toward the general conception of war as a *combat between combatants*. . . . The historical specifications of [this] principle are, however, conventional in character, and the war rights and obligations of soldiers follow from the conventions and not (directly) from the principle, whatever its force. . . . War is a social creation.[4]

Walzer seems not to have grasped the fact that, consistent with his principle (but not with his conviction), the distinction between combatants and noncombatants may be conventionally and responsibly erased—for instance, as a result of prevailing technology and related support arrangements, or as a result of construing war as a contest binding on successive generations, or as a result of the informal and *ad hoc* character of the administrative organization of one or more of the warring parties. Walzer is candid enough to admit: "I am by no means sure what the [moral] foundations [of war] are." His own confidence lies rather in the range of the "practical morality" of actual wars, so that the principle enunciated is said to be acknowledged by all—although, presumably, how to answer the question of the possible justice of war under the erasure of the combatant/noncombatant distinction is nowhere made clear.[5]

We may take advantage of this lacuna to introduce a distinction that will be of considerable use in reflecting on the defensibility of nuclear war. Let us speak of *total* war wherever the distinction between combatant and noncombatant is discarded or rendered uncertain in a principled way (for instance on the grounds suggested), regardless of whether nuclear or nonnuclear weapons are used;[6] and let us speak of *totalitarian* or *absolute* war wherever there is a tendency to risk annihilating or radically injuring an entire hostile population, or the entire populations at war, or large populations not party to the war, or the entire population of the earth, or of the future generations of any of those populations, or . . . . We break off deliberately, to leave unfinished the sense in which the very question of defining and justifying totalitarian war—or of wars falling (if possible) between total and totalitarian war—becomes the proper focus of an entirely different kind of reflection. It is reasonably clear that modern warfare, well before the introduction of nuclear weapons, should have forced us to consider the defensibility of total war and of various approximations to it; and it is equally clear that nuclear war poses in the baldest possible way the question of defending totalitarian war. Furthermore, if we don't assume that morality and rationality must be coextensive (in effect, that evil need be irrational), then it is clear that total war need not be irrational or imprudent, no matter how evil we suppose it to be; but totalitarian war appears to be rationally as well as morally problematic, in the sense suggested at the outset. *Rationality*, we may suppose, signifies no more than a sustained, general congruity with the minimal, characteristic, species-specific interests and behavior of a given species—paradigmatically, the human species—or weakened approximations to this condition. *Morality*, operative only at the human level, is in this sense a rational concern. Any nontendentious summary of the interests of the race must include, prominently, those addressed to survival, and the reduction of pain, injury, deprivation, and the like—what are usually termed prudential interests. Morality, then, is rationally constrained, characteristically but *not* necessarily, generally but *not* point for point, by our prudential interests. These logical qualifications complicate the analysis of the morality of nuclear war.

To admit these distinctions provides a very natural way in which to isolate the conceptual and valuational puzzles of nuclear war, for it is very likely that the moral appraisal of nuclear war will be affected in a distinctive way by the threat of wholesale irrationality and imprudence of the sort the world must now consider. We may reserve the term *conventional*, then, for wars that manage reasonably well (whatever the type of weapons) to preserve the conventional distinction between combatants and noncombatants. The differences between conventional, total, and totalitarian war, then, concern the range or scope of intended or at least admissible human targets, and have nothing as such to do with the mere technology of warfare. This is not to deny that certain forms of killing are particularly monstrous, or that their extensive use is even more horrific, or that special moral questions are bound to arise regarding the combination of particular forms of technological warfare and particular kinds of war. It is only to ensure a certain conceptual convenience and clarity.

What advantages can we draw from our distinction, without supplying a really careful account of the full context of nuclear war, nuclear threats, nuclear deterrence, and the like? Perhaps the following tally will seem uncontroversial without being vacuous or trivial. First, total war does not as such entail totalitarian war, although the entailment holds the other way round: it may, of course, be that total war risks tactical nuclear weapons in a setting in which belligerent powers are known to be capable of absolute nuclear warfare and cannot be relied on to restrain themselves within the limits of total war; but then, neither could they, if (with such a capability) they engaged in conventional warfare that appeared, at least provisionally, to respect current distinctions between combatants and noncombatants. In fact, the distinction between tactical and strategic warfare is essentially indifferent to the kind of distinction we are pursuing here: it has nothing to do with the scope or destructive power (the "yield") of particular weapons; it has to do only with the "range" of, with (literally) locating, military objectives.[7] Second, the distinction between total and absolute war is not value-laden as such, although it bears on the essential moral questions of modern warfare; for instance, it poses but does not prejudge the issues of both the morality and rationality of absolute war, and it concedes that if modern warfare is to be defended at all it must be conceptually possible to defend total war (or significant approximations to it). Third, our distinction places the entire question of defending war in the larger context of rational conduct, which is likely to be threatened in quite different ways by the prospect of total and totalitarian war: in this sense, it disallows older war conventions from appearing morally fixed, morally secure and reliable, and from escaping the necessity of regular diachronic review; it concedes the full moral relevance of social and political change; and it features the putatively instrumental and variable functions of war itself. Fourth, our distinction permits us to examine the question of nuclear war under the most realistic conditions, namely, those in which the appetite for war (as well as the fear of war) shows no signs of abating in spite of the proliferation of nuclear weapons and nuclear capability; in which there is no real prospect (at present) of controlling or globally outlawing the production of nuclear weapons; and in which the differential use of nuclear weapons for total and absolute war (and even conventional war) is known to be technologically feasible.

To recite these distinctions is merely to remind ourselves (in an orderly way) of what all of us already know. The really critical questions concern (a) whether nuclear war cannot but be an irrational or unacceptably imprudent undertaking; (b) whether, on independent grounds, nuclear threats and deterrence can be defended, even if nuclear war is judged hopelessly indefensible; (c) whether nuclear war and/or threats can be compellingly shown to be immoral or incapable of being morally justified; and (d) whether nuclear weaponry is *sui generis* in some relevent sense, so that its use in any and all circumstances of war can be justifiably condemned on principled grounds that do not uniformly apply to the various forms of nonnuclear war.

The realities of the present global situation, as we are all aware, force us to consider whether, if the United States and the Soviet Union were unable to persuade the other to abandon nuclear armaments altogether, or to reduce and restrict the military capability of both well below the level for waging or threatening absolute war, or to decide unilaterally to abandon or restrict their own armaments—or if there were realistic grounds for fearing that other hostile powers were soon likely to achieve, or had already achieved, the capability for waging or threatening or "catalyzing" absolute war, *or* for incapacitating either or both of the superpowers with respect to being able to control decisions about such matters unilaterally or jointly between themselves—nuclear war and nuclear threats would still be justifiably judged irrational, unacceptably imprudent, or immoral. (Here, the sense of "unacceptably" or "unreasonably" imprudent, or "unreasonable" or "imprudent," suggests a threshold regarding the risk of moral or prudential values beyond which, on either moral or rational grounds or both, it becomes increasingly difficult or impossible to defend a given policy—where, precisely, it is already conceded that *some* range of such risk, as in total nonnuclear war, *is* defensible.) In short, is it conceivable (a) that the issue of nuclear war and nuclear threat and deterrence is inherently paradoxical;[8] or (b) that the provisional irrationality, imprudence, or immorality of such war and such threat *in a rational world* cannot preclude such a judgment's being *rationally overridden in a pertinently irrational, unreasonable, or immoral world*?[9] The point of pressing these questions is to indicate the sense in which reflecting on the proprieties of (absolute) nuclear war—the apparent redundancy is deliberate—may be fundamentally different (morally) from reflecting on the proprieties of all antecedent forms of war, including the grossest forms of total war.

We have in effect now managed to set the stage for considering two fundamental questions about nuclear war that are morally neglected in the heat of public dispute: first, *whether it is or is not possible or convincing to examine the morality of nuclear war and nuclear arms independent of the morality of contemporary non-nuclear war, and second, whether and in what way the morality of nuclear war and threat is substantively affected by the current state of global nuclear risk and the admitted irrationality of absolute nuclear war itself.* The two questions are decisively linked to a deeper question about the nature and moral viability of the modern state—which has actually generated increasingly totalized nonnuclear war, the very capability for nuclear war, and the present risk of total nuclear annihilation. But here, we are more narrowly concerned with the peculiarities of nuclear thinking.

THE CORPORATE NATURE OF WAR

These reflections may be given further point by considering the question of whether, if it is wrong to do *x*, it is necessarily wrong to threaten to do *x*. Paul Ramsey has formulated the puzzle for nuclear war precisely in order to *justify* nuclear deterrence, while at the same time condemning nuclear war itself. This may seem impossible, until we realize that Ramsey construes the mere presence of nuclear weapons, independently capable of sustaining an absolute war but incapable of being rendered impotent by another nuclear belligerent, as constituting a deterrent without involving any intended threat (and even in the absence of such a threat) on the part of the would-be deterring power. Ramsey explicitly says: "Whatever is wrong to do is wrong to threaten, if the latter means 'means to do.' . . . . If counter-population warfare is murder, then counter-population deterrent threats are murderous."[10] Walzer, who discusses Ramsey's principle, agrees with it, but disallows Ramsey's application—essentially for two distinct reasons: first, because Walzer is unwilling to concede the apparently tortured logic of admitting that a state could deliberately produce a nuclear deterrent without intending a nuclear threat; and second, because, on independent grounds, what we have called total war Walzer regards as immoral as such.[11]

We have already conceded that *if* nuclear war is to have any inning at all, we must allow for the possibility of defending total war on moral grounds; and we have also suggested that to disallow that possibility is simply to enshrine older standard views about conventional war that have not come to terms—or have refused to come to terms—with the actual realities of contemporary warfare. In effect, to concede this is to disallow the condemnation of nuclear war or nuclear deterrence *solely on the grounds of disallowing total (even if nonnuclear) war.* The first of Walzer's objections is fair enough, however: Ramsey's justification of nuclear deterrence rests on a dubious trick of moral psychology; in fact, one could say that it rests on a well-known (but utterly) inadmissible application of the principle of double effect. On that principle, an agent may be said not to intend what he knows is a necessary consequence (or an overwhelmingly probable consequence) of what he *does* intend, and so is not morally responsible for that consequence. There may be room for a verbal distinction between intending to do x and intending to do x with the full knowledge that x entails, or very probably produces or leads to, y, but it cannot be a distinction that entitles us to segregate one's moral responsibility regarding merely knowing about the connection between x and y from one's full responsibility regarding intending-to-do-x-with-the-knowledge-of-that-connection. Put somewhat fussily, it would be much less dubious, morally, to say that one intends to do (or intends to include within the scope of what one intends to do) what one knows is entailed by, or linked through an overwhelming probability to, what (in the unproblematic sense) one intends to do. But these adjustments utterly fail to challenge directly the uncertainty of Ramsey's original principle—which Walzer is quite content to accept. Walzer says:

> deterrence depends upon a readiness to [act]. It is as if the state should seek to prevent murder [through vehicular recklessness during the Labor Day weekend] by threatening to kill the family and friends of every [potential vehicular] murderer—a domestic version of the policy of "massive retaliation." Surely that would be a repugnant policy. . . . The immorality [of this] lies in the threat itself, not in its present or even its likely consequences. Similarly with nuclear deterrence: it is our own intentions that we have to worry about and the potential (since there are no actual) victims of those intentions.[12]

Fair enough. But that does *not* show that nuclear deterrence *is* immoral, or immoral under all imaginable conditions. Also, Walzer's objection does not touch at all on the moral import of the peculiar—even unique—circumstances of *nuclear reasoning* with regard to deterrence. Here, perhaps, is the most difficult issue of all.

Never mind Ramsey's odd reasoning regarding deterrence. The conceptual distinction between total and absolute war raises the distinct possibility that the two kinds of war are or may be morally discontinuous: hence, that the principle Ramsey and Walzer share cannot (thus far) be justifiably universalized. On the face of it, it is not unreasonable to suppose that a war that threatens to destroy or injure all or most human life, possibly all or most sentient life, possibly all or many future generations—or at least that level of life moderately or minimally acceptable to the warring powers themselves—is a war that poses moral problems fundamentally unlike *any* that are even possible within the range of normal prudential concerns. Can the case be satisfactorily put?

Two essential features of war, conceptually linked to the assessment of every war, unavoidably complicate matters. One is that war is ascribable only to corporate bodies; the other, that the rationale for initiating, responding to, or pursuing a war requires a coherent connection between the putative interests of those bodies and the interests of the aggregated humans caught up in such activity. Put in the form of a paradox: wars are fought only by states, peoples, classes, clans, and other collective entities, but there are literally no such entities (they are necessarily fictions favored by certain human populations who regard themselves as forming the parts of such entities); hence, human beings engage in war only insofar as they interpret their own behavior and that of their fellows as embodying the actions, intentions, interests, objectives, beliefs, and convictions of the fictional entities they invest (ideologically) with the real power to wage war.[13] Of course, to say that there *are* no states or the like is simply to say that so-called collective entities cannot rightly be ascribed ratiocinative or affective or interested powers, except derivatively or metonymically— from, and only from, what (ideologically) may be projected from the psychological powers of actual human populations. To speak thus is emphatically *not* to suggest that human beings can organize or maintain complex social practices without spontaneously "intending" such entities; or, to deny that the enormous investment and sacrifice they are bound to endure confirm that they clearly believe such entities and their interests to be real enough; or, to deny that human aggregates regularly engage in war. In short, to speak in this way is not to subscribe to methodological individualism. It is, rather, to hold both that only human individuals function as the *cognitively* apt agents of war and that real *social* attributes and relations are not reducible to attributes and relations ascribed to and between mere individuals. If these two notions be accepted, then of course the rationality of war could not in principle be computed solely by the application of any calculus of individual interests.

War, then, is an attribute humans rightly ascribe aggregatively to themselves in virtue of an intervening ideology they share, that enables them to initiate and interpret their own behavior accordingly. The essential point is that, assuming a set of prudential interests fitted to the species-specific uniformities of individual human existence—interests that contribute to a minimal, holistic model of human rationality (not binding in any essential way, capable of being overridden without necessarily jeopardizing rationality itself)—we are bound to see that *we simply cannot comprehend the rationality of even conventional warfare, without admitting the need of those engaged in war to adhere to some collective ideology, and without admitting that such adherence is characteristically sufficient to confirm one's rationality and the reasonableness of one's behavior* (in the face of radically risking standard prudential interests).[14] War, then, is bound to appear increasingly irrational as we move from conventional through total toward absolute war, *if* assessed solely in terms of prudential interests *not* supplemented by corporate interests and objectives.

Thus far, our argument may be put this way: as we move from conventional to total war, war itself becomes increasingly difficult, even impossible, to defend on utilitarian grounds; for, so seen, it becomes more and more irrational, in risking and destroying the favored life of larger and larger parts of the total populations assumed to be making rational calculations about their own advantage.

It is easier and more natural to confirm the rationality of war on the assumption of collective or corporate interests not reducible to those of any aggregate of human individuals. The reason is simply that increased losses of every significant sort (damaging to normal prudential interests) *can* be tolerated as rational only by introducing irreducible corporate objectives that individuals can share (in the limit, by fascist identification with the *Volk* or the like) or by radically altering the model of individual rationality (for instance, by cooperating in race suicide for the sake of interstellar peace). The question remains whether, within the boundary of plausible extensions of terrestrial prudence, it is possible, impossible, or extremely unlikely to defend the rationality or reasonableness of nuclear war, nuclear threats, and nuclear deterrence.

Since war is a corporate or collective activity, an activity of fictional entities somehow generated by prudential agents, there must be an upper threshold of tolerance regarding the sacrifice of the rational concerns of aggregated individuals to the pursuit of collective goals. But if there is such a limit, then it would not merely be irrational to pursue a war beyond it, it would be immoral as well. *It would be immoral to pursue a policy that radically threatened not only the most fundamental prudential concerns of aggregated human individuals but also whatever could be said to serve such concerns—war, in particular—however adjusted or attenuated by intervening corporate objectives.* (Here is an essential clue as to how to assess the moral standing and prudential functioning of modern national states, at least.)

THE RATIONALITY AND MORALITY OF WAR

It is *not* immoral to act irrationally. But it *is* immoral (in a rational world) to choose, apparently reasonably, to favor corporate objectives without regard to reconciling those objectives and attendant behavior with the prudential concerns of aggregated humans. It *is* immoral to favor what would be irrational or radically unreasonable or imprudent, or what, knowingly, cannot be convincingly justified by reference to any collective ideology. For instance, it would be irrational to pretend to save mankind by promoting a war overwhelmingly likely to destroy mankind; it would be a global version of that well-known—profoundly irrational—decision of an American officer regarding the Vietnamese town of Ben Tre: "We had to destroy the town in order to save it."[15]

Now, then, the question before us is whether absolute or totalitarian war—or threat or deterrence—is, or cannot but be, immoral in the sense specified.

One obvious—and ironic—consequence of putting things this way is simply that *if* nuclear war is to be construed as rational, the best case can be made by peoples (say, a Nazi, perhaps a Stalinist, society) that are least inclined to treat corporate or collective entities as fictional and most inclined to treat the objectives of such entities as overriding the prudential interests of whatever persons form their mereological parts. In short, modern totalitarian states have a far easier time supporting (or appearing to support) the rationality of nuclear war than states that adopt a frankly contractarian or analogous ideology; although admitting this does not bear directly on the moral defensibility of nuclear war itself—or even its rationality—it concerns only the morality of supporting nuclear war relative to the reasonableness of doing so *on* one ideology or another.

It seems plainly *unreasonable* to view collective or corporate entities as anything but fictional, in the sense supplied; but it is hardly *irrational* to be thus *unreasonable*. It may even be conditionally advantageous, in a world increasingly drawn to the threat of nuclear war. Put another way, it is reasonable, in an increasingly irrational world, to contemplate nuclear war and nuclear threats *if* one seriously resists treating the primary agents of war as fictional. But, *once it is admitted that the corporate agents of war are fictional*, it becomes impossible to treat nuclear war (that is, absolute war fought with nuclear weapons) within the pale of *rational* behavior.

There are many ways of trying to demonstrate the immorality of nuclear war. Our attempt, here, is frankly offered as a trade-off against presuming too much about substantive moral rules and principles—more strenuously disputed than their advocates would care to admit. So we have begun with very little. We assume no morally viable option can be permanently or radically or disproportionately contrary to the prevailing prudential interests of the human species and still remain rational. But we have also conceded a difference between morality and rationality, and we have not assumed that prudential concerns cannot be morally or rationally overridden for cause (as in a just war or when the state's interests are, on occasion, overriding). Put paradoxically, war would be utterly irrational were it not for the fact that human beings are prone to invest their energies and convictions—at the cost of extreme prudential risk—in furthering the objectives of "entities" that it is most unreasonable to regard as real.

It is, for this reason, impossible or very difficult to reconcile *absolute* war (even of the nonnuclear kind—biological warfare, for instance) *with normal prudential interests.* The notion of a just war obliges us to concede that, *at least intermittently,* immediate prudential interests may be overridden in order, ultimately, to serve some set of further prudential interests systematically linked to those at risk. Those who (reasonably) reject the reality of corporate entities, who construe discourse about corporate or collective objectives as a heuristic means of focusing complex but entirely real objectives for the sake of aggregative effectiveness, are bound to condemn absolute war (*a fortiori*, absolute nuclear war) as both irrational and immoral. And those who affirm the reality of corporate entities and who regard the goal of such entities as unconditionally overriding with respect to (mere) prudential objectives must commit themselves to a most unreasonable doctrine; although, in doing so, they do conditionally enhance the reasonableness of pursuing absolute or nuclear war. On the argument, then, it is either irrational or most unreasonable to promote or plan or seriously entertain pursuing absolute nuclear war—though it may not appear so to a certain fanatic subset of those who treat states and similar entities as real, and hold their interests to be permanently overriding.

Still, our argument remains conditional in a decisive way. For nothing so far said shows that war involving the use of nuclear weapons cannot but be a form of absolute war. This proves an advantage, however: for *any reasonable advocate of nuclear weaponry must be prepared to show that its use can be confined to conventional or total war, or at least to escape absolute war.* There probably is no possible way to show that. It's hard, in a world of nuclear belligerents whose ability to wage absolute war or whose counterstrike capabilities cannot be effectively neutralized, to imagine that any power would regard it as reasonable to "commit" nuclear war. Even those who regard the interests of collective entities as unconditionally and permanently overriding are likely to assign prudential interests to such entities— which of course, nuclear war would still radically disable (in destroying or harming the human populations on which they necessarily depend). Hence, *there can be no prudentially oriented policy that could hope to justify (absolute) nuclear war*: there are no grounds on which to assign to corporate entities mandates of any sort radically overriding both their own prudential interests and those of the human aggregates on which they depend. This is the strong reason that leads so many to regard nuclear war as utterly irrational.

WAR AND ITS UNDERLYING CAUSES

We come now to a final difficulty. For it has not yet been *shown*, if absolute nuclear war is either utterly irrational or radically immoral, that—in a world already subject to imminent holocaust—it would also be irrational or immoral *to risk absolute nuclear war, or to threaten or entertain the use of nuclear weapons in a range between conventional and total war, or to act to deter nuclear war and nuclear threats by another, by developing a counterstrike capability.* These distinctions are not always correctly grasped by those impatient with any seeming tolerance for absolute nuclear war. A tell-tale proviso in a recent discussion of the issue by George Ball confirms very neatly (however inadvertently) the viability of the options we are considering. Ball's concern, of course, is to strengthen the conventional forces of NATO vis-à-vis the Soviet Union. His entire argument depends on the feasibility of "conventional" parity between NATO and the Soviet bloc: "we should resolutely undertake to build a deterrent that can survive a test of wills—an adequate *conventional* force in Europe."[16] This, however, "does not mean," Ball adds, "that we should furl or throw away our nuclear umbrella; we shall continue to need it to deter a nuclear attack. What it does mean is that we should no longer rely on it to stop the Soviets from attacking with conventional weapons."[17] Ball's statement confirms two points: first, that it is impossible to separate rational planning with respect to conventional and nuclear war and weaponry; second, that, given present military realities, it cannot be irrational, unreasonable, imprudent, or immoral *sans phrase* to engage any or all of the options listed just above—or at least to do so, while also sincerely attempting to reduce our reliance on nuclear weapons.

Earlier, in considering Ramsey's thesis, we suggested that if, indeed, absolute war is conceptually unlike conventional and total war, in the sense that a world really under the threat of nuclear holocaust is an utterly unreasonable and imprudent world, a world bordering on irrationality or already irrational, then there *might* be a *reasonable*—even a morally viable—basis for nuclear risk, nuclear threats, nuclear postures of deterrence and the like. The question is not merely one of whether, while opposed to committing nuclear war, one could consistently prepare a counterstrike capability, but rather of whether, *if* committing nuclear war were wrong or evil, it would necessarily be wrong or evil as well—in a world already at risk—to develop such a deterrent capability under the prudential constraint (that Ramsey and Walzer endorse) that one must then be prepared to use that capability. The question is not essentially one of the psychology of military reasoning, although that, too, is hardly negligible and affects important issues.[18] It is rather a question that paradoxically concerns *reasonable or moral behavior in a real world threatened by utterly unreasonable, even irrational and immoral, political and military commitments.* It is not implausible to hold—almost no one denies it—that the world is drifting toward a condition of potentially irreversible threat of absolute nuclear war, although it is impossible to be sure that the principal nuclear powers are or are not prepared to commit nuclear war, or will or will not be opposed to such a commitment in the near future. For all intents and purposes, we are *now* in that extremely unreasonable, possibly quite irrational, certainly imprudent global state—and getting deeper all the time. Even so, it would be preposterous to argue that it must now, in principle, be impossible to examine reasonable options. Reasoning would have an air of paradox, to be sure, and would *be* paradoxical. But we cannot suppose that there are *any* sustained real-life situations in which one could not develop a pertinent extension of rational conduct.

Some, of course, see the prospect of reasonable, prudential, even moral alternatives in a much more sanguine way within the actual boundaries of nuclear war. Robert Jay Lifton and Richard Falk have collected what are by now the canonical examples offered by Edward Teller and Herman Kahn; they have even managed to add some extraordinarily recent specimens of the genre. One sentence of Teller's fixes that mode of thinking that sees nothing paradoxical in nuclear prudence, sees nothing but the continuity of, say, industrial and nuclear conflict. "This much is certain: Properly defended, we can survive a nuclear attack; we can dig out of the ruins, we can recover from the catastrophe."[19] Hence, we must acknowledge that there are serious, informed observers of the nuclear threat who do *not* admit that nuclear war is *sui generis*, utterly discontinuous with total war or conventional war; *and* that there is no compelling evidence that the populations of, say, the United States and the Soviet Union would be utterly opposed to risking such a war or would favor domination by the other to the uncertain benefits of nuclear war.[20] As Lifton argues, it is plausible that "the continuing nuclear weapons cycle in any country depends on the collusion, or at least compliance, of most of the people. It depends, that is, on maintaining the degree of collective numbing necessary for that compliance."[21] There is as yet no reason to believe that that phenomenon will not persist indefinitely, or even grow, under conditions of increasingly autonomous, automated nuclear decision procedures. There is also, frankly, the quite horrid possibility—which Lifton merely acknowledges and which Beres positively refines through careful scenarios[22]—that at least certain sorts of nuclear war (most likely *not* a direct confrontation between the superpowers) might well remain limited (though hardly reliably). Beres holds that the policy of nuclear deterrence cannot succeed because, on *rational* grounds, nuclear powers would be unwilling to use their own counterstrike capacity in support of an ally victimized by a *limited* nuclear attack. Ironically, against what Beres says, this would be a form of rational nuclear deterrence—not against *any* particular nuclear episode but against unlimited or absolute nuclear war. Also, under circumstances of nuclear proliferation, the very incapacity of any state to determine who might attack it anonymously argues the *relative* prudence of acquiring a nuclear capability just when, paradoxically, controlling the prospect of absolute war or of limiting nuclear war will seem most dim. Such developments may actually increase earth's appetite for nuclear arms—paradoxically, as a rationally favored form of what may be perceived as an irrational form of deterrence in an utterly unreasonable and imprudent world.[23] In any case, it is in shifting from the provisionally rational or reasonable world of conventional and total war to the irrational or profoundly unreasonable and imprudent world in which we are all at absolute nuclear risk that, as a matter of course, moral and prudential considerations threaten to behave paradoxically.

We cannot, therefore, rule out a counterstrike capability as unconditionally irrational, imprudent, or immoral, even though it be utterly irrational to think of winning an absolute nuclear war.[24] For all its humanity, therefore, Jonathan Schell's well-known objection simply misses the mark. Schell says:

> The central proposition of the deterrence doctrine—the piece of logic on which the world theoretically depends to see the sun rise tomorrow—is that a nuclear holocaust can best be prevented if each nuclear power, or bloc of powers, holds in readiness a nuclear force with which it "credibly" threatens to destroy the entire society of any attacker, even after suffering the worst possible "first strike" that the attacker can launch.[25]

On Schell's interpretation, the deterrent power of nuclear weapons is supposed to insure that "the threat of their use . . . will prevent their use."[26] But that is an utterly unreasonable and unreliable constraint. The notion of a reasonable deterrent, *now, in and only in a world at absolute risk,* cannot be more than the notion of *increasing the likelihood that a nuclear war* (capable of extinguishing the race, impossible to discount, threatening a world imprudent enough to have put itself at risk) *can still be effectively confined to a limited war.*

There is no question that this is a hateful alternative. It may *not* be feasible for nuclear belligerents to assure one another that they would be prepared to keep a nuclear conflict or strike or counterstrike from becoming absolute. In *that* case, they could not be entirely rational. They could, however, still behave reasonably and prudently within the terms of their irrational stance. It would certainly not be incoherent to hold that, in the irrational world we are imagining—namely, our own—it would be prudent or even moral for some power to risk nuclear annihilation *by* developing or maintaining a nuclear deterrent, *when the world was already at absolute risk.*[27] It would remain irredeemably irrational or immoral to begin an absolute war (by first strike or otherwise) or to respond to a war by means of an absolute counterstrike. But to risk such a war in a world thus risked *or* to be unable to confine a nuclear war, once launched, to a limited war could not *then* be similarly judged or so judged for similar reasons.

The options are certainly unpalatable. They presuppose that we are on the edge of countenancing a new form of war: a kind of nuclear war falling between total war and absolute war, what we have been calling *limited nuclear war.*[28] It is a form of war that affords an unacknowledged option of reason, prudence, morality under conditions that already exist and show no evidence of being effectively eliminable—an option that cannot be rejected out of hand as irrational, that addresses realities within the constraints admitted to bear on all lesser forms of war and threats of war, that other familiar options either do not cover or cannot disqualify. Of course, our concern is not to vindicate such war, but to map all the possibilities open to responsible military reasoning. What we are calling limited nuclear war would resemble conventional war in being an instrument of collective policy. It would resemble total war in rejecting the demarcation between combatant and noncombatant. It would resemble absolute war, of course, simply in risking absolute war.

The moral is elementary. It is not that we must countenance limited nuclear war; it is rather that we must understand why it is that *the analysis and assessment of modern warfare cannot be separated from the analysis and assessment of the modern state itself,* why it is that every effort to isolate the nuclear question drives us to intolerable paradox. This is what is being ignored in all the refined debates about the just-war concept. *There are no just wars any longer;* or if there are, there is no reliable way to exclude the legitimate use of nuclear weapons or the risk of nuclear disaster. This is what is missing from the bishops' pastoral letter. For the bishops fail to condemn (nonnuclear) total war, fail to acknowledge that modern warfare cannot escape being waged in that form, fail to admit the erasure of the conditions of the just-war doctrine,[29] fail to fix an *essential* distinction between nuclear and nonnuclear weapons, fail to justify the condemnation or impermissibility of using limited nuclear weapons, and fail to link the assessment of war and the fate of the just-war concept to their underlying causes. In fact, the bishops formulate *no* principled condemnation of limited nuclear war to match their explicit condemnation of the use of nuclear *weapons* in so-called "counter-population warfare" (against largely civilian or population concentrations) or of the use of such weapons in initiating war. They also never explain what we are to understand by the expressions "nuclear war" or "nuclear warfare."[30]

We are confirmed, therefore, in the gloomy conclusion that the unconditional condemnation of nuclear warfare rationally eludes us as the world's imprudence and irrationality deepen. It is conceptually hopeless to oppose any and all forms of nuclear war or any and all uses of nuclear weapons—short of absolute (nuclear) war itself—*unless* we can provide a suitable basis for effectively condemning total war involving "merely" nonnuclear weapons. The unwillingness of the world to apply the just-war concept to the condemnation of total war—what the bishops now appear to countenance as conventional war—signifies the utterly illusory nature of current efforts to improve arguments against the use of nuclear weapons. In fact, to take note of that truth is simply to take note of the incompatibility of condemning modern warfare and of legitimating modern states. What we are finally forced to see is the absurdity of attempting, in our own time, to try to recover an effective criterion of just war suited to the practices of contemporary states, that is, of corporate entities that pursue war essentially as a natural extension of policy.

We have been debating the wrong question.

NOTES

1. Cf. Louis René Beres, *Apocalypse* (Chicago: University of Chicago Press, 1980), pp. 148–50; Jonathan Schell, *The Fate of the Earth* (New York: Alfred A. Knopf, 1982). The entire confusion (though hardly the futility) of attempting to fix a reasonable notion of limited war, whether nonnuclear or nuclear, is decisively shown in Ian Clark's rather detailed account, *Limited Nuclear War* (Princeton: Princeton University Press, 1982). The final sentence of the book says it all: "In the last analysis, political philosophy provides no adequate chart for selecting a course between the Scylla of limited war and the Charybdis of nuclear holocaust" (p. 244).
2. "The Challenge of Peace: God's Promise and Our Response," (United States Catholic Conference, Inc., 1982), which appeared in the *National Catholic Reporter*, 5 November 1982, pp. 9–20.
3. Michael Walzer, *Just and Unjust Wars* (New York: Basic Books, 1977), p. 36.
4. Ibid., pp. 42–43.
5. Ibid., p. xv. Cf. also Clark, *Limited Nuclear War*.
6. Cf. Walzer, *Just and Unjust Wars*, p. 169, where Walzer uses the phrase "total war" (in a condemnatory sense) for another purpose; also Beres, *Apocalypse*, p. 106.
7. Beres points out, for instance, that tactical nuclear weapons are often significantly more powerful than so-called strategic nuclear weapons; see *Apocalypse*, p. 51.
8. Cf. Gregory S. Kavka, "Some Paradoxes of Deterrence," *Journal of Philosophy* 75 (1978); "Deterrence, Utility and Rational Choice," *Theory and Decision 12 (1980)*.
9. Cf. Robert Nozick, "Moral Complications and Moral Structures," *Natural Law Forum* 13 (1968).
10. Paul Ramsey, "A Political Ethic Context for Strategic Thinking," in *Strategic Thinking and Its Moral Implications*, ed. Morton A. Kaplan (Chicago: University of Chicago Press, 1973), pp. 134–35. The passage is cited by Walzer, *Just and Unjust Wars*, p. 272.

11. Cf. Paul Ramsey, *The Just War: Force and Political Responsibility* (New York: Charles Scribner's, 1968); also Walzer *Just and Unjust Wars*, chap. 17.
12. Walzer, *Just and Unjust Wars*. Ramsey, incidentally, does address the issue of double effect, responding to a critic's remarks, but his account is not satisfactory; see his *The Just War*, chap. 15.
13. I have explored this issue in a number of places: *Negativities: The Limits of Life* (Columbus: Charles Merrill, 1975), chap. 4; "War and Ideology," in *Philosophy, Morality, and International Affairs*, ed. V. Held et al., (New York: Oxford University Press, 1974); "The Problem of Revolution," *Philosophy in Context* 5 (1976); cf. J. J. Rousseau, *The Social Contract*.
14. The theme of such a model of rationality is central to Margolis, *Negativities*; see also Donald Davidson, "Mental Events," *Actions and Events* (Oxford: Clarendon Press, 1980).
15. The wording is Walzer's, *Just and Unjust Wars*, p. 192; see also pp. 188–96.
16. George W. Ball, "The Cosmic Bluff," *New York Review of Books*, 21 July 1983, p. 40; italics added.
17. Ibid., p. 41. He concludes, "Meanwhile, we should gradually raise the threshold for the use of nuclear weapons until it ceases to have meaning. That is the only prudent course available to us—and it will not remain available forever."
18. It might well be taken to be the most developed issue that Beres addresses in *Apocalypse*; see Kavka articles cited in note 13.
19. Edward Teller with Allen Brown, *The Legacy of Hiroshima* (Garden City, N.Y.: Doubleday, 1962), p. 244; cited in Robert Jay Lifton and Richard Falk, *Indefensible Weapons: The Political and Psychological Case against Nuclearism* (New York: Basic Books, 1982), p. 21. See also the rest of chap. 2; and Herman Kahn, *On Thermonuclear War* (Princeton: Princeton University Press, 1961).
20. Cf. Kavka, "Deterrence, Utility, and Rational Choice."
21. Lifton and Falk, *Indefensible Weapons*, p. 10.
22. Ibid., pp. 16–17. Cf. Desmond Ball, "Can Nuclear War Be Controlled?" Adelphi Paper no. 169, The International Institute for Strategic Studies, London (Autumn 1982); cited by Lifton and Falk. Cf. also Beres, *Apocalypse*, particularly pp. 77–98.
23. See Thomas Schelling, *The Strategy of Conflict* (New York: Oxford University Press, 1960); and Kavka, "Some Paradoxes of Deterrence."
24. A fair sample of recent thinking along this line is offered by Sir Nevil Mott, "European Opinion and NATO Policy," *The Bulletin of the Atomic Scientists* 38 (1982); and McGeorge Bundy, George F. Kennan, Robert S. McNamara, and Gerard Smith, "Nuclear Weapons and the Atlantic Alliance," *Foreign Affairs* 60 (Spring 1982).
25. Schell, *The Fate of the Earth*, p. 196.
26. Ibid., p. 197.
27. This, if I understand his argument correctly, is congruent with Kavka's analysis in "Some Paradoxes of Deterrence."
28. The following statement is offered by Schelling: "With the development of small-size, small-yield nuclear weapons suitable for local use by ground groups with modest equipment, and with the development of nuclear depth charges and nuclear rockets for air-to-air combat, the technical characteristics of nuclear weapons have ceased to provide much basis, if any, for treating nuclear

weapons as peculiarly different in the conduct of limited war." *The Strategy of Conflict*, p. 257. Cf. the rest of Appendix A, ibid.
29. Cf. ibid., p. 14 particularly.
30. Ibid.

8
NEW DIRECTIONS IN DETERRENCE THEORY

Patrick M. Morgan

When the Reagan administration came into office, there was a widespread feeling that deterrence was in serious difficulty, in general meaning that the West, particularly the United States, was in bad shape in terms of both forces and doctrines to continue deterring the Soviet Union. The administration made this the central preoccupation in its foreign and defense policies. But the uneasiness about deterrence had arisen even earlier, in some ways as far back as the Nixon administration; and in the Carter era real defense spending began to rise, the MX was approved, plans for new missile deployments in Europe were laid, and the Rapid Deployment Force was initiated. Thus Reagan policies rested on a broad feeling that deterrence was in trouble and that this called for action.

One aspect of the problem was the matter of extended deterrence; it was said that American threats to escalate to the strategic level in retaliation for a Soviet attack on our allies were of diminished, to the point of nonexistent, credibility. Henry Kissinger's 1981 address to assembled NATO officials raised all sorts of eyebrows on this point:

> it is absurd to base the strategy of the West on the credibility of the threat of mutual suicide . . . the European allies should not keep asking us to multiply strategic assurances that we cannot possibly mean, or if we do mean, we should not want to execute because if we execute, we risk the destruction of civilization [Kissinger 1982: 109].

Another aspect was the vulnerability of American land-based missiles to a Soviet attack. This was said to increase Soviet incentives to attack in a crisis, and led to the proposition that unless Soviet ICBMs were made equally vulnerable, the United States might be paralyzed to the point of not retaliating for a limited counterforce attack. Still another aspect was the divergence between Soviet and American thinking on deterrence. We were told to imitate the Soviets' appreciation that deterrence rests on a war-fighting capacity and military doctrine. Colin Gray has advanced the view, to which others subscribe, that "forces that do not lend themselves to politically intelligent employment in war are probably insufficient to deter" (Gray: 136).

Apart from these reservations, decisionmakers and analysts still reposed great confidence in deterrence as an instrument for manipulating Soviet behavior. The reservations had to do with the perceived inadequacies of our military posture. Deterrence would be fine if these deficiencies were corrected, and the chances of a deterrence failure would sharply decline. Of course, deterrence might still fail, but this also called for correcting the military imbalance and for expanding American military options for conducting wars.

There was not much new in this. "The nuclear strategy of the United States remains to this day essentially the same as the one worked out during the Kennedy Administration, and, indeed, is not very different from that adopted at the very beginning of the nuclear age" (Lodal: 157). Freedman's recent history of nuclear strategy finds no real progress or evolution over the years: "What is impressive is the cyclical character of the debates" (Freedman: xv).

It is quite true that deterrence had been in trouble, but not quite in the ways it is fashionable to suggest. The problems referred to above, and the circularity of the debates about them, resemble the puzzles in the sciences that, Kuhn tells us, accumulate until they provoke a paradigm shift. They are hard to grapple with if we remain within the framework of classic deterrence theory. That theory still supplies the intellectual basis for most of the discourse on major national security issues, and the current changes in the American military posture are designed to make deterrence, as traditionally conceived, work better. Worthy of more attention is the slow, steady erosion of that theory, based on a better understanding of governmental decisionmaking. We are on the verge of an absence-of-clothes-for-the-emperor situation, where the paucity of decent evidence to support the standard way of pursuing national security embarasses all concerned.

A different approach to understanding deterrence is beginning to emerge, one that does not proceed within the standard framework and moves beyond the recurring debates. It involves trying to ascertain just exactly what governments do in deterrence situations, primarily by case studies, as well as suggesting that certain contextual factors pertaining to the nature of the international system have a distinct bearing on the effectiveness of deterrence. Thus it has both a behavioral and a theoretical dimension. The former takes us into tracking the perceptions and actions of governments in crises and confrontations to assess better the impact of deterrent threats. The latter involves attempts to integrate deterrence into general theoretical appreciations of the nature and dynamics of international politics. This chapter offers a brief analysis of how the new approach differs from others that have long been available.

THE PROBLEM

Nuclear deterrence arose as the preeminent answer in our time to a terribly compelling question: how are we to prevent wars among great powers? Since early in this century it has been widely appreciated that great power wars, when the capabilities of major nations are fully mobilized, are intolerable in their consequences. They have the potential for catastrophic levels of destruction and loss of life in a general warfare so grievously harmful as to ravage the entire international system. The trouble is that wars among great powers have been a normal, and very important, part of the international system. As Anatol Rapoport has suggested, "war between great powers, far from being an aberration, is a normal activity of military establishments" (Rapoport: 403). From this readily arises the von Clausewitz view that war is awful but purposeful, an extension of the state's political objectives in coping with the international system; and the standard observation that the political/military struggles of the member states keep the system in some sort of equilibrium.

By the end of the 19th century it was being suggested that the military capacities of states were a growing source of insecurity and instability—that national security and international order ultimately depended on a resource (modern weapons and forces) and a recourse (war) that in themselves undermined security and order. One result was the emergence of early attempts at arms control, in the Hague Conferences and related activities, to codify rules of war and to outlaw the use of certain weapons: expanding bullets, poison gas, aerial bombing, submarines (Dupuy and Hammerman: 48–70). In short, there was an international effort to hold great power war within limits.

At the national level, a rather different approach to the problem was under way; a search for methods to conduct a great power war that would enable the costs to be kept within tolerable limits. States sought to exploit changes in warfare made possible by economic-scientific-industrial progesss so as, if necessary, to win overwhelming victories quickly and decisively. Plans proliferated for rapid mobilization, followed by decisive offensive thrusts on land, to bring the next war to a rapid and successful conclusion; plans were devised for the single grand naval engagement to shatter the enemy fleet; early theorists of air power offered what we now call strategic bombing as the true route to quick victory.

The near success of some of these measures in World War I and the fear that they would pose a greater threat in the future added to the perceived agenda for arms control. Renewed attempts after 1918 to put warfare under some restraint focused not only on types of weapons or practices in war (gas, naval armaments) but on states' capacities to mobilize quickly and to mount devastating surprise attacks. But the search for new ways to win quickly was eventually resumed. In planning for a future war both Germany and Japan developed approaches to utilize surprise and mobility to bring about the quick defeat of even numerically superior forces and to avoid the mutual exhaustion of 1914–18. And the resulting war once again escaped the limits arms control had sought to impose.

Thus, these two approaches to the problem were working more or less at cross-purposes. War among great powers remained a reasonable possibility, and states had to act accordingly. To prepare for it was to develop weapons and plans tending to undermine arms control. But short-war solutions seemed equally illusory, deficient on at least three grounds. First, there were no effective, feasible ways to halt the war if a rapid victory were not secured, and fighting continued to unprecedented levels of death and destruction in both world wars. Second, the possibility of losing quickly increased the insecurity of great states, particularly in a crisis, a significant factor prior to 1914 for great powers on the continent and in the reciprocal concern over a strategic surprise at sea in England and Germany (Tuchman; Wainstein). Third, if their plans worked out, great powers could smash their rivals, so they had little incentive to limit their wartime objectives, while the cost of a long war invited the escalation of those objectives. Such huge stakes made this warfare even less tolerable for sustaining the international system.

Of course, yet another alternative was a marked alteration in the system itself, some change that eliminated great power warfare as a necessary regulatory mechanism and prevented states from resorting to it. Wilsonian collective security, an effective great power condominium as envisioned in the design of the UN Security Council, or a program of general disarmament, were suggested for this purpose. Each proved either impossible to establish or a failure in practice. Governments do not any longer treat them as realistic possibilities, if they ever did.

The eventual outcome was a return to arms control, but of a radically different sort. When nuclear weapons were first developed there were fears that they represented the culmination of the search for quick and total victory, the perfect weapons for the triumphant surprise attack. Only gradually did they come to be seen as a solution to the problem. By making possible a level of retaliation that would make an attack pointless, they could eliminate states' vulnerability to a sudden defeat. Nuclear deterrence is arms control not by limiting the weapons of a great power war, but by piling them up and thus guaranteeing such enormous costs in that sort of war that it is never initiated. As such, it is the dominant solution of our time to the intolerability of those wars.

NUCLEAR WEAPONS AND POLITICS

The central concern in an analysis of deterrence in theory and practice is the relationship between nuclear weapons and politics. The relationship can be explored on two levels, the international system and the national government. At the international system level, the question usually raised is: have nuclear weapons altered international politics in a fundamental way? When nuclear weapons were first developed it was felt by many that they must. Late in World War II Niels Bohr mounted a personal campaign to convince the British and American governments that, if they were to survive, states had to compromise their sovereignty and put nuclear technology under international control. Other atomic scientists and some high officials in various governments also took this view (Sherwin). Churchill flatly rejected it, as did all the governments concerned, in one way or another. This lends support to the view that nuclear weapons have not really altered international politics at all, and it is clearly true that in many respects the behavior of states was unchanged. They remained autonomous, conflictual, and steadily competitive for power and influence. They continued to maintain significant military capabilities, to build coalitions, to engage in the balancing of power, and to resort to war.

Deterrence theory requires that we reject this view, however. Political conflicts among great powers have regularly led to war. To find such wars intolerable and to count on deterrence to prevent them is to assume that, in a fundamental way, the normal course of international politics can be frustrated indefinitely. This also means that nuclear weapons eliminate, if deterrence is successful, the main basis for managing the international system. This is the root of the frequently heard assertion that nuclear deterrence has the overwhelming virtue of having prevented World War III. Some such conception underlies the MAD approach to deterrence: once a sufficient capacity for destruction is in the grasp of great states, "superiority" becomes a relatively meaningless term, force becomes a much less useful instrument, and old ways of conducting international politics no longer apply. In effect, nuclear deterrence means the negation of international politics, to a certain extent.

Unfortunately, the evidence is insufficient to reject the first view and confirm the second. We do not know if nuclear deterrence is what sustains the peace or whether, in fact, deterrence only seems to work because the international system is currently in a configuration in which great power political conflicts are restrained at some point short of war. There is a frightening possibility that we have laid the destructive instruments of deterrence on top of a system that remains unchanged.

At the level of the national government, the relationship between nuclear weapons and politics is typically confronted by deterrence theory and its critics. An excellent starting point for a review of this is the Kennan perspective. George Kennan has developed a clear, consistent approach to the relationship between nuclear weapons and politics. He first broached these ideas in his days in the State Department, and a recent collection of his writings (Kennan 1983) demonstrates the continuity of his analysis. It is worth considering here as a path not taken. Kennan offered his views as an alternative to the reliance on nuclear weapons in American foreign policy that was to make necessary the development of deterrence theory. His thinking provides an intellectual case for rejecting deterrence theory in its entirety, precisely by addressing the relationship between nuclear weapons and politics.

For Kennan the essential fact about nuclear weapons is that they are monstrous. Their effects are necessarily so gross that a sane or rational government could hope to achieve no political purpose by resorting to them. Their use would be the negation and the failure of politics. Worse than this, they have a hypnotic effect, inviting a belief that they are useful and usable when they are not, and arousing a sense of security by their possession that is entirely unwarranted. Kennan has a strong sense of the fallibility of governments and decisionmakers, of their wickedness, irrationality, vulnerability to misperception, and miscalculation. Thus it is not that nuclear weapons cannot be used, only that they cannot be used for any reasonable political purpose.

The fact that they might nonetheless be used has led Kennan to press consistently for a pledge of no first use, then for cuts in nuclear arsenals, and finally for complete nuclear disarmament. If they have no political purpose, if their use would be the negation of politics, if their presence puts civilization at risk, then the proper relationship of politics to nuclear weapons is for political leaders to eliminate them from their arsenals.

But then how are we to prevent great power wars? The essence of Kennan's answer lies in his understanding of the nature of the Soviet-American conflict. He rejects the view of the Soviet Union as ideologically and politically driven to seek an endless expansion of its rule, by force when it can get away with it. That Moscow is always interested in expanding its power and influence he does not deny— what great power is not? But it has been relatively cautious and conservative, preoccupied with sustaining its sphere of control in an era when there have been and will continue to be serious limitations on its capabilities and resources. For this reason there are no fundamental conflicts of interest between the USSR and the US that should lead either to resort to war. Conflicts and frictions abound, but not of the sort to make war unavoidable or even likely.

Thus, war between the two can be prevented without the elaborate and terribly dangerous practice of nuclear deterrence, Kennan maintains. Not only are the conflicts that exist not such as to necessitate a war, but there have been and continue to be opportunities for political settlements and the better political management of the Soviet-American competition. These opportunities have been lost or insufficiently exploited, because the piling up of nuclear weapons and the tendency to treat relations between the two as mainly a problem in deterrence have helped inhibit the serious consideration of political solutions. Nuclear weapons have, by their presence, been allowed to eclipse politics (see also Gaddis).

Kennan left the government in large part because American policy was headed in the opposite direction. As John Gaddis has pointed out, there was a psychological dimension to the American concern with the Soviet Union that Kennan's view could not assuage. There was a fear of looking weak and irresolute, and the development of and reliance on nuclear weapons seemed to go some way toward easing it (Gaddis: 88). The overriding need was for a strategy that encompassed nuclear weapons, providing guidelines for their use in pursuit of national objectives. From Kennan's perspective there could be no such strategy; any proper appreciation of nuclear weapons caused the realization that they were incompatible with strategy.

Yet there is no abrupt dividing line between Kennan's position and what developed into American deterrence theory. Kennan admitted that possessing some nuclear weapons might be required, although only a few would be sufficient for deterrence. His analysis is echoed in the views of those who, down through the years, have advocated either a minimum deterrence posture or a pure MAD posture. These people have felt, pretty much for the reasons Kennan elucidated, that a deliberate decision by the Soviet government to initiate war with the United States was almost impossible, since it would be politically senseless. This would make unnecessary any elaborate conception of how deterrence works leading to a large and variegated nuclear arsenal, constant attention to the details of the nuclear balance, and the development of elaborate scenarios for the conduct of nuclear war.

CLASSIC AMERICAN DETERRENCE THEORY

Deterrence theory developed in another direction. It came to treat deterrence as a subtle, relatively delicate, psychologically complex phenomenon. And it proceeded as if it were entirely possible for a great power to initiate a war against other great powers under a variety of circumstances, making it vital to investigate deeply how this could be precluded, as well as how to conduct the war that would result if it nevertheless happened.

Those who set about developing deterrence theory did not refute Kennan's analysis. Instead, they more or less ignored it. Some critics of deterrence theory challenged this, arguing that American deterrence theory has been derived from a demonic image of the Soviet Union, which held it quite capable of, even eager to, launch an aggressive attack on this country and its allies whenever it felt it could do so successfully (Green: 55–59). It is true that devotees of deterrence have often held just such an image, and there are those who have never abandoned it, including many now associated with the current administration (see Thompson).

Deterrence theory developed apart from views of this sort, however. It derives from a broad assumption that states have always been willing to use force to advance their interest and are still willing today. Deterrence theorists made no effort to ascertain the political conditions that could lead to great power wars or to analyze the nature of the Soviet regime and the dynamics of the Soviet-American rivalry to determine the possibility of war. Their preferred focus was on the technical dimensions of the military situation: under what circumstances would an enemy be able to see a successful conventional or nuclear attack as physically and psychologically possible? How can the emergence of those circumstances be prevented? If they already exist, how can they be eliminated? The political motives and judgments that might prompt an attack were not of central concern.

How do we prevent a great power war? The answer supplied by deterrence theory is to prepare retaliation so severe that, in anticipation, the opponent will decide not to attack or, where possible, to prepare a defense so stout as to deny the attacker a victory, thereby discouraging the attack. (An analysis of deterrence by denial is found in Mearsheimer.) For this purpose both nuclear and conventional forces are deployed. This way of thinking about the problem takes more or less for granted the political conflict sufficient to generate a war; in effect, it assumes such conflict will continue. The object of deterrence is not to modify this, but to prevent its culmination in war.

Deterrence would be relatively simple if this was all there was to it. The problem is that we cannot simply assume that a government will fight and/or retaliate if attacked or if its friends are attacked. It might, but then again it might not. Retaliation may be very costly and dangerous, particularly where nuclear weapons are involved. Retaliating at a nonnuclear level may also appear too costly, particularly if the chances of escalation are significant. Put succinctly, retaliation may not be rational, and thus not credible. If it is not credible, how can deterrence be explained?

Kennan's analysis foreshadowed this problem. If nuclear weapons, and in fact modern warfare, were devoid of meaningful political purpose, this presumably applied not only to the state thinking of initiating a war, but to the state contemplating retaliation. Kennan himself did not ever quite say this. As noted, he accepted the possible utility, for purposes of deterrence, of a small nuclear arsenal. He also pressed for complete nuclear disarmament, and has argued that nuclear weapons are not things "with which one readily springs to the defense of one's friends" (Kennan: 7).

Deterrence theorists have wrestled with this question for years without finding a permanently satisfactory answer. One solution has been to treat credibility as a technical or signaling problem. It was a matter of finding the right ways to convey an image of resolve. For instance, we could treat commitments as interdependent when it comes to image: behavior with regard to one commitment conveys a message as to how a state would react if any of its commitments were challenged.

Here the complications mount. For one thing, there are few occasions for showing resolve when a commitment is directly, openly challenged. This has led, along with the fear of appearing weak in any form, to finding other occasions for doing so. Officials found it could be expressed rhetorically in conflicts short of an outright attack, it could be demonstrated by decisions on weapons systems, it could be signaled by how one approached negotiations, etc. As one example of many, Secretary of Defense Caspar Weinberger criticized the nuclear freeze proposal because it would send Moscow the wrong message. In other words, this concern for image has no natural limits.

A second difficulty is well illustrated by Vietnam. The justification for our involvement there was to sustain credibility, but the costs, recriminations, and regrets had the effect, if any thing, of eroding American credibility. This sort of situation can lead to numerous adventures for the purpose of sustaining credibility that eventually drain resources and will.

The final difficulty is that no necessary connection exists in logic or in fact between successfully upholding lesser commitments and the credibility of those that would involve grave, intolerable costs. Because of the vast scale of the potential consequences if nuclear weapons are involved, there is no reason to believe a state that fights at a markedly lower level of conflict will be ready to do so on the nuclear level.

Another solution has been to insist that there could well be conditions under which the use of nuclear weapons or the fighting of a major conventional war was acceptable, and that our forces be designed accordingly. This is the essence of flexible response. How can a state best convey the message that it would retaliate? By developing a plan, or set of plans, and the necessary forces for the conduct of war, including nuclear war. How can such a war best be conducted? Be developing options for doing so, allowing the conduct of hostilities at a level suitable for achieving the nation's interests and in such a controlled fashion as to limit the chance that a general nuclear war will result. Deterrence is not credible without sophisticated plans and capabilities for war fighting at all levels. A threat to respond at a low level will lack muscle if the opponent feels he can escalate with impunity; a threat to respond at a high level will lack credibility if the consequences would be overwhelming, so the opponent will feel free to act at lower levels.

Deterrence theorists have returned to this point repeatedly, which was originally emphasized in NSC-68. Ignored in the Eisenhower administration's conception of deterrence, it formed the focus of the critiques of that conception that fostered Kennedy administration policy. It was also the main preoccupation of the Gaither Report, which attacked Eisenhower defense policies. After the Kennedy administration had implemented its version of flexible response only to be followed by a retreat from it toward MAD, this concern for options was revived in the Nixon administration and has dominated national security policymaking ever since.

The ultimate exposition along these lines was initially presented by Herman Kahn in his insistence on preparing to fight and survive a nuclear war. It is continued today by analysts such as Colin Gray, and played a significant role in Reagan administration policy. Gray's constantly reiterated theme is that in the design of the nation's forces the objective should be victory, in the sense that the nation's political purposes can be sustained and the outcome is less favorable to the opponent than to the United States.

An alternative solution, and an equally influential one, was worked out primarily by Thomas Schelling. He admitted that retaliation was often of such cost as to make it difficult to promise credibly. He suggested that governments cannot guarantee to control their actions tightly, particularly in situations of high stress, great uncertainty, and bitter conflict, such as grave crises or after fighting at some level has already broken out. Governments can threaten to do things that it might not be rational to do, because governments are not always rational.

Much of Schelling's analysis is involved in American descriptions of how deterrence works. In the discussions of the Minuteman vulnerability problem, it is frequently suggested that the Soviets cannot count on the United States to not launch on warning; although this would be irrational, we might just do it. Or there is the frequent suggestion that the threat of escalation in response to a Soviet attack in Europe is not without weight, because that is what could happen amid the confusions and high emotions the attack would create.

Thus, deterrence theory came to have a schizoid quality when it came to rationality. Its classic expositions began by assuming rational decisionmaking. The Kahn-Gray wing pushed this to the point of asserting that only if one was rationally prepared to fight, survive, and win could one convince a rational opponent not to attack. But in the 1970s many analysts influenced by this view became alarmed with the state of the strategic balance: because the United States might not appear equal or superior (a lack of "perceived equivalence"), Soviet leaders might be so *irrational* as to see opportunity where none existed and be misled into excessive confidence in a crisis, heightened aggressiveness, and serious miscalculation of American will. On the other hand, those more attached to the Schelling version never explained why, if the United States could be so irrational as to retaliate, the Soviet Union could not be so irrational as to attack; and many of them also came to see any perceived inferiority as possibly crippling, politically and psychologically, even though this was very difficult to explain if "threats that left something to chance" were unavoidably credible.

Lawrence Freedman's history of nuclear strategy makes it abundantly clear that finding a rational basis for the use of nuclear weapons has been the critical problem all along. He notes that in the 1950s it led "prominent strategic and military figures" of both superpowers to advocate preemptive nuclear war strategies because parity would otherwise strip away the credibility of retaliatory threats. Then he traces the emergence of the Kahn solution and the Schelling solution. He concludes that the problem remains. No political or moral purpose appears sufficient to justify attacking with nuclear weapons, and no sufficiently rational basis for retaliation has emerged.

> The essence of the problem is the difficulty of attaching any rationality whatsoever to the initiation of a chain of events that could well end in the utter devastation of one's own security. . . . No means of controlling events to be sure of avoiding the worst outcome have been developed. In consequence any strategy that requires the threat of first use of nuclear weapons suffers from incredibility. Even threats confined to retaliation, which may achieve little except another volley from the enemy, suffer from this incredibility [Freedman: 397].

The same solutions are still around. Some analysts advocate preparing to fight and win a nuclear war; others often refer to uncertainty in explaining why the Russians are deterred. And the preferred solution is still that of developing flexible response options, making retaliation more rational by being able to hold it to a response in kind.

Does being able to respond in an equivalent fashion make retaliation more rational? It is widely believed that it does, and this is the basis of our current national security policy. Thus it is held that "a statesman who knew that he could fight a nuclear war with some chance of his society surviving could take a far more credible and robust stand" (Freedman: 374). Is this because retaliation is thereby made more rational? It is hard to see how this can be so. After an attack, the preeminent purpose for having the capacity to retaliate, namely to avoid being attacked, has been lost. Some other reason or reasons for retaliating must be found. Of course, a nation might wish to strike back simply for revenge, for retribution with no thought to the costs and consequences involved. But our concern is with the rational decisionmaker. What will he do?

Whether retaliation is rational depends on the results of weighing the benefits and harm that will result from not retaliating, retaliating in some limited and equivalent fashion, or retaliating in a massive way. If retaliating massively were to so paralyze the enemy's decisionmaking that no more attacks would occur, then that might be the best choice. But if it would provoke a huge counterretaliation, then all is lost. How is one to tell which would happen? That brings us to limited retaliation. If limited retaliation will not ultimately result in massive exchanges, maybe it would be best; if it forestalled any further attacks, then it would look better than a massive retaliation. But what if limited retaliation produced escalation to all-out war? Then not retaliating might result in the best outcome, if no more attacks occurred. How would a decisionmaker choose? How would the necessary cost-benefit calculations be possible?

In the past, retaliation for conventional attacks could be assessed in terms of the immediate outcome and the effect it would have on future confrontations against the same opponent (or others). But when the nation might well not survive physically and the requisite calculations cannot be made, then retaliation is not made more rational by multiplying options to reply in a limited fashion. Kissinger is certainly correct when he writes that

> in all likelihood, the problem of limiting the use of weapons whose power has no operationally definable limit will find no acceptable theoretical formulation in advance; as a practical matter, failure to achieve a consensus over a period of thirty years is a pretty good working definition of the impossibility of developing in the abstract a strategy of limited nuclear war [Kissinger 1982: 196].

The behavior of the great powers, as best we can observe it, certainly seems to reflect this view. Time and again those governments have conducted themselves as if escalation were a terribly dangerous possibility and that no rational way existed to calculate in advance just how things might go, if ever their soldiers could be seen deliberately killing each other even on a very small scale. Michael Mandelbaum summarizes the superpowers' behavior as "wary, cautious, moderate" (Mandelbaum: 217). Stephen Kaplan stresses the great circumspection of both superpowers in using military force where the other might be involved, each trying to avoid any direct or indirect military clash on even a very small scale (Kaplan: 667–77; see also Tillema and Van Wingen; Bundy; Friedberg). Nuclear powers with a clear superiority vis-à-vis other nuclear powers have not seized on this to attack, nor have they used blatant nuclear threats to get their way in serious confrontations. It is impressive that no nuclear power has ever openly used a nuclear threat against another nuclear power to force it to retreat from a position (although there may have been indirect or private threats of this sort). Even in the Cuban Missile Crisis, the American nuclear threat was only to retaliate for the firing of any of the Soviet missiles on the island.

SOVIET DETERRENCE

Americans and other Western contributors to the development of classic deterrence theory have not managed satisfactorily to relate nuclear weapons to politics in a way that supports the theory. How have the Soviets done? They appear to believe strongly in the necessity for deterrence, and they never fail to promise retaliation in the event of an attack. (Discussions of Soviet views can be found in Hoeber; Leebaert; and *Comparative Strategy* 1980.) They have consistently built up the necessary forces, apparently with an eye to obtaining a war-fighting to the point of war-winning capability.

The Soviets place great emphasis on the use of force as always being the servant of politics not only in efforts to deter hostilities, but in the conduct of them. Thus, it is most interesting that their analysis of deterrence allows no room for the dilemma that Western observers have argued must confront the political leader faced with a decision to use nuclear weapons. Instead there is an enormous rhetorical emphasis on the inevitability of retaliation and on the massiveness of the destruction it would bring in the wake of an attack on the Soviet Union. Not a scintilla of doubt about whether retaliation would in fact occur is ever allowed to appear in Soviet pronouncements, as far as I know. This allows the Soviet Union to commit itself to a no-first-use posture without fear that this will be taken as reluctance to use nuclear weapons under any circumstances, as something that would undermine the credibility of Soviet retaliatory threats.

Such a declaratory posture is linked, of course, to a huge military capability that reflects a traditional preference on the part of the armed forces (which can be seen in this country as well) for having as much of an advantage as possible if war occurs. There is little or no acceptance of the possibility of limited nuclear war (although some Western analysts see signs of a change here), apparently out of the same concern for credibility that requires the absolute guarantee of retaliation.

It is now customary to belittle the earlier American attitude that the Soviets were slow learners in deterrence thinking. This is usually coupled with the suggestion that we need to be learning from them about the value of strategic superiority and a war-fighting posture. This assertion needs to be challenged. The Soviets have no more solved the problem of the irrationality of retaliation than we have; they have not answered Kennan's assertion that nuclear weapons are unusable. They avoid confronting the dilemmas readily apparent to American analysts only by exercising total control over public discussion of such matters. They can readily threaten to unleash a massive form of retaliation without having to face domestic comments that this is surely implausible under a host of circumstances, immoral under others, and incompatible with the responsibilities of Soviet leaders for safeguarding their society. Americans can say this about the American government; the public Soviet posture is designed to discourage our saying it about them. But this can leave the Soviets looking like monsters and inhibit efforts in the West to find nonmilitary avenues to increase the security of both the Soviet Union and ourselves. And it is entirely possible that what is not discussed publicly is not all that much better discussed and understood privately. The Soviets may indeed have been slow learners in squarely facing the true dilemmas of the nuclear age and in failing to measure all the costs of their approach to deterrence.

A NEW APPROACH

There is another way to explore the relationship between nuclear weapons and politics and, on this basis, to try to better understand how deterrence works. Deterrence can be studied by expanding our understanding of how governments attempt to practice deterrence, how they bring themselves to the point of initiating a war, and how they behave when confronted with threats of retaliation. What do governments actually do in deterrence situations, and what factors appear to determine what they do? If we knew, we could better develop, test, and refine deterrence theory and derive from it a more satisfactory body of advice to the policymaker.

That this is a useful way to proceed has not been lost on a number of people. This is not to say that classic deterrence theory makes no reference to the behavior of states. Much of its appeal has rested on its persuasive account of statesmen's actions. The deterrence model took hold in the postwar era in part because of perceived lessons of the 1930s on the futility of conciliation, and similar considerations dominated the Soviet approach to deterrence, as well. There are other empirical elements in classic deterrence theory. The Cuban Missile Crisis and other events have been scrutinized in debates over the utility of strategic superiority. Schelling's exposition on credibility drew on numerous examples from daily life as well as from instances in international politics.

But in the main, deterrence theory came to be, as George and Smoke and Jervis have argued, essentially ahistorical and nonempirical. It lacked roots in a careful body of findings about the behavior of governments, and rested instead on key simplifying assumptions from which a deductive analysis flowed. This is not difficult to understand if we consider the difficulties that beset efforts to generate such findings, and remember that deterrence theory was attractive because it seemed to offer a way around them.

First is the question whether nuclear weapons make a big difference in the behavior of states. If they do, then the range of past state behavior that can be usefully canvassed is sharply limited. Analysts do not agree on this point, which has discouraged drawing on historical evidence from before 1945 or on cases since then involving states without nuclear weapons. Second is the difficulty of developing an adequate series of deterrence successes and failures for purposes of comparative analysis. It is not easy to identify a clearcut success, for it is always difficult to determine why something, i.e. an attack, did not occur. It is easy to see that when an attack has not occurred it may be for any number of reasons other than the threat of retaliation. Or it may be, indeed it is highly likely, that many factors affect the impact of threats of retaliation, so that a deterrent threat is only partly responsible for a deterrence success. Less well understood is the fact that it is also difficult to determine when deterrence has failed. There is a tendency to treat deterrence as meaning that when a state is militarily strong, other states will avoid doing all sorts of things it doesn't like. A failure of deterrence is then said to exist when it doesn't get its way, not just when it experiences an outright military attack, and this permits the analyst to incorrectly multiply examples of failure for study. Nor can an outright attack, particularly on allies or friends, always be deemed a deterrence failure, for there may have been no serious attempt made to deter it, yet examples of this sort are often cited. (These mistakes in classifying deterrence "successes" and "failures" can be found in Russett, George and Smoke, Organski and Kugler.)

Third, we are obviously, mercifully, lacking in cases of failures of nuclear deterrence. Given the simultaneous difficulty of knowing for sure when nuclear deterrence has been successful, we are left with only indirect ways of detecting its workings for purposes of developing a suitable theory. Obviously, this third problem is simply a combination of the first two, but it helps explain why deterrence theory has such a tenacious grip. Something has to be done about great power war. Nuclear deterrence may be the solution, but we lack conclusive evidence that it is or isn't. Such a situation generates a compelling need for a theory to tell us it is, but that same lack of evidence requires that we take the theory on faith. As many observers have noted, it is indeed a kind of faith complete with zealots, high priests, and the splitting of hairs in highly abstract and abstruse debates (see Fallows).

More progress in grappling with these difficulties might have been made if it had not been for the lure of current national security policy issues. Many academic analysts are now specialists in these issues, and much of their effort has gone into elaborating the ins and outs of policy matters that were currently prominent. Less appealing has been the task of reexamining basic assumptions and images via the careful investigation of state behavior. In effect, academics have been too often engaged in carrying coals to Newcastle, imitating work constantly done in and around the government. Debates about the merits of the MX or the B-1, the exact configuration of the strategic balance, and the like, are undeniably fascinating and not without importance, but they normally take place within settled convictions about how deterrence works. What has been needed is more probing of those convictions.

In particular, we need to contemplate and investigate the distinct possibility that it is not deterrence that induces sufficient restraint in the conflicts of great powers to prevent war, at least not by itself, but that various other factors are critical in establishing a degree of restraint that deterrence does not. Only in this way can we assess with more precision the risks we run in gambling our lives and the civilization on it daily.

In fits and starts we are beginning to do something about this. More scholars are interested in what needs to be done, and they are beginning to develop ways to construct a better picture of deterrence. No comprehensive summary of this work is possible here; instead, there will be a brief review of some interesting recent contributions.

ON THE DEFENDER

Studies of crises and confrontations have broadened our understanding of the difficulties confronting any government that might be attacked and hopes to prevent an attack by deterrence. Classic deterrence theory has had to struggle with the difficulty of making retaliation sufficiently probable in appearance to sustain deterrence. But the complications for the deterrer are more substantial than this.

Alexander George and Richard Smoke have made a major contribution here. Their massive study of American experience with deterrence demonstrates that commitments are often unclear for perfectly understandable reasons once the way a government works is taken into account, that they frequently need clarification and reassessment that becomes the order of the day only after some challenge to them has erupted. Challenges can be designed that work around them and make awkward the selection of a suitable response. Thus, what constitutes an "attack" is fuzzier in practice than one might expect, something the challenger can exploit.

Robert Jervis has summarized a number of findings that bear on the defender's conduct of deterrence. He emphasizes that governments are often a good deal more cautious than deterrence theory suggests, so that "decision makers . . . seem easier to deter than the theory implies" (Jervis 1978: 33). On the other hand, we now know more about how things can go wrong. Deterrence theory calls for governments to be highly capable and alert in assessing situations and developing strategies. Instead deterrers can and do misread their opponents' values and images of reality, misestimate their opponents' capabilities and options, and thus incorrectly or inadvisedly apply deterrence. Also, the pulling and hauling inside the government may block the creation and implementation of a precisely crafted strategy.

There has also been a reconsideration of the concept of a commitment, based on evidence that its credibility rests more on the interests at stake than on the tactics adopted to signal its existence (Huth and Russett), interests that may have little to do with some rational calculus. This makes credibility less subject to precise manipulation than theorists on deterrence have suggested (George and Smoke; Jervis 1978). It is also worrisome because there are signs that governments are not very good at estimating the depth or intensity of opponents' commitments.

On another matter, I have argued elsewhere that it can be hard to detect, and therefore suitably respond to, the onset of a deterrence situation (see Morgan). It can be difficult for leaders to realize or to accept the fact that their society may shortly be attacked, and to do so in time to generate a sufficiently explicit threat of retaliation. This is borne out by investigations of the phenomenon of strategic surprise attack, in which a government is subjected to an unanticipated blow of shocking, often devastating proportions (such as Pearl Harbor, the German attack on Russia in 1941, the 1973 Arab attack on Israel, etc.). Cases of strategic surprise have drawn considerable attention in recent years. (Nearly all the relevant works are cited in Knorr and Morgan.) One reason is that "Of the major wars in Europe, Asia, and the Middle East that have reshaped the international balance of power over the past several decades, most began with sudden attacks" (Betts: 3). Another is that nuclear deterrence is our foremost solution to the problem of strategic surprise.

A striking finding is that the attack has nearly always succeeded in catching the victim unprepared, even though it occurred after a period of crisis and considerable tension. In other words, the victim's leaders had good reason to suspect an attack could occur. On top of this, they usually had information suggesting an attack was imminent. Yet they typically failed to take last-minute precautions or other steps to convey the strongest possible deterrence threats.

Case after case demonstrates the existence of barriers to perceiving the need to attempt, or to bolster, deterrence. Some barriers are created by the attacker's secrecy and deception, while others stem from inconsistencies and ambiguities in available information. But the crucial factors are the erroneous preconceptions and defective cognitive processes of decisionmakers. They think they understand how the opponent sees things, but they don't; they think less of the opponent's military strength and propensity to take risks than they should; they are confident of obtaining ample warning, while misreading what is available. As a result, they don't attempt a last-minute tailoring of their military dispositions and threats.

There is also fear that calling alerts and taking related steps would incite domestic criticism (such as Nixon and Kissinger experienced for their alert in the midst of the Yom Kippur war), and that if this were done too often it would encourage a "cry wolf" attitude that would heighten complacency and diminish alertness. Alerts and mobilizations can also be economically expensive. All this points out that the burdens of practicing deterrence can be substantial enough to discourage attempting it.

This is reinforced when, as is not uncommon, the defender believes an alternative strategy (such as conciliation, negotiations, scrupulous neutrality, etc.) that makes deterrence unnecessary will prevent an attack. Thus victims of strategic surprise are often confident, right up to the day of the attack, that it will never come.

Another aspect is the possibility that a state may mount deterrence threats and bear the related burdens when this is unnecessary. In this case deterrence is illusory, a misperception sustained by a faulty cast of mind. Attention has been given to this in various ways. Robert Jervis outlines two broad images, the deterrence model and the spiral model, which may drive the analyses and policy preferences of officials in international conflicts (Jervis 1976: 59–113). Within the first, the opponent is aggressive, with an appetite for expansion. Therefore he must be confronted with a firm stance and resolve, including the use of threats of a forceful response. Concilia- tion won't work and in fact is counterproductive, encouraging the aggressor to per- sist. In the spiral model, states are caught in a dilemma. They must take steps to protect themselves, but in doing so they appear to each other as threatening, which incites suspicion and mistrust that lead to further efforts to bolster security and invite conflicts to spiral out of control. A conciliatory effort may break through this interac tion, whereas threats designed to intimidate are likely to reinforce it. Glenn Snyder and Paul Diesing draw a similar distinction between "hard-line" and "soft- line" officials (Snyder and Diesing: 297–310).

What if two governments basically satisfied with much of the status quo cannot avoid periodic conflicts and carry into them hard-line images of each other? We would expect even minor clashes to have a tendency to escalate into tests of resolve, with one or the other seeing the need to practice deterrence, although it would nor- mally be unnecessary and inappropriate. And it would appear to work, but suspi- cion and a sense of threat would be pervasive, and concessions would be made only grudgingly. From this experience the necessity for deterrence would appear to be repeatedly confirmed.

Imagine what studies of deterrence might be like in this situation if decision- maker images and the two states' status-quo objectives were not identified as the critical variables. Examination of the historical record would turn up no starkly consistent pattern in supposed deterrence situations. It would therefore be possible to turn out intricate theoretical analyses focusing on threat techniques, signaling strategies, crisis bargaining, and the psychological effects of the military balance. The debates could be endless because there would always be room for skepticism about any of the conclusions reached, and it would never be clear just when the national military posture was adequate. The two states would continue to believe deeply in the necessity for deterrence to regulate their relationship, finding little in their past dealings to sustain any other conclusion.

This hypothetical example resembles the postwar American-Soviet relationship at too many points to be simply rejected out of hand. Those governments watched the collapse of appeasement in the 1930s, which helped stamp their postwar images of interstate relations in the shape of a hard-line deterrence model. Each was forced into the war by a devastating surprise attack, inviting the reliance on deterrence, which they have pursued ever since, to ensure it would never happen again. It is at least possible that their preoccupation with deterrence will someday appear as a tragic interplay of interlocking misperceptions, if we survive long enough for histo- rians to do their work.

This would also help explain why it is not easy to find, by indirect measures, evidence that nuclear deterrence exists and works. For instance, various studies have failed to uncover any clear and consistent relationship between a state's posses- sion of nuclear weapons and its likelihood of prevailing in conflicts and confronta- tions (Kaplan; Blechman and Kaplan; Organski and Kugler). Huth and Russett conclude that even in cases of apparent deterrence success, "only a marginal contribution was made by the possession of nuclear weapons." Another line of inquiry concerns the strategic arms competition. For some time analysts have been suggesting the possibility that no such arms race exists, that superpower defense spending and arms acquisitions are driven not by action-reaction process, but by domestic political and organizational pressures. This has led some analysts to suggest that since "the builders of strategic arms have operated in almost totally closed systems," arms acquisitions have been rationalized as sustaining a deterrence that doesn't exist (Organski and Kugler: 201–2). While the absence of a true arms race, even if conclusively demonstrated, would not prove that nuclear deterrence does not exist, it is nonetheless disturbing. If deterrence depends on states being closely attuned to messages from opponents, anything suggesting that they are not always attentive to what an opponent is up to, or are so only in ways skewed by internal factors, must detract from out confidence in deterrence and complicate our explanation of how it works.

ON THE CHALLENGER

We are beginning to learn more about the behavior of governments who initiate confrontations that can result in war, knowledge that enhances our grasp of how deterrence works and fails. For purposes of illustration we can concentrate on evidence on the impact of various forms of misperception in shaping the onset and course of crisis situations.

One of the findings of Snyder and Diesing is that actors enter into confrontations with fairly elaborate theories about international politics and images of themselves and their opponents. The crisis arises because the two sides' views are divergent and in some ways incorrect. Often the challenger thinks, incorrectly, it can successfully coerce a satisfactory result by pressure.

Cases of strategic surprise also reveal a pattern of misperception on the part of the attackers. Incorrect views are found on such matters of critical importance to deterrence as relative military capabilities, the anticipated outcome of war, and the likelihood war would be necessary (Knorr and Morgan). An investigation of Egyptian decisionmaking during a series of conflicts with Israel, in which Egyptian officials considered initiating a war, finds that those leaders paid limited attention to Israel's interests, had consistent misestimates of the military balance and probable course of hostilities, and "grossly deviated from rational norms in making their decisions about the use of force" (Stein).

Richard Ned Lebow has examined 26 international crises from 1897 to 1967. More than half were "brinkmanship" crises, when one state directly challenged another's commitment. Why they did so is not surprising.

> Perhaps our most striking finding is the extent to which crisis strategies in the cases we studied were based on unrealistic assessments of how adversaries would respond to a challenge. In every instance brinkmanship was predicated upon the belief that the adversary in question would back down when challenged. But this expectation rarely proved justified [Lebow: 270–71].

Just as relevant is his conclusion that such misjudgments often occurred in spite of the available information:

As often as not, it appears, brinkmanship challenges were initiated in the absence of any good evidence suggesting that the adversary lacked the resolve to defend his commitment. In many cases, the available evidence pointed to just the opposite conclusion [Lebow: 93].

We need not conclude that a good approximation of rational decisionmaking is never achieved nor that the initiation of a confrontation or opting to launch an attack is necessarily irrational (see Stein and Tanter, for example). What is clear, however, is that if crises arise in part because of infirmities in governments' grasp on reality, it will not be easy to explain how deterrence works or fails by use of a rational decisionmaker model. We would have to be prepared to assert that once a crisis arrives and deterrence threats are issued, rationality blossoms and dominates the decisions that result, a conclusion that does not fit much of the evidence. That is why I have suggested elsewhere that an appropriate model of the decisionmaking involved should highlight the tendency for many types of governments to be extremely wary in crisis situations and to fear that they are vulnerable to serious errors, as the way to begin to explain how deterrence works when it is successful (Morgan).

Lebow finds that when a state did initiate a brinkmanship crisis, this occurred because its leaders felt a compelling need to change the status quo, because of domestic political pressures and/or perceptions of vital national interests. In this frame of mind leaders were highly likely to misperceive the opponent's commitment, because this clashed with a strong need to see their objectives as readily attainable. Accordingly, they were also prone to excessive confidence—even wishful thinking—as to how a war, if it occurred, would turn out.

With this in mind, deterrence becomes an attempt to put some unpromising students through a crash course on the potential errors of their ways. The potential attacker must learn to see things differently. But "learning during a crisis is likely to be hindered by the same impediments that caused the initiator to midjudge his adversary's resolve in the first place" (Lebow: 272). Janice Stein has derived a broadly similar picture of what makes a challenger hard to constrain successfully via deterrence.

Snyder and Diesing studied more crises that were resolved short of war, so their analysis would lead to more confidence that deterrence can work. They too describe a crisis as a situation in which learning must take place: "Strategy revision is initiated when a massive input of new information breaks through the barrier of the image and makes a decision maker realize that his diagnosis and expectations were somehow radically wrong and must be corrected" (Snyder and Diesing: 397). Yet the chances for such learning are affected by whether the actor is suitably primed for it, by whether the actor is "rational" or "irrational." The first has limited confidence in his initial view of the situation, therefore searches for new information and is receptive to it, and focuses in particular on what the opponent is up to. The second, on the other hand, has a rigid belief system and great confidence that he understands the situation and the opponent. His planned course of action therefore needs little reconsideration. It is not hard to identify the more-promising target for the "massive input of new information" that a deterrence threat is designed to supply.

To this can be added an interesting aspect of many instances of strategic surprise. Political decisionmaking normally is immersed in coalition building, bureaucratic politics, and related processes that tend to rule out radical departures, such as an attack. Nevertheless, cases of strategic surprise have often emerged from a combination of factors that made the attacker something like a unitary decisionmaker. Sometimes a single individual dominated the decision process; on other occasions secrecy severely limited the relevant decisionmakers to a handful of like-minded officials. In a few cases there was a powerful consensus on the diagnosis of the situation, which sharply restricted the chance an alternative policy would be adopted. The result was that normal constraints on the taking of the radical step of initiating war were circumvented and the decision was easier to make (Knorr and Morgan).

This body of evidence challenges a core assumption in the theory and practice of deterrence. Earlier, reference was made to the great caution and prudence nuclear powers have displayed in the postwar era. What is the connection between this and nuclear weapons? Are the latter responsible for the former? Numerous observers assert that they are (see, for instance Martin; Mandelbaum; Brodie; and Waltz). While there is undoubtedly something to this, it seems quite likely that to a significant degree the relationship also runs in the opposite direction, and that it is because the governments of great states in the postwar period have been prudent that deterrence with nuclear weapons has appeared to work as well as it has. From this perspective it is wise to conclude that "peace will depend, as much or more than it does on mutual deterrence, on the ability of the superpowers to avoid or control crises" (Bull: 18) because that is an excellent index of their continuing prudence. Governments so lacking in caution as to permit a serious deterioration in their relations would simultaneously put the reliability of deterrence in doubt:

> What is often forgotten in strategic studies . . . is that the balance of terror rests upon a particular arrangement of political relations as much as on the quality and quantity of the respective nuclear arsenals. Movements in these political relations could prove far more disturbing to nuclear stability than any movements of purely military factors [Freedman: 399].

What sustains this prudence of great states, their ability to avoid or control crises and maintain the stability of their political relationships? If states often blunder, miscalculate, and grope about blindly, and if this means that deterrence cannot be readily relied upon to work, then why haven't we had a third world war? This calls for brief speculation about yet another line of inquiry that is just getting under way. The classical theory and the practice of deterrence have been ahistorical not only in the sense referred to earlier, but also in ignoring the possibility that the incidence of great power wars depends on the development and configuration of the global political system. That system may pass through phases in which such wars are very likely because political relationships decay and deadly crises abound, and other phases in which those wars are highly unlikely. We may have been living, since 1945, in a favorable phase, when the exhaustion of the war and the relative satisfaction with the resulting distribution of territory, power, and status kept great power competition well below the level of war. This would mean we have been practicing deterrence in an era when it was unlikely to have been really put to the test. It would also mean that we need to do something to reduce our reliance on it before this era passes (Modelski and Morgan).

CONCLUSION

It is unfortunate that heavy reliance on deterrence in the contemporary international system is a self-sustaining, self-reinforcing phenomenon, particularly where nuclear weapons are concerned. It induces concerns over demonstrating resolve and not appearing to be weak that undermine attention to opportunities for negotiation and the settlement of outstanding issues. It incites vertical proliferation because of a persistent fear that war-fighting capabilities and options will be necessary both to make it work and if it fails. It converts arms limitation efforts into contests to secure the best relative military posture vis-à-vis the opponent, while strongly encouraging steps that design around or negate any limitations achieved.

This means it is not enough to enlarge our understanding of how deterrence works so as to proceed to suggestions that other resources of statecraft be given their day. Effort must go into investigating how states might break out of self-sustaining deterrence relationships, thereby building a bridge between deterrence theory and the use of other methods for preventing great power wars.

REFERENCES

Betts, Richard. 1982. *Surprise Attack.* Washington: Brookings Institution.

Blechman, Barry, and Stephen Kaplan. 1978. *Force Without War.* Washington: Brookings Institution.

Brodie, Bernard. 1978. "The Development of Nuclear Strategy." *International Security* 2, 1981. no. 4 (Spring): 65–83.

Bull, Hedley. 1981. "Future Conditions of Strategic Deterrence." In *The Future of Strategic Deterrence,* ed. Christoph Bertram. London: Macmillan. Pp. 13–23.

Bundy, McGeorge. 1981. "The Future of Strategic Deterrence." In *Strategic Deterrence in a Changing Environment,* ed. Christoph Bertram. Montclair, NJ: Allanheld, Osmun. Pp. 111–15.

Comparative Strategy 2, no. 1 (1980).

Dupuy, Trevor, and Guy Hammerman, eds. 1973. *A Documentary History of Arms Control and Disarmament.* New York: R.R. Bowker.

Fallows, James. 1981. *National Defence.* New York: Random House. Pp. 139–70.

Freedman, Lawrence. 1981. *The Evolution of Nuclear Strategy.* New York: St. Martin's Press.

Friedberg, Aaron. 1981. "A History of the U.S. Strategic 'Doctrine'–1945 to 1980." In *Strategy and the Social Sciences,* ed. Amos Perlmutter and John Gooch. London: Frank Cass. Pp. 37–71.

Gaddis, John. 1982. *Strategies of Containment.* New York: Oxford University Press.

George, Alexander, and Richard Smoke. 1974. *Deterrence in American Foreign Policy: Theory and Practice.* New York: Columbia University Press.

Gray, Colin. 1980. "Strategic Stability Reconsidered." *Daedalus* 109, no. 4 (Fall): 135–54.

Green, Phillip. 1973. "Strategy, Politics, and Social Scientists." In *Strategic Thinking and Its Moral Implications,* ed. Morton Kaplan. Chicago: University of Chicago Center for Policy Study. Pp. 38–69.

Hoeber, Amoretta. 1979. *Soviet Strategy For Nuclear War.* Stanford: Hoover Institution Press.

Huth, Paul, and Bruce Russett. Forthcoming. "What Makes Deterrence Work? Cases From 1900 to 1980." *World Politics.*

Jervis, Robert. 1976. *Perception and Misperception in International Politics.* Princeton: Princeton University Press.

_____. 1979. "Deterrence Theory Revisited." *World Politics* 31, no. 2.

Kaplan, Stephen. 1981. *Diplomacy of Power.* Washington: Brookings Institution.

Kennan, George. 1983. *The Nuclear Delusion.* Rev. ed. New York: Pantheon Books.

Kissinger, Henry. 1981. "NATO: The Next Thirty Years." In *Strategic Deterrence in a Changing Environment,* ed. Christoph Bertram. Montclair, NJ: Allanheld, Osmun. Pp. 107–11.

_____. 1982. "Strategy and the Atlantic Alliance." *Survival* 24, no. 5 (September–October).

Knorr, Klaus, and Patrick Morgan, eds. 1983. *Strategic Military Surprise.* New Brunswick, NJ: Transaction Books.

Leebaert, Derek, ed. 1981. *Soviety Military Thinking.* London: George Allen and Unwin.

Lodal, Jan. 1980. "Deterrence and Nuclear Strategy." *Daedalus* 109, no. 4 (Fall).

Martin, Laurence. 1979. "The Role of Military Force in the Nuclear Age." In *Strategic Thought in the Nuclear Age,* ed. Martin. Baltimore: Johns Hopkins University Press. Pp. 1–30.

Mandelbaum, Michael. 1979. *The Nuclear Question.* New York: Cambridge University Press.

Mearsheimer, John. 1983. *Conventional Deterrence.* Ithaca: Cornell University Press.

Modelski, George, and Patrick Morgan. Forthcoming. "Understanding Global War." *Journal of Conflict Resolution.*

Morgan, Patrick. 1983. *Deterrence, A Conceptual Analysis,* second edition. Beverly Hills: Sage Publications.

Organski, A.F.K., and Jacek Lugler. 1980. *The War Ledger.* Chicago: University of Chicago Press.

Rapoport, Anatol. 1972. "Can Peace Research be Applied?" In *Disarmament and Arms Control,* ed. Frank Barnaby and Carlo Schaerf. New York: Gordon and Breach Science Publishers. Pp. 391–404.

Russett, Bruce. 1963. "The Calculus of Deterrence." *Journal of Conflict Resolution* 7 (March): 97–109.

Sherwin, Martin. 1977. *A World Destroyed.* New York: Vintage Books.

Stein, Janice Gross. Forthcoming. "Calculation, Miscalculation, and Conventional Deterrence: The View From Cairo." In *Psychology and Deterrence,* ed. Robert Jervis, Richard Ned Lebow and Janice Gross Stein. Baltimore: Johns Hopkins University Press.

Stein, Janice Gross, and Raymond Tanter. 1980. *Rational Decision Making: Israel's Security Choices 1967.* Columbus: Ohio State University Press.

Thompson, W. Scott, ed. 1980. *From Weakness to Strength.* San Francisco: Institute For Contemporary Studies.

Tillema, Herbert, and John Van Wingen. 1982. "Law and Power in Military Intervention." *International Studies Quarterly* 26, no. 2 (June): 220–50.

Tuchman, Barbara. 1962. *The Guns of August.* New York: Dell Publishing.

Wainstein, Leonard. 1971. "The Dreadnought Gap." In *The Use of Force,* ed. Robert Art and Kenneth Waltz. Boston: Little Brown. Pp. 153–69.

Waltz, Kenneth. 1981. "The Spread of Nuclear Weapons: More May Be Better." *Adelphi Papers.* London: Institute for Strategic Studies.

9
CREDIBILITY AND BLUFF

John Hare

This essay will look at the suggestion that nuclear deterrence works by bluff; it will examine the connections between bluff and credibility; and it will conclude with a discussion of the difference it makes to the moral assessment of deterrence whether it works by bluff or not.[1]

A bluff is a threat not accompanied by the conditional intention to carry out the threat if the threat fails.[2] It may be of two types: either accompanied by the intention not to carry out the threat, or not accompanied by a conditional intention one way or the other. I may threaten my son that if he spills the milk one more time, he will be sent to his room, and I may intend to send him to his room if he spills his milk; that is not a bluff. But I may also have resigned myself to tolerating spilt milk again without punishing him, or I may not yet have made up my mind whether to punish him. In both these last two cases I hope that merely issuing the threat will be sufficient to deter him.[3] In the nuclear case, we will consider the claim that deterrence works by bluff of the second type. The first type is unlikely here; probably those who issue the nuclear threats have at least left open the decision about nuclear use. The second type of bluff requires only that they have not yet decided whether they would indeed carry out their threats.

It is true that the nuclear powers try to indicate periodically that they do have the intention to carry out their nuclear threats. For example, Khrushchev declared during the Cuban Missile Crisis that the United States was pushing mankind "to the abyss of a world missile-nuclear war" and that if any effort to stop Soviet ships were to be made, "we would be forced for our part to take the measures which we deem necessary and adequate in order to protect our rights. For this we have all that is necessary." Kennedy declared, "It shall be the policy of this nation to regard any nuclear missile launched from Cuba against any nation in the Western Hemisphere as an attack by the Soviet Union on the United States, requiring a full retaliatory response upon the Soviet Union." But these sorts of declarations, and international political rhetoric in general, have to be seen as instruments of policy. One can sometimes learn from a government's statements what it wants its intended audience to hear, although this is not straightforward. But one cannot often learn what the intentions of the government in fact are.

It may be argued that a strategy of bluff is possible only theoretically; that in practice those with the final decision must, when they come into office, think through the options and decide when they would authorize nuclear use. It is certainly hard to believe they would be able to make these decisions from scratch at the last moment, given the short time available for decision once nuclear use by either side has started. But there are three responses to this argument. First, from the historical record. The private presidential papers of those presidents of the United States in the nuclear age whose papers are now public reveal that not one of them had firmly made up his mind under what conditions to authorize massive retaliation. Eisenhower, for example, although pressed to make this decision several times, steadfastly refused. Kennedy, during the Cuban Missile Crisis, was constantly aware of the danger that nuclear weapons might be used, but does not appear to have decided under what conditions he would use them. His actions were motivated in part by the desire to *avoid* the necessity of making such a decision. One reason he decided against an air strike on Cuba was that if the Soviet Union answered by attacking Turkey, he would then have to decide whether he would order the use of nuclear weapons against the Soviet Union.[4] It is reported of Carter that when Brzezinski brought him examples of scenarios for nuclear use, he refused to settle the question of which scenarios would lead him to authorize the use of the weapons.

The second response is that conditional intentions are rare in politics much before an action actually has to be taken. Members of Congress, for example, if they know an issue well and have voted on it several times before, may know in advance which way to vote the next time around. But if the issue is a new one, and especially if it is new and momentous, the politician will often leave the decision until the last possible moment.[5] This is partly because of a desire to leave options open and preserve flexibility; partly it is due to a recognition that the nature of the choice depends on the immediate political environment, and this can change radically in a short period of time. What a politician *will* often want to know in advance is what the options are, and what the arguments and evidence are in favor of each option. This is why Carter had his national security advisor prepare the scenarios for nuclear use.

It is hard to know what a conditional intention for an institution like a government amounts to.[6] It is hard enough to know this for an individual. For example, the announcement that the United States would leave UNESCO in a year was accompanied by signals that this result could be forestalled if certain conditions were met. It is difficult to say if the United States' government had in fact formed the conditional intention to leave. A year was more than enough time for changes both at UNESCO and in the U.S. government. These changes were not predictable enough to allow much firmness in a decision one year ahead. The point is that the declaration of the intention is an instrument of policy, designed to secure certain kinds of political change, whether the conditional intention that is "declared" is in fact present or not.

The third response is that the strategic doctrine of both superpowers, insofar as this is public, rules out launch-on-warning or launch-under-attack. Indeed, one of the arguments made by the Soviets against the installation of Pershing II missiles in West Germany was that this would force them to move towards these strategic options. It has been argued that neither side would in fact ride out an attack before deciding whether or how to respond; but this is nonetheless the present doctrine. The reason for the doctrine is to allow a decision to be made on the basis of sufficient evidence, and not to leave it to the computers. This suggests, although it does not imply, that the decision has not already been firmly made under what conditions to launch a retaliatory response.

It may also be argued that nuclear bluff could not be credible. Certainly a strategy of bluff would not be adopted if it made it impossible to issue a credible deterrent threat. How, then, is the credibility of a threat to be measured? We can take the credibility of a deterrent military threat as dependent upon two variables--the relative military capabilities of the parties and the relative size of the stakes at issue between them.[7] If one country is to find the threat by another country credible, it must believe first that the second country has available the force it is threatening to use and, second, that this force might be judged by the second country appropriate to the value it attaches to the object at stake. The crisis over Hungary and the Cuban Missile Crisis provide interesting examples. In the case of Hungary, the Soviet Union faced the possible collapse of its inner ring of defenses just as the United States did in Cuba. The Soviet Union was as far in advance of the United States in local conventional capacity in Hungary as the United States was in advance of the Soviet Union in Cuba. It is significant that the United States did not threaten to use nuclear weapons against Soviet cities in the Hungarian crisis, although the administration was under pressure to do so, but it felt free to do so in the Cuban crisis. This difference is explicable in terms of the above analysis of credibility. A threat by the United States over Cuba was credible, whereas a threat over Hungary would not have been.

A distinction can be made between different levels of stakes. We can call "marginal" those stakes that pose the possibility of gains and losses but do not involve a hierarchical shift in the international system,[8] "landslide" those stakes that do not pose the danger of a hierarchical shift, and "survival" those stakes that threaten the very survival of a nation as a nation. Hungary and Cuba represented stakes in the intermediate or "landslide" range. Their importance was such that a defeat for the Soviet Union in the first case or for the United States in the second could have seriously disrupted the balance of power.

We might plot a graph with levels of force on the vertical axis and the size of stakes at issue on the horizontal. On the vertical axis the range would be from conventional force at the bottom, through chemical weapons, tactical and strategic nuclear weapons, to the entire arsenal of the superpowers at the top. On the horizontal axis, the range would be from marginal stakes, through landslide stakes, to survival stakes. A threat by the United States to use a certian level of force will be maximally credible relative to a certain size of stake. We might then plot a threat credibility curve (strictly, a cumulative probability distribution curve) that would probably be an S-shape: it would show a gradual rise as force was threatened in response to Soviet activity in Angola or Yemen, then a steep rise through attacks on members of NATO, especially if United States' troops were involved, and it would flatten out at the top over attacks on Minutemen or on U.S. cities. The threat to use the entire arsenal is not likely to be maximally credible even for the highest stakes, because of the possible stake in preserving "intra-war" deterrence.

This analysis of credibility sheds light on the difference between a strategy of bluff and a strategy of "simple deceit."[9] The pretense that there is an irrevocable commitment to retaliate, as with a "doomsday machine," or that one has lost all control over the final outcome, is a strategy of simple deceit.[10] It will not be easy to secure credibility for threats issued on this strategy. The purpose of pretending to make an irrevocable commitment, or pretending to give up final control, would be to enhance in the eyes of one's opponent the value one attributes to some object. But it will not be worth trying to do this for stakes such as national survival that it might be rational to *decide* to defend with maximum force. For the value of national survival is not enhanced in this way. But if our account of credibility is correct, any expression of an irrevocable commitment to defend with a level of force an object one would *not* have chosen to defend with that level of force is not likely to be believed. The opponent will be more likely to see through the "simple deceit" and suppose that one has retained control of the final decision while pretending to abandon it.

One policy implication of this analysis of credibility is that it is necessary to have available all the levels of force appropriate to the stakes for which one wants to be able to issue deterrent threats. This is not the place to try to analyze what these stakes are, but an argument can be made for parity at each level of force.[11] This would involve a country having available to it, or to its allies, the force at each level to counter the force available to its enemies. This is necessary if the country is to have the flexibility to make deterrent threats credible in relation to the whole range of stakes at issue with its opponents. If a country or an alliance does not have available to it, for example, conventional forces of sufficient size and scope to counter the conventional forces of its opponents, it will be forced either to escalate or to surrender in the face of a full-scale conventional attack.

The debate centers most often around the forces in Europe. it is a controversial question whether at the moment of NATO conventional forces do have parity. The conclusion of the specialists seems to be that there is some inferiority, but the overall conventional balance still makes military aggression unattractive.[12] This means, in effect, that the choice has been made not to put exclusive reliance on the threat of nuclear use. This is a change in emphasis from the interpretation of "extended deterrence" that minimized conventional forces in Europe during a time of western strategic superiority, and relied on the threat of immediate escalation. Moreover, a consensus is emerging that it would be desirable to rely less on the nuclear threat than NATO currently does, even though there is no consensus yet on how much more expensive it would be to rely on a conventional reponse to conventional attack, or on whether this additional expense is affordable.

The connection of our analysis of credibility with bluff is that neither of the two variables by which credibility is measured requires an intention to carry out the threat in the threatened circumstances.[13] Credibility, that is to say, may be independent of this sort of intention. Each side in a dispute measures the credibility of the other's threats by assessing the availability of the threatened force and the importance of the stake at issue to the other side. Deterrence can work as long as the judgment can be made that the threatener might choose to carry out the threat, since the force is available to him and it is appropriate to the size of the stake.

As stated earlier, there are two types of bluff. If an intention has been formed not to carry out the threat (the first type), this intention will in some cases be hard to keep invisible. The argument might be made that this kind of secrecy is possible in closed totalitarian societies, but not in open democracies. But the important case to consider for nuclear deterrence is the second type. Our analysis of credibility suggests that the absence of a visible conditional intention to carry out the threat does not significantly affect credibility. This may be clarified by a nonnuclear example. President Reagan has refused to rule out the use of U.S. military force in Nicaragua (leaving aside the question of covert activity). At the same time he has denied that there is currently any intention to use such force. The explicit refusal to rule out force is an instrument of policy, posing an implicit threat to the Sandinista government of invasion under unspecified circumstances. An astute observer of the political scene in the United States could determine that the mood in Congress and in the Pentagon is highly averse to such force being used, under present circumstances. But the Sandinistas claim, nonetheless, to fear invasion. The point is that the administration's intentions in this matter are invisible. But the force is available for an invasion of Nicaragua, and the Sandinistas have no doubt tried to calculate how large a stake Nicaragua represents to the administration. After Grenada, in particular, there is a credible threat to use force against Nicaragua under certain conditions (perhaps a Nicaraguan invasion of Honduras). The relevance of Grenada is that a certain level of force was deemed appropriate by the current administration to a certain size of stake in the region. Because the level of force would have to be greater in Nicaragua, the stake would have to be higher, but it is not inconceivable that it could become high enough. The Sandinistas need to assess not so much whether there is now a conditional intention to carry out an extremely vague threat, but whether (if the situation changes in certain ways) the mood in Washington might change, and a decision might be taken to authorize the use of force. What this example shows is that the conditional intention about what to do given, for example, a Nicaraguan invasion of Honduras is either not present, or is at least successfully hidden. Some members of the government or the Congress may be convinced that a counterinvasion of Nicaragua would be disastrous. On the other hand, contingency plans for such a course of action may well have been drawn up. But the government itself can hardly be said to have a conditional intention for this case, or at least to have one that is at all perspicuous. Threats here rely for their credibility not on this sort of conditional intention, but on the Sandinistas' assessment of the force available and the size of the stake to the current U.S. government.

The nuclear case is similar in that no one intends to use the weapons under current circumstances. The question is whether there is now a conditional intention to use them under any foreseeable circumstances. If a president and his advisors wanted to preserve deterrence and had decided not to use nuclear weapons under any circumstances, they would have to hide this from Congress and the American people as well as from the Soviet Union. But the case is different if there is no conditional intention one way or the other. Congress, the American people, and the Soviet Union will in any case be uncertain about the government's declarations of intention in this matter. Such declarations are known to be a necessary part of nuclear deterrence whether or not they are accompanied by the intentions they "declare." But this recognition does not destroy the effectiveness of deterrence. What makes the deterrent work is the residual uncertainty created by the mere existence of the weapons, coupled with the possibility that the stake might be high enough for a decision to be taken to use them.

How does this affect the moral assessment of deterrence? This analysis forestalls one form of attack.[14] Suppose it is assumed that no nuclear use can be morally justified (a large assumption, which will not be defended or attacked in this essay). Suppose it is also granted that whatever is wrong to do is also wrong to intend to do. Suppose, finally, it is agreed that a successful nuclear deterrence policy requires the intention to use the nuclear weapons under certain conditions (contrary to the argument of this essay). An argument can be made from these three premises that nuclear deterrence cannot be morally justified. But if we are correct, even if the first two premises are granted, the third can be denied. The possession of nuclear weapons, the issuing of implicit and explicit threats, and the training of personnel to "man" the deterrent may all be parts of the implementation of a strategy of bluff; they do not need to involve any conditional intention to use weapons.

There are at least three objections to this response. The first has been referred to elsewhere as "the objection from the rank and file."[15] Suppose it is true that the government of the United States has not formed a conditional intention to bomb Soviet cities, for example, in retaliation for an attack on American cities. Nonetheless, thousands of men and women in the armed forces have to be prepared to carry out the orders that would result in an attack on Soviet cities if the United States were engaged in the implementation of a strategy of use and not of bluff.[16] Is it not true that those "manning" the deterrent must have formed a conditional intention to fire the missiles, if so ordered? If so, a strategy of bluff may release the top military commanders from immoral intentions (granting that the intention to retaliate is immoral), while at the same time requiring these immoral intentions of the rank and file. For if it is immoral to intend massive retaliation, it is surely immoral to intend to carry it out if so ordered.

I know of no completely satisfactory rejoinder to this objection (to this reponse to this attack on deterrence). A partial rejoinder is that most of those "manning" the deterrent will not be in a position to know whether in obeying orders, through all the stages of alert, they are implementing a strategy of threat or of actual use. It would be morally preferable if the maker of the threat could be known to be the one who would eventually have to carry it out. Developments in communications technology have made this increasingly possible by allowing the centralization of command and control mechanisms. If this were possible, a satisfactory rejoinder would be available. Each of the innumerable antecedent decisions necessary for the use of the weapon could be taken in good faith by a member of the armed forces who supported a policy of threat, but not of use. But if there must be individuals (like the crew of the Enola Gay) who both know they are taking the last and irreversible step and who are not originators of the policy, then they are indeed being asked, for the sake of effective deterrence, to form the intention to obey immoral orders (again granting that these orders are immoral).[17] This is one moral cost of nuclear deterrence, even if deterrence is explained in terms of a strategy of bluff.

There are other such costs. The second objection is that the threat of nuclear warfare is immoral in itself, whether or not it is accompanied by the conditional intention to use the weapons. Many reasons could be given in support of this view, but I will mention only four. The point is that nuclear deterrence could still be deeply objectionable even if it is analyzed as a strategy of bluff.[18] First, there is the constant possibility that the threat may be carried out by miscalculation, accident, or madness. Second, the longer we rely on the deterrent, the more we become used to the idea of the destruction we are threatening against others and in the end against ourselves; we become dangerously less ready to move decisively toward arms control and disarmament. Third, the whole world has to live under the shadow of the possible destruction of civilization as we know it. Fourth, the maintenance of a credible deterrent threat requires diverting essential resources from meeting basic human needs.[19]

The third objection is that even if the nuclear threat is not necessarily accompanied by a conditional intention to use the weapons, the threat to use them still makes their use more likely.[20] But if it is wrong to do something, it is also wrong to make it more probable that one will do it. If it is wrong to intend to do something, then it is wrong to make it more likely that one will form the intention to do it. The development of the first atom bomb is instructive here. When Einstein and others first pressed for it, they feared that the Germans would develop the bomb first. But in the period from 1942 to 1945, it seems to have become accepted by almost everyone in a position of authority that the bomb would actually be used by the Allies if it were developed in time. Thus the work at Los Alamos went on at full speed even after the discovery that the Germans had not, in fact, been nearly as close as had been assumed. World War II saw the progression from Guernica to Warsaw and Rotterdam, Hamburg and Dresden, Tokyo, and then Hiroshima and Nagasaki. Moral sensibilities became progressively blunted as the war progressed and the technology developed.

There is no proof that new weapons will inevitably be used, only the fact that new weapons have usually been used sooner or later. In addition to the history of the first atom bomb (which is perhaps a bad example because the United States was engaged in a world war), there is the fear that the arms race is producing weapons that themselves make it much harder to keep deterrence stable (because they put a premium on preemptive use). There is also the fear that deterrence leads to the proliferation of nuclear weapons into less reliable hands. In any case, the assessment that nuclear states are in the end likely to use the weapons if they are available changes the moral calculation about deterrence. For if the assessment is that the system of mutual deterrence is likely to break down anyway, it is rational to risk more radical measures to dismantle the system before this happens. If the assessment is that deterrence has a good chance of remaining stable for the foreseeable future, this dismantling is less urgent.

It is not the purpose of this essay to discuss the empirical question of which of these two assessments is more likely to be right. But it is important to see that the moral assessment of deterrence depends (among other things) on how likely deterrence is to remain stable. This in turn depends on particular policies of particular governments. Deterrence therefore has to be evaluated morally in the light of its current political context. By the nature of politics, no exact possibilities can be attached here, but it can be argued that certain policies move deterrence toward stability and others move it toward breakdown. Emphasizing invulnerability, deemphasizing first-strike capability, and pushing for a comprehensive test ban treaty are policies likely to decrease the chances that anyone will use nuclear weapons. The connection with credibility is that they tend to increase the size of stake required for a credible nuclear threat in the eyes of one's opponents. On the other hand, emphasizing worst-case scenarios in procurement decisions, deploying systems with the rationale of prevailing in a nuclear war, and constantly expanding the areas of "vital national interest" are policies that tend to increase the chances of breakdown. They tend to decrease the size of stake required for a credible nuclear threat by one's own side. Lists like these tend to sound partisan, and the arguments for these conclusions have not been given. But such lists do illustrate one reason why our moral feelings about deterrence tend to be ambiguous. Unless we take the position that deterrence is immoral if there is any risk of breakdown at all (or that it is moral whatever the chances of breakdown), our moral assessment will vary with the continual and ambiguous shifts in government policy.

Because the policies just referred to need involve only capabilities and stakes, they can shift without requiring changes in conditional intention about nuclear use.

This suggests that conditional intentions may be relatively unimportant not only for credibility, but for the moral assessment of deterrence as well.

NOTES

1. Some of the argument will be taken from J.E. Hare and Carey B. Joynt, *Ethics and International Affairs* (London: Macmillan & Co., 1982), esp. pp. 101–24.
2. A conditional intention is an intention to do something given certain conditions, e.g., the failure of a threat.
3. See note 13. Barrie Paskins and Michael Dockrill, *The Ethics of War* (Minneapolis: University of Minnesota Press, 1979), pp. 236–44, claim that "bluff" cannot be used for the situation where no intention has yet been formed to carry out the threat or not to carry it out. This claim does not seem to be consistent with ordinary usage, in poker, for example, or with the dictionaries. But even if they are right about the word, the case of threatening without yet having formed a conditional intention whether or not to carry out the threat will be important for the analysis of deterrence.
4 Robert F. Kennedy, *Thirteen Days* (NY: W.W. Norton, 1969), p. 96.
5. It is dangerous to generalize in this way about politicians. Some are notorious for making up their minds in advance about what they are going to do and sticking to it, come what may.
6. We can say at least that a government can be responsible for its actions and hence can act intentionally. But the "intentions" here may not be independent of the actions. Thus, a government can issue a threat intentionally, but the intention here is the intention to issue the threat, not the intention to carry it out if the threat fails.
7. Carey B. Joynt, "The Anatomy of Crises," *The Year Book of World Affairs*, vol. 28 (London, 1974), pp. 15-22: and Hare and Joynt, *Ethics and International Affairs*, pp. 118–20.
8. For the concept of a hierarchical ranking, see G. Schwarzenberger, *Power Politics* (London: Stevens, 1951), chaps. 6 and 7.
9. "Simple deceit" is J.S. Maxwell's term. See Paskins and Dockrill, *The Ethics of War*, p. 211.
10. One of T.C. Schelling's suggestions was to delegate decisions about nuclear use to junior officers so as to increase the uncertainty faced by one's opponent. See his *The Strategy of Conflict* (Cambridge: Harvard University Press, 1960), pp. 261ff.
11. This essay attempts no precision about how the continuum of force should be split up into different levels.
12. *The Military Balance, 1982–1983* (London: International Institute for Strategic Studies, 1983).
13. If an intention is apparent, it may be relevant to credibility. This is probably the case with the child spilling the milk, which is why bluff is not encouraged in child-raising manuals. The child will know his parent well enough to know when the threat is a bluff, and even which type of bluff it is. But the argument of this chapter is that visible intentions are not necessary for credibility of military deterrent threats, even though governments have to "display" their intentions and "demonstrate" their resolve.

14. Gregory Kavka analyzes this form attack in "Some Paradoxes of Deterrence," *The Journal of Philosophy* 75, no. 6 (June 1978): 285–302. David Hoekema responds in "Intentions, Threats, and Nuclear Deterrence" in *The Applied Turn in Contemporary Philosophy, Bowling Green Studies in Applied Philosophy,* vol. 5(1983), ed. Michael Bradie et al. Because the Roman Catholic bishops did not consider the connection of deterrence and bluff in their pastoral letter, their conditional acceptance of deterrence is liable to this attack. See J.E. Hare, "Threats and Intentions" in *Evangelicals and the Bishops' Pastoral Letter* (Grand Rapids, MI: William B. Eerdmans Publ., 1984).
15. Hare and Joynt, *Ethics and International Affairs*, pp. 110–12.
16. Michael Walzer says that deterrence requires "thousands of men trained in the techniques of mass destruction and drilled in instant obedience" in *Just and Unjust Wars* (New York: Basic Books, 1977), p. 272.
17. It may be argued that the American armed forces, like the West German, have manuals that include an explicit instruction that all commands be evaluated morally before they are carried out. But in practice this will not often be done, and the system of military training and discipline is designed to encourage that it not be done. It is probably unrealistic to expect any widespread independence of mind in the matter of obedience to orders in an effective military force.
18. Any thoughtful proponent of deterrence is likely to have replies to each one. For instance, the danger of the use of nuclear weapons is decreased if both parties possess them, given that the only use so far has been against a nonnuclear power; popular commitment to arms controls seems to go in cycles, being higher now than it was five years ago; the shadow of the destruction of civilization is real, but so is the shadow of the destruction of the freedoms that are the fruits of that civilization; and an effective conventional deterrent, e.g., for Western Europe, would be more expensive than the present nuclear deterrent. The point is that none of these arguments is affected by whether or not deterrence is correctly analyzed in terms of bluff.
19. There are many such lists: e.g., Hedley Bull, *The Anarchical Society* (New York: Columbia University Press, 1977), pp. 124–26.
20. This is David Hoekema's point in "Intentions, Threats, and Nuclear Deterrence."

10
RISKING ARMAGEDDON

Russell Hardin

Moral concern with nuclear arms, like prudential concern, is primarily a concern with objective consequences and their risks. One cannot contribute much to the debate on the issue without addressing and assessing these consequences. The chief difficulty is their peculiarly subjective quality: they depend on what relevant decisionmakers think them to be. A large part of the complexity of the nuclear arms conflict, therefore, is that opposing leaders manipulate and otherwise affect each other's perceptions of risks. This is an inherent part of strategic interactions that are more complex than straightforward, pure conflicts.

To keep the issues clear, it is best to put them into the analytical framework for analyzing strategic interactions: game theory. Unfortunately, however, game thinking on these issues is often deceptively muddled. I wish here to set out the relevant game analysis of the strategic structure of the problem of nuclear arms, to relate it to the risks we face, and to relate both the game analysis and the risks to the morality of various arms policies.

The principal policies to be discussed are continuation of the present regime of high-level innovative armament, unilateral disarmament, and mutual disarmament (or arms reduction) down to levels of minimal deterrence. A further policy that is often posed as the moral ideal is complete mutual disarmament. Under present conditions I think this policy is not credible, and I will therefore discuss it only briefly. In general when I speak of mutual disarmament I will mean disarmament only down to minimal deterrence levels.

The positions most commonly held by moral philosophers in recent debates on nuclear arms fall into deontological and utilitarian classes. Deontologists generally conclude that the use of nuclear weapons is in principle wrong because many innocents would be killed. Utilitarians argue that the policy is best that entails the fewest expected deaths. They conclude that either unilateral disarmament or continued deterrence is right, depending on their account, often from stylized facts, of which

This essay has benefited from extensive commentaries by Avner Cohen, Steven Lee, and Henry Shue; and from a presentation by Professor Joseph V. Smith of the University of Chicago, "The Climatological Effects of Nuclear Explosions," to the Ethics and Politics of Arms Control Seminar of the American Academy of Arts and Sciences, Midwest Center, University of Chicago.

policy has the least grisly implications. My purpose here is to contribute to the utilitarian understanding of nuclear weapons policies. The issue therefore is whether unilateral disarmament, mutual disarmament, or continuing the present dynamic regime would have the best consequences.

Methodologically, to answer this utilitarian moral question requires the kind of analysis required to answer the prudential question whether the Soviet Union or the United States should disarm unilaterally or strive for mutual arms reductions. We may all agree that nuclear war would be worse than anything it was meant to accomplish or to avoid. And yet we may still disagree about the value of nuclear deterrence. Among the reasons for disagreement are different counterfactual assumptions from which we may argue.

This essay will discuss the plausible strategic structures of the problem of nuclear arms; the risks of the policies of unilateral disarmament, mutual disarmament, and continuing the present regime; other risks that might influence our moral choice of policy; and certain logical and moral objections to deterrence.

First, however, a few remarks on the confusions of game analyses of these issues may prevent misunderstanding. It is usual to simplify available strategies to a tractably small number, most often to two. In the games in Table 10.1, each superpower can choose to arm (A) or disarm (D). The United States is the row player, and the Soviet Union is the column player. The payoffs are ordinal for each player from most preferred (1) to least preferred (4). The first payoff in each cell is to the row player and the second to the column.

Aside from reducing the range of strategies, these games simplify the situation by supposing that each side has only one move. In real life the United States has thousands of relevant strategy choices (e.g., whether to add one more weapon to an existing complement). It also has a long sequence of moves (in 1983, for example, the United States began to deploy Pershing II and cruise missiles in Europe). We can generally correct for both these simplifications if we are attentive to them. The one to which analysts tend to be less attentive is the reduction of all moves over a long period into a single move. In general, if approximately the same situation faces us repeatedly, we can analyze the problem as an iterated game, for which the extant understanding is often very good, and for which the recommended solution may be quite different from that for the relevant single-play game.

The most grievous problem in the game representation of Table 10.1, however, is the determination of the payoffs. The strategy choices are whether to arm or to disarm. The payoffs are not clearly chosen in any meaningful sense: they are how many lives one loses or, rather, how many one can expect to lose in each given outcome. Unfortunately, how many lives one expects to lose in a particular joint choice of strategies is a function of choices one expects the other side to make, given that preliminary choice of strategies. Hence, the payoffs are inherently tied to the subjectivity noted above. Being mutually armed is risky—and hence costly—if we think it is. To stipulate payoffs in the game without bringing in this subjectivity would be wrong-headed.

Note that this problem of subjectivity is not merely that of the subjectivity of preferences. In the latter, I prefer oranges to apples, while you prefer apples to oranges. For the present analysis we may crudely suppose that if either side's objective expected payoffs were given, that side's preference ordering over those payoffs would be fairly easy to assess, because it prefers fewer expected deaths to more.

The subjectivity here is that the expected payoffs are not objectively ascertainable apart from the subjective intentions and beliefs of relevant parties on both sides.

One final note on the games that follow. In the matrices the disarmament strategy (D) means different things depending on whether the other side is also disarmed. If one side is disarmed while the other is heavily armed, the former will want to be demonstrably completely disarmed. If both sides are disarmed, both will want to maintain a modest force for minimal deterrence. Hence, again, mutual disarmament is disarmament only down to minimmal deterrence levels, while unilateral disarmament is complete nuclear disarmament (and probably much more). (We could easily expand the matrices of Table 10.1 to include two disarmament strategies; this would not change the analysis except to add pointless clutter.)

THE STRUCTURE OF THE PROBLEM

Elsewhere I have noted that the present superpower competition in nuclear arms has one of six possible strategic structures, if three plausible constraints on their preferences are met.[1] The constraints are:

1. That Soviet and American preferences over various outcomes are symmetric in the sense that we can switch the labels of the row and column players without changing the game;
2. That both sides prefer mutual disarmament down to minimal deterrence levels to mutual armament at high levels; and
3. That, if only one side be armed, each side prefers that it be the one to be armed.

Of the 78 strategically distinct ordinal 2 x 2 games, only six meet these constraints. These are shown in Table 10.1. In three of these games both sides rank mutual disarmament first, in two they rank it second; and in one they rank it third. Given the second constraint, they cannot rank it fourth.

To give some sense of how we would determine which game fit the facts of the nuclear conflict, consider Game 6 and then compare Games 4 and 5. In Game 6 (Nuclear Pax Romana), the likelihood of explosion in a mutually armed regime is evidently high. It is also relatively high even in the state in which both sides are disarmed down to minimal deterrence levels. If the likelihood of unintentional accidents that could escalate is very high, we may well be in Game 6.

Now compare Games 4, Prisoner's Dilemma (PD), and, 5, Chicken. One would see the conflict as Chicken rather than as PD if one expected greater harm in the mutually armed condition than in the unilaterally disarmed condition. But if one thinks deterrence is stable and that a single nuclear power would be despotically or prudentially brutal, one would see the conflict as PD. Americans and Russians seem generally to see their conflict as PD, although the current Reagan administration is reviving an earlier suspicion that the conflict is Chicken.

The payoffs in the games in Table 10.1 represent the prudential assessments of the peoples of the superpowers. What would be the assessment of a utilitarian? Clearly, in the three equal cooridnation games (Games 1, 2, and 3), the 1,1 outcome is preferred over all games by a utilitarian. And in the unequal coordination game (Game 6), the outcomes 1,2 and 2,1 are preferred over the others.

Table 10.1   Six Possible Structures for the Superpower Competition in Nuclear Arms

		Game 1 (Coordination) USSR				Game 2 (Coordination) USSR				Game 3 (Coordination) USSR	
		D	A			D	A			D	A
US	D	1,1	4,3	US	D	1,1	4,2	US	D	1,1	3,2
	A	3,4	2,2		A	2,4	3,3		A	2,3	4,4

		Game 4 Prisoner's Dilemma USSR				Game 5 Chicken USSR				Game 6 Nuclear Pax Romana (Unequal Coordination) USSR	
		D	A			D	A			D	A
US	D	2,2	4,1	US	D	2,2	3,1	US	D	3,3	2,1
	A	1,4	3,3		A	1,3	4,4		A	1,2	4,4

Without further information, however, we can say very little about which outcomes are utilitarian in Games 4 and 5. In Game 4, the outcome 2,2 is better than 3,3. And in Game 5, the outcome 4,4 is the worst of all outcomes. To say that mutual disarmament is best in either of these games requires assessment of expected losses in each of the three outcomes other than the dispreferred outcome. Of course, to say which of these six games we face also requires such assessment. But only in Games 4 and 5 may utilitarian considerations conflict with prudential considerations, although even in these games these considerations might not conflict.

Let us summarize the utilitarian conclusions. In Games 1, 2, and 3, mutual disarmament down to minimal deterrence levels is utilitarian. In Game 6 unilateral (complete) disarmament by one of the superpowers is utilitarian. In Games 4 and 5, perhaps mutual disarmament is, as is widely assumed, utilitarian, but perhaps unilateral disarmament is utilitarian. To say what the United States should do either prudentially or morally requires that we assess the expected outcomes of all four strategy pairs: (a) US and USSR disarm to minimal deterrence levels, (b) US arm and USSR com pletely disarm, (c) US completely disarm and USSR arm, and (d) both arm heavily.

Rankings of expected outcomes for each nation without aggregation across nations will be sufficient to decide which game we are in and which strategy is prudent.[2] At least crude aggregations will be required to say which of three outcomes in each of Games 4 and 5 and which of two outcomes in Game 6 is utilitarian. In many contexts one might object in principle to discovering more than ordinal rankings by each nation of its outcomes. But here we may perhaps presume that numbers of lives lost provide good measures of value, so that we have a quasi-cardinal measure of aggregate welfare. For example, one might be able to say that, in going from the lower-left to the upper-left cell in the PD Game 4, the gain in lives to the Soviet Union is greater than the loss to the United States. If a similar claim can be made for going from the upper-right to the upper-left cell, then the 2,2 outcome is utilitarian.

It should be clear that a utilitarian recommendation on whether to disarm unilaterally or to strive instead for mutual disarmament down to minimal deterrence levels depends heavily on an assessment of the likely risks of various arms regimes. If our conflict is as in the Nuclear Pax Romana, insisting on mutual disarmament is both imprudent and immoral. If the conflict is a Prisoner's Dilemma, unilateral disarmament is imprudent and possibly immoral.

I do not know enough to assert with confidence in which game we find ourselves. I think it fairly safe to conclude that prudent Americans would not think we are in one of the easy coordination games—1, 2, or 3. But that means we are in one of the games in which utilitarian assessments are most difficult and require the most care and in which errors in judgment can produce perverse recommendations. I am inclined to think that mutual deterrence at low levels of armament can be relatively stable and that a unilateral regime (under either superpower) would be relatively brutal, merely for prudential reasons. Therefore, I am included to think we are in a Prisoner's Dilemma rather than a Chicken or Nuclear Pax Romana. Perhaps that is the voice of my residual childhood chauvinism. But I think not, because I would dread a Nuclear Pax Americana about as much as a Nuclear Pax Sovietica. Perhaps, with its greater resources, the United States could better suppress nuclear arms around the world without resorting to nuclear strikes than could the Soviet Union, so that a utilitarian would have to prefer the American regime. If that is the case, then, although the conflict may be prudentially symmetric as in constraint (1) above, it is not morally symmetric.

Note that the game matrices in Table 10.1 fail to capture a very important aspect of the nuclear arms conflict. The Prisoner's Dilemma matrix shows that, if the United States were armed and the Soviet Union disarmed, then the Soviet Union would prefer to arm. In game theory parlance, the outcome in the lower-left cell is therefore unstable. In the world of nuclear arms, however, that outcome might be very stable despite the preference structure of the game, for the simple reason that the United States could perhaps effactually prevent the Soviet Union from arming. But whereas this might morally be an optimal outcome if the conflict is as in the Nuclear Pax Romana of Game 6, it might morally be a severely suboptimal outcome if the conflict is a Prisoner's Dilemma.

The problem with the matrices, of course, is that they represent abstract preferences over particular outcomes. They do not capture one's incentives to alter the status quo once an outcome has been achieved. Game theorists typically speak of unstable outcomes as though one had an incentive merely from one's preferences to switch strategies to move to an alternative outcome in which one's payoff is higher. Part of the appeal to the United States of the lower-left outcome in Games 4, 5, and 6, however, is that in that outcome the United States could coerce Soviet choices.

UNILATERAL DISARMAMENT

The chief risk to a superpower that chooses to disarm unilaterally is that its choice cannot easily be made credible. The other side might fear that any number of generals would be holdouts. Hence, if the United States were to disarm unilaterally, it would want to do so very thoroughly to reassure the Soviet Union that there was virtually no risk of hidden arms or of a sudden rearmament. This would require dismantling all rockets and rocket-launching facilities, all nuclear power plants and fuel-processing facilities, and many physics and engineering research facilities. In this era of cruise missiles, it might even require dismantling all aircraft and ship-building facilities as well as destroying or surrendering all military ships, aircraft, and larger land vehicles—anything that could possibly carry cruise missiles within range of the Soviet Union. (As Admiral Gayler has noted, "any airplane bigger than a Piper Cub can carry a nuclear bomb.")[3] Even then, there is some risk that disarmament could not be made credible. For this reason, the small size of American cruise missiles is distressing.[4]

One might suppose we could then rely on opening ourselves to inspection by permanently stationed Soviet observers with right of access. But this is easier to suppose than to achieve. Not only the United States would have to be overseen, but also most of Western Europe, China, and to a lesser extent Israel, India, Pakistan, Brazil, South Africa, Japan . . . —the list is long. The Soviet Union lacks the resources to carry out such a mission. And its leadership might not trust a world in which many of its best scientific personnel were stationed abroad. It seems likely that it would be far cheaper for the Soviet Union to destroy various installations and, far more important, certain communities of scientists and engineers than to attempt to control the employment of human capital. The cheapest way to do that would be with nuclear strikes on a modest number of targets.

It is almost inconceivable that anyone could be certain that all extant weapons under American control had been surrendered. One would always suspect that some—plausibly large—number had been squirreled away. Consequently, the Soviet Union might continue to be deterred from attacking American cities for a long time. But it might therefore choose to concentrate its surveillance on the United States and to obliterate Chinese, Indian, Japanese, and other nuclear facilities and man-power. Oddly, then, the Pax Sovietica might not be particularly onerous for Ameri-cans, but it might seem very grim nevertheless to utilitarians.

In any case, to make strong claims for the moral ranking of continued deterrence at lower levels of armament versus unilateral disarmament requires serious assess-ment of the plausible risks and consequences of the two regimes. I think it very easy to conclude with Naess and McMahan that unilateral disarmament by smaller states is both rational and moral. But one cannot so easily conclude that unilateral disarma-ment by one of the superpowers makes sense, as Lackey and Churchill suppose and Naess seems to imply.[5] It might make sense, but no one has adequately undertaken to work through the range of risks at stake.

Consider some of the facts that might influence one's judgment of the conse-quences of a superpower's unilateral disarmament. During 1953–54 the Eisen-hower administration considered whether to attack the Soviet Union to prevent its gaining the capacity to wage nuclear war against the United States.[6] In 1969 the Soviet Union reputedly felt out American officials on how the United States would react to a Soviet attack on Chinese nuclear weapons facilities.[7] More recently, Israel destroyed a French-made nuclear power plant in Iraq, evidently to forestall Iraqi development of nuclear weapons. All of these preemptive attacks were consid-ered or undertaken in contexts of what were then exceedingly primitive capabilities under development. If the United States were to disarm now, it could not usefully be compared to the Soviet Union, China, or Iraq in those years, because even after disarming its capabilities would be extraordinary. Indeed, they would be extraordinarily threatening. If there were incentives for the earlier preemptive attacks, there would be vastly greater incentive for the Soviet Union to do whatever best guaranteed that a disarmed United States would stay disarmed. Coercive Soviet governance of the United States might be radically more costly than coercive Soviet governance of Afghanistan. And if it failed, a handful of bombs on Southern California, Los Alamos, and so forth, might seem to be the most attractive option. The historical Pax Romama was achieved after the destruction and salting over of Carthage.

On this point, much of the debate has been misleading. Lackey supposes that the Soviet Union would be incapable of dominating the United States, and anyone who muses for a moment on the recent histories of Hungary, Czechoslovakia, Poland, and Afghanistan must concur. It is odd, however, that Lackey seems to think this means that the United States would prosper after unilateral disarmament.[8] Churchill similarly supposes that a disarmed United States could depend on the deterrent force of nonviolent defense. He concludes that "there appear to be no circumstances under which a nuclear attack on an unarmed nation would appear rational."[9] One may almost agree but still doubt that a single superpower would rest easy with its evidence that others are disarmed. Similarly, one may agree with Lackey that the Soviet Union would not wish to "dominate" the United States in the way it is trying to dominate Poland or Afghanistan. Rather, it would merely wish to deter the United States from ever rearming and thus threaten the Soviet Union again. It would view the United States as a Carthage, not as an Egypt or Dalmatia. The most grievous obstacle to having the Soviet Union view a disarmed United States as no longer threatening is the near impossibility of getting Americans to refuse nuclear arms and to adopt Churchill's nonviolent deterrence.

Perhaps I am wrong, and a unilaterally disarmed United States would be more nearly Greece than Carthage to the Soviet Rome. But it behooves anyone who fears mutual deterrence (on the ground that national leaders may be sufficiently foolish or vicious as to make nuclear war deliberately) to tell us why a single superpower should be governed by gentler, more reasonable folk. After all, the risks to a single superpower of occasionally using nuclear weapons would be negligible in comparison to the risks to one of two superpowers.

Despite some of Lackey's arguments in its defense, unilateral disarmament may nevertheless make moral sense, because it may imply fewer expected deaths than any regime of mutual armament. It is hard to imagine, however, that it could be prudent. In either case, the judgment necessarily turns on a relative comparison. For unilateral disarmament the most important comparison is to mutual disarmament down to minimal deterrence levels. Let us turn to the risks inherent in such deterrence.

MUTUAL DISARMAMENT

In the games of Table 10.1, the strategy of disarmament, D, may mean different things depending on whether the other side also disarms. As discussed above, a nation that disarms unilaterally will want to disarm completely and to make it very clear and credible to the other side that it has done so.

If both sides disarm under current conditions, however, it seems implausible that they would choose to disarm completely, since complete nuclear disarmament would entail grievous instability. Quick rearmament to levels of momentary superiority would be possible and even tempting. Complete mutual disarmament therefore does not seem desirable or politically feasible in present conditions. Hence, under a regime of mutual disarmament we can expect both sides to continue to be armed to some minimal deterrence level. What risks do we face in such a regime?

Clearly, as many have pointed out, we still face the risk of mutual annihilation—but that risk should be considerably smaller than under the present regime of extravagant overkill. The principal changes in going to a regime of reduced arms would be the removal of the most unstable systems and the end of the highly competitive development of new and, technologically speaking, "better" weapons. The latter would follow from the cessation of testing of radically new systems. These changes would depend on and would enhance a trend away from the current adversarial stance of the two superpowers.

We might also face a slight risk that one side would make a major technological advance to gain real superiority that would allow it to destroy the other side. This, however, is a rsk common to every plausible regime, and it might be smallest under the minimal deterrence regime, in which testing and research could be most effectively controlled.

Compare the risk in the unilateral disarmament and present regimes. By definition, of course, in a unilateral regime one side has such superiority. Whether it would actually use it to destroy much of the other side would turn on how thoroughly it thought it had the other side's nuclear potential under control. As for the present regime, one might suppose that it is increasingly stable because a first-strike attempt against the massive, diverse systems now in place would be suicidal (for reasons to be discussed below). It would be foolish, however, to suppose that technological progress will have benign effects. The present regime of rapid expansion and development of systems may lead to disastrous "improvements." At the very least, therefore, anyone convinced that the present regime is stable would want to put stringent controls on further developments. In addition, most of us are likely to agree that the scope for war by accident or mistake would be substantially less under minimal deterrence than in the present regime. Indeed, that scope might be particularly reduced by enhanced confidence that massive research were not underway to upset the present systems.

Perhaps by far the greatest risk of a regime of mutual disarmament down to minimal deterrence levels is that it would leave both superpowers free to change their policies back to massive overarmament. This is the only way in which the policy of mutual disarmament may be inferior to a policy of unilateral disarmament. A fully disarmed United States would face a strong incentive not to rearm if the Soviet Union were armed: the prospect of instant suppression, even destruction. Indeed, the only serious view of a unilateral regime may well be that the disarmed nation would be virtually incapable of any significant effort to rearm. In a regime of minimal deterrence, either side could unilaterally opt to return to a program of massive armament.

Finally, as compared to the alternative regime, what risks would a regime of minimal deterrence reduce? If tit-for-tat strategies of mutual disarmament were begun, the likelihood of war by accident or mistake might be substantially reduced at the outset, and should fall further thereafter. And a regime of minimal deterrence obviously has the advantage over a unilateral regime that it would deter either side from barbaric actions that a single superpower might take.

Many readers may be familiar with the "opera singer problem," a favorite joke among (conservative) Chicago economists. It concerns a midwesterner who is asked to judge a contest between two sopranos. After listening to the first soprano, he immediately awards the prize to the second soprano without bothering to hear her, because he is confident that she must be better. It is ironic that conservatism might be called the inverse of the opera singer problem: conservatives prefer the status quo to any alternative because they have no experience in the alternatives, and yet they are morally certain that the status quo must be better. Any defense of mutual deterrence against claims for unilateral disarmament may smack of conservatism in this sense.

The only respectable way to defeat conservative claims is to offer a very careful, well-reasoned account of why some alternative is superior to the status quo. It is relatively easy to offer convincing arguments about why mutual disarmament down to relatively modest levels is superior to the current status quo. Perhaps one could even offer good arguments about why unilateral disarmament would be superior to the status quo, although so far no one has done any more than convince us that the thesis is worthy of further thought and should not be dismissed out of hand.

Those who propose unilateral disarmament seem to think mutual arms reduction down to low levels is not so far removed from the status quo. But it may be the necessary first step on the only path that can lead to a world in which relations between the United States, the Soviet Union, and China approach the quality of relations betwen most of the nations of Europe or between Canada and the United States.

THE PRESENT REGIME

Because the regimes of complete unilateral disarmament and of mutual arms reduction down to modest deterrence levels greatly simplify the strategic interaction between the two superpowers, their risks are easily outlined even if not so readily assessed. The present regime of extravagant bellicosity and overarmament is far more complex. That it is grievously risky seems obvious enough. But it is not easy to say how risky, and the risks may change rapidly in the wake of the rapid changes in technology that continuous expansion and escalation will bring.

Rather than survey the range of risks we face in the present regime, I will focus on the problems inherent in a constant need for preparedness and on certain current developments in weapons systems. Let us first consider the problem of preparedness.

That states make outragous plans for odd contingencies is not proof of how they would actually act. Indeed, it is often true that one cannot know how one would act until or unless faced with a real decision. For example, poker played for pennies is likely to be very different from poker played for high stakes. It is comforting to suppose that the adolescent gamesmen in the Pentagon will not be in command when the moment comes to test their theories.

Unfortunately, however, decisions in a nuclear crisis may come too fast for anyone to be seriously said to make them. In these circumstances, decisions may be determined by the preparations taken for them. When there is more time to face the actuality of the decision problem, past preparation may play a much smaller role.

Hence, hair-trigger arrangements are doubly risky. They may allow the cowboy jingoists of the politicized strategic community to have their way by occluding the seriousness and caution with which grave decisions are usually taken. There is not only great difficulty ascertaining what the facts are and therefore the risk of reacting to no provocation, but also much greater likelihood that the worst decisionmakers will hold sway. The cowboys one fears in such moments are those who in Texas are derisively characterized as "all hat and no cattle." Perhaps they have never held greater sway than they hold today.

We have lived with the risks of the regime of heightened preparedness for at least two decades. Those risks are that war may happen by accident or by mistake. The sense that those risks are greater today than ever before may be a function of the neanderthal, belligerent tone of present leaders. But it is surely also a function of the radical changes now taking place in weapons systems.

Risk of accidental launch has probably been declining as systems have improved over the years. But new programs currently planned may greatly increase that risk by putting retaliation on a hair trigger. This risk is not symmetric, however, in the sense that the Soviet Union, with almost all its warheads on fixed, land-based missiles, must feel far more threatened by accurate, first-strike weapons than the United States, whose main force is on relatively invulnerable submarines. American deployment of weapons potentially capable of a first-strike therefore enhances the risk of a Soviet accident, while Soviet deployment of such weapons should not greatly affect control of American weapons. The perversity here, of course, is that it is generally assumed that Soviet monitoring and command and control capacities are woefully inferior to American capacities.

The dismal record of Soviet incompetence that resulted in the shooting down of KAL 007, the Korean passenger plane, should scare any halfway intelligent American out of wanting the United States to have first-strike capability. To deploy a full first-strike force is probably the riskiest action the United States could take short of war in the next decade or two. Such deployment may lead to the annihilation of the United States for no reason or any offsetting benefit. The idea of deploying such a force is so patently stupid that Reagan administration officials have not offered a serious rationale for doing so.

One touted rationale sounds like a paradox of administration reasoning. Robert Dean of the Department of State says it is credible that the Soviet Union would choose to attack our modest collection of ICBMs. Why? Because they could plausibly knock out 90 percent of them, "forcing the American President to rely on sea-based systems to undertake a strike against Soviet cities and industrial sites . . . . and then suffer in return a similar strike by the Soviet leadership." American retaliation would be suidical. Hence, Dean says, "a prudent and responsible policy for the U.S. is to preclude that option to the Soviet Union." Later he adds, "That would, of course, be an extreme situation, on the end of the probability curve. But that does not absolve us, given the possible consequence, of the responsibility of dealing with the possibility."[10]

The greater risk to American lives, surely, is that we may cause the Soviet Union to wonder whether we have serious first-strike capability. Many of the current American innovations may do just that. The new Pershing II, MX, and Trident II missiles will all be accurate enough to destroy Soviet ICBMs, the vast bulk of the Soviet nuclear force. A few years from now the Soviet Union will be within 20 minutes of losing almost its entire nuclear strike force. The Soviet Union could not handle flight 007 in two hours.

For all the technical sophistication of the American weapons, they are subject to the major weakness of depending on Soviet capacity to determine with certainty at all times that they have not been launched. What prudent leader would entrust our lives to a link in the chain that is so demonstrably weak? It has been suggested that perhaps the KAL pilot flew over Soviet territory because he would be rewarded for saving time and fuel. If so, he was a fool. He would have had to depend for his safety either on Soviet incompetence ever to spot his plane or on Soviet competence to recognize his plane as civilian if its were spotted. If our first-strike systems are deployed, we will likewise have to hope for Soviet incompetence to pick up many false signals and, when they do pick up such signals, their competence to read them as false. Who would be so foolish as to choose to enter the bizarre world of contradictory hopes in which flight 007's pilot took his passengers to their deaths?

Against this argument, American military leaders suppose that the most likely explanation of the attack on flight 007 was thoroughgoing Soviet incompetence, but that it is almost inconceivable that the Soviet Union could mistakenly suppose we were attempting a first strike. Why? The personnel who tracked and downed 007 had demonstrably failed to join with the plane until it was almost out of Soviet airspace. When they finally caught it, they were minutes from losing the right to deal with it and from being held personally responsible for letting what they thought was a spy plane escape. In a state of near panic they brought it down.

Detecting a missile attack is a completely different matter. It is so desperately important to do it well that much of the Soviet Union's limited resources in advanced electronics is dedicated to the task. Third-rate radar systems and personnel do not monitor American missiles, but state-of-the-art satellites and computers. And a panicked officer in the field will not decide how to respond to various signals. Those who will respond are people who, like American military leaders, are firmly convinced that a successful first strike is impossible. They therefore will discount occasional mistaken signals. When it comes to nuclear weapons, the American military trusts the Soviet Union, although their trust is almost always not for attribution.

Perhaps the American military are right. If so, their case should be a part of the public debate on the new first-strike weapons. I, and many Americans, think the new weapons are foolish, wasteful, and dangerous. It behooves those who think we are wrong to stop browbeating us and to try to educate us. After all, no one's interests are served by terrifying a large segment of the American public.

Almost everyone outside the most influential American circles seems to believe that the new, highly accurate missiles are destabilizing and risky. Another major technological advance, the cruise missile, may plausibly be stabilizing—indeed, too stabilizing. Because 3200 cruise missiles are to be borne by American B52 bombers and thousands more are to be borne by submarines, aircraft carriers, and trucks, there is virtually no chance that the United States could be disarmed by a Soviet first-strike. Implicit claims to the contrary are implicit efforts to deceive the American people. Indeed, cruise missile deployment now makes the MX obsolete for any use other than as a first-strike weapon.[11]

Fortunately, cruise missiles may be completely unusable except as a retaliatory weapon for the following reason: while they are supposed to be accurate within 30 meters and to have the capacity to destroy an extant ICBM, they are too slow for use as first-strike weapons. Hence, anyone under attack by significant numbers of cruise missiles would have the time and the incentive to launch ICBMs in order not to lose them. As a result, no one would be foolish enough to use cruise missiles in the first place, because their use would invite one's own annihilation. They *are* an ideal weapon for two purposes, however: terrorist or lunatic attacks on, say, New York, Moscow, or Tel Aviv, and retaliatory attacks on a superpower that has already expended its ICBMs.

On this account the cruise missile sounds too good to be true. Alas, it may, in Shaw's twist, be too true to be good. The cruise missile may be stabilizing in the extremely perverse sense of blocking substantial arms reductions by making verification harder. It does this for the same reason that it makes a successful first strike virtually impossible. Cruise missiles are so small and dispersible that they cannot be reliably located by an enemy.[12] Hence, they cannot all be reliably destroyed by an enemy and, alas, they cannot all be credibly destroyed by their possessor.

The most upsetting aspect of the cruise missile is that it is a new weapon based on highly innovative technologies that may be developing very rapidly. It is supposed that the current generation of cruise missiles may be obsolete before its procurement is even completed. With higher speed and greater range, the next generation of cruise missiles may give the United States clear superiority over the Soviet Union; indeed, it may give the United States a credible enough first-strike capacity to push the Soviet Union into a disastrous hair trigger regime.

Yet the problematic stability of the cruise missile could be overcome by leaders seriously intent on reducing risks. The United States and the Soviet Union could share technology for cruise missiles and destroy their other nuclear systems. The destruction of big missiles and submarines is relatively easily verified. But this is the regime of mutual arms reduction down to minimal deterrence. If we do not enter that regime, we are likely to see further technological advances, many of which will presumably add to the risks we face.

The problem of the cruise missile may be generalized. In the current, highly competitive regime, both sides strive for technological advances. Among the most remarkable advances in recent years have been radical improvements in guidance systems that render most new delivery systems and new generations of older systems capable of great precision. Hence, virtually all systems being newly deployed are capable of killing the other side's fixed, land-based missiles. Many other developments—such as antisubmarine, anti satellite, and antiballistic missile systems—in the works similarly will enhance counterforce capacity. Such developments tend to shift the nuclear conflict from deterrent to belligerent status.

It is at least conceivable—if unlikely—that the United States will so far outstrip the Soviet Union in such electronic innovations as to impose a Nuclear Pax Romana on the Soviet Union. It is also conceivable that such developments on both sides will push at least one side into a very fragile launch-on-warning regime. A regime of mutual disarmament down to lower levels with restrictions on testing of new weapons is probably the most sensible way to counter such destabilizing tendencies of competitive technological innovation.

OTHER RISKS

I have not discussed many other risks of the various regimes. For example, one might suppose that the the expected harm from terrorist or lunatic action might vary significantly among the three regimes. At least three other issues of great interest can be settled with only a serious risk assessment. They are (a) the issue addressed by Naess and McMahan, whether smaller Western states ought to disarm unilaterally; (b) the problem of other nuclear powers more generally; and (c) the politics of current armaments policies.

In general, the case for unilateral disarmament by Norway, the United Kingdom, and perhaps other European nations and the case for Japanese refusal to arm are compelling. It would be crazy for these nations to be armed if the United States unilaterally disarmed, and it may be pointless or crazy for them to be armed if the Soviet Union disarmed. Hence, it is probably at best pointless for them to be armed in any case.

It seems plausible, as Brian Barry not altogether facetiously remarks,[13] that the British have chosen to have their tiny island dotted with nuclear weapons largely out of a sense of fair play. If Americans are to be immolated, it is only sporting that the English be immolated along with them. Whatever the British motives, weapons on British soil may do little other than increase the scope of damage that a Soviet attack would cause. The value of those weapons as a deterrent to Soviet attack on Britain may be slight in comparison to their disvalue as a provocation in the event of a Soviet-American conflagration. McMahan's carefully argued defense of this claim is, I think, convincing.[14]

China poses different, probably more serious, risks. Because nuclear weapons can be quite inexpensive relative even to China's gross domestic product, it is hard to imagine that a regime of minimal deterrence would not soon include China as an effectively equal nuclear superpower. In one respect it would be less stable than a two-nation regime: there would be yet another nation in which yahoos might come to power and promote belligerent policies. But in another respect it might be more stable: the chance that one nation of three near-equals could expect to overcome both its enemies at once is substantially less than the chance that one nation could overcome a single near-equal.

As noted above, unilateral nuclear disarmament by the United States would, at any time in the near future, virtually mandate unilateral nuclear disarmament by China and all other nations. Continuation of the present regime may extend for a decade or two the period in which there are only two nuclear superpowers; but eventually China will join the group, perhaps with an order of magnitude less overkill capacity, but still with adequate capacity to deter either or both other superpowers. It might be more destabilizing to add a third party to the present regime than to the regime of minimal deterrence. This is an issue on which thoughtful analysis would add to the cogency of current discussion. A related issue not yet typically addressed is whether mutual disarmament would be easier to achieve before or after Chinese capacity vastly exceeds what would be needed for minimal deterrence.

Finally, in a similarly cursory fashion, let us consider the risks we, the people, face in the politics of current arms policies. A, perhaps the, major risk the American and Soviet peoples face is that arms manufacturers, generals, and politicians may view the nuclear conflict as a very different kind of game from those in Table 10.1.[15] They may see it as in their career and financial interests to seek high rather than low levels of armament. Hence, they may prefer the present regime to a regime of massively reduced armaments. Their cupidity may be our worst enemy.

This means that in the United States, where democratic control is not completely stymied, our leaders' cupidity is rewarded only by our gullibility. It may also mean that, next to Soviet and American leaders, ordinary American citizens are the people morally most culpable for the risks we and others currently face. Next to Soviet and American leaders, American citizens should be most capable of bringing about reductions in the moral risks American, and probably therefore also Soviet, weapons impose on the world. We should be ashamed of the support we have given to belligerent, imprudent, and immoral policies.

MAXIMIN AND MINIMAX REGRET

When the risks of various available strategies cannot be assessed adequately, we may find it impossible to estimate the expected values of the outcomes well enough to try to maximize our prospects. We may then resort to criteria for choice other than maximization. Two that are widely commended are Maximin (MM) and Minimax Regret (MMR); both have been used in considering policies on nuclear arms.[16] The MM principle grows out of the analysis of two-person zero-sum games. In such games, rational players cannot do better than to choose by MM—hence, it is a compelling principle of choice for such games. Under MM, one surveys all of one's strategies for their worst outcomes, then chooses the strategy whose worst outcome (minimum) is best (maximum); that is, one maximizes the minimum. Against a rational player in a two-person pure conflict game,[17] the result will be the best of one's worsts.

In games that are not zero-sum or pure conflict, MM generally does not make sense, because one may do better by colluding on another strategy. For example, in the PD, the MM strategy is to defect (to choose A in Game 4), but both players can do better by colluding on cooperation. Nevertheless, it is sometimes supposed that MM does make sense in games that are not pure conflict if we do not have enough information to calculate the expected values of choosing various strategies, as may be true, if, for example, we do not know enough about the other player's payoffs to predict that player's strategy choice. How would MM apply to the nuclear dilemma?

A consequence of arming the United States is that the Soviet Union may be destroyed. A consequence of arming the Soviet Union is that the United States may be destroyed. And, of course, a consequence of arming both is that both may be destroyed. A strictly prudential (that is, not moral) claim for MM does not make any recommendation on whether the United States should arm or disarm. If maximin reasoning is to apply, it must apply to moral claims. here is would follow that having both armed is potentially worse than having only one armed, since the former might bring about the destruction of both.

Now turn to minimax regret. MMR is generally applied to games with cardinally valued payoffs, that is, with payoffs in some units that can be properly added, subtracted, and multiplied. MMR recommends that one choose what to do by minimizing the greatest regret that one may experience afterward. For example, if I stay home from a picnic because I hate being out in the rain, I will regret my choice if the day turns out to be sunny. But if I go, I will suffer regret if it rains. If I have no idea whether it will rain, I may have no basis on which to choose except my sense of which regret I would rather avoid. If I hate rain enough, I should stay home. If I enjoy picnics enough, I should go.

Table 10.2 Minimax Regret Choice

Partial Game matrix				Partial Regret matrix			
		Column player				Column player	
		I	II			I	II
Row's	I	3	12	Row's	I	4	0
payoffs	II	7	2	regret	II	0	10

This is the usual account of MMR: that one must resort to it if one has no idea of the likelihoods of various outcomes and cannot calculate the expected values of one's strategy choices. The MMR choice rule is a version of the principle of insufficient reason. Arguments both for unilateral disarmament and for continued deterrence are often implicitly MMR arguments. To see how severe are the conditions that recomend MMR, consider the simplistic example in the partial game in Table 10.2 that shows only Row's payoffs. Suppose I am the Row player and you are Column. My payoffs are 3 units of something good, 12 units, and so forth. Suppose you choose your strategy I. If I choose my strategy II, my payoff of 7 is the best possible under the circumstances and I suffer no regret. But if I choose my strategy I, my payoff of 3 is 4 less than what I could have gotten given your choice. Hence, I suffer a regret of 4. The worst regret I could suffer would be when I choose II while you choose II. Applying the MMR criterion, I can minimize my maximun regret by choosing strategy I.

Note that MMR makes no more sense than MM if I know enough about the game I face. If I know that you are 99 percent certain to choose Column I in the game of Table 10.2, I can calculate my expected payoffs from each of my strategy choices. My strategy I yields

$$.99 (3) + .01 (12) = 3.09,$$

and my strategy II yields

$$.99 (7) + .01 (2) = 6.95.$$

It would be silly of me to choose other than strategy II, although in doing so I risk getting the worst of all payoffs and suffering the greatest regret. Note that, with such a large difference in expected outcomes, we need not have a very accurate sense of the probabilities we face—even crude estimates may suffice.

There is another ground on which one might argue for MMR. If one does not have a good cardinal measure of one's payoffs, one might follow MMR even though probabilities of the payoffs are clear. Without good cardinal measures one might not be able to calculate the expected payoffs, as I did for the game in Table 10.1 when I assumed that Column would choose strategy I with 99 percent certainty.

Consider the Homeowner's Insurance Game in Table 10.3 and its associated regret matrix. Suppose I know from local statistics that the likelihood of my house burning is only 1 percent. The expected payoff to me from insuring is -$200 (i.e., the cost of insurance). The expected payoff from not insuring is 1 percent of the value of a disastrous debt. I do not know how to compare the expected loss of $200 to the one-chance-in-a-hundred disastrous debt. Hence, I may simply opt to avoid the more grievous risk, even though I might know very well that my insurance company pays out in claims only half of what it collects in premiums.

Table 10.3   Homeowner's Insurance Game and Its Regret Matrix

	Insurance Game			Regret Matrix	
	Fire	No fire		Fire	No fire
Insure	down $200	down $200	Insure	0	$200
Not insure	disastrous debt	down nothing	Not insure	disastrous debt −$200	0

Again, however, we may reject MMR even for homeowner's insurance if the numbers change a bit. For example, suppose such insurance costs half one's salary to protect against the very unlikely event of ever needing to collect on it. An MMR argument in favor of buying the insurance then would make no sense. Somewhere well below half one's salary it seems to make sense. Are the likely consequences of unilateral disarmament so slight that the MMR criterion obviously should govern our choice? Perhaps—but the claim wants factually based argument.

Perhaps the nuclear conflict has in it both of the uncertainties here, that of probabilities and that of measures of consequences. For example, one might suppose that one of its risks is the obliteration of the human race in this century. How can one compare this, even at a low probability, to the destruction of ten or twenty million people at some perhaps far higher probability?

In fact, we act as though we could make such choices all the time. At the individual level we risk personal obliteration merely for the whim of going out to dinner or a movie. At the social level we risk obliteration of humanity when we seek technological solutions to such trivial problems as how to keep leftover food fresh —because the chemical technology may destroy the atmosphere, the ozone layer, our chromosomes, or our lungs.

If MM or MMR is to play a role in our utilitarian assessment of whether the United States should disarm unilaterally, it must follow that we are utterly uncertain whether it is more prudent of the United States to disarm or to remain armed. And our uncertainty must be due to a lack of *any* sense of whether disarmament is prudent, not merely because of our judgment that the issue is, say, a toss-up.

Do we lack any sense of whether disarmament is prudent? At the moment perhaps we do, possibly because no one has taken the issue seriously enough to weigh the prospects. Before we settle on an MM or MMR decision, we should attempt to weigh the prospects. For what it is worth, I suspect that American armament to far less provocative levels than the present administration seeks is prudent, because I believe that mutual deterrence at low levels of armament can be quite stable. Even if this is correct, the utilitarian judgment is not foregone, because more than American interests are at stake in that judgment. But in any case the judgment should not be reached by MM or MMR, since the conditions for MM or MMR choosing are not met.

The crucial issues are: what are the relative odds on nuclear war under various regimes? How bad will be the results of any nuclear war? Our answers to both these questions have changed over the decades. They may be in the course of especially radical change right now. The principal change is, in general, perceptions of how bad nuclear war might be. But, as usual in strategic contexts, this change may affect the odds on nuclear war.

THE NEW CONSENSUS ON THE EFFECTS OF NUCLEAR WAR

There is a growing consensus among diverse scientists—American and Russian—that a serious nuclear exchange would be suicidal to both nations. According to the scientists of the so-called TTAPS group, the dust and debris blown into the atmosphere and the smoke from urban firestorms would occlude the sun, reducing its light to the middle latitudes of the northern part of the globe to perhaps five percent of its usual level. Most plant life would die quickly in the nuclear winter.[18] Civilization might not die outright, but the grim world that remained would not bear comparison to the one that was destroyed.

Suppose this scientific view prevails and that every civilian and military official responsible for Soviet and American nuclear weapons believed that an attack on the other side would be massively destructive to the attacker, even if it were a technically successful first strike. What difference would such a belief make to our risk assessments?

One's first reaction is that the risk of nuclear deterrence is even graver than we thought. Hence there might seem to be all the more reason to disarm unilaterally. But note that the changed perception of consequences is almost certain to change the likelihood of actions as well. If it were widely known that guns were of such poor quality that half the time they would be as harmful to the user as to the intended victim, surely there would be fewer murders with guns. If *equal* harm to the user were certain, there would almost never be a gun murder. Granted, nations are not simply individuals, and they may behave more stupidly. But destruction by their own actions of everything they valued would be required of many actual individuals if a nuclear strike were effected. Indeed, the theory of deterrence is that the near-guarantee of its own destruction will deter a nation from certain kinds of actions. Presumably, no one thinks the motivational theory wrong. Hence, increasing the degree of certainty that a nation will suffer grievous harm that it could avoid should reduce the likelihood of its leaders undertaking the action that would bring it harm.

How do these two effects balance out? The risk of the regime of deterrence is the level of destruction it might bring, multiplied by the probability it will bring such destruction, minus the risk incident to not having the regime of deterrence. Let us ignore the latter risk. Many recent academics discussing deterrence and disarmament have concluded that the level of destruction nuclear war would cause is very high, that remnant human survivors would be reduced to Stone Age conditions of life. The new consensus therefore does not greatly change their assessment of the level of destruction of such a war. But if the new consensus changes the assessments of the better military leaders and of many civilian leaders, it may substantially reduce the probability of nuclear war between the superpowers.

Is it plausible that the new consensus changes the nature of the deterrence game we face? Yes. It may lead to a much lower level of expected destruction from the regime of mutual deterrence. The prudential losses from use of nuclear weapons may now so clearly override any possible prudential benefits as to reduce the risk of their use more than the overall effect of their use is perceived to have increased. But the incentive for a sole nuclear power to use very small numbers of weapons to ensure that no other power gains access to them is not massively reduced. Hence, it could be that the absolute value of the (negative) mutual armament payoff is significantly decreased relative to the (negative) unilateral disarmament payoff. If this is the case, the game we face may clearly be Prisoner's Dilemma, and not Chicken or Pax Romana. On the other hand, if a major part of the risk of a regime of mutual deterrence is from accidental or irrational war, the expected (negative) payoff for mutual armament may now seem to be much larger than it was previously thought to be. In this case, it is more likely than we might earlier have thought that we face the Pax Romana or even Chicken, and less likely that we face a Prisoner's Dilemma. One might suppose that acceptance of the new consensus would discredit further talk of nuclear war fighting, nuclear superiority, and vulnerability, and shift the focus of policy well away from plans for active use of nuclear weapons. Hence, for the short term we may suppose that war by accident and irrationality will be less likely than it has recently seemed. We may therefore be more inclined to think we face a Prisoner's Dilemma.

Will the new consensus make much difference? Any answer must be speculative, but it seems likely that it will. Recall the circumstances of the Limited Test Ban Treaty. The strategic argument for the treaty was essentially that it would be a cooperative resolution of the Prisoner's Dilemma of the race to produce ever more effective warheads. It is odd that many people who are smart enough to understand various difficult issues lack any understanding of such strategic arguments. So-called "statesmen" currently want the United States to be slow in agreeing on arms controls so we can "catch-up" with the latest Soviet developments. Many of these people are merely dishonest politicians, but many seem to be blind to strategic claims. Such people on both sides blocked any halt on testing until a new consensus on the harmfulness of the testing suddenly developed. The treaty was then signed, within months of the demonstration that American babies born in the age of American atmospheric testing were growing up with strontium-90 in their teeth.[19] Bureaucracies and nations may behave stupidly, but they can be moved to common sense by powerful evidence of massive harm to themselves.

The new consensus means that the current state of affairs approaches that in which an infamous Doomsday Machine would destroy the planet if a nuclear explosion were set off. In one respect we are better off than under the Doomsday Machine: a single lunatic who set off one bomb could not destroy us all. In another respect we are worse off: the less-than-perfect guarantee of self-destruction may not be strong enough to prevent someone from risking a use of the weapons. Perhaps, on balance, the new consensus is better than the Doomsday Machine: no band of lunatics or terrorists can destroy us all, and neither organization that can destroy us all will want to. Hence, the superpowers will be deterred from nuclear attack.

Americans can prudentially take some comfort in the thought that the Soviet Union may be even more completely vulnerable to collapse in a nuclear winter than the United States. Soviet agriculture, beset by its four enemies—spring, summer, fall, and winter—could not survive even a modest drop in temperature. A hard freeze during the growing season would bring mass starvation. If, as *Science* reports,[20] Soviet scientists are persuaded that substantial use of nuclear weapons will produce radical reduction in temperature for several months, we can feel increased confidence that the Soviet Union will avoid using the weapons.

Alas, the new consensus may not lead to disarmament down to lower levels, but may merely recommend that less-destructive but still-lethal weapons be developed. The chief ecological problems with current weapons are that their explosive force blows tons of debris into the stratosphere, and their thermal effects may start fire-storms that inject tons of smoke into the stratosphere. Knowledge of the harmful-ness of these weapons even to their user presumably will lead to a search for new technologies that avoid self-destructive harms. There may therefore never be a bet-ter time than now to strive for massive mutual arms reductions and the end of all weapons testing.

The TTAPS estimates may be greatly exaggerated. The stratospheric effects of a nuclear attack are not even approximately a linear function of total explosive power used. Atmospheric bursts of high-yield weapons over cities would cause radically greater stratospheric pollution per megaton than would groundbursts of low-yield weapons on weapons installations. Indeed, highly accurate low-yield weapons (well under a megaton) detonated at ground level in a counterforce attack might inject negligible amounts of pollution into the stratosphere. Hence, if the superpowers are to draw any inference from studies of the climatological effects of nuclear explo-sives, the inference may be that they should pursue counterforce, first-strike weapons and strategies. Thus the current technological trend toward greater coun-terforce capability may be exacerbated. Would we be better off as a result? As usual, it depends. We might run a higher risk of war, but any war that erupted might be less destructive.

THE LOGIC AND MORALITY OF DETERRENCE

My concern has chiefly been with the risks of various regimes in a utilitarian account of the nuclear dilemma. It would be odd, however, to put much effort into such a discussion if the logic or the morality of deterrence were seriously doubted, as they are in certain circles. One claim maintains that, loosely speaking, the notion of deterrence is logically flawed because failure is inherent in it. The utilitarian account is criticized as self-contradictory and immoral.

It is often claimed that the premise on which belief in nuclear deterrence is based is flawed because failure is inherent in the logic of deterrence. Failure does seem to be inherent in certain kinds of deterrent systems. For example, it may be necessary that some people commit crimes and suffer punishment under the criminal justice system for the threat of punishment to succeed in deterring anyone from committing crimes. But this is a function of the generalized nature of the system of criminal deterrence.

Consider for a moment the inherent complexity of the system of deterrent sanc-tions in criminal law. First, the sanctions cannot be brought to bear with certainty, but only with greater or lesser probability. The lower the probability, the more severe the threatened sanction may have to be to deter. Second, the sanction is rela-tively generalized. It must be threatened against all potential miscreants more or less uniformly; its severity cannot be tailored to match individual variation. A 50-50 chance of going to jail for a year might be sufficient to stop you from embez-zling, but not to stop me. A sure prospect of execution would deter virtually every-one from committing most crimes, while less-sure prospects of much milder penalties are sufficient to deter most of us. That the criminal sanction often fails to deter is not a matter of the logic of deterrence. Rather it is a matter of our choosing levels of enforcement and degrees of punishment that are inadequate to deter every-one, always.

No comparable inherent failure in the logic of deterrence governs many classes of very specific acts of deterrence. If you point a gun at me as I reach for your money and you say, "Don't touch it or I shoot," I will not need to be shot once to be deterred. The deterrent standoff between the nuclear superpowers resembles this example more than the deterrent system of criminal sanctions. Retaliation in the nuclear standoff can be instantaneous and sure because it can be confidently focused on the only nation that can provoke it. One of the reasons we fear nuclear proliferation is that deterrence in a world of many nuclear powers begins to have the problems of deterrence in criminal law: it cannot be so surely focused, and we may doubt that what might deter, say, Soviet leaders, would deter the leaders of other nations.

Even if deterrence makes rational sense, however, there is still a commonplace objection to supposing deterrence in such single-shot cases can be right, at least on a utilitarian account. Once the Soviet Union has attacked the United States, say, it can no longer serve anyone's interests in deterrence for the United States to counterattack. Hence, it would be immoral to counterattack. But this implies that a moral nation cannot meaningfully deter an adversary by threatening nuclear retaliation. Practically speaking, this argument is obviously specious, because the supposedly moral nation can arrange matters institutionally to guarantee a counter attack, or at least to make it extremely likely. Since the result of effective deterrence could conceivably be better than the result of not deterring, it may be moral to arrange for retaliation to happen under relevant circumstances.

Against this conclusion another familiar complaint is raised. It will be utilitarian to deter only if one can rely on nonutilitarian actions by certain people (particularly in the strategic defense corps). Hence, utilitarian theory is inherently contradictory if it prescribes deterrence. But this is a silly complaint. If everyone were utilitarian we would not face the appalling prospect of nuclear war. It is because many people are not utilitarian that nuclear deterrence is an issue. A utilitarian prescription of what we ought to do about nuclear weapons that did not take into account the way actual people behave in our world would be a stupid prescription. One that does take actual behavior into account can, without contradiction, recommend a system of deterrence that depends on ex post actions to retaliate.

Finally, consider the familiar complaint that, even if it is internally consistent, utilitarianism is immoral. It would be out of place here to try to deal systematically with this objection. But the problem of nuclear weapons and the possible consequences that may follow our policies concerning their employment poses the starkest real-life test of the generality of this objection to utilitarianism.

It is a peculiarity of much of philosophical ethics that it is almost exclusively personal and not political or institutional. In deed, philosophers often treat duties and rights as personal, not legal, political, or otherwise institutional problems. Certain intuitionist rights theorists, such as Charles Fried and Robert Nozick—as opposed to such a rationalist rights theorist as Alan Gewirth—seem to demoralize ethics into a concern with how-I-get-(and keep)-mine.

But even those for whom ethics is still a matter of morality often truncate their view and do not look past the moral agent into the realm of contingent facts. Most extant defenses of unilateral disarmament by the United States are deontological and agent-centered: they follow immediately from the claim that one ought not to be a party to using nuclear weapons. Germain Grisez notes simply, "When I say that the deterrent is morally evil, . . . I mean that we ought to dismantle the deterrent immediately, regardless of consequences. The end simply does not justify the means."[21] If the end is the expected net saving of tens of hundreds of millions of lives, can this view be tenable?

Alas, when concern with consequences enters moral judgment, it is often extremely hard to be dogmatic. Is it better to face a one-in-a-hundred chance of the destruction of the United States and 100,000,000 Americans, or a one-in-five chance of the destruction of southern California and parts of several other states and 20,000,000 Americans? How about one in a thousand versus one in fifty? Assuming one can answer such questions, what are the odds of how much damage under the mutual deterrence and the unilateral disarmament regimes?

Despite such difficulties, when the consequences are as grievous as they may be in various nuclear arms regimes, otherwise honorable concerns with perfection, virtue, rights, and the doctrine of double-effect simply give way. The difference between letting humanity or some large part of it be immolated and causing it to be immolated is a moral difference that pales into insignificance. The person who does either is heinous and immoral. Moral theory— rightly—risks the fate of Catholic doctrine in the age of Voltaire if moral theorists do not face this dreadful issue in a way that matters to the hundreds of millions of people whose lives are at stake.

Of course, this means that anyone in a position to affect nuclear policy necessarily has or risks having dirty hands. That is an inescapable fact of life in the nuclear age. Moral theory cannot dodge the fact and be credible. A moral assessment of alternative nuclear arms policies must be grounded in their alternative harms, not in a concern with moral agency.

CONCLUDING REMARKS

While it is surely true that the chief problem we currently face with nuclear weapons is the obstinacy and even stupidity of national leaders in their rhetoric of hostility, it is also true that the technology of nuclear weapons has become an almost autonomous force for harm. To create trust in the presence of these weapons will be extremely difficult.

It is an important fact about the present system of deterrence that the existence of current weapons technologies puts the two superpowers at risk just because they have underlying conflicts. It is not now in the power of either superpower to avoid both the consequences of unilateral disarmament and the consequences of some form of continued nuclear deterrence for at least the near term. Nor, alas, can both superpowers together likely avoid both sets of consequences.

In the easy coordination Games 1, 2, and 3 in Table 10.1, it is supposed that a United States disarmed to a minimal deterrence level would have nothing to gain but something to lose from suddenly rearming to a level adequate to suppress the Soviet Union. On the contrary, it is at least arguable—and one suspects many would firmly believe—that the United States would have much to gain from such rearmament. In particular, it would preempt the possibility that the Soviet Union would rearm. Hence, given that the weapons are easily manufactured and not easily disinvented, both sides probably prefer to be the only nuclear power over all other possibilities. In that case, Games 1, 2, and 3 cannot represent the state of affairs we face. The nuclear arms conflict is genuinely a conflict of the type shown in one of Games 4, 5, and 6, and not merely a failed cooperation. The optimal solution to Games 4 and 5 is most likely mutual disarmament down to levels of minimal deterrence. The optimal solution to Game 6 is unilateral disarmament by one of the superpowers.

For what it is worth, my view of what policy we should follow is somewhat ambivalent. I think it is almost surely true that mutual disarmament down to levels of minimal deterrence is far better than the present, lunatic regime. Unilateral disarmament might be better than either of these regimes, but it might also be worse than either. Its potential harms and benefits are harder to assess, because they involve social scientific claims about a kind of world of which we have no experience.

The overwhelming difficulty of a moral assessment of what to do about nuclear arms is captured in the question of which of these games fits our current predicament. To answer that question we must assess relevant risks, with all their contingencies. Simple analysis is insufficient—facts count uppermost. Philosophers seem to be painfully uncomfortable with facts, not least perhaps because they do not really believe in them. Social scientists, whose life is a struggle with presumptive facts, generally are analytically sloppy, and they have the crudest grasp of moral theory. On the issue of nuclear policy, however, it is essential to bring to bear jointly the strengths of philosophers and social scientists.

NOTES

1. Russell Hardin, "Unilateral Versus Mutual Disarmament," *Philosophy and Public Affairs* 12 (1983): 236–54, especially pp. 246–50.
2. It is possible that more than ordinal information would be useful. For example, with certain ranges of payoffs, the jointly optimal strategy in an iterated PD may be to alternate between the 1,4 and 4,1 outcomes. Moreover, if cardinal comparisons are possible, we might even conclude that the best joint outcome was, say, 1,4. Achieving it might require a side payment from the United States to the Soviet Union. Fortunately, these complications are probably pointless in the present context.
3. Noel Gayler, "Opposition to Nuclear Armament," *Annals of the American Academy of Political and Social Science* 469 (September 1983): 11–21, quote on p. 20.
4. See the photograph in Bruce Russett, *The Prisoners of Insecurity* (San Francisco: W.H. Freeman, 1983), p. 22.
5. Naess, Chapter 25, and McMahan, Chapter 17, this volume; Douglas P. Lackey, "Missiles and Morals: A Utilitarian Look at Nuclear Deterrence," *Philosophy and Public Affairs* 11 (Summer 1982): 189–231; Robert P. Churchill, "Nuclear Arms as a Philosophical and Moral Issue," *Annals of the American Academy of Political and Social Science* 469 (September 1983): 46–57, especially pp. 56–57.
6. David Alan Rosenberg, "The Origins of Overkill," *International Security* 7 (Spring 1983): 3–71, especially pp. 33–35.
7. Henry Kissinger, *The White House Years* (Boston: Little, Brown, 1979), p. 183; Marvin Kalb and Bernard Kalb, *Kissinger* (Boston: Little, Brown, 1974), pp. 226–28.
8. Lackey, "Disarmament Revisited: A Reply to Kavka and Hardin," *Philosophy and Public Affairs* 12 (Summer 1983): 261–65, especially pp. 263–64.
9. Churchill, "Nuclear Arms," p. 57.

10. Federation of American Scientists, *Seeds of Promise* (Andover, MA: Brick House Publishing Co., 1983), pp. 160, 164.

11. Harvard Nuclear Study Group, *Living with Nuclear Weapons* (Cambridge: Harvard University Press, 1983), pp. 174, 177–79; Michael Pentz, "The Threat of Nuclear War and the Responsibilities of Scientists;" pp. 63–80 in *Debate on Disarmament,* ed. Michael Clarke and Marjorie Mowlam (London: Routledge and Kegan Paul, 1982), especially pp. 70–71.

12. They are 18 feet long by 2 feet wide with their wings folded, and each can carry a 200 kiloton warhead (Harvard Nuclear Study Group, *Living with Nuclear Weapons,* p. 178; Pentz, "The Threat of Nuclear War," p. 71).

13. In commentary at the political theory workshop, University of Chicago, summer 1982.

14. Jeff McMahan, *British Nuclear Weapons: For and Against* (London: Junction Books, 1981).

15. See further, Hardin, "Unilateral Versus Mutual Disarmament," especially pp. 252–54.

16. See Gregory Kavka, "Deterrence, Utility, and Rational Choice," *Theory and Decision* 12 (1980): 41–60, whose "disaster avoidance principle" is a cousin to MMR; and Lackey, "Missiles and Morals," pp. 196–205.

17. Every constant-sum game is strategically equivalent to the relevant zero-sum game. Unfortunately, the usual convention for referring to the whole class is "zero-sum games."

18. *Science,* 18 November 1983, pp. 822–23. Also see Chapter 3 by Paul and Anne Ehrlich, this volume; R.P. Turco, O.B. Toon, T.P. Ackerman, J.B. Pollack, and Carl Sagan, "Nuclear Winter: Global Consequences of Multiple Nuclear Explosions," *Science,* 23 December 1983, pp. 1283–92; and Paul R. Ehrlich et al., "Long-Term Biological Consequences of Nuclear War," ibid., pp. 1293–1300.

19. Much more was going on at the time, but the educational campaign by doctors and others on the effects of our own tests on us seems to have been persuasive and important.

20. *Science,* 18 November 1983, p. 823.

21. Germain G. Grisez, "Toward a Consistent Natural Law Ethics of Killing," *American Journal of Jurisprudence* 15 (1970): 64–96, quote on p. 93. For a good, brief discussion of such views see David Hollenbach, *Nuclear Ethics* (New York: Paulist Press, 1983), especially chap. 6, "Deterrence—The Hardest Question," pp. 63–85.

11
BOMBS AND BIRDS' NESTS

Richard A. Watson

MAN AS A PART OF NATURE

Let us consider the thesis that man is a part of nature, that is, that human beings are animals and culture is natural. This is actually a rather trivial hypothesis and not much more than saying that what is, is natural. The main alternative thesis is that human beings have a supernatural element, such as an immortal soul or an intuitive sense, that provides access, say, to a realm of absolute values. In its religious expression, this view might include the provision that some of man's goals and behavior are undertaken with divine guidance or according to divine plan. I see little evidence for this alternative, but there is much empirical evidence for the view to which I subscribe, that all human behavior—both biological and cultural—is a result of natural processes.[1] And on this view, bombs are as natural as birds' nests. Just as natural as bombs, of course, are international treaties between nations for the elimination of nuclear war, and on this I base my hope for peace.

Before going on to this hope, I must discuss one problem stemming from man's being a part of nature. This is the biological fact that individual living things are subordinate to the species of which they are members, in the strict sense that all individuals die even though their species is perpetuated. (Similarly, species themselves evolve and become extinct as life itself goes on.) It then appears that the "importance" or "purpose" of individuals is to perpetuate the species (and of species to perpetuate life).

This suggests a species solution to current human problems. For example, Garrett Hardin recommends that large numbers of people selected primarily by geographic and historic circumstances be abandoned to a fate of early death.[2] Other human beings more favorably located will survive, and the human species will be perpetuated. Such a view is, obviously, hard on individual humans who, by accident, may be citizens of, say, Bangladesh. If such thinking is unfair, however, it is

The ideas expressed in this essay are the result of study and discussion during the years when the author was a Fellow of the American Council of Learned Societies, of the Princeton Center of International Studies, and of the Center for Advanced Study in the Behavioral Sciences at Stanford, California.

both expedient and practical. I turn now to the ecological facts on which it is based, and to a critique of the holistic ideology these facts might appear to support.

THE IDEOLOGY OF HOLISM

I am concerned with holism as it is suggested by an ecological argument that goes something like this: every individual living thing and every species on our earth are members of an ecological community. All may be, as far as we know, the only embodiment of life in the universe. This community of individuals is such that the good of any one of its members is linked with the whole; the survival of any one individual or species depends on its harmonious integration with the community. Thus, any given individual or species is subordinate to the ecological community as a whole. One conclusion that has been drawn from this is that it is anthropocentric and antiecological to work for the survival of the human species more than for the survival of any other species.[3] And as remarked above, Hardin argues that it is bad for the human species to spend resources on perpetuating the lives of individuals who impede species survival.

The primary conclusion of this argument is that any given individual or species is expendable. What is "important" is the good of the ecological community of life that does survive. Individuals essentially serve the community; the community incidently serves the individuals. Thus, this version of the ecological argument leads to the position that the good of an individual can always be sacrificed for the good of the ecological community. Environmentalists who argue in this way that we should live in harmony with and protect the ecological community have a tendency to support the ideology of holistic communalism. The argument supports the patriotic view that one should be willing to die for one's country. And it lies behind therapeutic programs designed to bring deviants into adjustment with community standards and practices.

A problem with this position is that even extreme communalists still pay homage to the view that individual human beings are important, and that the community or the state is in some large part meant to serve the needs of individuals. An argument against communalism is that the ecological community, the culture, the society, the state, and the human community are abstractions, just as are the species and life itself. They are basically sets of actual and possible relationships among actual and possible individuals, and to set them up as "important" or of value independent of the individuals that embody them is to subordinate actual, existing individuals to abstract entities. The good that a well-balanced ecological community does for the individuals that make it up is in fact the combination of goods that all the individuals in the community enjoy as a result of being interrelated in that particular way. The ecological community is not an entity that causes this good, just as species and life itself are not entities that cause individuals.

I am sure that human beings can live securely in harmonious integrated ecological communities and social relationships. These are kinds of holisms. But it is wrong to use these facts to support the communal ideology that the whole is more important or more real than the parts. Consider, for example, two interpretations of President Kennedy's plea to "Think not what your country can do for you, but what you can do for your country." Your country is not an entity that can do things; rather, the word "country" stands for social and political arrangements. In strictly individual terms, Kennedy was saying, "Think not what I can do for you, but what you can do for me." Or, more generously, "Think not about the community relations that would be best for you, but about the community relations that would be best for all Americans." The second interpretation stresses the fact that individual goods depend on communal interrelations.

This view of man as a part of nature, and of the perpetuation of the human species and of life itself as more important than individuals who appear to exist essentially to perpetuate the species, tends toward holistic thinking. Holistic thinking, in turn, sometimes leads to anti-individualistic, totalitarian, and fascistic political ideologies. Of course, there is no necessary connection, but thinking for a group sometimes leads to anti-individualistic group thinking.

But is the view any better that only individuals are important? Individualist thinking tends toward anarchy. Some claim that it sets man against man with no goals or goods other than the immediate gratification of desires. I cannot argue the point here, but it does seem as likely that individualistic human beings can come together in cooperation for the purpose of secure and harmonious human relationships for their own sake, as that communalists will attain the good life for all through subordinating themselves to an abstract entity, such as the community or the state or the species or life itself.

I have mentioned one example of species thinking, Garrett Hardin's scheme of triage. It is a basically passive plan in which the people of the "have" nations let the people of the "have-not" nations go under. Such might-makes-right thinking in this century has led to active genocide. A leader cries for living space for his people. The only way he can get it is by taking it away from others. And what is to be done with the dispossessed?

Our strength is in our quickness and our brutality. Genghis Khan had millions of women and children killed, by his own will and with a gay heart. History sees him only [as] a great state-builder. What weak western European civilization thinks about me does not matter. . . . I have sent to the east only my "Death's-Head units" with the order to kill without pity or mercy all men, women, and children of Polish race or language. Only in such a way shall we win the vital space that we need. Who still talks nowadays of the extermination of the Armenians?[4]

. . . Destruction of Poland in the foreground . . . Have no pity. Brutal attitude. Eighty million people [the Germans needing living space] shall get what is their right [by eliminating the Poles]. Their [the Germans'] existence has to be secured. The strongest has the right.[5]

Given the way food is produced and distributed, now, the earth is overpopulated with human beings. Perhaps everyone could eat well and live well if we all became vegetarians and gave up high-energy technology. But it is unlikely that this will happen. Even if it did, population would continue to grow for several centuries, and no animal species has ever been on such a geometrically rising curve without crashing. There will be a great reduction of population soon, in the next few tens or hundreds of years.[6]

Thinking biologically of man as a part of nature, one can ask: what use are the bombs? They are for reducing the population and opening living space. Thinking culturally, one might argue that the geniuses who conceived of, the technicians who designed, the engineers who built, and the politicians who may deploy the neutron bomb are working for the human species. They may reduce the human population to tolerable limits with only minimal long-run radiation effects, and without destroying property or living space. This is an example of thinking not for individuals, but for the species.[7]

Is it unthinkable? Most suggestions about how to avoid nuclear war ignore the fact that those who think they can win a nuclear war *can* win a nuclear war. It is a mistake to believe that a scenario in which half the people on earth are killed is a horror beyond imagining. Plenty of people—it would take only ten or a hundred— would be quite happy to preside over the rebuilding of the world after a nuclear holocaust. Look at the numbers. Reduce the world's population by half and we *still* have a population problem.[8]

What is the alternative? The course of action I propose depends on an individualist ideology, so I state here briefly an argument for individualism that I present in more detail elsewhere,[9] the claim that only self-conscious individuals can be moral agents. Only conscious individuals can have primary rights and duties—that is, they must know that they have them to have them in a primary sense—and thus morality applies in a primary sense only to individuals. When self-conscious individuals have ideas about what is good and bad and right and wrong, and when they can choose and act to one or the other end, then they can be moral agents in the sense of being responsible for what they do.

While entities other than human beings—dolphins, for example—might be moral agents in this sense, it is surely obvious that the community, the state, the species, and life itself are not. Hegelians may think that the state or the people are coming to consciousness, Jungians that mankind has an underconsciousness, and mystics that the universe itself has life and consciousness. I see no evidence for any of these hypotheses. And so by evidence and temperament I keep this discussion in the naturalistic context.

I agree that ecological holism is a proper model for viewing the place of the human species in nature, but we must avoid abstract holistic thinking on behalf of the environment, *the* human species, life *itself, the* nation-state, and even *the* individual. Instead, each and every one of us must act as an individual responsible for the decisions he or she makes. We must recall all other individuals—particularly those acting in the name of abstract entities and institutions—to their individual responsibility for the decisions they make. The future of the human species rests on decisions that will be made by identifiable individuals. These important individuals can be controlled only if they are identified and only if they can be held to personal account.[10]

In sum, holistic species thinking is a trap. It is not the species that is important, but rather each self-conscious person; not the person, an abstraction, but *each* concrete, conscious individual. There is no point for *nation-states* to pledge not to use nuclear weapons; nation-states are not moral actors. Only *individuals* can give pledges.

WHAT INDIVIDUALS CAN DO

Individual human beings make decisions whether or not to build and use nuclear weapons. So far, only President Harry S. Truman has decided to use them, in 1945. Since then, crucial decisions to make more nuclear weapons have probably been made by only a few hundred individuals. Several thousand more bear responsiblity for their influence in advising that more nuclear weapons be made. And millions are responsible for making them. But I am interested only in those individuals at the top who have the authority, and who are obeyed when they say: "Make those weapons. Drop that bomb."

They are very few in number. If we can influence them to continue to decide not to use nuclear weapons, and to begin to decide not to manufacture more nuclear weapons, nuclear disarmament will be on its way.

This thesis has a major objection. The motive forces in human affairs—this argument goes—are not individuals. The crucial determining factor in any major historical event is never a decision made by an individual, no matter how great his authority. Instead, forces of biological, environmental, geographic, demographic, economic, cultural, social, technological, ideological, or spiritual development determine the course of human history. It is not exactly that technology, say, is autonomous. The objection is not that individual decisions are determined in the sense that they could not logically be otherwise, but that individual decisions are made under pressure and influence of such force that given decisions must be made.

For example, this argument goes, if a president of the United States during the mid-20th century had decided to make accommodations with Russia, he would have been replaced by a president who would support the Cold War. The argument continues that if a leader of a major nation decided to stop producing nuclear weapons, his decisions would be ignored and he would be replaced by a leader who would order production to continue. This is a view best expressed by Leslie White: that individuals and individual decisions are not the motive forces of history, but are merely the instruments through which autonomous physical and cultural evolution takes place. [11]

Most great leaders believe that individual decisions are determinative. Here again is Adolf Hitler, on 22 August 1939:

> Essentially it depends on me, my existence, because of my political activities. Furthermore the fact that probably no one will ever again have the confidence of the whole German people as I do. There will probably never again be a man in the future with more authority than I have. My existence is therefore a factor of great value.

And he goes on immediately to say:

> But I can be eliminated at any time by a criminal or an idiot. [12]

I think the evidence shows that Hitler is right about the power of individuals. The assassination of Hitler in 1939 would have made a difference, as did the later death of Joseph Stalin (a man who probably did have more authority than Hitler). The conviction that individuals are important has led to the concept of "head-hunting" by state police forces, who try to eliminate or make ineffective the leaders of radical groups. I am suggesting a kind of head-hunting of leaders who can make decisions about the deployment of nuclear weapons.

Of course, for leaders to have influence, their decisions must be carried out. The authority structure of hierarchical organizations is set up so that decisions from the top *will* be carried out. Thus, it is too easy to say with the determinists that the times were ripe, that had it not been this leader making this decision, another leader would have made the same decision. In numerous instances of change, the major factor that stands out is change of leadership. A new leader makes different decisions than those of the old leader. Often there is no continuity of forces from old to new leader, only a discontinuity.

We must continually influence the continuously changing few hundred people in the world who have the power and authority to make decisions about nuclear weapons and war. Those of us who want to live in peace with modest goods must support those rulers, leaders, industrialists, and other powerful individuals who do not appear likely to initiate a nuclear holocaust. We have to strive to get our leaders to agree not to use nuclear weapons. And if they appear to be about to push the button, we must restrain them with force, violently if necessary.[13]

NOTES

1. This is argued for in detail in Richard A. Watson and Patty Jo Watson, *Man and Nature: An Anthropological Essay in Human Ecology* (New York: Harcourt Brace and World, 1969).
2. Garrett Hardin, *Promethean Ethics: Living with Death, Competition, and Triage* (Seattle: University of Washington Press, 1980).
3. For criticism of this view, see Richard A. Watson, "A Critique of Anti-anthropocentric Biocentrism," *Environmental Ethics* 5 (1983): 245–56.
4. Adolf Hitler. Quoted by William L. Shirer in *End of a Berlin Diary* (New York: Alfred A. Knopf, 1947), p. 253.
5. Ibid., p. 255. Speech of 22 August 1939.
6. See Paul R. Ehrlich and Anne H. Ehrlich, Chapter 3, this volume.
7. This possibility is raised by the Ehrlichs in ibid.
8. Ibid. The Ehrlichs' remark that in the worst case civilization would be destroyed, but the human species would survive.
9. Richard A. Watson. "Self-Consciousness and the Rights of Nonhuman Animals and Nature" *Environmental Ethics* 1 (1979): 95–129.
10. Something of this sort is implied by Jonathan Schell, *The Fate of the Earth* (New York: Alfred A. Knopf, 1982). See also Stephen Toulmin, Chapter 19, this volume.
11. Leslie A. White, *The Science of Culture: A Study of Man and Civilization* (New York: Farrar, Strauss, 1949).
12. Hitler, quoted in Shirer, *End of a Berlin Diary*, p. 248.
13. In "Hard Cases for Total Pacifists," *Peace Research* 14, no. 2: 21–28, Herbert Spiegelberg suggests that in the face of a serious threat it might be better to surrender than to bring on nuclear war. He remarks that after a few hundred years, even the authority of the Roman Empire petered out. I think any nation that disarmed unilaterally would be taken over or at least controlled by nations with nuclear weapons. Politics has to do with power, and probably will always involve violence and war. What we are trying to do now is to outlaw nuclear weapons in war and politics. Should we succeed, we must then quickly add chemical and biological weapons to the forbidden list. See also Jefferson McMahan, Chapter 17, this volume, and Arne Naess, Chapter 25.

PART IV

JUST WAR? MORALITY AND NUCLEAR WEAPONS

Nuclear weapons sharply challenge our traditional ways of thinking about the morality of military matters. The advent of nuclear weapons has changed military reality in a fundamental manner, and our traditional ways of moral thinking may not be adequate to accommodate the change. War and weapons of war have always posed special problems for our moral understanding, due to the difficulty of the tension war creates between our moral and prudential concerns. Yet large nuclear arsenals have raised the moral problems of war to a critical pitch. The unique power of nuclear explosions gives these weapons a moral uniqueness as well. The moral problems discussed in the next chapters all reflect, in one way or another, the confounding of our traditional ways of moral thinking by the special nature of nuclear weapons.

Four questions are addressed in the next eight essays. Is the use of nuclear weapons in war ever morally justifiable? Can the threat to use nuclear weapons—the policy of nuclear deterrence—be morally justified? What does the moral status of nuclear weapons policies imply for political action? Finally, what is the relation between morality and political decisionmaking regarding nuclear weapons? This last question, following naturally upon the discussion of nuclear thinking in Part III, is considered first.

The first two essays address different aspects of the relation between morality and nuclear decisionmaking. Gregory Kavka's essay investigates the relation between morality and politics through a case study of the Cuban Missile Crisis. Reflection on the crisis generates a "moralist's puzzle" that he seeks to resolve: why was the avoidance of nuclear war not given greater priority and weight in the crisis decisionmaking? He concludes that the politician and the moralist approach problems with different "mind-sets." Jean Elshtain's concern is how the divorce between morality and politics exemplified by nuclear decisionmaking has come to be, and how this divorce is reflected in the relations between men and women. The divorce between morality and politics, she argues, is a result of the success of the doctrine of realism, and this doctrine, and the inadequacy of the just-war response to it, is the focus of her examination.

The essays by Sidney Axinn and Terry Nardin discuss whether or not the use of nuclear weapons in war is morally justifiable. Both address this question in terms of moral codes or practices within which war has traditionally been considered and argue that these codes and practices rule out the use of nuclear weapons. Axinn considers the morality of the use of nuclear weapons in terms of the the code of military honor. The military practitioner is met on his own ground and shown that the moral code to which he is professionally committed implies that the use of nuclear weapons is morally unjustifiable. Nardin argues that because our traditions of moral reflection and discourse on war, including the just-war tradition, give primacy to categorical over instrumental or consequentialist constraints, the use of nuclear weapons is morally prohibited. His main concern is to criticize the one argument that could morally permit their use, the argument from extremity.

Nuclear deterrence, the topic taken up in the next two essays, raises two kinds of moral questions. First, is deterrence permitted by the kind of deontological constraints discussed by Axinn and Nardin? This question turns largely on the moral status of the intentions involved in the policy. Douglas Lackey examines three arguments that attempt to show that the intentions involved in nuclear deterrence are morally acceptable, and he finds all of them to be unsound. But, second, given the importance of the consequences of maintaining or abandoning nuclear deterrence, is the policy morally justified from a consequentialist perspective? Jefferson McMahan takes up this question, arguing that nuclear deterrence, while lessening the risk of domination by the Soviet Union, also increases the risk of nuclear war. After an examination of the risks involved, McMahan concludes that unilateral nuclear disarmament is morally preferable to the policy of nuclear deterrence.

The concern of moral reasoning to guide action is one focus of the essays by Edmund Pellegrino and Stephen Toulmin. Both consider what actions should be taken by individuals in the light of an understanding of the moral reality of the nuclear predicament. Pellegrino, examining the moral role of physicians, argues that they are morally obligated to educate the public about the medical consequences of nuclear war, but are not morally permitted to refuse to cooperate in plans for treating victims of nuclear war. Toulmin argues that the contemporary relevance of just-war analysis is fully seen only by examining the concepts of sovereignty and allegiance. His examination leads him to recommend two strategies. First, we should practice *counter-deterrence*, i.e., threaten to abandon our loyalty to the state should it ever use nuclear weapons. Second, we should recognize our *multiple loyalties*, such as those transnational commitments we have as human beings or as members of professions, in order to institutionalize an independent source of moral criticism against the claims of the nuclear-armed nation-state.

12
MORALITY AND NUCLEAR POLITICS: LESSONS OF THE MISSILE CRISIS

Gregory S. Kavka

Decisions about the development, placement, and use of nuclear weapons (and other weapons whose employment may lead to the use of nuclear weapons) have potentially enormous effects on the well-being of humanity. Wrong decisions in this area could even lead to the extinction of our species. Such facts tempt those of us trained in moral philosophy to view the formulation and execution of nuclear weapons policies as essentially moral problems. But nuclear weapons decisions are typically made by political leaders, who are greatly influenced by a variety of non-moral (e.g., political, military, and personal) factors. This prompts a number of questions about the role of morality in nuclear decisionmaking. Have moral considerations had any influence on nuclear weapons policy? If so, in what way? What factors, if any, have interfered with or restricted this influence? Might moral factors come to play a greater role in nuclear politics, and if so, how can moralists—philosophers, theologians, and others—contribute to their doing so?

To obtain tentative answers to some of these questions, I shall use an illustrative case study, the U.S. government decisionmaking during the Cuban Missile Crisis of October 1962. This incident has been selected for a number of reasons. Ample documentation of the decision process in this crisis, and even some theoretical studies of that process, are available. Also, it is clear that the decisionmakers in this situation were cognizant of the presence of the factor which renders all nuclear weapons decisions of great moral significance— the attendant risks of nuclear war. There was also a public intervention by a prominent philosopher, Bertrand Russell, which might provide some lessons about moralists' direct influence on nuclear decisions. Finally, a variety of particular facts about the missile crisis decisions suggest some interesting hypotheses about nuclear politics in general.

The missile crisis was in many respects an atypical instance of nuclear weapons decisionmaking. It was unusually important (because of the risks and stakes

---

This essay was written while I was supported by a fellowship for independent study and research from the National Endowment for the Humanities. I am grateful to the Endowment for its support, and to Steven Lee for his very helpful comments on an earlier draft.

involved), received extraordinary attention from high government officials, and involved the time pressures and psychological accompaniments of crisis (rather than routine) decisionmaking. So we should be cautious in extrapolating its lessons to cover more "normal" decisions about nuclear weapons development and deployment. At the same time, it would be highly surprising if the tensions and pressures of the missile crisis completely altered the tendencies present in normal nuclear decisionmaking situations. For example, it is clear from the record that the general tendency of decisionmakers to reflect the attitudes and perspectives of their own units or departments carried over into the missile crisis: Defense Secretary McNamara initially viewed the Cuba-based missiles in purely strategic terms, U.N. Ambassador Stevenson recommended a diplomatic approach, and high military officials urged forceful military action.[1] For these reasons, it does not seem inappropriate to treat the missile crisis as a source of suggestive hypotheses about nuclear weapons decisions and the role played in their formulation by moral considerations.

I begin by briefly reviewing the events of the missile crisis, including incidents of particular relevance to our concern with moral influences. I then proceed to discuss what should most puzzle moralists about U.S. decisionmaking: that avoidance of nuclear war (and risk thereof) was not given even greater priority and weight. A solution to this puzzle is then proposed, which rests on the claim that political decisionmakers and moralists typically approach decision-situations with different "mind-sets"—classes of background assumptions, ways of conceptualizing alternatives, etc. A review of the significant role moral considerations did have in missile crisis decisionmaking follows, in which the deontological form of such considerations is emphasized and discussed. Finally, I attempt to distill from all this some useful lessons about the possibilities for, limits on, and means of, future moral influence on nuclear decisionmaking.

EVENTS OF THE MISSILE CRISIS

Soon after taking office as president of the United States, John F. Kennedy approved a CIA-organized invasion of Castro's Cuba by armed exiles. The ill-fated "Bay of Pigs" landing of April 1961 was quickly crushed by Cuban forces. This fiasco caused extreme domestic and international political embarassment to the new administration; and at the June 1961 summit meeting in Vienna, although Kennedy admitted the incident had been a mistake, Soviet leader Nikita Khrushchev reportedly "bullied" him about it.[2]

As the congressional elections of November 1962 approached, Kennedy was continually attacked by Republicans for being soft on Cuba. One senator charged that the Soviets were installing missiles in Cuba, and while the available intelligence estimates and the assurances of Soviet diplomats indicated this was not so, the president made two public warnings in September 1961 that the introduction of "offensive ground-to-ground" missiles would not be tolerated by the U.S.[3]

Nevertheless, photographs of Cuba taken by U-2 planes on 14 October and analyzed on 15 October revealed that the Soviets were lying: medium- and intermediate-range ballistic missile sites were under construction. The president was notified the morning of 16 October and immediately called a meeting of an ad hoc group of high-level advisors, an Executive Committee that continued to meet frequently throughout the crisis, at first in the strictest secrecy. They initially considered six categories of alternative responses: doing nothing, a private diplomatic approach to the Soviets, a private diplomatic approach to Castro, a blockade of Cuba, a "surgical" air strike against the missile bases, and a full-scale invasion of Cuba.[4] Soon they narrowed the choices to two, blockade or air strike. Despite initial leanings toward the latter, a consensus for blockade developed, and the president decided on this course on 20 October. The main considerations that apparently influenced this decision were that (a) an air strike would kill Soviet military men and risk immediate Soviet escalation, (b) an air strike would—as Undersecretary of State George Ball and Attorney General Robert Kennedy (the president's brother) emphasized—be a Pearl Harbor in reverse, and would go against American traditions, (c) an air strike could not be sure to destroy all the missiles,[5] and (d) the blockade was a first step that could be followed by stronger action if necessary.[6] U.S. officials were well aware, however, that even the blockade was dangerous and could lead to nuclear war between the superpowers.

In preparation for public announcement of the blockade, the administration sent emissaries to major allies, prepared for a presentation to the U.N. Security Council, and made arrangements for an Organization of American States meeting to endorse the blockade, thus giving it a degree of legitimacy under international law.[7] In addition, military moves were made to enforce the blockade, to prepare for possible attack on Cuba, and to increase strategic readiness. After informing, but not consulting with, key congressional leaders, the president announced the existence of the Cuban missiles and the naval "quarantine" of weapons shipments to Cuba in a national address.[8] He had communicated the same message to the Soviets by diplomatic channels an hour earlier.

Less than two days later, the blockade was officially put into effect. The Soviets' immediate public and private response was that they would defy the blockade, which they considered illegal and provocative.[9] Both sides apparently put their strategic military forces on alert. Bertrand Russell sent telegrams to Kennedy and Khrushchev urging restraint by each, but condemning only the actions of the United States.[10] Chairman Khrushchev responded to Russell publicly, calling for a summit meeting and blaming the U.S., which he compared to a robber that needed to be taught a lesson.[11] President Kennedy also answered Russell personally, claiming that "your attention might well be directed to the burglars rather than those who caught the burglars."[12] Meanwhile, the extreme anxiety of American officials was eased somewhat when half the Soviet ships on their way to Cuba stopped outside the quarantine line. The president tried to manage the blockade carefully, drawing back its radius to give the Soviets more time to think, letting through a Soviet tanker, and first stopping and searching a chartered vessel of neutral registry. But U-2 photos showed the missile construction on Cuba proceeding even faster than before and indicated that some missiles would soon be operational. Tension grew again when a U-2 was downed over Cuba (Kennedy canceled previous orders for retaliation to such an occurence), another strayed over the U.S.S.R. due to navigational error, and pressure for an air strike grew within the administration.

Two letters from Khrushchev on 26 and 27 October offered different terms of settlement for inspected removal of the missiles. The first, a rambling personal message, called only for a U.S. pledge not to invade Cuba.[13] The second, more-formal letter required the removal of U.S. missiles in Turkey as well.[14] (President Kennedy had earlier ordered the dismantling of these missiles, but diplomatic complications had prevented this from being done.) Robert Kennedy's suggestion to accept the more generous proposal of the first message, while ignoring the second, was adopted and carried out. In addition, the president's brother personally told Soviet Ambassador Dobrynin, on the night of 27 October, that the U.S. would attack the missiles unless, by the next day, the Soviets agreed to remove them. He also indicated that the president had previously ordered the Turkish missiles removed and expected they would be gone soon after the crisis.[15] The next day Chairman Khrushchev agreed to withdraw the missiles under U.N. inspection, given the U.S. pledge not to invade Cuba.[16]

The missiles were withdrawn but had to be inspected on exiting ships, as Castro would not allow inspection of Cuba. A further snag concerned Illyushin bombers given to Castro. The Cuban leader initially refused the Soviets' request to return them, but President Kennedy, who considered them covered by the U.S.–Soviet deal, threatened to attack them if they were not removed. On 19 November Castro gave in to Soviet entreaties, and the last Illyushins left Cuba on 6 December, ending the crisis.[17]

UNJUSTIFIED RISKS

The actions of the U.S. government during the Cuban Missile Crisis risked a large-scale nuclear war with the Soviet Union. Given the magnitude of such a possible disaster, how could the risk possibly be justified? This question later worried Robert Kennedy, a central participant in the crisis, as well as some critics of administration conduct during the crisis.[18] In particular, a moralist looking at the record of American decisionmaking is likely to wonder why more serious consideration was not given to the more-pacific alternatives that might have avoided the risk of war—to do nothing or to make a private diplomatic approach to Khrushchev.

We cannot dispel the moralist's puzzlement by dismissing the president and his advisors as evil or irrational men—it is evident from the record that they were conscious of their awesome moral responsibility, were enormously concerned with doing the right thing, and planned their actions with considerable deliberation, ingenuity, and care. Nor will it resolve the matter to claim that American decisionmakers were concerned only about the American people, while the moralist is concerned about the well-being of all people.[19] For key officials did worry about the effects of their acts on non-Americans as well,[20] and, in any case, *either* concern would justify placing the very highest priority on nuclear war avoidance.

With this in mind, we may restate the moralist's puzzle. Why, during the missile crisis, did the Kennedy administration—composed of rational, decent, and well-informed men, and acting after careful deliberation—undertake unjustified risks of nuclear war? In this section, I will consider four ways of seeking to dissolve this puzzle by arguing that the risks were, in the circumstances, morally justified. These are based on the respective claims that (a) the risks were not significant, (b) there was no alternative, (c) all alternatives involved worse risks, and (d) the government followed an appropriate rational principle for risk-taking under uncertainty.

Was There Significant Risk?

Perhaps the imposition of the Cuban blockade would have been morally justified if it had entailed only a small or insignificant risk of nuclear war with the Soviets. But were the risks small? This is not the opinion that knowledgeable observers and participants expressed after the crisis. British Prime Minister Harold Macmillan later said, "the Cuban crisis . . . was the week of most strain I can ever remember in my life."[21] Bertrand Russell similarly reported that "never before in the course of a long life have I experienced anything comparable to the tense anxiety of those crucial hours."[22] Khrushchev spoke of "our [the Kremlin leaders'] anxiety, which was intense."[23] This war anxiety was behaviorally reflected in preparations by Soviet diplomats in New York to burn secret papers.[24] Secretary of State Rusk, a member of the Executive Committee, said to George Ball the morning after the president announced the blockade, "We have won a considerable victory. You and I are still alive."[25] Robert Kennedy wrote of a time during the crisis when "the feeling grew . . . that a direct military confrontation between the two great nuclear powers was inevitable,"[26] and of his brother, the president, that "the possibility of the destruction of mankind was always in his mind."[27] That the president viewed this possibility as genuine and of significant probability is evidenced by his having encouraged his wife to move closer to government war shelters,[28] and having later told his close advisor Theodore Sorensen that the odds of war had then seemed to him "somewhere between one out of three and even."[29]

It might be replied that the participants' perceptions of the risks of the missile crisis were wrong. Since both sides feared war and wished to avoid it, the likelihood of its actual outbreak was of necessity extremely low. But historical precedent suggests other wise. World War I began, as President Kennedy was well aware, with neither side wanting it.[30] And there were a number of not implausible scenarios by which the Cuban events might get out of control and escalate into nuclear war. (The president was so concerned about one of these involving U.S. missiles in Turkey, that he ordered those missiles defused at a key point in the crisis.)[31] In fact, certain incidents occurred that could well have set off escalation but for luck and caution on both sides—the U-2 downing over Cuba, another U-2 straying over Soviet territory, and U.S. Navy ships forcing Soviet submarines to surface (without the president's knowledge).[32] At the same time, certain U.S. military leaders were pressing for the use of nuclear weapons,[33] and it is not implausible to speculate that some of their Soviet counterparts may have been doing likewise. It thus seems clear that there was a real and substantial risk of escalation to nuclear war, had the Soviets rejected the ultimatum delivered to Dobrynin and had the United States carried out its planned attack in response.

A final piece of evidence concerning the real dangers of the missile crisis is the behavior of the superpowers in the more than two decades since then. Despite their continued political, ideological, and military rivalry, the U.S. and U.S.S.R. have managed to avoid direct confrontations between their military forces in any part of the world, have generally taken great care to do so, and have sought a partial detente with one another. This cautious behavior is frequently attributed to a desire to avoid crises like that of 1962.[34] The powerful aversion to such crises on both sides is strong evidence that, even in hindsight and from the perspective of considerable temporal distance, the governments of both the superpowers regard the missile crisis as having been fraught with extreme danger.

Perhaps President Kennedy's estimate of a one-third to one-half chance of war arising from the missile crisis was a considerable overestimate. Given, however, the testimony of decisionmakers on both sides, the cautious behavior of the superpowers since in avoiding military confrontations, the fact that historically there have been wars that neither side wanted, the fact that some high U.S. military officials wanted to use nuclear weapons during the crisis, and the fact that some military events did get out of the leaders' control during the crisis, it is clear that the U.S. course of blockade followed by ultimatum and, if necessary, conventional attack, carried a not-insignificant risk of resulting in nuclear war with the Soviet Union. What was it about the nature of the circumstances that might have justified pursuing a course of action that entailed such risks?

Were There Alternatives?

One possible justification for pursuing a dangerous course of action is that there are no alternatives. And Executive Committee members often spoke in language suggesting that this was so during the missile crisis. For example, Robert Kennedy used modal phrases such as "action was *required*," "the U.S. *could not* accept what the Russians had done," and "he [the President] would *have to* do something."[35] And Sorensen said Kennedy's previous "pledge to act was *unavoidable*" and "action was *imperative*."[36]

Yet it is clear that there were alternatives and that inaction was among them. In particular, at least two more pacific and initially less-dangerous alternatives than blockade were proposed and considered at early meetings of the Executive Committee. Defense Secretary Robert McNamara initially took the view that no action was a viable alternative, since the missiles in Cuba did not really much alter the strategic balance.[37] And private diplomacy *might* have caused Khrushchev to remove the missiles without the risk of a public and military confrontation.

Perhaps, however, these alternatives were not within the power of the president and his advisors to pursue effectively, for, as the president and his brother once mused, the president might have been impeached and removed from office if he had not taken strong action.[38] This is a possibility, of course, but hardly a certainty since a U.S. president had never been impeached, and a less-challenging course might still have resulted in the removal of the missiles from Cuba. Hence, while alternatives more pacific than blockade may have carried their own risks and disadvantages, they were genuine alternatives.

Were the Alternatives More Dangerous?

The most plausible justification for the blockade of Cuba is that the more-pacific alternatives of inaction and private diplomacy were, in the long run, even more risky. Forms of this justification are suggested by some of the U.S. decisionmakers and by knowledgeable analysts.[39] They appeal to two sources of long-run danger: changes in the international political situation, and domestic political changes leading to more-dangerous U.S. policies.

President Kennedy believed that if the United States did not act strongly in response to the Cuban missiles, U.S. prestige would suffer, the Atlantic Alliance would be in danger, and—most important—Soviet leaders would doubt our willingness to defend our interests and would engage in other aggressions even more likely to lead to war than a confrontation over Cuba.[40] But this belief derived from several questionable assumptions. First, Kennedy viewed the placement of missiles in Cuba as primarily a test of American will.[41] Thoughtful American analysts have suggested instead that stop-gap defense of the U.S.S.R. against an American first-strike strategic capacity and/or defense of Cuba were more likely motives.[42] Second, there is no evidence of any consideration of other ways of shoring up U.S. credibility that might pose less of a direct challenge to the Soviets—e.g., using the missiles in Cuba as a domestic justification for greatly increased defense spending, sending more troops to Europe, etc. Third is the assumption that private diplomacy would not get the missiles out of Cuba and would allow the Soviets to delay and play to world opinion. But, like the blockade, private diplomacy did not preclude stronger action later, and it would have allowed Khrushchev to "retreat" more gracefully. It would thereby have minimized the danger of irrational action by an embarassed adversary caught by surprise in public. Nor would private diplomacy preclude offers and ultimata of the sort that eventually ended the crisis. Given the weaknesses in these three key assumptions, it seems highly doubtful that pursuing a more-pacific path would have posed graver risks than did the blockade-ultimatum-attack strategy that was actually pursued.

Nuclear war could have resulted in another way from the administration following a more-cautious policy. The president might have been impeached for being too soft, or a Republican congress might have been elected that would apply irresistible pressures for future dangerous U.S. actions.[43] But impeachment would have resulted in a Democratic successor—Vice President Johnson. And a Republican congress, if elected, could not *force* Kennedy—if he stayed in office—to undertake foreign policy moves that he considered dangerous and provocative. So it is doubtful that this path would have led to a stronger probability of war than the risks encountered due to the blockade.

Finally, it may be worth noting that the blockade, too, may have carried long-range as well as short-run risks of war. Some believe that the Soviets' public retreat in Cuba led to their massive investment of resources in a strategic buildup over the two decades since.[44] If this buildup has increased the risk of nuclear war, such increase might be charged partly to our failure to adopt a less-challenging posture toward the Cuban missiles.

In summary, the blockade (and threatened air strike) may *conceivably* have been less likely to lead to nuclear war than the more-pacific alternatives. But the arguments for this are so weak that one must regard the quick dismissal of these alternatives as unjustified and hard to comprehend, if we view the decisionmakers as having been engaged in anything like rational, moral decisionmaking.

Rational Disaster Avoidance

The Executive Committee was operating under what I have else where called *two-dimensional uncertainty*[45]—not only did they not know the outcomes of the available courses of action, they did not even have reliable estimates of the probabilities and utilities of the various *possible* outcomes of each course of action. Further, they believed any alternative might result in a disastrous outcome: doing nothing or warning the Soviets privately might lead to the missiles staying in Cuba with a subsequent loss of prestige, credibility, and strategic advantage for the United States, while stronger actions (including blockade) might lead to nuclear war with the Soviets. But the probabilities were not the same. Severe political losses seemed likely to follow from choosing a pacific course, while the blockade may have risked nuclear war with probability of one-third to one-half, or less. So their choice

seemed to be between a greater likelihood of a lesser disaster (severe political-strate-
gic losses) and a smaller risk of a greater disaster (nuclear war). Elsewhere, I have
argued that for *some* choices of this form under two-dimensional uncertainty, it is
rational (or, at least, not irrational) to choose the alternative that maximizes one's
chances of avoiding disastrous outcomes.[46] Would it not follow that American
decisionmakers acted in a purely rational and justified manner in running a smaller
risk of nuclear war rather than a more-probable risk of severe loss of U.S. prestige
and credibility?

It does not follow, because there are restrictions on my principle that recommends maximizing one's chances of disaster avoidance under two-dimensional
uncertainty. This principle can be plausibly applied only when the disasters risked
are of roughly the same order of magnitude. (Otherwise the unknown but expected
probability gains will not offset the risk of bringing about the more disastrous outcome.) But it is doubtful that U.S. prestige and credibility loss is a disaster of even
roughly the same order of magnitude as large-scale nuclear war, whether we measure in terms of the welfare of the U.S. people, or people everywhere. Missile-
crisis decisionmakers might, then, have (implicitly) followed the principle of minimizing the probability of a disastrous outcome. But, if they did so, it was a misuse
of the principle, which could not appropriately serve to justify their choice.

Running Unnecessary Risks

The most plausible justifications of U.S. government actions during the missile
crisis are that these minimized the risk of war and/or of other disastrous outcomes.
In the last two subsections, I have pointed out some glaring weaknesses in these
justifications. Nevertheless, another fact clinches my case that we cannot plausibly
view their deliberations as a process of moral decisionmaking, the fact that the president ran *unnecessary* risks of nuclear war by prolonging the crisis to obtain marginally better terms of settlement. When it still looked like the Soviets might challenge
the blockade, he rejected the idea of an immediate summit meeting with Khrushchev, because "before a summit took place, . . . the President wanted to have
some cards in our own hand."[47] Later, instead of accepting the formal Soviet offer
for withdrawal of the missiles in return for a pledge of non-invasion of Cuba and the
removal of the missiles in Turkey, Kennedy chose the riskier course of an ultimatum
combined with, at most, an implicit promise about the Turkey-based missiles.
Finally, after the basic settlement he threatened to restart the crisis with military
action to remove the Illyushin bombers, which before the crisis the administration
had accepted as posing no significant danger to the U.S.[48]

In the case of the bombers, Kennedy perhaps ran no significant risk of war, as it
was clear that Khrushchev, who had already given in on the missiles, would not be
inclined to resist.[49] But the rejection of the idea of a summit, and the refusal of an
explicit pledge on the missiles in Turkey, came at the two points in the crisis when
war fears were greatest on the American side.[50] Nor would Kennedy have risked or
lost much by acting in a more conciliatory manner. He had already ordered the
missiles in Turkey dismantled, and ended up making something very close to an
implicit promise, through his brother, to remove them (which he did). Nor, by holding out on this point, was he establishing the principle that he would concede nothing under pressure from the Soviets; for, under pressure, he *did* pledge not to

invade Cuba. We may conclude that by holding out on certain particular points—especially the missiles in Turkey—the president probably ran *unnecessary risks* of nuclear war.

The Puzzle

We have seen that given their perception of the risks of nuclear war involved in blockade and military action, the missile crisis decisionmakers should have selected—or at least given much more lengthy and serious consideration to—the more pacific alternatives. This seems the relatively straightforward conclusion of a moral analysis. Given that they were not evil or unintelligent people, and that they appreciated the risks and consequences of nuclear war, why did American leaders act otherwise? This is the moralist's puzzle.

MIND-SETS, MORALS, AND POLITICS

I have suggested that President Kennedy and his key advisors were wrong to reject, especially so quickly, the more-pacific, possible responses to the placement of Soviet missiles in Cuba.[51] Yet I believe that, overall, Kennedy performed admirably in the situation, and that we were fortunate to have had him at the head of the U.S. government at the time.[52] This seeming paradox is understandable when we recall that Kennedy was a politician making a political decision. In such a position, he was atypically sensitive to the relevant moral issues and took extraordinary care in the formulation and execution of his policies, because of his perception of the enormous stakes involved and the dangers of the situation. In saying this, I am not simply adding a wrinkle to the old charge that Kennedy was just another calculating politician, making his decisions to help himself and his party in the next election.[53] (The added wrinkle would be that Kennedy was *less* like this than most politicians.) For in my view, *international* politics had as much, or more, to do with Kennedy's decisions than did domestic politics. And, even more important, in speaking of Kennedy's decisions as "political," I am not referring to the sort of ends he was deliberately trying to promote, but to the general *mind-set* with which he approached the decision.

This concept of a "mind-set" is the key to understanding the missile crisis decisionmaking. It refers to the general way of thinking and to the background assumptions, about both the world and the making of decisions, that decisionmakers bring to a problem situation. A decisionmaker's mind-set includes the ways in which he or she tends to (a) formulate and define a problem, (b) search for, define, select, and discard various alternatives for action or solution, (c) view certain constraints on action as absolute or nearly so, and (d) interpret the world, especially the acts and motives of other agents. It is obvious that peoples' mind-sets often influence the decisions they reach without the people themselves being aware that, or how, they do so. Individuals who are reflective and self-aware, and take the time and trouble to step back and think about their worldview and methods of decisionmaking, may be able to discern certain features of their own mind-sets. But, more typically, we bring our mind-sets to our decisions without being aware of their existence or their natures, and they influence the way we structure and decide issues without our even being aware that this is occurring.

When individuals or groups with different mind-sets consider a given situation or problem, they are likely to reach different conclusions, and may well be puzzled, confused, or angered by the other party's stance. For each side's mind-set is so natural and leads so directly to its own conclusions that, in an important sense, one side cannot understand what the other side is thinking and doing. Defining the problem and steps to its solution in its own particular way, and implicitly assuming that the other party must see the same problem and solution, one party can only interpret the other party's resistance as a symptom of irrationality, craziness, or perversity.

An interesting example of this sort of tension between mind-sets arose at a conference on philosophy and psychoanalysis, whose proceedings were subsequently published. [54] In one paper, a philosopher sympathetic to psychoanalysis struck a discordant note by analyzing the unconscious reasons that philosophers hold certain metaphysical positions. [55] (No doubt to many philosophers at the conference, this paper seemed at worst an *ad hominem* irrelevancy, and at best a gross instance of the genetic fallacy.) [56] But the interesting point, for our purposes, is that it was a clash between rather different mind-sets. Each side defined the question at issue and sought its solution in terms of the mind-set typical to its discipline. Hence, most of the philosophers applied logical analysis to the activities of the psychoanalyst, while their colleague put on the psychoanalyst's hat and sought after the unconscious explanation of their activities. Each may have been right from his own point of view, but each portrayed the other's analysis as a piece of logical, or psychological, pathology. But (unconsciously) structuring the key issues differently and adopting different methodological approaches to them, each side was unable to understand fully and appreciate what the other was doing.

A less extreme, but nonetheless significant, clash of mind-sets creates the moralist's puzzle about the missile crisis. The moral analyst finds it difficult to understand or appreciate the actions of the Kennedy administration, because he or she does not share the mind-set of the political decisionmaker. This is the mind-set that determined the quick dismissal of the moralist's preferred pacific alternatives.

President Kennedy, and most of the men around him, shared a basic mind-set toward making foreign and military policy decisions. This mind-set was fundamentally "political" in the sense that it was in many ways typical of the mind-set of political actors, and its content and structure were largely determined by its usual function of guiding agents to the satisfactory solution of political problems. Three distinguishable elements of the Kennedy administration mind-set contributed to the way it dealt with the missile crisis, including, in particular, its quick rejection of the more-pacific alternatives. These elements concern international politics, domestic politics, and personal politics.

International Politics

The missile crisis was primarily an international political crisis and, during it, President Kennedy's main concern, other than avoiding nuclear war, was to uphold the international political position of the United States. [57] The president and his men shared a certain mind-set about international politics as they approached the issue of Soviet missiles in Cuba. For our purposes, the most important features of that mind-set were certain norms concerning how great powers should or must act in international affairs, and certain beliefs about the motives of adversary nations.

The norms of great power behavior that seem to have greatly influenced American decisionmakers were that great powers (a) should not suddenly upset the status quo balance of power in the world, (b) should not launch surprise attacks on much smaller powers, and (c) should (even *must*) actively resist challenges to the balance of power and their own credibility. The first norm is reflected in the administration's view of what was, at bottom, wrong with the Soviet surreptitious placing of missiles in Cuba. In his address announcing the blockade, the president described the Soviet's action as a "provocative and unjustified change in the status quo,"[58] and insiders reported that this was his private view as well.[59] The second norm lay at the heart of George Ball and Robert Kennedy's arguments against an air strike on Cuba, which apparently had great influence on the president and others.[60] Norm three was accepted by the administration not only as a reason to respond forcefully to the Cuban missiles,[61] but also as a reason for avoiding actions that would pose a provocative challenge to the Soviets, e.g., military acts likely to produce Soviet casualties.[62]

Notice that these norms of international behavior restricted the administration's options on both ends of the scale of imaginable responses. The Soviets had blatantly attempted to violate the first norm, and—by the third norm—this called for a strong, i.e., more than diplomatic, response. But the second norm counted heavily against precipitate military action directed at tiny Cuba. United States action was also influenced by its leaders' perception of Soviet motives. The president and his advisors saw the Cuban missiles as a political challenge and a test of American will.[63] Instead, Soviet motives may actually have been primarily defensive—against another invasion of Cuba, and against the American's newly advertised first-strike capacity.[64] The Kennedy administration, not planning such an invasion or strategic attack even in its wildest dreams, would naturally have been more inclined to see serious aggressiveness behind Khrushchev's move. The traditional pattern of viewing one's own international conduct as benign, and one's adversary's as threatening, doubtless contributed to the quick American decision to go beyond acceptance or diplomacy in its reaction to the Cuban missiles.

Domestic Politics

Political leaders depend, for their continued power and effectiveness, on the support of key groups within their countries. This necessity of maintaining domestic political support is an accepted background assumption of decisionmaking, so that political leaders are strongly disinclined to undertake actions that cannot command significant domestic support or that would cause damaging criticism. And, since staying in power and remaining an effective leader is generally a dominant personal goal, as well as a necessary means for accomplishing one's policy aims, political leaders habitually and automatically tend to avoid loss of support and power.

Once we note this tendency, which is part of the ingrained mind-set of politicians, we can recognize that the domestic political situation in the United States influenced, and imposed constraints upon, decisionmaking in the missile crisis, even while we reject as misleading the charge that Kennedy manufactured the crisis—or exploited it—for domestic political reasons.[65] Domestic politics influenced the administration mainly in a negative way: rather than promising advantages or encouraging calculations of domestic gains and losses, it seems to have made administration officials perceive their options as more limited than they really were. In particular, it made the president and his advisors regard the more-pacific alternatives as unfeasible, partly because they would not satisfy strong domestic audiences and their pressures.

Prior to the crisis there had been strong Republican criticisms of Kennedy for not taking action against Cuba, and the president had issued two public warnings against Soviet missiles in Cuba. When the missiles were discovered, the president's "pledge to act was unavoidable."[66] As one noted analyst put it,

> This is a classic illustration of the effect of the "backdrop"—in this instance, the opposition and congressional committees—on policymaking in a crisis . . . . [T]he administration was pinned down on a response to Soviet offensive missiles in Cuba, and the President's *options were narrowed.*[67]

Two other incidents demonstrate the administration's sense of having "no options" because of domestic politics. Another Executive Committee member passed Sorensen a note indicating that operable missiles in Cuba would produce Republican congressional gains that "would completely paralyze our ability to react sensibly and coherently to further Soviet advances."[68] And the Kennedy brothers felt the president had to act to avoid impeachment.[69]

Thus domestic politics did seem to affect missile crisis decisionmaking, but not in the way critics charge. Kennedy did not choose blockade to obtain domestic political gains or to avoid domestic political losses. Instead, domestic politics apparently influenced what the president and his men perceived to be their feasible options. They operated according to an axiom of the typical political mind-set, which says "alternatives are not real options and should be eliminated from consideration, if they lack domestic support and seriously risk loss of power." As a result, they set aside the moralist's favored options of no action and private diplomacy.

Personal Politics

Political leaders are human beings. And insofar as they deal with other political leaders, there is bound to be a personal element in their official relationships and interactions. We all have certain ways of interpreting the behavior of those with whom we come in contact—ways of reading their motives, responding to their overtures, and influencing their subsequent behavior toward us. These tendencies, in political actors, form part of their mind-set for "personal politics," interactions with other politicians. When the politicians in question are heads of states acting in official or semiofficial capacities, the personal interaction between them may well be expressed in and through governmental decisions and policies.

So it was, apparently, in the missile crisis. President Kennedy, who had tried to improve U.S.–Soviet relations and establish them on a rational and predictable basis, apparently felt personally betrayed by the clandestine introduction of Soviet missiles into Cuba.[70] He felt that he himself was being challenged and tested by Chairman Khrushchev, who had already bullied him at Vienna. In fact, his initial reaction upon learning of the missiles is reported to have been, "He can't do this to *me.*"[71] Thus, Kennedy's mind-set on the problem of the missiles included the tendency to see the issue partly in personal terms, as well as the belief that a personal challenge must be answered. As one commentator put it:

> Kennedy had worried, both after the Bay of Pigs and after the Vienna meeting with Khrushchev, that the Chairman might have misjudged his mettle. This time Kennedy determined to stand fast. . . . The nonforcible paths—avoiding military measures, resorting instead to diplomacy—could not have been more irrelevant to his problem.[72]

At the same time, the personal aspects of the situation may have constrained Kennedy from resorting to a more dangerous action than blockade. He was influenced by his brother's appeal that the United States should not suddenly attack a small nation and inevitably kill many of its innocent citizens.[73] Perhaps, to the extent he saw the issue in personal terms, the president was as determined to resist becoming a bully himself as he was to resist Khrushchev's apparent bullying.

Contrasting Mind-Sets

We have seen how elements of the mind-set of the president and his advisors involving international, domestic, and personal politics converged to bring about what puzzles the moralist—the early elimination of the nonmilitary options. The Soviets had violated the perceived norms of great power behavior, and this demanded of the United States—as another great power—a forceful response. In addition, the domestic political atmosphere and the personal challenge by Khrushchev to Kennedy made an acquiescent or pacific response unthinkable.

As noted above, the possessors of a mind-set are typically unaware of it. It consists of precepts, rules, assumptions, and schemas for interpreting reality that are generally useful or necessary for arriving at decisions. Since one sees the world through one's mind-set, but usually does not see the mind-set itself, the rules, assumptions, etc., constituting it are seldom questioned, analyzed, or reexamined at the time of decisionmaking. This is true even for exceptionally important decisions. Thus, President Kennedy saw the missile crisis as sufficiently important to call for special procedures of decision and execution—formation of an ad hoc Executive Committee, personal direction of military moves, etc.[74] But he did not think to call for a critical reexamination of the fundamental precepts and assumptions of the political mind-set that he shared with his top advisors.[75] This oversight is understandable in view of the time pressures of the crisis, the difficulty of even being aware of having a mind-set, and so on. But it is also rightfully criticizable. One wants to say that with so much at stake, decisionmakers should exercise special care to take as little as possible for granted, to question all vital assumptions, and not to eliminate alternative courses of action from consideration too soon.

Consider, for example, the Kennedy brothers' reaction to the observation that the president might be impeached if he did not act forcefully to remove the missiles. They had been worrying about the dangers of military action, but possible impeachment served as a final and clinching argument that settled the matter in their minds.[76] They apparently accepted the simple rule that any option that leads to (a substantial chance of) impeachment is to be rejected. It is interesting that a similar, but broader, rule was invoked by Executive Committee member McGeorge Bundy when discussing Truman's decision to build the hydrogen bomb. After acknowledging that the United States would not have lost significant ground in the arms race if it had waited to see if the Soviets would make the first move on the hydrogen bomb, Bundy wrote:

> No American president could have avoided the heaviest kind of political damage if a unilateral decision to stay out of the thermonuclear race had been followed by an apparent Soviet breakthrough. On the issue as presented, I think the president made the right choice.[77]

Thus, three members of the Executive Committee, the Kennedy brothers and National Security Advisor Bundy, shared the assumption that an option that leads to the heaviest political damage, e.g., serious risk of impeachment, is itself a decisive reason for rejecting it. This seems a reasonable assumption in *normal circumstances*, since a president or other politician suffering such damage is likely thereby to have his most important personal and political goals shattered. But when undergoing the risk of massive political damage would or might save humanity from tremendous danger—a substantial risk of holocaust during the missile crisis or the dangers of an ongoing nuclear arms race in the case of the H-bomb decision—it clearly seems wrong simply to follow the normal political rule, rather than seriously to weigh and to compare the risks of the alternative courses of action.

Let us compare the more mundane situation of a college teacher who wants to keep her job. In normal circumstances, the fact that a certain action—e.g., giving a student a much higher grade than deserved to aid medical school admission—might well lead to loss of her job would count as a decisive reason for her not undertaking it. But suppose she had very good reason to believe that this student would kill himself if, and only if, he did not receive the higher grade. Then the danger of job loss would no longer be an obviously decisive consideration, and the teacher should open the matter up to serious moral deliberation (including, perhaps, searching for new alternatives that would preserve all the major values at stake). If she does not, but blindly follows the normal rule in this abnormal situation, she may rightly be accused of irrational "rule-worship,"[78] as may the members of the Executive Committee who did not recognize humanity-risking decisions as abnormal enough to require the reexamination of deep-seated political rules.

This moral criticism of the missile crisis decisionmakers does not show that they were bad people. They were not. Instead it reflects the difference in the mind-sets of the moralist and the political decisionmaker. The moralist has an analytical-critical mind-set that includes the principle of pausing to reconsider carefully one's own presuppositions and assumptions when one is confronted by a decision-problem carrying abnormally large stakes. Differences in mind-sets result from differences in experience and training, and also differences in function. Political decisionmakers are constantly making practical decisions, hence they generally need a relatively simple, useful mind-set that can repeatedly and effectively aid them in that task.

It may be useful to draw an analogy between the moralist's relation to the political decisionmaker and the latter's relation to military subordinates. Robert Kennedy writes of the military advice given during the missile crisis:

President Kennedy was disturbed by this inability [of representatives of the military] to look beyond the limited military field. When we talked about this later, he said we had to remember that they were trained to fight and wage war—that was their life. Perhaps we would feel even more concerned if they were always opposed to using arms or military means—for if they would not be willing, who would be? But this experience pointed out for us all the importance of civilian direction and control and the importance of raising probing questions to military recommendations.[79]

We have seen that the moralist looking at the missile crisis is likely to have a view of the political mind-set that is similar to President Kennedy's view of the military mind-set. To the moralist, since the politician often does not look enough beyond the political field to the wider (and moral) significance of his actions, "the importance of raising probing questions" about political decisions must be stressed.

We may use this analogy between the politician's attitude toward the military and the moralist's attitude toward the politician to clarify further our central claim about different parties possessing different mind-sets. One possible way to look at the relationship between mind-sets is to view them as *nesting* within one another. According to this view, the military mind-set is a simplified and specialized subset of the political mind-set, which is in turn a simplified and specialized subset of the moral mind-set. This means that the principles of decision embodied in the military mind-set are simplified rules of thumb guiding military decisionmakers toward correct or adequate decisions about "the right thing to do" in most situations they are likely to face, while the political mind-set embodies more-complex rules containing various exception clauses and reflecting sensitivity to a wider range of relevant considerations. The moralists' mind-set is broader still, in the sense that it subsumes political rules of thumb under yet more complex systems of moral rules, pays attention to more-relevant considerations (e.g., the well-being of humanity instead of the well-being of a nation), and employs the metaprinciples that prescribe adopting a critical stance toward one's own principles and assumptions. One implication of this view of the relationship of different mind-sets is that military, political, and moral decisionmakers are all really trying to decide the same thing—what it is morally right to do—and are simply using more or less sophisticated methods.

I believe, however, that the nesting view is misleading in certain respects and fails to convey accurately the relationship between moral and political mind-sets. It is better to think of different mind-sets as *overlapping* in the sense that only some of the various assumptions and principles embodied in them may appropriately be viewed as more-complicated (or simpler) versions of one another. Three reasons make this overlapping view preferable to the nesting view. First, it allows for the fact that the moralists' mind-set embodies controversial substantive principles and assumptions as well as the unassailable metaprinciple of critical self-examination. It is not *obvious* that in a world of independent sovereign states, such substantive principles (e.g., those requiring would feel even more concerned if they were always substantial consideration of the interests of all affected) should govern the actions of national decisionmakers. But the nesting view, in treating the moralists' mind-set as the all-encompassing one at the top of the hierarchy, suggests that its components are beyond criticism from the viewpoint of other mind-sets.

The second disadvantage of the nesting view also flows from this suggestion. There is tension, in the nesting view, between the metaprinciple of critical self-examination and the nesting view's implication that the moral mind-set already contains whatever is of value in other mind-sets. By contrast, the overlapping view correctly suggests that moralists may have something to learn from studying and coming to understand other mind-sets. Third, and finally, it seems doubtful that—as implied by the nesting view— military men, politicians, and moralists mean precisely the same thing by the question "What is the right thing to do?" Of course, they are all seeking directives for action in posing the question; but the substantive criteria they apply in answering it may be so different as to ensure that they are not answering the *same* question in any sense beyond this very minimal, formal sense of "sameness." Thus, for example, it is hard to imagine that moralists mean the same thing by "doing the right thing" in the Cuban crisis situation, as did the U.S. general who apparently believed it would be "right" to use nuclear weapons in an attack on Cuba, since our adversaries would use such weapons if they attacked the United States.[80]

It is worth noting, further, that even if the nesting view were correct, moralists would not be in a position to impose on others the decisions flowing from their more-encompassing mind-set, as President Kennedy was able to impose his more broadly based decisions on the military. Until there are philosopher kings, moralists, if they are to have any significant effect on policy, must try to understand the political mind-set and how to deal with it. Investigating the ways this mind-set does not fit within, or overlap with, the moralists' own mind-set is an important part of this task. This is not to say, however, that moral considerations do not as yet play any role in political decisionmaking. They did play a role in the missile crisis, and before we reach any final conclusions, we must consider what that role was.

THE ROLE OF MORAL CONSIDERATIONS

The moralist's view of the American side of the crisis is that the U.S. government should have given even greater priority and heavier weight to the avoidance of nuclear war, and pursued (or at least more carefully considered) a more-pacific diplomatic course. The substance of this view was implicit in a telegram to the president from the eminent philosopher Bertrand Russell. But instead of giving a clear and politically balanced statement of the moral case, Russell unfortunately hid it behind a harsh one-sided condemnation of U.S. actions.[81] Understandably, this provoked an angry response from the president and had no beneficial impact on American thinking or action. But even had the message been clear and even-handed, it is unlikely to have had a significant effect. For example, no evidence exists that a balanced statement from Pope John XXIII, published in the *New York Times* on 26 October and calling on "all rulers" to "save peace" and "accept negotiations, at all levels," had any impact within the administration.[82] And while Russell's much friendlier telegram to Khrushchev did receive a favorable public response from the Soviet leader, who exercised caution in challenging the blockade as the philosopher urged, Russell himself later admitted that he had no real influence on Soviet actions.[83]

However little effect Russell's moral intervention may have had, we have seen already that moral considerations did play a significant role in the deliberations of the Executive Committee. George Ball and Robert Kennedy argued that a surprise attack by a large nation on a small one, entailing many civilian casualties, would go against America's traditions.[84] This may reasonably be viewed as an appeal to such moral principles as the immunity of non-combatants from attack, and the unfairness of the strong attacking the weak. Certainly, though, most moralists would find exclusive concentration on these deontological principles as misguided, in a context in which a serious risk of nuclear holocaust is present. The primary moral concern, in such situations, should be the avoidance of the horrible *consequences* of nuclear war, with adherence to ordinary deontological principles being, at most, a second priority.

Thus, to the trained moralist, it was an oversimplified and misguided conception of morality—involving simple, general, prohibitory rules—with which the missile crisis decisionmakers operated. Yet, ironically, had they followed the theoretically correct procedure of giving more weight to *consequences* in such a context, they might have adopted a worse and more-dangerous course of action. For they might not have estimated and evaluated consequences in the moralist's preferred manner; rather, they might have followed the lead of hard-line Executive Committee member Dean Acheson, who observed that "[Robert] Kennedy seemed . . . to have been moved by emotional or intuitive responses more than by the trained lawyer's analysis of the dangers threatened and of the relevance of these to the various actions proposed."[85] Acheson seems to have been advocating proceeding via a consequentialist risks versus gains analysis, rather than by appeal to intuitively based deontological principles. But *his* consequentialist analysis, unlike the moralist's, led him to favor vehemently an air strike against the Cuban missiles.[86]

It is worth noting in passing that the Kennedy/Acheson dispute provides some confirmation for a seemingly paradoxical claim sometimes made by consequentialist moral theorists; namely, that it may have better consequences if people generally believe and try to act as deontologists rather than as straightforward consequentialists. This is because simple deontic rules are easier to learn and apply, lead to fewer coordination problems, and are less open to self-interested or self-deceptive manipulation than are consequentialist calculations.[87] The missile crisis deliberations lend support to this "paradox," because Robert Kennedy's deontological principles and arguments appear to have led to a safer course of action and a better outcome than the consequentialist cost/benefit analysis of Dean Acheson would likely have led to. If this was not purely accidental, the consequentialist paradox is sustained.

We may now draw some general conclusions about the role of moral considerations in the missile crisis decisionmaking. Moral intervention by outside "experts," such as Bertrand Russell and the Pope, had little, if any, influence. Moral considerations advanced by Executive Committee members themselves apparently had substantial impact, but primarily in the form of oversimplified and rigid deontological constraints, which were perhaps given greater weight than they deserved. On the other hand, the *really important* moral consideration—the avoidance of nuclear war—while given substantial weight, probably received much less than it should have been given, or else the pacific alternatives would certainly have received greater consideration.

MORALISTS AND NUCLEAR POLITICS

What do our observations about missile crisis decisionmaking suggest about the possible future influence of morality, and moralists, on nuclear weapons policy? The main lesson, I think, is that the differences between the mind-sets of moralists and political leaders are substantial and are likely to limit the manner and extent to which the former can influence the latter. Direct moral intervention by outsiders, even if packaged more diplomatically than Russell's messages to Kennedy, is highly unlikely to have any impact. This is not only because unsolicited advice is generally disregarded, but also because outsiders with different mind-sets are unlikely to address the problems as the decisionmakers perceive them.

Nonetheless, moral considerations are likely to affect nuclear weapons decisions in two ways. First, when they are introduced by insiders who share the basic political mind-set, but are concerned with certain moral dimensions of the problem at hand (as, for example, Robert Kennedy was concerned about civilian casualties and the ethics of surprise attack). Second, moral considerations and arguments may influence the domestic (and even international) political background, in the context of which political leaders frame, and decide, nuclear weapons policy. We have seen how the domestic background during the missile crisis served to inhibit Kennedy and his advisors from following the courses of action moralists would likely have preferred. Similarly, a different sort of political climate could close off, for politicians seeking (as nearly all do) to retain political support, certain bellicose and immoral options as unfeasible. Perhaps, for example, the peace movement in certain countries of Western Europe is already exerting influence in this way.

So if moralists are going to influence nuclear weapons policy, it appears that they are going to have to do so primarily in two *indirect* ways. First, through education, by which they can introduce future leaders and citizens to the moralists' method of analyzing problems (including adopting a critical attitude toward one's own assumptions), as well as to the substantive moral principles and issues relevant to nuclear weapons policy. Second, by political action, in the form of support for groups adopting a morally enlightened position concerning disarmament, the arms race, and related matters.

At this point a difficulty emerges. As I have emphasized elsewhere, the moral issues surrounding nuclear weapons policy are exceedingly complex and difficult and pose a number of unsolved puzzles and paradoxes. Yet, for purposes of political action (and for some educational purposes at some levels), oversimplification, papering over of relevant differences between positions, and ignoring significant objections are quite often required for effectiveness. Hence, for moralists dealing with nuclear weapons policy, there is a potential pragmatic conflict between the requirements for adequate analysis and the demands of successful politics. I close with a suggestion about one way in which the community of moralists concerned about nuclear weapons policy might deal with this conflict. Perhaps rather than all concerned trying to individually "synthesize" the conflicting elements, what is called for (and will be most effective) is some form of specialization. In this way some may devote their main energies in this area to moral analysis, some to education, and some to political persuasion, as their individual abilities and inclinations lead them.

NOTES

1. See Elie Abel, *The Missile Crisis* (New York: Bantam Books, 1966), pp. 36–37, 38–39; and Robert F. Kennedy, *Thirteen Days* (New York: W. W. Norton, 1971), pp. 26 and 97. On the theory of routine foreign policy decisionmaking, with special application to the issue of antiballistic-missile deployment in the

United States, see Morton Halperin, *Bureaucratic Politics and Foreign Policy* (Washington: The Brookings Institution, 1974).

2. Abel, *Missile Crisis*, p. 25.

3. Texts of Kennedy's statements are in David Larson, ed., *The "Cuban Crisis" of 1962: Selected Documents and Chronology* (Boston: Houghton Mifflin, 1963), pp. 3–4, 17–18.

4. Abel, *Missile Crisis*, pp. 48–50; Theodore Sorensen, *Kennedy* (New York: Harper & Row, 1965), p. 682.

5. This prediction by the military was based on faulty analysis and was later corrected. See Graham Allison, *Essence of Decision* (Boston: Little, Brown, 1971), p. 126. This book is a theoretical study of missile crisis decisionmaking.

6. Ibid., p. 60; Abel, *Missile Crisis*, pp. 78–79; Kennedy, *Thirteen Days*, pp. 26–27; Sorensen, *Kennedy*, pp. 684–85; Arthur Schlesinger, Jr., *A Thousand Days* (Greenwich: Fawcett Publishers, 1965) pp. 738–39; and Richard Neustadt and Graham Allison, "Afterword" to *Thirteen Days*, pp. 128–29.

7. For texts of U.S. Draft Resolution to the Security Council and Ambassador Adlai Stevenson's statement, see Larson, "*Cuban Crisis*," pp. 48, 66–81. The text of the O.A.S. resolution, adopted 23 October, is in ibid., pp. 64–66.

8. Text in ibid., pp. 41–46.

9. See, e.g., U.N. documents in ibid., pp. 49–54 and 90–102. See also Abel, *Missile Crisis*, pp. 116–17; and Kennedy, *Thirteen Days*, p. 44.

10. Bertrand Russell, *Unarmed Victory* (Baltimore: Penguin Books, 1963), pp. 31–32.

11. Text in ibid., pp. 36–38, and in Larson, "*Cuban Crisis*," pp. 125–27.

12. Russell, *Unarmed Victory*, p. 45; Kennedy, *Thirteen Days*, p. 52.

13. For paraphrases of the letter, see Abel, *Missile Crisis*, pp. 158–62; Allison, *Essence of Decision*, pp. 221–23.

14. Text in Larson, "*Cuban Crisis*," pp. 155–58.

15. Kennedy, *Thirteen Days*, pp. 86–87; Allison, *Essence of Decision*, pp. 65–66.

16. Text of Khrushchev's letter to Kennedy is in Larson, "*Cuban Crisis*," pp. 161–65.

17. On the Illyushin matter, see Abel, *Missile Crisis*, pp. 187—91; and Sorensen, *Kennedy*, pp. 719–21.

18. See Kennedy, *Thirteen Days*, p. 106 (Sorensen's note at the end of the text); Roger Hagan, "Righteous Realpolitik"; I.F. Stone, "What Price Prestige"; and Ronald Steel, "Lessons of the Missile Crisis," all in The *Cuban Missile Crisis*, ed. Robert Divine (Chicago: Triangle Books, 1971).

19. Thus, for present purposes, we need not determine whether, or to what extent, morality allows or requires national leaders to give priority, in their deliberations, to the welfare of their own people.

20. See, e.g., Kennedy, *Thirteen Days*, p. 84.

21. Abel, *Missile Crisis*, p. 128.

22. Russell, *Unarmed Victory*, p. 28. Ordinary people's reactions were similar. Abel reports (p. 146) that Prague housewives were panic buying. I myself remember this as the one time in my growing-up years that adults around me were genuinely worried about events in the political world.

23. Nikita Khrushchev, *Khrushchev Remembers* (New York: Bantam Books, 1970), p. 550.

24. Kennedy, *Thirteen Days*, p. 71.
25. Abel, *Missile Crisis*, p. 110.
26. Kennedy, *Thirteen Days*, p. 61.
27. Ibid., p. 105.
28. Sorensen, *Kennedy*, p. 693.
29. Ibid., p. 705. See also Schlesinger, *A Thousand Days*, p. 734.
30. Kennedy, *Thirteen Days*, p. 40.
31. Ibid., p. 76.
32. On the submarine incidents, see Allison, *Essence of Decision*, p. 138.
33. Kennedy, *Thirteen Days*, p. 26.
34. See, e.g., Dean Rusk, "Co-existence without Sanctimony," in *Detente*, ed. G.R. Urban (New York: Universe Books, 1976), pp. 245–46; and Bernard Brodie, *War and Politics* (New York: Macmillan, 1973), pp. 430–32.
35. Kennedy, *Thirteen Days*, pp. 9–11. Emphasis added.
36. Sorensen, *Kennedy*, pp. 674–75. Emphasis added.
37. Abel, *Missile Crisis*, p. 38; Allison, *Essence of Decision*, pp. 195–96.
38. Kennedy, *Thirteen Days*, p. 45. Compare Neustadt and Allison, "Afterword," pp. 115–16.
39. See, e.g., Abel, *Missile Crisis*, p. 35; and Neustadt and Allison, "Afterword," pp. 115–16.
40. In his televised speech of 22 October, Kennedy said the missiles in Cuba "cannot be accepted by this country if our courage and our commitments are ever to be trusted again by either friend or foe." See Larson, "*Cuban Crisis*," p. 43.
41. Sorensen, *Kennedy*, pp. 676–78.
42. See, e.g., Allison, *Essence of Decision*, pp. 47–55. Compare Khrushchev's own suggestion that these were his two motives, in Khrushchev, *Khrushchev Remembers*, p. 547.
43. See Sorensen, *Kennedy*, p. 688.
44. See, e.g., Divine, *Cuban Missile Crisis*, p. 155.
45. "Deterrence, Utility, and Rational Choice," *Theory and Decision* 12 (March 1980): 41–60, esp. 46.
46. Ibid.
47. Kennedy, *Thirteen Days*, p. 45.
48. On previous acceptance of the bombers, see Allison, *Essence of Decision*, pp. 236–37.
49. Abel, *Missile Crisis*, p. 187.
50. Kennedy, *Thirteen Days*, pp. 44–48, 72—75.
51. As the president had the final decisionmaking authority, I shall focus in this section on the factors influencing him. It is clear, however, that many of his top advisers shared his views.
52. Robert Kennedy once said of the members of the 14-man Executive Committee, "If six of them had been President of the U.S., I think that the world might have been blown up." Quoted in Steel, "Lessons of the Missile Crisis," p. 233.
53. See, e.g., ibid., pp. 217–20; Hagan, "Righteous Realpolitik," p. 74; Stone, "What Price Prestige," pp. 158–59; and Leslie Dewart, "The Kennedy Trap," in Divine, p. 169.
54. Sidney Hook, ed., *Psychoanalysis, Scientific Method, and Philosophy* (New York: New York University Press, 1959).

55. Morris Lazerowitz, "The Relevance of Psychoanalysis to Philosophy," in ibid., pp. 133–54.
56. See, e.g., "Philosophy and Psychoanalysis," Donald Williams's vigorous reply to Lazerowitz in Hook, *Psychoanalysis*, pp. 157–79.
57. See, e.g., Sorensen, *Kennedy*, p. 683; and Abel, *Missile Crisis*, pp. 35–36, 47–48.
58. Larson, *"Cuban Crisis,"* p. 43.
59. Sorensen, *Kennedy*, p. 683; and Abel, *Missile Crisis*, p. 171.
60. Kennedy, *Thirteen Days*, pp. 17, 27; Abel, *Missile Crisis*, pp. 66–67, 74; Allison, *Essence of Decision*, p. 203; and Neustadt and Allison, "Afterword," p. 128.
61. See references in notes 58 and 59. Also see Kennedy, *Thirteen Days*, p. 11; and Schlesinger, *Thousand Days*, p. 729.
62. Schlesinger, *Thousand Days*, p. 759; Kennedy, *Thirteen Days*, pp. 14, 102.
63. Schlesinger, *Thousand Days*, pp. 728–29; Sorensen, *Kennedy*, pp. 676–78.
64. See references in note 42.
65. See Dewart, "The Kennedy Trap," for the suggestion that the administration deliberately created the crisis.
66. Sorensen, *Kennedy*, p. 674.
67. Allison, *Essence of Decision*, pp. 189–90. Emphasis added.
68. Sorensen, *Kennedy*, p. 688.
69. Kennedy, *Thirteen Days*, p. 45.
70. Allison, *Essence of Decision*, pp. 193–94; Neustadt and Allison, "Afterword," pp. 122–23.
71. Allison, *Essence of Decision*, p. 193. (From Richard Neustadt, "Afterword: 1964," *Presidential Power* [New York, 1964], p. 187.)
72. Allison, *Essence of Decision*, pp. 194–95.
73. Ibid., p. 203.
74. See Irving Janis, *Victims of Groupthink* (Boston: Houghton Mifflin, 1972), chap. 6; and Allison, *Essence of Decision*, pp. 127–32. The Janis chapter is a theoretical study of missile crisis decisionmaking.
75. By contrast, an important false *factual* assumption about the feasibility of a surgical air strike was reexamined and corrected during the crisis. See Allison, *Essence of Decision*, pp. 124–26.
76. Kennedy, *Thirteen Days*, pp. 45–46.
77. McGeorge Bundy, "The Missed Chance to Stop the H-Bomb," *New York Review of Books*, 13 May 1982, p. 16.
78. On rule-worship, see J.J.C. Smart, "An Outline of a System of Utilitarian Ethics," in Smart and B. Williams, *Utilitarianism: For and Against* (Cambridge: Cambridge University Press, 1973), p. 10.
79. Kennedy, *Thirteen Days*, p. 97.
80. Ibid., p. 26.
81. See Russell, *Unarmed Victory*, p. 31, for the text of the telegram.
82. For the text, see Larson, *"Cuban Crisis,"* p. 142.
83. Russell said, "I don't suppose I have altered the course of events by a fraction of an inch," and wrote, "Probably Khrushchev only does what I ask if he had decided to do it anyhow." See Ronald Clark, *The Life of Bertrand Russell* (London: Jonathan Cape, 1975), p. 600.

84. At the time this argument was made and had its effect, the participants believed a surgical air strike against only the missiles themselves was not feasible, and that any attack sufficient to wipe out the missiles would entail large numbers of civilian casualties. See Kennedy, *Thirteen Days*, pp. 15–17; and Allison, *Essence of Decision*, pp. 123–26.

85. Dean Acheson, "Homage to Plain Dumb Luck," in Divine, *Cuban Missile Crisis*, p. 197.

86. Ibid., p. 199.

87. See, e.g., Richard Brandt, *A Theory of the Good and the Right* (Oxford: Clarendon Press, 1970), pp. 273–77.

13
CRITICAL REFLECTIONS ON REALISM, JUST WARS, AND FEMINISM IN A NUCLEAR AGE

Jean Bethke Elshtain

How did we get from Machiavelli to MAD?[1] Where do women fit within the political and theoretical universes constituted by realism and just-war doctrine? To answer these questions, I will examine realist presumptions in light of feminist questions, and then consider an alternative tradition, just-war doctrine, with the same imperatives in mind. The concluding section of this essay will take up feminism explicitly and show the ways in which several forms of contemporary feminism are indebted to the traditions of realism or just war,[2] followed by the beginnings of an alternative, drawing upon Hannah Arendt. One of my underlying concerns is that feminism may reproduce presumptions that make the feminist enterprise self-defeating—if one takes seriously its professed aim to chart a transformative course in our thinking and our politics. The problem of collective violence serves as a provocative nodal point for interpretation and critique. A second animating concern is my conviction that we are now set on a treacherous course, but that we have the capacity to draw back and rethink. By "we" I mean all of us, not just a few learned experts and strategic impresarios.

WHAT MAKES REALISM RUN

Rousseau insisted that those who wish to separate politics from morals will never understand either. Yet this is precisely the promise of realism: the creation of an autonomous political realm free from the chastening of moral judgment and limitation. Although the origins of realist thinking go back at least as far as Thrasymachus's cynical insistence that justice is but the imposed will of the stronger, or to the representatives of Athens who declared to their counterparts from Melos that "might makes right," the modern discourse of realism is most often traced from Machiavelli, through early theorists of sovereignty and apologists for *raison d'état* (Bodin, for example), to its ultimate expression in Hobbes's *Leviathan*. Modern realists locate themselves within a potent, well-developed tradition, and most feel secure in the knowledge that their discourse long ago "won the war." By that I mean the fact that alternatives to realism tend to be evaluated *from the standpoint* of realism, and all contrasting points of view are lumped together and labeled "idealism." To proclaim oneself or be labeled "idealist", is to disqualify oneself or be disqualified as an airy unrealist who is incapable of, or refuses to, face the tough "reality" of a tough world.[3] "Idealists" have been on the defensive for decades. But is the realist throne secure? I shall argue that realism failed to reflect human realities a long time ago.

Modern realism presupposes a world of sovereign states, each seeking to enhance its own power, driven either by an aggrandizing lust for more power ("revisionist" states) or a fear-riddled need for more security ("status quo" states). The upshot, in either case, is that force alone checks force, and struggle is endemic to the system. Modern realism is most often presented as a theory—or *the* theory, with multiple permutations—of *international* relations, an account of the behavior of states in an arena characterized as anarchic. By anarchy, the realist refers to a world order in which each state is the final arbiter of its own interest and the last court of appeal in its own behalf. But realism, historically, is much more: it involves a way of thinking (an epistemology, if you will); a set of presumptions about the human condition that bears implications for "domestic" politics, secreting images of men and women and the parts they play in the human drama; and a potent rhetoric.

Take, for example, the greatest and most uncompromising version of realism as articulated in Thomas Hobbes's *Leviathan*.[4] Hobbes's method, his theory of human nature, and his creation of a world in which each consents to be ruled absolutely on pain of death combine to forge a remorseless picture of the human condition. Hobbist realism offers an analogy between the "state of nature," a war of all against all, and organized states, whose relation to one another is a similar war, constrained only by the fact that power can check power. Just as the state of nature is characterized by a terrible equality in that each individual is capable of killing the others, the condition of states is characterized by a similarly terrible equality. As there is no overarching authority to compel states to behave decently, as there is in a domestic polity once individuals relinquish their primordial freedom and infuse power into an awesome, authoritarian ruler who commands order, there is no solution to the state of war between states.

Each aspect of the Hobbist universe requires or turns on several basic givens. One is the denial that relations between human beings are characterized by other than fear, force, or calculation in any sphere or sets of relations. A second is Hobbes's insistence that our *natural* condition is one of anarchy and enmity. A third is his understanding of power as a *force majeure* behind which is the club, the clenched fist, and the executioner's mask. Yet power wielded to check power is the only hope for social order, necessary to prevent a fall back into the most horrible possible fate: the original state of nature.

In the Hobbist world, men and women are deprived of a public-political voice. By that I mean that Hobbes's political vocabulary is stripped of terms of public moral evaluation—the language of justice, right, equality, liberty. In addition, women are deprived of their traditional role in moral education through mothering. The vocabulary of moral sentiment, affection, and emotion—love, mercy, compassion, kindness, concern—terms that describe and help to constitute relations of intimacy and responsibility—also go by the board as lacking all meaning. Under the terms of Hobbist realism, women enjoy the equality of the silenced and subjected, but they can be neither moral agents nor citizens. All human subjects are stripped of a capacity to reflect, to judge, to question, and to act, for these activities are constituted in part by language infused with moral terms.

The first thing to be said about Hobbes's world of abstract, hostile monads is that it is anthropologically false. The human race could never have survived if the relations of each to all were one of unrelenting fear and suspicion. From the simplest tribal beginnings to the most complex social forms, women had to nurture infants—no matter what the men were up to—if life was to go on in any sustained form. This point may seem embarrassingly trivial. After all, Hobbes did not deny that parents raised children; he just denied that the activity was intrinsically social, bore deep meaning, or need be laced through and through with moral imperatives. But the point is that the activity could not be sustained in the absence of precisely those features Hobbes sought to eliminate: uncalculating care, concern not reducible to "power-over," and so on. That important features of the human condition, particularly those aspects linked to maternity and sociality, are forced out of Hobbes's universe indicts his "realism" as a distortion, rather than a reflection, of the complexities of the human condition.

It is doubtful that most modern realists would endorse fully the constellation of Hobbist presumptions I have just outlined. They would likely reject his vision of the state of nature as extreme and his construal of family life as dire and unconvincing. Why, then, is it so easy to accept the wider conclusions Hobbes drew by analogy from the state of nature and domestic rule? I refer to his insistence that states are in anarchic relations with one another and that power alone is the name of the international game. If Hobbes omitted central features of human social life *internal* to civil society, perhaps he is similarly guilty of one-sidedness in his characterization of the world of states. Realists seem not to consider this possibility; indeed, when Hobbes is presented in academic courses in international relations, his anthropology is rarely examined in depth, and his views on family life are often completely ignored. In this way suppression and denial of female images and the imperatives linked traditionally to mothering and the creation of human communities are perpetuated in our thinking on "the real world."

My hunch is that most architects of our strategic doctrine and shapers of our foreign policy would, if pressed, locate themselves not as Hobbists but inside a Machiavellian tradition. This tradition proclaims the autonomy of the political realm as a world having its own norms, rules, and imperatives, which ill-suit it for evaluation by moralists who do not understand those imperatives and their legitimate and necessary function. What holds the Machiavellian world view together? Machiavelli begins, as did Hobbes, with a set of anthropological presumptions proclaiming human nature as both constant and bleak.

> For it may be said of men in general that they are ungrateful, voluble, dissemblers, anxious to avoid danger, and covetous of gain; as long as you benefit them, they are entirely yours; they offer you their blood, their goods, their life, and their children . . . when the necessity is remote; but when it approaches, they revolt.[5]

Machiavelli's understanding of human nature, his assessment of his own epoch, and his celebration of the pre-medieval civic past spurred him to articulate a theory of political action that could be justified from the standpoint of an ethic at odds with the constraints of Christian morality on individual and collective action. His ideal of civic virtue (*virtù*) required at its foundation "a good military organization," troops "well disciplined and trained" in time of peace in order to prepare for war. This "necessity" he drew from "every page of Roman history."[6]

For Aristotle's alternative classical vision of the male citizen as a participant coequal with other males in a *polis* animated by discourse of a particular kind, requiring ruling and being ruled in turn, Machiavelli substitutes the armed popular state. This "militarization of citizenship" (in the words of J.G.A. Pocock) is one of the potent legacies of Machiavellian realism *and* a doctrine that subverts consideration of alternative images of participation, citizenship, and civic virtue.[7] Military preparedness becomes a *sine qua non* of the state; the entire social order is bound up, directly and indirectly, with this central institution.

There is more. Machiavellian—and modern—realism is held together by a compelling version of a public/private split, with morality retreating into the private domain, the world of women. Within the realist public sphere, terms like power, force, coercion, violence, and strategic necessity roam freely, structuring political action and consciousness. On the other side of a conceptual chasm, softness, compassion, the gentler virtues, and emotionality are possible, but they must be contained. Citizenship having been armed, women cannot be "good citizens" in this scheme of things. Instead, the woman may serve either as a "mirror" to male warmaking (a kind of collective civic cheer-leader) or as an "other" who embodies the softer, domestic values and virtues out of place within, and subversive of, *realpolitik*. The instrumental clarity and calculatedness of politics contrasts with, but requires, the expressive emotion and "irrationality" of intimate life.

Within Machiavelli's universe, a man might well be a good ruler but a wicked person. If "private" morality, judging him as a person, also condemned him thereby as a ruler, it could auger ill for political survival. Rules of conduct appropriate to private morality ("privatized" might be the better term) were inappropriate to a morality of politics that turned on achieving one's ends through a strategic economy of violence and holding one's power through skillful and, if necessary, ruthless use of force. The voice of piety, womanly or priestly, could be heard as long as it carried no weight in a public domain characterized by armed virtue. What emerges from Machiavelli is a series of public and private mirror images that require one another and sustain his world. Out of the realist picture as political actors, women reflect it as "mirrors" or as "other"—a point to which I shall return.

If Hobbist realism squeezes out the notion of citizen altogether, a Machiavellian mode opens up space for citizenship, but on terms defined by the notions of armed virtue and collective will. Politics constituted by realist presumptions overemphasizes political and military images and necessity. To the extent that women play a political role, it is not as citizens but as collective "support troops," mirroring male war making or embodying those pieties and virtues on the other side of the Machiavellian divide. Immunized from political action, the "realist female" may honor the Penates at the hearth, but she cannot bring her values to bear on the public life of her society. Placed in a historically constituted double bind, she serves as a substructural support for that in which she takes no direct part. From time to time, the realist narrative draws the woman into the picture when she is needed as the occasion for war (we must fight to protect "her") or as a kind of silent Greek chorus, not so much commenting on the action as weeping over its effects.

I mention the force of the realist narrative and its images of male and female because I am convinced of their lingering, if implicit, power inside the worldview of modern realists. To be sure, we have moved from the male republican citizen of

Machiavelli's ideal state to the technologized soldier of the modern bureaucratic state. The "face of battle," in John Keegan's words, has changed dramatically, growing more and more horrific. But the terms through which we think about war, peace, and politics are repeated endlessly.[8] Because realism won the discursive war, becoming the "common sense" of nation-states and those who govern them, and becoming deeply and more broadly imbedded in our understanding of political and social life, we rarely bring its underlying structure for a close-up examination.

We accept the realist's characterization of himself as being in touch with mordant and often bitter truths of the human condition, and thus better prepared than the idealist to do the necessary, if sometimes regrettable, dirty work. I do not wish to deride realism simplistically as little more than the long tale of masculine self-valorization, punctuated with repeated acts of individual and collective brutality. The problem of "dirty hands" *is* a problem. We do not know, when we act in the world, what the full results of our actions may be, and we cannot forestall every tragic possibility. We may sometimes be compelled to do a determinate wrong in the name of an overriding right.[9] The critic can acknowledge all this and her case against realism is stronger if she does, yet go on to insist that realists make things too easy for themselves. Most have not had enough of a problem with "dirty hands"; they dirty themselves and plead necessity too blithely. President Truman's jaunty insistence that he lost no sleep at all over his decision to drop the atomic bombs on Hiroshima and Nagasaki is a case in point; if true, Truman's report is profoundly disturbing. Such decisions should be anguished.

Presuming the worst from every situation and the worst in the intentions and motives of others, realists invite the worst. Their discourse helps to structure a politics that conforms to their presumptions. Starting with the conviction that the world is divided between one's allies (or potential allies) and one's opponents (or potential enemies) and holding that one's opponents are prepared to take advantage of any sign of weakness, indecision, or slackness of will, the realist endorses strength, decisiveness, and staunchness of will. The statesman (whether male or female) can never seem "womanly," or soft. We have no choice but to prepare for the worst (says the realist) because "our opponents," lacking our moral compunctions, are assuredly doing precisely that. The world of the realist becomes self-confirming, with alternative reflection prevented by worst-case scenarios and unquestioned hypotheses. In the words of E.P. Thompson, modern realists, including many deterrence theorists, are "trapped within the enclosed circularity of their own self-validating logic."[10]

Two features of realism, or strong propensities that realism invites, are *abstractedness*, on the one hand, and *disassociation*, on the other. These are complicatedly related and difficult to characterize succinctly, turning on a number of philosophic concerns that plunge us instantly into very deep water. But let me at least suggest why a standpoint that proclaims its clear-sightedness when confronted with harsh truths in fact operates in a twilight zone of multiple denials. By abstractedness, I refer to a mode of thinking that oversimplifies human realities, overlooks pluralities and makes possible, in turn, disassociation from one's deeds.

The point here is not that all abstractions are to be avoided—we cannot think without them—but that the world of realists presents a dangerously oversimplified vision of human thought, emotion, and social and political life that, in turn, paves the way for the love and hatred of abstract collectives that predominate by definition in time of war. In his small masterwork, *The Warriors*, J. Glenn Gray reminds us that a basic aim of a nation-state at war, necessary to pursue the war, is to establish a picture of "*the* enemy" as absolutist and abstract as possible to distinguish as sharply as possible the act of killing from the act of murder: it is always *the* enemy, a universalist construction that appears concrete. We surrender our capacity to reason concretely to such abstractions, falsifying reality in the process. Eric Maria Remarque's protagonist in *All Quiet on the Western Front* kills a frightened French soldier who has leapt into the trench beside him in a panic to escape whizzing bullets. The man dies agonizingly from his bayonet wounds, and when he has died, Remarque's disillusioned hero speaks to him directly, "Comrade, I did not want to kill you. . . . But you were only an idea to me before, an abstraction that lived in my mind and called forth its appropriate response. It was the abstraction I stabbed."[11]

A second example—on a very different level—of abstractedness that invites disassociation but does not provide space for the rediscovery of the concrete (as does Remarque's novel) may be found in the following depiction of Western Europe by a strategic analyst: "Western Europe (like South Korea) amounts geographically to a peninsula projecting out from the Eurasian land mass from which large continents of military force can emerge on relatively short notice to invade the peninsula."[12] The abstractedness of this thinking facilitates treating "Western Europe" as a possible arena for a tactical nuclear exchange. After all, it is potentially expendable territory! All modern forms of game theorizing and computer simulation are similarly abstract and have, argues Hannah Arendt, "a hypnotic effect," blocking the human capacity to perceive and understand "reality and factuality."[13] Proclaiming that they are capable of "thinking the unthinkable," such realists are (again Arendt) not engaging in "thinking at all."

Realism's disassociated relation to reality is perhaps most evident in doctrines and strategies that posit nuclear war as the extension of war by other means. Realism, remember, presumes a tight relationshipship between holding and exercising power and violence or the threat of force. The apogee of this association is the nation-state itself in its "face" as the legitimate repository of violent means that may be deployed to the end of its own survival or ends deemed to be in its interest. But given nuclear technology, the idea that one might deploy such weapons to achieve the ends of one's state falls apart under barest scrutiny. The means of violence have so outstripped any rational (even romantic) end that one might suppose that realists would long ago have begun to question the relationship between power and violence in our times.[14] That this has not happened extensively or decisively reminds us of the depth of realism's abstracted and disassociated relationship to present dangers and possible future horrors, on the one hand, and to other features of human society that might, if "seen" and given weight, put pressure upon the realist *Weltanschauung*, on the other. Realism ignores a whole range of human capacities, possibilities, and goods: our kindness has no bearing, but our cruelty dominates; our compassion is hidden, but our spitefulness is center stage; our origins as vulnerable infants are forgotten, and an image of willful (male, for the most part) adults prevails.

Our present realist dead-end, then, turns on and requires severing politics from moral consideration and the privatizing of morality as part of a split between male and female images, spheres, and imperatives. Realism was also locked into place when older notions of *realpolitik* and armed civic virtue became fused with 18th-century rationalism and 19th-century nationalism. In a world organized along the lines of our present "realist" model, collective violence will remain the court of last appeal, and in this kind of world there are no easy ways out. Yet there is an alternative tradition, to which we have sometimes repaired, to challenge or at least to complicate the world realism claims to reflect but denies having in any sense wrought. I refer to just-war thinking.

JUST WARS AND MODIFIED REALISM

Just-war doctrine is a complex body of ethical and political thinking, a gerrymandered edifice composed over time and under pressure, which has served historically to question and chasten collective violence. From the beginning, just-war thinkers have reacted to a context set by the hard-nosed realists of their day. For just-war doctrine grew out of an implicit compromise between the absolute pacifism and withdrawal *from* the world of early Christian communities, on the one hand, and the unacceptable possibility that Christianity, as it became institutionalized, would mirror and reproduce the extant terms of the world, on the other. Opposing absolute pacifism, just-war thinkers acknowledged that violence might sometimes be necessary to protect the innocent from harm, although the resort to violence is always a grave matter and morally regrettable. The overriding presumption of just war from the early Christians to the present is in favor of peace. Peace, not war, is seen as the most characteristic, the "natural" (if you will) human activity. It follows that violence must always justify itself before the court of nonviolence.

The text that lay the discursive basis for all later just-war thinking was St. Augustine's 4th-century masterwork, *The City of God*. For Augustine, the *Pax Romana* was a false peace wrought by evil means, and he indicts Roman imperialist wars as paradigmatic instances of unjust war. "Consider the scale of those wars, with all that slaughter of human beings, all the human blood that was shed!" he cried.[15] But he goes on to defend, with regret, the possibility that a just war might be used in defense of a common good. The dictum that war is evil bears presumptive force. War is not an activity that forges and sustains civic virtue but, instead, a tragedy that may be required to protect the innocent from certain destruction and to defend a way of life that sustains a common good.

As developed over time by just-war thinkers, nearly all of them Christian theologians before the early modern era, non-combatant immunity gained a secure place as the most important of *jus in bello* rules, for justice must prevail in war's waging as well as in its inception.[16] By the time Martin Luther recast the central elements of just-war argument in the 16th century, it consisted of an interrelated list of general rules, primarily prohibitions: a deontology binding upon Christian men, women, and rulers.

I mentioned above that just-war thinking has been reactive, with other forces pushing and pulling it. Although I cannot trace that history here, one mark of this historic scarring is evident in 20th-century papal teaching. Given a world organized into sovereign states, with no overarching arbiter to settle disputes, the "right" of states to "self-defense" is recognized in Vatican II in these words: "As long as the danger of war persists and there is no international authority with the necessary competence and power, governments cannot be denied the right of lawful self-defense, once all peace efforts have failed."[17] Of course, *jus ad bellum* criteria must be brought to bear, and any conflict must be conducted by *jus in bello* rules.

We immediately detect the following: the stipulative requirements for pursuing war remain essentially unchanged from their earliest formulations, with noncombatant immunity the center pieces. *Jus ad bellum* considerations have altered, however, in this sense: the *context* has shifted to put greater weight on the "right" of extant states to "self-defense" with less focus on concepts of a "common good." The presumption may be that any modern state, no matter how rotten, bears at least some semblance or intimation of a common good; moreover, it is for the people in that society to transform it from within, rather than for others to alter its arrangements through violence.[18] What remains constant is the insistence that *moral* considerations must enter into all discussions of war and serve as a serious ground for making *political* judgments.

Just-war argument, like realism, is part of a total worldview that includes a vision of domestic politics. By that I refer to ideals of human social life in families as well as politics. St. Augustine begins from a presumption that realism denies: that human beings are innately social and that human life is laced through and through with a basic grammar of injunctions and prohibitions concerning the taking of human life, sexual relations, and the administration of justice. Rather than bifurcating the social sphere into rigidly demarcated arenas (the masculine "hard" and the feminine "soft") as Machiavelli was to do later, Augustine finds in the household "the beginning or element of the city, and every beginning bears reference to some ends of its own kind, and every element to the integrity of the whole of which it is an element, it follows plainly enough that domestic peace has a relation to civic peace."[19] The household and the city, public and private, do not diverge sharply but are aspects of a greater whole, which is borne into its parts even as the integrity and meaning of each part carries forward to become an integral part of the whole.

Women occupy an important role in this scheme of things. Both parents share responsibility for their children, although husbands are the "just rulers" of households, who must be neither arbitrary nor proud. Children first learn respect for the moral law within the family, in and through their relations with parents. Although Augustine's is a world in which men and women play important roles, the man, finally, is the prime author of the broader social narrative. The sexes are viewed as complementary not as segregated into two separate normative systems with different rules applying to human behavior, depending upon whether one is a public man or a private woman. A "people" overall is held together, not through coercion, or *cupiditas* (lust for dominion and economic gain), but by their "common agreement as to the objects of love." In this *societas Christiana*, women have a central role and are a moral force. Women and men can speak in the same moral voice, bringing shared imperatives to bear. I am not, of course, claiming that the just-war world—in Augustine's teaching or that of later just-war spokesmen—was one of sex equality. Indeed, that notion would have no meaning within the life and discourse of his age. Rather, I am claiming that just-war argument, unlike realism, recognizes our sociality and honors women's part in the human story by giving weight to her activities and purposes. Morality and politics, males and females are at least inside the same picture frame.

Where, then, is the problem? At the beginning of this essay I promised to suggest an alternative to realism *and* just-war thinking. Toward this end, I will explore the cultural images of male and female which are rooted in the just-war tradition and are inadequate, at present, if one's reference point is transformative possibility. I will also argue the just-war theory, in practice in our recent past, and in theory as recast in the United States Catholic bishops pastoral letter on war and peace, is inadequate to the nuclear realities we face.

Augustine's moral householders and his insistence that civic peace is but domestic peace writ large gave way, over time, to a sex-complementary order that more sharply divided males and females, their honored activities, and their symbolic resonance. As men became "just warriors," fighters, and defenders of righteous causes, women were transformed into a particular sort of dialectical "other" that I, drawing upon Hegel's *Phenomenology,* call "beautiful souls." As Christian theology and morality evolved (or devolved) into a received body of sentiments, the female beautiful soul is pictured as a collective woman who exemplifies particular virtues —she is self-sacrificing, frugal, and decent, and she eschews vanity, selfishness, and waste. She keeps the faith and serves, and there is genuine goodness in much of this. But in wartime, she cannot put a stop to suffering; cannot effectively fight the mortal wounding of sons, brothers, husbands, and fathers. Although women do have a social identity, and many women historically have empowered themselves on the basis of that identity, this female symbol too easily collapses into a sentimentalist celebration of womanly virtues and invites retreat into counsels of private goodness. Indeed, the collective woman may be the occasion for a just war; she may require protection by that collective male entity, the body politic.

The just warrior defends the body politic; he keeps it intact. The just warrior is a human being compelled to engage in the regrettable, but sometimes necessary, task of collective violence. The image of just war, as I have indicated, is rooted deep in our historic memory, and there has been genuine honor within that cultural form. But the modern face and reality of war quite literally explode our image of just warriors, fighting fair and square by the rules of the game. War is more and more a matter of remote control, with less and less possibility for acts of bravery, courage, and restraint. The beautiful soul can no longer be protected: she and her children are all vulnerable. Moreover, the lingering hope that somehow female qualities will transform the political arena, turning it from a play of force into a forum for decency, have worn thin with historic experience. The interlocked collective symbols of male and female leave us with imagery that goes nowhere, that disallows room to move in a search for alternative animating visions.

The problem with applied just-war doctrine is the question of slippage. I refer to the fact that modern just-war thinking, especially arguments that do not share the full ontological and moral commitments of the religious analyst, are subject to casuistic trimming. To be sure, the insistence holds that violence is always regrettable and devoutly to be avoided. But beyond that, many horrors may slip through the cracks of just-war doctrine in actual cases. For example: in Michael Walzer's *Just and Unjust Wars*, a complete contemporary treatment by a non-theologian, queries concerning past practice—the British decision to bomb German cities during World War II—and present policy—nuclear deterrence theory—revolve importantly on consequentialist criteria. That is in making his moral assessments, he brings to bear considerations that go beyond the deontological requirements of classic just-war teaching (e.g., noncombatant immunity). Thus Walzer justifies, with regret, the saturation bombing of German cities during World War II, given the nature of the Nazi threat and the predictable outcome should Britain have fallen to Germany. Present threat and future danger fused to override *jus in bello* rules, and the British made total war on the most densely populated areas of major German cities.[20] By decrying Nazism as an immeasurable evil, Walzer insists that the issues at stake can only take this form: should I wager a determinate crime against an immeasurable evil? Clearly, a condition of "supreme emergency" erodes the force of central just-war prescriptions.

The slippage to which I refer, then, is the way in which just-war thinking is subject to infusion of categories along the lines of a moral cost-benefit equation. By adjusting to the "realities" of total war, just-war thinking approaches a modified form of realism. I raise the example of World War II and total war in part because Walzer proclaims our present circumstance to be one of continuing "supreme emergency." Given this emergency, this unrelenting threat to our survival as a political community and a nation-state, deterrence is inexorable: it, too, is given. Walzer regrets his own conclusion, for he finds deterrence a

> bad way of coping with supreme emergency, but there may well be no other that is practical in a world of sovereign and suspicious states. We threaten evil in order not to do it, and the doing of it would be so terrible that the threat seems in comparison to be morally defensible.[21]

The argument that requires this conclusion concedes so much to the realist posture ("sovereign and suspicious states," "threatening evil . . . not to do it," etc.) that it seems nearly indistinguishable in most respects from a modified realist posture.

The just-war position, I am suggesting, too easily slips into a rationalization for our "tragic" choices. For example: as all serious just-war thinkers concede, it is notoriously easy to use and abuse the charge "aggression." Yet, determining who is an aggressor, hence an outlaw state, is central to the modern just-war assumption that states have rights that, like those of individuals, can be abridged or violated. Victim states may demand redress for grievances, and war is the ultimate form of self-help in one's own behalf. Few cases of aggression are as clear-cut as the German violation of Belgian neutrality in 1914; moreover, the language of "rights" and "aggression," the legalistic tone of much just-war discourse, is ill-matched when pitted against the realities of nuclear war. Walzer, again, expresses this concern. Opposing American use of the atomic bombs on Hiroshima and Nagasaki, finding them unjustified within his just-war frame, Walzer asks: "How did the people of Hiroshima forfeit their rights?"[22]

The language of "rights" and their forfeiture is impoverished in the context of nuclear war, and inadequate to characterize what happened on those dreadful days. Our language of moral reflection must be up to the task of conveying nuclear reality. Pope Paul VI seems closer to the mark when he speaks of "butchery of untold magnitude."[23] But his language and its animating ethos belong to a prophetic tradition not shared by most academic philosophers who take up just-war arguments. The language of "rights" comes easier to us who are heirs of Western social contract theory than a language of deep moral outrage and radical evil. But when outrage and evil are washed out of just-war thinking, it loses much of its heart and soul, receding instead into analytic maneuvers and stipulative fine-tuning.

In addition, there is a political concern. The modified just-war posture I question above may too easily lend itself to rationalization by the less than scrupulous; moreover, the way matters of war and peace decisionmaking are now joined, just-war conditions can be invented, at least initially, to fortify us for conflict. Citizens are placed in reactive postures. By the time the matter of whether a war is just or not is debated, and all information is released to the public, we may already be in the thick of things. Properly applied, just-war doctrine requires open, substantive debate. But debate of that sort may not even take place under present conditions, although one can predict that every attempt will be made to convince concerned citizens, in the absence of a debate that we "cannot afford" if we are to move efficaciously in a perilous situation, that the conditions and limitations of just-war concerns have been met, in the judgment of policymakers. The shakiness of just-war thinking, then, is forced upon us by "the nature of the modern state combined with the nature of modern total war."[24]

The strongest, most compelling, and most comprehensive review and restatement of just-war teaching in light of nuclear reality is the U.S. Catholic bishops pastoral letter on war and peace issued 3 May 1983. It is a brilliant and commendable exercise. The bishops condemn the arms race as a curse and an act of aggression against the poor; they endorse conscientious objection and express their admiration for pacifism; they declare that nuclear weapons cannot under any circumstance be used to destroy population centers; they perceive no situation in which the initiation of nuclear war is justified; they prohibit offensive war of any kind, conventional or nuclear; and they proffer comprehensive suggestions on ways to promote peace in and through all levels of civil society. But they retain a strong brief on the right to self-defense against "unjust aggression," and they offer cautious, provisional acceptance of deterrence "in current conditions" so long as deterrence is a "transitional strategy" toward the end of genuine arms reduction and control. As well, the bishops evoke "the principle of proportionality" as a moral brake on defensive responses to "unjust attack," whether "nuclear or conventional," and they express deep "skepticism" (rather than flat condemnation) concerning arguments in behalf of "limited nuclear war."

My concerns about the bishops' letter are twofold. First, continued use of the language of proportionality, discrimination, and so on, perpetuates terms of discourse more appropriate to an earlier, prenuclear era. Second, the bishops accept without question the "states-with-rights" view that dominates Walzer's discussion. I do believe a people has a right to self-defense, but I am concerned that the way they perceive that right and determine "aggression" is subject to distortion and abuse. The Soviets claimed threats to their security justified their intervention in Afghanistan; the United States has frequently given wide berth to its own understanding of the right to self-defense. By accepting the context of the present —a world of sovereign and suspicious states—and going on to view deterrence as the best of a very bad deal, the bishops are less radically deconstructive of the realist edifice than they might have been had they not, themselves, been compelled to hammer out a compromise statement.

The more passionate voice is too easily muted by the legalistic forms of just-war argument. Albert Camus wrote in 1948,

What the world expects of Christians is that Christians should speak out, loud and clear, and that they should voice their condemnation in such a way that never a doubt, never the slightest doubt, could rise in the heart of the simplest man. That they should get away from abstraction and confront the blood-stained face history has taken on today.[25]

Much of that blood-stained history is tied directly to the emergence and victory of the principle of nationalism. The state is not only the container for the common life of a people; it is also, or can be, a coldly calculating engine of death. War is deeply rooted inside the infrastructure of modern states; war is a major social system. If my claims are persuasive, or even plausible, it follows that critics of our present course must acknowledge the reality of the state system while simultaneously questioning its present forms and priorities. Otherwise one concedes too much at the outset to the realist paradigm.

This much, by now, should be clear: one's starting point, one's presumptions, and the imperatives they exude, set limits for one's discourse on war and on the relationship of men and women to war. Hard-line realism sanctions the use of coercion and force, having embraced these as lying at the very heart of individual and collective human existence, in a way just-war thinking, seeing us as social and moral, does not and cannot. Just-war argument requires that one be open to moral suasion, and insists that a genuine politics is about attempts to reach for a "common good" rather than merely to hold or seize power. Women are placed outside the realist frame (although the privatized female shadow lurks in the background). Women are inside the just-war picture but cast in historically constituted roles that make it difficult for women, *and* men, to break out of the dialectic of "beautiful souls" and "just warriors." If realism is increasingly abstracted from reality, just-war thinking, which makes contact with that reality, is now stretched to the breaking point. Realists take leave of reality, and just-war thinkers are overtaken by it. What, then, is an alternative?

REFLECTIONS ON WOMEN, WAR, FEMINISM, AND HANNAH ARENDT

Certain forms of contemporary feminist discourse are indebted to the realist and just-war presumptions I have just discussed. Within the current feminist universe one finds, for example, hard-line feminist realists who make generous use of military metaphors, conceiving politics as a power-riddled battleground in which the best advice to women is that they learn to "fight dirty." With Hobbes, these thinkers assume that men are compelled by nature to seek the oppression of others. By "men" they refer, of course, not to the generic human, but to biological males. "All men" becomes a natural category at odds with "all women." There is much tough talk about sex-war, and shock troops, and locating the enemy. Writes one: "Politics and political theory revolve around this paradigm case of the Oppressor and the Oppressed."[26] Another urges women to become "fully integrated" in the "national guard, our state troopers," up to and including full participation in military institutions. Only through combat preparation and integration into extant structures of power can women end their colonization.[27]

Such feminist realism, with its Hobbist precursors, is stuck inside a self-reproducing world of fear, suspicion, anticipated violence, and force to check-mate force. Realist feminist discourse is peppered with worst-case scenarios and presumptions of supreme emergency (for example, the recent suggestion that males and their reactionary female cohorts are at work planning future "gynocide," or mass destruction of women along the lines of the Holocaust). Men are set up as implacable foes against which women must defend themselves at every turn, and the possibility of genuine, mutual ties between men and women is denied, either absolutely and in principle or, for the time being, during the current state of sex-war. The similarities to hard-line realism are striking and usher into an analogous cycle of defense, escalation, and deterrence.

A modified feminist realism, more indebted to Machiavelli than to Hobbes, may be found in the legal brief filed by the National Organization for Women in 1981 as part of a challenge to all-male registration.[28] NOW claimed that compulsory, universal military service is central to the concept of citizenship in a democracy, thus buttressing notions of armed civic virtue. If women are to gain first-class citizenship they, too, must have the right to fight. Laws that exclude women from draft registration and combat duty perpetuate archaic notions of women's capabilities; moreover, devastating longterm psychological and political repercussions result from women's exclusions from the military of their country.[29] By endorsing without apparent qualm the military as an institution, the NOW brief unthinkingly reinforces "the military as an institution and militarism as an ideology."[30]

What the NOW case represents, in its deep structure, is a leap out of the female/private side of that public/private divide I outlined as essential to a Machiavellian worldview. But in this instance, NOW leaps straight into the arms of the dominant male whose sex-linked activities are affirmed and valorized thereby. Paradoxically, repudiation of "archaic notions of women's role" becomes a tribute to "archaic notions of men's role," although the brief fails to see any irony in all this. In practice, equal rights feminism has tended to mean, in these and other instances, an affirmation of extant structures of social privilege. Unaware of the deep indebtedness of their arguments and theories to worldviews and philosophic presumptions historically geared against acceptance of women and those values to which they are symbolically and historically linked, feminist realists, whether in their extreme Hobbist form or softer "armed civic virtue" embodiment, do not offer a serious challenge to theory-as-usual in considerations of women, men, war, and violence.

There are, as well, feminist variants flowing from just-war discourse. One involves a celebration of the "female principle" and a proclamation of the moral superiority of women and their forms of virtue. Such feminists find the NOW right-to-fight argument deeply disturbing. For them it represents a capitulation, *not* to the historically constructed features of our present order, but to a pre-given, ontological masculinist principle. In utopian versions of what is sometimes called "cultural feminism," women are often urged to withdraw into separate communities, to free themselves from the taint of the male surround, and to work for a world organized around the values they embrace. But in this scenario the female beautiful soul, rather than being in the picture, withdraws into a more privatized (if intensely communal) mode. No feminist who seeks to participate in peacemaking as a social and cultural activity of the greatest urgency, one that requires reaching out rather than drawing in, can unambiguously embrace the image of "caring" and "connected" females *in opposition* to "callous" and "disconnected" men. Sex segregation is deepened, not challenged, by such views—indebted to, yet much exaggerating, the beautiful-soul image located inside just-war thinking.

In contrast to the etherealized and abstract vision of sex-segregated beautiful souls, there is a second and more vital image linked to the just-war tradition. One might call it the "moral mother," although visions of militant Sparta might spring to mind, and that is not what I have in mind. Instead I am thinking about a more down-to-earth beautiful soul, a woman engaging a complicated and messy world, guided perhaps by basic principles, but open to new realities. This beautiful soul is very much in the world, not out of it. With those women whose views now coalesce to create the gender gap—the significant differences showing up consistently in survey data on male and female views on force, the use of force, and the threat of force—she seeks to bring her imperatives to bear on the social world in which she finds herself. Although the more earth-bound beautiful soul I evoke need not be a biological mother, she must be one concerned with mothering in a broader sense, with protecting the vulnerable without patronizing them, with the human dignity of all, especially those we tend to cast aside or repudiate, with fairness and decency and many other terms we academic analysts use rather embarrassedly. This modified beautiful soul does not accept the hard-line, gendered epistemology and metaphysic of absolute beautiful souls, but she does insist that ways of knowing flow from ways of acting and being in the world, and that hers has vitality and validity in both private and public ways.

Yet the modified beautiful soul exists in a surround that constantly pushes her toward mere sentimentalisms or naive abstractions. (I have in mind, "If only people would just learn to talk with each other because all people all over are the same and *mean* well," and the like.) It is ironic that the very qualities that make her sensitive to the abuse of the weak and the arrogance of the strong become the ground by which she is disqualified for the "tough" tasks of institutionalized power.

To suggest an alternative to the powerful discourses thus far assayed, and the male and female images they secrete or tend to sustain, I shall offer a brief, appreciative gloss on Hannah Arendt's *On Violence*, a text thus far overlooked by feminist analysts.[31] Arendt's suggestive discussion provokes us, if we can "see" her argument, into *re*-cognizing the present, beginning what must necessarily be a long process of disenthrallment from reigning, received notions. She helps us to "get at" our collective embrace, or our acquiescence in, a view of politics that situates violence as one among a number of ways that power manifests itself and, as well, as a particularly effective way for the powerless to gain political power.[32]

Arendt asks us, the heirs of the Western tradition, to put to ourselves this question: how did we arrive at the point where it is "natural" for us to assume that violence is sometimes necessary, even if it is to be regretted, in just-war fashion? (The violence Arendt has in mind is that of groups or collectives, not individual outrage culminating in the single violent act of Melville's *Billy Budd*.) One key assumption at work for and in us, she claims, is our belief that history has an underlying purpose, a teleology: history is "going someplace." The big word, of course, is *progress*. Both liberals and their Marxist opponents share the discursive terrain out of which progressivist ideology springs; they both see history as a story of progress, evolution, stages, and end-points.[33]

This sort of thinking bears us in certain directions. We all want to (need to) believe that some good must come out of any and all horrendous things; that somehow, in the long run, the end *will* justify the means. A repressive state apparatus is a necessary way-station on the road to classless society: containing and slaughtering the Indians is a necessary if sorry episode in the narrative of civilized progress (that Engels viewed American destruction of Indian tribes as a historic necessity indicates the epistemic ground shared by "progressivists" of all persuasions). Arendt invites us to consider the possibility that our infatuation with "progress," our often-inchoate yet nonetheless powerful conviction that history will somehow redeem itself, slides us into a way of thinking and being that compels us to assess individuals, peoples, and whole civilizations as either primitive or progressive, backward or developing, lazy or industrious, irrational and ignorant or open to reason and enlightenment. Hoping to manipulate the vectors of progress, including its human element, we fashion instruments to plan and dominate forces of nature and "laws" of social life. We do not acknowledge the potent will-to-power humming along as the restless motor of progressivist ideology.

Remember, Arendt continues, where there is a will to power as an urge to dominate there is also its shadow, its other: a will to submit, an urge to be dominated. The two go together. Arendt finds an *inner* connection between the compulsion to rule-over and the compulsion to be ruled, and this dominator/dominated construct of rule is rooted in the same presumptions as the teleology of historic progress. The dominated swell with *ressentiment*, seeking to dominate in turn. The *danse macabre* continues; we are locked into a thoughtless stalemate. The politics of such a world is no politics at all, she continues, but a form of structured violence that disempowers us. Authentic politics is at odds with forms of rule that require violence, hot or cold, to hold themselves intact. In a genuine *civitas*, rule is among equals, and one important step toward such politics is to refuse to accept the reduction of politics to the business of domination. Violence and power are not natural allies, or peas in the same conceptual pod, but "true opposites." Violence is never legitimate; it may, to be sure, defeat power, but it is *not* power. Violence is crudely instrumental. Power, however, like the Kantian subject, is an end in itself, just as politics is itself a human good and participation as a citizen is a mode of experience flowing from political being. The most likely result of violence is simply a more-violent world, not a more-just one. But power is what we experience as participants in a group that seeks to begin something anew, that forges commonalities out of a shared hope that it is possible to start, to initiate, to bring into being.

I fear all this sounds airily elusive. For most of us it seems strange, for we accept—it is the way the world is portrayed to us—that violence is one way to get things, including power. Arendt's essentially Aristotelian vision may strike us as nostalgic or heroic. We must live in the world, we murmur frustratedly, not in some eloquent elucidation of one. Yet that is precisely what Arendt sees herself as about—getting us to be "at home" in the world so we can, at least, understand the terms of our own predeterminations and recognize the symbolic foundations of our politics in images of *realpolitik* and armed civic virtue as well as in promises of freedom, equality, and rights.

Arendt's project requires nothing less than a new understanding of the political: a plenary jolt to received meanings and symbols that might shift the symbolic foundation for political life away from organized violence and armed civic virtue, images that either invite or justify war and destruction, to those of birth and hope. Understanding that narrow rationalist appeals rarely reach the human heart and lack the power to help us to transform ourselves, Arendt asks, implicitly, the Gospel question: Whence ariseth hope? Hope is the basis of any politics that can sustain us, that enables rather than frustrates our capacities for action. In *The Human Condition*, Arendt offers a radical suggestion. She embraces a potent, female-linked symbol that, were it to grow more powerful, might help us to transform our politics and to redeem, *not* history, but at least a portion of our own lives. Arendt writes:

> The miracle that saves the world, the realm of human affairs, from its normal, "natural" ruin is ultimately the fact of natality, in which the faculty of

action is ontologically rooted. It is, in other words, the birth of new human beings and the new beginning, the action they are capable of by being born. *Only the full experience of this capacity can bestow upon human affairs faith and hope, those two essential characteristics of human existence . . .* that found perhaps their most glorious and most succinct expression in the new words with which the Gospels announced their "glad tidings": "A Child has been born unto us."[34]

Thus far, being either too tough or too blind to the vulnerability of all new beginnings, we have failed to explore the full richness of Arendt's discussion. Yet the future of humanity in light of nuclear weapons, and the war systems that require and produce them, calls for us to dare to begin a new narrative; to say "no" to the great historic War Story and the parts it allows to women.[35] A new story begins with the birth of hope; the stone, once again, is at the bottom of the hill.

NOTES

1. MAD, as everyone knows, is the acronym for Mutual Assured Destruction, the strategic doctrine that promises utter annihilation to the "enemy's" territory, economic and governmental infrastructure, and population, should that enemy take steps that force the other side to go MAD. As mad as this is, some current strategists have gone even madder, proclaiming nuclear war "winnable" without the total annihilation threatened by MAD.
2. The interested reader will find a full, critical examination of the major theoretical frames of contemporary feminism as political discourse in Jean Bethke Elshtain, *Public Man, Private Woman: Women in Social and Political Thought* (Princeton: Princeton University Press, 1981), chap. 5.
3. It took me awhile in graduate school to rethink this division and to understand that the dichotomy does not occur neutrally, but is framed from the realist side.
4. Thomas Hobbes, *Leviathan*, ed. Michael Oakeshott (New York: Macmillan, 1962). For the discussions of Hobbes and Machiavelli, I am drawing upon portions of *Public Man, Private Woman*.
5. Niccolo Machiavelli, *The Prince and the Discourses* (New York: Modern Library, 1950), p. 61.
6. Ibid., p. 503. My views on Machiavelli are not universally, perhaps not even widely, shared among most political theorists who evoke his name as a father of civic republicanism. Concerned that Machiavellians and their opponents maligned and distorted the man and his work, revisionist appreciations of Machiavelli have been a necessary correction. But, having acknowledged that much, I must demur. I believe there is ample textual warrant for my interpretive claims.
7. J.G.A. Pocock, *The Machiavellian Moment* (Princeton: Princeton Unversity Press, 1975), p. 212.
8. See Gregory S. Kavka, Chapter 12, this volume, for a fascinating discussion of the ways in which debate and consideration of alternatives were shaped, constrained, and opened up during the Cuban Missile Crisis.
9. Of course, the example that immediately springs to mind is the war against Nazism. Saying this does not mean I endorse all actions taken by the Allies in pursuit of total defeat of Germany.

10. E.P. Thompson, *Beyond the Cold War* (New York: Pantheon, 1982), p. xx.
11. Erich Maria Remarque, *All Quiet on the Western Front* (New York: Fawcett, 1975), p. 195.
12. Cited in Thompson, *Beyond the Cold War*, p. 10.
13. Hannah Arendt, *On Violence* (New York: Harcourt Brace Jovanovich, 1976), p. 8.
14. Thompson asks: What could a nuclear war possibly be about? All the usual motives—defend one's borders, gain territory, protect an ally, extend one's sway, exploit a region, preempt a revolution—do not pertain.
15. St. Augustine, *The City of God*, ed. David Knowles (Baltimore: Penguin Books, 1972), p. 861.
16. Michael Walzer, *Just and Unjust Wars* (New York: Basic Books, 1977), p. 21.
17. "The Challenge of Peace: God's Promise and Our Response," *Origins* 13, no. 1 (May 19, 1983), p. 10.
18. Intervention might be justified under extreme circumstances, e.g., knowledge of genocide and the possibility that one might help to save lives.
19. Henry Paolucci, ed., *The Political Writings of St. Augustine* (Chicago: Henry Regnery, 1967), p. 151.
20. Walzer adds the caveat that such bombing went on far too long, well past the point of justification. A very different view of the process is found in Freeman Dyson, *Disturbing the Universe* (New York: Harper Colophon, 1979). Dyson served in the "Operational Research Section" of Bomber Command during the war, calculating probabilities for bombing raids with out much of a "feeling of personal responsibility. None of us ever saw the people we killed. None of us particularly cared" (p. 30). But his reflections after the fact are sad and bitter. He writes: "I began to look backward and to ask myself how it happened that I got involved in this crazy game of murder. Since the beginning of the war I had been retreating step by step from one moral position to another, until at the end I had no moral position at all" (pp. 30-31).
21. Walzer, *Just and Unjust Wars*, p. 58.
22. Ibid., p. 274.
23. Quoted in the Bishops' Letter, p. 13.
24. Gordon Zahn, *Another Part of the War: The Camp Simon Story* (Amherst: University of Massachusetts Press, 1979), p. 251.
25. Albert Camus, *Resistance, Rebellion and Death* (New York: Alfred A. Knopf, 1961), p. 71.
26. Ti-Grace Atkinson, "Theories of Radical Feminism," in *Notes from the Second Year: Women's Liberation*, ed. Shulamith Firestone (N.P., 1970), p. 37.
27. Susan Brownmiller, *Against Our Will. Men, Women and Rape* (New York: Simon & Schuster, 1975), p. 388.
28. My point here is not to argue either the fairness or the constitutionality of male-only draft registration, but to examine the kinds of arguments now brought to bear in the case.
29. The brief is available from the NOW Legal Defense and Educational Fund, 132 West 42nd St., NYC, NY 10036. See also the discussion in Cynthia Enloe, *Does Khaki Become YOU? The Militarisation of Women's Lives* (London: Pluto Press, 1983), pp. 16-17.
30. Enloe, *Khaki*.

31. This may be because (a) Arendt is a political theorist, a mode of discourse underrepresented in feminism; (b) Arendt is often regarded as either a foe of or no staunch ally of feminism because she is widely quoted as proclaiming that it makes little sense to see "woman" as a political category in some "natural" and inclusive way.
32. Arendt considers the dialectical notion that good will come from evil in history a dangerous and treacherous hope.
33. Arendt, *On Violence*, p. 10 ff.
34. Hannah Arendt, *The Human Condition* (Chicago: University of Chicago Press, 1958), p. 247.
35. Nancy Huston, "Tales of War and Tears of Women," *Women's Studies International Forum* 5, no. 3/4: pp. 271-82.

14
HONOR, PATRIOTISM, AND ULTIMATE LOYALTY

Sidney Axinn

MILITARY HONOR AND THE LAW OF WARFARE

Military honor is the response evoked by two demands. One was expressed by the French King Henry IV, and the other by Nietzsche. In a letter to one of his lieutenants, Henry wrote, "Hang yourself, Brave Crillon! We fought at Arques, and you were not there." Honorable comrades fight when they are needed, and are obligated to show courage, to take risks for proper objects of loyalty. Yet there are limits to the behavior that honor permits, and Nietzsche pointed out that members of the noble class take their revenge only within the circle of equals. Some targets are proper and some are not; some means of fighting are acceptable and some are not. And he adds (p. 466) the further, serious warning "He who fights with monsters should be careful lest he thereby become a monster." Honor requires sacrifice, but not without limits. In the first part of this essay I shall discuss the current significance of each of these aspects of the military tradition. After developing the concept of military honor, I analyze relationships between military honor, patriotism, morality, and nuclear weapons. My conclusion is that loyalty to individual nations must be replaced by loyalty to an international government. Otherwise military honor has no moral foundation. As Nietzsche had it, we would then become the monsters that we took the enemy to be.

Military Honor

Is the notion of honor a fraud to dupe the infantile, the stupid, or the romantic? Or is it "the ultimate protection of societies," as some insist?[2] Fascist governments have taken their conception of national honor most seriously, democratic governments hold the honoring of business contracts as a basic feature of their civilization, and no society seems able to give up some application of honor. I will limit this discussion to certain features of military and national honor, and discuss applications of the term and the moral progress of the conception of honor through history.

In a general way military honor refers to courage and fidelity. The role of courage is clear enough, as is willingness to do one's duty, e.g., to follow orders, regardless of danger (no desertion under fire). The notion of fidelity is more complicated.

"Fidelity" means a careful and exact performance of duties, but the term leaves open the matter of just what duties require this special role. For the military tradition, the duties are dual: to king or government, and to the military code. The military code, or law of warfare, is found in two places, and almost every nation (140, as of April 1976) has agreed to be bound by its strictures. It is explicitly and formally stated in the Hague and Geneva Conventions,[3] and in what FM 27-10 calls "the body of unwritten or customary law . . . firmly established by the custom of nations" (p. 4).

One of the purposes of the law of war is to distinguish between actions of armed robbery and the actions of honorable soldiers who are members of a militia. Actions of the latter sort satisfy four conditions (according to the Geneva Convention on POWs). The persons (a) are commanded by a person responsible for his subordinates, (b) have a fixed, distinctive sign recognizable at a distance, (c) carry arms openly, and (d) conduct operations in accordance with the laws and customs of war.

Each of these conditions is important. The distinction shown by (a) is that a criminal acts for his own selfish goals; a soldier acts for the sake of his commander and country. Since a soldier is not ashamed of what he does, he wears a sign (a uniform) to proclaim his loyalty and to openly warn his enemies, as (b) requires. Condition (c) shows that he hopes to win by open, honest, proud effort, not by deviousness or lying to the enemy. Condition (d), the requirement that the laws *and customs* of war not be violated, has its complications—but continues in the same spirit. The difference between a sneaky, selfish thief and a proud soldier lies in the open, honest willingness to sacrifice for the sake of others, and to do so without violating the agreements and precepts of the military code. Let's turn to some features of the code.

That there be a declaration of war before starting hostilities is an obvious requirement, the basis for which is in the idea of fairness. To attack without warning does not give the enemy a chance to respond effectively. It would initiate an unfair contest, and the honorable soldier takes himself to be essentially moral and takes pride in his morality. Our own FM 27-10 holds that the law of war requires that hostilities be conducted "with regard for the principles of humanity and chivalry" (p. 3). "Chivalry," which has come down to us from the feudal age, still matters very much. Chivalry means acting with courtesy, with gallantry, with special respect for the weak, and with decency toward the enemy. Those who find "chivalry" outdated may substitute "gentlemanly." Those who find no meaning in either term must be denied the uniform and the right to carry arms. The Army Field Manual uses "chivalry," and the traditional sense of that term is significant. Consider the situation if chivalry were not expected from our military. When a town is invaded by soldiers with no tradition of chivalry nor military honor, there would be no bar to raping the women and pillaging, nor any limit to robbery, destruction, desecration of cemeteries, mutilation of bodies of the enemy, etc.

The history of warfare contains examples of each of these atrocities. Yet the same history shows moral progress, and the conception of chivalry is a significant part of it. The Laws of War are vague in certain ways. These laws have had numerous reformulations and continue to have them. The taking of hostages was once allowed, but now is forbidden: it is unfair to seize an innocent person, even if such an act may have some military advantage. In the matter of weaponry, the history is hardly satisfactory; some weapons are outlawed, while even more damaging ones are invented and used. Yet the conception of chivalry—military honor—continues to develop and become more and more significant.

Of course, to note that the conception and the practice of military honor are expanding does not mean that individuals are becoming personally more honorable than individuals of previous centuries. Following Kant's philosophy of history, we can agree that military honor involves a wider scope in modern times than earlier—without making the error of thinking that the individuals of our times are somehow persons of better character or greater integrity. The history of civilization, of increasing democracy, and of military professionalism are responsible for the progress, which takes place even though we may be morally no better than our ancestors. Our laws and customs are more civilized, but our own characters are not made more pure. So, at any rate, Kant states it in his "Idea for a Universal History," and in other parts of his view of history.[4] That Lt. Calley was tried and convicted by his own side is an example of progress in the development of the role of military honor. That his superiors were not also brought before a court-martial is an example of the distance still to go.

In brief, the customary view of military honor is now under stood to require a declaration of a war. Military honor also prohibits attacking those who have surrendered, causing "unnecessary suffering" and the use of weapons that cause it, treachery, taking of hostages, and a series of acts called war crimes.

Defeat with Honor Versus Victory with Shame

Suppose that the view of the military presented above were completely discounted, and that our military could win a particular war by beheading all prisoners of war, raping captured women of all ages, and killing all the enemy children. Would our country be so disdainful of national honor that it would accept winning on such terms? Even if the political leadership of the country agreed to these means, there would remain the question of whether our military forces would prefer to win or to surrender. The tradition of military honor is supposed to produce soldiers who refuse to obey such orders, because their sense of chivalry requires courtesy, gallantry, and decency. That's why the Army must keep that term "chivalry" and have the courage to institutionalize it, teach it, and require it of all military personnel. Is this a serious or a romantic view of military honor?

Of course, this idealized view of honor is never completely attained in the actual world. There have been frequent violations, such as attacks without prior declarations at Pearl Harbor and in the Yom Kippur War. Nevertheless, the essential talent of military honor is like the view of law expressed by Roger Fisher:

> The essential talent of the law lies not in producing perfect order but in coping with disorder in an orderly way. Contract law, negligence law and criminal law "work" not in the sense of producing a society with no broken contracts, no negligence and no crimes, but by telling us how society should respond when things go wrong.[5]

In a similar way, the conception of honor and of the laws of war tell us *what* to be shocked at, and what to do about punishments.

Would we prefer defeat with honor, or victory with shame? Certainly, we don't want to be compelled to choose, so the proper move is to attack the question. The last part of this essay will propose a way of "overcoming" this question, for those who are not satisfied with either alternative. First we shall turn to some well-known properties of the law of warfare.

The Distinction Between Combatant and Noncombatant

A basic distinction that lies beneath much of traditional thinking about the laws of warfare is the line between those who announce themselves as combatants, and those who may sympathize with them but do not take part in combat. Is this distinction still of significance in the modern industrial world? In the present and recent past, those who maintain the economic base of a modern army are as critical an element in victory as almost any other. Without food and supplies, no army can operate. What is the position of the ordinary citizen during war?

The British *Manual of Military Law*, their edition of the Conventions, is helpful on this matter. During a war,

> every subject of the one state becomes an enemy to every subject of the other. It is impossible to sever subjects from their State, . . . it is no longer possible to say that international law protects the civilian population from injury which is incidental to attack upon legitimate objectives. Nevertheless . . . it is a generally recognized rule of international law that civilians must not be made the object of attack directed exclusively against them. The view that war is a relation not only between State and State but also between individuals must be read subject to that important qualification.[6]

Our FM 27-10 repeats, exactly, "civilians must not be made the object of attack directed exclusively against them" (p. 16).

Before a civilian-occupied area can be made a target, *special notification* and time for evacuation must be given. This goes back to the Hague Convention. As our FM 27-10 puts it, "commanders of United States ground forces will, when the situation permits, inform the enemy of their intention to bombard a place, so that the non-combatants, especially women and children, may be removed before the bombardment commences" (p. 20). Questions immediately arise: Were Hiroshima and Nagasaki legitimate military targets? And were the noncombatants in those cities given the information and the time to evacuate, before the cities were bombed by atomic weapons?

The information and the literature since the attack on the Japanese cities gives a variety of responses, but the obvious answer to these serious questions is, these cities were not proper military targets, and the warning to evacuate was not provided. A proper military target has a clear military function. Otherwise, in the language of the Hague Convention, "The attack or bombardment, by whatever means, of towns, villages, dwellings, or buildings which are undefended is prohibited" (FM 27-10, p. 19). Hiroshima and Nagasaki were apparently not defended. They would still have been legitimate targets if they were "ports . . . and other places devoted to the support of military operations" (ibid.). Yet according to the U.S. Strategic Bombing Survey, "The principal feature which detracted from the target value was the remoteness of the industrial concentration from the center of the city."[7] Furthermore, "Hiroshima . . . never became a highly industrialized city, and, at the time it was attacked with the atomic bomb, there were only three companies employing more than 500 persons."[8] According to FM 27-10, when an undefended place is bombarded, "loss of life and damage to property must not be out of proportion to the military advantage to be gained." Hiroshima was not an acceptable military target, by our own standards.

Three days later Nagasaki was bombed, a location also not an honorable target. As our FM 27-10 quotes the Hague Convention, "In sieges and bombardments all necessary measures must be taken to spare, as far as possible, buildings dedicated to religion, art, science, or charitable purposes . . . provided that they are not being used at the time for military purposes" (p. 21). On the Air Force map of the city of Nagasaki, the Urakami Roman Catholic Cathedral was located 600 meters northeast of the hypocenter.[9] Also within 2000 feet of ground zero were the Mitsubishi Hospital (Urakami branch), the Chinzei High School, the Shiroyama School, the Nagasaki prison, the Blind and Dumb School, and "miscellaneous small industries." The major industries were all outside this immediate area! In terms of the U.S. armed forces definition of military honor, the atomic bombings of the Japanese cities were war crimes.

Is there, then, a defense of the decision to launch the first attack with atomic weapons? Again, a large literature on the matter presents both viewpoints. That the attacks were legitimate is sometimes based on the reasoning that the war was shortened, and the total number of lives lost was diminished. This was President Truman's position. On the other side, the "strict constructionist" view holds that the attacks on these civilian populations were clearly forbidden by the war conventions. The utilitarian argument that the total loss of life was smaller as a result of the bombing overlooks several objections. One is that the awesome power of the new atomic weapon could have been demonstrated on a target free of civilians, such as a mountain, or a small offshore island. Second, our demand for unconditional surrender should have been reduced to conditional surrender, and by the time of the attack on Hiroshima, the war might have been ended without the loss of life and casualties that were involved in the course that President Truman took. Third, it is not the cost in American lives, or even in total lives, but the moral acceptability of the military means that is central to the debate. Even if torture of POWs could diminish the total length and cost of a war, it is not a means that can be used, according to the Convention. Military honor forbids it, according to FM 27-10. Conclusion: the attack on Hiroshima was a war crime, as was the attack on Nagasaki, three days later.[10]

The Dirty Hands Theory of Command

Some students of the matter agree with the last viewpoint, that the Hiroshima attack was a war crime, but hold the "dirty hands" theory of government. This is the position offered by Michael Walzer.[11] According to this position, there are desperate times in which crimes must be committed for some greater good, but those who commit such crimes should at least feel guilty afterward.

According to this viewpoint, the British terror bombing of Germany in World War II was a criminal activity. But during the period of Hitler's early victories, it was defended as necessary to avoid the unthinkable horror of a German victory against the Western Allies. Well, say certain commentators, this criminal activity was necessary, but since it was immoral, those responsible should be in "agony" (Walzer's term) afterward. They have morally "dirty hands" and should not feel justified about what they have done, but the rest of us are glad they did it.

What can be said about the view that it takes dirty hands to carry on a war? There are rules of war; but, it is held, war is not a game, and these so-called rules are never respected absolutely. Winning the war is of greater importance than the rules. Therefore, the rules are a sham, perhaps meant to impress and calm the civilians. The rules must be broken on certain critical occasions, and if this is having dirty hands, then war requires that commanders be willing to accept this.

It is a centerpiece of military ethics to insist that what is called "military necessity" is not an acceptable excuse for breaking the laws of war. In the language of 27-10, "Military necessity has been generally rejected as a defense for acts forbidden by the customary and conventional laws of war" (p. 4). Well, say critics, this merely establishes that certain acts are immoral. Even though some apologists maintain that dirty acts are sometimes needed to gain desirable goals, the evidence for the *need* for dirty hands is far from clear. The need to attack Hiroshima was certainly not obvious, nor the need to fire-bomb Dresden. Is the need to torture prisoners obvious? It may be convenient, but there are other sources of information, and actions are often based on incomplete information. The German army did not have to fire on civilians leaving Leningrad, nor bomb the cathedral at Coventry. We have always to consider the great capacity that humans show for inflicting pain on others, and the apparent enjoyment that this can sometimes give (whether or not it is wrapped in righteousness and sanctimony). Conclusion: while dirty hands can often speed up an operation, it is by no means clear that they have been *required* to win conventional wars in the past. If it takes dirty hands (war crimes) to win, an honorable soldier should not win. At least, that's what the international agreements on warfare require. The *honorable* path is often clear.

While dirty hands may be more convenient or faster than the honorable route, the results in many historical cases would have been no different. The difficult question is this: if we understood that honor would very likely lead to surrender, but that dirty hands might bring victory, how should we choose between them? If the question is serious, momentous, we will need to analyze and weigh the key terms "dirty" and "surrender." How dirty? And what is lost by surrender?

Killing an innocent civilian is a war crime, but killing several such civilians is even worse. Mutilation of the body of an enemy soldier is another war crime; mutilation of many of the enemy is still worse. Likewise, a crime committed by the intention of one soldier is not as terrible as the same act done by the intention of many. When compensation is paid by one nation for certain war crimes, the greater the number of crimes, the greater the compensation. So it is not frivolous to ask, how dirty must we be to win? How much of a loss of honor will it take? The second half of the problem is the matter of the gain. What is the difference between victory and defeat, what is to be gained by paying the price?

Nuclear Warfare

The question of nuclear weapons must be considered in terms of the "dirty hands" defense for at least two reasons: (a) these weapons do not discriminate between military and nonmilitary targets; and (b) even if such weapons were confined in their total effects to military targets, they cause what FM 27-10 calls "unnecessary suffering." Heretofore unnecessary suffering has forbidden chemical and biological warfare, glass particles in shells, dum-dum bullets, etc.

The 1956 edition of 27-10 has one sentence on atomic weapons. This holds that atomic weapons, as such, cannot be regarded as violative of international law "in the absence of any customary rule of international law or international convention restricting their employment" (p. 18). The point is that the use of this weapon, as any other weapon, is limited by the general laws of warfare. These laws forbid such practices as attacks on hospitals marked by the Red Cross, attacks on civilians, attacks on neutrals, assassinations, unnecessary suffering, taking of hostages, etc. It seems monstrous that 27-10 should specify the illegality of "lances with barbed heads, irregular shaped bullets, and projectiles filled with glass" (p. 18) but not atomic and nuclear weapons. The extra terror factor is not an honorable means. On this basis, atomic and nuclear weapons seem to have at least as much unnecessary suffering as irregular shaped bullets, and therefore ought to be unacceptable weapons. It is impossible to imagine a use of nuclear weapons that would not violate the Hague Convention against the employment of "poison or poisoned weapons" (27-10, p.18), as well as the Hague provision against unnecessary suffering.

The bombing of Nagasaki on 9 August 1945, three days after the bombing of Hiroshima, involved clear violations, as reported above. Houses of worship, hospitals, and schools are legitimate targets only if they are used for military purposes, such as storing weapons. Following the example of the West German reparations payments to Jews, the United States should now be paying reparations to the civilian victims at Hiroshima and Nagasaki. Military honor and national honor forbid exactly what occurred. Civilian populations were attacked without warning, and with a weapon calculated to produce unnecessary suffering. Reparations to the *hibakusha*, as the survivors are called, is a response required by honor.

To be legitimate weapons, atomic and nuclear weapons must be able to be restricted in their effect to military targets, and must not cause "unnecessary suffering." We have no serious basis for either assumption. The wind-carried fallout and the long-time aftereffects on both the human targets and the environment make even the smallest nuclear bomb a dishonorable weapon. It is disappointing to note that the military profession has not yet insisted on this position. Unless it finds its voice, military honor is reduced to political opportunism.

Reprisals

If a weapon is not acceptable, is it acceptable as a reprisal against war crimes by the enemy?

An act of reprisal is retaliation for a prior act by the other side. This is the ancient idea of *lex talionis*, the law of retaliation: it is justified to inflict a similar injury upon one who first inflicts an injury. The Old Testament expresses the idea that fairness requires the equal balancing of harm caused and harm received in the well- known passage (Exodus, xxi, 23-25) "if any harm follow, then thou shalt give life for life, eye for eye, tooth for tooth, hand for hand, foot for foot, burning for burning, wound for wound, stripe for stripe." Two points must be noted: first, that it is acceptable to retaliate when someone else causes harm; and second, that justice requires that the retaliation be exactly equal in harm, but no more than equal.

Is this idea of retaliation, of responding to injury by inflicting a similar injury, simply an old, barbaric custom? Has it been outgrown in a civilized age, or is it still an essential feature of justice? The arguments on the morality of the death penalty show that there are still advocates of each side in this matter. On the one hand, if something is so disgusting as to be forbidden as an act of war, it is, at the very least, inconsistent to commit such an act to show that such an act should not be committed. On the other side is the notion of *lex talionis*, that fairness calls for equality in anything important and particularly in the infliction of serious harm. The Geneva Conventions are an effort to gain some of the advantages of both moral styles. Certain acts are forbidden, regardless of previous patterns, e.g., hostage-holding. We must make moral progress, and we do. Yet *lex talionis* is still allowed, providing it is a last resort after five carefully specified steps have been taken. But such a reprisal must be no more harmful than its provocation, and the responsibility for it must be clearly assumed by proper command. Even so, certain forms of retaliation are forbidden, regardless of provocation: reprisals against POWs or the wounded and sick, collective penalties, and punishment of protected civilians.

Suppose the enemy commits acts that are clearly war crimes: they are maltreating dead bodies, e.g., cutting off their heads. May this act, or another forbidden act, be committed in retaliation? The answer to our question in FM 27-10 is that a forbidden act reprisal may be chosen, but only after the following conditions have been met:

1. Other means of making the enemy stop illegal action must be tried, such as direct appeal, reporting to neutral third powers, and reporting to the International Red Cross. In other words, the weapon of publicity is to be used first and given a chance to produce results.
2. Reprisals "should never be employed by individual soldiers, except by direct orders of a commander" (27-10, p. 177).
3. The commander is to give such orders only after careful inquiry into the alleged offense, since he is to assume responsibility. If the action is later found to have been unjustified, the commander himself is liable for punishment for committing a war crime.
4. Reprisals are permitted only against enemy troops who are not POWs. Reprisals against wounded or sick POWs and protected civilians are prohibited.
5. In the language of 27-10, "reprisals are never adopted merely for revenge, but only as an unavoidable last resort to induce the enemy to desist from unlawful practices" (p. 177).

There is one further consideration. The reprisal must not exceed the degree of violence of the act or acts against which it is directed. Conclusion: reprisals are legitimate, and they may consist of acts that would otherwise be forbidden, but they are legitimate only after the five restrictions have been met. And they must be no stronger than the provocation, and never against hostages. (Since hostages cannot be taken, it should be clear that hostages cannot be the target of reprisals.)

Suppose the legal framework, the limitation on reprisals, is agreed to; may nuclear weapons be used in reprisal? It was held, above, that such weapons are not legitimate under the customary laws of warfare. Nonetheless, even illegitimate weapons may be used in reprisal for the enemy's war crimes, after the five requirements have been properly met. But since the use of nuclear weapons would exceed the degree of violence of any other weapons, nuclear weapons are not acceptable in reprisal for war crimes.

Suppose the other side first uses nuclear weapons. May they then be used in reprisal? At first the assumption of *lex talionis*, the law of retribution, looks as if it justifies inflicting equal suffering on the enemy; therefore, a reprisal in kind with nuclear weapons might seem justified. The purpose of warfare must be kept in mind, however. This leads to an obvious but sometimes overlooked matter.

The goal of war is to win, for which the enemy must agree to terms of surrender. A war does not end unless the enemy can accept the terms of surrender, which means that they do not continue or plan to continue the fight. If one side behaves so treacherously that the enemy cannot trust any terms of surrender, the war has not ended, since neither side finds itself at peace. If one side makes it impossible for the other to agree to stop fighting, peace can be achieved only if all the enemy are exterminated. Even this goal of extermination is unrealistic: all the active enemy plus all those related and sympathetic may have to be exterminated. If those who are sympathetic also have friends who are sympathetic, the plans for extermination may have to include ever wider circles, with almost no end.

Assuming that the goal of war is to bring the enemy to accept terms of surrender, the strategy of reprisal by nuclear weapons makes the goal of war more and more difficult to achieve. Because nuclear weapons cannot be restricted to military targets, they must therefore be used, at least in part, against noncombatants. To increase the suffering and killing of noncombatants is to increase the resultant hatred and cause pointless destruction. In the language of FM 27-10, one of the purposes of the Law of War is "facilitating the restoration of peace" (p. 3). In several areas in the world mutual hatreds have continued for generations, and the wars are still not ended. Therefore, even as reprisals, nuclear weapons make the objective of war less likely to be accomplished because they must increase the level of hatred to be overcome.

It might be objected that the United States did use atomic weapons in World War II, and the goal of the war was not lost. In response, it must be noted that there were no such weapons at the disposal of the enemy; therefore reprisal in kind was not possible. Nations do commit war crimes and go on to victory. Nonetheless the current balance of military power and military threat does not establish that the U.S. behaved properly, even in terms of its own interests. A world without the precedent of Hiroshima and Nagasaki might be more secure than the world with the precedent. Our great anxiety lest an enemy develop atomic weapons was quite understandable; our use of the bomb was quite a different matter. Germany was then the only potential developer of the bomb, and Germany had surrendered.

Conclusion: Honor in warfare is defined by the Hague and Geneva Conventions and accepted by all civilized nations. Under these assumptions, nuclear weapons are not acceptable even as reprisals for enemy crimes. Such weapons don't discriminate between legitimate military targets and illegitimate targets, they cause unnecessary suffering, and they can make it even more difficult to bring the enemy to accept terms of surrender. Since the legitimate goal of warfare is the surrender of the enemy, not their extermination, the choice of weapon must be restricted. This has been done ever since the St. Petersburg Declaration of 1868, in which the signing nations renounced the use of certain explosives. The heroes at Hiroshima were not Americans.

PATRIOTISM AND MORALITY

The issues involved in nuclear war can be put in terms of a moral antinomy. An antinomy is a pair of statements that assert *opposite* positions, but positions such that *each* is attractive or impressive. By clearly distinguishing between a particular thesis and its opposite (or antithesis), and considering the advantages and disadvantages of each, it is sometimes possible to gain considerable clarity about a problem. In our case, we shall examine the antinomy between those who take patriotism to be the ultimate loyalty, and those for whom morality is more important.

The four terms "honor," "morality," "loyalty," and "patriotism" need to be reviewed before we look at the antinomy. Following the Kantian tradition, I have taken *morality* to mean treating everyone by the same set of rules. (I ignore, in this context, serious distinctions such as between intention and consequence, individual and group, etc.) *Honor* refers to the faithfulness with which one keeps promises and carries out duties, regardless of personal cost. For *military honor*, the promise and the duty are to act without violating the laws of warfare. Since the laws of warfare require that the *same set of rules* holds for all sides in a conflict, military honor is a special case of morality—the moral demand is that the same set of rules bind everyone. In sum, obedience to military honor is always moral, but all cases of moral behavior need not be military.

By *loyalty* one refers to a relationship between an individual and a beneficiary, such that the individual is willing to sacrifice at least something for the sake of the beneficiary. Varieties and degrees of loyalty may be distinguished in terms of the extent of the sacrifices and the goals of the beneficiary for whom they are made. For present purposes, we can specify fanatical loyalty as the case in which an individual is willing to sacrifice *anything* for *any* goal of the beneficiary. By an "ultimate loyalty," we shall mean loyalty to the one most important beneficiary in someone's life. Patriotism, of course, means loyalty to one's nation. The variety and strength of the loyalty can vary.[12]

> THESIS: *The moral response requires the sacrifice of anything needed to defend the interests of one's ultimate loyalty, one's nation.*
>
> ANTITHESIS: *The moral response requires that some things never be sacrificed, regardless of the goal at stake.*

Observations on the Thesis

To be without loyalty is apparently to be without honor. Since honor involves holding to one's commitments, there must be commitments or there is nothing to honor. In this sense, "loyalty" and "commitment" are synonyms. The ordinary image of loyalty is the case in which two friends are walking together. If one is attacked by bullies, the other is expected to come to his or her aid. To run off rather than sacrifice one's safety is to show that friendship, or that particular friendship, is not a serious loyalty. Most of the world's friendships are probably based on something less than the principle of "I would die for you." Loyalty can be measured by the degree of sacrifice that it is worth. There is an obvious difference between a casual acquaintance and someone who is willing to get his hands dirty to help a friend.

Two questions arise on the relationship between loyalty and patriotism. Are there limits to the sacrifice that is morally required to protect one's basic loyalties? And, second, is the nation a morally proper object of loyalty? The position of the thesis, above, is that moral value requires an absolutely basic and supreme loyalty. With no such absolute in one's life, all is reduced to the petty play of selfishness. We can understand selfishness, but we give it no honor. On this view morality means the willingness to sacrifice, and serious morality means the willingness to sacrifice anything for the sake of one's ultimate loyalty. We might call this position *moral monism*, from my viewpoint an unfortunate vestige of monotheism.[13]

Even if one accepted moral monism, the thesis forces consideration of a second question: what can stand as an ultimate attachment, an absolute loyalty? Historically, people have taken their basic loyalties to be their families, lovers, religious leaders, god or gods, king or fatherland and, recently, their political form of government. The term "nation" sometimes includes both the sense of one's countryland and also its political structure. (When a choice must be made between the land and the form of government, loyalties become sharpened, e.g., when a country is invaded but escape is possible.) (I have not included the ultimate attachment, to oneself, because it is considered to be opportunism, and usually [?] denied the moral vocabulary.) The debate over nuclear warfare can ignore most of the list of possible and actual loyalties and come down to the choice between one's nation and mankind.

The question becomes whether any single nation is worth the sacrifice of not merely one's own life, but of a significant part of mankind. To place such ultimate value on a nation is to hold the position that must be called the religion of nationalism, which is a variety of religious fanaticism. Let us consider the historical situation in which atomic bombs were used to protect our nation. Suppose that we had not used atomic bombs on Hiroshima and Nagasaki, and instead had negotiated a surrender of our country to the Japanese. First, a great many human beings would not have been killed in those two cities. And now, almost 40 years later, what would be the difference? Perhaps we would be selling our cars, cameras, and TV sets to the Japanese! If, instead of their surrender to us, we had surrendered to the Japanese emperor, we might have negotiated for many of the same changes in the Japanese government. Perhaps their renunciation of war might not have been made part of their constitution, and we would now not be embarrassed by the effort to persuade them to add their own military efforts to ours in the Pacific area (pacific?).

If one looks at a nation 20 or 30 years after a war, it is not always easy to understand whether it won or lost that war. The point is that whatever the characteristics of a nation, perhaps characteristics so morally sublime that they are worth making the nation an ultimate loyalty, time and the war itself will make changes in that nation. These changes may be so large as to alter the basis for bestowing one's highest loyalty. Of course, these observations are based on the history of essentially pre-nuclear wars. With atomic and nuclear bombs, the changes in any nation that remains after such a war must be enormous. Whatever the original foundation of loyalty, and however profound the basis for patriotism before a nuclear war, the entity that remains after such a war might be so dramatically different that one's pre-war love for his country might change to post-war hate.

Suppose that one contemplates a sacrifice of many human lives, but a sacrifice that results in preserving the patterns of government, the political, economic, and social structures that now exist. Would a sacrifice for that goal, maintaining exactly what we now have, be morally defensible? The very question seems empty and frivolous, because as soon as we frame it we realize that all of our structures undergo change. The serious question therefore becomes whether we are willing to sacrifice for one prospect of future change or another such prospect. Suppose we have a fantastic loyalty toward the U.S. Constitution. We understand that it has been and will be subject to amendments, but we would rather die than live under a different constitution. How different? Ours changes through different interpretations of the courts and administrative bodies, plus the differences made by repealing amendments and adding new ones. While it takes an expert constitutional lawyer to understand and predict the present and future applications of the constitution, we hope that all citizens understand certain broad features of our basic document. Our military, on induction, swear to uphold the constitution, and we hope that they have some understanding of what this means (we are either too confident or too worried to test that assumption). We avoid certain problems by ignoring the constitution in the further developments of military life after that moment during induction, at least in the military life of enlisted men.

My point in these considerations is that the nation is not a clear and acceptable moral absolute. *We can't accept the thesis*, the assertion that the nation is to be an absolute loyalty for us. That position is a romantic hangover from the image of a good slave or servant; it is undignified for a mature stage of mankind's history.

Observations on the Antithesis

According to the antithesis, morality must never be sacrificed. Morality means treating everyone by the same set of rules. (While the conception of morality has had many other interpretations, I shall assume that Kant was right about his analysis of the common and essential core of the idea.)

Since our antinomy is concerned with "the moral response," the choice between thesis and antithesis is a decision on what is to be taken as morality. For the thesis, morality may require that the same set of rules apply to all members of one's own nation, but not to citizens of other or "enemy" nations. For the antithesis, morality requires that at least some of the rules apply to all humans, regardless of citizenship. Further, the thesis may countenance different rules within the citizenship of the nation if that is needed for national defense (for example, lying to fellow citizens, unequal sacrifices by them, etc.). In order to hold to the thesis without embarrassment, nations at war regularly describe the enemy as less than human. If only "we" are fully human, then the antithesis may be empty and ignored. After a war nations rediscover the fact that the enemy is also human. I take this pattern to be consistent with the viewpoint above, the view that the thesis is not a morally acceptable choice.

The War Conventions are taken to express the boundaries of military honor, and they do so because they are a set of rules that apply equally to all parties. Military honor requires, on paper, an impressive level of honesty toward the enemy. I offer two examples from our FM 27-10, the specifications of "Good Faith," and of "Parole." After the Hague article 24 on permissible ruses of war, our Field Manual adds, "Absolute good faith with the enemy must be observed as a rule of conduct." This is followed by a long list of legitimate ways of

> mystifying or misleading the enemy against which the enemy ought to take measures to protect himself. It would [however] be an improper practice to secure an advantage of the enemy by deliberate lying or misleading conduct which involves a breach of faith, or when there is a moral obligation to speak the truth. For example, it is improper to feign surrender so as to secure an advantage . . . to broadcast to the enemy that an armistice had been agreed upon when such is not the case would be treacherous [p. 22].

The matter of parole is similar. U.S. military personnel are forbidden to give parole (their word that they will not escape), except for temporary purposes. If they do so, they are bound by the Geneva POW Convention "on their personal honour scrupulously to fulfill, both towards the Power on which they depend and towards the Power which has captured them, the engagements of their paroles or promises (p. 72). Conclusion: the accepted demands of military honor require that we choose the antithesis. Morality insists that some rules apply to everyone, enemy or not.

Consequences of the Antinomy

Given the above viewpoint on morality, can conventional warfare be waged morally? If it is fought under the restrictions of the Geneva and Hague Conventions, conventions that apply equally to everyone, it can be carried on with honor. Honor, again, is the consistent commitment to agreed upon rules that hold for all. The urgent question since Hiroshima is the status of atomic and nuclear warfare. Such warfare violates the essentials of the "laws of warfare."

Four of the elements of war with honor are each at risk or obviously violated by nuclear weapons. First, the distinction between combatant and noncombatant is eliminated. Second, the distinction between belligerent and nonbelligerent nation is eliminated, since fall-out cannot be controlled. Third, the restriction on unnecessary suffering is eliminated. Fourth, the restriction on hostages is ignored, since cities become hostages. Conclusion: nuclear warfare violates the minimum demands of military honor.

CONCLUSIONS

What Would It Take to Prevent Nuclear Warfare?

Years ago, in his classic work on the theory of government, Thomas Hobbes gave us the basis for the answer to this question. In Chapter 21 of this volume, Edward F. McClennen presents Hobbes's analysis in a form that applies to the present. Nuclear war can be prevented only by an international government with the power, the military power, to settle disputes between nations. McClennen's conclusion, that Hobbes's analysis of the distinction between war and peace applies to relations between nations, is a new and compelling version of an old idea. It was involved in early proposals for a League of Nations. In 1793 Kant published the following:

No state is for a moment secure from the others in its independence and its possessions. The will to subjugate the others or to grow at their expense is always present, and the production of armaments for defense, which often makes peace more oppressive and more destructive of internal welfare than war itself, can never be relaxed. And there is no possible way of counteracting this except a state of international right, based on enforceable public laws to which each state must submit (by analogy with a state of civil or political right among individual men). For a permanent universal peace by means of a so-called *European balance of power* is a pure illusion, like Swift's story of the house which the builder had constructed in such perfect harmony with all the laws of equilibrium that it collapsed as soon as a sparrow alighted on it.[14]

One hears the argument that for almost 30 years the voluntary possession of atomic and nuclear weapons has kept the peace, and so international government is not needed. This is as persuasive as holding that if playing Russian roulette 30 times has allowed one to remain in good health, it should be continued. Hobbes and Kant are right: I think we all know it and expect that the religion of absolute nationalism must soon end. Nuclear weapons are not the only reasons for moving to an international government, but they are compelling.

Earlier we faced the question, "Which is preferred, defeat with national honor, or victory with national shame?" We avoid the question by moving from a system of sovereign nations to an international government. No war, no such question.

What Would It Take to Produce an International Government?

An international government means the end of conventional patriotism, the time-honored trust in the protection of one's own country. If our lives were in more danger by remaining with the pattern of national sovereignty than by giving up this kind of sovereignty, would we still remain patriotic in the old sense? How close and certain must death be before we shake off patriotism? Would we rather die defending our nation's right to keep its own military power, or give up our military on condition that the Soviets and the rest of the nations do the same? Then what? We are at the mercy of an international government. We are at peace with the Soviets, because we both have domestic police forces but no facilities for international war, and we are both in awe, in fear, of the military might of the international government. Suppose we are at peace with the Soviets: what will stop the undeveloped nations from voting themselves a large share of our wealth? Nothing but our own political and economic capabilities. Our power to produce food is most obvious. These capabilities may be our protection against the jealousy of the rest of the world. The developed countries are all in the same situation here; we, the Canadians, the Europeans, the Soviets, the Australians, and the Japanese have common political goals. Is the risk of being plundered by the Third World so terrible that we would rather remain with the risk of individual sovereignty? The rational choice is to protect our lives and those of our families and friends. The cost is that we must make friends with the rest of the human race. We must take the risk of democracy, the risk that the majority of people in the world will make themselves into a decent international government. These problems go beyond the scope of this volume, but the goals are involved in present assumptions about war.

The Future of Honor

I have held that military honor requires that nuclear weapons be forbidden. By parallel arguments, it can also be shown that the technique of area bombing in World War II was a violation of military honor. The result of the antinomy between patriotism and morality leads to the conclusion that loyalty must be transferred from separate nations to an international government. What, then, will be the scope of honor?

In addition to the loss of honor in directing unacceptable weapons to unacceptable targets, another aspect has been lost. The honor in risking one's person, one's own welfare, in the defense of king or country has been erased by technological development. To press a button from a remote location and deliver a blow to an enemy is now *to perform the basic military act*. What honor is this! How far from the acts of sacrifice, of personal bravery, of a decent *machismo*, that have deserved respect in the past. If one nation can purchase a more powerful computer and launching device than another nation, that nation's soldiers do not acquire more personal or military honor thereby. In modern nuclear war there is no honor—neither in the personal actions of the soldier nor in the results of those actions.

Human relations will always call for honor, but in new contexts. To be willing to press for an international government requires and will continue to require a willingness to sacrifice for a greater good. Any sort of international government will be, as all governments, a policing power. A police force, certainly, needs personnel whose behavior meets higher and higher standards of honor. The world needs more honor, not less. Immediately, it needs those in the military to take the honorable path and refuse to deal with what their own basic codes call dishonorable weapons and strategies.[15]

NOTES

1. Friedrich Nietzsche, *Beyond Good and Evil*, trans. Helen Zimmern, in *The Philosophy of Nietzsche* (New York: Modern Library, 1927), p. 581.
2. Alfred Vagts, *A History of Militarism, Civilian and Military*, rev. ed. (New York: The Free Press, 1967), p. 449.
3. Most nations publish editions with their own comments. I refer to the version published by the U.S. Department of the Army, *The Law of Land Warfare*, Field Manual (FM) 27-10 (July 1956). There have been revisions, but its principles are essentially unchanged since the Hague Convention of 1907.
4. Immanuel Kant, "Idea for a Universal History from a Cosmopolitan Point of View," in *On History*, ed. Lewis W. Beck (Indianapolis: Bobbs-Merrill, 1963).
5. Roger Fisher, *The New York Times*, 13 March 1974, p. 41.
6. The War Office, *Manual of Military Law*. Part 3: *The Law of War on Land* (London: Her Majesty's Stationery Office, 1958), p. 18.
7. U.S. Strategic Bombing Survey, *The Effects of the Atom Bomb on Hiroshima*, 3 vols. (1947). Unclassified 1 May 1950. This quote is from Vol. 1, p. 73.
8. Ibid., p. 71.
9. Some of the detailed "effects" are reported in the literature: *Hiroshima and Nagasaki: The Physical, Medical, and Social Effects of the Atomic Bombings* (New York: Basic Books, 1981): "Of the city's 20,000 Catholics, some 15,000 are said to have been concentrated in this area [Urakami]. About 10,000 of them are thought to have been sacrificed to the atomic bomb" (p. 382). In a

section of the same source titled "Radiation Effects on Animals and Plants," we find "It was said that rats remained the same before and after the explosion" (p. 81).

10. For some historians, "The evidence seems to point to the conclusion that use of the atomic bombs was not necessary to bring an end to the war, and, rejecting a number of other options, a decision was made to use the atomic bomb on cities whose population density was high. Thus it seems clear to many *hibakusha* (survivors) that the atomic bombings were big demonstrations aimed at influencing Soviet behavior" (*A Call from Hibakusha of Hiroshima and Nagasaki*, proceedings of the International Symposium on the Damage and After-Effects of the Atomic Bombing of Hiroshima and Nagasaki, July 21-August 9, 1977 [Japan National Preparatory Committee, 1978], p. 70).

11. Michael Walzer, *Just and Unjust Wars* (New York: Basic Books, 1977); also "Political Action: The Problem of Dirty Hands," *Philosophy and Public Affairs* 2 (1973): 160-80.

12. These varieties of loyalty are developed further in Axinn, "Loyalty and Ultimate Commitments," a paper delivered at the May 1983 A.P.A. meeting in Chicago.

13. I argue that such monism is a variety of fanaticism, in "Ambivalence: Kant's View of Human Nature," *Kantstudien*, No. 2 (1981), pp. 169-74.

14. "On the Common Saying: 'This May Be True in Theory, but It Does Not Apply in Practice,' " *Kant's Political Writings*, ed. Hans Reiss, trans. H.B. Nisbet (Cambridge: Cambridge University Press, 1970), pp. 91-92.

15. I owe thanks to Rosamond Putzel, Paley Library, Temple University for research on Henry IV.

15
NUCLEAR WAR AND THE ARGUMENT FROM EXTREMITY

Terry Nardin

To raise the question of the morality of nuclear war is to invite skepticism, regardless of the conclusions one might reach. For some, the question is too easy: they are surprised by the implication that nuclear war, which is an incomparable evil, is something about which much can be said beyond simple condemnation. A variation of this attitude is that the moral problems posed by nuclear war are not particularly difficult ones, and that all the really interesting questions have to do with nuclear deterrence. My own view is that the issues posed by nuclear war itself are not as straightforward as is sometimes assumed and, furthermore, that clarification of these issues is needed if progress is to be made on the question of nuclear deterrence.

Others are inclined to dismiss the topic as impossible. The doubt here is that anything intelligible can be said about the morality of nuclear war—either because nothing intelligible can be said about morality, or because moral judgments are irrelevant to war, or perhaps because the prospect of nuclear war somehow transcends the bounds of moral discourse as we have known it. Moral skepticism, however, is only rarely a well-thought-out philosophical position. More often it simply dismisses those traditions of thought and argument that make it possible to speak significantly about the rights and wrongs of nuclear war. Such skepticism commonly reflects a failure to attend to the actual experience of moral deliberation and judgment, which in turn may have something to do with unfamiliarity with the traditions of moral reflection and discourse. By drawing upon these traditions we can see precisely why the use of nuclear weapons, and perhaps also the threat to use them, is morally indefensible.

Not everyone accepts the teachings of traditional morality, however, and therefore I shall also address the question of the acceptability of nuclear weapons within the framework of essentially pragmatic or economic reasoning that is today widely

This essay was presented at the October 1983 meeting of the Inter-University Seminar on Armed Forces and Society, Chicago. I wish to thank Avner Cohen, Steven Lee, Jefferson McMahan, and Jerome Slater for their helpful criticisms of my argument.

regarded as providing the only rational basis for moral judgment. It is difficult to ground policies for using nuclear weapons under any circumstances within traditional moralities, according to which the pursuit of ends is governed by certain fundamental and categorical constraints, or within schemes of practical reasoning such as utilitarianism, according to which we are to choose actions (or, sometimes, to act according to rules) that have the best overall consequences. Contemporary usage notwithstanding, it seems to me mistaken to refer to utilitarianism or other consequentialist theories as "moralities," but instead of arguing this point, I shall explain why the military use of nuclear weapons is indefensible in any case by considering and rejecting an argument for keeping open the possibility of using weapons in certain unusual situations of supreme national emergency. This is the strongest argument for nuclear defense, one that has a certain appeal even to those who would reject the use of nuclear weapons in more ordinary situations. To expose its limitations is of practical as well as theoretical importance, for this argument, "the argument from extremity," is recurrently invoked against the categorical constraints of the traditional morality of war—constraints which stand today, along with the obvious imperatives of self-preservation, as one of the few remaining barriers against the folly of nuclear war.

THE JUST-WAR TRADITIONS

It is common when discussing the morality of war to speak of "the just-war tradition," but this expression is misleading in several ways. "Just" means that war is to be initiated and conducted within certain limits or constraints. But these constraints may be so restrictive as virtually to rule out war altogether, in which case the view that there can be just wars is replaced by pacifism, or else so permissive as to impose hardly any limits at all on military conduct, as in the doctrines of *compétence de guerre* and *Kriegsraison*. In the first case we have a standard of justice that forbids war in any circumstances; in the second, one indistinguishable from expediency. Just-war thinking, properly so called, eschews both of these extremes.

Nor is it accurate to speak of *the* just-war tradition, as if there were only one. It is especially misleading to identify just-war thinking, as many do, with the tradition of the Roman Catholic church. Catholicism has made room for other views of warfare, including both pacifism and essentially unlimited or "holy" war against enemies of the faith. Furthermore, just-war thinking can be found in other religious and cultural traditions, including those of other Christian denominations, of Judaism, of Islam, and of China both before and after Confucius. Just-war thinking has also passed into secular morality and law, although religious institutions still play an important and possibly indispensable part in keeping it alive.

Finally, there are differences even within particular traditions of just-war thinking, as the continuing debate within the Catholic church on the issue of nuclear weapons well illustrates. The existence of a tradition does not preclude diversity and disagreement. Far from escaping controversy, a moral tradition is shaped by it and provides a common vocabulary within which continued controversy takes place. The just-war traditions are traditions of disagreement as well as of agreement: they are identified as much by their recurrent questions as by their answers to these questions.

For these reasons it is perhaps best to use the phrase "just-war thinking," as I do here, recognizing that the understanding of war as an activity constrained, like all human activities, by moral considerations is one that can arise within quite distinct religious or cultural traditions. Such an understanding has the additional advantage of forestalling the common objection that concern with moral constraints on war is a kind of religious or cultural parochialism. This is not to say that the idea of the just war is universal, either in the sense that everyone accepts it or that it is known in every culture. Indeed, as the terrifying history of Christian Europe suggests, the hold of this idea is uncertain even where it is most deeply rooted. What is clear is that just-war thinking can be found outside the Catholic church, outside Christianity, and outside Western civilization, and therefore its central concerns are more or less independent of the particular theological or cultural premises of those traditions that have been most concerned with it.

A fundamental principle of morality governing the making and waging of war is that there are limits to the use of armed forces even for good ends. This principle is reflected in the requirement, common to many traditions of just-war thinking, that war should be undertaken only as a "last resort"—that is, reluctantly, after other remedies have been conscientiously tried and have failed—and with "right intention"—that is, in a sentiment of charity, humility, and moderation. It is also reflected in the requirement that hostilities are to be carried on by all sides within certain constraints, once the fighting has started, regardless of whose cause is just. Some of these constraints on the initiation and conduct of war are instrumental, others categorical. The precise relation between these two kinds of constraints constitutes a fundamental issue both in the morality of war and in the theoretical exploration of that morality.

The force of the rule that captors should not display and abuse captured enemy soldiers, or that an undefended town should not be leveled before being occupied, derives in part from instrumental considerations. Expressed as the principle of military necessity, such considerations discourage destructive conduct in war that is not genuinely related to the controlled and effective application of armed force. So understood, military necessity merely formalizes certain obvious maxims of prudence or expediency. Even more important is the principle of proportionality, which discourages methods of fighting so costly as to outweigh the benefits sought in employing them. Unlike military necessity, proportionality is not entirely a principle of expediency, if by that we mean efficiency in the pursuit of our own welfare, for the costs and benefits to be weighed need not be confined to the costs and benefits to our side only. Proportionality is therefore potentially a more severe constraint on the conduct of war than military necessity. Nevertheless, it does not categorically exclude certain kinds of acts, for any form of violence is permissible if it is supported by the correct cost-benefit calculations. And, of course, the principle of proportionality does not itself tell us what is to count as a cost and what as a benefit in making these calculations.

The character of the constraints embodied in the traditional principle of noncombatant immunity is very different. According to that principle, it is wrong to attack those not immediately engaged in fighting or in preparing to fight—"those who look on without taking part," in the words of an ancient Hindu text on the conduct of warfare. The line between combatants and noncombatants, those who take part and those who do not, is not always easy to draw, and there are always borderline cases: munitions workers, for example, or those who actively support partisan or guerrilla fighters. The laws of war as they have been understood in the West for several centuries classify as noncombatants not only civilians but prisoners of war, the wounded, and the shipwrecked. However the class of noncombatants is defined, its members are regarded as bystanders, and it is regarded as wrong to attack them directly and intentionally. They are not, however, immune from harm that is a foreseen but unwished for and unavoidable consequence of attacks on combatants and other military objectives. The underlying principle here, sometimes called "the principle of discrimination," yields considerations quite unlike those of necessity and proportionality in that the constraints on military conduct imposed by the former are not determined by the ends pursued or the consequences produced, but are to be observed regardless of the worth of those ends or consequences. Thus they are categorical constraints, in the sense that they define certain kinds or categories of acts as wrong, regardless of the good that is supposed to, or does in fact, come from doing them.

The various traditions of regulated warfare embody both instrumental and categorical constraints, emphasizing now one and now the other. The principle of discrimination, for example, has been central to Christian moral teaching on the conduct of war, while instrumental considerations have loomed large in military practice, and also in the positive law of war, which tends to be rather closely tied to military practice. Even so, the tendency in recent years has been to give increasing emphasis to the principle of discrimination. This can be seen, for example, in the general acceptance in military codes of the view that respect for noncombatant immunity is superior to the claims of military necessity. Thus it can be argued today that it is never lawful to deny quarter, to allow troops to pillage and rape, to make hostages of civilians, or to attack the survivors of a sunken vessel. These constraints, in other words, cannot be overridden by considerations of expediency or proportionality. On the contrary, they define the bounds within which cost-benefit calculations are permissible.

The view that the constraints derived from the principle of discrimination may be overridden as necessary or useful for the achievement of certain ends we may label "consequentialism." It exists in many versions. Both the Christian tradition and the secular tradition of international law have decisively rejected it as an ordinary principle of war. They are largely committed to the converse view that the principle of discrimination is superior to and therefore overrides considerations derived from the weighing of consequences. But consequentialism is nevertheless so deeply rooted in the way we now think about morality that the priority of the principle of discrimination is under constant attack—so much so that many of those who accept it as a general rule are prepared to suspend it in situations of extremity, as we shall see below.

MORALITY AND NUCLEAR WEAPONS

Just-war thinking often makes a distinction between permissible weapons and permissible targets. From time to time particular weapons—explosives, the expanding bullet, the airplane, poison gas, incendiary bombs, biological agents, and now nuclear weapons—have been condemned as inherently immoral. In fact this characterization is a shorthand way of saying that the weapon is one that cannot be used in morally permissible ways. But the claim is too strong, even for nuclear weapons. While it may be unlikely that the latter could be used without violating the constraints of proportionality and discrimination, the argument that they could never be so used is hard to sustain. If nuclear weapons were to be designed and deployed for use solely against military targets, if the destruction they caused could be confined to such targets, and if their use carried little risk of escalation, it might be possible to justify their use in war. But it is implausible that the nuclear weapons we have now would be used in morally acceptable ways. Therefore the theoretical possibility that nuclear war might be conducted both proportionately and in such a manner as to spare civilians is largely irrelevant to the present debate over the morality of nuclear war.

One can get an idea of how nuclear weapons fit into just-war thinking by considering how a particular moral tradition, that of Roman Catholicism, responds to the problems posed by their existence and potential use. The characteristic premises and arguments of Catholic just-war thinking are clearly displayed in the pastoral letter on nuclear arms approved in 1983 by the American bishops.[1] The letter relies on the instrumental principle of proportionality as well as on the categorical principle of discrimination, arguing that because it is extremely unlikely that any nuclear exchange could remain limited, the requirements of proportionality and discrimination would necessarily be violated. More pointedly, it implicitly condemns the present strategies of the superpowers as constituting an open challenge to these principles by sanctioning, in certain circumstances, the first use of nuclear weapons, direct attacks on civilians and on the fabric of civilian life, and the conduct of limited nuclear war.

The letter argues that it is clear beyond serious dispute that a direct attack with nuclear weapons on cities and industry would violate the principle of noncombatant immunity. Hence the judgment of the bishops is categorical: "Under no circumstances may nuclear weapons . . . be used for the purpose of destroying population centers or other predominantly civilian targets" (pp. 14-15). Cities may not be attacked even in retaliation, and especially not after one's own cities have already been destroyed. The letter acknowledges the existence of controversy over attacks on military targets that would involve "indirect" or "unintentional" injury to civilian life, condemning such attacks on the grounds that this injury would be disproportionate to any end to be gained by nuclear attack.

If it is wrong to use nuclear weapons either against cities or against military targets in such a way as to cause massive civilian casualties, it must also be wrong to rely on nuclear weapons to resist nonnuclear aggression, such as a Soviet invasion of Western Europe using conventional weapons. Nor can the use of nuclear weapons in what is hoped will be a limited exchange be defended. The objection in each case is that even on the unlikely assumption that nuclear weapons could at first be used in conformity with the principles of proportionality and discrimination, it is implausible to expect that escalation could or would be avoided. Indeed, the bishops' letter concludes that "the danger of escalation is so great that it would be morally unjustifiable to initiate nuclear war in any form" (p. 15). To begin a nuclear war on any scale and in any circumstances, the bishops argue, "is to enter a world where we have no experience of control, much testimony against its possibility and therefore no moral justification for submitting the human community to this risk" (p. 16).

The bishops' letter also raises grave questions about the moral acceptability of nuclear deterrence. Recognizing the difficulty of an issue that has been addressed within and outside the church since the beginning of the nuclear age, an earlier draft of the letter nevertheless reached the conclusion that because it is wrong to use nuclear weapons, it is also wrong to intend even conditionally to use them, and therefore to prepare to use them should the specified conditions ever be realized, which is what the policy of nuclear deterrence amounts to (unless one is just bluffing). This is not to say that the distinction between possessing and using nuclear weapons is not morally significant. Possession, the bishops argued in this draft, is a lesser evil—but it *is* an evil, because it is bound up with an intention to use these weapons in a manner that would almost certainly violate the principles of proportionality and discrimination, because of the significant danger that deterrence may fail and of the consequences of such a failure, and because of the intimate link between deterrence and an arms race that perpetuates "a relationship of radical distrust" among nations while consuming resources desperately needed elsewhere. Still, the argument that nuclear deterrence has so far served to prevent nuclear war, though unprovable, cannot simply be dismissed.[2] Therefore, the draft letter concluded, a policy of deterrence precisely tailored to preventing the use of nuclear weapons is provisionally permissible, provided (a) that the search for nuclear superiority, the development of a war-fighting capability, and the introduction of new weapons that undermine rather than stabilize deterrence be clearly and decisively repudiated, and (b) that efforts to eliminate reliance on nuclear deterrence be conscientiously and energetically pursued.

The final version of the bishops' letter upholds and extends these conclusions regarding the policy of nuclear deterrence, but it drops the argument that deterrence may be justified as the lesser evil. I mention the inclusion of that argument in the earlier draft because it demonstrates how mistakes can be made within a tradition and how they can be corrected. For as the bishops' cancellation of the lesser evil argument suggests, it is indeed doubtful that nuclear deterrence can be defended in this way within the framework of Christian morality, according to which the weighing of consequences is constrained by certain categorical prohibitions. The bishops' original conclusion—that for the time being we must accept deterrence as the lesser evil—would seem to contradict St. Paul's principle that evil is not to be done that good may come of it (Romans 3: 7-8), which has been taken to mean that one may not violate the categorical constraints that constitute the core of the moral law for the sake of any possible benefits to oneself or to others. That principle must therefore forbid continuation of or participation in a policy of nuclear deterrence, if indeed the policy is itself evil. The principle that one should choose the lesser evil is a principle of instrumental reasoning, not a categorical principle. One should act to promote one's own well-being and the well-being of others, and avoid injuring oneself and others so far as that does not require one to act unjustly. But one may not act unjustly—that is, violate categorical prohibitions—to promote good or avoid bad consequences. To promote good is a conditional, or as some say, an "imperfect" duty. One should promote the good so long as one does not have to act wrongly to do so. Not to murder, on the other hand, is a categorical or "perfect" duty, one to be observed whatever the consequences. The principle of lesser evil provides a way of ordering imperfect duties, but it cannot (consistent with the Pauline principle) be invoked to override perfect duties, for that principle requires that we seek to promote good and thus to fulfill our imperfect duties within the bounds of categorical constraints and the perfect duties derived from them. If to possess nuclear weapons for the purpose of deterrence is to violate such a duty, then possession cannot be justified by appeal to the principle of lesser evil.

Without the lesser evil argument, it is no longer clear on what basis the policy of nuclear deterrence is defended, even as a provisional measure, in the final version of the bishops' letter. Its authors are barred by their own premises from pursuing the line, common to many treatments of the deterrence question, that nuclear deterrence need not be regarded as intrinsically wrong provided it is linked with a policy of attacking only military targets. According to this line of reasoning, there is a morally relevant distinction to be made between attacking a country with the direct intention of destroying its civilian population and attacking its ability to wage war even though the population is thereby indirectly destroyed. But can the deaths of a very large number of civilians in a counterforce attack with nuclear weapons really be described as incidental and excused as unintentional? It is doubtful that destruction on such a scale is properly regarded as indirect or unintended in the sense required to maintain the integrity of Christian morality as, in its fundamentals, a system of categorical constraints. Nor can the threat of such destruction—which, because of the indiscriminate character of nuclear weapons, is implicit in their very existence and therefore necessarily infects the policy of nuclear deterrence—be defended plausibly as unintentional.[3]

The usual rejoinder to this objection is to argue that in the case of deterrence our real intention is to prevent aggression and to ensure that nuclear war will never occur. Nevertheless, our chosen means to these ends (if they are indeed the ends that actually underlie present nuclear policies) entails threatening civilians with total destruction. Perhaps, according to some definitions of intention, we do not intend to destroy them, but we do intend to threaten to destroy them—that is, we hold them hostage. And this threat is itself immoral, even if we never carry it out. It follows that to pursue a policy of nuclear deterrence is to do evil that good may come of it, and thus to violate a fundamental precept of the moral tradition.

It is sometimes argued, at a less sophisticated level that we (that is, any nuclear power confronting a nuclear-armed adversary) do no wrong in possessing or, if we are attacked, using nuclear weapons, for *they* have lost their rights not to be subjected to nuclear threats or attacks by antecedently threatening or attacking us. But the argument is obviously invalid. First, it relies on a primitive theory of collective responsibility according to which an entire people, including its children and future generations, are held culpable for the policies of its present regime. The people are not the aggressor, and they have not lost their rights. They are no different than those bystanders in other countries who must also live under the nuclear sword and who are going to be destroyed if we retaliate. Second, the argument assumes that the nuclear weapons we have today are like other weapons, useful means for securing victory or avoiding defeat. Indeed, the argument harkens back to the justifications offered for obliteration of German and Japanese cities during World War II, which some have defended as an effective if not just response to German and Japanese aggression. But to use nuclear weapons in response to a conventional or nuclear attack under present circumstances would simply magnify the scale of disaster for everyone. That is the irony of "prevailing" in a nuclear war. The argument from reciprocity cannot be used to justify a response that is so wholly disproportionate as well as indiscriminate. The moral argument for nuclear deterrence is similarly flawed, although here the objection would seem to rest more heavily on discrimination than on proportionality. Our policy of deterrence may be a response to their own policies, but in pursuing it we threaten a much larger class of persons than those who are actually threatening us. Our being prepared to take the rest of the world with us into the abyss is preferable to actually doing so, but that doesn't make it right.

MORALITY IN EXTREME SITUATIONS

Those who defend the possession or, in certain carefully specified and doubtless very rare circumstances, the actual use of nuclear weapons tend to argue in one of two ways. The first is to deny altogether the moral force of categorical principles, and to adopt the consequentialist principle that the decision whether to keep or use nuclear weapons should, like any other rational decision, be made by weighing the probable costs and benefits of alternative courses of action. In some versions of this argument general rules may be permitted to constrain these calculations, but only as a matter of convenience—that is, as a substitute for a more comprehensive calculation of actual or expected consequences, and not as a categorical constraint possessing moral significance apart from its contribution to the realization of good ends.

Another approach is to recognize the independent force of categorical constraints such as the prohibition of direct attacks on the innocent in ordinary circumstances, but to argue that these constraints are inapplicable in extreme situations—typically, situations in which fidelity to categorical principles appears almost certain to have catastrophic consequences. The argument thus embodies the traditional structure of just-war thinking up to a point: although categorical principles ordinarily constrain the calculation of consequences, these constraints may themselves be overridden in extreme situations in which certain ultimate values (still to be specified) are at stake. We do no wrong in violating categorical moral rules in such situations, because those rules contain an implicit escape clause that permits us to do in extremity what is normally forbidden. Considerations derived from categorical princi ples are, in the face of imminent catastrophe, but only then, to give way before consequentialist considerations. Thus, although the authority of categorical rules is recognized for all but a small number of hard cases, the addition of an escape clause immediately distinguishes the morality containing it from a truly categorical morality, one in which consequentialist calculations are made only within the bounds prescribed by categorical principles. Underlying the escape clause idea is an essentially instrumental conception of morality, according to which moral rules are themselves justified by the good they promote (and the bad they help us to avoid), and whose authority is therefore only provisional. Respect for categorical principles and for the rights and duties derived from them is thus confined within bounds set ultimately by the calculation of consequences.

I shall refer to this view that the traditionally acknowledged moral rules ought not to be taken as a guide to conduct when to do so would be likely to have catastrophic consequences as "the argument from extremity." Before considering its implications for nuclear war and deterrence, however, I want to explore its application to war generally by considering a version of the argument put forward by Michael Walzer in *Just and Unjust Wars*. Walzer's acceptance of the extremity argument is qualified in a number of ways, for he would not say that the ordinary constraints on military conduct are in extreme situations no longer applicable, or that we do no wrong in departing from them. On the contrary, these constraints, although overridden by the demands of necessity, remain in force and continue to provide a ground for moral judgment. The burden of his argument is that sometimes, "in very special cases," we must act in ways that violate the normal constraints of just-war morality. These are situations of supreme emergency in which a political community is faced not merely with defeat, but with disaster. If the community really is threatened by disaster at the hands of an aggressor, it may use any expedient means to defend itself, even at the cost of transgressing the most fundamental restraints on the conduct of war, such as those prohibiting direct attacks on neutrals, civilians, and other bystanders. Those who make war on behalf of the community may not, of course, fall back on gratuitous violence—on senseless attacks that bear no reasonable relation to defense. Considerations of necessity and proportionality continue to apply, even though those of discrimination and noncombatant immunity may have to be ignored. When "what is being defended is the state itself and the political community it protects and the lives and liberties of the members of that community" (p. 230), utilitarian calculation may force us to violate the rules of war.

Because the principle propounded here is clearly subject to abuse and therefore dangerous, Walzer is careful to qualify it. A genuine "supreme emergency" is, first of all, one in which the consequences of defeat are not merely bad in ways in which any defeat is likely to be: dishonor and humiliation, loss of some territory, or payment of indemnities to the victor. The danger, Walzer argues, "must be of an unusual and horrifying kind" (p. 253). He relies upon the example of Nazism to make the point that although one must be skeptical about claims that one is fighting for national survival or for the defense of civilization, situations occasionally occur in which these values are indeed threatened. The threat posed by Nazi Germany to the rest of Europe was one of enslavement and extermination, a barbaric assault on national independence, on personal liberty and security, on justice and the rules of law, on the most elementary principles of decency and human dignity. But the Nazi threat was in fact worse than required to trigger the argument from extremity: political communities can be threatened with destruction in other, perhaps less horrifying ways. When this happens, Walzer thinks (though "not without hesitation and worry"), there is at least a case to be made for overriding the rights of the innocent. "The survival and freedom of political communities . . . are the highest values of international society" (p. 254), and extreme measures are sometimes necessary to resist the destruction of those values.

Defensive measures that violate the rules of war cannot be regarded as necessary, however, unless the threat is not only grave, but imminent (p. 252). The threat to supreme values must appear as an emergency—a danger that has arisen suddenly and unexpectedly, leaving the community exposed to disaster and with few options for avoiding it. Britain's situation during the period of "phony war" before the successful German invasions of Norway, the Netherlands, Belgium, and France was not yet desperate, for these terrifying events were still part of an unknown and uncertain future. Therefore, when Churchill attempted, in April 1940, to disrupt German shipping by mining the coastal waters of Norway, a neutral country, he violated the rules of war unnecessarily. But when, a few months later, Britain began to bomb Germany, and began to move toward a policy of making German *cities* the main target of the bombing, the situation had been transformed into a true crisis by Hitler's victories and his preparations for an invasion of the British Isles. "The decision to bomb cities was made at a time when victory was not in sight and the specter of defeat ever present. And it was made when no other decision seemed possible if there was to be any sort of military offensive against Nazi Germany" (p. 258). In these circumstances, the British use of the only significant weapon available to them, their strategic bomber force, in the only manner in which it could be used effectively, for area bombing, was (until 1942, when alternatives again became available) both necessary and in some sense right.

I say "in some sense right" because Walzer is not very clear about precisely how we are to regard such violations of the rules of war. I shall return to this in a moment. But first I want to point out that the argument from extremity provides no grounds for condemning the threat or use of nuclear weapons apart from those that rest on the calculation of consequences. Thus, if the conditions Walzer prescribes for bombing cities were met, there would not appear to be any intrinsic objection to nuclear attacks that do not apply equally to conventional ones. Nor is nuclear deterrence categorically distinct from a comparable policy of nonnuclear threats. Not only to threaten nuclear attacks but, just conceivably, to carry them out may be justified if a political community is threatened with destruction, provided the use of nuclear weapons can pass the consequentialist tests of necessity and proportionality. I don't think this argument opens the door very wide to nuclear warfare, and clearly neither does Walzer. But that it opens it too far I have no doubt.

The difficulties raised by the extremity argument are both conceptual and practical. Conceptually, the argument is hard to accommodate within the structure of traditional morality because it reverses the priority of categorical and consequentialist considerations. The argument from extremity constitutes a departure *from* rather than an extension *of* traditional morality. It collapses the distinction between authoritative and instrumental constraints and thereby destroys what has traditionally been regarded as distinctive of the moral point of view. The practical difficulty, as I shall argue below, is that the argument from extremity is unpersuasive as a guide to action even on consequentialist grounds.

The conceptual problem arises because from the perspective of traditional morality the rightness of an act depends upon considerations embodied in a moral practice. Such practices come into being where persons who do not necessarily share the same values are nevertheless related to one another by their mutual acknowledgment of the authority of common constraints on their behavior, although these constraints may not be liked by those to whom they apply, nor conducive to their particular ends. In other words, the authority of these common constraints or rules is independent of their desirability. They have the force of moral law, prescribing rights to be respected and duties to be fulfilled as a matter of obligation rather than discretion.

It is because of its stress on the authoritative rather than instrumental or utilitarian character of moral rules that the traditional conception of morality is sometimes said to be a "law conception." And indeed this feature is evident in the structure of positive law. Whatever the implications of a particular legal system for human welfare and happiness, the authority of its laws and the legal obligations it imposes are determined by standards internal to that system and not by considerations derived from other practices or from external values that, according to one theory or another, the legal system is supposed to serve. This is the central insight of legal positivism: that the authority of a law depends upon its pedigree rather than its content, and that while there may be moral or other grounds for disobeying a law, such disobedience cannot be *legally* justified within the legal system of which it is a part. Morality, according to the traditional understanding—one deeply embedded in the Hebrew-Christian tradition and receiving its most influential philosophical expression in Kant's ethical writings—also displays this structure. Moral authority and obligation are determined by considerations internal to a moral practice and not by those derived from external goods such as individual and collective happiness. In this respect the determination of moral right and wrong resembles the determination of correct and incorrect linguistic usage, which is a matter of the phonetic and grammatical rules of a particular language and is entirely independent of considerations such as whether speech produced according to those rules is pleasing or persuasive.

This insistence on the priority of constraints over ends distinguishes the traditional understanding of morality as an authoritative practice from theories such as utilitarianism, which are in effect proposals to reinterpret morality as an instrumental practice shaped to the fulfillment of certain overarching ends (commonly identified by formulas such as "the greatest happiness of the greatest number," "the general welfare," or "what's best, all things considered"). The traditional understanding postulates no such ends; on the contrary, it presupposes the existence of persons ("individuals") engaged in the separate and collective pursuit of a multiplicity of ends of their own choosing and related to other persons similarly engaged, and imposes considerations of justice and propriety on the relationships of exchange, cooperation, and competition in which they may become involved. It therefore reflects a complex and highly pluralist conception of human good, one that gives weight to the pursuit of "nonmoral" goods such as happiness or the reduction of suffering, as well as to moral (that is, practice-regarding) goods such as justice, fidelity, and truthfulness. But that an act is aimed at the realization of some nonmoral satisfaction or good, even one so valuable as individual or communal survival, does not necessarily make it right. An act cannot be right if it violates the authoritative constraints of a moral practice, notwithstanding the fact that it may have good consequences, for while the consequences make the act "good," only conformity to those constraints—to what used to be called "the moral law"— can make it "right."

Unfortunately, the manner in which terms such as "right," "ought," "justice," and of course "moral" have come to be used reflects a failure to distinguish clearly not only between the judgments of traditional morality and those of consequentialism, but among judgments made within different moral traditions. To judge is to judge according to the standards of some particular practice. Unless the practice is specified or otherwise clear, the judgment is unintelligible. Therefore the argument from extremity, where it takes the form of a claim that a certain act is right, or just, or moral, even though it offends traditional morality, is unintelligible until the particular moral or instrumental practice according to which the act is being justified is made clear.

When this is attempted, the result is often paradoxical. Suppose we urge that it is sometimes right to break the law, and that by "right" we in fact mean "lawful" according to that same body of law whose violation we wish to defend—say, Massachusetts law. (This is not, of course, the usual argument for civil disobedience or other lawbreaking.) Our claim is then that it is sometimes lawful under Massachusetts law to break Massachusetts law, which makes no sense. Nor can we save our proposition by pointing out, if it is true, that Massachusetts law provides certain exceptions covering the sort of act we wish to justify, for then we cannot say that the act is unlawful. The same reasoning applies in the case of moral judgments: because it is the considerations of a moral practice that determine whether an act is morally right, the claim that it is sometimes morally right to ignore these considerations amounts to the claim that it is right to do that which is not right. This is absurd. How can it be right to act wrongly? And similarly for other moral terms: how can it be that we ought to do that which we ought not to do? How can it be just to act unjustly?

The way to avoid the paradox of appearing to claim that it is right to do wrong is to make it clear that the term "right" as it is used or implied in making such a claim has two meanings. The statement "it is right to do that which is not right" then becomes "it is $right_1$ to do that which is not $right_2$," where $right_1$ and $right_2$ are different senses of right. For example: "it is $right_1$ (morally right) to do that which is not $right_2$ (permitted by Massachusetts law)." Or: "it is $right_1$ (has the best consequences) to do that which is not $right_2$ (conforms to the moral rules)." We avoid the paradox by making it clear that the two senses of right invoked by the argument from extremity refer to different practices or schemes of practical reasoning. We cannot intelligibly say that it is morally permissible to do what is morally forbidden, but it is certainly intelligible (though it may be false) to say that it is sometimes morally permissible to violate the positive law or legally permissible to violate the moral law, that justice requires what may be inexpedient, or that it may be expedient to bomb cities even though unjust.

The paradoxical character of the argument from extremity is acknowledged by Walzer when he formulates his version of the escape clause, which he argues is required by the morality of war, as the proposition "do justice unless the heavens are (really) about to fall" (p. 231). If the political community really is threatened with destruction, then its leaders are to violate the rules of war if doing so reasonably appears to be prudent in the effort to avoid that catastrophe. In other words, if the heavens are really about to fall, one may—indeed, must—do injustice to prevent that from happening. Walzer does not say that the categorical rules and the rights embodied in them are no longer without moral force: "These rights . . cannot be eroded or undercut; nothing diminishes them; they are still standing at the very moment they are overridden: that is why they have to be overridden" (p. 231). The destruction of noncombatants is "a kind of blasphemy" (p. 262), and those responsible must bear a "burden of guilt" (p. 231)—even, Walzer suggests, "the burdens of criminality" (p. 260). In short, Walzer evidently shares the traditional view that if what we do to avoid catastrophe violates the moral rules, it is by definition wrong, however good the consequences. He accepts the judgment that some acts are intrinsically, that is, categorically, wrong or unjust.

The argument from extremity, then, is intelligible only on the assumption that the "ought" in the proposition that sometimes unjust acts ought to be done is not what the moral tradition would recognize as a moral ought. It is, rather, a hypothetical or instrumental ought; certainly Walzer's version of the argument from extremity is instrumental, as his name for it ("the utilitarianism of extremity") implies. The end that demands the necessary murder of noncombatants is the survival of the political community. Whatever the defects of his conclusions, Walzer does not obscure the issue by shrinking from calling the thing by its correct name. Those who intentionally attack noncombatants in conditions of extremity are "murderers" (p. 323). But because they are murderers in a good cause, even Walzer is attracted by the view that their action is somehow right. But it is not right—merely expedient (one hopes it is at least that) in the pursuit of its postulated end. To hold otherwise is to slip back toward the confusion of names represented by the all-too-common failure to distinguish clearly between the considerations constituting a moral practice and those derived from the pursuit of particular substantive ends.

The very general moral terms, like "right" and "ought" and "moral," have been least able to escape this confusion. More specific terms, like "courage" or "truthfulness," are less easily distorted. Given the way in which the word "ought" has come to be used, for example, I might be able to make a case that in certain circumstances one ought to deceive a terminally ill person about his condition, but there is no way I can correctly characterize this action as truthful. The terms "justice" and "just" seem to fall somewhere in between: they are often used today as synonyms for "morally right" in its blanket sense, yet still cling recalcitrantly to their ancient association with the idea of fidelity to positive and moral law. And this is why even now it is implausible to claim that it could never be "just" intentionally to convict and punish a person known to his prosecuters to be innocent, or to defend as "just" the deliberate destruction of cities and their inhabitants for the sake of military advantage, even in a just cause. These are paradigm cases of injustice. Such acts might be defended as desirable by appealing to the end they are supposed to serve, but to call them "just" is a linguistic and factual as well as a moral mistake.

Sometimes, to violate the categorical constraints that are at the core of the traditional morality of war may be the best course—that is, the most effective and attractive course—given certain values or ends. But to defend such actions as "morally best" is to confuse the desirable with the obligatory, the "good" with the "right". By confusing the pursuit of good ends with a conscientious respect for the categorical precepts of a moral practice, it obscures what has traditionally been regarded as distinctive of the moral point of view. It is therefore subversive of morality as a distinctive form of thought and conduct. A morality is not a comprehensive scheme of practical guidance or judgment that tells us what to do or what is best, all things considered, but rather one kind of practice among others, a practice within which we determine what is morally right. Our lives are shaped by an indefinite number of activities and practices and ideals, and so an indefinite number of grounds—legal, religious, economic, aesthetic, and moral—exists for choosing or judging any action. Given the diversity and incommensurability of human ends, it is an illusion to think that there can exist any single or comprehensive "best" ground, or that it is reasonable to expect morality to provide such a ground.

THE UTILITARIANISM OF EXTREMITY

From the standpoint of traditional morality, the argument from extremity does not qualify as a moral argument. All it can hope to show is that sometimes to act immorally is best, given certain ends. But as a maxim of instrumental rationality, the argument from extremity leaves much to be desired, for at least two reasons. First, the conception of the good underlying the goods usually postulated when the argument from extremity is invoked or defended is suspect. And second, the assumptions made by the extremity argument concerning the calculation of consequences are faulty. Doubts about the kind of reasoning presupposed by the extremity argument become all the more grave when that argument is invoked in controversies over the use of nuclear weapons.

In the context of discussions of war, those who fall back on the argument from extremity often postulate the good of a particular political community as the end that calls for, if it does not justify, violation of the traditional moral constraints. Walzer's version of the extremity argument takes this form. Nazi aggression constituted a threat not only to Britain but to all Europe, perhaps even to all mankind and to civilized values everywhere. But the threat to Britain alone was sufficient to justify that country's decision to bomb German cities (p. 254). In general, "political leaders can hardly help but choose the utilitarian side of the dilemma. That is what they are there for. They must opt for collective survival and override those rights that have suddenly loomed as obstacles to survival" (p. 326). This is a strong variant of the view of the political leader as trustee of the people, charged with the defense of their interests and their rights. But there are limits to what a trustee can do, and the role is not one we ordinarily regard as legitimizing illegal or immoral acts for the sake of the beneficiary. The statesman, like the trustee, is "there" for more than the good of those immediately served. Even if statesmen, like trustees, have a particular responsibility to those they serve, the conclusion that even in extremity the rights of others can be sacrificed for the sake of that responsibility does not follow. Surely it is arbitrary simply to assert that the community whose good is served need be no more inclusive than that of a single state. Perhaps the inclusion of this wider good in the calculation of utilities is intended, by those like Walzer who make this argument, to be covered by the notion of proportionality. But as Walzer himself acknowledges, proportionality is an uncertain guide and a weak constraint.

The good of a community includes not only the well-being of the group but the perpetuation of its identity, not only the lives and happiness of its members but the continued existence of their laws and traditions and entire way of life. Those who have invoked the argument from extremity are quick to point out that the benefits to be secured at the price of injustice include more than physical survival. The laws of the political community must give way to the demands of necessity when the independence of the community is in danger, because only in that way can the laws themselves, as well as the happiness of those who live by them, be secured. Versions of the extremity argument, such as Walzer's, extend this reasoning to include violation not only of positive law but of morality. For a moral community the argument from extremity is an invitation to sacrifice the moral life for the sake of its survival as a community. The individual who attempts to purchase continuation of life through immoral conduct makes an understandable, though hardly honorable, choice. Is not a community also degraded when it secures its survival—its continued independence and the lives and liberties of its members—through the deliberate destruction of noncombatants? The good for the sake of which such a crime is committed is immediately diminished by the commission of that crime. Let us count the full cost of such actions, if we are going to calculate.

As it is typically deployed in the context of controversies over the morality of war, then, the argument from extremity can be seen to rest on questionable assumptions concerning the good. The skeptic is surely entitled to ask *whose* good and what *kind* of good is being appealed to in the defense of moral enormities. The dangers of nuclear war make the provision of compelling answers to these questions all the more imperative. The virtual certainty that the consequences of a nuclear exchange would be dreadful for the attacker and for all mankind, as well as for the immediate victim, radically alters the cost-benefit ratio. Between the major powers it is scarcely conceivable that any reasonable calculation of consequences could support a decision to use nuclear weapons, even, because of the risks of escalation, on the most limited scale— though it is wise to bear in mind that this is not a judgment shared by some of those who may one day make this decision to use them. The state that uses nuclear weapons in an effort to avert catastrophe simply invites an even worse catastrophe.

Between a local nuclear power and its nonnuclear adversaries, on the other hand, it is at least conceivable that circumstances approximating those in which Britain found itself between 1940 and 1942 might occur. Improbable, to be sure: one would have to imagine a truly murderous aggressor, one willing to risk not only defeat but destruction, the existence of conditions in which the danger that the conflict might escalate to nuclear war would be very small, and so forth. But the more such assumptions we make, the closer we edge toward acceptance of at least tactical nuclear defense, with huge civilian casualties should there be no way to avoid them. Even here, however, it is hard to imagine even remotely plausible circumstances in which a direct attack on cities comparable to those of World War II would be expedient even for national ends, much less for the good of the human community. Once we have opened our minds to the argument from extremity, however, there is nothing to bar engaging in such macabre calculations, and nothing to preclude a catastrophic miscalculation.

To make a case for nuclear deterrence based on the extremity argument would appear to be easier, for the costs of deterrence are less than those of war—or appear to be less, for our calculations may be wrong about this, too. Certainly the competition in arms, the growth of the national security state, the increasing risk of nuclear madness or terrorism, the recurrent waves of fear and hatred that all of this breeds, the continued danger of nuclear war as nuclear arsenals proliferate, and the prospect of universal destruction should such a war occur must be taken into account, along with the costs of alternative policies. Still, many of us are prepared to rely on the argument from extremity to reconcile deterrence with conscience. To threaten other nations with annihilation is certainly wrong, but what choice do we have? Caught in the vice of necessity we dare not abandon our nuclear weapons and our plans for using them, even though we know that, given the dangers and uncertainties of nuclear war, to use them would be pointless as well as evil. This is the way in which nuclear deterrence is commonly defended by those who grant that the making of nuclear war is inherently wrong. They share Walzer's conclusion that in our nuclear world "supreme emergency has become a permanent condition" (p. 274), although perhaps too hastily, for it is not clear that a nuclear state choosing to abandon deterrence through unilateral action would be in any *imminent* danger of destruction. (Recall that there is no supreme emergency, according to Walzer, unless the danger is both serious and imminent.)

Whatever its implications for nuclear deterrence, the argument from extremity provides little practical guidance for deciding whether in a particular situation nuclear weapons should ever actually be used. For the argument is at its *most* plausible in the context of the judgments we reach as observers, rather than as makers of decisions. As observers we consider historical cases whose outcome we know, or we engage in the imaginative exploration of hypothetical cases whose outcomes we control. But the moral traditions, though shaped by the past, are concerned primarily with the direction of our present and future conduct. And although moralists like to explore the implication of principles for conduct in imaginary situations, including situations in which the survival of a nation depends upon someone's telling a lie or taking an innocent life, the moral traditions are concerned with guiding conduct in the actual, not in an imaginary, world. And their common conclusion, distilled from centuries of reflection upon the responses of countless individuals and commu-

nities to innumerable personal and community emergencies, is that the consequences of keeping faith with the moral tradition will not be catastrophic. This has
never been taken to mean that the consequence of acting morally will always be
better for the agent than those that might be brought about by violating the moral
rules. Clearly, the consequences of acting rightly are often disagreeable and sometimes tragic. But not catastrophic: the maxim "let justice be done though the
heavens fall" expresses the confidence of the ages that in fact the world will not
come to an end, although individuals and even communities might be destroyed, as
a consequence of obeying the moral law. Shall we abandon our moral traditions
because nuclear weapons now make it possible for us to bring the world to an end?
The conclusion hardly follows, for the world is endangered not by mankind's fidelity to these traditions, but by its rejection of them.

Unlike many other consequentialist arguments, the argument from extremity
asks us to dispense with the guidance of traditional morality and to calculate consequences only in situations of looming catastrophe. The argument is in effect that
we should rely on moral rules in making ordinary decisions when there is time
for careful and dispassionate deliberation, but that in situations of crisis we must
fall back on morally unaided reason. But the argument from extremity is doubly
defective as a guide to practice, for it provides no adequate criterion for deciding
when the moment to override the categorical constraints has actually arrived, and
no grounds for confidence that the calculations we will make in a moment of
unusual and horrifying danger will be rational ones. It is hard to believe that the key
notions upon which the argument relies—"supreme emergency," "imminent catastrophe," "immeasurable evil," and the like—would be correctly applied by those
for whose guidance they are intended. The extremity argument proposes a rule for
spectators, not players. Rational decisions are not likely to be made in circumstances of international crisis—and, as we know, political leaders often make
errors in judgment, even in ordinary situations. Their judgments in emergencies
are also often mistaken, and mistaken in predictable ways. They confuse the bad
consequence for themselves of acting morally with bad consequences for their
nation or for what they regard as "civilization." They are prone to mistake defeat in
war for the end of the world (for it may be the end of *their* world), and the success
of their enemies for the triumph of evil. The real danger is not that we may find
ourselves in a situation in which the heavens will fall unless we use nuclear
weapons, but rather that in a nuclear crisis those who make the fateful decisions will
act stupidly.

The attractions of the arguments from extremity are purely theoretical. To rely
on it in practice would not only be immoral by traditional standard, but also futile.
Nor is the case for accepting the extremity argument as a principle of practical
reasoning persuasive even if our standard is a utilitarian one, for it is highly doubtful that any adequate utilitarian defense of the proposal to qualify the morality of
war with a utilitarian escape clause could be constructed. Those who are skeptical
of the utility of such a proposal may be unable to prove conclusively that the overall
consequences of adopting it would be worse than sticking with an unqualified morality, but if so its defenders are equally prevented from demonstrating the utility of
accepting it. The burden of proof, however, is unquestionably on the latter.

NOTES

1. U.S. Catholic Bishops, "The Challenge of Peace: God's Promise and Our Response," *Origins* 13 (1983): 1-32.
2. Early draft of essay cited in note 1, *Origins* 12 (1982): 316-17. For another, secular, version of the lesser evil argument, see Michael Walzer, *Just and Unjust Wars* (New York: Basic Books, 1977), p. 274: "We threaten evil in order not to do it, and the doing of it would be so terrible that the threat seems in comparison to be morally defensible."
3. Douglas Lackey considers alternative conceptions of intention and their implications for the ethics of nuclear deterrence in Chapter 16, this volume.

16
THE INTENTIONS OF DETERRENCE

Douglas P. Lackey

The American nightmare, circa 1957: somewhere in Russia there is a button; if a choice is made, the button will be pushed; if the button is pushed, New York City will be destroyed. The American nightmare, circa 1984: there are 2,000 such buttons. Presumably American leaders wish to reduce this threat. But if the buttons are pushed, there is no way that the cities can be saved; and if the choice is made, there is no way to stop the buttons being pushed. The Americans have no recourse but to work upon the choice.

They have two options. They can reward the Soviets for choosing not to push the buttons, or they can punish the Soviets for choosing to push them. We have a Cold War and punishments are favored over rewards. But punishment after the fact would come too late, so the threat to punish must work beforehand. And the punishment threatened must be probable enough and severe enough to negate whatever the Soviets hope to gain from the destruction of American cities. Parity suggests itself. If the Soviets destroy New York the Americans will destroy Moscow; if the Soviets destroy Chicago the Americans will destroy Leningrad, and so on. But is it moral to make such threats?

One line of reasoning is this. It is morally wrong to kill innocent people. Most of the people in Leningrad and Moscow are innocent, regardless of what the Soviet leaders do. Therefore it would be immoral to destroy Moscow or Leningrad. A second line of reasoning says that it is morally permissible to protect innocent people from deadly assault. The people of New York and Chicago are innocent, and their only protection is deterrent threats. Therefore it is permissible to threaten to destroy Moscow and Leningrad. The conclusion seems to be that it is moral to threaten to destroy Moscow but not moral to destroy Moscow. Some philosophers call this "the paradox of deterrence."

An easy resolution suggests itself. We will do only what is moral. We will threaten to destroy Moscow, but if New York is destroyed we will not destroy Moscow. Our bluff will have been called,and we will do nothing. But this resolution is too simple to be satisfactory. If the threat to Moscow is to reduce the threat to New

The author wishes to thank Professor Harold Hochman and the Baruch Center for the Study of Business and Government for released time during the period in which this essay was written.

York, it must be credible. For the threat to be credible there must be some chance that it will be carried out. Thus, if we make a credible threat, we foresee that there is some chance that we will carry it out.[1] Now in law, what we foresee as a consequence of our acts is what we intend by our acts. Thus if the threat is credible, we must intend that Moscow be destroyed or, at least, we must intend that there is some risk that Moscow be destroyed. But is it moral to have such an intention?

Over the years, American officials who have taken the trouble to supply moral justifications for American strategic policies have advanced or implied three arguments to the effect that American strategic intentions *are* morally acceptable.[2] The three arguments are:

1. The policy of the United States calls for the use of strategic nuclear weapons only in the event of nuclear attack on the United States or its allies. It follows that if strategic nuclear weapons are ever used, not the United States but some other, aggressor nation will have used them first. Thus, the intention behind the American policy of deterrence is not an aggressive intention. On the contrary, the American intention is to combat aggression. (We will call this the aggressor-defender argument.)

2. The American policy of deterrence is designed to prevent the Soviet Union from attacking the United States. This policy has succeeded for 35 years and will continue to succeed. There is very little chance that the Soviet Union will launch a nuclear attack on the United States. It follows that there is very little chance that the United States will attack Moscow. Thus the United States is not now intending to attack Moscow, since we do not believe that we will ever attack it. The intention to attack is a conditional intention, and we do not think that the conditions of this intention will ever be fulfilled. Our main and unconditional intention is to prevent a nuclear attack on the United States. That intention is morally acceptable, since a nation has the right to take such steps as are necessary to prevent attacks on itself. (We will call this the conditional intention argument.)

3. Strictly speaking, the United States does not intend to attack Moscow even conditionally. Our strategic weapons are targeted on Soviet military forces, not on cities or other populated areas. It is true that if the U.S. launched a nuclear attack, many innocent civilians would die, but we would bring about the death of these civilians with regret. If we could find a way to destroy the Soviet military forces without killing innocent civilians we would do so. (We will call this the double-effect argument.)

These are serious moral arguments. They do not appeal merely to the national interest, nor are they obviously unsound. Nevertheless, they are all unsatisfactory. In the course of my showing that they are unsatisfactory, it will emerge that the intentions behind the present policy of deterrence are not morally acceptable.

Each argument contains three sorts of assumptions. First, it contains assumptions about matters of fact: what our strategic policy actually is and what its effects actually are. Second, it contains philosophical assumptions, particularly about the nature of intentions and their role in the moral evaluation of policies. Third, it contains moral assumptions about what is morally acceptable and what is not. Each argument contains a false assumption of one sort or another.

THE AGGRESSOR-DEFENDER ARGUMENT

To get a grip on the aggressor-defender argument we must first clarify American policy regarding the first use of nuclear weapons. It is the policy of the United States never to use *strategic* nuclear weapons—B-52s, ICBMs, submarine-launched ballistic missiles—until some other nation has already used nuclear weapons in the course of waging war. On the other hand, it *is* the policy of the U.S. to use smaller nuclear weapons—tactical nuclear weapons, and intermediate-range nuclear weapons such as the F-111 and the Pershing II—against an enemy who has not yet used nuclear weapons. For example, it has been NATO policy since the early 1950s to repel possible attacks by Warsaw Pact forces with tactical and intermediate-range nuclear weapons, even if Pact forces do not use them first. So the policy of the United States is "no first use" of strategic nuclear weapons, coupled with a policy of "first use" of tactical and intermediate-size nuclear weapons.

Defenders of the present policy will note that these observations do not affect the force of the argument. For even if the United States is the first to use nuclear weapons, it is committed to using them only for defensive purposes. The general argument holds that the U.S. does not intend to use its nuclear weapons for the purposes of aggression.

One would perhaps be impressed with the official reasoning if the United States combined its commitment to "defense only" with some clear definition of the concept of aggression. But neither the U.S. nor anyone else has a clear definition of aggression. Most nations that engage in war claim they do so for purposes of defense. If we look at a concrete situation in which the U.S. might have used nuclear weapons first, it is very difficult to determine who was the aggressor and who the defender. Suppose, for example, that the Soviet Union had responded to the American blockade of Cuba in 1962 by sealing off Berlin—a possibility to which John Kennedy assigned more than minimal probability.[3] In this possible world, as in 1948, American planes fly to the relief of the city, but *this* time Soviet fighters intercept the planes and shoot them down. A relief column approaches the East German border and is thrown back by Soviet troops, some of whom, in the course of fighting, cross over into West Germany—at which point tactical nuclear weapons are authorized to halt the Soviet advance. Who is the aggressor and who is the defender? Certainly the Soviets had the right, under international law, to supply their ally Cuba with weapons Cuba considered helpful to its own defense. On the other hand, the United States had very little right, under international law, to stop Soviet boats on the high seas. Arguments about who struck the first blow tend to migrate backward in time.

It is usually very difficult to determine who is the aggressor and who is the defender when war breaks out. By contrast, it is easy to determine who has used a nuclear weapon first. Because of the consequences from the first use of nuclear weapons, the question of who uses nuclear weapons first looms larger on most people's moral horizons than the question of who is the aggressor. For such people, a "nonaggressive first-use" intention is morally more reprehensible than an "aggressive second-use" intention.

There is a further difficulty with the aggressor-defender argument, and this one takes in strategic nuclear weapons. Suppose the unlikely situation that the United States launches an attack on the Soviet Union using conventional weapons, an attack which, in the eyes of all concerned, is clearly aggressive (although for some noble purpose). The Soviet Union responds with a strategic nuclear attack, and the U.S. responds with a nuclear second strike against the U.S.S.R. By hypothesis, in this case, the U.S. is the aggressor, so the Soviet nuclear strike, by the aggressor-defender principle, is not an act of aggression. But if the Soviet nuclear strike is not an act of aggression, then the American second strike cannot be characterized as a response to aggression. So "we will use strategic nuclear weapons only in response to aggression," and "we will use strategic nuclear weapons only in the event of a nuclear attack on the United States or its allies" are two quite different principles, and neither implies the other. The conclusion is that the intent of policy based on the latter principle cannot be justified according to the aggressor-defender argument, even if we had some clear idea of what aggression is.

THE CONDITIONAL INTENTION ARGUMENT

The thrust of the conditional intention argument is that current American strategic policy has two intentions, an unconditional intention to prevent attack and a conditional intention to retaliate if struck. The argument affirms that the unconditional intention is the morally decisive one, and that the conditional intention should be ignored by moralists, since there is every reason to think that the conditions of this intention will never be fulfilled.

Let us assume that the two intentions are indeed associated with the present policy of nuclear deterrence. Nevertheless, these two intentions are in logically different categories. The unconditional intention *to prevent attack* is the main purpose of the policy. The conditional intention *strike-if-struck* is not the purpose of the policy. The formation of this intention is part of the means by which the purpose is achieved. We cannot assume, then, that if the unconditional intention is morally acceptable that the conditional intention must be morally acceptable, unless we are prepared to assume that an intended end always justifies the intended means.

We must, then, consider the conditional intention in and of itself. Our intention is to issue a nuclear strike if we suffer a nuclear attack. If we issue such a strike, millions of innocent people will be killed. Such a strike would be morally wrong, in Paul Ramsey's phrase, "the most unloving act in the history of mankind."[4] How then can we justify such an intention? Two arguments suggest themselves.

1. We might argue that the formation of this intention is justified because its formation produces some good consequences and no morally unacceptable ones. But when we consider this argument we must consider all the consequences, not just the intended ones. One of the consequences, many people believe, is a diminished chance of Soviet nuclear attack on the United States. But there are other consequences as well. Since the formation of this intention creates a disposition to proceed with a nuclear second strike, it probably increases the chance of accidental, unintentional, or unauthorized nuclear war. What is more, the formation of the intention to strike-if-struck increases the chance of an American nuclear attack on the Soviet Union; thus it puts innocent people in the Soviet Union at increased risk. (Certainly people in the Soviet Union are more at risk if we form the intention to strike-if-struck than if we form the intention not to strike-if-struck.) I would argue that this increased risk inflicted on innocent people in the Soviet Union is a violation of their rights, for which there is no justification. (Self-defense will not do, since self-defense can only be directed at the attacker, and the people in the Soviet Union

are attacking no one.) Thus, it cannot be argued that forming the conditional intention is morally acceptable because it has only morally acceptable consequences.

2. This leaves the argument that forming the intention is morally acceptable because the intention is conditional. Yet the conditional character of this intention might justify its formation in a number of different ways:

i. One might argue that if the conditions of the intention are never fulfilled, we should retrospectively judge that it was not morally wrong to have formed the intention. Since no evil has come of it, the formation of the intention was not wrong. The trouble with this argument is that it is at least partially happenstance whether or not the Soviet Union launches a first strike. It hardly seems proper for us to claim moral credit for good luck. Suppose a driver is so drunk that he would hit anyone who happened to be on the road. Fortunately no one is on the road. The drunk driver cannot claim that his driving was morally acceptable simply because he injured no one, nor can the United States claim that the intention to strike-if-struck is morally acceptable on the grounds that no one in fact is injured or will be injured by the formation of the intention.[5]

ii. One might argue that the formation of a conditional intention is morally acceptable if those who form it *believe* that the conditions of the intention will never be fulfilled. By this argument, a person who forms the intention to kill innocent people if attacked has acted improperly if he believes that he will indeed be attacked, but he has not acted improperly if he believes that he will not be attacked. (The act in question here is the formation of the conditional intention—a mental act.)

There is a grain of truth in this argument. Most people would consider it more wicked to form an intention to commit murder if one believes that one will commit this murder than to form an intention to commit a murder if one believes that one will not commit this murder. But even though the intention may be less wicked, it does not follow that it is morally acceptable. Both intentions may be morally wrong, and the morally proper course of action would be to avoid both.

My own view is that a person's belief that he will not perform a wicked act that he conditionally intends to do will not serve as an excuse for forming such an intention. Consider the following scenario: Jones believes everything Olga, the fortune teller, tells him, and Olga tells him the sun will not rise tommorrow. Jones's friends deride him for accepting Olga's prophecy, and Jones angrily promises that if the sun rises tommorrow, he will murder the first person he meets. Jones is a man of his word, and he has really formed a conditional intention to do this murder. Certainly we have a poor moral opinion of Jones, even if we think that Jones sincerely believes that he will not commit the murder. We feel, on the epistemological side, that Jones should not have this belief and, on the moral side, that he should not form such an intention.

iii. The defenders of the present policy of deterrence will object that their beliefs about the fulfillment of the conditions of their conditional intentions are different from Jones's belief, because his belief that the sun will not rise tomorrow is irrational. The belief of American leaders of state that the U.S.S.R. will not launch a first strike provided the U.S. guarantees destruction in return is (allegedly) a rational belief. Certainly many people, including those who do not like nuclear deterrence, believe that the chance of a Soviet first strike on the U.S. in the coming decades is not great. Does this make a moral difference?

The principle suggested here is this:

> *It is always morally permissible to form an intention to do W if C provided that one has good reason to believe that C will not occur even if W is a wicked action which would be morally wrong to perform if C occurred.*

The principle is general, and one tests such principles by considering specific cases. These show the principle to be false. Suppose that Smith, after reading anti-Semitic literature, forms the conditional intention "If I ever meet a Jew I'll spit in his face." Suppose, furthermore, that Smith believes with good reason, that he will never meet a Jew (he is stranded on a desert island, perhaps). Smith is hurting no one, nor in his circumstances is he likely to. If the formation of his intention is a crime, it is a victimless crime. Is it morally acceptable for Smith to form such an intention? I think not.

To find the reason why it is wrong to form a conditional anti-Semitic intention, we must reach beyond our present repertoire of moral concepts—justice, rights, the common good, etc.—to older moral concepts involving character and the virtues. We should attempt to resurrect the notion of "defects of character," and I can think of no better definition of a defect of character than to say that a defect of character is a disposition to do a wicked thing. A person who has formed the intention to spit in someone's face has formed a disposition to do a wicked thing, and thus has exhibited a defect of character. Since the formation of this conditional intention springs from a defect of character, the formation of the conditional intention is not morally acceptable.

This discussion may sound strange when it is dissected logically, but it corresponds to the everyday procedures of moral judgment. We do not judge the character of people simply on the basis of what they do. We judge their character on the basis of what we believe they *would* do under various circumstances. And we persist in these judgments even if we feel that these various circumstances are unlikely to occur.

What we have said here about the anti-Semite who does not expect to meet any Jews applies to the practitioners of nuclear deterrence. These are people who would kill millions of innocent people if the circumstances called for it. If they are so disposed, that disposition is a defect of character. It remains a defect of character even if the circumstances that would provoke the killing of millions of innocent prople are unlikely to arise.

In all the preceding discussions we have assumed that what people have good reason to believe will not occur will, in fact, not occur. But this assumption is too strong. "Good reasons" can only assure that there is a high probability that a certain event will happen. Even if there are good reasons to believe that there will be no Soviet first strike if the United States maintains deterrence, we can ask, and should ask, what the probability is that there will be no first strike. Some would set the probability as high as 99 percent; some might set it at 90 percent; others might set it at 66 percent. But is a 90 percent probability a high enough probability to justify forming the intention? Is a 66 percent probability high enough?

What we will consider to be an acceptable level of probability depends on the moral gravity of the act we are conditionally intending to perform. It is one thing for a person to say he will steal a book if he gets the chance when there is only a 5 percent probability that he will get the chance, and quite another thing for a person to say that he is prepared to kill millions of innocent people if the circumstances are right when there is "only" a 5 percent chance that the circumstances will be right. When someone forms a conditional intention to kill millions of innocent people, *at a minimum* we will demand that it be *nearly certain* that the conditions of the intention will not be fulfilled. But few are prepared to say that it is *nearly certain* that the Soviets will not launch a first strike if the United States continues to practice deterrence.

To form a conditional intention to do a wicked thing is not the same thing as to do the wicked thing. But it does involve an internal commitment to doing the wicked thing. I have meditated for almost a decade on how to evaluate such internal commitments.[6] My feeling now is that the moral status of the formation of an intention to do W if C is the same as the moral status of *binding* oneself externally to doing W if C. In the case of nuclear deterrence, the internal commitment to strike-if-struck is morally equivalent to binding oneself to strike-if-struck—to creating a doomsday machine that will automatically launch a second strike. Suppose that the chance of a Soviet first strike if deterrence is practiced is 5 percent over the next 40 years. Would it be morally permissible to construct a doomsday machine that will *automatically* kill millions of people in the Soviet Union if the United States is attacked, if the chance of such attack is 5 percent? I think not. But if it is not morally acceptable to construct such a machine, then it is not morally acceptable to form the corresponding intention to strike-if-struck.

THE DOUBLE-EFFECT ARGUMENT

We advance, then, to the third line of argument for the moral purity of American intentions: the argument that our weapons are aimed at military targets, not civilian targets. According to this argument, we intend with our nuclear weapons to destroy only military forces and enemy soldiers, and not enemy civilians.

The intention to destroy enemy forces in a just war is a morally acceptable intention. Therefore, it follows that the intentions behind the posture of deterrence are morally acceptable. This argument has three parts: (a) an empirical claim about American targeting policy; (b) an inference from American targeting policy to American intentions; and (c) the moral claim that these intentions are acceptable. We will consider each in turn.

Targeting Policy

In a letter to the National Council of Catholic Bishops, National Security Advisor William Clark wrote:

> For moral, political, and military reasons it is not our policy to target Soviet civilian populations *as such*. Indeed, one of the factors that has contributed to the evolution of U.S. strategic policy is the belief that targeting cities and populations was not a just or effective way to prevent war. This being said, however, no one should doubt that a general war would result in a high loss of human life, even though our targeting policy does not call for attacking cities per se.[7]

The key phrase in Clark's statement is *per se*. What does Clark mean by *per se*? If all he means is that the United States does not have bombs targeted for "Moscow," but for "main train station, Moscow," then the *per se* should be dismissed as irrelevant, as mendacious as Truman's announcement to the American people of the bombing of Hiroshima: "Sixteen hours ago an American airplane dropped one bomb on Hiroshima, an important Japanese Army base."[8]

But I believe that Clark's *per se* means more than this. The American people have been told little about American targeting policy. We know there is a Single Integrated Operational Plan (SIOP) for American strategic forces. We know there is a National Strategic Target List. We know that since the Schlesinger regime in 1974-75, the president has been provided with many different suboptions within the general format of the SIOP. But unless we have a security clearance, our best evidence about the structure of the target list comes from published but censored testimony before the Senate Armed Services Committee. In 1980, the committee published a list of typical targets on the National Strategic Target list, with the numbers of each type of target blotted out:

1. *Soviet nuclear forces:*
   ICBMs and IRBMs, together with their launch facilities (LFs) and launch command centers (LCCs)
   Nuclear weapons storage sites
   Airfields supporting nuclear-capable aircraft
   Nuclear missile-firing submarine (SSBN) bases
2. *Conventional military forces:*
   Caserns
   Supply depots
   Marshalling points
   Conventional airfields
   Ammunition storage facilities
   Tank and vehicle storage yards
3. *Military and political leadership:*
   Command posts
   Key communications facilities
4. *Economic and industrial targets:*
   a. War-supporting industry
      Ammunition factories
      Tank and armored personnel carrier factories
      Petroleum refineries
      Railway and yards and repair facilities
   b. Industry that contributes to economic recovery
      Coal
      Basic steel
      Basic aluminum
      Cement
      Electrical power[9]

Milton Leitenberg has suggested that the listing of the target categories in this order implies a targeting *sequence*.[10] If so, then in a multistage nuclear war our intention is to strike Soviet strategic weapons first and Soviet economic targets (read: cities) last. Furthermore, Desmond Ball reports that the SIOP is divided into four general catagories of attack options, and that within each of these classes of options there are some targets listed as "withholds."[11] Four types of "withholds" were revealed in 1979: population centers, national command and control centers, particular countries targeted in the main SIOP (e.g., East Germany and other Soviet satellites), and "allied and neutral territory." When William Clark says that "the U.S. does not target cities," I take him to be referring to the fact that, in the SIOP, Soviet population centers are "withholds."

There is good news and bad news in these leaks about "withholds." The good news is that the United States seems to be making *some* effort to avoid dropping bombs on Soviet cities, at least in the initial stages of nuclear war. This is a big step beyond the planned SAC raids of the 1950s, which were designed to leave all Russia a "smoking radiating ruin in less than two hours."[12] The bad news is that if population centers are labeled as "withholds" in the targeting plan, it follows that they are *still* listed in the targeting plan, and at some stage in a nuclear war Soviet cities stand to be bombed. This contradicts the claim that "we do not target cities as such."

One would like to know more about what is involved in the Pentagon policy that "population centers" are "withholds." Does this mean merely that Soviet population centers not located near significant strategic forces are not targets in the early stages of nuclear war? Or does it mean that Soviet population centers near significant strategic forces are also off-limits in the early stages of a nuclear war? I suspect that only the former is true. My evidence is Herbert York's affirmation that Leningrad is considered a strategic target because it is an important port facility, that Kiev is a strategic target because it is an important transportation center, and so on.[13] Common sense also indicates that it is highly likely that the Pentagon will attempt to destroy any unfired Soviet ICBMs in the course of a multistage nuclear war, even if these ICBMs are placed near populated areas. The best inference that can be made from the available data is that Soviet cities not near Soviet strategic weapons will not be struck at the beginning, but would be struck at the end of a multistage nuclear war. Soviet cities that are near Soviet strategic weapons would be destroyed in the early stages of a nuclear war, though technically they would not be the designated targets of an American nuclear strike.

American Intentions

If my assessment of SIOP "withholds" is correct, in the early stages of a nuclear war millions of innocent people in the Soviet Union will be killed by American strategic weapons. In the later stages, which may be reached very quickly, tens of millions will be killed. What do the facts (if they are facts) tell us about American intentions?

We must first define the word "intention." In one sense, our intentions are what we bring about intentionally; they are the foreseeable consequences of our deliberate acts. In this sense of intention, if we launch a nuclear strike which we foresee will kill millions of Russians, then we intend that these Russians be killed. Clearly, this is not the sense of intention that William Clark and others have in mind when they deny that we intend to kill innocent civilians. What Clark and others must mean by intention is what we mean by "purpose"; in this sense our intentions are the *desired* consequences of our deliberate acts.

The argument then proceeds to observe that when our second strike kills millions of innocent Soviet citizens, we do not desire to kill these innocent millions. It follows that we do not intend to kill them; our intention remains pure. I disagree. There is a rule as old as Aristotle that whoever desires an end desires the means as well. What is the end, the goal of the United States, should a nuclear war begin? Secretary of Defense Caspar Weinberger, in his latest annual report, says:

> Should deterrence fail, our strategy is to restore peace on favorable terms. . . We would seek to deny the enemy his political and military goals and to counterattack with sufficient strength to terminate hostilities at the lowest possible level of damage to the United States and its allies.[14]

Notice that he did not say that it is the goal of the United States to act so as to produce the least damage *to the world* or the smallest number of deaths of the innocent. If a large number of innocent deaths of Soviet citizens would "restore peace on favorable terms," that would serve the purposes of the United States. It is a plain fact that the deaths of millions of Soviet citizens would encourage the Soviet leadership to surrender. So those deaths, caused by American strategic weapons, are a means to the American end. But if they are means to the American end, they are desired, even if the desire is tinged with regret. If these deaths are desired, they cannot be excused or justified as unintended, on any interpretation of the concept of intention.

The Principle of Double-Effect

Let us suppose that the conclusion of the previous section is wrong and that the United States truly does not desire to kill innocent Russians, that their deaths would be regrettable but unintended side effects of attempts to destroy Soviet military forces. Would such killings then be morally justified? According to the traditional principle of double-effect,[15] which is being invoked here in defense of deterrence, it is permissible to produce an unintended side effect only if one's action has some other effect which does more good than the bad effect does bad. In the case of a second strike, it is permissible to produce millions of unintended Russian deaths only if one's act produces some good side effect which more than compensates for these deaths. The only good that could plausibly outweigh millions of lives lost is millions of lives saved. So an American second strike can be morally justified only if it saves more people than it kills. It is difficult to imagine a plausible scenario for a second strike, massive or limited, which would save more people than it killed. (Caspar Weinberger did not even pretend that the American second strike would save lives overall; he implied merely that it would save American lives.) Consequently, even if the intention behind the second strike (destroy enemy forces) were pure, the strike itself is not pure. If so, it is not morally acceptable to intentionally adopt it.

INTENTIONS AND CAPACITIES

The intentions claimed for the American policy of deterrence are of different sorts. Some of these intentions, I have argued, are not really involved in the policy of deterrence. Those that *are* involved are not morally acceptable. But even if the intentions behind deterrence were morally acceptable, it does not follow that the policy is morally acceptable. To judge the policy morally, we must consider not merely the intentions behind the policy, but its actual effects in the world—the unintended consequences and the unwanted risks of deterrence. This important phase of the analysis of deterrence I must leave for the other contributors to this volume.

NOTES

1. All persons who have spoken officially on the subject of deterrence stress that American deterrent intentions are not bluffs. The report of the President's Commission on Strategic Forces, chaired by Brent Scowcroft, stated: "Deterrence is not, and cannot be, bluff. We must not merely have weapons; we must be perceived to be able, and prepared, if necessary, to use them effectively against the key elements of Soviet power" (*New York Times*, 12 April 1983). General George Seignious, former Chief of the Joint Chiefs of Staff, testified in 1979, "I find such a surrender scenario irresponsible—for it sends the wrong message to the Soviets. We have not built and maintained our strategic forces, at the cost of billions, in order to weaken our impact by telling the Russians and the world that we are going to back down—when we would not" (quoted in Herbert Scoville, *MX: Prescription for Disaster* [Cambridge: MIT Press, 1981], p. 78).
2. The first two of these arguments were presented by Caspar W. Weinberger in his Shattuck lecture, the third by National Security Advisor William Clark in a letter to the National Council of Catholic Bishops. See Caspar W. Weinberger, "Remarks by the Secretary of Defense to the Massachusetts Medical Society, 19 May 1982," *New England Journal of Medicine* 307, no. 12 (16 September 1982); and William Clark, letter in *Origins*, 28 October 1982, p. 327.
3. See Robert F. Kennedy, *Thirteen Days* (New York: Signet Books, 1969), pp. 35-36, 58, and 60.
4. Paul Ramsey, *War and the Christian Conscience* (Durham: Duke University Press, 1961), p. 170.
5. Thomas Nagel, in his essay on "Moral Luck," *Mortal Questions* (Cambridge: Cambridge University Press, 1979), pp. 24-39, argues that we should not penalize persons for their good moral luck. But the argument here is not that we should treat the person who intends to strike-if-struck the same as we treat the person who has actually struck, or that we should treat attempted murder as if it were murder. The argument is that we should not treat the man who intends to strike-if-struck on a par with the man who intends to not-strike-if-struck.
6. See Douglas P. Lackey, "Ethics and Nuclear Deterrence," in *Moral Problems*, ed. James Rachels (New York: Harper & Row, 1975).
7. William Clark, letter quoted in *Origins*, 28 October 1982, p. 327.
8. Barton J. Bernstein and Allen J. Matusow, eds., *The Truman Administration, A Documentary History* (New York: Harper & Row, 1966), p. 39. I have a recording of Truman's announcement, which to my ear is different from their text. On the recording Truman says, "The world now knows that the first atomic bomb was dropped on Hiroshima, a military base."
9. U.S. Senate, Committee on Armed Services, Hearing on Department of Defense Authorization for FY 1981 (Washington, D.C.: Superintendent of Documents, 1981), sec. 5, p. 2721.

10. Milton Leitenberg, "Presidential Directive 59 and American Nuclear Weapons Targeting Policy," *Journal of Peace Research* (1981).
11. Desmond Ball, "U.S. Strategic Forces: How Might They Be Used?" *International Security* 7, no. 3 (Winter 1982-83).
12. David Alan Rosenberg, "A Smoking Radiating Ruin at the End of Two Hours: American Plans for Nuclear War With the Soviet Union 1954-55," *International Security* 7 (Spring 1983).
13. Herbert York, *Race to Oblivion* (New York: Simon & Schuster, 1970), p. 43.
14. Report of Secretary of Defense Caspar W. Weinberger to the Congress on the FY 1984 Budget (1 February 1983), p. 32.
15. Francis Connell, "Double Effect, Principle Of," *New Catholic Encyclopedia* (New York: McGraw-Hill, 1967).

17
NUCLEAR DETERRENCE AND FUTURE GENERATIONS

Jefferson McMahan

THE ARGUMENT

People's views about nuclear weapons tend to reflect the ordering of their fears. A crude generalization might be that those whose position is characterized primarily by opposition to nuclear weapons tend to fear nuclear war more than they fear the Soviets, while those who are disposed to support nuclear weapons tend to fear the Soviets more than they fear nuclear war. This in part explains why opponents of nuclear weapons often try to support their position by describing the probable effects of nuclear war and by deemphasizing the Soviet threat, while supporters of nuclear weapons stress the threat from the Soviet Union and the evils of Soviet communism, and maintain that nuclear war would be "survivable." In short, each group seeks to evoke in others the fears that motivate its own position, and to quieten fears that underlie the opposing view. Of course, many defenders of nuclear deterrence may also believe that only the threat of retaliation prevents the Soviets from attacking Western countries with nuclear weapons, and so they could legitimately appeal to the fear of nuclear destruction in support of the retention or acquisition of nuclear weapons. But the fact that they do not ordinarily do this suggests that they recognize that fear of nuclear destruction leads naturally to opposition to nuclear weapons.

The conflict between these two basic attitudes is most strikingly manifest in the old debate about whether it would be better to be "red" or dead. Of course, this debate greatly oversimplifies the issue, since no choice between policies presents us with a stark choice between Soviet domination and nuclear war. But the comparative evaluation of these two outcomes does have a place in one interesting type of

An earlier draft of this essay was read at the California Institute of Technology,the University of Illinois at Chicago, and the University of Chicago. The discussion following each reading was very helpful in my revisions. I have also benefited from written comments by Robin Attfield, Robert McKim, Jan Narveson, and Derek Parfit. My greatest debt is to Steven Lee, whose penetrating comments caused me to make a number of important changes in the argument.

consequentialist argument in which probabilities are also taken into account. For example, someone who believes that it would be better to be red than dead might argue, on the basis of that assumption, that it would be preferable to adopt a policy which, in comparison with the present form of nuclear deterrence, would decrease the probability of nuclear war, even if it would increase the probability of Soviet domination, as long as the increase in the latter probability would not be significantly greater than the decrease in the former.

The assumption about whether it would be better to be red or dead as it would appear in such an argument might be interpreted in different ways, some more defensible than others. The assumption might simply express a personal preference; that is, it might express nothing more than that one would, or would not, find life under Soviet domination worth living. So interpreted, the assumption would be absurdly narrow as the basis for a consequentialist argument. The assumption might, however, be more generously interpreted as expressing a view about whether it would be better for one's country *as a whole* to suffer nuclear destruction or to fall under Soviet domination. But even on this broader interpretation, an assumption of this sort would still be too narrow to serve as a premise in a plausible consequentialist argument, because it would still exclude from consideration the interests of persons in other countries—both enemy countries and countries not directly involved in the conflict. The interests of Americans are not the only interests that count. Nor, indeed, are existing generations the only generations that count. Thus, perhaps the most important reason why an assumption about whether it would be better to be red or dead is too narrow is that it fails to take account of the effects of nuclear war on future generations.

For these reasons, a consequentialist argument against nuclear deterrence based solely on the claim that it would be better to be red than dead would be implausible. But an analogous argument can be constructed on a broader foundation. The foundation would still consist in a comparison between the two outcomes: nuclear war and Soviet domination. But the comparison would take into consideration the interests of existing people everywhere, and would also take account of how future generations might fare in each of the two outcomes. The main aim of this essay is to present and discuss this analogous argument and, in particular, to defend its central assumption: that it is of the utmost moral importance to ensure the existence of future generations.

The argument, stated fully, is as follows:

1a. Nuclear war would be a greater evil than Soviet domination where future generations are concerned.

1b. Nuclear war would be worse than Soviet domination for people in the US and for people in allied countries which would also be directly involved in the war.

1c. Nuclear war would be worse than Soviet domination for people in countries not directly involved in the war, and it would also be worse for the Soviets and their allies.

2. It is therefore considerably more important to prevent nuclear war than it is to prevent Soviet domination.

3. The present policy of nuclear deterrence has a high probability of preventing Soviet domination, but it also has a significant probability of leading to nuclear war, even with the relatively near future—say, within the next 30 years.

4. The abandonment of nuclear deterrence by the US and the adoption of a policy of nonnuclear defense would decrease the probability of nuclear war, but would also increase the probability of Soviet domination. It would not, however, increase the latter probability by significantly more than it would decrease the former. Indeed, it might increase the latter by *less* than it would decrease the former.

5. Any other negative effects of this change in policy, even when considered together with the increase in the probability of Soviet domination, would not be sufficient to outweigh in importance the decrease in the probability of nuclear war.

6. One of two policies is superior if it would, when compared with the other policy, reduce the probability of a very bad outcome, even if it would also increase the probability of a significantly less bad outcome, provided that the increase in the latter probability would not be significantly greater than the decrease in the former, and provided that the adoption of the policy would not have other undesirable effects which, together with the increase in the probability of the less bad outcome, would outweigh the advantage of decreasing the probability of the very bad outcome.

7. A policy of unilateral nuclear disarmament by the US, combined with a policy of nonnuclear defense, would be superior to continued reliance on the present policy of nuclear deterrence.

(This argument also applies, *mutatis mutandis*, to the Soviet Union; but, since it is intended as a contribution to an essentially Western debate, it is preferable to direct the argument against the US, whose policies we are in a better position to influence.)

It is important to notice that the conclusion of the argument is *not* that unilateral nuclear disarmament would be the best policy for the US to adopt. That may well be true, but it is not entailed by the argument. The conclusion of the argument is only that unilateral nuclear disarmament is preferable to the present policy of nuclear deterrence. This leaves open the possibility that there may be some further alternative that would be superior to both—for example, a policy of minimal deterrence (that is, a policy that would aim to deter a nuclear attack, and nothing else, with the smallest arsenal that would be sufficient to guarantee deterrence).

The argument rests on a number of controversial claims, each of which might be challenged. My own view, however, is that each is defensible. Although I shall argue at some length in support of premise 1a, spatial constraints make it impossible to provide a thorough defense of any of the premises. I hope to say enough in support of each premise to show that the argument as a whole is indeed plausible. But my main aim must be simply to illuminate the structure of the argument, and to suggest what considerations are relevant to the assessment of the premises.

CONSEQUENCES FOR PRESENT GENERATIONS

It is primarily premise 1a—that nuclear war would be worse than Soviet domination where future generations are concerned—that makes this argument against nuclear deterrence distinctive. As we shall see, this initial premise is based on the assumption that it is considerably more important to ensure that future generations exist than to ensure that, if they exist, they will not exist under Soviet domination. Since my argument in support of this assumption is lengthy, controversial, and more distinctively philosophical in character than the discussions of the other premises of the argument, it merits a separate section to itself, which I shall reserve until after I have discussed and defended the other premises of the main argument; for it will help to see how the argument as a whole works before we focus on the justification of this one premise.

It might be suggested that premises 1b and 1c, which together assert that nuclear war would be worse for existing people than Soviet domination, would themselves be sufficient to establish premise 2—the claim that it is considerably more important to prevent nuclear war than to present Soviet domination. In that case, it might be thought that premise 1a would be superfluous. That would be a mistake. Premises 1a, 1b, and 1c work together to support premise 2. The more support there is for each of the first three premises, the stronger premise 2 will be—that is, the greater will be the relative importance of preventing nuclear war over preventing Soviet domination. And the greater the relative importance of preventing nuclear war is, the more readily and decisively will the argument carry through to its conclusion. (For the greater the relative importance of preventing nuclear war, the greater will be the increase in the probability of Soviet domination that we would accept in exchange for a fixed decrease in the probability of nuclear war.)

Bearing in mind this fact about the structure of the argument, let us provisionally grant premise 1a, and go on to consider premise 1b—the claim that nuclear war would be worse than Soviet domination for people in the US and allied countries. This claim is supported by several lines of argument. Since any two-sided nuclear war would be unlikely to remain limited,[1] nuclear war would probably result in the deaths of most people in the US and in allied countries. If most people would find life under Soviet domination worth living, then it follows that, for most of those who would be killed in a nuclear war, nuclear war would be worse than Soviet domination. And indeed it seems plausible to suppose that most people in the West would find life under Soviet domination worth living, just as most people do who presently live under Soviet domination.

Suppose that, contrary to this conjecture, many people would personally prefer death to life under Soviet domination—that is, they would not find life under Soviet domination worth living. Would this show that Soviet domination would be worse than nuclear destruction? Not necessarily; for the view that Soviet domination would be worse than nuclear destruction would presumably be based on a claim about the overriding importance of liberty, but the view is itself less attentive to the demands of liberty than the contrary view. It ignores the preferences of those would would prefer life under Soviet domination to death. But the view that nuclear destruction would be worse respects the preferences of those who would prefer death to life under Soviet domination, for Soviet domination would allow these individuals to choose death rather than submit to domination by the Soviets.[2] In short, while nuclear war would be worse for those who would prefer life under Soviet domination to death, Soviet domination need not be worse for those who would prefer death to life under Soviet domination.

What about those persons in the US and allied countries who might survive a nuclear war? Would life among the radioactive ruins of the US and Western Europe be preferable to life under Soviet domination? What primarily distinguishes life in many Western countries today from life in Soviet-dominated countries is that people in the West enjoy political, social, and economic freedoms denied to people in the East. These would not survive a nuclear war. Michael Howard has claimed that, from the point of view of the survivors of a nuclear war, "the political, cultural and ideological distinctions that separate the West from the Soviet Union today would be seen, in comparison with the literally inconceivable contrasts between *any* pre-atomic and *any* post-atomic society, as almost insignificant."[3] His main reason for this claim is that any regime that might emerge in the US after a nuclear war would be inescapably authoritarian, and thus would, in this crucial respect, resemble the regime that governs the Soviet Union today.

What about those who, in spite of this, would prefer life amid the postwar ruins to life under Soviet domination? The short answer is simply that, while Soviet domination would of course deny them their preference, it is by no means clear that nuclear war would satisfy it, for survival in nuclear war cannot be guaranteed.

Together these arguments provide strong support for the claim that nuclear war would be worse than Soviet domination for people in the US and in allied countries. Let us turn, then, to the claim that nuclear war would also be worse for people elsewhere in the world. It is, of course, completely uncontroversial that nuclear war would be worse than Soviet domination for people in the Soviet Union and allied countries. It is, however, less clear that nuclear war would be worse than Soviet domination for people in countries not directly involved in the war. One reason why this comparison is more difficult is that it is uncertain what the effects of nuclear war would be in neutral countries. It is arguable that nuclear war would result in the deaths of most, if not all, of the people in these countries.[4] In that case nuclear war would be worse for these people than Soviet domination, for the same reasons that it would be worse for people in the US and allied countries. But suppose that the effects would be more limited—for example, that they would consist primarily in a certain number of immediate deaths from fallout, and in environmental damage, increased rates of cancer and birth defects, and severe political and economic dislocation. Even in this case the upheaval in these countries would be enormous, and would be likely to give rise to authoritarian political structures no less repressive than those in Soviet-dominated countries today. Thus it is difficult to believe that life under these conditions would be better than life under Soviet domination.

For many of the world's people, life in a world dominated by the Soviet Union might be no worse than life is at present. It is difficult to substantiate this claim, however, partly because it is difficult to predict what a world dominated by the Soviet Union would be like. Conditions would undoubtedly be different in different places. But, if it is permissible to extrapolate from our knowledge of life today in Soviet-dominated countries, the claim has some plausibility. Life in Soviet bloc countries today seems, in general, no worse than life in many other countries—some of which are effectively under American domination. To see the force of this point, one might ask oneself, for example, whether one would prefer to be a dissident in Poland today or to have been a dissident in Iran under the Shah. While American governments have shown far greater respect than Soviet leaders for the rights and liberties of their own citizens, their concern for the rights and liberties of citizens of Third World client states has been no greater than that shown by Soviet leaders toward the citizens of Soviet client states.[5] To say this is not to present an apology for Soviet efforts to control the affairs of other countries, but only to provide a *comparative* evaluation of the possible consequences of Soviet domination for people outside the US and Western Europe.

The foregoing arguments provide strong support for the claim that nuclear war would be worse for existing people than Soviet domination. If we provisionally grant that nuclear war would also be worse where future generations are concerned, then it seems clear that nuclear war would be a far greater evil than Soviet domination, and therefore that it is considerably more important to prevent nuclear war than to prevent Soviet domination. In other words, premise 2 is true.

Let us turn, then, to premise 3. Defenders of the present policy of nuclear deterrence will not, of course, object to the claim that this policy has a high probability of preventing Soviet domination. But they will deny that there is a significant probability of nuclear war in the relatively near future under nuclear deterrence as it is currently practiced. Strictly speaking, the argument does not actually require the claim that nuclear deterrence is likely to lead to nuclear war; all it requires is the claim that an alternative policy would have a *lower* probability of leading to nuclear war, without having a significantly higher probability of leading to Soviet domination. Nevertheless, there are several reasons for including the claim that nuclear deterrence as it is presently practiced is likely to lead to nuclear war. One is that, if correct, the claim provides the argument with additional urgency. Premise 6, in particular, seems most cogent in cases in which the worse outcome is highly probable under the alternative policy. Another reason for including the claim is that the arguments that support it will help to show why the shift to a policy of nonnuclear defense would greatly reduce the probability of nuclear war. A brief critique of the present policy of nuclear deterrence will set the stage for a defense of an alternative policy. But the most important reason for including the claim that the present policy of nuclear deterrence has a significant probability of leading the nuclear war is that, without this claim, the argument would be less likely to go through. For, if the probability of nuclear war under nuclear deterrence were very low, then there would be little scope for reducing it by shifting to a policy of nonnuclear defense. And since, as I have conceded, the probability of Soviet domination under nuclear deterrence is low, the scope for increasing it by shifting to a policy of nonnuclear defense is considerable. Given this combination of background conditions, it might seem more reasonable to suppose that the shift to a policy of nonnuclear defense would increase the probability of Soviet domination by significantly more than it would reduce the probability of nuclear war.

Nuclear deterrence as it is presently practiced has a significant probability of leading to nuclear war, for at least five reasons. All five are familiar, and thus require little elaboration here.

1. The practice of deterrence has led (some say necessarily) to the development by both sides of counterforce weapons and the adoption of counterforce strategies. The characteristics necessary for counterforce weapons are the same as those necessary and sufficient for first-strike weapons. Thus, each side's deployments now pose a threat to the other's retaliatory capability. As each develops its counterforce capability, it will have an increasing incentive to use this capability in a first strike of its own. The fears generated by each side's sense of ever-increasing vulnerability, combined with other pressures to insure that deterrence remains "credible," in turn lead to yet more destabilizing new deployments.

2. The practice of nuclear deterrence leads inexorably to competition in the development of new technologies. Each side feels it must press forward with its own research; otherwise the other side might arrive unilaterally at technological discoveries that would provide a decisive strategic advantage. This technological side of the arms race leads not only to fears and suspicions about the sinister projects the other side may be pursuing, but also to the development of dangerously

destabilizing technologies—both of which aggravate the threat of war. For example, early research on ballistic missile defenses led to the development of MIRV's, which have in turn (in conjunction with increases in missile accuracy) given rise to fears of a first strike.

3. The possession of nuclear weapons in large numbers makes it not unlikely that a nuclear war will start by accident or mistake. This could happen in various ways. The most likely is that one side might launch its missiles under the mistaken impression that it is itself under attack. False alarms are in fact a disturbingly frequent occurrence.[6]

4. Nuclear deterrence both sanctions and encourages nuclear proliferation, and nuclear proliferation increases the probability of nuclear war. Nuclear deterrence sanctions proliferation because most of the arguments supporting the possession of a nuclear arsenal for purposes of deterrence are universal in their application; they do not refer to unique features of any particular country's situation. Deterrence also encourages proliferation in at least two ways. The possession of nuclear weapons for purposes of deterrence provides continuing testimony to their value. It also poses a threat to the security of nonnuclear countries, which these countries, following the logic and the example of the threatener, may attempt to meet by developing nuclear arsenals of their own. Thus, fear of the US and the Soviet Union prompted China to develop its arsenal, and fear of the Chinese arsenal at least partly motivated the development of India's nuclear capability. Fear of the Indian capability has now spurred Pakistan's efforts to acquire a nuclear arsenal.

5. Nuclear deterrence stimulates and, indeed, requires the mutual fear and hatred that are more likely than anything else to lead eventually to war. Politicians often find it necessary, as Senator Vandenberg once advised President Truman, "to scare the hell out of the country" with visions of the "communist menace" to whip up public support for expanded arms programs. Even in the absence of this calculated manipulation of our fears, we would naturally fear and hate those who perpetually threaten to incinerate us. But we may also find it psychologically necessary to hate anyone whom we threaten with annihilation. Our consciences may require that we cast our potential victims in evil and dehumanizing roles, as President Reagan did when he described the Soviet Union as "an evil empire" and claimed that communism is "the focus of evil in the modern world."[7] Under deterrence, these attitudes cannot be significantly relaxed. Thus, E.P. Thompson writes that, "by maintaining each part in a posture of menace to the other, nuclear deterrence fixes indefinitely the tension which makes the resolution of differences improbable."[8]

With these five points as background, let us now turn to the defense of premise 4. This premise makes several factual claims. The first is that the adoption of a policy of nonnuclear defense would reduce the probability of nuclear war. A nonnuclear defense policy would require complete unilateral nuclear disarmament and a reliance on various types of nonnuclear forces for the country's defense. It might, for example, involve greatly strengthening the US's conventional forces; it might involve the reintroduction of conscription (with, one hopes, more generous provisions for conscientious objection than in the past); it might involve the formation of a territorial militia; or it might involve a greatly expanded civil defense program. These are just some of the possibilities. The important point is that, while such a policy would require unilateral nuclear disarmament, it would *not* leave the US defenseless.

The adoption of a nonnuclear defense policy would reduce the probability of nuclear war, for at least six reasons. Five of these refer back to the reasons why nuclear deterrence as presently practiced is likely to lead to nuclear war.

1. The adoption of a nonnuclear defense policy would reduce the probability of a preemptive first strike virtually to zero. Nuclear disarmament would deprive the U.S. of the *ability* to launch a first strike, and it would deprive the Soviet Union of its primary *target* for one. It is sometimes suggested that the Soviets might be tempted to attack the US to prevent the possibility of American nuclear rearmament. But to achieve this aim they would have to attack and destroy all the many nuclear reactors in the US, and they would surely be deterred from such an attack by the fact that it would produce a vast amount of global fallout. It might also be objected that American nuclear disarmament would remove the major obstacle to a Soviet preemptive strike against the Chinese. But, if the Soviets were tempted to attack the Chinese, they would presumably be restrained more by an awareness of the damage such an attack would do to their international reputation than by fears of American retaliation, which would be extremely unlikely.[9]

2. A policy of nonnuclear defense would slow the competition in the development of nuclear technologies by removing one of the two main competitors.

3. A nonnuclear defense policy would greatly reduce the probability of an accidental nuclear war. It would eliminate the possibility of an accidental or unauthorized firing by the US, and would also eliminate the possibility that an accidental firing by the Soviets would lead to retaliation and uncontrollable escalation.

4. A policy of nonnuclear defense might have an inhibiting effect on proliferation. It would presumably restrict the transfer of nuclear materials from the US to other countries. Since it would also fulfill the US's obligations under the Non-Proliferation Treaty, it might help to revitalize the treaty. Finally, just as the present policy of nuclear deterrence testifies to the value of nuclear weapons, so the abandonment of nuclear weapons by the US would testify to the dangers that attend the possession of nuclear weapons.

5. The adoption of a policy of nonnuclear defense would serve to reassure the Soviets about American intentions, and so would help to dispel the fears, suspicions, tensions, and animosities that presently constitute the single most important factor dragging the world toward war.

6. The adoption of a policy of nonnuclear defense could lead the Soviets to reciprocate by greatly reducing the number of their nuclear weapons. This might occur as the natural result of the relaxation of tensions consequent upon the change in American policy. Or, more cynically, it might happen because the Soviets would not wish to be seen as relentlessly militaristic in comparison with the US. They would, in any case, have little to lose by dismantling a large number of their weapons for, given that a significant percentage of their nuclear weapons are at presented targeted on American missile silos and bomber bases, the elimination of the US's nuclear arsenal would deprive most of the Soviet missiles of their targets.

At this point it may be objected that these arguments either ignore the deterrent effect of the possession of nuclear weapons, or else assume that Soviet intentions are wholly benign. A policy of nonnuclear defense would deprive the US of the ability to deter a nuclear attack, and thus, it might be argued, would *increase* the probability of nuclear war rather than decrease it.

In response to this objection we need to ask what reason the Soviets would have for a nuclear attack on the US if the US had renounced the possession of nuclear weapons. Since the US would no longer pose an offensive threat to the Soviet Union, they could have no defensive reason for attacking, and the idea that the Soviets might attack out of sheer malice seems excessively cynical. The most plausible suggestion is that they might make selective nuclear strikes in an attempt to achieve domination or conquest. In particular, actual or threatened nuclear strikes might be used in an effort to coerce the surrender of the US, and thereby to establish the global dominance of the Soviet Union.

It would seem, then, that what is really being claimed when it is said that the abandonment of nuclear deterrence would increase the probability of nuclear war is that the abandonment of nuclear deterrence would increase the probability of Soviet nuclear blackmail. But the limited, coercive nuclear strikes the Soviets *might* make in an effort to achieve domination over the US would not constitute nuclear war in the sense intended in the premises of the main argument. These premises presuppose a conception of nuclear war such that nuclear war would involve the relatively extensive use of nuclear weapons, and would result in widespread destruction. Otherwise—if one or two nuclear strikes would count as a nuclear war—the first four premises of the argument would presumably be false.

Given this understanding of what counts as nuclear war, the adoption of a policy of nonnuclear defense would clearly reduce the probability of nuclear war: it would greatly reduce the probability of the extensive use of nuclear weapons. The real objection to the adoption of a nonnuclear defense policy, then, is that it would increase the risk of nuclear blackmail, and thus would increase the probability of Soviet domination. Since the US would certainly be able to defend its borders under a policy of nonnuclear defense, Soviet domination could probably be achieved only through some form of nuclear coercion, involving either actual or threatened nuclear destruction. Thus, a limited amount of nuclear destruction in the US should be counted among the possible costs of Soviet domination. (It might be objected that, if we assume that Soviet domination might involve a limited amount of nuclear destruction, this will weaken the case for premises 1a through 2. I think, however, that careful reflection on the arguments for those premises will show that they are not undermined by this assumption. If Soviet domination would involve a limited amount of nuclear destruction, that would of course make it worse than it would otherwise be, precisely because it would then involve some of the evils characteristic of an even worse outcome—all-out nuclear war.)

How likely would it be that the US, if it were to give up nuclear weapons, would be subjected to nuclear blackmail leading, if successful, to Soviet domination? The answer depends in part on our assessment of the motives and goals of the dominant Soviet leaders. If, as is arguable, Soviet military policies are motivated primarily by defensive concerns, then the abandonment of nuclear deterrence would not significantly increase the probability of nuclear blackmail or Soviet domination. It would, however, be unwise to rest the argument on sanguine assumptions about Soviet motivations. So we should assume that the familiar allegations about the Soviets' aggressive designs have some plausibility. And we must therefore concede that the abandonment of nuclear deterrence might significantly increase the probability of nuclear blackmail and Soviet domination. But, even if the Russians would no longer be restrained by fear of nuclear retaliation, they would still have other reasons for refraining from attempting nuclear blackmail. One is that nuclear threats or an actual nuclear attack would almost certainly provoke an effort at nuclear rearmament by the US. Moreover, the Soviets could not hope to subdue the entire world simultaneously, and other countries with a potential nuclear capability might be frightened into developing their own nuclear arsenals, which would then be arrayed against the Soviet Union. For an attempt at subjugating the US through nuclear blackmail, the Soviet Union would probably pay a high price in the creation of a large number of determined enemies. Finally, even if the effort at nuclear blackmail were to succeed, the Soviets would still face what I think would be predictably insurmountable problems in trying to subjugate and control the United States, a large country, both geographically and in terms of population, whose population is remarkably united in its hostility to Soviet communism.[10]

In short, while shifting to a policy of nonnuclear defense would undoubtedly increase the probability of nuclear blackmail and Soviet domination, how much it would do so is a matter of speculation. But, given that the shift to a policy of nonnuclear defense would *greatly* reduce the probability of large-scale nuclear war, it is hard to believe that it would increase the probability of Soviet domination by *significantly more* than it would decrease the probability of nuclear war. If it would not, then that is all that the argument requires.

We have so far compared the present policy of nuclear deterrence with a policy of nonnuclear defense with respect to two possible outcomes: nuclear war and Soviet domination. Either or both of these policies, however, might lead to other possible outcomes. If we were to compare the two policies with respect to all the possible outcomes, the argument would become hopelessly complex. Thus premise 5 has been introduced to eliminate the need to conduct a series of detailed comparisons. It asserts that the apparent superiority of a policy of nonnuclear defense over the present policy of nuclear deterrence where nuclear war and Soviet domination are concerned is not outweighed by the superiority of nuclear deterrence where other possible outcomes are concerned.

The strongest challenge to this premise lies in the claim that the shift to a policy of nonnuclear defense would greatly increase the probability of conventional war. While it is unlikely that the Soviet Union would be tempted to launch a conventional attack against the US, it might be less inhibited about initiating conventional war elsewhere in the world—for example, in Western Europe. At present the possibility of escalation to all-out nuclear war helps to deter any type of attack on the US or its allies. Since the adoption of a policy of nonnuclear defense would eliminate this threat, the risks of conventional aggression might then appear acceptable.

This is an important challenge, but I think it can be met. There are three relevant points. One is that the possibility of American nuclear rearmament would have a deterrent effect. But a more important point is this. There are two ways to dissuade a potential aggressor from attacking. One is to threaten him with punishment if he does attack, so that the benefits he might derive from attacking would be outweighed by the harm he would suffer. Nuclear deterrence attempts to influence a potential attacker's calculations in this way. The other way is to arrange things so that, whatever his aim in attacking, he would be unable to achieve that aim. This second form of dissuasion is often referred to as "deterrence by gain denial" or "defensive deterrence."

Unlike strategic nuclear attacks, conventional attacks can be effectively deterred by defensive means. Indeed, the threat of "gain denial" is in general a more *credible* deterrent to conventional attack by a nuclear-armed aggressor than the threat of retaliation, since defensive measures do not involve the same risks that retaliation involves. Already there is a strong movement of opinion in Western Europe favoring a policy of defensive deterrence in Europe. Since the total gross domestic product of the European NATO countries alone is substantially greater than that of the Warsaw Pact (including the Soviet Union), there is no doubt that collaboration between the European NATO countries and the US could lead to the development of nonnuclear forces amply sufficient to defeat, and therefore to deter, a conventional Warsaw Pact invasion.

At this point it may be objected that the Warsaw Pact could overcome NATO's nonnuclear defenses through the use of tactical nuclear weapons, so that the likeliest consequence of America's abandonment of nuclear deterrence would not be a conventional attack on Europe, but a *combined* conventional and tactical nuclear attack. This objection assumes that tactical nuclear weapons provide strong or perhaps even decisive tactical advantages. This assumption seems to me to be false. Spatial constraints prevent me from challenging it here, although I have done so elsewhere.[11]

The third point that can be made in response to the charge that American nuclear disarmament would increase the probability of conventional war is in part an *ad hominem* point. Many of those who argue that nuclear weapons are needed to deter conventional war claim that the deterrence of conventional war is nearly as important as the deterrence of nuclear war, for modern conventional war would be only marginally less terrible than nuclear war. But, if it is true that conventional war would be that destructive, then it follows that the threat of conventional destruction should be virtually as effective a deterrent to conventional war as the threat of escalation to nuclear war.

The possibility of American nuclear rearmament, the threat of effective "gain denial," and the terrible destruction potential of modern conventional warfare could together provide a strong deterrent to conventional war. Thus, if the adoption of a policy of nonnuclear defense would increase the probability of conventional war, it need not do so by much.

Even if we assume that the adoption of a policy of nonnuclear defense would have other negative effects than the increase in the probability of Soviet domination, these other effects would at least in part be cancelled out by certain other positive effects of the change in policy. Among these positive effects would be a significant decrease in the production of nuclear wastes, a significant reduction of the probability of a serious nuclear accident, and the elimination of the threat posed to civil liberties and democratic institutions by the possession of nuclear weapons. All things considered, it seems likely that a policy of nonnuclear defense could satisfy the condition stated in premise 5.

As I have suggested, premise 5 is intended to deal with the fact that negative outcomes other than nuclear war and Soviet domination are relevant to the comparison between nuclear deterrence and nonnuclear defense. At this point it may be objected that my argument gives insufficient attention to the main *positive* outcome relevant to the comparison of the two policies—the continuation of the status quo, or the avoidance of *both* nuclear war and Soviet domination. For it is surely relevant to the comparison of the two policies to ask which has the greater probability of avoiding both these disastrous outcomes.

In an important paper on the subject of nuclear deterrence, Gregory Kavka proposes and defends a principle he calls the Disaster Avoidance Principle. The principle asserts that when choosing between potential disasters under two-dimensional uncertainty [that is, "the chooser has no reliable quantitative estimates of the relevant utilities and probabilities, but has confidence in his judgment of their ordinal rankings"], it is rational to select the alternative that minimizes the probability of disaster occurrence.[12]

Kavka claims that this principle supports nuclear deterrence over unilateral nuclear disarmament (or nonnuclear defense) since, of the two policies, nuclear deterrence offers the greater probability of avoiding both relevant disasters, nuclear war and Soviet domination. He claims that, because of this, the policy of nuclear deterrence is superior, even though it has a greater probability of leading to the worse of the two disasters. This argument directly challenges the plausibility of the principle stated as premise 6 in my argument.

Kavka's claim that nuclear deterrence offers the greater probability of maintaining the status quo is based on the assumption that the probability of nuclear war under nuclear deterrence is less than the probability of Soviet domination would be under unilateral nuclear disarmament. I think that my earlier arguments show that this assumption is very much open to doubt, although it is compatible with the main argument of this essay. But, even supposing that his assumption is correct, it is not sufficient to establish that nuclear deterrence offers the greater probability of disaster avoidance. To establish this conclusion, it is necessary to make the further assumption that the probability of nuclear war under unilateral nuclear disarmament would be greater than (or at least not less than) the probability of Soviet domination under nuclear deterrence. For, if the probability of nuclear war under unilateral nuclear disarmament would be *less* than the probability of Soviet domination under nuclear deterrence, then, given Kavka's assumption that there are no reliable quantitative estimates of the relevant probabilities, we could not know which of the two policies would provide the greater probability of disaster avoidance.

It is not implausible, moreover, to suppose that the probability of nuclear war under unilateral nuclear disarmament *would* be less than the probability of Soviet domination under nuclear deterrence. I have already suggested why I think that the probability of nuclear war under unilateral nuclear disarmament would be very low. And, although I have conceded that the probability of Soviet domination under nuclear deterrence is low, even the most ardent proponents of nuclear deterrence have argued that the probability is not insignificant. They have argued that any number of apparently insignificant weaknesses in the American strategic position could give the Soviets a psychological advantage and enable them to coerce the US to surrender.[13]

Of course, nothing I have said so far has been sufficient to prove the falsity of either of the assumptions necessary to show that nuclear deterrence offers a greater probability of disaster avoidance. But I think enough has been said to show that neither assumption is obviously true. This being the case, it is not clear whether Kavka's Disaster Avoidance Principle is actually applicable to the comparison between nuclear deterrence and unilateral nuclear disarmament (or whether, if it is applicable, it actually favors nuclear deterrence). This suggests that, in comparing these two policies, it is *at least* equally plausible to appeal to my premise 6 as it is to appeal to the Disaster Avoidance Principle.[14]

A further objection to my argument that might be mentioned here is that, since each of us would (one hopes) be willing to risk death to defend his country,[15] we should all be willing to risk nuclear destruction by supporting nuclear deterrence, in order to prevent Soviet domination. Yet, there are important differences between risking individual death and risking collective death. One is that to risk collective death is to put future generations at risk as well. If it matters whether future generations will exist, then each individual may be willing to risk his own life only on the assumption that failure will not entail the death of all. Thus from a willingness of each to risk his own life we cannot infer a willingness of all to risk the lives of all.

The foregoing arguments, while not conclusive, should be sufficient to show that premises 1b through 6 are not obviously implausible. It remains to be shown that premise 1a is also defensible.

CONSEQUENCES FOR FUTURE GENERATIONS

The main reason for thinking that nuclear war would be worse than Soviet domination where future generations are concerned is that nuclear war could lead to the extinction of the human race, and it is considerably more important to ensure that future generations will exist than to ensure that, if they exist, they will not exist under Soviet domination. Of course, it is by no means certain that nuclear war would lead to extinction. On the contrary, most scientists seem to agree that extinction would be unlikely. On the other hand, it seems uncontroversial that a large-scale nuclear war (which is probably the only possible kind of nuclear war) would greatly reduce both the number of future people and the future quality of life. It will become evident that, because of this, the explanation I shall offer of why extinction would be a terrible tragedy will also imply the truth of premise 1a even on the assumption that nuclear war would not lead to extinction. Thus my argument in this section will support the claim that nuclear war would be worse than Soviet domination where future generations are concerned regardless of whether or not nuclear war would lead to extinction—although the extent to which nuclear war would be worse than Soviet domination will be greater the more likely it is that nuclear war would lead to extinction.

The claim on which premise 1a rests, and which I hope to establish in this section, is that it is of the utmost moral importance to ensure the existence of future generations. Many people feel intuitively that this claim is correct, but are nevertheless unable to find arguments to support their conviction.[16] Others believe the only moral reasons for ensuring the existence of future generations are those that arise from the fact that we, the living, prefer that there should be future generations—because, for example, we desire to have children.[17] After all (it might be argued), preventing the existence of future generations could not be worse for future generations themselves, for nothing can be worse for people who never exist; so preventing their existence would not be against *their* interests or violate their rights. If those who argue in this way are right and the only reasons we have for ensuring the existence of future generations are ones that appeal to our own interests, then premise 1a will contribute nothing to support the claim that nuclear war would be worse than Soviet domination which is not already provided by the claim that it would be worse for existing people.

This challenge to premise 1a might be developed in the following way. It is only on the condition that future generations will exist that we can affect their interests. Thus, a concern for their interests cannot provide a reason for ensuring their existence. On the other hand, a concern for their interests can and, indeed, does provide a reason for ensuring that, *if* they exist, they will not exist under Soviet domination. In the words of one recent writer, "if we believe that the risks of deterrence are worth taking for ourselves than we need not shrink from taking them . . . for our descendants."[18] This is so (it might be argued) because, while *we* have much to lose if the gamble fails and the race is exterminated, future generations would, strictly speaking, lose nothing at all.

This argument rests on a mistake that has been exposed by Derek Parfit.[19] Suppose that, as a result of American nuclear disarmament, the Soviets were to dominate the world. This would obviously have widespread effects on people's lives everywhere. There would be important contrasts between life under Soviet domination and life as it would otherwise have been. One important contrast, often ignored, is that different people would meet, and different marriages would be made, so that different children would be born. Even in those marriages that would be the same, children would be conceived at different times and thus would develop from different genetic materials. As Parfit has shown, this would in fact be sufficient to make them different children. In short, if the Soviets came to dominate the world, this would dramatically affect who would subsequently exist. As time passed, the proportion of people who would not have existed had the Soviets not dominated the world would increase until eventually there would be no one in existence who would also have existed had the Soviets not dominated the world. There would, therefore, be relatively few future people of whom it could be said that they were affected for the worse by American nuclear disarmament and the subsequent domination of the world by the Soviets. Assuming that the others would have lives worth living, they could not claim to have been affected for the worse by Soviet domination, since, were it not for Soviet domination, *they* would not have existed.

This shows that, in the case of most future people, our reason for ensuring that they will not exist under Soviet domination cannot derive from a concern for their interests. Our reason must instead be more impersonal in character. But from a more *impersonal* point of view it must surely be more important that future generations exist, if their lives would be worth living, than that they do not exist under Soviet domination—especially since Soviet domination could not be expected to last forever.

I shall reinforce this conclusion with several arguments for the claim that, while preventing the existence of future generations would not be against their interests, it is nevertheless of the utmost moral importance not to prevent their existence. One such argument appeals to the fact that our lives would be impoverished by the expectation that we will be the final generation. At present our lives are enriched by the assumption that they will be linked in various ways with the lives of future people. We rely on future generations for the furtherance and completion of projects we have begun or taken over from our ancestors; we depend on them to preserve and enrich our culture, and to help fulfill our ideals; and we hope that they will benefit from and appreciate our works, providing us with posthumous recognition. If we were to suppose that there would be no future generations, many of our present activities would be robbed of much of their meaning.[20]

These are undoubtedly important reasons for ensuring the existence of future generations. Again, however, if the force of these points is *only* that it would be worse for existing people if there were to be no future generations, then these points will contribute nothing to the larger argument against nuclear deterrence that is not already provided by premises 1b and 1c. It is, however, equally plausible to suppose that there is *independent* value in, say, the evolution of our culture, so that it is important for our culture to continue to develop quite apart from the fact that *our* lives would be impoverished by the belief that the evolution of our culture were at an end. If this further claim is accepted, we have a reason for ensuring the existence for future generations that is independent of the interests of existing people.

Another and perhaps stronger argument for the claim that it is morally important to ensure the existence of future generations also makes no appeal to the interests of existing people. This argument moves from the claim that there is a principle of non-maleficence that provides a moral reason not to bring a person into existence if his life would be worse than no life at all, or "worth not living," to the claim that there is a principle of beneficence that provides a moral reason to bring a person into existence if his life would, on balance, be worth living. The argument takes as its first premise the claim that it would be wrong, other things being equal, to bring a person into existence if his life would predictably be worth not living. This seems uncontroversial. But how can we best explain *why* it would be wrong? It is tempting to appeal to side-effects, to the fact that it is normally worse for existing people if a person who is utterly wretched comes to exist. But this explanation is excluded by the *ceteris paribus* clause. And in any case the appeal to side-effects could provide only a partial explanation of why it would be wrong to bring a miserable person into existence. For it is only contingently true that it is worse for existing people when miserable people come into existence. There could be cases in which this would be better for existing people.

A second possible explanation is that to bring a miserable person into existence is worse *impersonally*, since it would involve a net increase in the amount of misery in the world. The argument could in fact be run on the basis of this explanation, and the conclusion would be substantially the same (although it would differ in form). But this second explanation seems less plausible than a third: that it is wrong to bring a person into existence if his life would be worth not living simply because to do so would be bad for that person—not just impersonally bad, or bad "from the point of view of the universe," but bad from the point of view of the person himself. To bring such a person into existence would be to *harm* that person. Of course, in order to defend the view that it would be wrong to bring a person into existence if his life would be worth not living, we need more than the simple claim that to bring such a person into existence would be to harm him. We also need the further claim that, other things being equal, it is wrong to do what will harm people. This too seems uncontroversial. Most people accept as part of their morality a principle of non-maleficence.

The next stage in the argument is to point out that, if to bring into existence a person whose life is worth not living is to harm that person, then to bring into existence a person whose life *is* worth living must be to benefit that person.[21] If, in addition to a principle of non-maleficence, we also accept a principle of beneficence, then it follows that there is a moral reason to benefit people by bringing them into existence.

Now, there are several ways of resisting this conclusion which are compatible with the assumption that to bring into existence a person whose life is worth living is to benefit that person. The most obvious is to deny that there is a moral reason to benefit people. If there is a moral reason not to harm people but no moral reason to benefit people, then it follows, given our assumption that to be brought into existence can be either a benefit or a harm, that it would be wrong, other things being equal, to bring a miserable person into existence, but not wrong not to bring into existence a person whose life would be worth living.

While it is commonly assumed that it is morally more important to prevent or alleviate misery than to promote happiness, the claim that there is *no* moral reason to promote happiness—*no* general reason to benefit people—seems unacceptably strong. Among other things, it implies that it would not be wrong to fail to prevent a dramatic decline in the quality of life, as long as the decline involved only the loss of certain sources of happiness, and not an increase in suffering or misery. It implies that this would not be wrong even if the decline could be prevented at little or no cost to the agent. This seems unacceptable.[22]

Another way of denying that the expectation that a person would have a life worth living provides a moral reason for bringing him into existence is to appeal to the view that there is a moral asymmetry between *doing* and *not doing*—the view that we are morally more responsible for what happens as a result of what we do than we are for what happens as a result of what we do not do. If a person's coming into existence can be either good or bad for that person, then the coming-into-existence of a miserable person and the not-coming-into-existence of a happy person are both undesirable outcomes. Bringing a miserable person into existence is a case of *doing*; not bringing a happy person into existence is a case of *not doing*. Thus, assuming that there is a moral asymmetry between doing and not doing, it follows that to bring a miserable person into existence is worse than not to bring a happy person into existence.

Again, however, this view will have to take an unacceptably strong form in order to imply that it is not wrong, other things being equal, to fail to bring into existence a person whose life would be worth living. It would have to assert that, except in the case of special obligations, such as those derived through promising, we cannot be held responsible for what happens or fails to happen as a result of our not doing something. Since this view implies that it cannot be wrong, other things being equal, to fail to prevent a person from being harmed, I shall assume that it is unacceptable.

A third and seemingly more plausible way of denying that there is a moral reason to benefit people by bringing them into existence is to appeal to the principle that an act cannot be wrong unless there is or would be someone for whom that act would be bad, or worse. Call this principle the "Complainant Requirement." Since we are assuming that to bring a miserable person into existence would be bad for that person, the Complainant Requirement is compatible with the claim that it would be wrong to bring a miserable person into existence. Moreover, if we assume that it is worse for a person to fail to receive a benefit, then the Complainant Requirement is also compatible with the view that there is a moral reason to benefit people. But it also implies that it cannot be wrong not to bring into existence a person whose life would be worth living, even though to bring him into existence would be to benefit him. For, if we do not bring him into existence, there will be no one for whom that will be worse (unless, of course, it would be worse for some existing person). In short, the Complainant Requirement takes account of the important fact that, if we fail to bring a potentially happy person into existence, that cannot be bad for someone who never in fact exists.

In spite of its apparent plausibility, the Complainant Requirement is unacceptable. To see why, consider the following case.[23] Suppose that we are confronted with a choice between two social policies. One policy (the "short-term policy") would provide certain marginal benefits for existing people, but would also cause a decline in the quality of life in the further future. This decline would not be so severe that people's lives would not be worth living, but the quality of life would be significantly lower than it would have been had we adopted the other policy (the "long-term policy") instead. The long-term policy would provide no benefits for existing people, but it would allow us to sustain a high quality of life indefinitely. It seems clear that it would be wrong to adopt the short-term policy.

The Complainant Requirement, however, implies that it would not be wrong to adopt the short-term policy. Recall the earlier claim that the identity of a person depends on the timing of his conception. Since the implementation of the short-term policy would have widespread effects on the details of people's lives, it would affect who would subsequently exist. After a certain time, there would be no one in existence who would have existed had the short-term policy not been adopted. Thus the people who would exist in the further future when the quality of life has declined would not have existed had the short-term policy not been adopted. Since their lives would be worth living, the adoption of the short-term policy cannot be worse *for them*. Since it would be better for existing people, the short-term policy is not worse for anyone who ever lives. So, according to the Complainant Requirement, it cannot be wrong to adopt the short-term policy. If we believe it *would* be wrong to adopt the short-term policy, then we must reject the Complainant Requirement.

A final possibility might be to appeal to some theory of rights. While a case can be made for thinking that one can have violated a person's rights by bringing him into a predictably miserable existence, it cannot be claimed that one would violate a person's rights by *failing* to bring him into existence. But, while the appeal to rights excludes the possibility that one could have a duty, based on a respect for people's rights, to bring into existence a person whose life would be worth living, it does not exclude the possibility that there might be some *other* moral reason for bringing him into existence. To support the conclusion that it cannot be wrong, other things being equal, not to bring such a person into existence, one would need the further claim that an act cannot be wrong unless it violates a right, which is absurd.

I know of no other way in which we can accept that to be brought into existence can be a benefit and at the same time deny that there is a moral reason to bring a person into existence if his life would be worth living. By default, therefore, I think we must accept that there is a moral reason to bring a person into existence if his life could be expected to be worth living. There is a principle of beneficence that requires us, if other things are equal, to benefit people by bringing them into existence. While this conclusion may initially seem counterintuitive, it draws further support from the fact that it helps to explain the widespread conviction that it is morally imperative to ensure the existence of future generations. Our moral reason to ensure the existence of future generations is at least in part a moral reason to provide, or not to prevent, the enormous benefits of life for the enormous number of people who might exist in the indefinite future.

This conclusion does not, however, fully account for the common belief that it is of the utmost moral importance to ensure the existence of future generations. To see this, let us compare two choices. The first is the choice between human extinction and the perpetuation of the human race. The second is a hypothetical choice between perpetuating the human race only on earth and perpetuating it both on earth and on some other planet. In this second choice, the alternative that involves populating another planet would, we may suppose, roughly double the number of people who would exist in the future. And we may suppose that life on the other planet would be of the same quality as life here. Thus the first alternative in each of these two choices would involve denying life to roughly the same number of people: extinction would deny life to a large number of people who would have benefited from being alive, but so would the failure to populate another planet. Our intuitive conviction is that the failure to ensure the survival of the species would be far worse than the failure to populate two planets rather than one, but we cannot account for this conviction by appealing to our moral reason to benefit people by bringing them into existence. If other things were equal, our principle of beneficence would imply that the failure to populate two planets rather than one would be just as bad as the failure to ensure the survival of the species.

This problem can be solved by appealing to our first two arguments for the conclusion that it is important to ensure the existence of future generations to explain why it would be worse to fail to prevent the extinction of the species than to fail to populate two planets rather than one. The failure to prevent the extinction of the species would deprive the lives of existing people of much of their meaning and would also bring the evolution of our culture to an end, while the failure to populate two planets would not. For these reasons the failure to prevent extinction would be worse than the failure to populate two planets.[24]

There is, however, a further objection to my argument. It is an objection to the claim that a partial explanation of why it is important to ensure the existence of future generations lies in the fact that there is a moral reason to benefit people by bringing them into existence. I shall conclude by briefly stating this objection and sketching a possible solution to it.

It is natural to assume that, when we benefit a person and other things are equal, this leads to a better state of affairs. Thus we could in principle continue to improve a state of affairs, *ceteris paribus*, just by increasing the number of lives worth living. Consider a world in which everyone has a life worth living, but of a relatively low quality. This world would become better and better the more people it contained, other things being equal. Thus, if it were sufficiently populous, it could in principle be better than *any* world with a finite number of lives, all of which would be well worth living. This has, for obvious reasons, been called "the Repugnant Conclusion."[25]

As long as we assume that there is value in increasing the number of lives worth living, we will be threatened with the Repugnant Conclusion. But my claim that the expectation that a person would have a life worth living provides a moral reason for bringing him into existence does not *necessarily* imply this conclusion. My earlier argument does not imply that our moral reason for benefiting people by bringing them into existence must be of a certain strength, or must override other conflicting reasons for action. It is therefore compatible with the following view.

Quality of life and quantity of life are separate values. There is no compelling reason for thinking that trade-offs between them must always be arranged so as to maximize total utility. There is, in fact, *no* objectively correct set of trade-offs between the two values. But the following principles for the determination of trade-offs seem plausible, and they allow us to avoid the Repugnant Conclusion. First, increasing or preserving the quality of life in general matters more than increasing the number of lives. The force of this claim is that it always takes an *increase* in the total utility derived through increasing the number of lives to make up for a decline in the quality of life. Second, as the quality of life gets lower, it takes an increasingly larger gain in the total utility derived through increasing the number of lives to make up for a fixed decline in the quality of life. Finally, once the quality of life drops to a certain point, there is *no* gain in the total utility derived through increasing the number of lives which could make up for a further decline in the quality of life, even though there is still value in increasing the number of lives worth living. In short, at this point the value of preserving the quality of life and the value of increasing the number of lives worth living become incommensurable. It follows that a world in which the quality of life is below the threshold at which incommensurability begins cannot be better than a world in which the quality of life is high. This will be true even if the world with the lower quality of life has a vastly greater total utility.

This is only the crudest sketch of how I think the Repugnant Conclusion might best be avoided. The further elaboration of this view will have to be the work of another essay.

* * *

As I mentioned earlier, the argument of this essay leaves open the possibility that some policy other than the present policy of nuclear deterrence or a policy of nonnuclear defense may be superior to both. If, for example, the strategic arguments of this paper are correct, then a policy of minimal deterrence might be justified purely on Pareto grounds, in the sense that it would be better than the present policy in some respects, and worse in none. My arguments in support of the claim that a policy of nonnuclear defense would reduce the probability of nuclear war could also be cited, with relevant changes, to show that the shift to a policy of minimal deterrence would also reduce the probability of nuclear war. (It would certainly reduce the probability that nuclear war would lead to extinction.) And, provided that it would allow for a series of counterstrikes, and provided that the weapons could remain both effective and largely invulnerable to preemption, it is arguable that the shift to a policy of minimal deterrence would not weaken deterrence, and so would not increase the probability of nuclear blackmail or Soviet domination. At least as an interim policy, minimal deterrence has much to recommend it. Indeed, the shift to a policy of minimal deterrence would be an essential preliminary to the adoption of a policy of unilateral nuclear disarmament, for it would provide an important test of the desirability of unilateral nuclear disarmament. This is because the Soviets' reaction to a unilateral shift by the US to a policy of minimal deterrence would provide important evidence of what their likely response would be to the adoption by the US of a policy of unilateral nuclear disarmament.

Alternatives such as minimal deterrence need to be more carefully explored. Because it fails to consider these other alternatives, the argument of this essay is of limited significance. But it will have served an important purpose if it has at least shown that the case for nuclear deterrence cannot be regarded as unassailable. Consideration of unilateral nuclear disarmament as a viable option can no longer be excluded from "responsible" discussion in the US.[26]

NOTES

1. Desmond Ball, "Can Nuclear War Be Controlled?" *Adelphi Papers* no. 169 (London: International Institution of Strategic Studies, 1981); and Ian Clark, *Limited Nuclear War* (Princeton: Princeton University Press, 1982).

2. Compare Bertrand Russell, "A Counter-Reply," in *Ethics and Metaethics: Readings in Ethical Philosophy*, ed. Raziel Abelson (New York: St. Martin's Press, 1963), pp. 17 - 72.

3. Michael Howard, "On Fighting a Nuclear War," *International Security* 5, no. 4 (1981): 14.

4. Jonathan Schell, *The Fate of the Earth* (New York: Alfred A. Knopf; London: Jonathan Cape, 1982).

5. Noam Chomsky and Edward S. Herman, *The Washington Connection and Third World Fascism* (Boston: South End Press, 1979); Edward S. Herman, *The Real Terror Network* (Boston: South End Press, 1982); and Jenny Pearce, *Under the Eagle: U.S. Intervention in Central America and the Caribbean* (London: Latin American Bureau, 1982).

6. Jefferson McMahan, *British Nuclear Weapons: For and Against* (London: Junction Books, 1981).

7. *New York Times*, 9 March 1983.

8. E.P. Thompson, *Zero Option* (London: Merlin Press, 1982), p. 2. Published in the U.S. as *Beyond the Cold War*.

9. These two objections were suggested to me by Russell Hardin.

10. For further discussion of the problem of nuclear blackmail, see Jefferson McMahan, "Nuclear Blackmail," in *Dangers of Deterrence: Philosophers on Nuclear Strategy*, ed. Nigel Blake and Kay Pole (London: Routledge and Kegan Paul, 1983).

11. McMahan, *British Nuclear Weapons*.

12. Gregory S. Kavka, "Deterrence, Utility, and Rational Choice," *Theory and Decision* 12 (1980): 46 and 50.

13. See, for example, Paul Nitze, "Deterring Our Deterrent," *Foreign Policy* 25 (1976-77).

14. There are other reasons for preferring premise 6. For example, Kavka concedes that, if the probability of nuclear war under nuclear deterrence is high, then "Disaster avoidance is a rather forlorn hope and its importance pales in comparison with the goal of disaster minimization", ("Deterrence, Utility, Rational Choice," p. 51). While Kavka thinks that this probability is low, I have argued that it is significant. If I am right, then this constitutes another reason for appealing to premise 6 rather than to the Disaster Avoidance Principle. Of course, there are conditions under which it might seem reasonable to be guided by the Disaster Avoidance Principle rather than by premise 6. For example, if, as many people believe, the probability of Soviet domination under unilateral nuclear disarmament would be close to 1, then, even if unilateral nuclear disarmament would not increase the probability of Soviet domination by significantly more than it would decrease the probability of nuclear war, it might be rational to prefer nuclear deterrence. (This case was suggested to me by Robert McKim.)

15. Here and elsewhere in this essay, "he" and "his" should be understood to mean "he or she" and "his or her."

16. See, for example, Jonathan Glover, *Causing Death and Saving Lives* (Harmondsworth: Penguin Books, 1977), pp. 69-70. Like Glover, Schell (in *The Fate of the Earth*) tries to *explain* why it is morally important to ensure the existence of future generations; but since the crucial assumptions in his explana-

tion are both controversial and undefended, his explanation cannot be considered a justification.

17. Jonathan Bennett, "On Maximizing Happiness," in *Obligations to Future Generations*, ed. R.I. Sikora and Brian Barry (Philadelphia: Temple University Press, 1978); Joel Feinberg, "The Rights of Animals and Unborn Generations," in *Philosophy and Environmental Crisis*, ed. William Blackstone (Athens: University of Georgia Press, 1974); Jan Narveson, "Future People and Us," in Sikora and Barry, eds., *Obligations to Future Generations*; and Peter Singer, "A Utilitarian Population Principle," in *Ethics and Population*, ed. Michael Bayles (Cambridge, MA: Schenkman, 1976).

18. David Watt, "Trying to Balance on the World's Nuclear Tightrope," *The London Times*, 7 January 1983.

19. Derek Parfit, "Future Generations: Further Problems," *Philosophy and Public Affairs* 11, no 2 (1982), sect. 1.

20. This point is eloquently made by Schell, *The Fate of the Earth*, in chapter 2. I leave aside the question whether it would be worse for existing people to be the final generation even if they were not *aware* that they were.

21. For a rebuttal of certain objections to the claim that to be brought into existence can be a benefit, see Jefferson McMahan, "Problems of Population Theory," *Ethics* 92, no. 1 (1981): 104-9. In that paper I also argue that people benefit from being brought into existence to the full extent of their lifelong balance of utility.

22. See James Griffin, "Is Unhappiness Morally More Important than Happiness?" *Philosophical Quarterly* 29 (1979).

23. I owe this example to Derek Parfit.

24. In a review of Schell's book in the *London Review of Books* (1-14 July 1982), I unjustly criticized Schell for being unable to solve this problem. The ideas on which the solution I have proposed is based are implicit in Schell's narrative.

25. Parfit, "Future Generations."

26. This essay was written in the spring of 1983. At that time the theory of the "nuclear winter" had not been developed. Since then, however, the theory has gained increasing credibility, and the scientific community now believes that the probability that nuclear war would lead to human extinction is much greater than has hitherto been suspected. For obvious reasons, therefore, the nuclear winter findings have strengthened the argument of this essay.

18
THE PHYSICIAN, NUCLEAR WARFARE, AND THE ETHICS OF MEDICINE

Edmund D. Pellegrino, M.D.

You must not abandon the ship in a storm because you cannot control the winds. . . . What you cannot turn to good, you must make as little bad as you can.

Thomas More, *Utopia*

INTRODUCTION: SOME MORAL PARADOXES

Since the beginnings of medical history, the physician has been pledged to a special role in society—to treat the sick, to prevent illness, and to advance the knowledge of both. When his knowledge and skills cannot effect cure, the physician is obliged to relieve the pain and suffering of the incurable, the disabled, and the dying. In civilized societies, these pledges transcend age, sex, nationality, social and economic status as well as political and religious belief, and self-interest. They extend to prisoners, opponents of the regime, and enemy soldiers. Military as well as civilian physicians commit themselves to these same ideals, as the Geneva Conventions of 1949 attest.

Physicians owe a loyalty to all humanity because illness and injury are common to the human condition. The sick or wounded person is a vulnerable, dependent, and exploitable human being.[1] That fact demands a higher degree of empathy, altruism, and moral sensitivity than we expect in ordinary human affairs. It is that fact, also, that lies at the heart of the special status society has always accorded the good physician.

Medical knowledge, moreover, is shared, not proprietary, knowledge. Physicians draw freely on the discoveries and research of colleagues in all countries. Medical knowledge belongs to no one people. For this reason the physician owes an obligation to all who are sick or injured, whether or not they are his countrymen.

This transcending loyalty accounts for the exchange of medical information between countries with opposing political ideologies, that unites physicians when epidemics and catastrophes occur anywhere in the world, and explains why the first contacts often sought between hostile nations are through the exchange of medical knowledge and personnel. It accounts, too, for the general agreement on international ethical codes like the Hippocratic Oath, the Declaration of Geneva, the codes of Helsinki or Nuremberg, the Geneva Conventions of 1949, and the United Nations Principles of Ethics. The commitment of the majority of the world's approximately four million physicians to a common set of ideals is one of the rare examples in this troubled world of a genuine and effective international bond.

What is not confronted directly in these codes and conventions is the inherent tension between the humane and humanitarian ends of medicine and the deliberate destruction of human life that war of any kind entails. The preponderance of current ethical opinion justifies military service by physicians on the basis of loyalty to country and the medical needs of the wounded, civilian and military. None of the existing codes makes the prevention of war a specific obligation of physicians, civilian or military, or forbids their indirect participation in planning for its eventuality. [2]

But it is precisely this question that has been raised by the real possibility of nuclear war. Granting that physicians must under all circumstances treat the casualties of a nuclear war, do they not have the additional obligation to use their knowledge of the virtual impossibility of an adequate medical response to work actively for its prevention? To what extent may the physician cooperate in preparations and plans for treating civilian and military casualties? Does such participation make a nuclear war more or less likely? Is the physician's first loyalty to national interests or to the prevention of world disaster? Do the unique threats of nuclear warfare require fundamental alterations in the traditional presuppositions of medical ethics? To what extent may one cooperate in a complex society in acts one deems immoral without the loss of one's own moral integrity?

Questions of this kind have been focused recently by two concerted actions taken by physicians in response to the increasing probability of the world disaster that would follow on the use of even a fraction of the world's megatonnage of nuclear bombs. One event was the meeting in Cambridge, England, in April 1982 sponsored by Physicians for Social Responsibility. Physicians from 30 countries met to spell out the medical impossibility of meeting the national emergencies of a nuclear attack, and thus to rouse popular opinion against the arms race, and the contemplation of nuclear warfare. [3] The second event occurred in October 1981 in a California community whose physicians refused to pledge a number of that community's hospital beds for the care of military casualties injured outside the country as part of a Civilian-Military Hospital Contingency Plan.

In both cases physicians held that nuclear war is akin to a disease of pandemic proportions, that it is categorically different from conventional war, and that it is medically impossible to deal with the casualties it will produce. Also, it is argued that the very nature of nuclear war calls for a change in the traditional political neutrality of physicians and indeed, because of their special knowledge, imposes upon them a role of leadership in arousing public opinion against the use of nuclear armaments. Finally, it is argued that cooperation in plans to deal with the victims of nuclear warfare is not only useless but morally unsound, because it encourages a false sense of security, and might be misinterpreted by potential enemies as preparation for a preemptive first strike.

The ensuing debate has engaged some of medicine's most eloquent and influential medical spokesmen. For the most part the resulting discourse has been carefully reasoned; some of it, however, is polemical and hortatory, and some primarily political. Given the enormity of destruction this "last epidemic" would visit upon humanity, the intermingling of political philosophies, polemics, and ethics is understandable. But that intermingling must not obscure the ethical issues or sanction the use of nonethical arguments to make points in ethics.

This essay reviews the ethical arguments currently advanced to justify political action by physicians to deter the possibility of nuclear warfare, and to justify non-cooperation in plans for civilian defense should nuclear war occur despite efforts at prevention. Two moral paradoxes are examined: (a) how to remain faithful to the transcendent ideals of the profession at the same time that one fulfills the obligations owed to one's country, and (b) how to maintain personal moral integrity while cooperating with policies and programs whose ultimate ends one may deem immoral.

Like all moral dilemmas, these two cannot be resolved with finality. The issues are embedded in a matrix of debate about the morality of the just war, mutual deterrence, preemptive first strike, limited nuclear engagement, unilateral disarmament, and the like. Other chapters in this volume cover these issues in depth. This essay limits itself to the moral obligations of physicians, *qua* physicians, given their special roles in society and the sharp politico-philosophical differences among them on what is, or is not, consistent with the traditional ethics of medicine.

As responsible moral agents, physicians must decide how they will act, and how they will justify their actions in the face of the real possibility of global immolation by a nuclear war. I maintain, on grounds of morality and prudence, (a) that, *as physicians*, we have a positive moral obligation to educate the world to the impossibility of an adequate response to the mass injuries nuclear war would inflict; (b) that, *as citizens* in a democracy, physicians are obliged to take political positions and actions on the morality of nuclear armaments and war; and (c) that, *for physicians*, a policy of non-cooperation in civilian defense plans is morally dubious and pragmatically self-defeating.

Physicians can cooperate with plans to deal with casualties without loss of moral integrity (a) if they simultaneously undertake vigorous worldwide efforts to educate people to the full extent of the medical disaster a nuclear holocaust would produce and to the impotence of medical resources to deal with it; (b) if they simultaneously disabuse policymakers and the public of any notion that cooperation in any way sanctions nuclear warfare, or makes a first-strike policy a morally viable option; and (c) if none of the actions they take are intrinsically wrong.

The undeniable uniqueness of nuclear warfare as a threat to humanity does not justify any radical change in medical ethics, nor does it endow physicians with any special sanction to foster radical changes in the political structure of democratic societies.

THE FACTUAL FOUNDATIONS OF THE DEBATE

Most of the facts in the controversy can be taken as givens. One may argue about whether or not a one-megaton nuclear blast will generate a firestorm and whether its BTUs per mile will be more or less than the Dresden firestorm. One may cite different experts about numbers of casualties, or even possibilities of survival of a first strike. Some may hold that improved technology can pinpoint military targets so accurately that the damage to noncombatants will be limited. But what is incontrovertible is the overwhelming number of casualties; the severity of burns, trauma and radiation sickness; the contamination of food, water and air; the disruption of transportation; and the devastation of medical personnel, facilities, supplies of blood and medications.

Photographs of the demolition of Hiroshima and Nagasaki, the accounts of the survivors, an assessment of the injuries, and subsequent studies of the physical forces released all give eloquent testimony of the environmental, emotional, and social damage we can expect and which will be multiplied in any future nuclear conflict.[4] No amount of technical debate about the degree of damage or the physician's lack of expertise in such technical matters can eradicate the fact that nuclear warfare represents a jump of many orders of magnitude in violence over conventional war. Particularly pertinent are the inevitabilities of mass casualties among noncombatants and the contamination of the whole globe as a human habitation.

Given its unprecedented devastating potential—unlike any war humanity has ever experienced—nuclear warfare challenges the traditional presuppositions of medical ethics. As persons specifically ordained by society to use their knowledge for humane ends, what specific obligations fall upon physicians? Are those obligations encompassable within the framework or traditional medical ethics?

AROUSING WORLD OPINION

Certainly, one clear and impelling moral responsibility of physicians as physicians is to disseminate their knowledge about the topic in which they are expert: the medical horrors of nuclear war, and the practical impossibility of an effective medical response. Hiatt and Lown succinctly summarize the argument.[5] In their view, physicians are committed not only to treat disease, but to prevent it. Nuclear war is likened to an untreatable disease that is still preventable. If the people of the world apprehend its imminent dangers and its horrendous outcome, they can influence their leaders to avoid such a catastrophe. Physicians therefore are morally compelled, by the nature of their calling, to sound the alarm, since the threat is of pandemic proportions. This is a straightforward and logical extrapolation of the traditional medical ethics of the Western world.

Those who argue against this view do not deny the *prima facie* obligations of physicians to prevent epidemics or other medical disasters. Rather, they pose the counterobligations of loyalty to country as preeminent; the physician as a citizen owes loyalty to his country for the benefits it affords him. In a free country that debt is not lightly set aside. Those who oppose a physician campaign to arouse world opinion use several arguments. First, they argue, physicians are neither military nor technical experts: they may overestimate the dangers of nuclear war and thus mislead the public to take steps toward arms limitation or disarmament that could imperil the security of the free world. Second, they hold that the physician is not privy to the secret information governments possess or to the intricacies of international diplomacy, and thus may unintentionally undermine carefully laid plans for mutual deterrence or disarmament. Third, physicians may unwittingly become dupes of the enemy. By placing trust in the sincerity of their professional counterparts in the Soviet Union, for example, they may become the unwitting victims of a plan to lull our country into passivity and pacifism. Finally, it is argued that the authority and influence of physicians are so great that exposing their own helplessness to deal with a nuclear attack may promote despair and undercut government efforts at readiness and civilian defense, or even induce a "better red than dead" attitude.

Leaving aside name-calling, accusations of bad faith, or militarism, on the one hand, and communist conspiracy on the other, how do these arguments measure up? Both sides agree on the physician's obligation to disseminate knowledge of ordinary epi demics or impending medical disasters. Both agree that physicians must treat casualties should they themselves survive a nuclear attack. The disagreement centers on the degree to which physicians are obliged to influence public opinion against nuclear warfare, and the degree to which their cooperation with civilian defense plans encourages acceptance of nuclear warfare. Both sides want to serve national interests, but they differ markedly in what they interpret as those interests.

On balance, I believe the argument for widespread dissemination of knowledge about the medical disaster of nuclear war is more compelling. For one thing, physicians are in fact more expert than others in assessing the conditions and the possibility of an adequate medical response. They need not be military tacticians or physicists to make what is fundamentally a medical assessment. No one questions that the damage of megaton bombs would be greater than anything the world has yet seen in warfare. This being the case, it would be contrary to the whole spirit of a democratic society to withhold such knowledge from all of us who would be potential victims. The knowledge in question is not and must not be a military secret. It is already a commonplace topic in the media, in private conversation, in meetings, and in periodicals. All too often it is treated sensationally and inaccurately. The need for accurate information is urgent.

It is essential, therefore, that information on the medical disaster of a nuclear war be disseminated accurately, honestly, and authoritatively by those physicians equipped to do so. If the result were such worldwide revulsion that the people of the nuclear nations moved their governments away from the present course of mutual destruction, the "final epidemic" might indeed be averted. Free societies are built on the conviction that truth and the freedom to express it are the essentials to participatory democracy. Truth remains the citizen's major protection against political manipulation and oppression. Moreover, there is the real likelihood that the knowledge will be more unsettling to the totalitarian regimes than to the democracies. In democracies the issue should be accurate information, not freedom of access to it. Accurate information widely disseminated is still the gravest threat a totalitarian regime can face.

It is ultimately sounder to build nuclear armament policies on the reactions of an informed public than on the presumptions of even presumably benevolent governments. Government leaders have historically shown no greater sensitivity to human values than ordinary individuals. A matter as urgent as nuclear war provides an ultimate test of the viability of the concept of democratic government. In any case it is hard to argue that public ignorance of the medical outcome of atomic wars is preferable to a realistic appraisal of their dangers.

Likewise, it would be hard to argue that an appraisal that might lead to prevention of nuclear war is not in the national interest—indeed, in the interest of every nation. On balance, then, it seems that the physician's obligation, as physician and as loyal citizen, is best fulfilled by taking leadership in providing accurate and realistic assessments of the medical dangers of nuclear war. That knowledge must be transmitted honestly and without exaggeration if it is to prove effective in mobilizing people to policies of restraint and war prevention. Political means consistent with the requirements of a democratic society will necessarily have to be used. There is not, nor has there ever been, a contradiction between a physician taking a stance on public matters, and his dedication to the traditional obligations of medical ethics. In fact, most current professional codes speak of the physician's social responsibilities.

The precise extent to which any individual physician is compelled personally to devote his energies to the dissemination of knowledge and the sensitization of public opinion is difficult to say. The obligation clearly does bind the medical profession as a body, however, by virtue of its corporate convenant with society to advance the public's health. It applies especially to all those physicians whose duties bring them closest to the issues: official spokesmen, officers of the major professional organizations, physicians in the military and other government service, and those engaged in voluntary health organizations, radiation safety, public health, environmental medicine, and the like. The prevention of nuclear war is such a grave responsibility that every physician should be involved in some way. Given this obligation, the physician must refuse to engage in deception or to cooperate in the dissemination of false or misleading information to coerce public opinion for, or against, nuclear war or disarmament. This poses a particularly grave paradox for physicians in military and government service.

COOPERATION IN PREPARATIONS RELATED TO
NUCLEAR WAR: TWO CASES

The second specific situation in which medical ethics seemingly comes into conflict with the realities of nuclear warfare involves cooperation in plans for treatment of civilian and military casualties should nuclear war actually occur. Physicians at the Contra Costa Hospital in California were asked, as other community hospitals were asked, to pledge a certain number of beds for the care of military casualties who might be injured in nuclear engagements. This was part of a government civilian contingency hospital system. The physicians refused to do so, as did physicians in some other communities, on the ground that cooperation with a government program of this type encourages planning for nuclear war. The arguments against cooperation are well summarized by Geiger and Murray,[6] and for cooperation, by Bisgard and Johnson, all in the April 1982 issue of *The Hastings Center Report*.[7]

Geiger bases his argument for non-cooperation on two things: First, that no adequate medical response is possible to meet the medical demands following a nuclear attack. To participate in planning for such a disaster would be "a suspension of professional judgment and abandonment of reliance on medical and scientific data that cannot and should not be sanctioned even in the name of patriotism."[8] His second reason was that participation may actually increase the risk of nuclear war by lulling the public into a false sense of security—into believing that it can be limited, is survivable, and has effects that could be handled medically.

Murray, like Geiger, argued that cooperation would make nuclear war more acceptable to the public. He justified the California doctors' refusal as a means of alerting "the public to what they saw as the intolerable horrors of nuclear war."[9] He then contends that the physician is obliged to be a "moral leader" in dramatically bringing the issue of defense planning before the public to counter the "hegemony" of the Defense Department. "A physician's dedication to health is not limited to repair after illness or calamity has struck."

Both Geiger and Murray made a distinction between planning for nuclear war and treating the casualties of such a war should it occur. Both agree that physicians cannot refuse treatment to wounded persons, civilian or military. Their objections, however, leaving aside some polemics, were based on the false sense of security physician cooperation might give to civilian defense planning. On their view, to comply would be to cooperate directly with an evil intent.

Bisgard, on the other hand, challenged the contention that there is a connection between preparations to treat casualties and increasing the likelihood of nuclear war.[10] The physician's first responsibility, he argued, is, as it always has been, to treat the sick and injured regardless of the physician's personal values and beliefs about the morality of war. Moreover, not to cooperate in plans for a Civilian Hospital Contingency System is, in his view, to do positive harm by failing to prepare for the care of casualties. The preparations are not in themselves intrinsically evil; it is noncooperation that is evil.

Johnson also emphasizes the centrality of the physician's obligation to care for the wounded.[11] He saw contingency planning as part of that obligation, whether or not a war is just. Physicians, he argued, have a moral obligation to counter the erosion of the protection of noncombatants that modern war has already engendered. By incorporating the needs of noncombatants in contingency planning physicians reassert the special care that society owes the noncombatant, military or civilian.

Geiger's first argument, that participation in contingency planning is an abnegation of the physician's fidelity to scientific probity, does not seem very sound. This argument would hold only if the physician, in the face of overwhelming data to the contrary, were to minimize or falsify the destructive force of nuclear blasts and were to offer unsubstantiated promises of being able to handle the casualties. A few proponents of limited nuclear war have, in fact, minimized the number and extent of casualties. Their position is so contrary to the present preponderance of evidence and medical opinion that Geiger's criticism does apply to them. But it is not applicable to those who state the case accurately.

Geiger suggests that the contingency plan is poorly conceived and unrealistic. That may well be the case, but it is not a warrant for noncooperation. We do not cease looking for cures for cancer because our present therapies are poorly designed. The physician's cooperation is necessary if any improvement is possible. The Civilian Hospital Contingency System may not be the acme of human or medical ingenuity, yet the proper scientific attitude is not to abandon the quest for a better plan, but to work diligently to find one. The aim of an improved plan is not to make nuclear war a survivable possibility, but to treat casualties better, should it occur. As long as Geiger admits that the surviving physicians, if there are any, must treat casualties, he is compelled to admit that they ought to prepare to do so as well as possible, even if the odds are overwhelmingly against success.

Geiger's second argument (and Murray's argument, too)—that participation by physicians in contingency plans will give a false sense of security to the public— seems equally weak. First, this is unlikely to occur if physicians make it their business to warn the public about the horrifying medical effects of nuclear warfare, in as graphic, as detailed, and as accurate ways as possible. Part of that warning is to alert everyone to the virtual impossibility of an adequate mobilization of medical resources. A sense of false security would result only if the facts were not told or were misrepresented. These difficulties could be exposed by the "searching inquiry" into contingency plans that Geiger himself urges in his closing words.[12]

Geiger and Murray both fail to take into account that damage to public morale that would occur in response to a widespread refusal by physicians to even consider contingency plans. Rather than generating resistance to nuclear war, people would feel morally abandoned by the one group on whom they have traditionally depended in disasters of all kinds. The public could easily fall into a paralysis of anxiety that would leave all the decisions to the military, or to those physicians willing to cooperate. If physicians do not participate in planning, the vacuum will be filled by others with less knowledge. Moreover, to label any Civilian Defense Plan as hopeless is to preclude the possibility of new ways to deal with the disaster. One can always work to deal with the consequences of evil without condoning evil itself.

Murray advanced the additional argument that physician noncooperation is justified because it will dramatically alert the public to the awesomeness of nuclear war. This is hardly a morally tenable position. It proposes a morally dubious and questionably effective means to an end that is achievable in a morally more-defensible way—by accurate public information. Noncooperation cannot be used even for good political ends without undermining the credibility and motivations of honest efforts at public education.

One can heartily agree, therefore, with Murray's plea that doctors should become "moral leaders" in the effort to avert nuclear warfare, without condoning his policy of noncooperation. The conscientious objectors who serve in the medical corps do not interpret helping the wounded as a moral compromise with their hatred of war. There is no logical connection between working to avert a catastrophe and preparing to deal with it should mankind succumb, as so often in the past, to temptations to use the most lethal weaponry. The ardor of Geiger's and Murray's sentiments against nuclear war is shared by many, but their logic in behalf of noncooperation is weak and self-defeating.

One additional point in the Contra Costa case. The physicians assumed that they had a moral basis for withholding the commitment of community hospital beds on their own initiative. But is this the case? The hospital, if it is a nonprofit community hospital, belongs to the community, not to the physicians. The disposition of its beds and services rests not with the physicians, but with the community. Physicians are free to withhold their personal services but not the use of a community resource, unless that is the community's will.

In the case of a proprietary hospital wholly owned by physicians, there might be a case for physicians making the decision. But even if a hospital is proprietary, it takes on the character of a community resource *de facto*, if not *de jure*. Even the proprietary hospital is not simply the physicians' private property. It is more like a public utility, held in private hands but operated in the public interest, since it serves needs vital to public safety that ordinary businesses do not. Unless we succumb completely to the idea that medical and health care is nothing more than a commodity transaction, we must regard hospitals and doctors as national and community resources. As such they can justifiably be mobilized in a national emergency.

The arguments in favor of physician noncooperation are morally dubious at best. The good ends they hope to achieve can be attained by other, less questionable means. A physician can be faithful to his prime duty to care for the sick and wounded, and to that end cooperate in plans for civilian defense. And he can, at the same time, be faithful to his duty to alert the public to the dangers, the horror, and the awesomeness of the medical problems of a nuclear war. If he chooses, he can campaign actively against nuclear war as a citizen of a free and democratic society.

He can oppose the policies of his government. While protesting, he is still duty-bound as physician to participate in plans designed to deal with the disaster he fervently hopes to avert, should his efforts at prevention fail.

Physicians may, as individuals, disagree on the degree to which they should alert the public to the human destructiveness of nuclear war. They can disagree as citizens on the morality or immorality of particular defense policies. But as physicians, they must remain faithful to their age-old pledge to society to treat, to heal, to help, to assuage pain and anxiety—to ameliorate the human condition, no matter how difficult the problems, how culpable the victims, or how hopeless the effort may seem.

Medicine has an obligation to act as a constructive critic of the lifestyle of the society it serves. No one argues seriously that physicians ought not to inform and warn about smoking, overeating, lack of exercise, abuse of alcohol and drugs, occupational hazards, abuse of children, or environmental hazards. This does not eradicate the obligation to treat or ameliorate the effects of a deleterious lifestyle. This same obligation extends to the most fearful pandemic of them all—mutual destruction by a nuclear holocaust.

The obligation of the physician to use his knowledge for human good is based in the principles of benevolence, beneficence, truth-telling, and justice. In a matter of such unprecedented gravity as the prevention of nuclear war, these principles are in conformity with the traditional pledge of medical ethics to serve the good of others. This obligation extends beyond one's own nation, because all people will be affected by atomic war.

These fundamental principles also are pertinent to cooperation in civilian defense planning. Beneficence and non-maleficence require that physicians do everything possible to help those who need help; justice requires that medical knowledge be available to all humans; truth-telling, that physicians make clear their motives in cooperating with defense plans. Noncooperation would be construed by the public and patients as moral abandonment—a failure to make whatever small effort is possible to ameliorate suffering, pain, and disability.

To use the power of medicine to alleviate suffering as a political lever is to go counter to the expectations society holds of physicians. It is a morally unacceptable kind of paternalism. Respect for the autonomy of patients or the public is essential in a democratic society and in medical ethics. We must not violate that autonomy even to compel a people or their government to make the political decisions we think morally acceptable. Morality takes precedence over other considerations. But to use immoral means to advance a moral end, or force morality on others, is in itself immoral.

There is one condition under which participation in planning for the treatment of military casualties in civilian hospitals would be immoral. I refer to a situation in which civilian patients or casualties would be displaced or deprived access, and military casualties given priority. There is no claim in justice for such a preference. It would, therefore, be obligatory for physicians to refuse to cooperate if such preference were part of the plan, or until such a provision were eliminated.

The arguments advanced for noncooperation in civilian defense planning do not require drastic changes in the fundamental principles traditional to medical ethics. They underscore a sharp difference in the way these principles are interpreted and the way they relate to each other. But differences in the interpretation of moral principles do not vitiate the principles themselves.

The physician's credibility will gain, and not suffer, if he maintains his fidelity to his ancient moral charge. His efforts to instruct, to warn, and to urge public action and to influence world leaders will have cogency only if his logic, motivation, and ethics are not bent to ideological ends. Granting the loss of moral credibility the profession has suffered through the failings of its own members, its strength nevertheless remains a common dedication that transcends self.

AN ETHICS OF COOPERATION: SOME ASPECTS

I have argued that there are circumstances under which one may cooperate in actions that may have morally dubious and even wrong or harmful purposes and consequences. This is not the place to develop a full-blown, tightly-reasoned ethics of cooperation. But some outline of a framework for morally valid cooperation is appropriate in order to examine further the moral paradoxes under consideration.

In an imperfect world, in which we ourselves are imperfect and in which we are often inequitably linked to the actions of others, we are all likely, sooner or later, to become party to some action about which we may have serious moral doubt. Our involvement may result from geographic locale, economic necessity, or our place in institutional authority structures; from personal, family, or national loyalties; or from social ties or professional functions. Few people today could withdraw from every possible morally dubious activity in which they might have a distant part. To do so would isolate them from public life and institutional life and perhaps do harm to others. Each of us therefore needs guidelines for our decision to participate or withdraw from actions that may be morally questionable but which conflicting obligations do not permit us to eschew completely.

Some would make us partners in all the world's tyranny, poverty, violence, or injustice simply because we are members of the human race. Others would hold us guilty only for the evil done in, or by, the countries, institutions, or groups to which we owe allegiance. Others regard each person as an isolated and free agent, independent of what happens to others, and responsible only for his or her own immediate and direct actions.

None of these views seems completely realistic in a participatory democracy, or in an institutionalized society. Participation to varying degrees in actions whose morality may be dubious is a fact of contemporary life. Whether we are equally guilty with the primary actor, less guilty, or not guilty at all will depend upon the interplay of at least the following factors: the moral nature of the act itself; the intent of the primary actor and the degree to which it is shared by the person cooperating; the closeness of the cooperation to the performance of the act; its necessity for the completion of the act; and the harm that might come to the cooperator, or someone else, by the refusal to participate.

Cooperation in an act that is itself morally wrong, and in which participation is direct and necessary to its completion, would never be morally admissable. An example would be holding the gun on a robbery victim while an accomplice takes his wallet. Here the act itself is wrong, the cooperation is direct and immediate, the evil intent of the primary actor is shared, and the participation is necessary to achievement of the wrongful end. If the one cooperating were acting under threat to his own life or his family's, however, his act would be less guilty or not guilty at all, although still wrong. If, under threat of harm, the cooperator were to shoot the victim, then he would be guilty of murder, though under mitigating circumstances.

Here the evil act is a direct and intended consequence of the evil intent of the primary agent, and the guilt is shared with him.

On the other hand, one might participate in another's wrongful act at a distance, so to speak, without sharing the wrongful intent of the act. Here the cooperator's action, while itself morally neutral or even good, nevertheless provides assistance in the wrongful act of another. The cooperator does not will the wrong. Instead, the primary agent really uses a good or morally indifferent act for a wrong purpose.

One can think, for example, of the resident assisting at remunerative but unnecessary surgery performed by a competent but unscrupulous surgeon. The resident's acts of assistance are in themselves morally neutral or even good. He does not intend to exploit the patient, but his own job depends upon cooperation in the operation. If the resident is competent the patient will be assured of a safe, if unnecessary, procedure. By refusing to participate, the resident would endanger his own career; he would not deter the wayward surgeon, who would get another assistant. If no replacement were available the resident might do more harm to the patient by not assisting.

The degree of the resident's guilt would depend upon a careful analysis of the factors of the immediacy and necessity of his cooperation, the nature of the act, and its intent. If, for example, the resident were to assist the unscrupulous surgeon outside his regular duties while moonlighting for profit—he would be equally guilty with the primary surgeon. He would be less guilty if he were in a remote hospital where other assistants were unavailable or less competent.

The situation would be different again if the resident were asked to assist at an abortion he sincerely believed to be equivalent to murder. Here the intrinsic evil of the act—as perceived by the resident—would preclude cooperation even to save his job. The same might be true if the surgeon one assisted were grossly and repeatedly incompetent and a threat to the patient.

Distance, immediacy, and the degree of sharing in the intent of an act are important factors. The nurse who assists is one step further removed in her cooperation than the resident and less culpable, and the person who sterilizes the instruments, even further; the maintenance man who fixes the lights in the operating room, further still.

On the other hand, the chief of the professional staff, whose responsibility it is to monitor quality of care, may have a very direct and binding responsibility to stop unnecessary surgery. So, too, with the hospital administrator, who has been delegated the authority to monitor the quality of care in the hospital. Remoteness from the harmful action does not in itself absolve one from responsibility when one has the duty to prevent an evil action. Here we are dealing with negative cooperation—failing to intervene in a wrongful act when one has a duty that requires intervention. The most recent AMA code of ethics requires that physicians "expose colleagues who are deficient in character or competence." Most frequent instances of wrongful cooperation are of this negative sort—failures to act to avert harmful actions.

These examples only touch the periphery of the considerations that govern the morality of cooperation in wrongful or morally dubious acts. Numerous complex situations that we cannot analyze here bear closer analysis. Can a physician work for a for-profit hospital corporation that skims off the profitable patients and refuses to treat the less affluent? How accountable is a clinical teacher who fails to supervise students and residents whose judgment he doubts? How responsible is a hospital trustee, as surrogate for his community, for the ethical behavior of physicians, administrators, nurses, and staff in his hospital? How long can nurses or medical students remain silent if they see the rights of patients consistently violated?

I have chosen to illustrate the principles of cooperation with specific examples from clinical medicine. The analogies with situations in family life, school, business, and government are obvious. In the case of the physician's cooperation with preparations for dealing with casualties in a nuclear war, we can be more specific. Here, the act itself is morally neutral or even good—its intent is to help the victims no matter whether the war is just or unjust. Such action is consistent with the covenant to heal that binds the physician to society. The physician's cooperation is direct and immediate in the sense that he is an active and, indeed, a crucial participant in any disaster plans. His participation is intentional since, in our society—at the moment at least—no penalties are exacted from those who refuse to participate. His intent is to help casualties, not to facilitate a first-strike strategy, nor mislead the public into believing that a nuclear war is survivable or less horrendous than it is. Public misconstrual of the physician's intent, or official misuse of it, does not vitiate the physician's intent to help. The harm that might result from the physician's cooperation, i.e., a false sense of security about nuclear war, is remote; it does not result directly or immediately from his action, and it comes about by the misuse or distortion by others of what would normally be a good act—preparing to treat casualties of a mass disaster. The physician's cooperation is wrongful only if he shares in any intent to deceive the public about the survivability of nuclear war.

There is no firm evidence that physician cooperation in civilian defense plans would delude any majority of citizens into a sense of false security. Moreover, there is little evidence, beyond supposition, that our government is in fact using physicians as instruments for its own ends or could do so even if it wished. Undeniably, some government officials actually believe, against all factual evidence, that nuclear war might be survivable. Undoubtedly others might deliberately deceive the public. Still, there is no evidence that the public is so gullible that it will interpret the physicians' traditional dedication to helping the sick and wounded as evidence that they are dupes of the government.

Moreover, even if this were the case, there are other methods available for disabusing the public of its mistaken notion. Physicians can speak out with authority against nuclear war politics; they can educate the public in the horrors of a nuclear holocaust. This is not inconsistent with making themselves available simultaneously to help, should the cosmic madness of a nuclear war finally overcome our rationality. Indeed, by participation the physicians will have even more opportunity to warn against the terrible horrors of mass injuries as it becomes painfully apparent how pitiful are our means to deal with them.

On practical grounds, the goal of arousing public opinion might be better served by participation than non-participation. For one thing, the public would retain its confidence in the moral credibility of its physicians. They would listen more willingly if they did not think their physicians were primarily political ideologues. Alienating themselves from large segments of the public, on practical grounds alone, would be self-defeating to the purposes of those who oppose nuclear armaments. Moreover, it is unlikely that all physicians would boycott participation. Those committed to the use of nuclear weapons could end up making all the decisions about disaster plans, without the restraints provided by those physicians who oppose their use.

The distinction between the obligations of the physician as physician and physician as citizen is an important one. Like any other citizen, the physician may take political action, and cooperate in such action, to advance his personal political beliefs. But as a physician, he is a citizen with special knowledge and skill, and he has a special covenant with society. He cannot use that special status for primarily political ends. To fuse politics and medicine, even for a good end, is to confuse categories of moral obligation that must remain distinct. If we fuse them we risk yielding all our political and value decisions to experts; in a technologically structured society, that can only lead to a new kind of oligarchy or tyranny destructive to a democratic society. The distinction is admittedly subtle, but its subtlety does not extinguish its reality.

These questions of cooperation must be faced in every walk of life. They are particularly difficult for physicians because of the inherent conflict between the usual aim of medicine, which is to help, and the usual aim of military activity, which is to inflict injury. In authoritarian or morally homogenous societies, these questions are submerged. But in a democratic and free society they pose genuine quandaries. They confront, particularly, the career medical officer who has freely chosen a life of military service, as well as the conscripted physician who serves in a time of national emergency.

It has been argued, for example, that modern war could not be waged without physician participation, because physicians are needed to keep armies healthy, to deal with casualties, and to develop new modes of treatment for complicated war injuries.[13]

The physician is not as necessary in waging nuclear war as he is in a conventional war. In nuclear war it is no longer a question of keeping a fighting force in the field, but of destroying enemy missiles and missile silos or entire cities and their populations. Treating injured soldiers, or returning them to battle, would be meaningless, since massive mutual destruction would result in hours or days.

Even if all physicians were to refuse to serve on both sides of a conflict, governments would still wage war. Once caught in the fervor of their self-righteousness, governments would wage war without physicians. They would even knowingly run the risk of the additional casualties to pursue their military goals. There is no evidence that nuclear war would not be waged if there were no civilian defense plan in place. Therefore, it cannot be argued that the physician's cooperation is necessary to planning or carrying out the aims of nuclear warfare.

What about more direct forms of cooperation? For example, physicians are necessary for various aspects of the design, discovery, and testing of the agents used in chemical and biological warfare. Here, physician cooperation is directly linked to the intent to do harm. To use one's medical knowledge and ingenuity this way is to go counter to every ethical precept of medicine. One could argue, however, that participation in the research directed to combat the effects of biological or chemical warfare is justifiable. But it could not be argued that physicians, even for motives of patriotism, are justified in using medical knowledge to devise new nuclear or biological weapons. Here the cooperation in the intent and use of instruments of human destruction is too direct, and the act itself is immoral.

A particularly noxious example of the direct kind of immoral cooperation is the use of psychological and pharmacological techniques to brainwash or break down the resistance of prisoners of war. Here the degree of harm done is great, and the physician's participation is direct, necessary, and intentional. Equally reprehensible is the Soviet practice of falsely labeling political dissidents or prisoners as psychotic to explain away their dissent or to incarcerate them in mental institutions. This kind of prostitution of medical knowledge to evil purpose is too obvious to require a sophisticated critique.

SOME OBJECTIONS AND SOME RESPONSES

The proponents of noncooperation might be expected to level several objections at the positions I have taken. These deserve some anticipatory response. First, it might be objected that I have not addressed the need for a radical departure from the traditional medial ethic of political neutrality, that the uniqueness of nuclear war demands political action, and that it is impossible to separate medical and political acts under these circumstances. Indeed, it will be argued, the physician's loyalty to all mankind transcends national interests and obliges him to be a catalyst in generating world resistance to nuclear warfare.

To this I would reply that much depends upon the meaning of the word "political." If we can take it in its etymological sense, it includes almost all our civil relationships with each other and the state itself. In that sense, any action physicians might take to alert world society to the dangers of nuclear war is by definition political. In this sense, there has never been a contradiction between medical ethics and political affairs.

Political action can also mean to politicize, i.e., to make medical knowledge and practice an instrument primarily to advance political parties and ideologies or force some change in a political system. On this definition there is a clear conflict with medical ethics because it implies the use of medical knowledge outside the covenant with society.

For example, it is held by some that the unique nature of nuclear war demands a radical reexamination of the relationships between governments and their citizens. In this reexamination the physician, because of his transcending loyalty to mankind, is presumed to have a special role. Yet the decision to pursue a policy of nuclear armament is not tied to the way governments and their citizens relate to each other. Both the democratic and the totalitarian systems have caught the same suicidal nuclear disease, each blaming its infection on the other. Nor is any political system or intermediary between them likely to be immune from the same.

If it is suggested that loyalty to unjust or immoral governments can be suspended, this limitation has been recognized in Western political theory at least since St. Thomas Aquinas's *De Regimine Principum*. It is the motivation for the Bill of Rights and the American Revolution. The uniqueness of nuclear war does not alter this obligation nor relieve individuals of their personal moral responsibility to oppose an unjust government.

It is often contended that the nature and gravity of nuclear war, and the importance of its prevention, "transcends" politics. In one sense, this can be taken to mean that the loyalty of physicians to the well-being of all mankind transcends neutrality or makes it morally untenable. On this point I would agree. There is a second sense, however, in which transcending politics seems to be taken and that is, that physicians must also change the status quo or political institutions. The latter interpretation goes far beyond the first and does not follow from it. It suggests that the physician's medical expertise entails a special expertise in knowing what forms of government are more just than others. On this point, the physician has no more expertise than other citizens. In a democratic society he can propound his view as a citizen, but it would be a distortion of medical ethics to implant the responsibility for radical changes in government into medical ethics. Such an assertion will confuse and alienate many who would otherwise accept medical opinion about the uniqueness of the massive and overwhelming medical effects of nuclear warfare.

Another objection may be that I have not presented strongly enough the argument against cooperation, which is based on the fact that civil defense planning is a part of counterforce strategy because it presumes that enough people will survive to prevail or engage in counterstrikes. Thus, civilian defense planning might be interpreted by the enemy as part of preparation for a preemptive strike, and thus lead the enemy to its own preemptive strike. There is no question that a moral paradox exists here. Physicians are morally required to take all measures possible to prepare to treat the sick and injured, no matter how they become sick or injured, whether because of war or pestilence. Yet, in preparing for the catastrophe of nuclear war, the physician's actions could be misinterpreted by another nation and could result in the very calamity he wishes to avert.

Like all paradoxes this one cannot be resolved completely. After all, the argument could just as easily be turned another way— that noncooperation could also encourage the enemy to a preemptive strike. If he thought a nuclear war were winnable, the enemy could presume that we were not prepared to handle casualties. If they were so prepared, more of their citizens would survive than ours. They would then conclude that they could attack us and "win" the war.

We can engage in an infinite regress of presumptions about the enemy's presumptions, about our presumptions about their presumptions. Too much of international policy is based on such labyrinthine guessing games. The more reasonable answer is to take measures to treat those who might survive, while at the same time making clear that such preparations are at present almost certainly doomed to inadequacy.

Another moral paradox is more apparent than real and involves the potential conflict between loyalty to national interests and the loyalty of the profession to the welfare of humans to prevent pandemic threats to the well-being of all of humanity. If one interprets national interests narrowly as limited to prevailing over the enemy, then there might be a conflict. But the prevention of nuclear warfare is in every human being's interests—the individual patient's, the nation, and the world. It is unquestionably in the national interest to prevent nuclear disaster, and the physician's traditional ethical obligations are, therefore, not in opposition to national interests in the best sense, but favor them. If the national interest is interpreted narrowly, then again the physician, as citizen, has a moral obligation to participate in resetting and redefining the national interest. In this respect, the physician is a citizen with special expertise essential to redefining national interests, but with no more authority to do so than other citizens.

The moral paradoxes of cooperation and noncooperation are difficult to resolve. Much depends upon the interpretation physicians put on their own government's motives in preparing for civilian defense and on the presumptions opposing governments might put on those motives. In a Byzantine chess game with such grisly alternatives, the game of guessing about motives might best be kept to its simplest form. Strengthening, not weakening, the democratic processes of government in times of crises is the only way to assure the openness that defeats the misuses of political power.

On the whole, the traditional ethics of medicine, centering in the care of the sick, the prevention of illness, and the promotion of health, remain the physician's over-riding moral imperatives. If he is critical in his application of the criteria of morally licit cooperation, he can retain his moral integrity. He can oppose war and work for its abolition, but he must also serve as helper and healer. Whether the patient is ill because of his own personal misbehavior, or whether his illness and injury are the result of the social insanity of war, the physician's primary role is to stand ready to heal. The physician's task is like that of Rieux in Camus's great novel *The Plague*. He must avoid the extremes of pessimism or optimism; he must help contemporary man make his choices between peace and life, death and destruction.

Confronted as he is daily with the awesomeness of the death of individual persons, the physician has learned how to hope even when his patient's world is dissolving. His great contribution, even in the nuclear age, is to combat the moral plague of nuclear war, and at the same time to stand ready to help all who fall victim to this final and fatal irony in the drama of human existence. Only that example will prevent him and others from becoming morally fatigued and falling into a fatal quietism. "The true security problem of today," as Eisenhower saw it, "is not merely man against man, or nation against nation. It is man against war."[14] The physician should fight war, but in doing so he must not forget that his first charge is to help man, even if the valiant effort to avert war fails.

NOTES

1. E.D. Pellegrino, "Being Ill and Being Healed: Some Reflections on the Grounding of Medical Morality," *Bulletin of the New York Academy of Medicine* 57, no. 1 (January-February 1981): 70-79.
2. One exception is the exhortation of the Medical Association for the Prevention of War. "Medical Ethics in Relation to War," cited in Robert M. Goldwyn and Victor Sidel, "The Physician and War," in *Ethical Issues in Medicine*, ed. E. Fuller Torrey (Little, Brown, 1948), p. 338.
3. Howard H. Hiatt, "Preventing the Last Epidemic: II," *Journal of the American Medical Association* 246, no. 18 (6 November 1981): 2035-36; "Final Epidemic," *British Medical Journal* 284, no. 6323 (17 April 1982): 1140-41; International Physicians for the Prevention of Nuclear War, "Proceedings of the First Congress," *Contact* 64 (November 1981): 12-17; and Bernard Lown, "Physicians and Nuclear War," *Journal of the American Medical Association* 246, no. 20 (20 November 1981): 2331-32.
4. Eric Chivian, Susanna Chivian, Robert Jay Lifton, John E. Mack, eds., *The Medical Dimensions of Nuclear War* (San Francisco: W.H. Freeman, 1982).
5. Hiatt, "Preventing the Last Epidemic"; and Lown, "Physicians and Nuclear War."
6. In the *Hastings Center Report* 12, no. 2 (April 1982): H. Jack Geiger, "Why Survival Plans Are Meaningless," pp. 17-19; and Thomas H. Murray, "The Physician as Moral Leader," pp. 20-21.
7. In the *Hastings Center Report* 12, no. 2: Jay C. Bisgard, "The Obligation to Care for Casualties," pp. 15-17; and James T. Johnson, "The Moral Bases of Contingency Planning," pp. 19-20.
8. Geiger, "Survival Plans."

9. Murray, "Physician as Moral Leader."
10. Bisgard, "Obligation to Care."
11. Johnson, "The Moral Bases."
12. Geiger, "Survival Plans."
13. Morris Fishbein, *Doctors at War* (New York: E.P. Dutton, 1945), p. 3; and cited in Goldwyn and Sidel, "The Physician at War," p. 326.
14. Dwight D. Eisenhower, letter to President Richard L. Simon, Simon & Shuster, 4 April 1956. Quoted by David S. Broder, *Washington Post*, 7 September 1983, p. 17.

SUGGESTED ADDITIONAL READINGS

"The Arms Race." *Lancet* 1, no. 8266 (30 January 1982): 290.

Bates, Donald G., and Ian Carr. "Avoiding Nuclear War: Ultimate in Preventive Medicine?" *Canadian Medical Association Journal* 125, no. 8 (15 October 1981): 923-24, 929-30.

Bingham, Jonathan B. "Doctors Organize to Prevent Nuclear War." *Congressional Record* 127, no. 49 (26 March 1981). H 1194-95.

Bingham, Jonathan B., and Richard A. Knox. "No Medical Defense to a Nuclear Attack." *Congressional Record* 127, no. 1 (5 January 1981). E 12.

Boffey, Philip M. "Preventive Medicine for Nuclear War." *New York Times*, 6 December 1981. E 9.

"Doctors Against the Bomb." *New Scientist* 92, no. 1284 (17 December 1981): 788.

"Doctors Unite Against Nuclear War." *New Scientist* 90, no. 1247 (2 April 1981): 5.

Fish, Hamilton. "First Congress of the International Physicians for the Prevention of Nuclear War." *Congressional Record* 127, no. 49 (26 March 1981). E 1380.

Fouts, David W., and Robert Shepherd. "Nuclear War." *Journal of the American Medical Association* 247, no. 5 (5 February 1982): 581-82.

Holden, Constance. "Physicians Take on Nuclear War." *Science* 207, no. 4438 (28 March 1980): 1449 ff.

"International Physicians for the Prevention of Nuclear War." *Lancet* 1, no. 8223 (4 April 1981): 790-91.

Korcok, Milan. "Physicians Rally Against the Threat of Nuclear Epidemic." *Canadian Medical Association Journal* 123, no. 5 (6 September 1980): 418 ff.

Kornfield, Howard. "The Prevention of Nuclear War as a Medical Priority." *Western Journal of Medicine* 134, no. 4 (April 1981): 365-66.

Lown, Bernard, et al. "The Nuclear-Arms Race and the Physician." *New England Journal of Medicine* 304, no. 12 (19 March 1981): 726-29.

"MDs Asked to Speak Out Against Nuclear War." *Medical World News* 21 (3 March 1980): 23.

Meredith, Christopher, M. Hartog, J.H. Baumer, P.J. Fleming, M.J. Hall, Stewart Britten. "Doves in False Garb." *Nature* 296 (1 April 1982): 386.

Michaels, Evelyne. "Medicine Would Be Helpless in Nuclear War Say Concerned MDs." *Canadian Medical Association Journal* 126, no. 3 (1 February 1982): 315-16.

"Preparations for Nuclear War," *Lancet* 1, no. 8269 (20 February 1982): 443.

Relman, Arnold S. "Physicians, Nuclear War and Politics." *New England Journal of Medicine* 307, no. 12 (16 September 1982): 744-45.

Sidel, Victor W., and Mark Sidel. "Biomedical Science and War," in *Encyclopedia of Bioethics*, vol. 4. New York: The Free Press, 1978. Pp. 1695-99.

Smith, Chandler. "Nuclear War and the Physician." *Postgraduate Medicine* 70, no. 2 (August 1981): 33, 36.

Vastyan, E.A. "Medicine and War," in *Encyclopedia of Bioethics*, vol. 4. New York: The Free Press, 1978. Pp. 1695-99.

_____. "Warriors in White: Some Questions About the Nature and Mission of Military Medicine." *Texas Reports on Biology and Medicine* 32, no. 1 (Spring 1974).

Watts, Malcolm S.M. "Prevention of Nuclear War." *Western Journal of Medicine* 135, no. 3 (September 1981): 233-34.

Wells, Robert J., et al. "The Nuclear Arms Race and the Physician." *New England Journal of Medicine* 305, no. 4 (23 July 1981): 222-23.

Woods, David, "Physicians and the Bomb." *Canadian Medical Association Journal* 125, no. 12 (15 December 1981): 1350.

"World Doctor Group for Nuclear Freeze." *Medical World News* 23, no. 11 (10 May 1982): 76.

19
THE LIMITS OF ALLEGIANCE IN A NUCLEAR AGE

Stephen Toulmin

In recent years, the traditional debate about "the just war"—i.e., about the special conditions on which a resort to war, or its subsequent conduct, can be morally justified—has won fresh attention. Up to now, Michael Walzer's *Just and Unjust Wars* is the most striking academic product of this revival, but it is only the tip of an iceberg. Meanwhile, in the public arena, the U.S. Catholic Bishops' pastoral letter on War and Nuclear Weapons is firmly rooted in earlier traditions of "case reasoning" about moral matters.

Either way, the outlines of the just-war analysis are, by now, once again familiar; so, instead of spending needless time on historical exposition, I will state a few commonplaces, and then move to the specific issues raised by the development and use of nuclear weapons. To state certain traditional conclusions concisely:

— The use of violence against the person is in itself immoral, injurious or unjust, and can be justified only when it can be shown that the situation in question is exceptional: e.g., if the violence is the only available means to preserve one's life against attack, and so is the lesser evil. That much is true of state action, quite as much as it is of the actions of individuals.

— War is the use of violence by one sovereign or state against another, as a means of achieving the political goals of that sovereign or state.

— If legitimate and necessary goals of a sovereign or state (e.g., self-defense) can be gained without war, then war ought to be avoided; if this is not so, then at least the resulting war ought to be conducted in a just rather than an unjust manner.

— A war is conducted justly if and only if the violence used is a necessary means of achieving legitimate goals, its use is discriminating, and no more violence is used than is proportionate to the situation: i.e., if and only if it is the only way to achieve those goals, it is aimed exclusively at targets that obstruct this, and its scale is not disproportionate to their value.

— Citizens who owe allegiance to a sovereign state are morally bound to take part in its properly declared wars to the extent—but only to the extent—that the wars are conducted in a just manner.

— If the authorities of a sovereign state wage unjust wars persistently, or as a matter of policy, the moral claims of allegiance binding the citizens to the state are loosened, and may be overridden by other loyalties.
— In extreme cases, citizens may even have the moral duty to resist the state authorities, and restrain them from continuing to wage an unjust war.

Calling these statements "commonplaces" registers the fact that the traditional debate accepts them as beyond question. Serious argument begins only beyond that point, when one seeks to apply them to ambiguous practical situations: asking (e.g.) what room the claims of allegiance to the modern nation-state leave for the distinction between "combatants" and "noncombatants," or on what conditions a "liberation organization" (say) is morally entitled to act as a state authority.

Some contemporary writers assume that the very existence of nuclear weapons renders the just-war analysis of the morality of warfare irrelevant to our situation. That assumption is hasty and unhelpful. The traditional analaysis was, of course, formulated in another age, and its terms apply unambiguously only to the situation at that time. Still, even now it remains one of the few available starting points from which to survey our own moral territory; and, despite all the military innovations and horrors that face us today, we can find some important continuities between "then" and "now." So, the older analysis has not become flatly irrelevant. We need only take special care in extending its conclusions to our own problems, and in identifying the special difficulties that arise in bringing its application up to date.

Three terms particularly need to be exemplified: (a) that of "disproportionate" force, (b) that of a "sovereign" state, and (c) that of "allegiance" to the nation-state. The just-war analysis was formulated long before the development of modern explosives, to say nothing of military aircraft, in an age of crossbows, swords, and simple cannon. The doctrine of necessary, proportionate, and discriminating force was first addressed to such questions as, "How violently may artillery be used to bombard a besieged city?" It was also a time when the locus of sovereign authority was not hard to identify: an age of monarchs, whose rights and powers were defined and understood. Conversely, the claims of allegiance, too, were well-defined, and limited in the well-understood ways. The claims that a monarch could make on the life, time, or property of his subjects—or on those of his "lieges," which was not the same thing— was limited. At that stage, the romantic totalitarian claims of 20th-century nation-states and superpowers had not yet been conceived.

The definitive statement of the just-war analysis evolved during the 16th and 17th centuries, because they were a time of turmoil. Both the overseas expansion of the European powers, and the wars of religion between Catholics and Protestants nearer home, posed new and serious moral problems: "Do the traditional rules of war apply in fighting pagans or barbarians? What about heretics?" Still, up to the year 1800, one could still wage war in the spirit of Mozart's aria, "Non piu andrai." The first step backward toward the *dis*proportionate, *un*necessary and *un*discriminating violence characteristic of our own century seems to have been taken only as a result of the *professionalization* of warfare initiated by Napoleon Bonaparte.

Living as we do in a time of nuclear weapons and heedless nationalism, we cannot help seeing our ethical problems as vastly graver than those of the 18th century or even the Napoleonic Era. Still, it will be helpful here to consider them in traditional terms. Indeed (I shall argue) the novel difficulties posed by nuclear weapons can be stated with real precision *only* in those terms: viz., as questions about proportionality, sovereignty, and allegiance. Specifically, then, let us address the following questions:

1. Given the destructiveness of nuclear weapons, could their use ever be proportionate to a legitimate goal of state action? If it could not, will not any war in which nuclear weapons are actually used become, *ipso facto*, an unjust war?
2. Given the unlimited violence of nuclear weapons, can their use ever be presented as a legitimate means of self-defense? If not, has not the development of nuclear weapons made the standard assumptions about national sovereignty obsolete?
3. If nuclear warfare makes injustice unavoidable, and renders the claims of national sovereignty hard to sustain, does it not also make a citizen's allegiance to a nuclear power or superpower equally qualified and ambiguous?
4. When we take all these considerations together, how does the existence of nuclear weapons oblige us to reevaluate our loyalties, as between (say) the claims of sovereign nations, our professions, and humanity at large? And what new institutional restraints should we consider setting in place, to reflect the changing pattern of loyalties and allegiances?

PROPORTIONALITY, NECESSITY AND DISCRIMINATION

Technically speaking, the effects of nuclear bombardment exceed anything known from the use of conventional weapons. But, morally speaking, the objections to using nuclear weapons are not without conventional parallels. One may compare them, for example, with the objections raised against the obliteration bombing campaign, using high explosives and fire bombs, against the cities of Germany and Japan (notably Dresden, Hamburg, and Tokyo) executed by the Allies during the closing phase of World War II.

At the time, some people on the Allied side, who knew with some accuracy what was being done in their names, had scruples about this policy, and those scruples are worth recalling. They were of two kinds. They sprang immediately from the fact that the bombardment was *indiscriminate*—most of the victims were civilians, not soldiers—and from a conviction that, even during so-called "total war," the distinction between combatants and noncombatants ought not to be wholly ignored. More generally, however, they also had to do with the lack of restraint (i.e., *proportionality*) characteristic of the campaign: the fact that no serious attempt was made to limit damage from the bombardment to "what was unavoidable to bring about the legitimate goals of State action." Even at the time, it was not clear that the mass destruction of civilian housing promoted any legitimate goal of state action; and, in retrospect, this is even less arguable. While the Allies may have been justified in pursuing the war against Nazi Germany with resolution, and with all legitimate technical means, calling the resulting conflict "total war" did not justify removing all traditional moral restraints from the ways in which it was conducted; and 40 years later, some of us are still ashamed to recall how little we actively challenged the obliteration bombing, while it was still going on.

Is that sense of shame merely personal, idiosyncratic, and overscrupulous? Not at all. Once the indiscriminate character of the bombing was more widely understood, there was a widespread revulsion against it, not least in Britain, which had itself been on the receiving end of mass air attacks, on a smaller scale. Thus, Air Chief Marshall Sir Arthur Harris, the commander-in-chief of R.A.F. Bomber Command responsible for carrying out this obliteration policy, was one of the few major British commanders who did not receive a peerage after the war. Why was he discriminated against? That is a matter for historical debate. But, certainly, with the passage of time—and especially after Hiroshima—there was a general sentiment among people in Britain that the mass bombing policy had not been "their finest hour"; and Sir Arthur Harris himself emigrated to Rhodesia, to become one of the more eminent supporters of Mr. Ian Smith and his white-separatist "unilateral declaration of independence."

Physically and medically, the damage and casualties produced by a single nuclear weapon may be unique in horror and scale, but the line between defensible and indefensible ways of conducting warfare was already crossed, long before the issue of nuclear warfare arose. Indeed, the fact that the obliteration bombing of Germany and Japan in 1943-45 was already open to strong, though conditional, moral objection adds force to the argument that the use of nuclear weapons is *unconditionally immoral*. Given that the material damage and civilian suffering at Hamburg or Dresden were already disproportionate to any legitimate goals of state action, how much more clearly will this be the case about any use of nuclear weapons?

By setting the effects of nuclear weapons alongside those of conventional weapons, we make it clear that the burden of proof— already in doubt at the end of World War II with the growing violence of modern total war—has by now shifted decisively. Whether the casualties and damage produced in the bombing of Dresden, Hamburg, and Tokyo were excusable is a matter about which disagreement is still possible. Given its historical context, residual doubt is also possible about President Truman's decision to drop nuclear bombs on Hiroshima and Nagasaki without a prior "demonstration" of the new weapons. But, with all that we know now, any serious analysis of the issue must surely lead to the same conclusion as that of the U.S. Catholic Bishops.

To put the point concisely:

— No one has yet formulated *any* legitimate goal of state action that can be gained *only* by the actual use of nuclear weapons. So the moral presumption against such undiscriminating and disproportionate violence remains in place.

This is not the place to pursue the vexing question of whether the possession of nuclear weapons, as instruments of deterrence, is either morally acceptable in itself, or practically compatible with the acknowledgment that it would be morally *un*acceptable to put those instruments to actual use. There is no satisfactory way of dealing with that question briefly, and the discussion in the Catholic Bishops' letter is a useful starting point for any fuller discussion. But we must here consider one possible objection to the present argument: namely, that, in conceivable circumstances, it might be necessary and legitimate to use tactical nuclear weapons against a large-scale attack in Central Europe by conventional forces of the Warsaw Pact.

As to that, one may reply that those who advance this objection in full seriousness need to spell out for themselves, in specific and concrete detail, what the immediate character and likely effects of their actions would be, keeping in mind the nature of the actual terrain of Central Europe, the distribution of population in the region, and the long-term sterilization of the land that would follow from that use. If we reflect once again on the indiscriminate and disproportionate nature of the violence that this suggestion proposes, we shall see that its plausibility is similar to that of the World War II obliteration bombing policy. It looks like a neat way of solving an undoubted military problem; but it is a technique whose actual employment—even if it apparently "worked" in the short term—would become the object of retrospective shame and regret, in a similar way and for similar reasons to those which have, in retrospect, discredited the obliteration bombing policy of World War II.

Why are people so ready to contemplate this possibility, as a matter to be considered coolly, in a spirit of moral equanimity and political realism? If we study the rhetoric of this argument carefully, to see how the balance is tilted, we cannot wholly overlook the continuing influence of cold war demonology. The rivalry of the superpowers remains a major obstacle to any moral critique of contemporary political issues: on either side of this great divide, it is sufficient to hold up the possible victory of evil over good, i.e., of them over us, in order to give the color of justification to even the most inexcusable of policies. On both sides, fanaticism distorts political perception, both of the intrinsic character of the policies discussed and of their long-term consequences and implications: notably, what kinds of policies they will be seen to have been, and what their broader consequences will be perceived as having been (pardon the phrase) "once the dust has settled."

The issue is not a new one. In their passion for conquest, the 16th-century European invaders of the Americas resented the pope's insistence that the Native Americans were human beings, and so entitled to the same consideration as other human beings. Enthusiastic participants in the 16th-and 17th-century wars of religion likewise saw their victims' heresies as excusing any brutality toward them. At the present time, some people are equally tempted to banish communists (or terrorists, or counter-revolutionaries, or imperialists, as the case may be) outside the moral pale, and beyond the reach of all human consideration. So, when holders of public office talk like Alexander Haig, as though we may legitimately use nuclear weapons against the foes of righteousness, we must beg them to consult their consciences, and consider whether they are not yielding to fanaticism.

To put the issue in these terms is not to attribute motives to Alexander Haig or anyone else. (Who can imagine what morally serious state of mind people are in, when they accept the idea of a "limited nuclear exchange"?) It is merely to reformulate the central point that, as matters stand, the presumption (or moral burden of proof) against any use of nuclear weapons is vastly too high to be surmounted by any of the excuses advanced up to now. Many of us, indeed, are unable to think of any considerations that could excuse, or even palliate, the pain and destruction that would unavoidably result from any future use of nuclear violence, and are confident that the moral presumption against the use of nuclear weapons will remain unrebutted. From this point of view, it would even be morally inexcusable to repeat the obliteration bombing of 1943-45 if none but conventional weapons were employed; and that is *a fortiori* the case of nuclear weapons, with their vastly greater power to destroy, injure, and poison living things of all kinds.

Putting the point as moderately as the gravity of the issues permits, let me summarize it as follows: *In the absence of fresh rebuttals ("excuses") far more powerful than any offered up to now, there is at present no reason to believe that any future use of nuclear weapons will be anything but gravely immoral.*

SOVEREIGNTY

At this point, we may step back. The just-war analysis was first addressed to a situation in which political relations, as much as military technology, were much simpler than they now are. In the Middle Ages, local lords made war against their neighbors using military forces that comprised both horse-riding knights, who were their feudal dependents and sworn "liegemen," and paid mercenaries, who volunteered to "die for a living." The damage these forces were capable of doing was quite limited, and there was no stronger power that could prevent them fighting at all. So a comprehensive moral injunction against all wars would have had no effect: it was more urgent and more realistic to regulate and moderate the wars, by drawing some first lines (e.g.) between those people who were, and those who were not, justly at risk in the associated violence. In legal terms, the knights were justly open to injury and loss, because their feudal oaths implied an assumption of risk: the mercenaries accepted the same risks voluntarily, as explicit or implied terms of their contracts of employment. (Hence the moral weight that was initially attached to distinguishing military or "combatant" from civilian or "noncombatant" personnel.)

With this first context in mind, we can see why the just-war account emphasized the kinds of considerations it did; and also, in consequence, why social and political changes since the 18th century (no less than changes in military technology) oblige us to reconsider the terms of that analysis, before we apply it to our own times and problems. These social and political changes affect all the parties to military violence: the "sovereign" authorities at whose instance the war is carried on, the military or combatant forces who are the actual agents of violence, and the civilians, or noncombatants, who are the nonviolent contributors to, onlookers at, and/or victims of warfare.

As to the notion of "sovereignty": absent effective limits or institutional constraints on the actions of sovereign nations, international relations are organized as relations between nation-states. At least *de jure*, each of these states is accepted as having unabridged liberty to manage its internal affairs. True, it is understood that these states generally agree to conform to a range of agreements governing many of their interactions, the exchange of mail (say), or the regulation of deep-sea fishing. Such agreements are treated, however, not as formal abridgments on their "national sovereignty," but as voluntary restraints on their *exercise* of that sovereignty. Even the provisions to which member-nations of the European Economic Community are subject, with the associated sanctions, are no exception to that general statement. They were all accepted voluntarily, as a consequence of each nation's adhesion to the Treaty of Rome; and they can be legally avoided, by a free decision to secede from the community. (In the American sense, that is, there as yet exists no "United States of Europe.")

It was all very well to leave the claims of national sovereignty unabridged for so long as the exercise of sovereign rights had (and could have) only limited, controlled, and well-directed effects. In our own time, that is less and less the case, not merely because of the introduction of new military technologies, but more widely. The degree of interdependence between nation-states is generally increasing in the areas of ecology, agriculture, medicine, and elsewhere. To an increasing extent, for instance, any state that ignores responsibility for (say) the flow of industrial effluents from its factories, or the movement of smallpox carriers across its frontiers, risks finding itself an outlaw in the community of nations. *De facto*, if not yet *de jure*, such a state increasingly exposes itself to sanctions at the hands of other nations.

As yet, of course, the "supranational" republic of nations lacks formal institutions capable of imposing sanctions on outlaw nations. To that extent, the powers by which the nations jointly restrain such outlaws rest at most on agreements to pool their forces and institutions in the service of common interests. But, just as state power did not always begin as centralized power, so too "supranational" power may first take shape, not through the deliberate creation of a world state, but through the tacit acceptance of decentralized modes of supranational collaboration. Long before it is abandoned *de jure*, which will be a long time happening, the hitherto unrestricted "sovereignty" of the nation-state will be hedged in by voluntary limits and restrictions, to such an extent that it loses, at least *de facto*, most of the probability of its being gravely misused.

This general statement calls for qualifications. It assumes that on the international level, as within particular states, greater interdependence makes it increasingly disadvantageous for states to act as "outlaws," even in advance of formal machinery for the enforcement of international law. On certain occasions, of course, certain states still tend to calculate that the potential gains from the outlawry are worth their price; to that extent, the risks to humanity at large from the survival of "national sovereignty" will remain grave for many years. But, as Vico and the Epicureans both foresaw, the pragmatic demands of the actual situation may nonetheless lead to the progressive crystallization of supranational institutions and constraints, without any prior need for the sovereign nations involved to agree explicitly on any formal treaty or contract.

What is the relevance of this general argument to nuclear weapons and warfare? It reminds us that in form, if not degree, the problem of developing institutions for the control of new and threatening technologies is one that humanity has successfully dealt with before. One legacy of that victory is the myth of Prometheus. Many people wonder why Prometheus, the benefactor of humanity, was sentenced in folk memory to be crucified and disemboweled. The answer is not hard to guess. Those who saw what power Prometheus had put into the hands of malefactors—e.g., how they could use fire to burn down their neighbors' crops and houses—found the very name of fire as alarming as the word "atom" is to some people today. In their eyes, the destructive threat of fire outweighed all the blessings of controllable heat; and all the good that Prometheus had thought to bring the human race was apparently canceled out by the risks to which his discovery had exposed them.

What brought the technology of fire under human control was a *legal* invention: the concept of "arson." The use of fire was safely naturalized into human life through the development of new institutions and public attitudes, by which the *misuse* of fire was stigmatized as antihuman and punished as a crime. And, if effective ways of controlling nuclear power have so far eluded us, that represents a failure of our institutional imaginations. Lacking the means to police, arraign, and restrain the governments of nation-states, we risk the worst arson ever perpetrated, with neither police protection nor judicial process.

In these circumstances, the intensification and spread in *all* nations of public sentiment about the threat from nuclear weapons, about lack of care in the siting, construction, and management of nuclear power plants, and about the disposal of nuclear wastes are probably the best instruments immediately available to prepare for the emergence of the novel institutions we need. As Henry Maine observed on the national level, the *fiat* of a sovereign can be fully effective as law only where its execution recruits the support and sentiment of the subjects. So here, the breadth and intensity of general public sentiment about nuclear issues, as about environmental ones, will in the long run force the hands of the authorities of nation-states, by creating constraints that will limit *de facto* the practical exercise of powers which those states, as "sovereigns," technically (*de jure*) still possess.

Is that hope realistic? Or are there special reasons why developments that were effective in earlier cases cannot work in the nuclear case? As to that, we should not underrate the beneficent effects of historical obsolescence. The Holy Roman Empire existed in theory, long after it lost any practical role in European politics. This fact was no doubt very *untidy*, but any attempt to abolish the empire formally, with the agreement of all the parties concerned, would have done more harm than good: it was better to let it sink into irreversible impotence. Under its fading umbrella, there grew up the smaller, individual nations that eventually took over the powers that Charlemagne's successors (like those of Alexander before him) retained only in name, not in effect.

During the 1970s, there were similar hopeful signs that the so-called "super-powers" were losing their dominance over world affairs, as smaller regional group-ings began to tackle local problems in their own ways, over which America and Russia no longer had a controlling influence. In the 1980s, this hopeful tendency has (it is true) been checked, but that check could well be transient. In time, the diseconomies of scale that now hamper the dinosaurs of the industrial world may well make political superpowerdom, also, irrelevant to the everyday conduct of international affairs. In that case, smaller powers will see that the nuclear strength of both superpowers rests on an element of bluff, and they may develop the courage to call that bluff.

ALLEGIANCE

Once we move beyond this point, the argument becomes more radical. A just-war analysis obliged subjects to take part in a sovereign's wars only *conditionally.* If the sovereign were in grave or repeated breach of those conditions, their duty became to resist, restrain, or depose him. Persistent violation of the moral restraints on military operations, *ipso facto*, made a war an unjust war; and a sovereign who persistently involved his subjects in unjust wars dissolved those bonds of allegiance that required his subjects to obey his commands.

Thus, feudal allegiance was conditional. Knights were open to injury and loss because of their feudal oaths, mercenaries because they were under contract; in both cases there was a *quid pro quo*. The sovereign owed mercenaries whatever was due under their contracts and, although such contracts were usually verbal, they were nonetheless binding on men of honor. To his knights and liegemen, the sovereign owed something more: his support, his protection, and a share in the fortunes of his realm, on account of their obedient collaboration. Still, subjects of neither kind were bound to obey unjust commands. The relations of liege and liegeman, sovereign and subject, mercenary and lord were two-way relations, and the obligations so created could be breached by the sovereign as much as by his subjects. So, quite apart from all matters of prudence, a medieval monarch (like a pirate chief) had a standing obligation to keep "in" with his subjects and to "deliver the goods." Embroiling his subjects in unjust wars was just one way in which the sovereign could fail in his duties, and put his subjects' "allegiance" at risk.

What protection did this situation provide to the civilians or noncombatants who were not direct parties to the contracts or oaths of obedience? The answer to that question survives to this day in the traditions of "common law," which coincided with those of current "common morality." Both oaths and contracts have an effect only within broader limits set by morality. Neither the consequences of an oath nor the provisions of a contract can—even now—be insisted upon or enforced where they violate those moral limits. (Gambling debts are matters of honor, and neither morally binding nor recoverable by law; prostitutes are under neither a moral nor a contractual obligation to provide sexual services, etc.) When attempts are made to extend the scope of contracts or promises beyond morally acceptable limits, courts will refuse to enforce them, on the ground that their effects will be "unconscionable," i.e., against conscience.

No doubt, in actual practice, this doctrine gave medieval civilians little protection and left them highly vulnerable—especially since they were under pressure to place themselves, too, in a subject position, and accept obligations within the larger social hierarchy. But the moral position was quite clear: it was never a knight's (or a mercenary's) moral duty to rape or pillage, even if his lord ordered him to do so. At that point, the lord's orders overreached their standing limits, and must be set aside as unconscionable.

How does the traditional notion of "allegiance" apply to the citizens of a modern nation-state? And how can we apply to those citizens the aspects of a just-war analysis that hang on this notion? Those questions do not have clear or obvious answers. In the United States, the political education of schoolchildren is confused by the ceremony of pledging allegiance to the flag. (That phrase is at best a romantic figure of speech: there is no intelligible sense in which a flag can undertake to perform the obligations of a "liege lord.") In any other respect, the term "allegiance" figures rarely in modern life and thought. Instead, romantic communal enthusiasms are permitted to conceal the fact that the moral obligations that arise from the bonds of loyalty to any state are conditional on the conduct of its officials, and can quite easily be forfeited by them.

Still, despite all the changes in social organization since the Middle Ages, a citizen's obligations do remain conditional. By itself, the mere fact that the officials who exercise a state's sovereign powers were dramatically elected, and not imposed on the state by an hereditary ruling group, by a single dominant party, or by naked force, does nothing to exempt them from the traditional obligations of a sovereign to his subjects. Nor are those officials free to demand that subjects obey any and all of their orders, just and unjust alike. That much will be familiar to all readers of Thoreau's essay *Civil Disobedience*: here, we may just pursue the special implications of the point for the issues raised by nuclear weapons and war.

In discussing "proportionality" and "discrimination," we saw that a just-war analysis leads to three conclusions:

1. No legitimate goal of state action which is urgent and important enough to excuse the suffering produced by the use of nuclear weapons could be achieved *only* by the use of those weapons.

2. In no foreseeable circumstances can nuclear weapons be the necessary means to any legitimate goals of military action; and

3. A war in which nuclear weapons are actually used will thus, *ipso facto*, be an unjust war.

We can now add the fourth conclusion:

4. Any actual use of nuclear weapons by a state will at once dissolve the bonds of loyalty and call into question the duty of obedience otherwise binding on the citizens of that state.

In short: as matters stand, *one immediate effect of any actual use of nuclear weapons by the governing authorities of a modern state will be to justify its citizens in disobedience.*

Taken in an isolated and general form, that conclusion is too weak and theoretical to be of use. Once a nuclear exchange between two states has actually begun, what good will it do for a few citizens on either or both sides to declare themselves in a state of disobedience? Still, if we carry our analysis a stage further, two practical suggestions are worth considering:

1. The threat of widespread, morally based disobedience in the event of actual nuclear war will be a healthy check on the military planning of any Nuclear Power. (We may refer to this as the doctrine of counter-deterrence.)

2. A redirection of people's loyalties, away from the nation-state and toward other independent moral claims, can provide a parallel check on the reckless or irresponsible conduct of governments. (We may refer to this as the doctrine of multiple loyalties.)

The Doctrine of Counter-Deterrence

Imagine that the citizens of the nuclear powers unambiguously require the state's officials to acknowledge the moral situation. In future, they insist, any use of nuclear weapons must put the organs of the state irretrievably in the wrong. Once this has happened, the citizens will declare the bonds of national loyalty dissolved; they will be released from the moral claims of allegiance to their former nation-states; and, as they rebuild their towns and their lives, they will be free to organize themselves into fresh political entities from the ground up. Under a just-war analysis, the nation-state will have forfeited its authority and abdicated its sovereignty. That being so, its citizens may take public affairs into their own hands and order them according to their own decisions.

Surely, that declaration will have little practical effect: even the effect of threatening it will be little greater than the effect of the current state policy of nuclear deterrence. But neither nuclear deterrence nor counter-deterrence (which is its mirror image) addresses the actual situation: both resort to hypothetical scenarios to make points of political rhetoric.

When, for instance, representatives of the nuclear powers present their policies, either in diplomatic contexts or as exercises in public relations, they always take care to add pious disclaimers. They do not really foresee using those weapons: they retain them only because they are in danger from the nuclear weapons of their adversaries. Under the theory of deterrence, rival powers are held back from nuclear war by a fear that springs from the threat of actions that, at the same time, both sides disclaim as unthinkable. Unfortunately, their disclaimers are no more self-interpreting than a broad wink. No hearer can be entirely sure which to take seriously: the threat to use nuclear weapons in hypothetical circumstances, or the disclaimers that accompany this threat. Nor can onlookers ever be fully confident that the officials who formulate these policies are clear about them in their own minds. The U.S. nuclear freeze movement, in fact, got a major boost from things that Alexander Haig said as secretary of state. These provoked the reasonable fear that he himself no longer knew when he was winking and when he was serious. He had apparently talked himself beyond mere deterrence, and now thought of nuclear weapons as morally tolerable instruments of war.

If the state doctrine of deterrence is based on governmental posturing, therefore, it is no objection to a citizens' doctrine of counter-deterrence that it, too, rests on histrionics. In the world of political rhetoric, the sham of deterrence can only be answered by an equally striking countergesture. If the state authorities build up nuclear arsenals that they plan to use only on "hypothetical" conditions, their citizens are entitled to insist in reply that one further consequence of that hypothetical scenario will be the moral suicide of the state concerned.

At this point, an historical sidelight can be helpful. The medieval balance of church and state placed a check on willful and impetuous monarchs or barons; but, from the 16th century on, that check was lost. Fragmentation of spiritual authority and secularization of the state brought into being a new world of absolute sovereigns, who were viewed as God's political agents. Soon enough, of course, the claim of these individual monarchs to unrestricted sovereign power was challenged by their subjects; but that challenge merely shifted the same unrestricted sovereign power from the individual autocrat to other larger, oligarchic or democratic parties and assemblies. From 1650 on, the locus of sovereignty moved from the king to other estates of the realm, but its moral exercise remained effectively unchecked by any countervailing institutions.

True, the new institutions of representative government were supposed (*inter alia*) to speak as the moral voice of the people's conscience. But it was not easy to combine this task with that of being the political voice of larger constituencies: in actual practice, parliaments and congresses have been more effective in their political functions than in their moral ones. Instead of standing aside and serving as moral critics of the sovereign authorities, they have competed for a share of sovereign power. As a result, the political operation of modern nation-states has no more been restricted by institutionalized moral criticism than were the decisions of 17th-century absolute monarchs; and the resulting state of affairs has persisted for some 300 years, punctuated only by a series of revolutions, in the British North American colonies, France, Russia, and elsewhere, whose spokesmen always chose to justify the resulting shifts in political power as fulfilling, also, important *moral* goals.

Once again, however, the compromise on which this 300-year interregnum rested is undercut by the development of nuclear weapons. In their roles as the moral critics of nation-states, parliaments, congresses and supreme Soviets alike share a common failing: they, too, are committed to a belief in unqualified national sovereignty. Yet the claims of morality cannot be kept within the frontiers of any single state; and the voice of moral criticism can be—and often has been—raised across national boundaries. That is why, for lack of a better forum, we so often see the organs of the United Nations used as a locus for moral declarations and denunciations.

The Doctrine of Multiple Loyalties

So far, the kernel of our argument has been that 20th-century nations, states and communities are laying claim to rights and loyalties as unlimited as those of absolute monarchs: meanwhile, the facts of life, death, and power in a nuclear age make it morally proper and vitally necessary to find a way of restricting the scope of those claims.

Given the moral authority of the medieval church, monarchs and barons were open to external criticism, and could no longer claim to be in the right when they acted unconscionably. It was no doubt annoying for a monarch to find his authority challenged: in this respect, the conflict of wills between King Henry II and Thomas Becket, represented in T.S. Eliot's *Murder in the Cathedral*, was merely typical. Nowadays, when the conduct of affairs falls into the hands of unscrupulous or willful generals, presidents, and party leaders, we have no such defense. In our pluralistic society, there is neither a generally accepted source of moral criticism, nor a common standard against which their conduct can be measured; as a result, the state authorities can defend their claims to authority against external criticism by appealing to nationalistic passions— i.e., by "wrapping themselves in the flag."

Historically, then, the current reaction against the claims of nationalism, and the rise of morally based pressure groups, have a longer-term importance. Taken together, they can even be seen as first steps toward a renewed system of civil religion. Sometimes alongside, and sometimes in alliance with, the churches, a coalition of "movements" (devoted to environmental protection, nuclear freeze, consumers' rights, and similar issues) is engaged in restating that consensus about the human interests underlying moral arguments, which, ever since Aquinas, has been seen to carry conviction with "the natural reason" of all humans alike. And when industrialists and politicians find these pressure groups irritating, the reasons are once again familiar: recall King Henry II's heartfelt cry, "Who will rid me of this meddlesome priest?"

There is no occasion to relax this pressure. Whoever is its current occupant, the White House can never be a bed of roses; nor can major political decisions be exempt from moral appraisal and criticism. When, for instance, Richard Nixon spoke neither of the people, nor of the Constitution, but of *himself* as "the Sovereign," his hearers well understood that, in his fantasies, the powers of the president were those of an absolute monarch. If the authorities of nation-states have been able to elevate themselves above criticism, as the sole judges and guardians of "the national interest," that is because, in the countries of the industrialized world, the earlier consensus has fallen into disorder. So the central question becomes: *In the name of whom, or what, can this external criticism of the modern nation-states—its governors, officials and functionaries—be conducted? In a largely secular society, what other loyalties can counterbalance the unqualified claims of nation, community, or state?*

This is where the issue of multiple loyalties is crucial. The medieval church spoke in the name of a God whose authority no one, however great his temporal power, was ready to challenge. Faced with the exaggerated claims of the modern nation-state, individual citizens need other foci of loyalty and interest, in order to counter those claims. The issue is both complex and delicate, and we can land ourselves in trouble by tackling it on too abstract a level. The French revolutionaries, for instance, saw the problem clearly; but their counterreligion of reason and humanity quickly degenerated into authoritarian idolization. Rival groups of Marxist, Leninist, and Maoist ideologues today speak, with passionate intensity, about the interests of the workers, and the policies that will (in their views) promote those interests. At once, however, moral conflicts arise: by some preestablished harmony, those policies are always ones that guarantee the ideologues themselves positions of great political power. So, we need to find foci of loyalty that are as powerful as those of nationalism, but also less abstract, more familiar, and associated with values that are less easily corrupted.

One such focus is the loyalties and values we encounter in professional life. Commonly, these loyalties and values have a transnational, or even international, scope and institutional expression. (The USSR views the World Psychiatric Association with the same jaundiced eye that Henry II turned on Becket.) In the history of the nuclear freeze movement, one supranational forum within which the antinuclear case has made real progress has been the professions, most notably the medical profession. Physicians, preeminently, have special reason to recognize other moral claims besides those of nation-states; and, to a lesser extent, the same is true of all professionals. So, if groups like Physicians for Social Responsibility have had a major role in the public advocacy of a nuclear freeze, that is no accident, owing (say) to the charismatic personalities of some individual speakers. Rather, it reflects the multiple loyalties to which physicians are essentially subject, as being not merely citizens, but also humans and professionals.

Professionals of many kinds—physicians most of all—can understand the consequences of a nuclear exchange and explain to their fellow citizens the catastrophic implications of current policies in all the nuclear powers. If any alternative focus of loyalty can serve today as an immediate check on the unqualified claims of the idolatrously "sovereign" nation, it is the duties that are well known to all professionals: duties toward clients, patients, and fellow-humans in general, whose scope carries across the boundaries between different nations and states. An American physician or Russian psychiatrist, an Israeli lawyer or Danish mathematician faces his own built-in ethical conflicts. Between purely national duties to a state and (say) the supranational duties of a physician to all sick human beings, such conflicts are to be expected. So there is special room for professional people to band together and use their shared commitment to the values of their disciplines as a ground to question authority and "think otherwise."

To sum up: The claims of the nation-state over the citizen have increased, are increasing, and ought to be diminished. As professional people, for instance, we are not merely entitled to weigh our loyalties as professionals against our loyalties as (say) Russians or Americans; we are morally obliged to do so. If we find these professional obligations overriding those of national affiliation, so be it. *It is in fact a professional duty for people to measure their national loyalties against their human and professional consciences, and to question the judgment of politicians and other spokesmen for "the national interest," whenever their factual knowledge or their moral perceptiveness requires.*

In both of these directions—both counter-deterrence and multiple loyalties—critics of current nuclear weapons policy in the nation-state are already following, intuitively, the route that a just-war analysis legitimates. A world in which people still act on the maxim "My country, right or wrong" is a world headed for self-destruction; for any worship of the nation can blind us to the conditional claims which are all that sovereign power—even, that of a beloved country—can justly make on us.

We can win back our souls, and have a reasonable chance of preserving our bodies, only by fighting against the idolatry of the nation; since, in the last resort, the claims of human survival must override the claims of sovereignty and nationhood. As human beings and professionals, we must oppose the unjust acts—above all, the unjust wars and threats of war—conducted by our own nation-states. And, if this means threatening disobedience, then, once again, so be it. Along that road, we shall at least be traveling in excellent company.

PART V

THE NONNUCLEAR FUTURE: TOWARD A REFORMATION OF SOCIAL AND POLITICAL REALITIES

The maxims of philosophers concerning the conditions under which public peace is possible shall be consulted by nations armed for war.

Immanuel Kant, *Perpetual Peace*

What can be done to remove the nuclear threat? To answer this we must move from ethics to politics, seeking a political solution to a political problem. But the kinds of political solutions considered should not be limited to familiar maneuvers within existing political structures. A conventional political solution to the nuclear threat may not be possible; fundamental political change may be required. This would not be surprising: the radical difference between nuclear and conventional weapons may fundamentally challenge our traditional political thinking as much as it does our traditional military thinking. In keeping with our theme of examining fundamental questions, this part offers different approaches to removing the nuclear threat that involve fundamental political change.

A strong interest in nonconventional political solutions arose in the late 1940s, as Milton Fisk points out. Then the shock of the invention of nuclear weapons was still fresh, and the radical difference between nuclear and conventional weapons was easily perceived. Over the intervening decades the sense of shock has been dulled, and the radical difference is perhaps less apparent. This is suggested in present counterforce drift of nuclear strategy, which is increasing the tendency to view nuclear weapons as usable, hence more like other weapons. This loss of perception of difference has two consequences: the nuclear threat may itself be greater, since what is seen as more usable is more likely to be used, and we are less likely to recognize that basic political change may be needed to deal with it.

Nuclear weapons pose a serious threat because their possession is seen as necessary to maintain national security. Thus, before the threat can be removed, an alternative basis for national security must be found. Because nuclea ·eapons are such a fixture of our current social and political attitudes and instituti ⅃ arrangements, it seems likely that only basic change in these attitudes and institutions could establish such an alternative. The kind of fundamental change required is a question on which the authors in this section take a range of positions.

Dietrich Fischer argues that national security is best achieved by replacing nuclear deterrence with a policy he calls *dissuasion*. Whereas deterrence policies seek to reduce the likelihood of aggression by making war more costly for one's opponent, dissuasion emphasizes the three other kinds of disincentives: reducing the gain from war, increasing the gain from peace, and reducing the cost of peace. The policy of dissuasion, Fischer argues, could be adopted unilaterally to the advantage of either side.

Edward McClennen, on the contrary, argues that national security can be achieved only by multilateral change, the creation of a *world government* to enforce basic rights by law. To break the logic of "prisoner's dilemma," nations must agree on a coercive central authority. Louis Beres disagrees, arguing that a coercive central authority would still have to rely on nuclear deterrence, and that nuclear deterrence in any form cannot be the basis of long-term security. The proper path to world-order reform Beres calls *planetization*, the formation of a cooperative, international, political climate. Beres's position seems to emphasize primary changes in attitudes rather than in institutional structure.

Arne Naess also emphasizes changes in attitude, but the changes he recommends—leading to a national policy of nonviolent resistence—seem quite different than those Beres has in mind. Naess, bringing an important European and "Green" perspective to the discussion, argues that only unilateral disarmament can avoid the risk of nuclear war. The worst that could happen under such a policy is foreign occupation, and the deep cultural changes necessary to accept unilateral disarmament are those needed to adopt nonviolent resistance as the proper response should occupation occur. Naess, like McClennen, takes the task of maintaining national security out of the hands of the state, but instead of internationalizing the security function by world government, Naess *privatizes* it by putting it in the hands of individual practitioners of nonviolent resistance. In either case, states would no longer need to rely on nuclear weapons for national security.

Removing the nuclear threat by privatizing national security is also recommended by the final two authors, but each insists that prior consideration be given to fundamental change in political institutions. Richard Falk claims that most proposed solutions to the nuclear threat lack an understanding of how existing state/society relations constrain efforts to reverse the arms race. We must alter these relations by revitalizing democracy, eroding the state's ability to make war by taking the security function into our own hands through mobilization for militant nonviolent resistance. Milton Fisk argues that the state itself, by striving for military superiority over other states, is responsible for the arms race. To reverse the arms race, we must change the state structure through social revolution to one of genuine equality. Such a state, not seeking military superiority, would have to be defended by popular resistance.

20
DISSUASION: TOWARD AN ACTIVE PEACE POLICY

Dietrich Fischer

With the goal of maintaining national security, the United States and the Soviet Union have, over the last four decades, gradually built the capacity for human extinction, without anyone deliberately wanting it and, until recently, without our being quite aware of it. (How we have been sliding into the present situation is described in Chapter 2 by John P. Holdren. The other nations possessing nuclear arms probably do not yet have an arsenal sufficient to bring about human extinction, but they are approaching it.)

The discovery of the phenomenon of nuclear winter was more or less a coincidence (Sagan 1983). When the U.S. spacecraft Mariner 9 circled Mars in 1971, it observed a cooling of the Martian surface caused by a dust storm in the atmosphere. This observation led scientists to calculate the temperature changes on the earth's surface that would result from the dust and smoke clouds covering the earth after a nuclear war. The cooling was found to be so severe, on all continents, that any human survivors might starve to death. (The only way to know for certain would be to try it out.)

Without this accidental discovery, a nation might have brought about human extinction, without anticipating it, in a futile attempt to save itself by destroying the nuclear forces of its opponent in a preemptive strike. Yet Colin Gray and Keith Payne (1980; 25) have advocated such an "intelligent U.S. offensive strategy, wedded to homeland defenses, [which] should reduce U.S. casualties to approximately 20 million." They criticize the thought that "because the United States could lose as many as 20 million people, it should not save the 80 million or more who would otherwise be a risk" (p. 27). They declare that "nuclear war is unlikely to be an essentially meaningless, terminal event. Instead it is likely to be waged to coerce the Soviet Union to give up some recent gain" (p. 26).

It has now become apparent that even if a surprise counterforce strike aimed at destroying the nuclear forces of an opponent were 100 percent "successful," even if the other side were rendered incapable of retaliation, the ensuing changes in the

I wish to acknowledge support from the Ford Foundation under Grant No. 845-0345, which facilitated preparation of this chapter.

global climate would probably destroy the attacking nation as well, and all the other nations of the earth. In that sense, nuclear weapons have now been recognized as being similar in their effect to biological weapons. Biologically active killers could multiply and spread around the earth, sparing no country from their effects if they were used on a large scale. This insight made it relatively easy to conclude the 1972 treaty banning biological weapons (SIPRI 1982; 227). No nation would choose to use weapons that obviously would also kill its own population.

At least we have now become better aware of the far-reaching consequences of the use of nuclear weapons. Of course, this knowledge alone by no means guarantees that we will not use nuclear weapons to bring about human extinction. But at least we can no longer claim ignorance.

Almost everyone (except, perhaps, Gray and Payne) agrees that a nuclear war must be avoided. Opinions diverge as to how this is best to be done. Some emphasize national security as the overriding goal and advocate higher arms expenditures. Others stress the need for peace and advocate arms reductions, even if unilateral. One almost gets the impression that a choice must be made between security or peace. But there is no security without peace in the nuclear age. Both goals must be, and can be, pursued simultaneously. We will see that the crucial issue is not simply one of quantity, whether to spend *more* or *less* for defense, but of the *type* of defense that is most effective in achieving a secure peace.

A number of approaches aimed at preventing nuclear war will be examined in the following. To be effective, a clear understanding is needed of each method's promises and risks, the support it enjoys, and the opposition it faces. Some approaches can be taken independently by either side, while other approaches require mutual cooperation. Independent measures are, in a certain sense, easier to implement, because they do not depend on the uncertain outcome of complicated negotiations with an adversary. They can also buy time to give us a better chance to work out the more fundamental changes required in the international system to prevent nuclear war, and war in general. But independent strategies are usually less far-reaching, and cannot give as lasting security as measures based on mutual agreement.

Among steps requiring mutual agreement are, in the short term, various bilateral arms control and disarmament proposals. In the longer term, they must include the development of mechanisms to resolve international conflicts in other ways than through war. Even total mutual nuclear disarmament will be insufficient to guarantee against a nuclear holocaust. If nations continue to settle their differences through war, the temptation will always remain that one side or the other might build nuclear weapons again, to avert defeat. The knowledge of how to make these weapons cannot be eradicated as long as civilization exists.

The dispute whether short-term or long-term measures are more important is futile. As Jonathan Schell (1984) has aptly put it, such a dispute is comparable to an argument over whether the victim of an accident bleeding slowly to death needs an ambulance or major surgery. Obviously, he needs both.

This chapter will be limited to a discussion of some *independent* strategies that have been proposed for nuclear powers to protect their national security: defense, deterrence, preemption, and dissuasion. We will examine which strategies may help reduce the likelihood of nuclear war, and which of them may actually increase it.

DEFENSE

The concept of defensive arms has attractive aspects. Such arms are useful to prevent aggression, but by themselves cannot be used to carry out aggression. If a country builds conventional antitank and antiaircraft weapons, but no tanks and bombers, a neighboring country will not feel threatened by such purely defensive weapons. As long as the neighbor has no plans to invade the country so equipped, it has nothing to fear. If a country builds bomb shelters for its civilian population, its people are somewhat protected against conventional bombing raids, but such shelters do not threaten anyone else.

There are, indeed, very good reasons to concentrate on purely defensive equipment in the area of conventional arms, and to avoid deliberately the construction of offensive arms that must be perceived as a potential threat by adversaries, regardless of any declared intentions as to their use. The best way to prove purely defensive intentions is not to acquire the objective capability for offense. A concentration on defense alone does not generate mutual fear, and therefore has much less tendency to stimulate an arms race than a buildup of offensive arms. If we possess the capacity to carry out offensive military operations, no matter what our intentions may be, potential opponents will see us as a threat to their security and will seek ways and means to eliminate that threat. This, in turn, will reduce our own security.

Can concentrating on pure defense also serve to protect a nation against a potential nuclear attack? Ronald Reagan, in his so-called "star-wars" speech of 23 March 1983, proposed that the United States develop space-based beam weapons that could destroy nuclear missiles in flight. He even offered to share such a defensive technology with the Soviet Union at some future time. He added, "I have become more and more deeply convinced that the human spirit must be capable of rising above dealing with other nations and human beings by threatening their existence . . . Would it not be better to save lives than to avenge them?"

The underlying idea is praiseworthy, but the proposal has some serious flaws. First, let us try to imagine the U.S. reaction if the Soviet Union announced it was going to develop a space-based defense against nuclear missiles (while keeping its own missiles). The US would be frightened, and would have reason to be: such a technology could theoretically enable the USSR to subject the US to nuclear blackmail with no threat of retaliation. Even if the USSR promised to make that technology available to the US, the US would (and should) hesitate to base its security on such a promise. The US would probably want to increase its nuclear arsenal so it could penetrate any Soviet defense and maintain its potential to deter a Soviet attack. And it must be assumed that the Soviet reaction to the proposed US development would be exactly the same.

Second, laser or particle beams in space can be effective only against ballistic missiles that leave the atmosphere. The United States has already developed the counterweapon to such a defense: the cruise missile, which follows the ground at low altitude. It must be expected that the Soviet Union will soon possess an equally advanced cruise missile program. This renders space-based beam weapons ineffective against the latest generation of missiles.

Third, the space stations that would be used to emit laser or particle beams to destroy missiles could themselves be destroyed by hostile beams. They would be extremely vulnerable. During a crisis, each side would first want to destroy the other's space stations before their own were destroyed. Therefore, such a technology would add a new element of instability. This problem would be particularly serious, since one such space station could emit many beams and could potentially destroy several of the opponent's stations, thus giving an "advantage" to the side that would strike first.

Therefore, such plans to develop a "nonthreatening" defense against a nuclear attack, as attractive as they may sound, will not work. Indeed, no effective military defense against nuclear weapons is known today. Blast and fallout shelters can give only limited protection and that only at a great distance from a nuclear explosion; they offer no protection against a direct hit. Most important, they offer no protection against the nuclear winter. Antiballistic missile systems of any degree of reliability would be extremely difficult to construct, and it would be much cheaper to circumvent them with more ballistic missiles.

The main concern, however, is not that defense against a nuclear attack is not sufficiently effective. That alone would be no reason to pursue research in that area, in the hope of being able to develop an effective defensive scheme sometime in the future. More serious is the fact that any defense, even a partial one, if combined with offensive arms, makes the combination of the two more threatening than the offensive arms alone. Nuclear missiles combined with a defense against missiles are more threatening than nuclear missiles alone. No sane leader would ever want to initiate a nuclear war so long as he knows that his country is vulnerable to retaliation. But if there is some protection against retaliation, the first use of nuclear weapons might become conceivable to certain people under certain circumstances. Even if the "defense" were not effective in reality, if some people believed it effective, this might lead them to take irrational steps.

Nuclear weapons not combined with any defense will serve only the function of deterring others from using them—through the threat of retaliation. But if a nation that possesses nuclear arms begins to build up a massive civil defense program, whether in the form of shelters, evacuation plans, or beam weapons in space, an adversary has reason to wonder whether that nation is preparing itself to launch a first strike. This is the reason why many oppose civil defense against nuclear weapons. Not only do such plans deceive the public by giving it the false impression that protection against nuclear war is possible, but they may make nuclear war more likely by giving the impression that the nation is preparing itself to launch a nuclear attack. (The situation is different, of course, if a country that does not possess nuclear weapons and has no plans to acquire any builds civil defense shelters. Such measures may turn out to be useless in case of a major nuclear war; but at least they are harmless, since they cannot possibly be misperceived as preparations to initiate a nuclear war.)

Since defense is not feasible as protection against a nuclear attack, alternative methods have been devised. Three of them can be briefly characterized as follows:

— Deterrence: the threat to retaliate in kind against a nation launching a nuclear attack.
— Preemption: destruction of an opponent's nuclear weapons before he can use them against us.
— Dissuasion: convincing a potential opponent, without evoking fear, that peaceful relations are more attractive to both sides than war.

These three methods will be examined in the next three sections.

DETERRENCE

The basic idea behind deterrence is that even though we cannot physically prevent an opponent from attacking us with nuclear weapons, we may be able to keep his finger from the button by the realization that we could retaliate if he were to attack us first.

Bernard Brodie is considered the founder of this concept, although he did not use the word "deterrence." He recognized that the invention of nuclear arms had fundamentally altered the nature of war. In 1946 he wrote, "Thus far the chief purpose of our military establishment has been to win wars. From now on its chief purpose must be to avert them" (quoted in Schell: 52). Robert Oppenheimer failed to anticipate that. "Rightly observing that nuclear weapons could not be defended against [he] called them inherently 'aggressive' weapons and predicted that they would inevitably be used in lightning-swift aggressive war" (Schell: 64). Brodie replied that when a potential aggressor realized his opponent possessed the same weapons and was ready to retaliate, this would stop the aggressor. This insight has become the foundation of much of current nuclear strategy. Brodie stressed that this was not an end in itself, but only a temporary measure to gain more time to work out a radical restructuring of the present world system toward world government. Albert Einstein believed that world government was the only method to save the world from nuclear destruction.

An idea that may appear closely related to the concept of deterrence is that we must intimidate an opponent and instill fear in him so that he will not dare to attack us. Richard Pipes (1982) correctly observed that Soviet leaders are far more frightened by U.S. discussions of a counterforce strategy (aimed at destroying Soviet nuclear missiles) than they are by a countervalue strategy (aimed at destroying Soviet cities in retaliation against a nuclear attack on the United States). He seemed to imply from this observation that therefore a counterforce strategy was a more effective deterrent than a countervalue strategy, because the Soviet leadership was more afraid of it. A similar argument maintains that we should deliberately leave a potential opponent in the dark about our intentions, to make him constantly worry what we might or might not do. During his 1980 presidential campaign, Ronald Reagan refused to rule out the possibility of a preemptive nuclear strike by the United States, arguing that the US should never guarantee to an enemy what it won't do. He said, "Don't you open up the possibility of being hit by a surprise nuclear attack far more if you assure the rest of the world that under no circumstances would you ever be the first to fire those bombs?" (Scheer 1982: 240-41). We will come back to these concepts, but first we will examine the essence of deterrence somewhat more closely.

Basically, deterrence means to avert a hostile threat by posing a counterthreat *in response*. There are logically four possible ways of responding to threats, not all of which meet the criterion of deterrence:

1. We can threaten an opponent if he threatens us, and not threaten him if he does not. This is the only posture that should properly be called "deterrence."
2. We can threaten an opponent regardless of whether or not he threatens us. This is a sort of extreme "hardline" posture.
3. We can refuse to threaten an opponent under any circumstances. This is a sort of "pacifist" posture.

4. We can threaten an opponent when he does not threaten us (when he appears weak) and not threaten him when he threatens us (being cautious and retreating when he appears dangerous). This posture is the logical opposite of deterrence and may be called "appeasement." Instead of deterring aggression, it invites aggression.

Equating deterrence with threatening an opponent is too ambiguous; it is necessary to specify when an opponent ought to be threatened. If we threaten him under the wrong circumstances, we may inadvertently provoke aggression. The popular idea that if an opponent feels threatened he will not dare to attack is too simplistic. How important it is, for our own security, not to threaten an opponent as long as he does not threaten us, does not yet appear to be widely understood.

In a computer tournament of repeated plays of a prisoner's dilemma game, as reported by Douglas Hofstadter (1983), Robert Axelrod (1984) found that the winning strategy, which was most successful in soliciting cooperation from an opponent, was "TIT FOR TAT": cooperate if the other side does, and retaliate with a one-time move of noncooperation if the other side refuses to cooperate on the preceding move. In general, he observed that the strategies that did well had the following four characteristics in common: (a) they never initiated noncooperation; (b) they did not passively accept noncooperation, but retaliated immediately; (c) they did not retaliate excessively (and thus escalate "hostility"), but immediately cooperated again after retaliating once; and (d) they were simple and transparent, making it easy for the opponent to discover how he would respond. The same four principles also seem to make sense for an effective strategy of deterrence (although we cannot afford to learn from repeated mistakes, as in a computer simulation).

In the real world, we do not normally face simple dichotomies like "cooperation" or "noncooperation" on the part of an opponent. Should a nation, for example, retaliate with nuclear weapons against conventional aggression, or only against a nuclear attack? NATO's current policy is one of "extended" deterrence, implying the threat of using nuclear weapons first in case of a Soviet conventional attack on Western Europe. Bundy, Kennan, McNamara, and Smith (1982) have advocated a transition to a policy of no-first-use of nuclear weapons, after strengthening NATO's conventional defense. They emphasize that in an age of rough nuclear parity between the United States and the Soviet Union, an escalation to nuclear war would clearly be suicidal and might therefore no longer be credible.

There are some benefits and risks associated with each course of action, and which one is favored depends on how those in power assess the various costs and risks. The threat of relying on the first use of nuclear weapons, if the opponent believes it, no doubt contributes to reducing the likelihood of conventional aggression; but it increases the likelihood of a nuclear war. A policy of no-first-use without a strengthening of conventional defense would increase the likelihood of conventional war, but reduce the likelihood of a nuclear war. A policy of no-first-use, combined with a stronger conventional defense, would reduce the likelihood both of nuclear war and also of conventional war (because there is less reason to doubt that conventional defense would be used—it is more credible). On the other hand, such a posture might involve somewhat higher defense expenditures.*

Those who think that a conventional war is almost as serious as a nuclear war and is quite likely unless deterred by the threat of first use of nuclear weapons will

---

*In Fischer (1984; 164ff) evidence is offered to show that a purely defensive mili-

favor a policy of first use. Those who consider a nuclear war far more serious, and who expect that an opponent would retaliate with nuclear weapons against a nuclear first strike, rather than capitulating, will favor a policy of no-first-use. Those who consider war in general to be probable will favor higher conventional defense spending. (As mentioned in the previous section, it is important that these expenditures are for defensive, not offensive conventional arms.) Those who consider aggression to be very unlikely will prefer reduced defense expenditures.

It should be clear that a policy of no-first-use is a strong deterrent against an opponent's use of nuclear weapons, because he knows that as long as he does not use nuclear weapons, he will not suffer a nuclear attack, but that if he uses them, he faces the prospect of nuclear retaliation. If we threaten to use nuclear weapons first, deterrence against a nuclear attack is undermined.

Of course, more is needed than a mere pledge not to use nuclear weapons first. Nuclear forces must be restructured so their first use would never make any military sense, for either side. It has been said that even though the Soviet Union made a no-first-use pledge, it could not be trusted, and therefore the United States should not commit itself to a no-first-use policy. But there is no need to trust the other side in order to adopt a no first use policy. It is in a country's own interest to pursue such a policy, and make it as convincing to an opponent as possible. A mere pledge adds little to one's own security. A commitment to no-first-use that is believed by the other side, because we follow it up with a removal of first-strike weapons, adds much more to effective nuclear deterrence and thus to a country's own security.

To spare the efforts required for a credible conventional defense, some pursue a policy that risks a nuclear holocaust, which might lead to human extinction. I personally find their arguments unconvincing.

The threat of the first use of nuclear weapons in case of a conventional war does not necessarily deter a conventional war. Wars can sometimes escalate rapidly from a small incident, and there is usually no agreement between the two sides concerning who made the first move. Each side tends to claim, and probably often believes, that the other side started the war. There is always *something* the other side did first. Unless we put a clear firebreak between conventional and nuclear war, a small misunderstanding could escalate to a nuclear holocaust.

If deterrence intended to prevent the other side's use of nuclear weapons is to be effective, it must be credible. An exaggerated threat may suffer in terms of credibility. The threat to launch a full-scale counterattack in response to the firing of a single missile would widen the catastrophe, instead of containing it, and might not even be believed, since it would obviously be suicidal by destroying the earth's environment. Bundy (1982) has emphasized that to deter a nuclear attack, it is not necessary to threaten retaliation on the same scale, or even an increased scale. He writes, "the losses that would be sustained in receiving an attack of 100 megatons far outweigh any 'gains' in delivering ten times as much to an enemy."* A nuclear power may not want to encourage nuclear blackmail by totally acquiescing to it; but

---

tary posture is, in fact, less expensive than an offensive posture, contrary to a widespread assumption.
*We now know that even attacks of 100 megatons, about 1 percent of the superpowers' nuclear arsenals, could result in a nuclear winter. But the principle that the threat of lesser retaliation is a more than adequate deterrent remains valid.

it will certainly not want to escalate the conflict further through excessive retaliation if ever the nuclear threshold should be crossed, and instead will seek to convince the aggressor to terminate the war as rapidly as possible. A lesser retaliation is probably a more effective way to prevent an opponent from using nuclear weapons, because there will be less doubt in his mind about the resolve to carry it out, if necessary. An exaggerated threat is less believable.

In order to offer credible deterrence against a nuclear attack, it is not necessary to possess the same number of nuclear weapons as an opponent. All that is necessary is to be able to convince him that he would not be able to totally destroy our retaliatory force in a surprise attack. Solly Zuckerman (1982) has pointed out that even though the British and French nuclear forces are much smaller than those of the Soviet Union, they are sufficient to deter a nuclear attack on those countries, because even a lesser retaliation would still be a formidable punishment. This concept is called "minimum deterrence."

The recent discovery of the phenomenon of nuclear winter has shown a large-scale retaliation to be potentially suicidal, because it could destroy the life-sustaining environment. The likely result of this insight will be a gradual shift by the superpowers away from the very powerful hydrogen bombs they now possess to weapons with much lower yield, which are less likely to trigger a nuclear winter and cause self-destruction.

It is even conceivable that a new deterrence strategy based on highly accurate missiles with conventional warheads may emerge. Such retaliation against a nuclear attack would probably be aimed at such critical assets as communication centers and the bunkers hiding top government officials. This strategy of "decapitation" could be defended on the ground that it would make clear to top leaders that launching an attack would endanger themselves, not only others. But it may not be wise to carry out such a threat, because there might be no leaders left with whom to negotiate a rapid end to a war. The result, again, could be human extinction.

A saner approach to the prevention of war than such horrendous schemes of mutual threats is dissuasion, which will be discussed below. But first we have to consider an even more dangerous strategy, which has seriously been proposed.

PREEMPTION

A preemptive first strike seeks to destroy an opponent's nuclear forces before they can be launched.

The Harvard Nuclear Study Group (1983) discusses what it calls the "usability paradox": to serve the role of a credible deterrent, nuclear weapons must be "usable," but they must not be so usable that they might be launched by accident or miscalculation. The group writes:

> Threats to destroy each other's populations are so suicidal in a world of mutual vulnerability that they are simply not credible for all types of deterrence [presumably including "extended" deterrence] against a conventional attack. Threats against military targets have a greater credibility that has the virtue of enhancing deterrence [p. 108].

Obviously, a U.S. nuclear attack on Soviet cities in case of Soviet aggression against NATO would lack credibility, because the Soviet Union could then retaliate against U.S. cities. Such a threat would be credible only as a desperate response to a Soviet nuclear attack on U.S. cities. This lack of credibility is indeed a problem with "extended" (or overextended) deterrence.

Would a threat to attack Soviet nuclear missile silos help the situation because it is more credible, as Richard Pipes (1982) has claimed? In fact, a threat of a preemptive counterforce strike will not deter an attack, but rather provoke one. A counterforce strike against missile silos requires a credible first-strike capacity, the ability to disarm the opponent in a surprise attack by destroying all (or almost all) his nuclear forces. It would be suicidal to launch a partial attack, which would cause certain retaliation. Since not every nuclear warhead can destroy its target with certainty, more nuclear warheads are needed for a preemptive counterforce strike than there are targets to destroy. This has led to an intense arms competition, with each side trying to possess enough warheads to pose a credible threat against the nuclear forces of the opponent. The invention of MIRVs (Multiple Independently-targetable Reentry Vehicles) has greatly increased the chance of a successful first strike, and has brought increased instability.

A common notion holds that strategic stability is enhanced by parity. If both sides have about equal nuclear strength, neither could "win" a war, and the situation is stable, because both sides are deterred from starting a war. If one side has superior forces, it could "win" a nuclear war and is therefore not deterred, which leads to instability. We will see that this notion is incorrect. (A related notion holds that what guarantees peace is military superiority—of one's own side, of course. One's own side is seen in the role of the police force, the other side as the criminal. The stronger the police, the more peaceful the world is. But when both sides believe this, a rapid arms race results.)

I will show that parity (or a "balance of forces") is neither necessary nor sufficient for stability. Let us consider a hypothetical situation in which two opponents possess only land-based nuclear missiles whose accuracy is so high that a nuclear warhead can destroy its target (a missile in its silo) with a 90 percent probability. We will look at two cases, one without parity but stability, and another case in which there is perfect parity and yet great instability.

Assume first that one side has 2000 missiles, each with a single warhead, and the other side has only 1000 missiles with a single warhead each. Although there is a great imbalance, neither side could destroy the other side's nuclear missiles in a surprise attack. The side with fewer missiles could not destroy more than half of the other side's missiles. The side that can aim 2000 warheads at 1000 missiles can target two warheads at each missile, increasing the probability of destroying a particular target to 99 percent. But the probability of destroying all 1000 missiles is very low, $(.99)^{1000}$ or less than 10^{-4}. Thus neither side could preempt the other, and there is a certain measure of stability, despite the absence of parity.

With MIRVs, we can have a situation where each side can destroy the other's nuclear forces totally, provided it strikes first. Assume that each side possesses 1000 nuclear warheads on 100 missiles with ten warheads each. Each side can now aim ten warheads at each missile of the opponent. This increases the probability of destroying a given target to almost a certainty (99.999 999 99 percent). The probability of destroying all 100 of the opponent's missiles is also extremely high, 99.999 999 percent. Whoever strikes first can disarm the opponent; whoever waits takes a grave risk. Such a situation is obviously highly unstable, despite the perfect balance of forces. (Of course, these situations assume the use of very "low-yield" nuclear warheads, or the nuclear winter could destroy the aggressor, even without any retaliation.) This shows that parity does not guarantee, nor is it necessary for, stability. Far more important than to strive for "parity" is to maintain stability.

The traditional obsession with "parity," "balance of forces," "superiority," and "inferiority" has become obsolete with nuclear weapons. It is still true that numerical superiority can cause "psychological" instability—the other side's desire to "catch up"— and should be avoided for that reason. But such superiority cannot usually be translated into any military advantage, as along as the other side possesses a survivable capacity to retaliate. On the other hand, if the nuclear forces of both sides are highly destructive and at the same time vulnerable (such as MIRVs), then *neither side* may possess a survivable deterrent, despite a perfect balance. In that case, there can be instability even *with* parity.

One strategy that has been proposed to save stability even in the presence of MIRVs is "launch-on-warning." But such a strategy could bring even greater instability, given that there have been numerous false warnings of a nuclear attack in the past. Such a strategy could lead to an accidental nuclear war. During the debate following the television film "The Day After" in November 1983, Henry Kissinger and Robert McNamara agreed that a strategy of launch-on-warning was too dangerous. But while McNamara proposed that the U.S. government categorically say so, Kissinger thought it would be more prudent to leave the Soviet Union with the impression that the United States might consider a launch-on-warning, to deter the Soviets from attempting a preemptive strike. If a policy is too risky, how can it be credible? Even worse, if the Soviet leaders believed that the US had adopted a launch-on-warning policy (as Kissinger would like them to believe), the Soviets might feel under pressure to adopt the same strategy, so as not to "fall behind" the US. This could have disastrous consequences for civilization.

Fortunately, we are not yet in such a dangerous situation, despite the introduction of MIRVs. Both the United States and the Soviet Union also possess nuclear submarines, which cannot yet be reliably detected, and so provide an invulnerable deterrent force. But strenuous efforts on both sides to develop antisubmarine warfare capability, are moving us toward a strategically highly unstable situation. It is useless to destroy a submarine after it has launched its missiles, so the only sensible application of antisubmarine warfare is preemptive.

The development of a counterforce capability has been defended with the argument that "of course, we would never strike first, but if they hit us with some nuclear missiles, we would certainly want to make sure that they cannot follow up." This kind of reasoning credits the opponents with only a low level of intelligence by assuming they would launch only a few missiles and open themselves up to a massive counterforce strike against their remaining missiles. (This is as if someone encountered a sleeping lion and instead of escaping quietly or seeking to kill him instantly were to sting him with a needle.)

A strategy of "nuclear war fighting," of seeking to "prevail" in a nuclear exchange through counterforce targeting aimed at "damage limitation" to one's own side, is a departure from mutual deterrence in an extremely dangerous direction. A strategy of nuclear deterrence is not necessarily the same as "mutual assured destruction" (MAD). Such a strategy would deter only an all-out attack, and would have no credible response against a limited nuclear attack. It has therefore been rightly criticized. There is a need to possess a credible deterrent against attacks on any scale. Retaliation on a lower scale may be aimed at military bases or military industries—but it must *not* be aimed at nuclear missiles, since that would invite a nuclear attack rather than deterring it.

How can an adversary determine whether his opponent's missiles are aimed at his military industries (e.g., oil refineries, munitions factories, etc.) or at hardened missile silos? If a country has the *capacity* to destroy missiles in their silos, the other side must assume the worst, and may thus be tempted to launch a preemptive counterforce strike during a grave crisis. To prove that it has no intention to launch a preemptive strike against nuclear missiles, it is in a country's own interest not to acquire that capability, e.g., by possessing a relatively small number of warheads that could not destroy all the opponent's nuclear forces, or by possessing weapons with relatively low accuracy. To destroy an oil refinery does not require extreme precision, as does the destruction of a hardened missile silo.

There are in fact two different types of counterforce strategies. One is purely retaliatory, but is aimed at the opponent's military assets, with the exception of his nuclear missiles. The other strategy (which requires very precise nuclear warheads in large numbers) is aimed at the opponent's nuclear forces. This strategy is not available for retaliation (after the opponent has launched his nuclear missiles) and therefore makes sense only for a disarming surprise attack. Yet this second extremely dangerous and destabilizing strategy rather than the first is what is normally understood by a "counterforce" strategy.

It should now be clear why Soviet generals are more frightened by a counterforce strategy (against missiles) than by a countervalue strategy (against cities) on the part of the United States, as Pipes (1982) has emphasized. The reason is not that they put greater value on their missiles than on their citizens, but that they know the United States would never launch a surprise attack on their cities, which would inevitably provoke retaliation. But if missiles are aimed at missiles, a surprise attack is more credible. This does not imply that a counterforce strategy is a more credible deterrent. On the contrary, it could frighten the Soviet Union into attempting a preemptive strike.

Even if the Soviet Union has adopted a counterforce strategy, as Pipes claims, the US should not imitate such folly. A strategy of preemption is the logical opposite of a prudent strategy of deterrence. Instead of deterring an attack, it invites one. It signals to an opponent, "if you destroy us, you are safe, but if you leave us alone, you are at risk of being destroyed." A country that pursues a strategy of preemption with nuclear weapons endangers all of us, and possibly all future generations. If the person in command of the United States nuclear arsenal believes in the effectiveness of a preemptive counterforce threat (even without the intention of actually carrying it out), there is reason for profound concern.

DISSUASION

The key to an effective policy of dissuading aggression is the recognition that it is not sufficient to make war disastrous for a potential aggressor; it is equally important to make peace as attractive for him as possible. If the status quo appears unbearable to an adversary, his incentive to maintain peace is weakened.

War can be made less attractive in two ways, by increasing an opponent's losses in case he attacks, and by reducing any gains he might expect from his aggression. Similarly, peace can be made more attractive in two ways, by increasing an adversary's gains if he keeps peace, and by reducing any losses he may perceive to suffer.

Gains and losses should be understood in a much broader sense than involving only economic and military assets, or even the loss of lives. Such intangibles as prestige or humiliation, or the adherence to religious or ideological principles, are often high on the list of values of national leaders. (Underestimation of the importance of such values can lead to unfortunate misunderstandings.) There are thus four basic approaches to dissuading aggression. Military defense and deterrence have concentrated only on the first of these four possibilities. Johan Galtung (1968, 1984) has called the last three options "nonmilitary defense."

Increasing an opponent's losses in case of aggressive actions is usually considered a purely military task. But even here diplomatic and economic sanctions can be applied. For example, when Iran took some 50 U.S. diplomats hostage after the United States had admitted the former Shah of Iran for medical treatment, the United States froze Iranian bank accounts in retaliation. But the expectation that a combination of military threats and the promise of financial rewards would change Khomeini's mind turned out to be a miscalculation. Money held little attraction for the ascetic Khomeini, who had been deeply offended by the U.S. hospitality extended to the Shah, under whose regime he had been imprisoned. Yet this should not be too surprising. Even the U.S. government is more attached to certain high principles than it is inclined to bend to threats and material rewards. It would have been inconceivable for the U.S. government to extradite the Shah under Iranian pressure. Why should the US have expected Khomeini to react any differently?

A more successful use of nonmilitary sanctions, with some admirable features, was practiced by the Sandinista rebels in Nicaragua, based on their realistic assessment of the US political process and public psychology. When in 1979 Samoza's troops, in cold blood, killed a US journalist who had been reporting on their atrocities, this was shown on US television, and weakened US support for Somoza.

Reducing the gains an aggressor may hope to win can involve sabotage in occupied territory. Such measures are hardly applicable to the superpowers, who are more concerned about a potential nuclear attack than about an invasion of their territory. But such methods may be effective in dissuading aggression in other parts of the world that could spread to a superpower confrontation. For example, even if Saudi Arabia may not possess the military forces to keep out an invasion, it could threaten to blow up its oil wells and pipelines to keep them from foreign occupation. Similar tactics were used successfully by Sweden during World War II, which deterred a German invasion by threatening, among other things, to blow up its iron ore mines. Switzerland had no useful natural resources for that purpose, but it threatened to blow up its Alpine tunnels. If U.S. allies can deter aggression by such strategies, their dependence on U.S. intervention will be reduced, thereby increasing the security of the United States as well. On the other hand, threatening the first use of nuclear weapons in case of a Soviet move into the Persian Gulf region (the so-called "Carter doctrine") lacks credibility, because this would, according to Richard Barnet (1981: 77), "vaporize the oil along with the civilization that depended on it."

Not only possession of physical assets, but also control of the population (perhaps as a workforce for war industries) may be an aggressor's objective. To frustrate such aims, the population can offer passive resistance. No government can function without a minimal amount of voluntary cooperation from its subjects. This applies also to an occupation regime. Such tactics were used successfully by Norway's teachers, who went on strike in 1942 to protest a planned nazification of the schools. Quisling, the Norwegian prime minister, threatened to execute some teachers, but in the end had to give up the plan, as it would only have further alienated the Norwegian population from his pro-Nazi regime (Sharp 1973: 88–89).

To make peace more attractive, one can avoid subjecting an adversary to economic pressures, humiliation, or threats as long as he keeps peace. It is counterproductive to exert a "steady" economic pressure on an opponent. For example, if the United States were to "declare economic and technical war on the Soviet Union . . . as a peacetime complement to military strategy" (from "Pentagon Draws Up First Strategy for Fighting a Long Nuclear War," *New York Times*, 30 May 1982), as advocated in the 1984–88 U.S. defense guidance plan signed by Reagan's Defense Secretary Caspar Weinberger, this would reduce the Soviet Union's incentive to keep such a peace, instead of increasing it.

The imposition of heavy war reparations payments on Germany in the 1919 Versailles Peace Treaty made it easy for Hitler to campaign on the promise of abrogating that peace treaty. Lord Keynes, a member of the British delegation to Versailles, warned that such a heavy economic burden would cause social instability, but was ignored. The United States pursued a more successful peace policy after World War II, by granting economic assistance to its former enemies, Germany and Japan, as well as to other countries, in the form of the Marshall Plan.

If a country wants to keep peace, it should abstain from actions it would consider to be acts of war by the other side. For example, the "rescue mission" in Grenada was hailed as a U.S. success, freeing the island from Cubans who were allegedly building a Soviet/Cuban military base in the Western Hemisphere. But imagine the U.S. reaction if the Soviet Union had "rescued" the island of Diego Garcia in the Indian Ocean from U.S. forces who were building an American military base in the "Eastern Hemisphere." (If a superpower allows its military forces to be drawn into conflict by unpredictable political events in any small country, such as Grenada, Lebanon, or Afghanistan, this is analogous to connecting a powderkeg to dozens of fuses, any one of which could be ignited at any moment.)

To increase an adversary's gains from keeping peace, mutually beneficial trade and scientific and cultural exchanges may be set up, as well as assistance offered in case of natural disasters. There is always room for substantial mutual benefits from closer U.S.–Soviet cooperation in such fields as medicine, energy research, exchange of new manufacturing techniques, and joint space exploration. Unlike physical resources, knowledge is not lost when given away. The drastic improvement in U.S.–Chinese relations came about through mutually beneficial contacts. China gained U.S. technology, and U.S. corporations gained access to the huge Chinese market. Numerous Americans have visited China since the resumption of relations, and thousands of Chinese have come to study in the United States. China has begun to experiment with a more market-oriented approach to economic management, and some Americans have begun to study the Chinese public health system. If the United States had sent marines and bombers into China, and scholars and symphony orchestras into Vietnam, instead of the other way round, U.S. relations with these two countries would probably be the reverse of what they are today: friendly relations with Vietnam, and rather tense relations with China.

The use or threat of force is not only immoral but counter-productive to a country's true interests. Relying mainly on threats to pursue foreign policy goals and to maintain national security invites counterthreats, creates fear and anger, and is likely to lead to mutual escalation. With nonmilitary forms of defense, there is no fear of escalation; on the contrary, we would wish for mutual escalation. If others tried to be more secure by making peace more attractive for us, we would welcome such steps. We need not wait for reciprocity, but can initiate such measures independently, in our own interest.

Cooperation with an opponent may seem to be a dangerous form of appeasement, but in fact it is the exact opposite. Appeasement means to yield to an opponent when he behaves aggressively, and in this way to encourage more aggression. If we cooperate with a potential opponent as long as he keeps peace, and make it clear that such cooperation would cease in case of war, aggression is discouraged.

In today's highly militarized world, an exclusive reliance on nonmilitary defense is not sufficient. But nonmilitary defense measures can certainly add to a country's security, without posing any threat to other countries. Any nation that neglects to supplement its military defense with such nonmilitary strategies takes an unnecessary risk to its security. A broad range of redundant measures, all aimed at making peace more attractive and war less attractive for a potential aggressor, provides a higher degree of security than concentration on "the" most effective method alone.

CONCLUSION

It is necessary with all efforts to pursue negotiations toward disarmament and toward the establishment of an effective legal system at the global level. But it would be risky to rely solely on negotiations to achieve greater security, given the poor record of negotiations in the past. It is also necessary to take steps that any nation can take independently, without risk, without having to wait for agreement on reciprocity from other nations. As Kenneth Boulding once said, agreement is a scarce resource, and whenever we can do without it, this is preferable.

What measures can a nation take on its own to reduce the risk of nuclear war? We have seen that *defense* against nuclear weapons is currently infeasible; even worse, it could be destabilizing and actually increase the danger of war. *Deterrence* has worked up to now, but is too risky an approach in the long run. If it were to break down, the consequences could be apocalyptic. "Extended" deterrence has lost credibility, since the first use of nuclear weapons would most likely be suicidal. A policy of no-first-use ought to be combined with a stronger conventional defense to protect against conventional aggression. A strategy of "nuclear war fighting" and "damage limitation" through *preemption* invites a preemptive nuclear attack from the other side, rather than deterring it. It should be abandoned out of self-interest.

Those advocating a preemptive strategy may be victims of a linguistic confusion. The word "strength" has two different meanings, which are not always clearly distinguished. "Strength" can mean the ability to inflict harm on others, or the ability to prevent others from harming oneself. While the second form of strength is helpful, the first form is counterproductive. What is needed is a second-strike capability, and the *absence* of any first-strike capability. A second-strike capability is offered by a *survivable* retaliatory force, widely dispersed, possibly mobile, which cannot be wiped out in a surprise attack, but which is itself insufficient for a disarming first strike. A typical first-strike arsenal consists of nuclear weapons that are extremely destructive but vulnerable (e.g., with multiple warheads), so that they would either have to be used first or be lost.

Greater security depends not on higher or lower military spending, but on a *different* security strategy. The most effective independent strategy to prevent war is *dissuasion*, a combination of a broad range of measures that not only seek to punish aggression, but also to reward peaceful cooperation. Until mutual nuclear disarmament can be achieved, such a policy will include minimum nuclear deterrence against any nuclear attack, in the form of *lesser* retaliation against military targets (not against civilians, and not against nuclear forces—since this could be misperceived as a preemptive strategy by an opponent). But such a policy will deliberately avoid any effort to achieve nuclear "superiority." Talk of "winning" a nuclear war is self-defeating. It only puts pressure on the opponent to lay to rest such dangerous illusions with a massive nuclear buildup.

The more an opponent is faced with threats, humiliating verbal attacks, and unacceptable economic pressures, the less attractive the status quo will appear to him, and the weaker will be his incentive to maintain peace. Only a formidable threat in case of war can then make war seem even less attractive. On the other hand, the greater the efforts to make peace more attractive, through economic and diplomatic approaches, the less reliance need be put on deterrence to maintain peace. (England and France, for example, maintain such close economic, political, and cultural relations that nuclear deterrence plays no role in their mutual relations, even though both could destroy each other totally.)

A comprehensive policy of dissuasion is *robust* in the sense that it will work under a wide range of different assumptions. Other national security doctrines may be based on specific assumptions, and will fail if those assumptions do not hold. For example, a search for military superiority provides security only if the other side accepts inferiority. Unilateral steps toward disarmament bring the desired result— reciprocity—only if the other side is motivated by fear alone; it fails if the other side has aggressive intentions. Dissuasion works regardless of whether the opponent is motivated by aggressive intentions, by fear, or by a desire to cooperate, and regardless of whether the opponent's offensive capabilities are strong or weak. (Hong Kong is extremely weak militarily compared to China, but by providing China with a large portion of its foreign exchange earnings, Hong Kong has made it more attractive for China not to seize it by military force.)

Dissuasion is an active, positive peace policy, not merely a reaction to threats, as deterrence is.

Conflicts will probably always be with us, but this does not mean that international conflicts need to be resolved through war. Better mechanisms exist. Some have suggested that we should learn from sports, a ritualized form of conflict, in which certain rules ensure that neither side is fatally hurt. But we can do even better. In sports, the idea still prevails that in order to win, one has to defeat the opponent. Businessmen have a different approach. Unless a business deal is beneficial to both sides, it will not be realized. In approaching international conflicts, we could learn much from business mentality.

To dissuade aggression, it is necessary to make it clear that aggression cannot succeed. But it is equally important to recognize the legitimate desire of other nations also to be secure. If we pose a threat to the security of others—or even if we only allow them to perceive us mistakenly as a threat—they will naturally seek ways and means to eliminate that threat. Threatening others can be suicidal in the nuclear age.

REFERENCES

Axelrod, Robert. 1984. *The Evolution of Cooperation*. New York: Basic Books.

Barnet, Richard. 1981. *Real Security.* New York: Simon & Schuster.

Bundy, McGeorge. 1982. " 'No First Use' Needs Careful Study." *Bulletin of the Atomic Scientists*.

Bundy, McGeorge, George F. Kennan, Robert S. McNamara, and Gerard Smith. 1982. "Nuclear Weapons and the Atlantic Alliance." *Foreign Affairs* 60, no. 4: 753-68.

Fischer, Dietrich. 1984. *Preventing War in the Nuclear Age*. Totowa, NJ: Rowman & Allanheld.

Galtung, Johan. 1968. "On the Strategy of Nonmilitary Defense: Some Proposals and Problems." *In Peace and Justice: Unity or Dilemma?*, ed. Bartels. Catholic University of Nijmegen, Institute of Peace Research. Reprinted 1976 in Galtung, *Essays in Peace Research*, Vol. 2. Copenhagen: Christian Ejlers, 378-426.

_____1984. *There Are Alternatives! Four Roads to Peace and Security.* Chester Springs, Pa.: Dufour.

Gray, Colin S., and Keith Payne. 1980. "Victory Is Possible." *Foreign Policy* 39, pp. 14-27.

Harvard Nuclear Study Group. 1983. *Living With Nuclear Weapons*. New York: Bantam Books.

Hofstadter, Douglas R. 1983. "Computer Tournaments of the Prisoner's Dilemma Suggest How Cooperation Evolves." *Scientific American* 248, no. 5 (May).

Pipes, Richard. 1982. "Why the Soviet Union Thinks It Could Fight and Win a Nuclear War." In *The Defense Policies of Nations*, ed. Douglas J. Murray and Paul R. Viotti. Baltimore: Johns Hopkins University Press.

Sagan, Carl. 1983. "Nuclear War and Climatic Catastrophe." *Foreign Affairs* 62, no. 2: 257-92.

Scheer, Robert. 1982. *With Enough Shovels: Reagan, Bush and Nuclear War*. New York: Random House.

Schell, Jonathan. 1984. "The Abolition." *The New Yorker*, 2 and 9 January.

Sharp, Gene. 1973. *The Politics of Nonviolent Action*. Boston: Porter Sargent.

SIPRI. 1982. *The Arms Race and Arms Control*. Stockholm International Peace Research Institute.

Zuckerman, Solly. 1982. *Nuclear Illusion and Reality.* New York: Viking Press.

21
THE TRAGEDY OF NATIONAL SOVEREIGNTY

Edward F. McClennen

HARDIN'S THESIS

The thesis of Garrett Hardin's influential article "The Tragedy of the Commons," which was published fifteen years ago, is that some social problems do not have a *technical* solution. By this he means that some problems cannot be resolved by persons simply trying to do their best in terms of their own interests, as isolated individuals or groups of individuals, with the knowledge and technological resources available to them. These problems require for their solution highly coordinated activity on the part of all who are affected. In particular, he argues, we

> can make little progress . . . until we explicitly exorcize the spirit of Adam Smith . . . the idea that an individual who "intends only his own gain" is, as it were, "led by an invisible hand to promote . . . the public interest." . . . Adam Smith . . . contributed to a dominant tendency of thought which has ever since interfered with positive action based on rational analysis, namely, the tendency to assume that decisions reached individually will, in fact, be the best decisions for an entire society. . . . If the assumption is not correct we need to reexamine our individual freedoms to see which ones are defensible.[1]

Hardin focuses on an example that provides him with the title for his article:

> Picture a pasture open to all. It is to be expected that each herdsman will try to keep as many cattle as possible on the commons. . . . As a rational being, each herdsman seeks to maximize his gain. Explicitly or implicitly, more or

---

For inspiration in writing this paper, I am indebted to Polly Marlowe, of Peterborough, New Hampshire, and the late Margaret P. Welch, of Framingham, Mass. I stand in deep admiration of the exemplary commitment each has made in her life to those humanitarian and internationalist principles whose foundations are the preoccupation of this paper.

less consciously, he asks, "What is the utility *to me* of adding one more animal to my herd?" This utility has one negative and one positive component. (1) The positive component is a function of the increment of one animal. Since the herdsman receives all of the proceeds from the sale of the individual animal, the positive utility is nearly + 1. (2) The negative component is a function of the additional overgrazing created by one more animal. Since, however, the effects of overgrazing are shared by all the herdsmen, the negative utility for any particular decision-making herdsman is only a fraction of − 1. Adding together the component partial utilities, the rational herdsman concludes that the only sensible course for him to pursue is to add another animal to his herd. And another; and another. . . . But this is the conclusion reached by each and every rational herdsman sharing a commons. Therein is the tragedy. Each man is locked into a system that compels him to increase his herd without limit. Ruin is the destination toward which all men rush, each pursuing his own best interest in a society that believes in the freedom of the commons. Freedom in the commons brings ruin to all.

In defense of the use of the term "tragedy" in this context, Hardin offers the following quotation from A.N. Whitehead: "The essence of dramatic tragedy is not unhappiness. It resides in the solemnity of the remorseless working of things." To this one can add, in keeping with the Greek conception of tragedy to which Whitehead alludes, that the term *tragedy* is properly reserved for situations just like this, in which "the remorseless working of things" is set in motion by the deliberate choices of human agents.

All this will be familiar to those who have read Hardin's article. But I suspect that few will recall that Hardin opens his article with an allusion to a quite different example of the same type of tragedy. The opening paragraph is devoted to a quotation from an earlier article by J.B. Wiesner and H.F. York:

"Both sides in the arms race are . . . confronted by the dilemma of steadily increasing military power and steadily decreasing national security. *It is our considered professional judgment that this dilemma has no technical solution.* If the great powers continue to look for solutions in the area of science and technology only, the result will be to worsen the situation."[2]

Despite this quotation, the problem of the search for national security in a world organized in terms of sovereign nation-states is treated by Hardin only *en passant*. The Wiesner and York quotation serves merely to introduce the idea of a problem that has no technical solution. Hardin's preoccupation is with the two distinct problems of pollution and population growth.

HARDIN'S THESIS AND NATIONAL SECURITY

Hardin's preoccupations need not be ours. The argument to be found in "The Tragedy of the Commons" provides us, I believe, with a compelling diagnosis concerning what is wrong with the way in which nation-states pursue national security. Moreover, Hardin's own prescription for resolving such a "tragedy" is equally applicable to the problem of national security.

Consider how national security is presently pursued. We are now in a period in which the "spirit of Adam Smith" is once more dominant in the area of international affairs. What little gain was made after World War II in creating an international political and legal order has been all but completely eroded. While we continue to teach our children that the rule of law is essential to a peaceful, stable society, the United Nations is increasingly ignored as a potential keeper of anything but the minor peace between some of the smaller nations. As individuals we accept the idea that in disputes with neighbors we must not take the law into our own hands. But as a nation we are a law unto ourselves, and what we have taken into our hands is an awesome arsenal of weapons.

Central to this is the idea that if we look to our own defense, and others look to theirs, the result will be best for all. Our strategy has been to provide for ourselves, as an individual nation, and for such alliances as we have voluntarily entered into, the best defense system we can, in accordance with the latest advances in science and technology. For decades our overwhelming preoccupation has been with technological proposals for dealing with the problem of national security. B1 bombers, IRBMs, ICBMs, the Trident sub, multiple warheads, hardened silos, MX missiles, race track and dense pack deployment, neutron bombs, laser defense systems, cruise missiles, etc.

Security is a function of the force and counterforce capability one has managed to acquire relative to the other side's capability. In principle, security is supposed to depend upon having achieved at least parity with the other side. The argument is that with parity one can effectively resist aggression. Moreover, awareness of the adversary's capability is supposed to act as a deterrent. But each side has to work within the limits of error. In particular, with respect to defense against aggression, one must guard against underestimating the intentions and capabilities of the other side and, with respect to maintaining the deterrence value of one's own forces, one must guard against the other side's underestimating one's own capabilities.

Prudence mandates, then, a bias toward overestimating the advantages enjoyed by the other side and, consequently, a more or less constant concern with improving one's own defenses. "Overestimating" in this sense, while it may be economically costly, has no adverse effect either on one's ability to resist aggression, or on the deterrence value of one's destructive capability. If one's estimates turn out to be correct, the incremental improvements that one instituted would have been mandated anyway by security considerations. If one has in fact overestimated, then the incremental improvements simply enhance one's defensive capability and serve to provide one with an even more effective deterrent.

This rationale for "overestimating" applies symmetrically to both sides. The result is a form of strategic interaction, the logic of which is not hard to discern. If both participants are fully rational, there will be continual incremental additions to the destructive capabilities of each side. Given that security is a function of relative capability, and given a prudentially mandated bias toward overestimating the capabilities of the other side, and underestimating the deterrent effect of one's own system, at any given point in time one or the other or both sides will have rational grounds for improving their destructive capabilities. But the other side or both sides will recognize this and will have rational grounds for responding in kind. Nations thus find themselves locked into an upwardly spiraling competition for improved techniques of force and counterforce.

This suggests, of course, the same pattern of interaction Hardin discerned in the problem of the commons. Of course, there are differences between Hardin's commons and the arms race. But the differences are overshadowed by the fact that the logic of the two situations is the same. Both are instances of what game theorists call a "prisoner's dilemma" situation: mutual restraint would leave both sides better off than mutual lack of restraint, but each side stands to improve its position by not restraining itself, regardless of what the other side does.

Consider first the commons problem. If others add to their herds, our best response is to add to our own herd; if others do not add to their herds, we still stand to gain in terms of net financial position, and so the rational choice is to continue to add to our herd. Eventually, however, this must lead to overgrazing, a state in which both are worse off than they would have been had they practiced some form of mutual restraint.

At some earlier stage, before the ecological limit of the commons is reached, both can increase the size of their herds to their individual advantages. At some point, this will be no longer the case: the limit will have been reached. Unfortunately, the logic of the situation is such that rational agents must pass right through that limit point and continue the process of incremental additions to their respective herds. Ecological catastrophe must occur eventually: the overgrazed grass can no longer renew itself, and the pasture resource is destroyed. Hardin, with his flair for the dramatic and his eye on the theme of ecological disaster, focused on the ruin down the road, the ruin toward which all men rush. But the tragedy takes place much sooner, at the point at which mutual additions register net loss when compared to mutual restraint. From that point onward, it is all downhill.

Note, finally, that in the dilemma of the commons, to use Thomas Schelling's terminology, "the costs of using or overusing. . . are in the same 'currency' as the benefits." Each adds to his herd with a view to improving his net financial position. Once the limit is passed, mutual additions result in financial loss to both. But it continues to be the case that while others are increasing the size of their herds, it is financially advantageous to increase the size of one's own herd. At this point, the advantage is only relative: adding to one's own herd is simply a way of avoiding an even greater financial loss.

Consider the arms race. If others improve their force and counterforce capabilities, our best response is to improve our own; if others do not, we still enhance our security by self-improvement. Either way, we do better in terms of security by incremental improvements in our own capabilities. A commitment to improvements is thus rationally mandated. Given, then, a projected upward spiral in force and counterforce capability, what can we say about the net effect for each side in terms of the "currency" of national security? Do both sides, in so acting, eventually worsen the situation, as Wiesner and York projected many years ago?

Many would disagree. The typical argument is that the resultant balance of terror serves to keep the peace and, hence, offers each nation the security it desires (if only by means of programs that are very costly in any number of respects). On this view, the benefits are in the currency of security, while the costs are in terms of economic efficiency and other values. If this is true, then the logic of the commons and the arms race are not the same.

I believe that Wiesner and York are right in concluding that if the great powers continue to look for solutions in the area of science and technology only, the result will be a worsening of the situation. But the line of reasoning they employ to reach this conclusion is imperfect. In particular, it is vulnerable to the rebuttal mentioned above. Wiesner and York reason that security must decline if both sides continue to increase their capability to destroy the other side.[3] This presupposes that an increase in the destructive capability of the other side is a sufficient condition for a decline in one's own security. But this is incorrect.

In the early stages of an armaments buildup, a nation might reasonably estimate that its own capacity to inflict destruction on the other side is not great enough to serve as an effective deterrent. Some might argue that the ideal situation would be one in which that nation could effect a significant improvement in destructive capability without a corresponding buildup on the other side. But this argument is not easy to sustain, given the logic of defensive security. A rapid, unilateral buildup can destabilize the peace in two important respects. First, as the gap becomes greater, there will be increased pressure to move from a defensive to an offensive posture or, at the very least, to exploit that advantage in some manner or other. Second, the other side, perceiving that possibility, will have to give serious consideration to an immediate preemptive attack before the armament gap becomes too large, while it might still have some chance of prevailing. The logic of defensive security may require, then, sufficient increase in armaments on both sides to ensure that both possess threats significant enough to deter the other side. In this context, improved destructive capability on both sides may enhance, as opposed to detract from, security. The situation here is parallel to that which obtains in the case of the commons: we may suppose that at some previous point in the process, both sides stood to gain by mutual increases in their destructive capabilities.

The point here is that security is a function not only of the level of destructive capability possessed by one's adversaries, but the probability that such destructive capability will be employed. If an increase in destructive capability on the part of both sides leads to a decrease in the probability of either side resorting to armed conflict, then, in balance, security may have been increased rather than decreased, even though there has been an increase in destructive capability on both sides. For present purposes, it is unnecessary to consider what the trade-off should be between destructive capability and the probability that it will be used. All that is required here is that security be characterized so as to take account of the level of *expected*, as distinct from merely *possible*, destruction. This is the distinction Wiesner and York fail to make in their article.

The crucial question now is whether, over the last few decades, both sides have continued to improve their security position, or whether, in contrast, at some point a critical breakpoint was passed (as in the case of the story of the commons) and what we now face is a situation in which continued incremental improvements on both sides result in a mutual decline in security. Consider once again the history of the arms race since the end of World War II. By the end of the 1950s, both sides had stockpiles of nuclear weapons and delivery systems that were capable of inflicting unacceptable losses on the other side. The situation was one in which mutual assured destruction functioned as an effective deterrent and, hence, there was a relatively low probability that either side would launch an attack against the other side.

Now, 25 year later, what is the situation? Let us grant the estimates of our most pessimistic policy advisors. Let us suppose that at the present time an enormous window of vulnerability has opened for us, so that there is a real danger that the USSR will launch a preemptive strike (or seize the advantage in some other way). If such is the case, then one can argue in terms of the currency of security that more resources should be committed to building up our force and counterforce capability. We can acknowledge, then, that under such circumstances security considerations will call for an improvement in one's defensive position (just as we can acknowledge that any given participant in the commons tragedy will have rational grounds for adding to his herd).

Suppose, however, we do whatever is necessary to close this window of vulnerability. When parity is finally achieved again, what will be the situation? At best, we will have arrived once again at a state in which the probability of nuclear attack by the other side will be minimized. In the meantime, given the buildup over the last 25 years (including whatever incremental adjustments are made by the present administration in response to the "window of vulnerability" scenario discussed above), the destructive capability of both sides will have increased significantly. But if destructive capability goes up and the probability of its use has not decreased in comparison to what it was decades ago, the net result is an increase in expected destruction and, hence, a worsening of the security situation for both sides.

I conclude, then, that the logic of the arms race conforms to that of the tragedy of the commons. At some point in the past, it may well have been that both sides stood to gain from increasing their capacities for destruction so as to provide themselves with an effective deterrent. But that point was reached long ago. Since then, while it has been true that at every stage of strategic interaction along the way, one or the other side has had rational grounds for incrementally increasing its armaments commitment, the net result has been a vast increase in destructive power, with no improvement over the long haul with respect to deterrent effect. Thus, in terms of a measure of security that incorporates both the destructive capability of the other side and the probability that it will be used, security has declined. In terms of the very currency used to characterize the ends for which all this unilateral action has been undertaken, namely, national security, the unilateral approach has proved to be self-defeating.

A NONRETALIATORY DEFENSE IS NO SOLUTION

It might be argued in rebuttal that the dilemma we now face is the result of a policy of defense through the threat of massive retaliation, as opposed to a policy directed more at simply reducing the amount of destruction that the other side could hope to inflict upon us. The argument here would be that what really contributes to escalation of the arms race is that a capability to deter through the threat of massive retaliation is also essential to the development of a preemptive offensive capability. Since from a prudential perspective neither side can afford to completely discount the possibility of a preemptive strike by the other side, the result is that each side is bound to view a massive retaliatory capability on the other side as posing a serious threat, one that calls for a redoubled effort to achieve a more favorable balance of power. According to this argument, a return to a more traditional defense posture could serve to reduce tensions and start the process of deescalation.

It is unclear, however, that concentration on nonretaliatory defensive measures would really help. A serious problem of ambiguity arises with respect to the classification of weapons systems, not between those that are "deterrently defensive" and those that are "conventionally defensive," but between those that are "defensive" and those that are "offensive." A strong defense against a first strike by the other side also serves as a strong defense against a *retaliatory* strike by the other side and, hence, is plausibly perceived by the other side as a key part of an essentially offensive policy. Where such an ambiguity exists, there is little reason to expect that an announced shift to a more conventional defense will significantly reduce fears on the other side with respect to our offensive capabilities and intentions.

Even leaving this problem to one side, it is hard to construct a case for a conventional defensive approach. Wiesner and York offered compelling arguments against it nearly two decades ago. The destructive power of nuclear weapons is so great that even if a defensive system had a very high degree of reliability, the inevitable margin of error would leave any nation vulnerable to unacceptable losses. Moreover, one cannot anticipate in advance all the possible offensive and counter-countermeasures that could be developed, so that the reliability of any given defensive system will be drastically relativized to our own imperfect estimates of the offensive and counter-countermeasure capability of our adversaries. This, when coupled with the consideration that any such system requires great lead time to full deployment, implies that a purely defensive policy will, as Wiesner and York put it, always "start the race a lap behind."[4] But an approach to security that leaves one perpetually behind offers no security at all. It would seem, then, that if nations must look to their own security, it will prove rational for those who have nuclear weapons to exploit their deterrence potential, that is, to threaten to use them in retaliation against a nuclear attack by the other side.

Wiesner and York's remarks concerning the limitations of a defensive approach also provide a basis for disposing of another possible rebuttal. It might be thought that the massive overkill capacity of both sides is a more or less temporary phenomenon that arises because, at a given point in time, neither side has quite perfected its countermeasures. But, given the "margin of error" and "lap behind" problems, one must expect that the "perfection" of defensive systems will only very infrequently, and then only for a temporary period of time, result in any significant reduction in overkill capability.

HARDIN'S SOLUTION

What remedy does Hardin propose for the problem of overgrazing on the commons? We must, he argues, institute a system of private property rights, which will force each owner to bear the full costs of overgrazing caused by additions to his own herd. But this in turn means, of course, that there will have to be some form of government—if only a "night watchman" state—to delineate appropriate personal and property rights and settle the disputes that will inevitably arise. In short, persons will have to accept an arrangement under which they are no longer at liberty to do whatever they happen to judge to be in their own best interest. They will have to accept limitations on their personal "sovereignty" and accept the liability of having coercive measures applied against them, given a judicial finding that they have failed to keep to the terms of the social contract. Hardin, rather than shrinking from this conclusion, makes it central to his own proposal. Social arrangements are needed to guarantee responsible behavior on the part of participants:

> The social arrangements that produce responsibility are arrangements that create coercion, of some sort. Consider bank-robbing. The man who takes money from a bank acts as if the bank were a commons. How do we prevent

such action? . . . we insist that a bank is not a commons; we seek the definite social arrangements that will keep it from becoming a commons. That we thereby infringe on the freedom of the would-be robbers we neither deny nor regret. . . . Coercion is a dirty word to most liberals now, but it need not . . . be so. . . . To many, the word coercion implies arbitrary decisions of distant and irresponsible bureaucrats; but this is not a necessary part of its meaning. . . . The only kind of coercion I recommend is mutual coercion, mutually agreed upon.[5]

Is the need for coercive social arrangements confined only to maintaining a traditionally defined system of private property rights? Hardin's own view is that such arrangements are needed in other contexts as well. Among other things, he argues that rational interaction within the framework of private property will in certain instances cause serious problems, problems whose solution will require that traditional property right boundaries be redrawn and additional coercive measures be adopted. As a case in point Hardin cites the problem of pollution:

The tragedy of the commons reappears in problems of pollution. Here it is not a question of taking something out of the commons, but of putting something in—sewage, or chemical, radioactive, and heat wastes into water; noxious and dangerous fumes into the air; and distracting and unpleasant advertising signs into the line of sight. The calculations of utility are much the same as before. The rational man finds that his share of the costs of the wastes he discharges into the commons is less than the cost of purifying his wastes before releasing them. Since this is true for everyone, we are locked into a system of "fouling our own nest," so long as we behave only as independent, rational, free-enterprisers.

The tragedy of the commons as a food basket is averted by private property, or something formally like it. But the air and waters surrounding us cannot readily be fenced, and so the tragedy of the commons as a cesspool must be prevented by different means, by coercive laws or taxing devices that make it cheaper for the polluter to treat his pollutants than to discharge them untreated. We have not progressed as far with the solution of this problem as we have with the first. Indeed, our particular concept of private property, which deters us from exhausting the positive resources of the earth, favors pollution.[6]

Hardin thus regards the pollution problem as a version of the prisoner's dilemma. Each firm doing what it judges to be in its best interests leads to a worsening of the situation for all. Once again, the proposed solution is mutual coercion mutually agreed upon, that is, some system of coercively enforced rights and duties.

HARDIN'S SOLUTION APPLIED TO THE ARMS RACE

To what extent do Hardin's arguments concerning the need for mutual coercion carry over to the case of national security? A pressing matter here, it must be noted, is that many of those who have been attracted to Hardin's analysis of the problem of the commons have tended to resist any extension of that argument. Some would even resist the extension to the pollution problem. While granting that there is a need for well-defined property rights, the story they propose to tell is that once property rights have been fixed, if there is a potential for mutual gain through cooperation, markets and marketlike forms of voluntary negotiation and bargaining should emerge to enable the parties involved to realize these mutual gains. If persons are really concerned about pollution, one would expect to see some sort of arrangement worked out by all the parties involved.

The arms race dilemma naturally invites comparison with the pollution problem. Not only has the technological approach to national security proven self-defeating but, in a deeply worrisome sense, the nuclear nations have managed to poison our whole environment: the threat of destruction hangs over all of us. Since all are adversely affected, however, it would seem that all should have an incentive to cooperate in some fashion to improve the situation, through arms limitation or disarmament agreements.

Here, then, is a brief for permitting the spirit of Adam Smith to move freely at this level. The strategy is to agree that some kind of coercively enforced system of basic property rights is essential—but to resist any attempt to extend this argument and use it as a rationale for coercive institutions other than the "night-watchman" state. With respect to the arms race problem, the implication is that if unilateral approaches to national security prove to be self-defeating, then nation-states should have sufficient motivation to negotiate bilateral or multilateral agreements on arms limitation and reduction.

This brief is inadequate in a number of respects. One problem concerns whether it would be rational for any nation to agree to a freeze in the development and deployment of such weapons and, subsequently, to some kind of phased reduction of weapons stockpiles. The freeze fixes the level of deployment for the two sides and thus determines the relative bargaining power of each side in any future negotiations, including negotiations for staged disarmament. Thus each side has a significant interest in entering negotiations from a position of advantage or superiority; moreover, as already noted, it is quite rational, from the perspective of prudence, to err on the side of overestimating the relative power of the other side. If both sides have formed reasonable estimates of their relative positions, with a prudentially mandated bias on the side of overestimating the advantages of the other side, both sides will not find it rational to agree to the freeze.

The problem with bilateral and multilateral agreements goes much deeper, however. Consider, first, the problem confronting individuals who try to realize gains through mutual trade. As Thomas Hobbes saw so clearly more than 300 years ago, where there is no system of effectively secured basic personal rights, the "natural" state of competition is a war of all against all.[7] In such a world, we find not a marketplace in which mutual gains are possible through trade, but a form of interaction governed by the principle "to each according to his threat advantage." It is not a world of efficient agreements but of tragically inefficient hostility, in which individuals can have no reasonable expectation of securing their most basic interests. It is implicit in the account that Hobbes gives that the system of rights must be framed so as to offer guarantees with respect to certain basic interests of the individual: bodily integrity, a certain measure of autonomy, and the means to ensure not simply bare survival, but some reasonable level of well being.[8] Moreover, that system of rights must be effectively secured by coercive power. There must be a system for adjudicating disputes over such personal rights, backed by sufficient coercive power to ensure that individuals will no longer have effective recourse to private means of violence and deceit to ensure their cause. In this respect Hardin's argument concerning the need for "mutual coercion, mutually agreed upon," simply echoes the central thesis of the *Leviathan* concerning the need for a sovereign power.[9] On this account, then, there is no natural harmony of interest, no beautiful coincidence of individual and collective interests arranged by an invisible hand (may the spirit of Adam Smith rest in peace!) without some framework of coercively enforced rights that guarantee the personal integrity and basic interests of each participant.

Is there any reason to suppose that it is different for nations? The considerations we have just rehearsed apply to the concerns of nations with regard to national security. National security pertains, by definition, to the objectives of any structure of basic rights and duties itself, as defined with respect to sovereign states in their dealings with one another. National security concerns the territorial, political, and economic integrity of the nation-state. But these objectives precisely parallel the objectives of the system of basic rights and duties pertaining to individuals in their dealings with one another: bodily integrity, autonomy, and the achievement of a reasonable level of well being. Where an international system of national rights and duties does not yet exist, there is no possibility of nation-states starting from a position in which each is secure in its basic rights, to explore how best to secure potential mutual gains and avoid potential mutual losses.

I do not mean to suggest that before there is any kind of international order there must be a fundamental guarantee of national territorial, political, and economic integrity. One can imagine—this is what we live with now—an arrangement in which various secondary rights pertaining to, e.g., international trade, extradition, etc., are more or less regularly settled by international courts. The point is simply that this cannot be understood as anything more than a *de facto* arrangement. As long as the structure of basic rights has not been secured, one cannot expect compliance with the court's rulings except in cases where the nations involved believe that no basic interest of theirs will be compromised. Nations that have to look completely to their own resources to protect their territorial, political, and economic interests simply cannot afford to pursue any other policy.

It is impossible, I believe, to overestimate the need for a system of rights that will govern nations in their dealings with one another and that will be guaranteed by an international organization possessing adequate coercive power. A model according to which voluntary agreements between sovereign states will take care of inefficiencies simply cannot bear the weight that is expected of it. In regard to the conditions for efficient interactions between nations (no less than interactions between persons), one must reckon with the fact that a laissez-faire approach to security has proved, and will continue to prove, to be self-defeating. But beyond this we must reckon with another fact. This is the extraordinarily disruptive force of the sense of injustice experienced by those who view their relationships to others as arising, not from agreements into which they have freely entered from secure positions, but from "arrangements" forced upon them under conditions of disadvantage and vulnerability.

This is part of what the spirit of Adam Smith has bequeathed to the present community of nations: a sense of the injustice of past colonialism and continuing economic imperialism. It may be doubted whether, given this legacy, there is any possibility of a peaceful world order. But it is hard to imagine any other possibility except through an international order in which the rights of nations are secured by coercive means.

The conclusion is that nations have no choice but to create an international community, predicated upon a set of basic rights and duties of nations toward one another, enforced and adjudicated by a coercively backed international legal order. What is needed, if we are to overcome the national security dilemma, is an end to the system of absolute national sovereignty.

THE LOGIC OF INTERNATIONAL SOVEREIGNTY

Many will be inclined to resist this conclusion. Some will argue that the costs associated with coercively limiting the sovereignty of nation-states may be prohibitive. One such line of reasoning seeks to exploit the very Archemedian point on which we have tried, following Hobbes, to construct the argument: a prudential concern to ensure the future way to the fulfillment of certain basic interests. The suggestion is that Hobbes's own argument, concerning the need for individuals to relinquish the sovereignty they possess in the state of nature and to create by social contract a supraindividual sovereign body, tends to undercut itself. Even if it would serve the interests of peace and security to have a sovereign power that forced us to keep the terms of the social contract, would it really be rational for us to fashion such a Leviathan? How could we be sure that having made it, and set it to rule over us in the world, it would not turn, or be turned by others, against us?

It must be emphasized that the problem arises not simply for those who are narrowly self-interested. Even those who are directly concerned with securing the well-being of others must consider, from the prudential perspective (which requires that they take care not to compromise seriously the realization of those goals) whether or not a deliberate decision to create the Leviathan is justified. The prudential case *for* the Leviathan is that it offers the way out of the state of nature—a state that threatens any prospect one has of realizing one's objectives. The prudential case *against* the Leviathan is that to create it is to create something which can threaten one's prospects even more than they are threatened in the state of nature. In the state of nature some protection derives from the fact that power is either diffuse or, where it is concentrated, subject to continual alteration. The Leviathan, by way of contrast, constitutes an extraordinary concentration of power that is likely to be relatively stable and that can be used with crushing effectiveness against any participant. It can pose, then, a threat to the survival and integrity of the individual participants.

Hobbes glosses over this problem. His overwhelming preoccupation is with the evils of civil anarchy, not oppressive governments. He tends to favor monarchy and is content to insist (somewhat unconvincingly) that the worst that can happen to one under civil government compares favorably with what one must expect in the state of nature. As it turns out, however, a distinction can be made here (and in fact Hobbes himself makes it) between the principle of sovereignty and sovereign power, on the one hand, and the particular institutional expression of sovereignty, on the other hand. Hobbes's position is that individuals must enter civil society and in so doing abandon the status they had as independent sovereign beings in the state of nature; he also holds that the institutions defining this civil order must be backed by coercive force. But both of these points can be conceptually separated from the issue concerning what particular institutional form such arrangements should take.

Hobbes argues that we must abandon the state of nature in which each participant's reasoning powers set the standards for its judging case by case what is to be done, standards based upon the concept of self-preservation and promotion of its own objectives and interests (as it perceives them). We must move to a state in which each participant is bound by rules. To be bound by a rule means that each participant is no longer at liberty to act case by case in terms of what it judges to be the best course of action available to it. Thus, to leave the state of nature is to renounce one's right to act unilaterally in the light of one's own judgement of what is the best course of action. That individuals have such a liberty-right in the state of nature and do not have it in the state of civil society Hobbes unequivocally asserts in *De Civa* (the earlier version of his famous *Leviathan*):

> in a civil government the reason of the supreme, that is, the civil law, is to be received by each single subject for the right; yet being without this civil government, in which state no man can know right reason from false, but by comparing it with his own, every man's reason is to be accounted not only the rule of his own actions, which are done at his peril, but also for the measure of another man's reason, in such things as do concern him.[10]

The polemical character of the *Leviathan* version of Hobbes's argument tends to obscure the conclusion to which he has in fact driven the argument. His emphasis there on the notion that "covenants without the sword are in vain" (that coercion is needed) blurs his central point about the principle of sovereignty. What we must give up, if we are to escape from the state of nature, is the "right" to act in that manner which we judge to be right, on a case-by-case basis. We must, in short, submit ourselves to a rule of law—to a legal order under which we no longer have the right to act simply on our own lights. This is the essence, for Hobbes, of an individual's acceptance of the principle of civil sovereignty. In one passage in the *Leviathan* Hobbes expresses this pure principle of civil sovereignty with great force and clarity:

> when there is a controversy in an account the parties must by their own accord set up, for right reason, the reason of some arbitrator or judge, to whose sentence they will both stand, or their controversy must either come to blows or be undecided for want of a right reason constituted by nature, so is it also in all debates of what kind so ever. And when men that think themselves wiser than all others clamor and demand right reason for judge, yet seek no more but that things should be determined by no other men's reason but their own, it is as intolerable in the society of men as it is in play after trump is turned to use for trump on every occasion that suit whereof they have most in their hand. For they do nothing else that will have every of their passions, as it comes to bear sway in them, to be taken for right reason, and that in their own controversies, betraying their want of right reason by the claim they lay to it.[11]

What we have here, it can be suggested, is Hardin's whole argument raised one level higher. On this interpretation, what is urged is not the political counterpart to a technological fix, that is, some coercive mechanism that will alter the conditions under which we pursue our primary goals and our second-order prudential goals. Instead, it is recommended that we transform our very way of deliberating and deciding upon a course of action. It is an invitation to think of ourselves and those others with whom we interact as capable of engaging in a new form of activity, in which our choices are constrained by rules whose claims upon us we no longer have a right to refuse (even if it lies within our power and in our interest to refuse them). Were these suggestive remarks of Hobbes to be fully developed, it might call for a transformation of our conception of rationality itself and its relevance to the questions of rights and duties. However this might work out, one point would still remain central: Hobbes's claim that it is the familiar concept of rationality as prudence that demands our submission to the rule of law, and that, in this sense, the ground or basis of rights and duties lies openly before us, in the human condition and in our most pressing prudential concerns. Prudence, paradoxically, demands that we abandon thinking of ourselves as autonomous beings bound merely by rules of the prudential calculus. It demands that we discipline ourselves to the rule of law.

This is the core of Hobbes's argument about the principle of sovereignty. This view together with the view he shares with Hardin, to the effect that such a form of coordination between people must be enforced by coercion, needs to be separated from his more particular beliefs concerning what would be the most effective institutional form of sovereign power. The problem of prudence arises, with respect to the issue of institutional embodiment, both for individuals contemplating forms of civil society and nation-states contemplating an international order. It is not the rule of law or its reinforcement by coercive power that sets the problem for prudence, but the way in which that power is embodied and exercised.

The prudential problem is real enough, and the community of nations will have to take up the question of how the coercive powers of an international order can be so established that each member has more rather than less assurances that it will not be unfairly turned against it. But why should the community of nations doubt its ability to satisfy the reasonable concerns of prudent member states? We have, collectively, extraordinary experience to build upon in this regard. We have a sense not only of the need for forms of democratic representation, constitutional constraints, and separation of powers, but also of the need for mediating principles of economic and social justice, if the territorial, political and economic integrity of each participant is to be assured.

IS THERE HOPE IN EVOLUTION?

Some will be prepared to agree in principle with what we have argued here. But, speaking from a "realistic" point of view, they will urge that an international order is likely to be realized only in the fullness of time, as the result of much experimentation. The suggestion will be that as groups of nations continue to gain experience about the benefits of cooperation on more formal terms and the costs of failure to so cooperate, something like an international order will finally evolve.

But may we wait any longer to let nature take its course? There is too much truth (if little comfort) in Hardin's theme that "ruin is the destination toward which all men rush, each pursuing his own best interest in a society that believes in the freedom of the commons." Given the technology of destruction that each side now possesses, we must be concerned that ruin is the destination toward which all nations rush, each pursuing its own best interest in an international community that believes in absolute national sovereignty. The real possibility exists that the consequences of letting nature take its course will be completely unacceptable.

In the great debate over the nature of evolutionary change, the battle lines are drawn between those who are deeply committed to the view that *natura saltus non facit* (nature does not make jumps) and those who think the key to understanding evolution lies in the idea of short periods of explosive, catastrophic change. We need not settle this issue here. For our purposes it suffices to think of each of these models as outlining a possible evolutionary path to a more promising future.

One view is that the ability to agree to mutual coercion surely has survival value, and that gradually and over the very long haul those groups of nations who effect such arrangements will survive to inherit the earth. The trouble with this line of reasoning, however, is that we cannot be sanguine any longer about the prospect that natural selection will be able to work its magic. It may not be possible to undertake the necessary series of experiments. What is called for is a long period during which certain groups of nations manage to remain in a state of nature vis-à-vis one another and thereby suffer the consequences, while other nations manage to work out systems of enforced cooperation, to their own great relative advantage. Time is not what is lacking. The problem is that we lack the means to ensure that these lessons will be internalized. We have no way to guarantee that those who fail to coordinate will bear the costs and that those who do work out systems of mutual coercion will enjoy the benefits. We have no way to make sure that we are not all destroyed by the experiments.

The other view is that, in certain cases, people must undergo some great shock or significant catastrophe, after which the logic of the situation will be driven home to them and they will be prepared to act. It is true, of course, that some do manage to transform themselves when the shock is great enough. The existence of such a trait is due, no doubt, to natural selection. But our competitive drive and our extraordinary capacity to find technological solutions—traits we also possess as the result of a process of natural selection—have finally overreached us. We can hope for some contained catastrophic shock to bring us to our senses, but given the weapons systems we now possess, we can no longer have any assurance that it will happen this way. We must face the real possibility (I will out of stubborn idealism refuse to say "real probability") that the occasion for our transformation will also be the occasion of our destruction.

Our task, then, is most pressing. It is not simply that we must establish an international order so as to escape from the mutually disadvantageous pattern into which we are presently locked. That international order is also indispensable if we are to escape from the extraordinary risk to which we have exposed ourselves and others. Surely it lies within our power to accomplish this. We have managed many transitions, from tribal groups to small societies, from in formal arrangements to complex forms of civil order. Each transition has meant a transformation not only in our social existence, but in the nature of human individuality. No doubt, the hand of natural necessity can be discerned in all of this. As the conditions of interdependency have increased—an increase that itself is the result of the extraordinary success of our technology for survival—many of those cultures that failed to make the transition lost out. But such a theory of natural necessity is compatible with the notion of deliberate choice. The international community of nations can *choose* to meet the challenge that now confronts it.

The logic of the argument to be found in Hobbes and Hardin is clear. We have no choice but to transform ourselves once more. As individual states, we must take up the chains of obligations, one to another, together with all that such a commitment implies. We must establish a true international order and thereby put an end to the system of absolute national sovereignty. Only in this way can we escape from the self-defeating and awesomely dangerous situation that now confronts us, in which each nation is disposed to use for trump that suit whereof it has the most in its own hand.

NOTES

1. Garrett Hardin, "The Tragedy of the Commons," *Science* 162 (13 December 1968). Quote from p. 1244.
2. Ibid., p. 1243. Quoted from Jerome B. Wiesner and Herbert F. York, "National Security and the Nuclear-Test Ban," *Scientific American* 211, no. 4 (October 1964): 27-35. The specific quote is from p. 35 (emphasis in original).
3. Wiesner and York, "National Security," p. 35.
4. Ibid., p. 33.
5. Hardin, "Tragedy," p. 1247.
6. Ibid., p. 1245.
7. Thomas Hobbes, *Leviathan*, Part I, chap. 13.
8. At the end of ibid., Hobbes argues that it is "fear of death, desire of such things as are necessary to commodious living, and a hope by their industry to obtain them" that incline men to the social contract. The Laws of Nature that are characterized in Part I, chapters 14 and 15, and that spell out the terms of this social contract, are framed explicitly in terms of the notion that persons are concerned not only with bodily integrity and well-being, but also with giving up only that amount of autonomy necessary to secure peace.
9. See, in particular, Part I, chapters 14, 15, and 17 of the *Leviathan*.
10. Hobbes, *De Civa*, chap. 2(1), footnote.
11. *Leviathan*, Part I, chap. 5.

22
PREVENTING THE FINAL EPIDEMIC

Louis René Beres

All I maintain is that on this Earth there are pestilences and there are victims, and it is up to us, so far as possible, not to join forces with the pestilences.

Albert Camus, *The Plague*

CURRENT U.S. NUCLEAR POLICY

Despite its institutionalized expressions of support for controlling nuclear weapons, the United States continues to pursue a strategic policy that identifies American security with a provocative emphasis on counterforce targeting and renewed arms racing. Threatening to undermine the already fragile foundations of a peace based on reciprocal threats of obliteration, this policy is designed to fulfill military tasks at a level far exceeding the requirements of "minimum deterrence." Current U.S. nuclear policy, based on the foundations of Presidential Directive 59, which was signed by President Carter on 25 July 1980,[1] goes beyond the legitimate objective of survivable and penetration-capable strategic forces to steadily accelerated preparations for nuclear war fighting.

The essential rationale of this policy is twofold: First, it is expected to strengthen nuclear deterrence. Faced with what is perceived as a relentless buildup and refinement of Soviet strategic forces in alleged preparation for nuclear war, the present administration suggests a compelling need for revising the principles of "Mutual Assured Destruction" (MAD). Rather than be faced with an intolerable choice between all-out nuclear war and surrender, it argues, the United States requires a

---

The medical imagery of this chapter title is borrowed from the title of an important book by physicians and scientists on nuclear war: Ruth Adams and Susan Cullen, eds., *The Final Epidemic* (Chicago: Educational Foundation for Nuclear Science, 1981). According to the book's introductory statement by Dr. Howard Hiatt, Dean of the Harvard School of Public Health: "An inescapable lesson of contemporary medicine is that when treatment of a given disease is ineffective or where costs are insupportable, attention must be given to prevention." Dr. Hiatt's reference, of course, is to the "disease" of nuclear war.

new set of retaliatory options. These options have already been incorporated into plans that stress the destruction of Soviet command authorities and the deployment of intermediate-range theater nuclear forces in Europe.

Second, current U.S. nuclear policy is expected to permit U.S. forces to "prevail" if deterrence fails. Anticipated by former Secretary of Defense Brown's statement that "we are necessarily giving greater attention to how a nuclear war would actually be fought by both sides if deterrence fails,"[2] this policy counsels preparations for a nuclear war that may be protracted and carefully controlled. Apparently accepting the position of certain think-tank analysts that the United States "must possess the ability to wage nuclear war rationally,"[3] this policy reflects the understanding that a combination of counterforce targeting, crisis relocation of urban populations, and ballistic missile defense could make nuclear war "cost-effective."

Both parts of the policy rationale are misconceived. Based upon a series of erroneous assumptions and upon disregard for synergistic effects between American and Soviet strategies, it codifies a set of initiatives that can only hasten the arrival of nuclear war. Ignoring the reality that the delicate balance of terror cannot endure indefinitely, it compels the Soviet Union to match each American move with an escalatory countermove. The resultant *folie à deux* must inevitably heighten the insecurities of each superpower. It can never produce peace.

America's current nuclear strategy is based upon a confusion of the requirement of survivable nuclear forces with the employment of counterforce targeting doctrine. While it is clear that the former requirement is essential to stable deterrence, a provocative targeting doctrine is not only unessential, it is counterproductive. Considered together with America's failure to ratify SALT II, its continuing reliance on a policy of nuclear "first use," its program to improve long-range theater nuclear forces, and its renewed commitments to Ballistic Missile Defense (BMD) and Civil Defense, this country's intent to place a large percentage of Soviet strategic forces (and military and civilian leaders) in jeopardy actually provides our adversary with a heightened incentive to strike first.

Why should the American policy of "first use" appear threatening to the Soviets? After all, it has always been the official policy of the United States not to launch a nuclear strike as an initial, offensive move of war. Is a nuclear strategy provocative that does not exclude the *retaliatory* use of nuclear weapons to stave off defeat in a conventional conflict? The answer to this question lies in the fact that the distinctions between the "first use" of nuclear weapons and a nuclear "first strike" are, in practice, meaningless. Once the United States had determined that an adversary had committed an act of aggression, any intended U.S. nuclear response would certainly be characterized as a "first use" rather than as a "first strike," and the determination that an act of aggression had taken place would necessarily be made by the United States rather than by some specially constituted central arbiter.

Taken together with the consequences of NATO's conventional force inferiority, the policy of "first use" is especially unsettling to the Soviet Union since it is a policy that (a) allows for rapid escalation to nuclear conflict, (b) allows for the possibility of disguising a "first strike" as a "first use" either by deliberately creating conditions that lead to acts of "aggression" or by falsely alleging that such acts have actually taken place, and (c) joins with a targeting doctrine that focuses on Soviet strategic forces.

Hence, the American policy of "first use" offers incentives to the Soviet Union to undertake a preemptive nuclear strike against the United States. Moreover, this policy creates incentives for other nuclear powers to adopt hair-trigger strategies for protection against possible preemptive strikes. And these risks are incurred by the United States with little real benefit in terms of deterrence, since any American nuclear retaliation would almost certainly draw a Soviet nuclear response. In view of the enormously high probability of Soviet nuclear counterretaliation and the terrible destruction that would be visited upon allies, Soviet strategists must entertain grave doubts about American willingness to use theater nuclear forces.[4] We should not be surprised, therefore, when Soviet spokesmen continue to characterize current American nuclear strategy as a move toward an eventual American first strike.[5] In assessing this characterization, one cannot ignore the fact that a second-strike counterforce strategy is largely a contradiction in terms. A counterforce capability is apt to serve only the nation that strikes first. Used in retaliation, American's counterforce-targeted warheads would hit only empty silos.

Our purpose in placing Soviet military and civilian leaders in jeopardy is to destroy the Soviet leadership's ability to exercise political control during a nuclear war.[6] Yet, this purpose is clearly contrary to the essential rationale of a countervailing nuclear strategy: that is, preserving the prospects for limited, controlled nuclear conflict. Indeed, in view of this country's current inability to support its countervailing strategy with advanced weapon systems,[7] the expanded personal targeting of Soviet leaders actually increases the likelihood of a Soviet first strike in the near term.

Curiously, nothing in our current nuclear strategy suggests a plausible connection between nuclear war and politics. Why, exactly, are the Soviets getting ready to "fight and win" a nuclear war with the United States?[8] What conceivable postwar prospect can be associated with alleged Soviet plans for a first strike against the United States? Why should the Soviets be expected to disregard the Clausewitzian principle that war should always be conducted with a view to sustaining the overriding "political object"? According to Clausewitz:

> War is only a branch of political activity; it is in no sense autonomous. It cannot be divorced from political life— and whenever this occurs in our thinking about war, the many links that connect the two elements are destroyed, and we are left with something that is pointless and devoid of sense.[9]

The dangers of assessing Soviet nuclear intentions *in vacuo* are considerable. By assuming that their *Staatspolitik* offers no homage to plausible relationships between nuclear war and national political goals, our own nuclear policy creates a bewildering expectation of first-strike scenarios that in turn produces a staggering array of provocative tactics and deployments. As if these weaknesses were not enough to demonstrate the inadequacy of current American nuclear strategy, the present administration has founded this strategy on preparations to "prevail" in a nuclear war. Substantial evidence now supports the conclusion that such preparations comprise a pyramid of fantasies, a configuration of superimposed illusions that will collapse like a house of cards in the face of reasoned evaluations.

The understanding that preparations to prevail have no place in a nuclear war is as old as the Atomic Age. In one of the first major theoretical treatments of the subject of nuclear war, Bernard Brodie wrote: "Thus far the chief purpose of our military establishment has been to win wars. From now on its chief purpose must be to avert them. It can have no other useful purpose."[10] Long before the Atomic Age, philosophers and military strategists probed the idea of victory with sensitivity and prescience. Machiavelli, for example, recognized the principle of an "economy of violence" that distinguishes between creativity and destruction:[11] "For it is the man who uses violence to spoil things, not the man who uses it to mend them, that is blameworthy."[12] With respect to war, Machiavelli counseled that victory need not be in the best interests of the prince, and that it might even produce an overall weakening of a state's position in international affairs.[13]

Unlike proponents of current U.S. nuclear strategy, Machiavelli understood the difference between violence and power. More recently, Hannah Arendt has reflected on this distinction, elucidating a situation wherein the technical development of the implements of violence has now outstripped any rational justifications for their use in armed conflict. Hence, war is no longer the *ultima ratio* in world politics, the merciless final arbiter in international disputes, but an apocalyptic chess game that bears no resemblance to earlier games of power and domination. In such a game, if either "wins" both lose.[14]

Still another problem with the idea of prevailing in a nuclear war is the unpredictability intrinsic to all violence. Contrary to the anesthetized expectations of strategic thinkers who anticipate near-perfect symmetry between human behavior and their own strategic plans, violence harbors within itself an ineradicable element of the unexpected. As Hannah Arendt has observed; "nowhere does Fortuna, good or ill luck, play a more fateful role in human affairs than on the battlefield."[15]

In this connection, Arendt's concern for the uncertainties of violence has roots in Tolstoy's, Schopenhauer's and Joseph de Maistre's views about the chaos and uncontrollability of battles and wars,[16] and stands in marked opposition to the ranks of all passionate systematizers who deny the essential irregularity of battlefield activity. In the fashion of modern historians who seek "laws" to explain and predict the vagaries of human conduct on a global scale (e.g., Bossuet, Vico, Herder, Comte, Hegel, Buckle, Marx, Spengler, Toynbee and McNeill), the strategic mythmakers transform imperfect mosaics of military behavior into a structured "logic of events." Entangled in metaphors and false assumptions, advocates of the possibility of nuclear victory display a singular failure to understand the nonrational springs of action and feeling, and an unreasonable degree of faith in game-theoretic systems of rational explanation.[17] If only these strategic mythmakers could learn to appreciate how little humankind can control the disorderly multitude of factors involved in war. If only they could learn to understand what presumptuous hazards are associated with a strategy that seeks to impose order on what must inevitably be a heightened form of chaos.[18]

Students of world affairs would do well to consider Thucydides' account of the Peloponnesian War, where they would learn that the wellsprings of strategic behavior lie in the irrational and impulsive recesses of the human psyche. Here, they would encounter a memorable recitation of affairs in which the blind drives of honor and recklessness take precedence over considerations of safety and survival, a recitation that prefigures the consequences of excessive faith in rational models of nuclear warfare.

The conditions that arose in Classical Greece after the death of Pericles and the ascent of Cleon and Alcibiades in Athenian affairs have been repeated in countless episodes of human history. The appraisals and prescriptions of the Reagan administration point to an overweening pride and arrogance in counseling preparations for nuclear warfare, a pattern of *hubris* that underscores the urgency of Albert Einstein's warning at the beginning of the nuclear era: "The unleashed power of the atom has changed everything except our thinking. Thus, we are drifting toward a catastrophe beyond conception. We shall require a substantially new manner of thinking if mankind is to survive."[19] To create such a "new manner of thinking," students of world affairs must learn to disassociate any idea of benefit from considerations of nuclear war. As we have already seen, even Clausewitz understood that war must be conducted with a view to postwar benefit and that the principle of "utmost force" must be qualified by reference to "the political object" as the standard for determining the amount of effort to be expended.

SHORT-TERM CORRECTIVES

As we have seen, America's current nuclear strategy is sorely misconceived. To reverse this strategy, we require a rapid and far-reaching disengagement from developing patterns of counterforce targeting and from expanded preparations for nuclear war fighting. Only when such disengagement is complete can a viable arms control agenda for the eighties be implemented. Hence, only in the aftermath of such disengagement can we expect genuine movement to an improved world order.

To accomplish the necessary revisions in American nuclear strategy, the US must move immediately to restore the relatively promising principles of minimum deterrence. Minimum deterrence refers to a concept of reciprocal nuclear threat based on the ability of each superpower to inflict unacceptable damage upon the other after absorbing a nuclear first strike. Unlike the rationale of this country's developing "countervailing" nuclear strategy, which ties deterrence to a nuclear war fighting capacity, minimum deterrence rests only on the maintenance of survivable and penetration-capable nuclear forces. Hence, it is linked to a targeting doctrine that stresses cities and population centers rather than military "hard" targets.

Although it is sometimes argued that minimum deterrence is not credible because any retaliation would carry an overwhelmingly high probability of all-out nuclear war, this argument fails to understand that any U.S. counterforce reprisal would carry the same risks. This is the case because the "collateral damage" from such counterforce attacks would include tens of millions of fatalities and because a rational Soviet adversary could not possibly afford to conform to American strategic rules concerning a "limited" nuclear war. Indeed, Soviet policy continues to threaten the United States with all-out nuclear war once American counterforce reprisals have been launched. It follows that the alleged "flexibility" of current U.S. nuclear strategy is illusory, offering no advantages over a strategy of minimum deterrence. Current nuclear strategy does, however, carry serious comparative *disadvantages*. Since the American search for a nuclear war fighting capacity heightens Soviet fears of an American first strike, it simultaneously *degrades* this country's security. Moreover, American nuclear weapons that are counterforce-targeted to conform to nuclear war fighting doctrines of deterrence will have a measurably reduced deterrent effect, since their use in a second strike would produce substantially less damage to the USSR than would extensive countervalue attacks.

The overriding objective of such a move to minimum deterrence must be to reduce Soviet fears of an American first strike while preserving the survivability and penetration-capability of this country's strategic forces. This objective can be served by abandoning plans for further deployment of nuclear weapons with hard-target kill capabilities; abandoning plans for any ICBM–basing mode that assumes deployment of a ballistic missile defense system; abandoning plans for crisis relocation of civilian populations; abandoning plans for deployment of a new generation of medium-range missiles in Europe; and abandoning plans for stepped-up attacks on Soviet command, control, communication and intelligence (C³I) facilities. With such stabilizing moves underway, the superpowers could begin to make progress toward a START accord, which—in turn—would allow for negotiated limitations on long-range theater nuclear forces in Europe and on antisatellite weapons systems. Moreover, the realization of a START agreement would further the objectives of the Limited Test Ban Treaty and the Nuclear Nonproliferation Treaty.

The ultimate objective of START must be a follow-on agreement wherein both sides undertake substantial reductions in strategic forces. Before this objective can be realized, the above moves toward minimum deterrence must be augmented by a US renunciation of the right to "first use" of nuclear weapons—a renunciation that would parallel the Soviet declaration before the UN's second special session on disarmament. To support such a renunciation, this country must abandon production of the neutron bomb, discontinue NATO plans for the modernization of intermediate-range nuclear weapons in Western Europe, redeploy theater nuclear forces away from frontiers, and, ultimately, remove these forces altogether. These steps must be accompanied by efforts to strengthen U.S. and allied conventional forces relative to the Soviet Union in order to preserve a sufficiently high nuclear threshold. For its part, the Soviet Union must agree to steps imposing far-reaching curbs on its own theater nuclear weapons delivery capability and on Warsaw Pact ground manpower and tank forces.

Disarmament cannot be pursued seriously amid the precarious cross-currents of international belligerence and mistrust. Rather, it must await the achievement of a more harmonious nuclear regime, one founded on the kinds of strategic revisions and arms control agreements already discussed. With the appearance of such a regime, the START process could proceed to the negotiation of actual reductions in strategic forces, and meaningful disarmament negotiations could be extended on a fully multilateral basis.

However urgent it is to initiate what has come to be known as "real reductions" in strategic forces, it would be a serious error to seek these reductions prematurely. As revealed by the unsuccessful Vance mission to Moscow in 1977,[20] an improved nuclear regime must be constructed incrementally. While it would be a monumental error to abandon disarmament for less ambitious arms-control remedies, it would be just as debilitating to seek disarmament before such remedies are in place. Before states can be expected to trust that disarmament measures will be generally respected, they will require antecedent assurances of strategic cooperation and good will. In this connection, the American decisions to sell lethal weapons to China and to produce neutron weapons are manifestly counterproductive.

It is with this understanding that we can examine the recent proposals by George F. Kennan for a 50 percent reduction in U.S. and Soviet nuclear arsenals. According to Kennan:

> What I would like to see the President do, after due consultation with the Congress, would be to propose to the Soviet government an immediate across-the-board reduction by 50 percent of the nuclear arsenals now being main-

tained by the superpowers—a reduction affecting in equal measure all forms of the weapon, strategic, medium range, and tactical, as well as all means of their delivery—all this to be implemented at once and without further wrangling among the experts, and to be subject to such national means of verification as now lie at the disposal of the two powers.[21]

While Kennan's proposal flows from an acute awareness of the terrible urgency of planetary danger, it offers no real hope for real security. Although the situation is certainly as desperate as Kennan suggests, there is no reason to believe that the superpowers can move from *realpolitik* to world order overnight. Before any of these proposals can be implemented, a full-fledged transformation of current American nuclear strategy must take place. Such transformation is the essential primary arena of nuclear war avoidance. However slow and painstaking it will be to accomplish, it cannot be bypassed.

A WORLD GOVERNMENT?

What is the best long-term solution to the threat of nuclear destruction? One frequently discussed proposal is that we seek to overcome the antagonisms that may lead to nuclear war by abolishing national sovereignty through the establishment of a world government. Through the centuries, the idea has persisted that decentralized global politics cannot provide world order reform, and that true security requires nothing less than the replacement of balance-of-power dynamics with world government. In a world system teeming with the implements of apocalyptic destruction, isn't this idea valid? Why not world government?

The questions surrounding world government are enormously complex. But the fundamental transformation it would require in the existing pattern of military force and sovereign authority is not an appropriate path to nuclear war avoidance. With the creation of world government, nothing would change the "threat system" dynamics of the prevailing balance of power; and world government would still continue reliance on the logic of deterrence. True, threats would be issued from "above" rather than laterally, but the underlying notion of security through fear would not be eliminated. With today's enormously destructive weapons technologies, it is imperative that national decisionmakers learn to appreciate that the allegedly "realistic" approach to security (an approach that "ties" security to relative power position) is actually unrealistic, and that long-term security via nuclear deterrence is a contradiction in terms. This is the case whether threats of retaliatory destruction originate "horizontally" from other states (the classical balance-of-power arrangement) or "vertically" from a specially constituted world public authority.

But might not the practice of nuclear deterrence by the world government be less objectionable than such practice by states? After all, wouldn't individual states look differently upon the legitimate central repository of nuclear weapons than upon one another, and a situation be created with significantly greater promise for stability than that of the extant nuclear threat system?

In considering these questions, we must first understand that the shift to a nuclear-armed world government would not represent a shift to world law. The existing system of international relations, however decentralized, *is* a system of international law. Within this system, the threatened reprisals of individual states against prospective aggressors constitute authoritative efforts at law enforcement that are no less lawful than a pattern associated with world government. This argument has its roots in the Grotian conception of international society and international law, and can be rejected only by those holding narrowly "positivistic" notions of jurisprudence that limit legal order to the presence of a commanding sovereign.

We must also understand that the effectiveness of decentralized or self-help systems of law needn't be inferior to that of a centralized legal system. The fact that weapons wielded by duly constituted institutions and officials in domestic legal systems are generally perceived as authoritative and necessary does not always ensure widespread compliance. Even a cursory glance at the American criminal justice system reveals an extraordinarily low level of effectiveness, one that is low even in comparison to the effectiveness of international law.

In deciding whether or not to comply with specific directives of the world government, individual states would be influenced not only by their perceptions of authoritativeness, but also by their judgments of effectiveness. The world government would need to be perceived as commanding an adequate measure of force and as willing to use such force. In this connection, the threat of nuclear reprisal by the world government might appear even less credible than the threat of interstate reprisal in the present world system. This is the case because the prevention of nuclear war would be the very *raison d'être* of the world government.

If the separate states were to believe that the world government would abhor the actual execution of a threatened nuclear sanction, they might understandably doubt its willingness to inflict reprisals. On the other hand, if the separate states were to believe that world government decisionmakers regarded the preservation of their credibility as an overriding preference, then they might believe its stated willingness to carry out nuclear sanctions.

Perceived willingness may also depend in part upon the structure of the world systems, i.e., the prevailing distribution of global power. It might be argued, for example, that in the view of the separate states, the world government's valuation of its perceived resolve increases as the system moves from multipolarity to bipolarity. This is the case where states believe that (a) the extent to which the decisionmakers of the world government value their image of resolve varies in accordance with the perceived consequences of failed resolve in number-of-state terms, and (b) the perceived consequences of failed resolve in number-of-state terms deteriorate as the system moves from a multipolar to a bipolar condition. This second assumption is itself derived from two other assumptions: (c) the perceived consequences of failed resolve in number-of-state terms worsen as the states in the system become more and more aligned with fewer and fewer "blocs" (each bloc has a leading state which forms a "pole" of the system)* and (d) the states in the system become more and more aligned with fewer and fewer blocs as the system moves from a multipolar to a bipolar state.

---

*The argument here is that the number of states likely to be influenced by the recalcitrance of other states (i.e., to become recalcitrant themselves) increases in accordance with the number of states the delinquent state is likely to affect, and that this number is largest (excepting unipolarity) in the bipolar system.

Even were states to believe the nuclear forces of the world government to be substantially invulnerable, perceived willingness might also depend in part upon state perceptions of (e) the disutility the world government attaches to whatever destruction it might still suffer (to forces or otherwise) as a consequence of implementing a threat, and (f) the likelihood that the world government would feel compelled to anticipate incurring such disutility as a consequence of threat implementation. If, for example, states believe (1) that the world government has defined a level of destruction that it deems unacceptable, and (2) that the world government feels it would incur such a level of destruction if it chose to make good on a nuclear threat, then states will probably believe that the world government would not carry out its threat. Perceived willingness will thus depend in part upon the world government's ability to convince states not to believe 1 and/or 2 above. As it is difficult to imagine a situation in which the world government would not consider a certain level of destruction to be unacceptable, the world government must convince potential offenders that making good on a nuclear threat would not be risking an unacceptably damaging counterstrike.

In view of the foregoing discussion, we must note that even in a world system wherein the world government has the ultimate right to make decisions about the use of force between states, and where it supports this right by an amount of force deemed sufficient to inflict unacceptably damaging punishment, centralized nuclear deterrence need not necessarily be effective. This is so because such effectiveness also requires the belief on the part of states that the world government is willing to make good on its threats to use nuclear force, and the world government's capability to implement such threats is not vulnerable to preemptive attack or to active defense. These extraordinarily complex requirements are generally overlooked by advocates of world government, who feel that their only proper efforts should concern problems of attainability.

But what of the conceptions of world government that envision disarmed states and a lightly armed world government force? Clark and Sohn call for "universal and complete national disarmament together with the establishment of institutions corresponding in the world field to those which maintain law and order within local communities and nations."[22] And the World Federalists, USA, consistently call for a schedule for universal and complete disarmament rather than for a system whereby order is maintained by, the perpetual threat of retaliatory destruction.

Even these conceptions, however, are not immune to the foregoing critique of a world government. How would such a program for disarmament be accomplished without a prior transfer of strategic and conventional military force to the specially consti tuted world government center? If so, what reasons exist to believe that individual states will calculate, first, that the benefits of disarmament will exceed the costs if all other states are willing to disarm and, second, that all other states *are* willing to disarm?

Unless the specifically constituted world government operates on the basis of threat-system dynamics supported by the capability to yield "assured destruction," each state contemplating disarmament would entertain grave doubts about the reciprocal behavior of all the other states. Since the prospect of its disarmament can be considered gainful by each state only if the other states disarm as well, these doubts would have fatal implications for the success of disarmament. Without a prior transfer of military force to the world federal government, individual states would have every reason to calculate that the prospective costs of compliance with the decision to disarm would outweigh the prospective benefits.

What all this means is that even those conceptions of world federal government that rest upon designs for disarmament must take into account our earlier criticisms. Disarmament simply cannot be wished into being; rather, it must be accomplished incrementally. The primary stages of disarmament necessarily require conditions whereby the world government center is in a position to influence effectively the decisional calculi of states such that the prospective costs of failing to disarm appear intolerably high. And this necessarily requires a continuation (however temporary) of the long-standing threat system dynamics of deterrence. *A world government that fulfills the requirements of a credible deterrence posture in the nuclear age is an essential precursor to a world government superintending a disarmed world with light "police-type" forces.* Hence, the weakness of the former conception cannot be overlooked by those who favor the second.

But perhaps we are mistaken! Perhaps the world government authority might not require the threat of military force. Isn't the distinction between *auctoritas* (authority) and *potestas* (power) well established in political theory? Indeed, since Plato, whose concept of all authority was founded upon the absence of compulsion, it has often been argued that force *cannot* be the basis of authority. In this view, not only *can* sovereign authority emanate from sources unsupported by force, it *must* secure obedience without the threat or use of force.

For example, Hannah Arendt has suggested that the authority relationship between those who command and those who obey rests upon "the hierarchy itself, whose rightness and legitimacy both recognize and where both have their predetermined stable place."[23] Similarly, Bertrand De Jouvenel emphasized the volitional core of authority relations: "Authority is the faculty of inducing assent. To follow authority is a voluntary act. Authority ends where voluntary assent ends."[24] It follows from these views that the margin of obedience won through force demonstrates the failure of authority.

These arguments raise the possibility of effective action by a world authority without the threat of force. Isn't it clear, after all, that a world order depending upon force as its *ultima ratio* must be a permanent source of struggle rather than stability? Didn't Grotius make it clear in *The Law of War and Peace* (1625) that authority in the world system must necessarily derive from the claims of morality on the minds of people?

But what "forceless" principles of obligation might be appropriate to effective world government supervision of disarmament? Here we may turn to Plato for guidance. In the analogies that occur again and again in the political dialogues, the appropriate basis of authority is *special knowledge or expertise*. In the relations between the captain of a ship and the passengers or between the physician and the patient, for example, special knowledge or expertise provides the basis for compliance. The threat of force is not necessary. The obligation inheres in the relationship itself.

Could a "forceless" world government secure the essential compliance of states on the basis of some special claim to knowledge or expertise, namely, some commonly felt need for centralized management? And if such need must be the compelling element in the relationship between states and the world government, how might national leaders be encouraged to value it highly? Here, the principal question concerns the rank occupied by this need in the preference orderings of states as well as the scope of its claim.

Just how high a position would have to be assigned to the need for centralized management? And just how commonly felt must this need be? Even a few powerful states that would not concede the importance of centralized management might make its implementation impossible. Let us first consider the position that states might assign to the centralized management of force. If states were to believe that such management were essential to their survival, they might assign this need a very high rank. If the value assigned to self-preservation by states is always higher than that assigned to any other preference or combination of preferences, the need for centralized management of force would be allotted the highest possible position. This is true if the preference for self-preservation is tied to the need for centralized management.

To make such an assumption, however, would be foolhardy because it would assume that states identify their own prospects for survival with the prospects for the creation of a particular organizational scheme of decisionmaking for the world as a whole. Although such an identification might appear eminently reasonable from the view of an hypothetical "outside" observer, from the point of view of individual states it is not justified. States do not form their own preferences by first considering the security needs of the entire system; nor do they order their preferences in accordance with these needs.

States "behave" in this way because each lacks confidence in the others' willingness to work toward realizing a common objective. Moreover, states might fear that even if such willingness were assured, the new arrangement would not be conducted in an accept able, predetermined manner. Thus, even if states did not fear that centralized management would fail because other states would violate the spirit of such an agreement, they still might feel that the resultant distribution of authority would not be equitable and secure. This is because states might fear that without the instruments of violence, the world government would not be able to assure their safety.

States, then, assign a low probability to the securing of security advantages through world government, a probability so low that the prospect of exclusive security advantage would be preferred even where its perceived value is exceeded by that of security advantages through centralized management. We see, then, that states would not tie the need for centralized management of force to the preference for self-preservation. Consequently, this need would not be assigned the highest possible position in states' preference orderings. The conclusion is obvious: right without force is ineffective in the centralized management of world power. There is no apparent reason to suppose that power would be more effectively managed by a forceless world government than in the prevailing balance of power system.

This does not mean that world government could never succeed with disarmament in the absence of military force. We might arrive at a different conclusion concerning compliance with a "forceless" world government by substituting a different set of assumptions. Consider the following:

Assumption 1. Each state believes that the cost of individual compliance must be less than the benefit to it if at least some critical number of states comply with the world government.

Assumption 2. Each state believes that the cost to a state of complying is greater than the benefit to it of complying if less than some critical number of states comply.

Assumption 3. Each state believes that each state does better if at least some critical number of states comply than if none complies.

Assumption 4. Each state believes that each state knows that what it knows about the other states is paralleled by what the other states know about it, and each state believes that each state knows that the other states are rational.

It would follow from this particular set of assumptions that general compliance is the preferred outcome. Yet, these assumptions currently require far more of states than we can prudently expect. Before each assumption can be offered plausibly, a number of primary changes would need to take place in world politics. Such changes might include a reduced number of state actors, homogeneity of state governments, and "tight" conditions of bipolarity in which the ratio of power between the two blocs is roughly equal. Taken together, such changes, *inter alia*, could contribute to overcoming the central impediment to cooperation with forceless world government: the expectation of states that their own willingness to seek disarmament will not be universally (or at least widely enough) imitated. But such changes are hardly to be expected, at least in the foreseeable future.

It is exceedingly unlikely that either conception of world government—that with or that without centralized military force—will come into being. We need only to remember that states are presently unwilling to accept even the most marginal sorts of arms control remedies. Of course, centralization might be achieved coercively as well as volitionally, and Caesarism as a path to world peace through world government need not be dismissed out of hand. At the same time, it is a path that, as Rousseau recognized long ago, is likely to occasion the very kinds of conflicts and calamities that world government is designed to prevent.

A LONG-TERM SOLUTION

In a world wherein American nuclear strategy continues to rest upon an implausible set of assumptions and on a misunderstanding of interactive effects, an accelerated arms race can lead only to oblivion. In such a world, only a far-reaching disengagement from all form of strategic competition can provide the policy needed for survival. Time, as St. Augustine wrote, is more than the present as we experience it and the past as a present memory. It is also the future as a present expectation, and this expectation harbors within itself the seeds of its own verification.

Understood in terms of the overriding imperative to prevent the final epidemic of nuclear war, St. Augustine's wisdom suggests expectations of a new global society, one based on a more advanced stage of world evolutionary development. To encourage such expectations, appropriate initiatives must be taken within states by general publics, which comprise the essential starting point for world order reform. Since national leaders can never be expected to initiate the critical changes of direction on their own, the new evolutionary vanguard must grow out of informed publics throughout the world.

Once established, such a vanguard must seek to end international competitiveness founded upon egoistic definitions of national interest. The replacement of the power of the individual state by the power of the entire global community must not be the coercive military power one encounters in recommendations for world government, but the power of a universalized and new consciousness, a clear vision of reality that substitutes wholeness and convergence for the fatal instinct of "narcissism."

To better understand this vision, we might return to the central understanding of Freud's great work, *Civilization and Its Discontents*. Just as any civilization requires a renunciation of certain private instincts, so an organic world society requires a renunciation of certain "instincts" of states. Just as civilized man has exchanged a portion of his possibilities of happiness for security, so must states exchange a portion of their "egoistic" preferences for a chance at survival. In a struggle that Freud describes as a conflict between Eros and Thanatos, between the instinct of Life and the instinct of Death, states must enter into the service of Eros, satisfying their vital needs in a spirit that recognizes the interrelatedness of their fates.

The task, then, is to make the separate states conscious of their emerging planetary identity. With such a revisioning of national goals and incentives, states can progress to an awareness of new archetypes for global society. Since all things contain their own contradiction, the world system based on militaristic nationalism can be transformed into a whole and "related" world society.

Will it work? Living at a juncture between world order and global disintegration, can we seriously expect states to slough off the shackles of outmoded forms of self-interest? If, indeed, a latent oneness lies buried beneath the manifold divisions of our fractionated world, can states be expected to act in genuine communion with all other states and replace competitive power struggles with spirited cooperation? Perhaps not! But there is surely no other way. The Talmud tells us, "The dust from which the first man was made was gathered in all the corners of the world." By moving toward planetization, states can have a last opportunity to reaffirm the sovereignty of Reason over the forces of disintegration.

There is nothing fanciful, mystical, or utopian about this recommendation. States that begin to act on the basis of binding obligations in their relations with each other would do so *in their own interests*. By building upon the understanding that it is in the best interests of individual states to develop policies from a systematic vantage point, national decisionmakers could take a major step toward world order reform, not by abandoning their self-interested pattern of action, but by rerouting this pattern to a global orientation. To apply the vision of Pierre Teilhard de Chardin, no state can prosper and grow except with and by all the others with itself.

To move toward planetization will require broad and intensive involvement by informed publics, both here in the United States and abroad. Says E.P. Thompson, the distinguished social historian and writer:

We must protest if we are to survive. Protest is the only realistic form of civil defense. We must generate an alternative logic, an opposition at every level of society. This opposition must be international and it must win the support of multitudes. It must bring its influence to bear upon the rules of the world. It must act, in very different conditions, within each national state, and, on occasion, it must directly confront its own national state apparatus.[25]

The theoretical underpinnings of such a protest are contained in a recent article by Richard A. Falk.[26] Examining normative initiatives that challenge the root assumptions of militarization, Falk links these initiatives to actual and promising social forces. In connection with this effort, primary attention is focused upon "the Third System," i.e., "The system of power represented by people acting individually or collectively through voluntary institutions and associations, including churches and labor unions; a system oriented around challenging the domestic manifestations of militarization.[27] The Third System is "the main bearer of new values, demands, and vision," and it must contend with the constraints of "the First System" ("the system of power comprised by the governing structures of territorial states.")[28] and "the Second System" ("the system of power comprised by the United Nations, and to a lesser extent by regional international institutions").[29]

Falk's Third System is, of course, the essential primary arena for nuclear war avoidance and world order reform. Since the First System stands firmly behind the "logic" of militarization and the Second System is essentially a creature of the First System, we require a Third System movement for demilitarization. Based upon the emergence of a planetary consciousness "that is alive to the interlinked dimensions of militarization,"[30] this movement must be geared to changing the orientations of First System leaders by building upward pressures from the Third and Second Systems.

Understood in terms of the overriding global imperative to delegitimize nuclear weapons, Falk's proposal calls for a normative initiative on a global scale to create all varieties of denuclearization. Citing the examples of two documents drafted and endorsed by private citizens from around the world—the 1978 Delhi Declaration for a Just World and the 1980 Lisbon Declaration on Denuclearization for a Just World—he encourages the continuing development of a Third System consensus on the menace of nuclear weaponry. To promote such development, special responsibility lies with citizens of the superpowers, who must encourage demilitarizing imperatives through opposition to specific weapon systems, such as MX and Trident II, and through the struggle for human rights.

While some of Falk's prescriptions are potentially contradictory (e.g., a successful movement against draft registration might heighten reliance on nuclear weapons), his underlying thesis is markedly important and warrants widespread attention: There is a personal imperative to reverse the arms race and create a more harmonious configuration of planetary political life. For such a configuration to come about, this imperative must be widely felt and collectively manifested through coherent and well-articulated transnational movements. By displaying the kind of higher loyalty contained within the idea of a Nuremberg obligation to resist crimes of the state, individuals across the world can endow this strategy of world order reform with real potency.

CONCLUSION

In his book *Janus: A Summing Up*, Arthur Koestler identifies the polarity between self-assertive and integrative tendencies as a universal characteristic of life. Order and stability can prevail only when the two tendencies are in equilibrium. If one tendency dominates the other, the result is an end to the essential delicate balance.

This balance must immediately be restored among states in world politics. To create the necessary equilibrium, these states must begin to fashion their foreign policies on a new set of premises that defines national interest in terms of what is best for the world system as a whole.[31] By supplanting competitive self-seeking with cooperative self-seeking, and by renouncing the "everyone for himself" principle in world affairs, states can begin to move away from the social-Darwinian ethic that would otherwise assure our oblivion. By building upon the understanding that each state's best interests mandate developing foreign policy from a systematic vantage point, and by defining national interest in terms of strategies that secure and sustain the entire system of states, our national leaders can begin to match the awesome agenda of world order reform with effective strategies of response. With such a starting point, the prevention of global nuclear catastrophe could draw its animating vision from the wisdom of Pierre Teilhard de Chardin:

> The egocentric ideal of a future reserved for those who have managed to attain egoistically the extremity of "everyone for himself" is false and against nature. No element could move and grow except with and by all the others with itself.

The false communion of nation-states is inwardly rotten, time-dishonored, close to collapsing. A communion based on fear and dread and the resulting mighty efforts at producing increasingly destructive weapons have occasioned a deep desolation of the human spirit. The world has conquered technology only to lose its soul.

"The world, as it is now," Herman Hesse once wrote about the first quarter of the present century, "wants to die, wants to perish—and it will." No doubt, were he alive today, Hesse would see no need to change that observation. Indeed, as an anticipatory vision of what lies ahead, it is more exquisitely attuned to the present moment than to its intended time. To render this vision inaccurate, thinking and feeling human beings will have to learn to develop their potential for cohesion with others to ever more distant boundaries. Much higher reaches of planetary interaction exist than we are currently prepared to appreciate. Only when we begin to seek and cultivate these reaches will an appropriate transformation of international society become possible.

We must aim to realize a unique and fulfilled state in harmony with all others, a coherent vision sparked by the impulse of human singularity. With the manifestation of the one in the many, each individual state may begin to pursue a progressive development of consciousness to ever-higher levels without disregard for its cumulative effects. The world order consequences of this principle could embrace the beginning of a new world politics.

Alas, what reasons do we have to believe that such development can ever come to pass, that states can ever free themselves from self-imposed inconscience? If, as Schiller points out, "The law of the world is the history of the world," there is certainly very little cause for faith in human progress. The ancient and medieval people had no conception of such a faith, an idea, in fact, widely disavowed before Fontenelle and Condorcet offered it to the 18th-century world of letters. Even during the Renaissance, the conviction was widespread that man's development after a glorious antiquity has been regressive rather than progressive. The path of late Renaissance disillusionment was clearly marked out by Luther, Montaigne, Machiavelli, and Galileo.

During the 19th century, a thread of increasing hope in human progress emerged to characterize the poetry of Tennyson and the writings of Herbert Spencer, a thread that was to be broken by the incomparable barbarisms of our own century. That thread has yet to be mended. Today, we stand in a condition of near desperation, sustained not by the hope that we can do better, but by the wish that perhaps, somehow, we can still avoid the worst. In our profound sense of impotence, we have given new meaning to Pope's comment, "Whatever is, is right."

If it is important that states learn to care for themselves and each other at the same time, they must begin to restore the broken thread of hope and to rally around its circular throne. But this is only a beginning. Once "done," this must be followed by states learning to supplant their misconceived separation of national interest and world interest with an ongoing commitment to *planetization*. Only this commitment can endow the search for preventing the final epidemic with real hopefulness.

NOTES

1. P.D. 59 was clarified by former Secretary of Defense Harold Brown in a speech at the Naval War College on 20 August 1980. Derived from a war plan known as National Security Decision Memorandum 242, formulated in the closing months of the Ford administration, P.D. 59 represented the latest major retreat from the doctrine of "massive retaliation" first defined by John Foster Dulles in January 1954. The Reagan administration's "countervailing" nuclear strategy actually goes beyond P.D. 59 principles in its advocacy of "atomic superiority" and its overriding commitment to build a capacity to fight nuclear wars at any level. At present, the essential elements of this strategy are embedded in Secretary of Defense Weinberger's defense guidance plan to expand U.S. strategic forces so that they might meet the requirement of nuclear war fighting. Leaked to the press in May 1982, this plan would have American military leaders prepare for nuclear counterattacks against the Soviet Union "over a protracted period." Reflecting the strategic mythmakers' notion of "escalation dominance," the document stated that American nuclear forces "must prevail and be able to force the Soviet Union to seek earliest termination of hostilities on terms favorable to the United States." (See Richard Halloran, "New Atom War Strategy Confirmed," *New York Times*, 4 June 1982, p. 7.)
2. See Harold Brown, remarks delivered at the Convocation Ceremonies for the 97th Naval War College Class, Naval War College, Newport, Rhode Island, 20 August 1980, p. 6.
3. See Colin Gray and Keith Payne, "Victory Is Possible," *Foreign Policy* 39 (Summer 1980):14.
4. Significantly, these doubts are not dispelled by the U.S. decision to embark upon production and stockpiling of the neutron bomb. In fact, enhanced radiation weapons could only enhance deterrence if the Soviet Union were to believe that the American leadership is *irrational*. This is the case because the Soviet Union continues to threaten this country with all-out nuclear war once the nuclear threshold has been crossed—*whatever the character of the particular nuclear weapons involved*. It follows that the asymmetry in limited nuclear war doctrine between the superpowers thwarts the "logic" of the neutron bomb.
5. See, for example, "Soviet Charges Reiterated," *New York Times*, 21 August 1980, p. A8. In this connection, it should be understood that Soviet images of

the U.S. as a nuclear adversary have long been founded on the expectation of an American first strike. For examples of such images, see V.D. Sokolovsky, ed., *Soviet Military Strategy*, 3rd ed., ed. H.F. Scott (New York: Crane, Russak, 1968), pp. 56–57; A. Grechko, "V.I. Lenin i stroitel'stvo sovetskikh vooruzhennykh sil," *Kommunist* 3 (February 1969): 15–26; and William D. Jackson, "Soviet Images of the U.S. as Nuclear Adversary 1969–1979," *World Politics* 33, no. 4 (July 1981): 614–38. Nonetheless, since late 1979 the Soviet leadership has expressed heightened alarm over the U.S. quest for strategic counterforce planning and theater nuclear force improvements.

6. See Jeffrey T. Richelson, "The Dilemmas of Counterpower Targeting," *Comparative Strategy* 2 (1980): 226–27.

7. See, for example, the published concerns of CINCSAC General Richard Ellis, in Drew Middleton, "SAC Chief Is Critical of Carter's New Nuclear Plan," *New York Times*, 7 September 1980, p. 19.

8. This assessment, which was endorsed by Vice President Bush during the presidential election campaign and is now embedded in Secretary Weinberger's defense guidance plan, is now seen almost regularly in the journal and popular literature. See, for example, Leon Sloss's comment that, "All the evidence suggests that we confront an adversary who appears to believe it is possible to fight and win a nuclear war." (Commentary on article by this writer, "Presidential Direction 59: A Critical Assessment," *Parameters* 11, no. 1 [March 1981]: 19–28, appearing in *Parameters* 11, no. 2 [June 1981]: 90. Mr. Sloss, now with SRI International, directed the nuclear targeting policy review for the Department of the Defense in 1978.) See also Richard Pipes, "Why the Soviet Union Thinks It Could Fight and Win a Nuclear War," *Commentary* 64, no. 1 (July 1977); and Gray and Payne, "Victory Is Possible," pp. 14–27.

9. See Carl von Clausewitz, *On War*, Book 8, chap. 6B, "War Is an Instrument of Policy" (Princeton: Princeton University Press, 1976).

10. See Bernard Brodie, ed., *The Absolute Weapon* (New York: Harcourt, Brace, 1946), p. 76.

11. See the discussion of this principle in Sheldon S. Wolin, *Politics and Vision: Continuity and Innovation in Western Political Thought* (Boston: Little, Brown, 1960), pp. 195–238.

12. See *Discourses*, I, cited in ibid., p. 221.

13. See *Discourses*, II, cited by Wolin, *Politics and Vision*, p. 222.

14. See Hannah Arendt, *On Violence* (New York: Harcourt, Brace and World, 1970), p. 3. A similar argument is advanced by Arthur Koestler in the Prologue to his *Janus: A Summing Up* (New York: Random House, 1978).

15. See Arendt, *On Violence*, pp. 4–5.

16. See the discussion of these thinkers by Isaiah Berlin, *The Hedgehog and the Fox* (New York: Simon & Schuster, 1957).

17. The best treatment of the dangers of game-theoretic strategic thinking is still Anatol Rappoport's *Strategy and Conscience* (New York: Schocken Books, 1964).

18. For an illuminating argument on the indeterminacy of history, see Jacques Barzun, *Clio and the Doctors: Psycho-History, Quanto-History, and History* (Chicago and London: The University of Chicago Press, 1974).

19. Taken from a 1980 advertising supplement to *The Bulletin of the Atomic Scientists*.

20. Early in 1977, the Carter administration undertook a detailed interagency review of unresolved SALT issues. In the hope of reaching significant strategic arms limitations, Secretary of State Vance and Ambassador Warnke presented a comprehensive proposal to the Soviet Union in March 1977 that called for major cuts in the Vladivostok ceilings, as well as limits on the number of land-based ICBMs equipped with MIRVs and the number of very large, or "heavy," ICBMs. This proposal, which also called for restrictive limits on the testing and deployment on new types of ICBMs, was rejected by the Soviets, as was an alternate deferral proposal under which the SALT II agreement would be based upon the Vladivostok numbers. In the Soviet view, both proposals were inconsistent with the agreement of Vladivostok.

21. See address by George F. Kennan on the occasion of his receiving the Albert Einstein Peace Prize, 19 May 1981, *East-West/Outlook*, the American Committee on East-West Accord, Vol. 4., no. 3. (July/August 1981): 4. Mr. Kennan's proposal can also be found in *The New York Review of Books* 28, no. 12 (16 July 1981): 14–16.

22. See Grenville Clark and Louis B. Sohn, *World Peace Through World Law*, 3rd ed. (Cambridge: Harvard University Press, 1966), p. xi.

23. See Hannah Arendt, "What Was Authority?", in *Authority*, ed. Carl Friedrich (Cambridge: Harvard University Press, 1958), p. 82.

24. See Bertrand De Jouvenel, *Sovereignty: An Inquiry Into the Political Good* (Chicago: The University of Chicago Press, 1957), p. 33.

25. See E.P. Thompson, "A Letter to America," *The Nation*, 24 January 1981, p. 91.

26. See Richard Falk, "Normative Initiatives and Demilitarization: A Third System Approach," *Alternatives: A Journal of World Policy* 6, no. 2, (July 1980): 339–56.

27. Ibid., pp. 343–44.

28. Ibid., p. 343.

29. Ibid.

30. Ibid., p. 348.

31. For an elucidation of this perspective, see Louis René Beres, *People, States and World Order* (Ithasca, IL: F.E. Peacock, 1981); Saul H. Mendlovitz, ed., *On the Creation of a Just World Order* (New York: The Free Press, 1975); and Richard A. Falk, *A Study of Future Worlds* (New York: The Free Press, 1975).

23
CONSEQUENCES OF AN ABSOLUTE *NO*
TO NUCLEAR WAR

Arne Naess

In this essay I do not write as a kind of politician or advisor to politicians, but as a plain member of humanity—except for my special obligations due to my education and other privileges. If I were to advise a member of a government, I would first consider his or her position, the local power structure, and the narrowness of alternatives for that particular person at that moment. Why is it the duty of a philosopher to speak up on nuclear arms and the future of life, not only human life but, equally importantly, nonhuman life? A philosopher, by training, has value-priorities and maximally wide perspectives in time and space—a total view, however tentative and imperfect. Philosophy is a search for wisdom, the integration of reflection and action, not merely a search for knowledge. A philosopher is not a logician, an epistemologist, a political philosopher. Specialization leads nowhere. In our mammoth industrial societies, a philosopher must fight for the reestablishment of intrinsic, ultimate values in life and against the dominance of the merely instrumental. Increasing militarization is one aspect of the irrational belief that instruments and the pursuit of "power-over" can save us in the long run. To threaten with nuclear gadgets is to threaten Mother Earth and is inconsistent with every wide perspective.

No philosophy of great standing gives priority to the accumulation of material possessions, nor does any favor "power-over" when compared to "power-to," nor means over ends, nor non-ultimate ends over ultimate ends. Philosophers have advocated as part of wisdom a life simple in means and rich in the enjoyment of intrinsic values—values which are values in themselves, not mainly means to a further end. No decision, no policy, no technology is rational if it is not conducive to fundamental, ultimate ends and values. In what follows I take this as axiomatic.

Wise proposals are often characterized as unrealistic because people, while acknowledging their wisdom, are unable to act on them. Such a lack of personal integration is a product of the culture in which we live: our industrial societies do not foster our ability to act from our deepest feelings and broadest knowledge.

I assume, however, that individuals, given the opportunity to develop normally in an environment not degraded in obvious ways, are (sometimes) able to recognize wise decisions and act on them. And I assume that we are consciously able to change trends— political, social, and general cultural—at least to some extent. There are reasons to doubt this, but to reject this presupposition is self-defeating and pessimistic.[1] (The "we" I refer to are responsible citizens of nations which today possess nuclear weapons and those who live in industrialized states in general.)

What kind of policy could eliminate the roots (both causes and motives) of nuclear threats?

THE NATURE OF THE PRESENT NUCLEAR PERIL

The hostility between the two main nuclear powers has reached a high degree of intensity; nuclear war is a threatening possibility. It may start with a limited exchange of bombs and could stop at that, but it is just as likely to explode into a major nuclear exchange. The short- and long-range consequences of such an explosion would affect not only the belligerent countries, but mankind and living conditions on the planet in general. Such a war could not possibly serve fundamental, ultimate values of life. The situation is of vast planetary concern.[2]

No political objective, no goal such as "making the world safe for democracy and freedom" or "making the world safe for communism" could be achieved through a major nuclear war. And since our planet is not the property of the owners of the bombs, nor of mankind in general, we have *no right* to threaten with bombs.

The nuclear arms of a nation do not deter if an enemy believes that the nation will under no circumstances use them. It must always be credible that under certain circumstances the nation will use nuclear weapons within limits and go all out in their use *in extremis*. For the sake of credibility every nation must resort to clear threats, and increasing threats must be met with increasing threats.

The moral permissibility of ultimate full-scale retaliation cannot be upheld. The old way to defend the moral soundness of retaliation was to refer to the principle of just retribution: those responsible for the disaster had to be punished. But the chance of killing those really responsible for a nuclear disaster would be slim. Millions of nonbelligerents and innumerable other beings would suffer, while people at the top of the power pyramids would likely escape.

The danger posed by nuclear weapons would not be removed even through negotiated disarmament. If nuclear disarmament were realized through international treaties, threats to rearm would probably replace the present threats, and the technological race would then focus on means to rapid nuclear rearmament. Therefore, the threat of nuclear war would not decrease substantially as a consequence of nuclear disarmament among mutually hostile nations. Something more basic than nuclear disarmament must occur, something that has to do with nuclear cultures *as a whole*.

Until recently armaments of different nations could be roughly compared because rough quantification was possible. Now, with many different kinds of weapons, and different kinds of sophisticated inventions related to speed of delivery and other factors of major importance, even a rough comparison between the US and the USSR is difficult. Consequently, the governments are able to make increasingly alarming and *untestable* claims about one being behind the other and thus accelerate a race already feverish in its intensity. To call this self-accelerating race a "policy of deterrence" is to name it in accord with its intended, but unlikely, result. Basically it is a policy of military mobilization, making full-scale war possible within minutes.

So-called deterrence, I argue, cannot be a way to avoid catastrophe in the long run. Intense physical and mental mobilization for war has rarely been called off; it is more often a prelude to war. The state of mutual deterrence, if continued into the indefinite future, will almost certainly break down eventually. But my argument does not require so strong a claim. It is enough to accept the thesis that there is at least a fair chance that the arms race, if continued for a decade or more, will, accidentally or otherwise, lead to a major nuclear exchange. To avoid this possibility, we must move beyond the policy of nuclear deterrence.

My proposal starts with the observation that if one of a pair of mutually hostile nuclear powers unilaterally disarms, little motive remains for the other to use nuclear bombs. If a military move is made, it will be in the form of occupation or some form of domination from a distance. Thus, demilitarization is the surest means of avoiding nuclear war. It better deserves to be classed as a policy of deterrence than does the continued physical and mental mobilization that goes by that name.

If one side adopts a policy of unilateral disarmament, the worst that could happen is that it would be occupied by the other power. Of course, occupation itself would be seen as a great catastrophe, and here the role of mental mobilization is apparent. The desperate effort to win the nuclear arms race cannot be sustained without painting the consequences of military defeat and occupation by foreigners as worse than anything conceivable, both ethically and in terms of suffering.[3] But nuclear war would be far the greater catastrophe. I consider step-by-step unilateral demilitarization to be the proper road to follow. It must be step-by-step because time is required for the general populace to adapt to the value priorities involved.

In the part of the world where I live, Northern Europe, only one possibility of nuclear war is taken seriously: a war between the Soviet Union and the USA. But among politicians there is also a widespread fear of "Finlandization" if the arms race is not kept up; that is, a fear of dependence that could develop into domination or occupation. Finland is said to live "at the mercy" of the Soviet Union.

Left-wing groups today tend to be as critical of the way the Soviet Union is governed, including its economic system, as right-wing groups. But the significant difference is that the moderate left has a strong tendency to consider Soviet foreign policy as basically defensive, which would make it easier to accept Western unilateral disarmament. I agree with this leftist view, but find it unacceptable to take the thesis of defensiveness as a kind of axiom. The hypothesis should be taken seriously that the Soviet Union, at least as much as the US, is bent on a kind of world-policing. Each power is trying to prevent the development of regimes that could strengthen the other. The policy I recommend assumes, for the sake of argument, that the Soviets intend a kind of world-policing. With this assumption and thus the possibility of Soviet occupation, we should note the difficulties that a Soviet attempt at worldwide policing would involve. The way the Soviet Union has tried to protect itself through dominance in Eastern Europe since 1945 is obviously ineffective as a police method on a wide scale. If the US adopted unilateral disarmament, what would a Soviet government bent on world policing do? No one thinks that a physical occupation by the Soviets would be feasible, nor the establishment of Soviet communism through the very few communists in the US. (Some authors argue, by the way, that a communist USA would be even more frightening to Russian nationalists than a communist China.) I think that world policing is impossible in the long run by any military means.

While the Soviets might try, through military exploits, to dominate some new territories, there are strong reasons to suspect that large expansion would be extremely difficult. First, their domination of Eastern Europe was established through strong communist minorities, and in part through a rather weak attachment on the part of Eastern Europe to the Western European social system. Today Soviet communists are extremely few the world over, and the regimes that try to develop through Soviet help would rather be helped by the US. Second, the vast material and mental effort of the US to keep the arms race going would, in case of disarmament, be used to help those very regimes, and more generally, to foster social justice of a kind that could be furthered by Soviet military intervention.

A world in which the Soviet Union were armed and the US were not would have many problems. For instance, two minor states at war might ask for Soviet weapons and become politically dependent upon the Soviet Union, thus increasing the territories dominated by it. But history does not support the belief that empire-building solely by such means would last long.

Let us return to the assumption that occupation is possible. Even if the slogan "better dead than red" is not often heard in Europe, people seemed to hold until the late 1970s that there was nothing worse than being occupied and "conquered" by the Soviet Union. It is, however, of decisive importance that the populace of Northern Europe has started seriously to compare the two evils, nuclear war and occupation. And the consequences of living with the grave risk of such a war are being broadly discussed. Whereas it once took months or years to amass the materials necessary for a decisive wartime attack, technological invention has drastically narrowed the time between a decision and colossal, indiscriminate destruction. Long-range social and cultural activities cannot thrive where there may be nothing the next day to care about. People at the grass roots have started to contemplate these things.

The destructive effect of nuclear war on the conditions for life on the planet and the lack of ethical justification for such a destruction have not yet been widely enough considered.[4] The destruction cannot be justified on the basis of human political rivalry. This presents a sufficient reason for an absolute NO to nuclear war and the consequent adoption of a policy of unilateral disarmament. Most people, if given time and opportunity to assess the destructiveness, stupidity, and ethical depravity of nuclear war, will come to see that occupation and "conquest" of one's country is the lesser evil. I think they will also see that it is ethically unacceptable to participate in preparation for nuclear war in order not to be conquered.

Some would respond to this argument by claiming that, although foreign occupation or domination may be preferable to nuclear war, another, much better way of avoiding nuclear war that leads neither to foreign occupation nor domination is bilateral nuclear disarmament through treaty. But, as I have argued above, this would not solve the problem: threats to rearm would replace nuclear threats, and the carrying out of the former threats would again create the risk of nuclear war. The only solution is for one side to take the initiative to demilitarize.

The absolute NO on ethical grounds is contested on the grounds of the relative weight of bad or good consequences. But the above argument has shown that the possession of nuclear armaments cannot be justified on utilitarian grounds. In addition, an absolute NO is supported on deontological grounds as well. I cannot go into discussion of this point, but only refer to another area where an absolute NO is fairly well established: the NO to participation in torture. It implies a refusal to consider the hypothesis that one can save ten from torture through merely preparing for the eventuality of torture. The above argumentation against preparation for nuclear war rests on a double basis, one utilitarian and one deontological.

CULTURAL EVOLUTION

Saying "yes" to a credible threat of massive, nuclear retaliation implies a long string of "yeses." First, it implies a yes to the nuclear arms race, because the "enemy" naturally seeks to improve his forces to counter one's own. It also implies an arms race in other than nuclear forms and a more generalized technological race in support of the nuclear developments. A kind of nuclear culture is implied. In democracies as well as in dictatorships, continuous moral support of gigantic military spending is a necessity. In democracies it requires even greater conformity of opinion than in dictatorships about the utter necessity of continued arms race.

In short, a yes to the use of, or the threat to use, nuclear weapons affects cultures as a whole. It affects competitiveness, education, social relations, technological development, the economic system, ethical value priorities, religious teachings, political centralization, organization size, attitudes toward nature, and foreign relations, including relations to the Third and Fourth Worlds. In continuing the arms race we must say "yes" to these undesirable side-effects.

The cultural situation is dangerous from another point of view. Not only does the nuclear arms race affect the culture, but the culture in turn promotes the arms race by creating the apparent need for a nuclear defense. Certain cultural traits in affluent industrial countries make us increasingly vulnerable and increase our desperate need to trust deterrence. I shall mention only a few:

1. *Largeness and centralization*: Large organizations can be destroyed more easily than small; large towns, requiring difficult and complex transport of energy, food, and water, are at the mercy of the occupier. Centralization of energy sources, and of resources in general, requires organization on a large scale. Smallness, on the other hand, requires general, basic skills and soft, local technology. Mutual help, group loyalty, and local resilience grow in an appropriate economy of decentralization. Clinging to lifestyles that require largeness and centralization increases the tendency to see only two possibilities: successful, purely military defense, or complete chaos and death. Nuclear deterrence leaves a meager but real chance of survival, so why not place our trust in nuclear weapons? This way of thinking, taking certain complicated ways of life (never "enjoyed" in any culture until now) as a rock-bottom presumption, fosters an acceptance of nuclear weapons and shows a kind of parasitic relationship between recent cultural development and the arms race.

2. *Cultivation of means rather than ends*: Perpetual economic growth requires strong motivation to invest and strong motivation to buy what is produced. This involves progressive complication and vulnerability of means used to attain desired, intrinsic ends and values. The "good life" requires, to an increasing degree, a gigantic, vulnerable apparatus of organization. Explosive national and economic rivalries must be maintained to continue "progress."

3. *Cultivation of "power-over" rather than "power-to"*: By the term "power-to" I mean the power by which one can directly realize intrinsic values, and by "power-over," the power of access to means considered useful to secure intrinsic

values. Individuals and organizations have material riches and coercive or dominating power over other individuals and organizations, fighting to get as much as possible. But the relation of such power to intrinsic values may remain obscure, sometimes even forgotten. Competition tends to center on power-over rather than on power-to. Every great philosophy, whether of the East of the West, has insisted that the really powerful are those who are rich in power-to.

The wealthy, industrial cultures invite us to compete for power-over, the sophisticated means to satisfy desires, not real needs. This favors an identification of a loss of freedom with a loss of power-over, rather than a loss of power-to. This again favors postures of expansion, domination, violence and, ultimately, the use of threats of nuclear war to avoid decreased power-over. It also works toward destruction of the institutions of mutual aid, mutual concern, local sharing and solidarity.[5]

A successful campaign against threats of nuclear war thus requires deep cultural changes, so deep that the process may be called cultural evolution. If industrial societies are not capable of such evolution, the future of this planet is indeed bleak, for humans and for other forms of life.

THE WAY OF NONVIOLENCE UNDER OCCUPATION

It is a strange, but not inexplicable, coincidence that the policies adapted to the demilitarized status of society are substantially the same as those recommended by the green pole in European politics. Also, but to a lesser degree, the Deep Ecology movement in Europe and the United States proposes policies connected with these peace efforts. The way of cultural evolution envisaged in this essay is essentially the kind of way advocated by the Greens and Deep Ecologists. (Their philosophies and methods are set forth elsewhere in many publications.)[6] While only a minority of Europeans have confidence in the replacement of military by nonviolent methods, the minority is not insignificant and is increasing. According to a recent public opinion poll in France, "17% declared they would be ready to *rely* on a system of defense based on nonviolent resistance; only 18% had any confidence in the French strike force as a means of defense."[7]

I want to concentrate on a subject that is rarely discussed: preparation, especially in small industrial nations, for *occupation* in the context of a larger conflict involving threats of nuclear war. My main reason is the earlier point that it should not be taken as axiomatic that demilitarization would not lead to occupation by a militarized power. Here I speak in terms not only of nuclear disarmament, but of complete military disarmament or demilitarization. Beyond an absolute NO to nuclear weapons, we must seek to avoid the use of any form of large-scale, organized violence.

Two developments must proceed together: demilitarization and education in militant nonviolence. The term "militant" is used because it requires many soldierly qualities: self-discipline, loyalty, organizational solidarity, physical (but even more civil and mental) courage, and training. The word "respectful" might be added to "militant" because of the essentially respectful attitude fostered in relation to any human being. Person and action are distinguished: a person as such has the right to be respected. Yet this distinction can be drawn only if one adopts the way of nonviolence. The distinction cannot be effectively made by those who equate violence with effective resistance. As preparation for nonviolence proceeds, a gradual demilitarization can be undertaken.

According to some, demilitarization virtually invites the USSR or the US to its coercive power. They consider occupation of small nations like Norway a certainty. In deference to this perhaps mistaken but widespread opinion, realistic training in behavior under occupation should be instituted. It involves:

1. Training in communication with each other without access to the mass media and the many technical facilities we now use.

2. Training in communication with the occupation forces; i.e., learning the English and Russian languages, and acquaintance with the kind of "official" justification the occupier is likely to use and how he conceives his own history and culture. (Lack of such knowledge in 1940 in Norway made it necessary for the Home Front to warn against discussion with the Germans: the latter were likely to win too many points!)

3. Acquaintance with the rules of survival in prisons and concentration camps (survivors are eager to teach us, if invited to do so); acquaintance with the processes of deportation.

4. Acquaintance with the rules of noncooperation and coexistence with the occupier. Occupied people should welcome personal communication at every level, but refuse absolutely to assist in any kind of military work or work that in other ways are auxiliary to the occupation. They should refuse to accept what is patently untrue or to conform to rules inconsistent with their sense of honor.

5. Training in how to continue teaching children in the absence of schools. If the occupier takes over *all* major organizations, schools will probably have to be shunned. In general, information is needed on how all essential institutions of a community can function and be maintained on the microlevel when they are destroyed on the macrolevel. History shows that even 100 years of occupation have not obliterated a culture nor seemingly destroyed its quality of life.

6. Training in local self-reliance. Under occupation it may be necessary to dismember all major organizations, including the economy.

As already mentioned, I strongly objected to the tendency to treat the basic defensiveness of Soviet policy as an axiom. As an axiom it justifies the neglect of an unpopular and frightening theme: what *if* the Soviet Union proceeded to occupy the smaller disarmed European industrial countries? There should be a frank and widespread discussion of how the advocates of nonviolence propose to act under occupation, and how people could retain the essentials of their way of life. Reflection about what constitutes those essentials is, at the very least, required today.

Although I have accepted the assumption that the Soviets would move to occupy countries in the West that demilitarized, and thus that we must pursue training in militant nonviolence, I must repeat my earlier point that such a move would almost certainly be unsuccessful in a major industrial power such as the US.[8] Even in Eastern Europe, occupation *by Russians* would have been practically impossible. But large local communist parties believed that the Soviet system was inevitable, and a substantial number of people were willing to police the rest in a crude and brutal way. There is an atmosphere of civil war rather than of occupation. The Russians are unable and probably also unwilling to occupy. In places in the West where Soviet occupation is unlikely to be possible, my argument for unilateral disarmament is even stronger. But discussion of the possibility of occupation is valuable in any case, for it points to features of our culture that need to be changed if disarmament is to be possible.

The first reaction of many people to the requirement of increased preparedness for occupation is a grave doubt that the populace as a whole would be willing. If less than the total populace cooperated, various minorities might worsen the situation: a fanatic or heroic minority opposing the occupier with violence, a minority of Quislings, or a substantial minority of passivists sabotaging the essential, microorganization work. This is why training in militant nonviolence is needed to prepare the way for disarmament.

Any occupation force that tried to run a country would ultimately rely heavily on the cooperation of the occupied. Their benevolent but consistent noncooperation would place a great burden upon the occupier. If Norwegians in 1940 had said to the Germans, "I think your pay is excellent but, alas, I shall refuse to work for you" (that is, to make airfields, submarine bases, etc.), it would have taken longer to occupy Norway, and many more Germans would have had to work there throughout the war.

If ten top people in major organizations have ten immediate subordinates, and these again have ten each, it would require a million people to take over the six upper levels of the structure. In Eastern Europe a sufficient number of collaborators means the occupier does not have to control all the way down to the levels of the neighborhoods and local community.[9] I am convinced that two million more or less ideologically uninterested occupiers could not subdue a country of ten million decentrally organized resisters.

There is another factor to consider: It is an understandable policy of the Soviet Union at all costs to avoid contact between its own people and those of any country with a higher standard of living. This makes it imperative to limit the number of their people in foreign industrial countries to highly trained, constantly supervised officials, and to soldiers safely contained in barracks. To mingle freely and take over jobs in the economic life of an occupied country is out of the question.

In the past, people being occupied have usually prepared some kind of violent resistance in advance. This response is expected by the occupier and elicits a violent reaction. Moreover, the occupied people usually try to restore their large central institutions, and this inevitably provokes a massive response by the occupation power. (The fate of Solidarity is instructive.) Institutions must be maintained on the microlevel until the occupier is convinced that nothing is gained from the costly occupation. Why is it so costly? Resistance of the conventional type during occupation is not focused on economies: the occupiers print vast sums of paper money with which they pay the populace to work for them. Nonviolent resistance is less heroic but costs the occupier much in the long-run. The occupied do not accept the new money, and the occupier must pay the bureaucracy needed to occupy.

Of course, there are many objections to the policy of nonviolence. The advocate of the use of military power asks: what would a nonviolent resister do in a particular contemporary warlike situation, for instance 100 meters in front of advancing tanks? On the other hand, the defender of militant, benevolent nonviolence tends to argue more abstractly and from history. For example: "How could Hitler have been stopped through non-military means?" The defender of military power asks rhetorically how armies can be stopped nonviolently: "by lying down in front of them?" The defender of nonviolence invites us to consider a train of events since, let us say,

1918, or even earlier. A minority sought to help the German democratic politicians by providing food for the hungry (not shutting the flow off, as happened in the winter of 1919). Also, a minority attacked the financial abandonment of Germany by the West when the great economic crisis happened in the early '30s. The defender of militant, benevolent nonviolence resorts to history, saying: "If a minority favoring a certain nonviolent policy had been stronger, then the question of a military solution would not have arisen." Both ways of arguing have weak and strong points.

A similar polarity of argumentation makes itself felt concerning the consequences of actions: the first group stresses immediate consequences; the second, long-range consequences. This essay stresses the long-range consequences of a continuing arms race and the continuing adaptation of the whole culture to participation in nuclear war. The two groups have a slogan in common: freedom. But the term has many shades of meaning, and here they differ.

It is common in industrial democracies to identify a gain in level of freedom with a gain in individual influence over social arrangements, rather than a gain in self-realization, that is, an increase in the power of the whole personality to realize basic, intrinsic values.[10] Again, there is confusion of power-to with power-over. The tension between Nehru and the Indian nationalists on the one side, and Gandhi on the other, is an example of this and of great significance for world history. For the first group the key slogan *swaraj* (self-rule) meant political independence. For Gandhi, political independence was never treated as an ultimate, intrinsic value. For him *swaraj* included the eradication of mutual threats between religious groups. *Swaraj* required a level of maturity that could make political independence work to the best for the nation as a whole. In the West we must keep in mind that the self alluded to in Gandhian *swaraj* not the abstract ego, but the eminently, socially engaged, mature self.

Participation in plans of nuclear retaliation to maintain political freedom neglects the concept of freedom as understood by Gandhi as well as by central Western philosophers. To invoke love of freedom as the motive for the nuclear arms race is to debase the very ideals of freedom.

The discussion of freedom and resistance under occupation invokes the question of the essentials of a way of life. In spite of differences in ways of life today among those who feel they lead a good or satisfactory life, *kinds of* requirements are held in common.[11] Easiest to define are the biological and physiological requirements, such as food. Psychological requirements are much more difficult to define, and their presence much more difficult to test, but would include felt security, being loved and loving, being respected, self-fulfillment, engagement, meaningfulness, etc.

In discussing the hardships under dictatorships, "felt security" is foremost of the psychological factors. Declared opponents and their families may never be sure that the policy of some terrorists hired by those in power will not suddenly arrive and drag them from their homes. (An example is the British definition of non-dictatorship: you know it is only the milkman making a noise at the door at 6 a.m.) But *felt* security today is perhaps no greater than under occupation.

The evils of occupation, as experienced during the Nazi occupation of 1940 to 1945 in Scandinavia, were those of restricted public communication: everything printed was censored. A large amount of opinion and information only could be communicated to large groups "illegally." People caught in production and distribution were imprisoned and sometimes tortured. Schooling, a kind of communication to large groups, was interfered with. There was a pressure to change the content of the communication. Again, resisters were prosecuted. But clearly, those evils, which resulted in laborious organization and development of networks of small-group communication, could not compare with what is likely to happen after a nuclear war. The population's mental health and degree of satisfaction with life was not very much lower, I have reason to think, during the occupation of Norway than now. The fundamental evils of prolonged occupation by a state like the Soviet Union are likely to be social, cultural, and mental, rather than physical.

But again, the effects of nuclear war, and the kind of society likely to develop after such a war, represent losses of an entirely different order and evils of a completely different ethical kind. Whereas nonviolent resistance under occupation tends to heighten the morale of the populace, strengthen their will, draw people of different classes together, and deepen their consciousness of their own culture, the vision of territories after nuclear war is one of extreme demoralization.

CONCLUSION

In a poor Indian village it is more rational for each farmer, as an individual, to have five sons rather than one, but for the village as a whole, this is deadly. For each nation, taken separately, security, as conventionally defined, rests on competition and the arms race, but for mankind and the planet this is absurd, since their security in the case of an arms race inevitably decreases.

Unilateral demilitarization takes the opposite course and starts with the planetary view. Security, as conventionally defined, is zero or very low, to the extent that occupation is a possibility. But security, when defined in terms of power to defend the essentials of a way of life, is not zero or low. How high it is depends in part upon the material requirements of the essentials, the degree of unattractiveness of occupation, and the tendency among other nations to take the planetary rather than isolationist view.

The likely effect of a full nuclear war is such that one has to say absolutely NO. This implies saying "no" also to participation in the current preparations for nuclear war, that is, to the policy of nuclear deterrence. It implies a no to conventional armaments, which, within a short time, can be developed into nuclear armaments. It implies a policy of gradual unilateral disarmament.

Countries that unilaterally demilitarize have to take seriously the possibility of occupation. Defense means, in this case, defense of the basics of a way of life. The only promising way to assure this is the militant nonviolent way. But it implies deep cultural changes that cannot occur as long as there is preparation for participation in nuclear war. Therefore, the first step is the rejection of participation, whatever the circumstances.

The work for this long-range goal does not exclude wholehearted participation in present peace movements with more limited goals.

NOTES

1. Many scientists seem to reject this presupposition: they think that civilizations with the capacity for destroying themselves through nuclear force are likely to do so within 50 to 100 years.

2. For comprehensive treatment of this subject see Jonathan Schell, *The Fate of the Earth* (New York: Alfred A. Knopf, 1982). I have also profited from the publications of the Stockholm and the Norwegian peace conflict research institutes (SIPRI).

3. The consequences of black-painting were clear in World War II. The government of Germany was able to keep the war machine going in 1944 and 1945 largely by announcing that defeat would result in *definitive* subjugation of the German people.

4. On destruction of the natural environment see A.H. Westing, *Weapons of Mass Destruction and the Environment* (London: Taylor and Francis, 1977, for SIPRI); and idem, *Warfare in a Fragile World* (London: Taylor and Francis, 1980, for SIPRI); and Joseph Rotblat, *Nuclear Radiation in Warfare* (London: Taylor and Francis, 1981, for SIPRI). For a short, excellent outline, see Johan Galtung, *Environment, Development and Military Activity* (Oslo: Universitetsforlaget, 1982), pp. 34–40. The unacceptability of treating the nonhuman world morally indifferently is well argued in R. and V. Routley, "Against the Inevitability of Human Chauvinism," in *Ethics and the Problems of the 21st Century*, eds. K.E. Goodpaster and K.M. Sayre (Notre Dame, IN: University of Notre Dame Press, 1979), pp. 36–59. Human "light" living on earth promotes peace. Voluntary simplicity is indispensable; see Duane Elgin, *Voluntary Simplicity* (New York: W. Morrow, 1981).

5. Institutionalized mutual aid and concern are typical of most nonindustrial communities and cultures of moderate geographcal extension. It seems that the unique stress on material progress and growth in our societies requires aggressive, individual competition incompatible with an economy of mutual aid. An instructive recent example: the incompatibility of the competitive "welfare" state and mutual aid institutions among Greenlanders. See, for example, Bent Jensen, "Human Reciprocity: An Arctic Exemplification," *American Journal of Orthopsychiatry* 43 (1973):447–58.

6. The best articles and documents on Green economics and politics are written in the German and Scandinavian languages. Notable exceptions are some of the works of E.F. Schumacher, the "small is beautiful" prophet. They combine economic and philosophic issues. Hazel Henderson, *The Politics of the Solar Age: Alternatives to Economics* (New York: Anchor Books, 1981), is rather rhetorical but takes care of some of the Green positions. W. Leiss, "Political Aspects of Environmental Issues," in *Ecological Consciousness*, ed. R.C. Schultz and J.D. Hughes (Lanham, MD: University Press of America, 1981), is a good example of an American article on the politics of environmentalism. It occurs in an excellent anthology on philosophy of Deep Ecology. On this concept and its social and political relevance, see Arne Naess, "The Shallow and the Deep: Long-Range Ecological Movements," *Inquiry* 16 (1973).

7. *WRI Newsletter* 192, February 1983. On unilateralism see polls referred to in *Time* Magazine, 31 October 1983, p. 32.

8. This is more a consequence of the size and complexity of the US than of the likely success in implementing a policy of nonviolent resistance. When people from occupied Europe visited the US after the war, they asked: "To what extent would the people of the US be able (if willing) to carry out large-scale nonviolent noncooperation under occupation?" The answer by Americans was usually rather pessimistic because of the Wild-West tradition of shooting villains and

because of the inhomogeneity of the populace. (Local communication and loyal cooperation are more difficult among widely different cultural groups.)

9. It must be remembered that important sections of the populace in Poland and other Eastern European states were, in the decisive year after World War II, not resolutely and strongly in favor of the Western powers. I find the work of Czeslaw Milosz revealing in this connection. See *The Captive Mind* (New York: Vintage Books, 1955).

10. The Gandhian concept of freedom and self-realization is discussed in Arne Naess, *Gandhi and Group Conflict* (Oslo: Universistetsforlaget, 1974).

11. I here talk about felt quality of life, something different from quality of life defined in such a way that the opinions of B about the quality of life of A are relevant. For example, B might say that the life of A is profoundly unhealthy and will result in A's death, whereas A, if asked, would honestly maintain that his or her life is healthy and happy.

SUGGESTED ADDITIONAL READINGS

Berlin, Isaiah. 1969. *Four Essays on Liberty.* London: Oxford University Press.

Galtung, Johan. 1976. "On the Strategy of Nonmilitary Defense." In *Peace, War and Defense*. Copenhagen: Ejlers. pp. 378–426.

General and Complete Disarmament. Comprehensive Study on Nuclear Weapons. UN General Assembly, 35th session, 12 September 1980.

Leebaret, Derek, ed. 1981. *Soviet Military Thinking*. London: Allan & Unwin.

Naess, Arne. 1962. "Non-military Defense." In *Preventing World War III*, ed. Quincy Wright. New York: Simon & Schuster.

_____. 1967. "Non-military Defense and Foreign Policy." In *Civilian Defense: An Introduction*, ed. T.K. Mahadevan et al. New Delhi: Gandhi Peace Foundation.

Roberts, Adam, ed. 1967. *The Strategy of Civilian Defense*. London: Faber & Faber.

24
NUCLEAR WEAPONS AND THE RENEWAL OF DEMOCRACY

Richard Falk

*No public issue is more difficult than avoiding war; no public
task more noble than building a secure peace. Public officials
in a democracy must both lead and listen; they are ultimately
dependent upon a popular consensus to sustain policy.* [1]

It is typically the case that improving the prospects for peace in the world is associated with reforming the structure of international society (strengthening the United
Nations or, more ambitiously, establishing a world government), altering the ideology of the governing process in important states by replacing or eliminating extrem-
ism and crusading conceptions, or changing the way in which international security
is understood and defended (by exploring nonmilitary resistance and nonviolence).
Arms control and sometimes even disarmament are treated as largely autonomous
projects that can be pursued within the prevailing framework of international relations. The obstacles to peace are generally associated with geopolitical rivalries,
distrust, bargaining complexities and, to some extent, with the constraints brought
to bear on political leaders by pressure groups associated with the military-industrial complex.

In my view, such interpretations of the most promising directions for global
reform lack a necessary political dimension unless they also examine the relevance
of the relationship between the state and society with respect to the formation and
execution of policy in the war/peace area. By taking the particular situation in the
United States into account, I wish to show that the erosion of the procedures and
expectations of representative democracy in this area greatly impair the capacity of
the electorate to translate their growing demand that the government act effectively
to reduce the risks of nuclear war. Further, this impairment is not generally under-

I wish to thank my research associate, Cindy Halpern, for editorial and substantive
help, and the editors of this volume, who made valuable suggestions that I have
tried to incorporate in this revised text. An earlier, shorter version of this chapter
appeared in *Praxis International.*

stood, leading the bulk of the peace movement to seek "solutions" that cannot hope to achieve more than nominal results because of the character of bureaucratic control over national security policy. As a concrete example, the effort to rely on Congress and on a more enlightened elected leadership in the White House to end the arms race is naive in the extreme or, what amounts to the same thing, "utopian." The freeze movement as a *message* of concern is a brilliant political tactic, but conceived of as a *mechanism* for achieving results it is the gift of an innocent citizenry to a recalcitrant and essentially antagonistic bureaucracy.

In the advanced industrial world, a societal consensus has gradually taken shape that opposes the reliance by any government, including our own, on nuclear weapons for any purposes other than as an ultimate deterrent against nuclear blackmail or surprise attack. This opposition is of signal relevance to the possibility of avoiding nuclear war, and yet no major political candidate for the American presidency has been willing to endorse it. The explanation should not be surprising.[2]

As matters now stand, the effective leadership of both major political parties adheres to an idea of nuclear national security that is inconsistent with the directives of this societal consensus.[3] The essence of this bipartisan position is to accept a wider role for nuclear weapons, including their use to deter certain nonnuclear attacks and their use as threats to achieve diplomatic results; it includes, also, at the least, the development of nuclear warfighting capabilities and contingency plans for winning nuclear wars of different scopes. As such, the entire rationale of governmental authority based on "the consent of the governed" with respect to the most important question of human well-being has been sharply eroded, if not undermined.[4] Further, these official policies as to the use of nuclear weapons have also become questionable, if not illegitimate, to the extent they are increasingly perceived and have been analyzed as fundamentally inconsistent with relevant notions of law and morality.[5] In effect, the official, governmental posture toward nuclear weapons raises serious questions about the legitimacy of state power, and such questions disclose a deepening tension between the requirements of conscience and the normal duty of citizens to obey civic authority. As the Declaration of Independence affirms, and its governing political theory on society's right to overthrow tyranny confirmed, when a government fails to uphold its basic social contract with society, then as for the citizenry, in the Declaration's words, "it is their right, it is their duty, to throw off such government and to provide new guards for their future security,"[6] although it must be conceded that the context is the abuse of society by the state, not an excessive foreign policy.

Under present circumstances, without a revitalization of the present forms of representative government, there is little hope that any other approach to the reform of public policy can success fully challenge, except in a minor way, the current role of nuclear weaponry and related militarist dispositions in national security policy. The meaning of "revitalization" needs to be clarified in this policy context. It embraces a strategy of political action that falls short of making a revolutionary demand for the complete replacement of our governing process, and yet acknowledges the current crisis of political futility that confronts a peace-minded citizenry intent on ending the nuclear arms race and minimizing the role of nuclear weapons in the conduct of foreign policy.

This focus on nuclearism does not imply an indifference to the relevance of broader concerns either about the decline of democracy or militarism.[7] For one thing, nuclear preoccupations cannot be usefully treated in isolation. There is every reason to fear that a side losing a war waged exclusively with conventional weapons, but possessing nuclear weapons, would be tempted to threaten, and would be likely to use, such weaponry, especially if enemy encroachments on national territory and political independence were otherwise feared. The United States culminated its drive for victory in World War II by dropping atomic bombs on Japanese cities without even confronting threats to its core interests. Israel, faced with very real pressure early in the 1973 war, reportedly was ready to introduce nuclear weapons into the conflict rather than go down to defeat. Furthermore, non-nuclear war is also becoming ever more destructive and expensive, and is being fought with what Michael Klare calls "near nuclear weapons."[8] It seems dubious politically to have the concern with nuclearism make the world "safe" for unrestricted conventional warfare, or somehow to meet the charge of "pacifism" often hurled at the antinuclear movement by reassuring defenders of the national security status quo that existing interests could be protected by enhanced capabilities to carry on conventional warfare. Finally, in the United States since the Vietnam War there has existed grassroots resistance to military intervention in the Third World, hinting that the societal movement that has been mounted against nuclearism also could and should be extended to oppose interventionism, for the tactical, political reason of building the strongest possible antimilitarist coalition, if for no other reason.[9]

Analogously, the decline of democracy is of great independent concern aside from its dramatic expression in the war/peace setting. The quality of what is being secured depends to a significant degree on having a governing process that is responsive to an active citizenry, while at the same time it is mindful of minority rights. Democracy creates a beneficial framework for individual and group self-realization, as well as for the healthy connection between state and society. The participatory forms of democracy vary with the size of the state and popular expectations, but somehow it is essential that political energy flow upward and that leaders remain accountable to the people for their misdeeds. If these basic features do not operate at a behavioral level, their existence as a formal matter is of no significance. Virtually every country, however antidemocratic its daily reality, affirms its allegiance to democratic forms.

The peaceful bent of democratic and majoritarian sentiments cannot, of course, be taken for granted, as these are to be expressed through representative institutions and registered by way of elections and public opinion polls. There is generally a reservoir of anger and pent-up resentment against foreign states in the populace that can easily be mobilized and manipulated in an international crisis by politicians or clever pressure groups; as well, domestic frustrations can often be channeled into militarist overseas adventures and war fever. The calls to "nuke the Ayatollah" during the 1979-80 Iranian hostage crisis were a chilling expression of a widely supported demand by the public for American military action, however senseless it would have been in relation to its effects; and such sentiments were sustained even though the lives of the American hostages might thereby have been put in greater jeopardy. President Ford's handling of the Mayaquez incident or Prime Minister Thatcher's ardent embrace of the Falklands War both suggest that militarist responses can be very popular at home, despite losses of life sustained by fellow citizens. Public opinion polls indicate that a majority of Americans wanted President Reagan to take even tougher anti-Soviet action than he did in retaliation for the September 1983 shooting down of a Korean commercial plane overflying Soviet strategic territory. Public enthusiasm among the American people for the U.S. massive unprovoked intervention a month later in Grenada was even greater.

A tradition of informed thought about diplomacy regards the emotional elements of democracy and of public opinion as impediments to the rational maintenance of order in international society. Walter Lippmann was foremost among those who argued that the need of government in a democracy to mobilize popular support for its foreign policy inclines the behavior of these states toward undesirable extremes that lengthen and intensify wars, as well as leads them to introduce a kind of moralistic dimension into conflicts among nations that interferes with the prudent, professional management of diplomacy. This notion of professionalism hearkens back, nostalgically, to the 19th century and even earlier, when statecraft was generally an aristocratic undertaking insulated from democratic pressures and procedures. In that historical setting, affinities of class, even of family, made it feasible to negotiate differences among states quite cynically, if "adjustments" were needed to achieve peace or avoid war. As maneuverings on the diplomatic stage gradually became exposed to public scrutiny by the press, and as the expectations of democracy rose, so the argument runs, diplomats and politicians were forced to justify their claims in terms that could enlist the moral enthusiasm and political support of their citizenry. As a result, this process of democratization introduced irrational elements of national honor or adversary evil into the process, and made it more difficult to restrain or avoid conflict through rational methods.[10]

These factors act as qualifications on the generally held view that a constitutional order presupposes effective forms of citizen participation, especially in relation to war/peace decisions and national security policy. Indeed, the framers of the U.S. Constitution were preoccupied with the task of devising a scheme of separation of powers that would assure far wider participation in decisions to go to war than had been associated with the royal prerogatives of dynastic rule. And generally, Western political thought has proceeded on the Kantian assessment that since the burdens of war fall disproportionately on the populace, rather than the leadership, democratic control of foreign policy is positively related to the preservation of international peace, including a reluctance to take on those financial burdens associated with preparations for war.[11]

We need to question whether the underlying constitutional arrangements adopted by the United States in 1789 can any longer provide a democratizing framework for war/peace issues. After all, the Constitution was designed to operate in a sparsely populated, agrarian society far removed by oceans from potential enemies and minimally governed from its federal center in Washington. The new republic in its early days was committed to a foreign policy of neutrality and non-entanglement, outside the Western Hemisphere. Ideas of representative government, brilliantly synthesized by Madison in *Federalist Paper No. 10*, antedate sophisticated pressure group politics, the formation of a huge governmental bureaucracy with an extraordinary resource base, the struggle for leadership waged between two large national parties operating within limits established by pressure groups, large financial contributors, and the bureaucracy. Such conceptions were also formulated prior to the advent of a large permanent military establishment linked to powerful overseas corporate and banking interests. In other words, even aside from national security, a strong case could be made in the 1980s for rewriting the social contract that binds state and society. National security is only an acute instance of the fact that earlier constitutional conceptions, despite much stretching, no longer work to enable the functioning of political democracy. Within this relatively restricted domain of national security, reliance on nuclear weapons accentuates this loss of democracy.

These general considerations take on a more menacing character if interpreted in terms of the specific situation of the United States late in the 20th century. The government is largely insulated from diffuse popular pressures that might inhibit war-making. At the same time, the temptation of politicians to strengthen their domestic hand with a military victory remains strong and dangerous. Furthermore, the governmental machinery has itself become militarized in a manner than makes it especially *autonomous* in the national security field of action.[12] As a result, the challenge to a militarist orientation will have to come, if at all, from informal political forces generated by societal ferment, including such acute dissatisfaction with official policies and procedures as to prompt direct action and civil disobedience.

Governmental autonomy as a central attribute of state/society relations substantially insulates national security policy from shifts in public sentiments. The procedures of representative democracy (political parties, campaigns, elections, and the operation of the legislative process) are imperceptibly, yet deeply, constrained; at the same time a dominant segment of the public does not yet comprehend the relevance of the need for democratization to their policy concerns in these underlying structural terms.

My intention in this essay is to deal with a single aspect of this broad problem set—the problem of introducing changed attitudes toward the role of nuclear weapons in U.S. foreign policy. The analysis developed here also pertains to the more general problem of militarism and national security. Antidemocratic tendencies are a consequence of the buildup of the autonomous state and of the character of modern warfare and military technology, as well as a reflection of the dependence on nuclear weapons by leading states and the assumption by some of these states of a global policing role. These features are specifically associated with the two superpowers. Antidemocratic procedures and effects also flow from the status of subordinate alliance members, who have relinquished effective control over the execution of their national security policy in critical situations, and from the secondary effects of nuclear explosions, which make it impossible to achieve reliable security, no matter how peaceful a given foreign policy may be or how carefully defended the physical territory of a country. Switzerland is an instructive model of war avoidance in the nuclear age, but also of its limits, which are acknowledged in part by a strict and sensible war-mitigating civil defense program.

I will assume, as currently seems reasonable on the basis of public opinion polls and the expressions of moral conviction on this subject by religious leaders and institutions, that an unacceptable gap exists between official policies and the societal will on nuclear weapons policy. As indicated earlier, public sentiments can be inflamed in warlike directions, and antidemocratic procedures can operate in a moderating manner. In these respects, human nature, as the foundation of collective political behavior, is unpredictable and is influenced by such matters as cultural style and historical experience, as well as by various leaders, elite groupings, and pressure groups. Democracy of whatever form never operates in a political and cultural vacuum. The context is always crucial.

This general understanding needs to be qualified in terms of an existing state of mind with respect to nuclear weaponry and war. In this context, the effects of nuclear weaponry are such that even the most minimal human attachment to species survival produces fears and generates war avoidance pressures. In the West these pressures have been abated until very recently by a combination of leadership tactics designed to enliven a sense of threat from an ideological enemy and a set of reassurances that the weaponry will never be used. The characteristics of the new weaponry, especially the shortened time for decision in a crisis, together with heightened political rhetoric, especially that issuing from Washington, has broken down, temporarily at least, the structure of reassurance. The attempt to offset this breakdown by stressing the enemy threat has not succeeded with a majority of the populations in the NATO countries, including the United States. Whether this new societal attitude is firm and durable remains to be discovered. It is not very deep, and other concerns may allow leaders who defy the newly emerging societal consensus on war/peace issues to be reelected. As matters now stand, for instance, middle-class socioeconomic concerns with inflation and economic growth dominate the political process. A war scare could alter this situation in one direction, while Soviet aggressiveness could alter it in the opposite direction.

Our theoretical observation stands. Despite its ideological commitment to make the state responsive to societal will, the structure of the nuclear national security state creates formidable obstacles to that end. These obstacles are especially relevant now, when the new, emerging societal consensus seeks war-abatement postures and these sentiments are deflected and ignored. It needs to be kept in mind that such an adversary consensus can only take shape by overriding the passive and deferential attitudes promoted by pro-militarist state policies through a generally compliant media that exerts an enormous influence upon the "free" thought of the citizenry. The state has many other weapons, including the capacity to discredit challenges by identifying them as "naive" or "subversive," by using intelligence agencies and covert operations to disrupt and undermine oppositional activities, and by withholding and releasing information.

To pose the issue of constitutional order, however, it is not necessary to accept my empirical hypothesis. It is enough to inquire whether, if such a gap exists, it can be closed, given the way in which the state tends to deflect and ignore societal challenges.

In reformist terms, the issues can be phrased as follows: how can the American form of representative democracy be revitalized to enable an official realization of the societal will or conviction favoring a more restrictive role for nuclear weapons? Failing this revitalization, are there alternative ways to alter official policy, at least with respect to this crucial subject matter? In effect, what are the ways out of this apparent entrapment, often blamed partly on technological momentum and partly on bureaucratic rigidity and military orientation (for instance, critiques of "the military-industrial complex")?[13]

THE SPECIAL RELEVANCE OF NUCLEAR WEAPONRY

The loss of democratic control over foreign policy in the United States has been a cumulative process and has a variety of explanations. The expanded U.S. role after World War II meant a far larger share of governmental resources to be devoted to foreign policy during peacetime. As a result, governmental vested interests associated with an activist foreign policy increased, as did efforts to mobilize popular support. This circumstance was tied to an interpretation of the world situation, especially turbulence in the Third World, that emphasized military intervention in foreign civil strife. Sustained intervention was inconsistent with a leading political myth of the United States, that which affirmed self-determination as the basic right of all nations, and that fact led leaders to explain foreign policy in misleading terms to minimize popular opposition.

Of course, the alleged discontinuity of American foreign policy associated with recent times, say from 1945 onward, can be easily exaggerated. In the Western Hemisphere and across the continental expanse, the United States from the outset of its existence kept satisfying its geopolitical appetite for control and expansion. Yet, there was a new, greatly increased set of possibilities in the postwar world. The former core powers of international society were largely spent forces, whereas the Soviet Union, although devastated by the war, seemed poised to challenge the primacy of the West. The United States acted not only as a global leader in the postwar world, but it also acted to reconstruct the economic and political orders of the main defeated countries, and it acted to fill the alleged vacuum being created by the collapse of the colonial system of imposed order in Asia and Africa. This globalist role led to an expanded and expanding permanent place for military influence in the governing process. As well, the strain on U.S. resources, initially disguised by great economic strength, put an emphasis on cost-cutting, especially by way of reliance on mobility and high-technology weaponry, and on capital instead of manpower. This kind of reliance was accentuated as a result of the long ordeals of land warfare, first in Korea (1950–52), and later in Vietnam (1963-1973).

These policies, although subsumed under the rubric of the Cold War and explained to the public as essential steps to take in order to make "containment" work, became unpopular, especially as the dollar weakened and American lives were lost in the late 1960s. The latter stages of the Vietnam War exposed the shallowness of the foreign policy link between the government and the people in the United States. As a consequence, a "credibility gap" emerged, secrecy and the manipulation of information were used as devices to keep citizens from knowing what their government was doing or contemplating, and dissent beyond modest limits was harshly stigmatized.

Nuclear weaponry has a relevance to the decline of democracy throughout this period, although the relative weights of different, overlapping influences on the decline of democracy are impossible to measure accurately. The acquisition of nuclear weapons by a potential enemy, especially when combined with modern means of delivery, produces a permanent, prewar situation of anxiety and readiness. There is no longer a realistic possibility of demobilization so long as readiness to defend against a nuclear surprise attack is a, perhaps *the*, prime requirement of national security. Furthermore, war plans and decision procedures involving nuclear weapons are completely cut off from democratically agreed-upon guidelines or modes of accountability, much less citizen or even Congressional participation. The president has assumed, as far as we know, absolute control over nuclear weapons policy, the most significant decisional framework that exists at the present time for the U.S. government. Whether the president has actual authority in relation to the threats and uses of nuclear weapons remains, of course, untested and unknown.

The citizenry is kept completely in the dark, and is even deliberately misled by official pronouncements. In general, it has been deemed more important by our leaders to have a potential adversary believe that nuclear weapons will be unpredictably introduced into conflict than it is to inform the domestic polity about the real guidelines governing the use of nuclear weapons. In effect, intimidating Moscow takes precedence over informing and reassuring the American people. For instance, Robert McNamara wrote that when he was Secretary of Defense he had recommended to Presidents Kennedy and Johnson that nuclear weapons never be used first by the United States, no matter what.[14] At the time, the public doctrine definitely appeared to contemplate the first use of these weapons, especially in a European setting.[15] At other stages, the public has been misleadingly reassured, as has happened when actual threats to use nuclear weapons have been conveyed to adversaries in secret.[16]

To legitimize this usurpation of the basic constitutional arrangement, including the serious dilution of the force of doctrines about the separation of powers and checks and balances, especially those pertaining to war/peace issues, justifications by officials stressing "national security," the need for secrecy, and the overall circumstance of persisting emergency. The death sentences imposed on the Rosenbergs during peacetime for allegedly conveying atomic secrets to the Soviet Union were indicative of this official attempt to convince the public that it was necessary for the government to exercise special protective and custodial authority. The inner warlike resolve of the governing elite to counter alleged Soviet designs to achieve world domination is vividly confirmed by the fervor of "secret" national security documents recently declassified; NSC 68, a fundamental official consensus statement made in 1950 by the National Security Council, is especially indicative of an ideological atmosphere that obviously subordinates state/society proprieties to the waging of a global struggle for survival against the Soviet Union.[17]

Over the years, also, an elaborate nuclear national security network has evolved, with importantly mutually reinforcing links joining Congress, weapons labs, thinktanks, defense industries, elite universities, media specialists, and foreign policy associations. This network vigorously supports reliance on nuclear weapons in the context of extended deterrence and is geared to support the necessity for continual innovation for improved nuclear weapons systems. To be sure, interservice rivalries persist about the best means to implement this nuclearist consensus, including various attitudes of support and opposition toward different forms of arms control, and there is some disagreement on an individual or organizational basis as to the character of the Soviet threat and how best to respond to it. The nuclearist consensus, in other words, places limits on the range of debate, rather than embodying a rigid dogma that can be used to resolve every issue of nuclear weapons policy. The nuclearist consensus is, in a sense, set off against the emerging societal consensus mentioned earlier. An agreed set of attitudes and beliefs within government, concentrated in the national security bureaucracy, as to the legitimate role of nuclear weapons in the pursuit of national interests, constitutes the nuclear consensus. The societal consensus is more amorphous, less stable, and still emerging; it reflects a dominant opinion among the public on the overall unacceptability or illegitimacy of nuclear weapons, except as a weaponry of last resort to ward off, and possibly respond against, nuclear attacks by an enemy state.

This formidable structure of ideological support for nuclearism constrains competitive politics by establishing informal, but highly effective, boundaries on serious public discourse, electoral politics, and the institutions of representative government. Political candidates cannot hope to gain office, nor leaders to govern, without the tacit acquiescence of this nuclear national security establishment. If individuals or positions are seen as threatening to the nuclearist consensus, then official and quasi-official assaults on "credibility" mysteriously occur with devastating effect. Without credibility of this kind an American politician is virtually finished. Henry Wallace, Eugene McCarthy, Fred Harris, Harold Hughes, Jerry Brown, and George McGovern are a few examples of how rather diverse political figures lost their credibility and were thereby rapidly moved to the margins of the American political scene.[18]

Let me summarize my argument this way. Nuclear weapons are held by the armed forces for potential use at the sole discretion of the president or some official delegated to act on his behalf. In effect, no representative institution or procedure is given a role in sharing the responsibility for establishing advance guidelines or initiating a use of nuclear weapons. Even if such a role were established, by way of consultation or membership on a crisis committee, its exercise would likely be nominal, given the probable weight of military and intelligence "advice." Perhaps this situation is partially unavoidable, at least at the outer limit of responding to a surprise attack. Unless a country like the United States were prepared to accept its nuclear vulnerability without creating a capability to retaliate immediately or even preemptively, then it must have in being a method to assure rapid decision and response. In fact, this plausibility of immediate or preemptive response has been taken as essential for the proper functioning of deterrence, and without deterrence, it is argued, war becomes more, not less, likely, by tempting the adversary to strike first.

Nevertheless, this dimension of living with nuclear weapons could be mitigated, if the nuclearist consensus were so inclined. If nuclear weapons were strictly reserved to a role of retaliation against a prior nuclear attack, and this was made unambiguous to rivals, then a considerable effort could be made to achieve a survivable second-strike capability that allowed a sufficient pause between attack and response to enable a procedure for collective, one that might include meaningful participation by congressional leaders and, conceivably, even involve some form of consultation and assessment of public sentiment. Of course, any postattack decision process is bound to be laden with the absurdism of *any* contemplation of large-scale nuclear weapons use.

Of course, a variety of practical obstacles hinder democratizing the decision process pertaining to nuclear weapons. First, an untestable concern fears that entrusting the decision even in part to the legislative process would deprive deterrence of its main requirement for effectiveness—namely, credibility. The reasoning here is that an enemy would realize that such a deliberative procedure would expose the irrationality of making any nuclear response and, because of this realization, the process would make the option of nuclear attack more attractive, especially if a sufficient number of weapons were held in reserve further to deter retaliation. Such a logical view of credibility does not seem descriptive of how such decisions would actually be made by a government but, perhaps, more empirical evidence is needed for informed judgment as to the character of nuclear decisionmaking in general and in the particular settings of given leaders and leadership patterns. At the very least, wider participation by representative institutions in initiating uses and threats of nuclear weapons seems justified, because, as our argument shows, the democratic process should preclude such uses and threats, given the character of the antinuclearist societal consensus, as well as the morally and legally dubious status of these weapons.

An opposite danger is implicit in any move toward democratization of the decision process. Either in a situation of aroused tensions, or in the event the emerging societal consensus weakens or disappears (after all, American society overwhelmingly accepted the original justifications associated with the use of atomic bombs against Japanese cities in 1945), then representative procedures might lead to policies and attitudes more nuclearist than those currently advocated by the national security establishment, which at least tempers its reliance on nuclear weapons with sophisticated cost/benefit/risk notions. Such a concern about the dangers of democratization is definitely not fanciful, especially if it is understood that the nuclearist consensus will continue to deploy its considerable resources, including influence upon the media and the electoral process, to realign the societal consensus, by making it passive or submissive. In this situation, at a moment of crisis, democratized procedures of nuclear decisionmaking could add to the risks. We are faced here with an issue about the limits of representative democracy, and the relative risks and costs over time of antidemocratic and democratic procedures. In the end, the desirability of democracy being extended to this vital context rests on the quality of the citizenship (that is, education and moral sensitivity) and of the political leadership at all levels of government. There are no easy, assured answers.

Nor does it resolve such issues of choice to argue that present arrangements have avoided recourse to nuclear weapons since 1945. Any decision process, given the enormity of the consequences and the general abhorrence associated with weapons of mass destruction, is weighted against the use of such weaponry. The proper critical question is whether it is *sufficiently* weighted to that end, and what is the best mechanism for so weighting it, in light of an overall approach to political reality. My view, expressed here and elsewhere, is that the sole reliable orientation toward the weighting of choice involving nuclear weaponry depends upon their unconditional repudiation, except possibly in the context of retaliation against a prior nuclear attack. Such a view rests, this should be clear, on the willingness of a nuclear power to avoid recourse to nuclear weapons, even for threat purposes, in all settings of nonnuclear warfare. It also implies a willingness to accept defeat in warfare. It is possible to argue that the United States has walked the tightrope between threat and use in this regard, making threats, as in Korea (1952) and in relation to the defense of Western Europe, but refraining from use, as in Vietnam. The Vietnam context is ambiguous, as it is not clear that the use of nuclear weapons could have reversed the military/political outcome, nor that defeat was an anticipated consequence of restricting warfare to nonnuclear engagements.

In any event, the present centralization of this secret power of decision over the use of nuclear weapons stabilizes an antidemocratic "core" in the governing process, obscures the absurdity of the use of such weapons, and consigns the most momentous of all possible subject matters to unknown and unknowable response mechanisms. It also tends to nullify both electoral politics and official institutions that rest their claims to act upon the powers of representation. What also seems evident is that without fundamental shifts in the organization of international society, or without restricting somehow the availability of technological capabilities for war-making, there is no acceptable way to overcome altogether these antidemocratic features of nuclear weapons policy.

Beyond this general circumstance of necessity, nuclear weapons have been relied upon as an instrument of American diplomacy in a variety of Cold War settings. On some 20 occasions threats to use nuclear weapons have been seriously made, or such uses seriously considered, by U.S. leaders.[19] U.S. strategic doctrine and war plans continue to rely on nuclear weapons to achieve "extended deterrence," that is, to inhibit Soviet or other adversary nonnuclear provocations by the prospect of a nuclear response. As already mentioned, the United States reserves the option of a nuclear response to nonnuclear attack or hostilities in Europe, Korea, or indeed, wherever vital interests engaged and nonnuclear capabilities prove insufficient. These roles for nuclear weapons, quite inconsistent with prevailing views on law and morality, have never been candidly acknowledged to the citizenry or endorsed by the institutions and procedures of representative democracy.[20]

WHAT CAN BE DONE? SOME IMMEDIATE PRIORITIES

Having spent seven years as Secretary of Defense dealing with the problems unleashed by the initial nuclear chain reaction 40 years ago, I do not believe we can avoid serious and unacceptable risk of nuclear war until we recognize—and until we base all our military plans, defense budgets, weapons deployments, and arms negotiations on the recognition—that nuclear weapons are totally useless—except only to deter one's opponent from using them.[21]

Conceived in the abstract, partial denuclearization (minimizing risks, reducing tensions) should be a plausible response to the dangers of the nuclear arms race. Such a response would not, by its nature, require any alteration of state/society relations or even of the level of resources allocated to the military. Indeed, it is quite possible that segments of liberal leadership in the West would be receptive to an exchange of partial denuclearization for increased militarization. At this point, however, even partial nuclearization seems blocked by the nuclearist consensus. Therefore, some measure of revitalization of democracy operates as a precondition for any changes at all. The freeze movement and the Bishops' Pastoral Letter have achieved, at least for the present, increased pressures on the nuclearist consensus. In this atmosphere, former adherents of nuclearism can take stands in favor of partial denuclearization and propose nuclear/nonnuclear tradeoffs (that is, increased conventional force to offset decreased roles for nuclear weapons), instead of confining tradeoffs to various aspects of the nuclear arms race (that is, increased qualitative advances in new systems to offset quantitative ceilings, as in SALT I and II). Thus, democratization is relevant at all stages of denuclearization, even if its effect is only to loosen the nuclearist consensus and widen the orbit of acceptable public debate.

We will next explore the programmatic content of democratization as it regards nuclear weapons policy. The argument rests on the convergence of normative and pragmatic considerations—that societal well-being could be enhanced by taking certain steps, if the institutions of representative democracy were able to operate to reflect an emergent societal consensus. Taking these steps would also promote the restoration of political legitimacy by reducing the gap between nuclear national security policy and applicable notions of international law and morality. Such reforms are consistent with nonidealist (or realist) assumptions about international politics.[22]

The mainstream deterrence theorists keep reminding us that we must learn to live with nuclear weapons, and not pretend that we can generate the political will to recreate the world according to some pacific design. This position has a surface plausibility. It is virtually impossible to contemplate nuclear disarmament without some guarantee against risks of cheating by others,[23] and such a guarantee seems unattainable. States and, for that matter, the underlying political communities of citizens that constitute separate states, seem unready to accept the potential vulnerability to nuclear threats or attacks by others that is implicit in total nuclear disarmament, whether achieved unilaterally or by agreement. In this central respect, there is no early prospect of establishing a universal political community that would effectively do away with existing patterns of national security consciousness, structures, and capabilities (although some qualifications will appear in the next two sections).

Given this fixed societal resolve as to the horizons of possibility, reformist energies have naturally been focused upon *particular* steps that would minimize the risks arising from current arrangements and that would reduce to the lowest possible level the prospects of the threat or use of nuclear weapons.

The peace movement, for purposes of coalition building and for principled reasons, has mainly concentrated on particular steps thought to have a minimizing potential: opposition to the deployment of weapons systems with first-strike potential or those that diminish crisis stability (e.g., Pershing II in West Germany, cruise missiles in NATO countries, Trident II submarines, MX missile system); opposition to strategic postures, deployment patterns, and war plans that rely upon initiating uses of nuclear weapons (e.g., unconditional no-first-use pledges or pledges restricted to specific theaters of operation, say Europe); proposals to exempt certain geographical regions or domains from nuclear weapons deployment (e.g., nuclear weapons free zones for Central Europe, the Indian Ocean, Latin America, Africa, Pacific Islands; denuclearization of Antarctica, the moon, ocean floor, and outer space); support for unilateral and negotiated steps to end the nuclear arms race (e.g., a mutually verifiable freeze on production and development activities); proposals for ceilings and reductions on different categories of nuclear weapons to improve the stability of the existing arsenal and to diminish current so-called "overkill" capabilities (e.g., SALT process). The emphasis of these particular steps is upon risk reduction, and upon the central appreciation that nuclear weapons are, in McNamara's words, "useless weapons" when it comes to foreign policy and statecraft.[24] Much of the danger in the world arises from the fact that this simple *grund-norm* has never been accepted by policymakers, strategists, and leaders, especially in the United States.[25]

Correlative to this direct approach to denuclearization are the more indirect possibilities of toning down geopolitical rivalry. This toning down could take two principal forms: renouncing interventionary diplomacy, and seeking to reestablish detente in East-West relations.[26] Part of the nuclear temptation is bound up with America's post-1945 geopolitical overcommitment—a range of involvements that cannot be satisfied at acceptable costs without relying to some extent on the nuclear option.[27] These involvements rest, in part, on the dubious assumption that the United States must stand ready to oppose national revolutions in a wide range of Third World countries. Tensions in East-West relations also heighten suspicions and encourage hostile interpretations whenever "an incident" occurs. Past wars have originated in local incidents, giving rise to pressures that culminate in full-scale confrontation. In other words, ending the Cold War as definitively as possible and renouncing Third World interventionism would remove many occasions and pretexts for military action and reduce the dangers of escalation that are now implicit whenever East-West interests collide.

The cumulative effects of these steps would be of great significance in advancing the cause of denuclearization. It is arguable that under certain patterns of circumstances there could be one adverse effect of such denuclearization: heightened prospects of nuclear proliferation, especially by governments no longer able to rest their security under an American nuclear umbrella (most significantly, West Germany, Japan, South Korea). It is by no means clear that such results would occur. Indeed, with careful diplomacy by *both* superpowers there is every reason to believe such results could be avoided. In any event, the United States cannot hold its own future "hostage" to a position of great danger and immorality when it comes to nuclear weapons policy. My purpose here is not to make a specific substantive case around an overall strategy of partial denuclearization, but only to suggest that a wide range of particular steps deserve debate and support far beyond what is now possible under current conditions of constrained democracy.

Of course, a particular initiative, such as the freeze, or an opposition to a given weapons system, is plausible even within the current framework, but its effects will be blunted or neutralized by having to pass through the filter of the national security bureaucracy, which exercises a virtual veto power over free working of the political process. What has normally happened, partly in response to popular pressures for arms control, is that a kind of tacit bargain has been struck—for example, opposition to the Limited Test Ban was neutralized by the assurance of unlimited underground testing and an enhanced commitment to "qualitative improvements" in weapons, such as MIRVing. Even McNamara's plea for a NATO no-first-use posture is coupled in his formulation with an unexamined endorsement of the need for increased overall defense expenditures to achieve a comparable deterrent with conventional weaponry; in effect, increased militarization is the minimum price that the national security bureaucracy would be expected to exact for decreased nuclearism.[28] Such "bargaining" is endemic in politics, but it creates a dangerous illusion that democracy is alive and well in the national security sphere. The illusion takes the form of supposing that with sufficient public and congressional support it is possible to move *cumulatively* against the arms race and militarization. Exposing this illusion helps us understand the very limited sphere for freedom of action retained by the forces of political democracy.

REDEMOCRATIZATION AND THE REDEFINITION OF THE REAL: THE ABOLITIONIST QUEST

I had always resisted the suggestion that war, as a phenomenon of international life, could be totally ruled out. . . . I am now bound to say that while the possible elimination of nuclear weaponry is of no less vital import in my eyes than it ever was, this would not be enough, in itself, to give Western civilization even an adequate chance of survival. War itself, as a means of settling differences at least between the great industrial powers, will have to be in some way ruled out; and with it there will have to be dismantled . . . the greater part of the vast military establishments now maintained with a view to the possibility that war might take place.[29]

The nuclearist camp is pursuing an effort to limit "responsible" debate to argumentation about how best to live with nuclear weapons and to invalidate abolitionist perspectives, whether directed toward nuclear weaponry, or more generally, toward war.[30] As is implicit in the Catholic Bishops' Pastoral Letter and a variety of other religious and moral formulations, it is not possible to reconcile reliance on nuclear weaponry, or for that matter modern warfare, with minimal standards of human decency, nor with the pursuit of self-interested collective behavior. At best, a provisional irreconcilability could be acceptable, if it were to be seriously combined with a search for total disarmament and the creation of positive peace or a durable world order system. Granted that the security of national societies against foreign enemies will remain a vital concern for the indefinite future, it still seems possible to work toward the realization of arrangements over the years and decades ahead that could eventually make modern warfare as marginal to conflicts among groups as slavery has become to the organization of work within society. Such abolitionist goals do not suppose any kind of perfectionist potential in either the collective or in individual human beings. Conflict, even violence, would likely remain widespread and multifaceted, as would scarcity and gross disparities between rich and poor.

The displacement of war in its modern aspect requires a different sort of evolutionary process, one that is closely associated with the revitalization of democracy. The only feasible way to abolish war is for societal forces to reclaim and relocate the security function under direct citizens' control as part of their repudiation of war as the preserve of statecraft. As long as security is primarily entrusted to the state, it will presuppose a high-technology, centralized management of internal and external power relations, and this will necessarily include war as a natural limiting option. The idea of enlarging the public arena to encompass the planet does seem utopian, unless a prior inward build-down of the national security bureaucracies occurs at the state level. If such a build-down took place to an impressive degree, then one could imagine a greater willingness to endow collective security mechanisms, as contemplated by the UN Charter, with sufficient capabilities and autonomy to be a significant peace-keeping presence in world affairs. The essential step, however, is to fashion a citizenry effectively trained and mobilized for nonviolent, but militant, civilian resistance, so as to make conquest and occupation an unattractive option for a potential aggressor.[31] Governments under these circumstances would no longer be expected to undertake the violent defense of territory and independence through the centralized control over a military establishment.

The case for and the limits of nonviolence are both complicated and familiar. My assumption is that the advocacy and application of nonviolent approaches would come about by stages, and not without some implicit conditions (for example, the mode of resistance against a genocidal ruler or enemy—"the Hitler problem"). If this notion of security could be coupled with a strengthening of societal consensus around the sacredness of life, there would be no reason to associate nonviolence with weakness or passivity. The problems of demilitarizing security are properly associated with such other vital issues as capital punishment and abortion. There is considerable merit, as some Catholic thinkers have recently argued, in adopting a unified "pro-life" position built around the sanctity of life and around the biblical injunction "thou shalt not kill."

Obviously, the process of demilitarizing the security function—and separating it from centralized state power—could probably only occur by confidence-building stages. Its pace would be deeply influenced by public sentiment, which in turn would be strongly affected by the presence or absence of reinforcing steps taken by adversary states. The essence of the process, in a sense, is a capability to assert a new set of democratic prerogatives on behalf of the people, the citizenry. Such a dramatic result would almost certainly require a substantial, sustained grass-roots movement leading to the formation of strong demands for drastic constitutional reform.

At some stage, it may be time to issue a Declaration of Peoples Security drafted and discussed by assemblies of anti-statists, setting forth a new vision of state/society relations, and leading to the articulation of a relevant set of principles and rationales, possibly distributed at first by committees of correspondence and gathered together in a collection of "Peoples Security Papers." Whether such a call for constitutional renewal would be viewed as a subversive and illegal movement is unclear, but it would certainly create deep chasms in public opinion and would encounter every type of opposition from the various instruments of persuasion and coercion available to the modern state.

In essence, to realize the vision of an end to war does not depend upon contriving international mechanisms to facilitate disarmament. It calls for reestablishing state/society relations in such a way as to confer a much greater role upon the citizenry to work out new forms of defense and security appropriate to the special features of the nuclear age.

To the extent that the present analysis is correct, it does mean that moving the security framework beyond "stability" depends on the democratization of *all* major states. The existing transnational peace movement, if it intends to address underlying issues, cannot realistically hope to achieve results merely by working toward enlightened state/state relations. Enlightened intra-state and transnational relations are indispensable, and thus the growth of peace movement activities, independent of state control in the Soviet Union, Eastern Europe, and elsewhere, cannot be circumvented as a precondition for radical denuclearization and the pursuit of abolitionist ends in international relations generally. The war system reflects a certain character of state/society relations with respect to national security policy that centrally embodies war making and inevitably confers autonomous authority upon the political leadership of the modern state, with greater and greater adverse consequences, including the cultural consequences of "waiting helplessly" for nuclear war. Such a structure, regardless of its ideological habitat, is incompatible with achieving security-without-war.

NOTES ON PROSPECTS

Naturally, a detached assessment of the evidence yields little encouragement at the present time. The state remains firmly in control of the security function everywhere, and only very rarely are denuclearizing proposals or tactics associated with readjusting state/society relations. For minimizing strategies, as discussed earlier, there has generally been no challenge really directed at the existing array of responsibilities of the state for security, but only the suggestion that these responsibilities can be as effectively met while greatly reducing the role of nuclear weaponry. To go further and conceive of a positive peace system, as the Pastoral Letter does, if the effort is undertaken at all, is most commonly identified with generating support for a global governmental authority—an enhanced United Nations that has the characteristics of a limited world government—that will remove warmaking from the level of the sovereign state:

There *is* a substitute for war. There is negotiation under the supervision of a global body realistically fashioned to do its job . . . The hope for such a structure is not unrealistic, because the point has been reached where public opinion sees clearly that, with the massive weaponry of the present, war is no longer viable.[32]

This centralized peace system will apparently continue to conceive of security as a matter of warmaking, but hopefully with the balance of forces being held by the global arrangement and exercised on behalf of the world community as a whole. The approach taken here toward denuclearization and the abolition of war is instead decentralist and antimilitarist in emphasis, and rests on the potential capacity of the citizenry to be largely self-reliant when it comes to upholding societal security.

There are some reasons to be hopeful if the time-frame is stretched out over several decades. The state is losing its legitimacy in the national security sector, especially in relation to nuclear war. Societal forces are beginning to realize that the state is itself locked into warmaking as both a victim and abettor of technological momentum. It seems likely that as the critique of the state and the state system proceeds, the reformist focus will shift to an understanding of the impermeability of the national security bureaucracy to a societal consensus relating to nuclear weapons and war. Already seeds of such an understanding exist, as in the suggestion and warning made by President Eisenhower in his Farewell Address about the menace of "a military-industrial complex." But this warning was largely rhetorical; it did not constitute a political challenge. The national security consensus has easily outlasted and outwitted temporary failures of public confidence, and has usually struck back effectively by way of well-orchestrated scare tactics.[33]

At the same time, however, there is now some renewed realization that only a social movement with the staying power of the bureaucracy of the state can mount a societal challenge. The entry of churches into this struggle is crucial, as it gives citizens vital institutional backing, normative reassurance, and a tradition of continuity.

A variety of religious perspectives have also inspired individuals to undertake exemplary actions of a variety of kinds—for instance, blocking a train carrying Trident warheads, or seeking symbolically to interfere with the production of first-strike weapons. These actions express urgency and deep personal conviction (putting one's body in the path of danger and accepting the punishments of law), but more fundamentally, they express a loss of faith in national security as defined by the state and reinforced by the overall workings of representative democracy.[34] Groups engaged in nonviolent resistance are emerging at a rapid rate, although most still consist only of small knots of committed individuals, often part of religiously oriented experimental communities. Their political consciousness is devoted mainly to negating the claims of the state to subject our lives and the future of the planet to a destiny of nuclear apocalypse. Yet there are glimmerings that beyond the denial lies an affirmation of people's security based on the extraordinary potential for the empowerment of citizens to work out a variety of arrangements for the security of society without dependence on weapons.

Three phases of civic consciousness can be distinguished. Each overlaps with the others, even within the experience of a single citizen, yet in an optimistic interpretation of the future these three can be envisaged as stages in a scenario for revitalizing political democracy in the United States, especially as it pertains to war/peace issues.

1. *Resignation*: a basic sense of despair about ending the nuclear arms race, avoiding nuclear war, and eliminating the shadow of nuclear danger overhanging daily existence. Without an emphasis on redemocratization, despair persists in the form of unavoidable disappointment even for those who, responding to the encroachments of nuclear weaponry, seek various kinds of reform by way of arms control and disarmament. The nuclear national security state has sufficiently immobilized the institutions and procedures of representative democracy to render them almost completely ineffectual when it comes to challenging the fundamental content and framework of official policy in the war/peace area.

2. *Resistance*: a basic sense that the struggle against nuclearism has to be waged outside, and almost in defiance of, the normal constitutional order, although constitutional channels are used to the extent that they seem available. In such circumstances, nonviolent, symbolic acts of resistance operate to redefine the meaning of good citizenship. Participation in political campaigns, party politics, and elections become meaningful almost only to the extent that their failure to address basic grievances about nuclear national security is exposed. Resistance tends to be mainly negative in its political energy, although not in its human motivation, and this enables the resister to believe in the possibility, often created by and with a deeply held religious view of reality, of a possible national political community based on love, fearlessness, and sharing, rather than hate, fear, and possessiveness.

3. *Renewal*: a basic shift in emphasis from negation to reconstruction. The citizen is liberated from any illusions about political democracy as it has been handed down, and understands the impossibility of forging solutions within old problem-solving frame works. At this stage, the diagnosis of what is wrong becomes heavily concentrated on a broad collective effort to reconstitute the nature of security in international relations. As explained previously, the struggle now emphasizes new constitutional arrangements that transfer predominant responsibility for security downward from the state to the individual, local, and semilocal level. This transfer can only be premised upon conclusive disillusionment with militarized, centralized, high-technology security systems. The plausibility of such a transfer rests upon the creativity of the citizenry in designing various types of "peoples security" and in renewing the overall relationship between state and society so that political democracy can flourish again.[35] Implicit in such a process is not only a localizing, decentralizing spirit, but also a more cosmopolitan attitude toward the future, one that acknowledges a global political community as natural and necessary, including the persistence and benefits of political diversity. This diversity is a positive attribute of the global political community, provided only that the main subcommunities find ways to democratize the relationship of state and society in the war/peace context.

NOTES

1. "The Pastoral Letter of the U.S. Bishops on War and Peace," *Origins* 13, no. 1 (19 May 1983): 1–32, at 29–30.
2. Cf. an earlier piece of mine, "Nuclear Weapons and the End of Democracy," *Praxis International* 2 (1982): 1–11.

3. For elaboration of this critique of bipartisanship see Falk, "American Foreign Policy at the Crossroads: Lifting the Curse of Bipartisanship," *World Policy Journal* 1, no. 1 (1983): 127–57.

4. It is true that the liberal tradition in political theory seems to have been unconcerned about imposing constraints on the foreign policy of heads of state. The U.S. Constitution shows concern in the form of placing warmaking powers within the framework of checks and balances and by positing international law as "the Supreme Law of the Land," coequal in status with acts of Congress. Nevertheless, diplomatic practice sustained by judicial interpretation has given the president virtually unrestricted power over foreign affairs, with very little evident obligation of accountability. In recent years, avoidance of formal declarations of war have enabled extended military conflict to proceed on the basis of presidential fiat, further reinforced by way of restricting the access of the citizenry to information. There is a real question as to whether "the consent of the governed" pertains to foreign policy, except in the most general sense.

5. On problematic legal status see C. Builder and M. Graubard, "The International Law of Armed Conflict: Implications for the Concept of Assured Destruction," RAND Publication Series R-2804-FF, 1982; see also Special Issue on Disarmament, *McGill Law Journal* 28 (July 1983), esp. articles by Vlasic, Falk, Weston, and Paust.

6. For a stimulating recent exploration of the Declaration's outlook see Garry Wills, *Inventing America* (New York: Vintage Books, 1973).

7. See Robert Jay Lifton and Richard Falk, *Indefensible Weapons: The Political and Psychological Case Against Nuclearism* (New York: Basic Books, 1982).

8. Michael Klare, "New Arms Technology" issue, "The Conventional Weapons Fallacy," *The Nation* (9 April 1983), pp. 438– 44.

9. See Falk, "American Foreign Policy," pp. 141–47.

10. For argument to this effect see Gordon A. Crain and Alexander L. George, *Force and Statecraft* (Oxford: Oxford University Press, 1983), esp. pp. 60–72.

11. For a significant reinterpretation of this standard view of the Kantian perspective that discloses an interventionary disposition, see Michael W. Doyle, "Kant, Liberal Legacies, and Foreign Affairs," Parts 1 and 2, *Philosophy & Public Affairs* 12, nos. 3 and 4 (1983): 205–35, 323–53.

12. Formulation influenced by Eric Nordlinger, *On the Autonomy of the Democratic State* (Cambridge: Harvard University Press, 1981), esp. pp. 1–41.

13. For satiric treatment see *The Report from Iron Mountain on the Possibility and Desirability of Peace*, Special Study Group, with Introduction by Leonard C. Lewin (New York: Dell Publishing, 1967; London, Macdonald & Co., 1968; New York, Dial Press, 1967).

14. Robert S. McNamara, "The Military Role of Nuclear Weapons," *Foreign Affairs* 62 (1983): 59–80, at 79.

15. See Richard J. Barnet, "Annals of Diplomacy," Part II, *The New Yorker*, 10 October 1983.

16. For a helpful overview on the evolution of *actual* nuclear strategy see David Alan Rosenberg, "The Origins of Overkill: Nuclear Weapons and American Strategy, 1945–1980," *International Security* 7 (1983): 3–71.

17. For a useful collection of declassified internal documents revealing the character of national security consciousness in the early postwar period, see Thomas H. Entzold and John Lewis Gaddis, eds., *Containment: Documents on Ameri-*

can Policy and Strategy, 1945-1980 (New York: Columbia University Press, 1978); for text of NSC 68, see pp. 385-442.

18. Incidentally, overzealousness on national security policy can also lead to a loss of "credibility," as was the experience with Joseph McCarthy, Barry Goldwater, and George Wallace. The national security consensus, therefore, should not be confused with rightist politics, although it is much more "penetrated" by the right than the left.

19. Desmond Ball, "U.S. Strategic Forces: How Would They Be Used?" *International Security* 7 (1983): 31-60, at 41-2.

20. See sources cited notes 5 and 14; cf also the Pastoral Letter of the U.S. Bishops on War and Peace, pp. 1-32.

21. McNamara, "The Military Role of Nuclear Weapons," p. 79. Emphasis in original.

22. For discussion of international prospects from this perspective see Craig and George, *Force and Statescraft*, esp. pp. 146-53.

23. See David Deudney's discussion of "transparency revolution" for the relevance of technological breakthroughs in monitoring capabilities to the much greater viability of disarmament in a world of acute distrust between rival superpowers. See Deudney, "Whole Earth Security: A Geopolitics of Peace," *Worldwatch Paper* 55, July 1983, pp. 1-93, esp. 20-32.

24. See also to the same effect George F. Kennan, *The Nuclear Delusion*, rev. ed. (New York: Pantheon, 1983).

25. There have been ups and downs on attitude toward nuclear weaponry, ranging from Dulles-Eisenhower "massive retaliation" to McNamara-Kennedy-Johnson operational minimization. For more extended discussion see sources cited notes 16 and 19.

26. I have argued at length to this effect in source cited note 3.

27. For recent pro-nuclearist reformulation in relation to global array of commitments, see Lawrence W. Beilenson and Samuel T. Cohen, "A New Nuclear Strategy," *NY Times Magazine*, 24 January 1982, pp. 34, 38, 39.

28. McNamara, "Military Role of Nuclear Weapons."

29. Kennan, *The Nuclear Delusion*, p. xxviii.

30. See, e.g., writing of Wiesentelier, Mandlebaum, McGeorge Bundy, to this general effect; contrast Kennan, ibid., pp. xviii-xix, where he argues that sustainable denuclearization cannot be achieved without ending war as a human institution; cf. McNamara, "Military Role," where partial denuclearization is offset by increased nonnuclear militarization.

31. See Report of the Alternative Defence Commission, *Defence Without the Bomb* (Taylor and Francis, 1983); see also Michael Albert and David Dellinger, eds., *Beyond Survival: New Directions for the Disarmament Movement* (Boston: South End Press, 1983).

32. See "The Pastoral Letter of the U.S. Bishops on War and Peace", at pp. 29-30. For earlier conceptions of positive peace, see Grenville Clark and Louis B. Sohn, *World Peace through World Law*, 3rd rev. ed. (Cambridge: Harvard University Press, 1966), and Falk, *A Study of Future Worlds* (New York: Free Press, 1975).

33. For a telling perceptive account of this process, see Jerry W. Sanders, *Peddlers of Crisis* (Boston: South End Press, 1983).

34. Richard Falk, "The Spirit of Thoreau in the Nuclear Age," unpub. ms., August 1983.

35. For a comprehensive study of experimental possibilities along these lines, see Gene Sharp, *The Politics of Non-Violent Struggle* (Boston: Porter Sargent, 1973); idem, *Social Power and Political Freedom* (Boston: Porter Sargent, 1980), esp. pp. 195–378.

25
THE LOGIC OF THE ARMS RACE

Milton Fisk

The nuclear arms race goes on despite warnings of extinction, despite moral appeals, and despite massive mobilizations. The usual spurs to reform prove ineffective. This suggests that the difficulty posed by the arms race takes us back to basic social and political facts. The thesis argued here is that the state itself is responsible for the arms race. Thus, to deal with the arms race it becomes necessary to breach the norms of political strategy that assume the state.

The key point to be made about the state is that, in the competitive struggle with other states, it must accept the imperative of achieving superior force by itself, or at least in conjunction with allied states. This is not a new imperative, but it becomes a more frightening one in the nuclear age. The actual course of the arms race since 1945 illustrates the workings of the principle of superiority. But the principle is itself more than an empirical summary of the facts. For it is rooted in the need of the state to gain acceptance within its domain of its monopolization of the means of violence. The logic of the arms race cannot be turned around without changing the thrust toward superiority and hence toward a monopoly of force; in short, ending the state as we have known it and, hence, ending those social conditions on which it is based.

The familiar response to such a claim is that we have no time to deal with the big political and social issues; if we don't stop the arms race, we will be incinerated before we can ever enjoy a better world order. This impatience is understandable but misguided. It refuses to reckon with the obstacles in the path of disarmament simply on the grounds that disarmament is urgent. It would be an equally grave mistake to ignore the arms race on the grounds that the struggle for political and social change is all that counts. Rather, the urgency of ending the threat of nuclear war should become a key part of the motivation for the task of ending the state, and the social inequality and repression on which it is built.

This perspective is foreign to the nuclear disarmament movement of the 1980s, but in the immediate post-World War II period a sizable section of the disarmament movement saw the necessity of confronting the existence of the state. A spectrum ran from emphasis on cooperation among states through the United Nations, to emphasis on sacrificing state sovereignty altogether by transferring state power to a world state. The Oppenheimer and then the Baruch plans of 1946 chose the former route in advocating the international control of atomic weapons.[1] Einstein was a spokesperson for the latter route, which was that of the world federalists.[2] In the current period, Schell has revived the attack on state sovereignty advocated by Einstein and by Bertrand Russell, but although the moral tone of his work has been applauded, the present disarmament movement doesn't know what to make of his attack on the state.[3]

These attacks on the state have one important flaw: they isolate the treatment of the state from the social context of the state. Their appeals to curb state sovereignty are empty without appeals to change the conditions of inequality and repression within which state sovereignty grows. They suppose that the necessary changes can be made in the state without touching existing social conditions that would block those changes. Just as disarmament cannot be isolated from curbing state power, so too curbing state power cannot be isolated from revolutionizing social structure.

THE SUPERIORITY PRINCIPLE

When out of power a number of statesmen, politicians, and state advisors have argued that a modest deterrent force suffices. But in power their contributions have added to the thrust toward superiority in U.S. nuclear weaponry. The official state positions are not always that superiority is the aim, but it is hard to look at the course of the arms race and see it as anything more than a trajectory for gaining, maintaining, or regaining superiority. After the first Soviet atomic bomb test in 1949, there was a debate within U.S. ruling circles over whether to develop the hydrogen bomb. The Joint Chiefs of Staff said that "the public expects the Department of Defense to take action necessary to regain the favorable balance previously held."

But what about the Soviets? If one looks only at the early years of U.S. monopoly and then predominance in nuclear weaponry, it seems wrongheaded to claim that the Soviets were striving for superiority. But the Soviet trajectory must also include the recent years when the logic of the competition between the major powers has made clear a mutual striving for superiority. This point becomes confused if we try to inject into it considerations about whether the Soviet stance has been purely defensive, whereas that of the US has been consistently offensive. It is not a question of intentions at all. Superiority is a posture needed to gain the advantage, to win, to prevail, to frighten off the adversary in conflicts initiated by whatever side. "Defensive" and "offensive" are terms of apologetics and thus presuppose partisanship among states. (I am talking about what states must do in conflict situations, and leave comparative assessments of defensiveness and progressiveness to those who accept the state system and hence the arms race.)

First, it is important to give some basis for the principle of superiority. The state's monopoly of the more destructive means of violence is agreed to by a wide variety of theories of the state. So we are appealing to no very special view of the state by appealing to the state's monopoly of coercive power. What exactly is involved in this monopoly? Its crucial characteristic is that it involves more the state's *right* to a monopoly of coercive power than an actual monopoly itself. The state often exists without such a monopoly, but it is in real trouble when there is widespread refusal on the part of its citizens to recognize that it has a right to a monopoly. In what way, then, can such a refusal be met by the state? The relevant factor is the connection between the means of violence and the interests of the state. On the one hand, the means of violence monopolized by the state are to be used to advance the interests of the state and not more specialized interests. On the other hand, the means of violence, when monopolized, are to be adequate to realizing state interests. What is of interest to us is the requirement of the adequacy of the means of violence. Recognition of the right to monopolize the means of violence will be withdrawn if monopolizing the means of violence still leaves the state incapable of realizing state interests. We needn't be concerned yet about what the state's interests are; we assume only that they are widely enough accepted, for good or bad reasons, to give up private violence for their realization. Still, there will be reluctance to recognize the state's right to a monopoly of the means of violence if, once it is granted that monopoly, it fails to realize state interests with it.

Here, then, we have the basis for the principle of superiority. To assure that its right to a monopoly of force is recognized, the state must strive to arm itself adequately to realize its interests in conflict with other states or in internal conflicts. The French Resistance of World War II arose as a rejection of the prewar government that proved unable to defend France. This challenge was ultimately crushed by de Gaulle, but only with international help. The USSR agreed to rein in the French Communist Party, which was a major force in the local liberation committees and the patriotic militias, and the US and Great Britain provided the needed military force to awe the Resistance. The slogan of PCF leader Thorez, "One state, one police force, one army," helped legitimate the Gaullist state's claim to a monopoly of force.[4] Likewise, a state that disarms its people but then cannot defeat an internal insurgency in a civil war will have difficulty maintaining the allegiance of those who are not part of the insurgency. They will either arm themselves, thereby setting themselves up as a popular power, or replace the existing regime with one that promises to end the insurgency. The monopoly of force resulting from the initial disarmament of the people lacked the adequacy to serve the state.

Now for some qualifications. Not all states have the same ability to develop military might. Lack of capital, of resources, or of industrial capacity limits most states. To avoid subjection they are forced to group themselves with more powerful states. By open or implicit alliances superiority is achieved, and hence the right to monopoly control of force at home is not denied. The French do not prefer an open alliance with the US through NATO, and would like the world to think their own *force de frappe* is adequate security. There is, of course, an implicit alliance forced on them by the limitations of a purely deterrent force. The use of France's deterrent force in isolation from that of NATO in response to an attack on France by the USSR would only provoke France's total destruction through a Soviet counterstrike. This is enough to inhibit the French from using the *force de frappe* except as part of a mightier collective security force. The French state's right to a monopoly of force is recognized in view of the wide belief that the back door to collective security has not been irresponsibly barred.

Another qualification concerns perceptions. A state need not be superior; it need only attempt to be superior. Moreover, it need not be endeavoring with real success or likelihood of success; to be superior it need only be perceived by its citizens to be endeavoring with real success or likelihood of success. After all, several states may have no trouble gaining recognition for monopolizing force, but not all of them can be superior to the others. Also, at this point in the nuclear arms race, there may no longer be such a thing as real success or likelihood of success in the task of endeavoring to be superior. Let us mean by being superior something weaker than being able to realize some positive gain through hostilities. Instead, let superiority mean the ability to destroy enough of the adversary's military potential that he lacks the ability to mount a serious response. Such an ability is a first-strike capacity when realized at a single blow, or a war-fighting capacity when realized through protracted war. I will call it first-strike capacity, but whatever the name, the reality is not assured, and thus we can at most speak of perceptions of superiority.

The principle of superiority holds, then, that a state will attempt to be perceived by its citizens as endeavoring to achieve military superiority either through its own efforts or through alliances with other states. The result is that conflict will engender an arms race, for only by increasing arms can a state hope to be perceived as endeavoring to achieve superiority. The derivation of the principle rests on the need of states to be recognized for their right to have a monopoly of the means of violence within their domains. Without the recognition of such a right, it becomes less likely that a state will actually be able to maintain a monopoly. The failure of monopoly through absence of superiority is illustrated by a number of feudal states. In the 17th century, the Tokugawa Shogunate united Japan without ending the privatization of coercive power. The largest rival barony to the Tokugawa could field almost as many samurai in battle as the Tokugawa could by the early 18th century. Lack of superiority undermined monopoly. In feudal Europe, superiority reemerged through the absolute state with its emphasis on a professional military.[5] The privatization of coercive power in the hands of the nobles had become incompatible with the suppression of internal uprisings and the defeat of external aggression.

But isn't everything changed in the nuclear age? The principle of superiority is still central, nor has it been pushed aside by the doctrine of deterrence. No state has stopped with a minimal deterrent, when it was able to go further. The US and the USSR would have stopped the arms race more than 25 years ago if deterrence were the central fact. Even parity was reached a decade ago, but each side still looks for a way to gain the advantage.

Critics of the arms race may grant that superiority has been the determining factor, but many of them argue that it need not be, even in the context of sovereign states. (By "a sovereign state" we mean one that maintains a monopoly of force in its own domain and uses it to pursue its own state interests.) These critics will claim that a minimal deterrent or parity is adequate for sovereign states in the nuclear age. Aside from their inability to account for the actual arms race, these critics are faced with a number of objections.

We begin with a "prisoners' dilemma" argument showing that deterrence— either minimal or in the form of a parity of forces—is always secondary to superiority. Assume states face one another without compromises to their sovereignty. They don't let other nations in on their local monopoly of force. The best joint situation for them might be for neither to go further than a nuclear deterrent force—up to and including a parity of such forces. Each, though, suspects the other may try to develop a first-strike capacity. Under this suspicion, neither will give away the right to develop a first-strike capacity in so-called arms limitations agreements. Despite such agreements, each ends by choosing in a way that leads to a joint situation that is worse than deterrence: each ends up striving for superiority.

To get around this objection to the adequacy of deterrence, it is necessary to reject the assumption of sovereignty. This would mean tampering with the monopoly of force on which superiority is based. But the critics have staked their position on no change in the state. Weakening sovereignty would, however, be a major change in the state to avoid the centrality of the superiority principle.

We turn now to a "lottery paradox" argument made popular by Reagan administration advisors Richard Pipes and Colin Gray.[6] The argument shows that a deterrent may be too porous unless it is a force capable of winning wars from the most limited on up. It is irrelevant to answer this argument with the pious claim that we don't want to fight wars anyway. However bellicose its authors' intentions may be, the argument shows deterrence is not a tenable middle ground. If you don't want to search for a war-fighting capacity, you can't stop with deterrence. You need to look for a way to change the state and hence society, the last thing most proponents of deterrence want to face.

To begin the argument, suppose the adversary initiates a limited conventional aggression. Escalation is a real possibility, and it could involve nuclear weapons. There may be several stages in this possible escalation. We suppose that at some stage one cannot threaten the use of a nuclear force that is superior in relation to the force of retaliation. (This could be the case even if one's forces were at parity with those of the adversary.) The escalation *might* stop short of this stage, but there is a real risk that once it is started it will not stop short of this stage. Continuing the escalation through this stage will provoke retaliation involving unacceptable losses on one's side. With this conditional certainty of an unacceptable outcome at some stage, one may decide, instead, not to use nuclear weapons to deter aggression at any stage. One would fear that such a use would precipitate, at perhaps the next stage, an exchange in which one would suffer unacceptable losses. The possibility of this self-inhibition means that deterrence cannot be expected to be fully effective. The gambling-spirited adversary hopes for self-inhibition, and he may advance with impunity from limited to less-limited victories, and finally to total victory, simply through threat and without the actual use of nuclear force. In short, an effective deterrent rests on superiority, that is, on a first-strike capacity.

SERVING STATE INTERESTS

Let's take a closer look at the derivation of the superiority principle from the state's claim to a monopoly of force. The derivation went through by using the idea of state interests as the link. The monopoly of force was legitimated only because the state could use that force to advance state interests. And not just any force would be adequate for the advancement of state interests; it had to be a superior force, or a force that the state is endeavoring to make superior, or at very least a force that the state is perceived to be endeavoring to make superior.

Again, haven't things been drastically changed in the nuclear age? Many critics of the arms race agree on the uselessness of nuclear weapons once at least two powers have them and have them in large quantities. The Russell-Einstein declaration of 1955, signed by nine Nobel prize-winners, held that "the governments . . . purposes cannot be furthered by a world war."[7] And the same thought was expressed in 1981 by George Kennan when he said, "I deny that the nuclear explosive is a proper weapon. . . . It can serve no useful purpose. It cannot be used without bringing disaster upon everyone."[8] If, indeed, these critics are correct, the derivation of superiority from monopoly comes into question. Gaining nuclear superiority is no help in serving state interests, and thus it cannot reasonably be demanded of a state which wants to make good its claim to a monopoly of force. Since superiority in conventional weaponry can only be an invitation to an adversary to use nuclear weapons, superiority in conventional weapons cannot be demanded as a substitute.

There are two ways one might go with this. One either accepts the monopoly of force and concludes that it is simply wrong to try to derive superiority from it (the approach of those who want to say that the problems of the arms race can be dealt with without tampering with state sovereignty), or one insists the derivation of superiority goes through and concludes that since there is, in fact, no superior force that serves state interests, we must undercut state sovereignty by denying the claim to a monopoly of force. This is the approach of either the Russell-Einstein declaration, which calls upon states to give up their right to fight wars, or of Einstein and Schell, who call for a transfer of coercive power to a world government.

In all of this there is an overly hasty rejection of the usefulness of nuclear weapons. One of the reasons the thrust toward superiority is so strong is that there is a use for nuclear weapons. Before trying to account for the thrust toward superiority, which is undeniably there, by appealing to evil, to irrationality, or to a nuclear technology that has an immanent development in the manner of an Hegelian concept, we should inquire whether or not the bomb has some instrumental feature. I shall try to show that it has, and thus that neither the derivation of superiority from monopoly nor the monopoly itself need be rejected due to lack of instrumentality.

What kinds of state interests are in question? Let's examine some of the interests that might be served and then see whether, in fact, nuclear weapons are too destructive to serve those interests. What are the interests that might be served by the mere possession of nuclear weapons and what are the interests that might be served by the actual use of nuclear weapons?

Mere possession lacks the drawbacks of physical and human destruction. Thus it is initially plausible that the possession of nuclear weapons is useful. How might they be useful? First, there is nuclear diplomacy—the use of the threat of nuclear destruction to pursue state interests. The early use of nuclear diplomacy was far from a success. The success of the threat in the case of the Cuban Missile Crisis antedated the condition of rough parity in nuclear destructive capability, which we are assuming in this discussion of instrumental value. Under this condition there is little evidence of the usefulness of threats.[9]

Second, there is the arms economy. Spending on nuclear arms, at least in a capitalist country, can have an antirecessionary effect, yet this has no bearing on the relation between monopoly and superiority. The same is true of the usefulness of arms spending in forcing an adversary to undermine the production of socially useful items. The arms economy has no bearing because neither its positive nor its negative effect bolsters the claim to a monopoly of force. What it does is bolster the state's claim to a rightful role in intervening in the economy. The arms economy would have the effects it has even if the arms produced were turned over to private armies, thereby undermining the state's monopoly of force.

Third, there is deterrence—the prevention of aggression through the willingness to use nuclear weapons in response. This faces us with one of history's weightiest counterfactuals. So much hinges on it, yet so little has been done to establish it. Some would argue that since Western Europe was not overrun and since the Persian Gulf area was not overrun, the Soviets were deterred.[10] This has about as much credibility as arguing that because the match in the box in the pantry has not burst into flame since it was put there last month, it was wet all the while. Where there was no proven aggressive intent, we cannot assume aggression was deterred. Moreover, this point receives considerable confirmation beyond bare logic from fact. A number of aggressions *were* undeterred by nuclear arsenals. Soviet-supported actions in Vietnam were not deterred by U.S. arsenals, and U.S.-supplied forces in the Israeli invasion of Lebanon were not deterred by Soviet arsenals. As cases in which nuclear arsenals do not deter pile up, it becomes less and less credible to argue that they have deterred in cases where there was no manifest aggression.

Finally, there is awe—the effectiveness of nuclear weapons to wrench from a populace its recognition of the state's right to a monopoly of force simply by their dreaded power. Among the interests of a state is the reflexive interest of maintaining its own power, and thus it must have an interest in having its monopoly of coercive power recognized. Allegedly, nuclear weapons serve this interest. Nuclear weapons are like capital punishment. Conservatives tend to argue for capital punishment on the grounds that it awes the citizen into acceptance of the state's right to order a community through its law. The argument rests not on the negative fact of deterrence but the positive fact of community.[11] In each case—nuclear weapons and capital punishment—a basis is laid for incorporating the alienated citizen into the state. One might wonder why nuclear weapons are useful if the state can deal condignly with oppositions by conventional means, such as are employed in capital punishment. But one cannot ignore the factor of legitimation in building a coercive force that is superior to all internal oppositions. An erosion of the state's ability to ward off external threats will show up in demoralization, sabotage, and fraternization in the effort to build a superior internal force. It looks then as though the awesomeness of nuclear forces has instrumental value. The hitch is that once it gets out that this force can't be used, the awe turns to ridicule. Capital punishment can be used without destroying the society it is supposed to support, but mere possession of nuclear force is not enough to generate awe unless that force can be used without destroying the society. To say that the possession of nuclear force is useful because it is awesome, we must wait to see whether nuclear force is useful when actually employed.

And so we turn to the actual employment of nuclear weapons. This could be either massive or limited. A war in which the equivalent of 10,000 million tons of TNT are exploded would end the species and hence end all states. If in entering such a war the central interest of the US were the strengthening of capitalism by the destruction of Soviet society as it exists, then that interest could not be served by the war. Capitalism would not exist in any form after the war. All-out nuclear war has no instrumental value.

But are there interests that could be served by a limited war? A limited war might be one fought with superior force, in which case the adversary's control system, nuclear forces, and major conventional forces would be severely damaged, destroying his military potential. This would be done with forces short of species-destroying forces, a possibility resulting from focusing on decapitation, that is, on the destruction of political and military command, control, communication, and intelligence systems. The adversary would be forced to come to terms, and something like the old hope (expressed in the 1948 National Security Council Report 20) of a decommunization of Soviet society would be realizable. The Reagan Defense Department's Single Integrated Operational Plan-Six embodies the strategy of winning a war in this way. SIOP-6 tells us little about the damage done to the winner of such a contest. In even the most optimistic calculations it would be enormous. The result of the war cannot be characterized rosily as a vast expansion of capitalism to include the markets and resources of the USSR. At best it can be characterized as the survival of capitalism in the US, a capitalism too weak to begin the exploitation of the devastated, decommunized land mass to the east. If there were a state interest to be realized by such a war, it would be the state's interest in the survival of a social structure, which is judged to be in peril. Concern about the survival of the social structure is shown in plans to store records of debts in mountains, to have a supply of currency available, and to establish a postal system that can reach people in their fallout retreats.

We come, I think, to a similar conclusion about limited nuclear wars that stop short of bringing an adversary to defeat. In 1974 Secretary of Defense James Schlesinger spoke about the possibility of limited wars that would redress the particular military situation at issue while providing the adversary with an incentive to back down before destruction became widespread. Schlesinger thought he had framed the idea of limited nuclear war so that it was easy to see how escalation would be managed and controlled. But even in this case the damage would be enormous, and the idea that any great gains could be made is incompatible with controlling escalation. Aside from the loss of life within a restricted area, there would be thousands and perhaps millions of incidents of leukemia, thyroid disorder, and miscarriage resulting from fallout in a vastly wider area. But even if these losses can be ignored by being incurred mainly outside the territory of one of the conflicting states, what has that state to gain? It can at best prevent losses that it sees as threatening to its social system. If it takes the chance of using nuclear weapons to acquire a significant political or economic addition to its power, it must be prepared to face an even more serious nuclear response. Taking such chances is not part of what Schlesinger meant by managing and controlling escalation. Again, the interest to be served by the use of limited nuclear force that does not aim at defeat of the adversary is an interest that arises due to a threat to survival of the social structure.

In sum, the interests served by nuclear weapons are the interests of the survival of social structure or interests derived from these. Such interests are served by the use of nuclear weapons, and the possession of nuclear weapons serves interests—such as legitimation through awe—only because the use of nuclear weapons serves interests. Kissinger was right when he said, "The major nuclear powers are capable of devastating each other. But they have great difficulty translating this capability into policy except to prevent direct challenges to their own survival."[12] The feudal ruling class, which was based on the use of the land, fought wars to obtain more land. Later, mercantile and entrepreneurial classes benefitted from wars that expanded their markets. Here we have gains that can be parceled out or can be used as a whole by members of a victorious nation. Nuclear war has changed this, at least. It can only promise the survival of a social structure, which is not something people use either by parceling it out or by gaining access to it as a whole. Rather, the social structure is more basic, since it determines how the parceling out of gains is to be made among the people and how much access different people are going to acquire to gains that can't be parceled out but can only be used as wholes, such as an educational system, a judiciary, and a highway system.

Nuclear war is then reduced, as previous wars were not, to preserving class structure. For the feature of social structure that distributes gains and rights is its class structure, which plays a central organizing role within it. In the social structures on which states are built, gains and rights will be unequally distributed, and this is characteristic of class societies. In the nuclear age, the state interests on which the monopoly of power is based and which are to be realized with superior force are the interests of maintaining the class structure. Those in the lower classes who feel they have no interest in maintaining a class structure that disadvantages them have all the basis they need for feeling that they have no interest in the continuation of the nuclear arms race.

It does not follow from all this that adversaries in the nuclear age must have different social structures. States with similar social structures can attempt to defeat one another, and in the process one of them may lose its social structure. Yet the major cleavage in the world today is between opposed social systems—the capitalist and the bureaucratic. Each represents a different class system, a different system of inequality, and hence different relationships to work. This is nothing new in history: Tartar pastoralists devastated feudal Russia in the medieval period, and feudal Spain in the 16th century destroyed Aztec despotism. The fact that the cleavage today is once again between opposed societies allows for intensifying the pace of the arms race through the addition of ideological appeals to save one class system from its opposite.

But is nuclear war after all so destructive that even the interest of social survival cannot be served by it? Is it devoid of instrumental value? We need now some general remarks on the conditions of having instrumental value.

Some means to ends may have effects that block those ends. This cannot be an inevitable consequence of using those means, or they would not be genuine means. But genuine means can run the risk of having effects that block their ends. A 10,000 MT nuclear exchange is not a genuine means to state interests, since it inevitably blocks those interests. But a 1,000 MT nuclear exchange could realize those interests, even though it runs the risk of escalating into a 10,000 MT exchange. But running the risk of blocking an end is quite different from actually blocking it.

The risk may, however, be so great that there is no willingness to choose it. If this is the case the means involved is not a genuine means. There is a complication here that must not be ignored. People in different situations will have different ideas about what risks to take, so we will need to specify here that we are talking about the state or its authorized agents when we are talking about the willingness to choose a means to realize state interests. Someone else may feel that the state's standard of acceptable risk is irrational. This would mean that even when a means had instrumental value in relation to state interests and state agents, it would lack such value in relation to state interests for other agents. Only state agents are relevant here, because we are talking about the ability of the state to use its monopoly of coercive power to realize state interests. It is assumed that there is a monopoly of power in the hands of the state, and thus that if nuclear force is to have instrumental value it will depend on the standard of acceptable risk adopted by the state.

With these points about instrumental value in mind, let us turn to consider strategies for limited war, the only ones that hold out hope of realizing state interests. The risks are of course tremendous. The war-fighting strategy of SIOP-6 presupposes that nuclear delivery systems and weapons will perform with degrees of reliability and accuracy that are doubted by military engineers. A serious miscalculation about high performance could lead to retaliation and escalation that would destroy the societies of the adversaries. This outcome becomes all the more possible with the emphasis on the initial destruction of control and communication centers, centers which would be vital for moderating retaliation and controlling escalation. The risks would not be as great with the Schlesinger strategy of limiting nuclear war by pinpointing particular military situations. There is, after all, no psycho-political law of inevitable escalation, and there are factors that reduce the likelihood of escalation, such as a clear rejection of a war-fighting strategy. What critics of strategies like Schlesinger's contend is not that escalation is inevitable, but that they involve too great a risk of uncontrolled escalation for them to elect to take. Somehow, though, when such critics get around to expressing these reservations, they are no longer in a position of state agents, and thus their standards of acceptable risk are no longer relevant to the instrumental value of nuclear weapons.

The question then is not whether strategies for limited nuclear war would inevitably block the realization of state interests. They would not, because although there is a risk of escalation to all-out war, this risk falls short of an inevitability. The question is rather one about taking that risk. Only if there is a willingness to take the risk can the chance to further state interests by nuclear hostilities be realized.

The dreadful willingness is there in the state. We may find it hard to imagine that people are so monstrous that they are willing to risk species extinction to save a class system. People may not be born or even raised with such a willingness, but our adult state institutions have refashioned them. The plan for a redivision of the world through World War II made men willing to kill noncombatants through saturation bombing. And those men were then willing to build and deliver the first atomic bombs against the Japanese. Based on that willingess, plans were devised to fight wars with nuclear weapons, wars involving destruction many times as great as anything before. As nuclear arsenals grew, these official plans came to involve the use of nuclear weapons at some point in the development of hostilities in a way that risked escalation to total destruction. SIOP-6 is only the latest of such plans. These plans are expressions of a collective resolve on the part of the National Security Council and the Department of Defense to take extraordinary risks in the national interest. The president, as the apex of this collectivity, is conditioned to respond to external developments with an iron will. His willingness to take the risk becomes an expression of the resolve of the ruling military collectivity. His personal revulsion at the possible consequences are not to affect his institutional will. Beginning with World War II, the U.S. government has prepared an institutional framework for a disposition to choose means to state interests that risk species extinction.

It should be clear that such a disposition to choose to follow a strategy of limited war does not mean that the choice will always be made as the strategy dictates. It is only a disposition, but that is enough to ensure instrumental value to strategies of limited war. Such strategies can realize state interests, and in addition there is a disposition to choose from among them in given circumstances. This disposition is compatible with the possibility of self-inhibition on any given occasion. In discussion of the lottery paradox-style argument, we saw that deterrence is seriously weakened by the possibility of self-inhibition. We are not here excluding the possibility of self-inhibition, but postulating a general willingness to choose even where great risk is involved.

The instrumental value of nuclear weapons resolves the doubt about the derivation of the superiority principle from the claim to a monopoly of force. A superiority based on nuclear weapons can still be of service to state interests, and can then be exactly what is needed to legitimate the state's claim to a monopoly of force. We needn't, on the one hand, deny that superiority is based in the monopoly. And we needn't, on the other hand, say that the monopoly of force must be abandoned since it can no longer be supported by the usefulness of force. Rather, my call for a modification of the state and of existing social structure rests on the continued usefulness of force to the state. Since the force is useful it may well be used, yet any such use involves risks for which those outside the state, and those in the lower classes, in particular, have no real reason to take.

THE BROAD STATE

The state will have to be changed to avoid the arms race. How can we or should we try to change it? Benefits can be derived from a modification of the state that involve neither compromising sovereignty by transferring coercive force to a world government nor eliminating the state altogether. Whereas there is something less utopian-sounding about this less drastic modification, it still leaves us with problems, since the modification brings along certain instabilities. This modification in the state will result when there is a trend toward equality in the society. This trend toward equality changes, but does not eliminate, the state's monopoly of coercive power. With that change the basis for attempting to reach superiority is undercut. The modified state will be called the broad state.

The dangers of a rigid essentialism, on the one hand, and of a directionless empiricism, on the other hand, are hard to avoid in discussing the state. Essentialism would want to make the principle of superiority applicable to all states. Empiricism, by emphasizing the malleability of states, would allow for an escape from the arms race without socially unsettling changes. The essentialist approach ignores historical variations in essence; the empiricist approach ignores constraints upon variations in states.

Essentialism is misleading as an underpinning for a disarmament movement. It implies that the state in any conceivable social and economic circumstances will push toward superiority. To avoid an arms race we are limited to a stateless society. But states show important variations in different social and economic frameworks. Conceivably some such frameworks are the basis for states which do not pursue arms races.

The political dangers of the empiricist approach are more serious. The malleability of the state called for by the empiricist makes it possible to modify the state to satisfy popular protest without having to change the social and economic framework. So for empiricists it is diversionary to talk about the need to change society to end the arms race. Constraints are ignored, and the popular movement is left unprepared for inevitable defeat.

The modification of the state I am describing involves a historical change in the state's essence, a change based on the social change to a trend toward equality. It departs from essentialism by presupposing that the state has no fixed essence. Yet it departs from empiricism by presupposing that it is necessary to change the social relations to ones with greater equality in order for the state to avoid the arms race. Thus we are examining a possibility between the extremes of essentialism and empiricism.

The state is to be so modified that it is appropriate to call it the broad state, since many are incorporated into its activities. With a trend toward equality in the society, there will be at some point a change to a state that incorporates within itself many organizations of popular control. The state is no longer an institution for the rule of a few, but has become an institution for the rule of many. To the extent that there is still opposition to the trend toward equality, the state remains an instrument for dealing with conflict, and those who participate fully in it will tend to support, rather than oppose, the trend toward equality. Yet without broad rule there would be a strong current set up against the trend to equality by the state itself. For there would be centers of power within the state beyond popular control, which would defend the special benefits of that power against the equalizing trend.

Of crucial interest is the change in the monopoly of power in the broad state. This monopoly of power has the same objective that it has in the narrow state; it focuses coercive power on the realization of state interests, away from the realization of the special interests of individuals and groups. In the broad state, though, the interest of preserving the trend toward equality will be one that the monopoly of power will have to serve. The monopoly of power will have to be fashioned so that it can serve this interest. Here the standard of popular control that is applicable in all branches of the broad state will replace the standard of control by a few. The military and the police will incorporate popular militias and the role of regulars in the military and the police will be changed both by a democratic internal organization of the police and the military and by popular control of each of them from the citizenry.

The point to be emphasized is that the monopoly of force has to do with the concentration of force for state interests. This focusing of force can take place either under narrow or broad control. Broad control does not mean an abandonment of the monopoly. For example, only when the use of militias proved ineffective in smashing the railway strike of 1877 did a real push begin to give dominance to a professional and hierarchical military in the US.[13] This did not imply that the previous militias of the individual states of the Union were exceptions to the monopoly of force by the state as a whole. What it implied was that a broader form of control within the monopoly of the coercive power in the US no longer served the interests of the state. Among those interests were the interests of maintaining inequality in a period of intensified class struggle.

Now it is time to return to the superiority principle. Previously, we derived the superiority principle from the state's need to legitimate its claim to a monopoly of force. In fact what we did was to derive superiority from monopoly in the narrow form. The link between superiority and monopoly is broken when the context is the broad state and hence monopoly in the broad form. Breaking with essentialism makes it possible for us to see the importance of the social trend toward equality in the attempt to derive superiority from monopoly.

How is the link broken? Consider some of the imperatives of the effort to gain superiority. First, suppose superiority has to be achieved by an alignment with a major power. We are immediately projected outside the arena of popular control. A dominant factor in the control of the state becomes the policy of the major power in the conduct of world conflict. The very fact of unequal relations between such states dictates a major role for the external power in the affairs of aligned states.

Second, suppose a broad state attempts to achieve superiority itself. Several factors about such an attempt need to be noted. On the one hand is the economics of an arms race. The materials, the plant, and the labor that must be committed compromise, to a greater and greater extent and for a time that has no natural limit, a people's ability to achieve a meaningful equality through the elimination of poverty. In a period of economic boom, this adverse effect on the elimination of inequality is modified, but certainly not eliminated. With an arms race, such as the present one, that endures through economic crests and troughs, the long-term effect on the reduction of inequality is negative. Adding to this effect is an inevitable enrichment—both in tangible gains and in rights—for those in controlling positions in the arms industry. Their services are at a premium, and the urgency of the arms race ensures them ample incentives. Thus, the economics of a competition for military superiority is at cross-purposes with a social trend toward greater equality.

On the other hand is the secrecy of an arms race. The very effort to conduct an arms race in the open would generate so many handicaps that it would be deemed futile in advance. U.S. citizens are constantly reminded that even the modest channels open for popular reaction to U.S. military policy can hinder the speed with which the U.S. can advance the arms race. The purpose of such reminders is merely to hide the undemocratic character of U.S. military policymaking. The National Security Council is a covert dual-state that makes foreign and military policy in isolation from public review. The same act that set up the NSC in 1947 also set up the CIA to be used exclusively by the executive for national security. The Atomic Energy Act of 1946 institutionalized secrecy as a norm for government offices dealing in any way with the atom.[14] A broad form state could not avoid the demands of secrecy in a serious effort to gain superiority. It would then be forced to restrict the popular control that characterizes its monopoly of force. This in turn would counteract the trend toward equality.

Even though the derivation of superiority from monopoly breaks down in the context of the state that serves equality, the stability of such a state is questionable. How can it face a militarily superior force? One alternative is to attempt to put on hold the demands for equality and the consequent demands for a state of popular control. Military preparedness becomes the supreme imperative, and state power gravitates into the hands of the few. This elite will either attempt to develop a credible military force within the nation, or will attempt to develop it through alignment with a mightier power. The history of such attempts to put the revolution on hold has been a disastrous one, beginning with the Bolshevik attempt to fight off the Whites and the invading Allied armies. When the dust settles and the revolution is taken off hold, it has already expired.

The other alternative is an untested one. The best way to defend the trend toward equality may be to renounce the effort to mount a militarily superior force. Instead, the popular organization of the state can be used as the basis for preparing a popular resistance, should state power have to be relinquished in the face of a militarily superior force. The right point at which to relinquish state power will be determined on the basis of the standard of equality. At what point has the will to resistance to the forces of inequality reached such a pitch that it can motivate a prolonged popular resistance without the framework of state power? At what point will continuing the struggle within the framework of state power so compromise the social drive to equality that it will not be recoverable at a later stage?

The motivation behind this alternative is the conviction that holding state power is important only as long as it continues to serve the interests for which it was set up. The broad state was set up to serve the interest of furthering equality. When the survival of the state becomes incompatible with that interest, other means than state power should be employed to further that interest. The popular resistance that would continue to serve this interest after relinquishing state power would be primarily a political opposition that would attempt to increase its numbers nationally and internationally. As an international political opposition, it would have the potential for regaining state power not in just one, but in many nations, thereby making it less vulnerable to military defeat. Also, as an opposition, it would not grant the right to a monopoly of force by the state once it had relinquished state power. It would reserve the right to constitute itself as a military power to sap the basis of the hostile state above it.

The broad state is unstable, since its confrontation with superior force ends in its demise. This is true on each alternative for confronting such a force, because a broad state cannot use its monopoly of force to pursue superiority in force. The condition for stabilizing the broad state is to make it the dominant form of state in the world, but then, perhaps, the resultant reduction of conflict would make the state altogether unnecessary.

A WORLD STATE

The argument for a world state of the sort envisaged by Einstein and Schell is an essentialist argument. It takes the superiority principle as part of a fixed essence of states, at least of those that belong to a system of many states. Thus to avoid the arms race between states, the system of sovereign states must be done away with. Coercive power must be lodged with a state which is not among other states, a world state. The entities that have been deprived of their sovereignty may be called states by courtesy, but they are not really states since they lack sovereignty. If I am right and the essence of the state is historically variable, then the aim of avoiding the struggle for superiority can be realized with the broad state, which is a state among other states.

But the point of the present section is not to show that there is an alternative to the world state. It is to emphasize the lack of consideration of the social and economic framework in the strategic thought of world statists. For them the world state can be formed and the system of many states dissolved without changing social and economic conditions. This is a repetition of the empiricist line of thinking that the arms race can be ended without changing the familiar social and economic framework in an unsettling way. Thus, essentialism in the analysis is combined with empiricism in the reform.

In November 1945, Einstein wrote in *Atlantic Monthly,* "It should not be necessary, in establishing a world government with a monopoly of authority over military affairs, to change the internal structure of the three great powers [the US, the USSR, and Great Britain]. It would be for the three individuals who draft the Constitution to devise ways for collaboration despite the different structures of their countries." In reply to a group of Oak Ridge scientists who felt that the economic and social gulf between certain countries precluded immediate formation of a world government, Einstein wrote, "The freedom of each country to develop economic, political and cultural institutions of its own choice must be guaranteed at the outset . . . . In fact I believe the sole function of a world government should be to have a monopoly over military power." And behind all this was a faith in reason's ability: "Just as we use our reason to build a dam to hold a river in check, we must now build institutions to restrain the fears and suspicions and greeds which move peoples and their rulers. . . We do not have to wait a million years to use our ability to reason. . . We can and must use it now, or human society will sink into a new and terrible dark age which may last forever."[15]

In the conditions that existed after World War II, social and economic cleavages were being expressed through the various states in a threatening way. Without dealing with those cleavages first, world government was a pipe dream. The architects of American policy were convinced that the success of the postwar U.S. economy depended on expansion, and of course the key to economic expansionism was stopping the spread of the centrally planned economy with a military force within which the A-bomb was seen as the winning weapon.[16] But how could the U.S. economy be given freedom to develop in this expansionist way by a world government? After all, by 1949, the centrally planned economy was preventing the entry of the market economy not just into the USSR, but also into Eastern Europe and into China.

Members of the Soviet Academy of Sciences responded to an open letter addressed by Einstein to the United Nations. They said the appeal for a world government was nothing more than a fig leaf over U.S. imperialism. They correctly observed that before 1917 Russia had been exploited by foreign commerce, investment, and finance, and that independence was not achieved by allowing French and British capital free rein. It was achieved after the revolution through a state that effectively walled off the USSR from the world market to prevent a deepening of underdevelopment. Was Einstein suggesting that this state be dissolved so that, with the blessing of a world state, the stronger economies of the West could turn the USSR back into a source of cheap labor and a granary?[17] One can imagine a similar worry about a proposed world state from the newly independent countries of the Third World a decade or so later.

The Soviet economy has grown and become less isolated from the West. But this does not make the world state idea any more plausible for the 1980s. The predicted convergence of the Western and Eastern economies seemed warranted by detente, but by now has lost all warrant. To each side an invasion of the basic principle of ownership of the other side would rightly be regarded as a disruption of its dominant relations of production. The loss of control in matters of production resulting from such an invasion would imply nothing short of a restructuring of the class system of the invaded society. It is enough to say that in the absence of a clear winner in the global struggle between the private and state ownership systems, that struggle itself would make it impossible for a world state to function.

Perhaps, within the private ownership camp itself, the conditions are ripening for a world state. The multinational corporation transcends the state not only in production and sales, but also in ownership. The capital of several countries is fused in some key corporations. This, though, is not a sufficient basis for undercutting the nation state, or even the need the corporation has for it. States still intervene to protect "their" corporations against competitors in periods of crisis. The effect of the large multinational corporation has been to shift the centers of competition from the states themselves to continents. The axes of competition now lie between Japanese, North American, and West European capitals. Without eliminating the need for state sovereignty, it opens the possibility of states based on continental rather than narrower units.[18] Such a possibility falls considerably short of a world state.

The possibility of a world state would need to rest on what Kautsky, on the eve of World War I, called ultraimperialism.[19] Kautsky thought that just as competition between big firms led to cartels, so national cartels would lead to international cartels; they would pursue growth in indifference to the national origins of the capital they used; and these international cartels would compete but in a way that would allow "a federation of the strongest, who renounce their arms race." The actual persistence of national and continental competition indicates that the stage for ultraimperialism has not been set.

These considerations cast a dark shadow over Schell's claim that, "Just as we have chosen to live in the system of sovereign states, we can choose to live in some other system."[20] For him, only a political revolution is required to produce a world state, and so the choice is simply a choice of political system. From what has just been said, however, steps are needed to transcend the cleavage between the private and the state ownership systems, and also to transcend the economic rivalries between Japanese, North American, and West European capitalism.

Ultimately, the sort of social revolution needed for a world state would introduce a tendency toward greater equality. To reach a world state one would first have to go through the broad state discussed in the previous section. For only when the pursuit of equality becomes stronger than the pursuit of competitive advantage, both between social systems (such as the capitalist and the bureaucratic) and between large corporations with continental bases, is there any hope of relinquishing state sovereignty. But since the broad state based on the trend to equality avoids the struggle for military superiority, one can stop with it without going on to the world state. The instability of the broad state is avoided by its becoming the dominant form of state and not by overcoming the broad state in a world state.

IGNORING THE STATE

We have discussed political revolution in which the nature of the state would be changed to end the arms race. It is time to consider a response that calls for less, an empiricist response that supposes the arms race can be ended without changing the state. This empiricist response has great appeal to organizers in the peace movement who think success requires a broad appeal. Political revolution is a divisive issue, and thus a successful peace movement needs to adopt an empiricist response that leaves the state untouched. The British peace activist E.P. Thompson offers the latest version of the empiricist response.[21]

He starts with the view that the arms race does not serve state interests. Rather, the arms race is autonomous in respect to the state. Indeed, it has become a self-generating process with weapons calling forth newer and more powerful weapons. For this reason weapons can no longer be thought of as mere things: their internal logic has become the logic of military decisionmaking. As a consequence, the arms race lacks a rationality defined by goals outside itself. It is then irrational, and its internal logic is exterminist.

How does this view affect the strategy of the peace movement? A part of the military apparatus is the bearer of the autonomous arms race. This cancerous part of the military can be excised from the state without doing away with the military altogether. The state as a monopolizer of coercive power would not then be altered. Thompson proposes to excise the cancerous part by isolating it from the rest of the state. The first step in isolating the arms race is the development of a movement for non-alignment among current allies and clients of the US and the USSR. In particular, the nations of Europe would "resume autonomy and political mobility." This step would admittedly take place against the resistance of the two major powers. The second step is the development of international links between the people, not the officials, of the two blocs, including those of the major powers themselves. This step has faced resistance in the form of arrests of Soviet peace activists and refusals of the State Department to admit certain international peace activists into the US. With the threat of the breakup of the two blocs and with growing grass-roots disruption, the self-generating competition would end. At least, it would be ended in Europe, which is Thompson's focus. But if it can be ended in that torrid arena, an extension of these methods should end it altogether.

Thompson's overblown conception of autonomy dictates this policy of isolation. The state is left untouched, since the arms race is autonomous. That there is a self-generating aspect to the arms race is not to be denied. But this insight needs to be combined with the view that autonomy is never more than relative. Thompson is impelled toward an absolute view of autonomy by his fear that a vicious reductionism hides behind every effort to explain the arms race. I wish to show that Thompson's mystification of the arms race is not the only alternative to reductionism.

To show this it is essential to distinguish between the identification of causally crucial antecedents and the identification of a context within which such antecedents can be efficacious. Identifications of the former sort are the substance of an historical narrative that explains how we get from one place to another. Identifications of the latter sort serve an altogether different explanatory role; they set such a narrative in a context that lets it roll on without having to be pushed. Events that lead to certain others in one context need not lead to them in a different context. But the context provides only the form of a narrative and not the addition of substantive causes.[22]

This distinction allows us to avoid reductionism without giving up the claim that there is a primary level of historical explanation. This is possible since the distinction allows us to develop a new sense of primacy in historical explanation. We no longer need to say that, for there to be a primary factor in explanation, there must be events of a limited kind that alone qualify as antecedent causes in historical narratives. Such a view of primacy is manifestly reductionist, because it unduly limits the kinds of antecedents to which we can refer in an acceptable narrative. The eclectic alternative to this reductionism is to put no limits on the kinds of causes and thus to conclude too hastily that nothing is primary in history. Here is where the distinction between identifying crucial antecedents and identifying contexts for narratives comes in. Crucial antecedents can, to be sure, be events of any kind; but there is still primacy if the smooth unfolding of the narrative must be couched in a context of only one kind. Every scientific endeavor emerges, through conflict, with its preferred context.

How does this apply to the arms race? An aspect of self-generation can be brought out in a narrative that ignores all factors other than the strictly military, but still makes sense. For example, Poseidon submarine-launched missiles of intermediate range began to be deployed off Spain and Scotland in 1971. This led to a deployment of SS20 IRBMs in the Warsaw Pact in 1977, until rough parity with the Poseidon warheads was reached.[23] The NATO ministers in December 1979 then agreed to deploy U.S. Pershing II and cruise missiles in Western Europe, beginning in 1983. The narrative unfolds as a sequence of military causes and effects unmixed with diplomatic and economic causes. It is not necessary to chart diplomatic and economic curves for the 1970s to make a credible story. This is the self-generating and relatively autonomous aspect of the arms race.

But how does the narrative have the pull we all feel? Another way of asking this is to ask how the causes in the narrative appear as causes at all. There is an implicit context for the narrative, the context of state rivalry based on sustaining credible monopolies of force. Adding the context does not bring in further stimulus causes than those already in the narrative. It is strictly a formal element that enables those causes to be causes at all. The primacy of the political over the military and the technological is not due to the predominance of political causes in the narrative. They don't even appear in the narrative. The politics of state rivalry has primacy over the military since it provides the context for military causes; and the autonomy of the military is limited by this political context. This limitation is incompatible with Thompson's absolute autonomy for the arms race.

This undercuts Thompson's strategy for the peace movement, which was based on the possibility of isolating the exterminist elements of the state. A strategy of isolation would stand a chance if, indeed, the exterminist elements were involved in an autonomous process serving no state interests. In my account the state is a catalyst in the arms race, but not an inorganic one. For the state has its interests, and the arms race unfolds in the context of the state's pursuit of those interests. These interests will in fact discourage efforts at isolating exterminist elements. Insofar as exterminist elements are the architects of power blocs, the state will protect them, since it has an interest in alignments. Insofar as exterminist elements are the architects of the destruction of a genuine international peace movement, the state will protect them since it has an interest in the arms race.

Since the state makes possible the development of the arms race, a confrontation with it is inevitable. On the one hand, the states aligned with the major powers are responding to the principle of superiority by being so aligned. Breaking alliances with the two major states will face a double opposition. The major states will resist the breaking of alliances since each such alliance is an increment to its own power. The secondary states will resist non-alignment because of the need for collective security. Thus they could "resume autonomy and political mobility" only if they are transformed by the advent of a viable internal tendency toward equality. In the secondary states an effective peace movement will be able to challenge alignments for collective security with one of the major powers only while transforming those states from within.

On the other hand, the major powers themselves are responding to the principle of superiority by refusing to renounce their arms race. No strategem will work to isolate their arms race from their interests. Rather, the chances are that as fissures develop in their respective blocs and as peace movements span the cleavage between them, the resulting desperation that they will feel will express itself in even further intensifications of the arms race. No short cut to ending the arms race can avoid changing the states that inevitably engage in it. Surely, we chance being incinerated before the state can be changed. But this chance is smaller than the certainty that without attempting to transform the state, the arms race will continue.

THE ARMS ECONOMY

There are two ways to give economic matters a decisive importance in regard to the arms race. The first is the straightforward way of making economic crisis management the cause of the arms race: here cause is taken in the sense of an antecedent in an historical narrative. The second way is to employ the economic structure of the society as a context for such a narrative: here the economic context is appealed to to provide a basis for the connections in the historical sequence. I shall show that a causal account of the arms race in purely economic terms is incomplete. Whatever the importance of economic factors, political factors relating to the state's monopoly of force have an irreducible role in explaining the arms race.

This criticism of economist accounts of the arms race does not apply to attempts to use economic structure as the ultimate context for causal narratives. The reasons for this were given in the last section. They were, on the one hand, that such a context is a formal matrix for causal connections and is not itself a supercause and, on the other hand, that causes of a multiplicity of kinds can be effective within a context of a single kind. Thus political and other causes may be indispensable for the arms race, even though the ultimate context is economic.

The thrust of this chapter has been to emphasize the indispensability of the political for the arms race. At a further level, though, it would be important to emphasize that the vital role of the state is itself embedded in an ultimate economic context. This embedding has nothing to do with economist accounts of the sort to be criticized here, for the economist accounts try to eliminate all but economic antecedents in the narrative of the arms race. Embedding the logic of the state's monopoly of force in an ultimate economic context starts from the assumption that there are crucial noneconomic causes. In respect to an ultimate economic context, our discussion in the last section was only provisional. In that section I spoke of a political context for relatively autonomous military developments. This was appropriate here where our analysis goes no deeper than the political level. Had we pushed on to an economic context to give a full picture, the features appealed to in the political context would become an addition to the causal repertoire.

On economist accounts of the arms race, the state is taken to be a mechanism for intervening in the economy. It is exhausted by its functioning for the economy. Behind state military spending of the enduring sort since the beginning of World War II is an effort to deal with stagnation within monopoly capitalism. It is the nature of monopoly capitalism to create unused industrial capacity and unemployment. The arms economy is an effort to take up the slack in this unused capacity.[24] Some give the matter an additional twist by adding the element of economic imperialism. Thus Baran and Sweezy say that "it would be quite impossible to understand the role of armed force in capitalist society without placing the international character of the system at the very center of the analytical focus."[25] The international character of the system is caused by the monopolist producers who seek to reduce surplus capacity by developing foreign markets and investment outlets. These foreign markets and investments call for military protection. Unused capacity is still at the root of the arms economy, but the link is now economic imperialism.[26]

The difficulty with adding imperialism is that it contaminates the argument right from the start with a noneconomic element. Why is protection needed for foreign ventures? The context presupposed is that of states ready to defend the interests of their own dominant classes. Without this presupposition we must fall back on the argument that arms take up the slack in monopoly capitalism by arms production, rather than that arms protect imperialist ventures. So let's focus on the ability of arms to take up slack.

A crippling difficulty arises from the fact that the Soviet economy, whatever its basic nature, has not been in the grips of a crisis of unused capacity. Arms production is, rather, a drain on its growth of needed capacity. There seems to be no plausible way out of this difficulty. It might be said that the arms race is started by the effort to use surplus capacity in the West and completed by a catch-up response in the East. To get this linkage with the East, the terrain of economism has to be given up. The East's response is made on the basis of the state's need to keep its monopoly of force credible by being able to cope militarily with its adversaries. The asymmetry of the linkage then becomes incredible. If the East's response is on traditional grounds of state power, is it possible that the West's provocation has nothing to do with state power, but is the by-product of the otherwise innocent aim of crisis management? Surely, at least once the East has caught up, the response of the West is dictated not by the requirements of crisis management, but by a strategy of a military nature for regaining superiority.

This difficulty about linkage with the East points to a more basic difficulty with the economist's logic having to do with the nature of functional explanation. The arms economy may well play a functional role in countering the tendency toward stagnation. (In some respects it may also be dysfunctional, but such contradictions are not of themselves a basis for rejecting a functional argument.) Is such a functional role an adequate basis for saying that an arms economy will exist? In addition to the functional role of the arms economy, there must also be circumstances that play an active role in bringing about the arms economy. Teleology must be bolstered by agency in order to be effective, otherwise there would be something magical about teleology. Take an example from the welfare sector of the state. Old-age benefits, disability benefits, and Medicare serve the goal of legitimating capitalist society among its members. But to get these Social Security measures involves building political coalitions with sufficient power to make them part of the state. The political coalitions, in conjunction with people's actual needs, provide the agency for bringing about the functional measures. The conditions for building an effective political coalition become as vital for the existence of state welfare as does the functionality of state welfare for capitalism. And we cannot then overlook them in a full account of state welfare.

The political coalition behind the arms economy has been one of the most powerful as well as one of the most stable. Like most powerful coalitions, it is quite diverse. On the one hand, it is comprised of the large corporate military contractors, Congressmen anxious to increase industrial investment in their constituencies, universities tied to military research, unions benefiting from military contracts, and the Keynesian economic bloc. But the coalition would lack definition if this were all; it would find itself at cross purposes by wallowing in diverse interests. On the other hand, the coalition is comprised of the Pentagon, the think-tanks of the Department of Defense, the militarist faction of the Congress, the International Department of the AFL-CIO, and the Committee on the Present Danger. This aspect of the coalition provides it with a unifying perspective essential for its effectiveness. It has organized military spending around the concept of national security so effectively that the spectrum of economic interests ranging from the most self-serving to the Keynesian's concern with the economy as a whole comes forth as so many aspects of national security.

The condition for the power and the stability of the arms coalition is to be found in the need for superiority that flows from the monopoly of force. How might the defender of economism respond? On the one hand, it might be said that political coalitions are merely a device by which humans delude themselves into thinking that they have control of history. Actually, the ruthless march of economic necessity suffices. Thus the functionality of arms spending for the economy is sufficient to bring about the existence of arms spending. But we have already criticized this mode of thinking, indicating that teleology needs to be bolstered by agency to be effective. On the other hand, it might be said that the appeal to national security is a lie that somehow effectively unites people. The state really does not need superiority, but since people think it does they can be rallied to action around the slogan of national security. This only pushes us back to trying to explain the illusion of national security. If they accept this lie because they see economic benefits ahead in the effort to achieve national security, then they would have formed an arms coalition purely on an economic basis, and the lie about national security would have been unnecessary. But this is precisely how economism would account for the lie. Since the arms coalition can't be formed just on an economic basis, we had best grant that the effectiveness of the appeal to national security is based on what the state actually is.

In sum, the functionality of the arms economy is a factor in its existence. But a full account calls for more; it calls for the agency of a political coalition that has its power and stability through the appeal to national security, which is a noneconomic factor. Thus the superiority principle is behind the formation of such a coalition.

CONTRADICTIONS OF THE STATE

The analysis offered here will promote a more explicitly political strategy for the peace movement today. It puts the state itself at the center of the arms race. Politics, in the narrow sense of seeking solutions within the present state, has to be transcended. This recognition is similar to that behind the world state strategy that politicized a wing of the disarmament effort immediately after World War II. The difference is that today it should be clearer than it was then that a social revolution must also accompany a political revolution.

Some conditions today favor social revolution, but they are conditions fraught with a contradiction. Social revolution is favored by the inability of either capitalist or bureaucratic society to hold out a promise of a better future. This very inability, however, is a source of desperation that seeks an outlet in an accelerated arms race and in irresponsible bellicosity. So another race runs alongside the arms race, that between the human republic of equality and what Schell calls "a republic of insects and grass."

The conditions that favor social revolution are showing up with the growing number of threats of disruption within the major blocs and the major states of the world. These threats are connected with the pace of the arms race and with the slide toward wars. The stability of the Warsaw Pact has been threatened by repeated revolts, capped by that of 10 million workers under Solidarity in Poland in 1980–81. Just as the US thought it had effectively brought the Americas into its camp with an increasing number of dictatorial regimes, the serious threat of defections rose at several points in Central America. By 1970 chronic economic stagnation became the hallmark of both capitalism and the bureaucratic social system. By the 1980s the arms race itself was recognized as a source of significant losses in productivity and growth in both economies. The generalized stagnation has put a stop to rising standards of living. Cutbacks in welfare and wages have driven home the point that the ability of these societies to attack inequality and want is limited.

At present, neither system promises a future of greater human realization. Instead each hopes to penetrate its own imperial gloom by the drama of the race for nuclear superiority. Earlier empires often spent the days of their decline on compensatory military outlays. Unable to avoid economic stagnation, popular indifference to state mobilizations, rage against imposed austerity, and nationalist revolts, the US and the USSR pursue military superiority with accelerated intensity and intensified warlikeness. The risks the state is willing to take become greater and greater as the society's ability to improve life becomes more and more restricted.

Collective welfare ceased long ago to be a possible aim of military adventures. It has been replaced by the narrow aim of preserving the social structure. For the US, the defense of capitalism becomes the goal of foreign and military policy. For the USSR, the defense of the bureaucratic system becomes the goal. And so military policies have come to serve class societies that are proving retrograde in regard to human advancement. Societies such as these are too insecure to open themselves up to a new and less tragic principle of force; they retain the old principle of the monopoly of force in the hands of the few. This monopoly is the other side of social inequality and the instability it promotes. In an unstable situation the state's monopoly of force is more likely to be challenged. Superiority in force becomes a way of preempting the challenge.

The transition to states supporting a trend to equality will mean an end to the two major social systems of the world today. It will mean an end to the domination of weaker nations and will involve a recognition that to defend the struggle for equality will not be to ring it with arms. But we must be aware that the same conditions that promote such a transition will engender a desperation that is already producing a more dangerous arms race.

One cannot avoid the conclusion that we must still struggle for a new and broader form of state by hoping that other contradictions within the state can be resolved. Each contradiction involves a good and a bad pole. Why not just pluck the bad pole out, leaving a basically good state? Then one would not have to risk the possibility that in the effort at political and social revolution the state's bellicosity would develop in a lethal way. First there is the contradiction of security: one pole is the state's commitment to protect the common good with deterrent means; the other is the greater risk of holocaust due to the arms race. But the state as a force monopolizer is committed to the pursuit of superiority, even if it means risking the common good. Second is the contradiction of welfare: one pole is the commitment to improve the lot of the people; the other is the ever-greater expenditure of resources on the military. But when the perpetuation of class society is at stake, the state is free to sacrifice welfare to warfare within limits of political stability. Third is the contradiction of democracy: one pole is the recognition by the state that in all great modern republics the people are sovereign; the other is the secret organization by an elite of the effort to reach superiority. But in an unequal society the state's commitment to popular sovereignty is always conditional upon the needs for the defense of inequality. The futility of trying to resolve these contradictions within the context of states as we have experienced them points to the need for a new form of state.

NOTES

1. Gregg Herken, *The Winning Weapon* (New York: Vintage Books, 1982), pp. 155, 163.
2. *Einstein on Peace*, ed. O. Nathan and H. Norden (New York: Schocken, 1968), p. 471.

3. Jonathan Schell, *The Fate of the Earth* (New York: Alfred A. Knopf, 1982), p. 194.
4. Fernando Claudin, *The Communist Movement* (Harmondsworth: Penguin, 1975), pp. 321ff.
5. Perry Anderson, *Lineages of the Absolute State* (London: Verso, 1979), pp. 31, 215.
6. Colin Gray and Keith Payne, "Victory Is Possible," *Foreign Policy* (Summer 1980): 14–27.
7. *Einstein on Peace*, pp. 633–34, 681.
8. George Kennan, "Two Views of the Soviet Problem," *The New Yorker*, November 1981, p. 61.
9. Daniel Ellsberg, "A Call to Mutiny," *Monthly Review*, September 1981, pp. 5–6.
10. Michael Mandelbaum, *The Nuclear Revolution* (New York: Cambridge University Press, 1981), p. 174.
11. George Will, *The Washington Post*, 12 March 1981.
12. Henry Kissinger, *American Foreign Policy*, 3rd ed. (New York: W.W. Norton, 1977), pp. 59–60.
13. Stephen Skowronek, *Building a New American State* (New York: Cambridge University Press, 1982), chap. 4.
14. Sidney Lens, *The Day Before Doomsday* (Boston: Beacon Press, 1978), chap. 8.
15. *Einstein on Peace*, pp. 349, 354, 378–79.
16. Herken, *The Winning Weapon*, p. 237, the letter from Forrestal.
17. *Einstein on Peace*, pp. 443ff.
18. Ernest Mandel, *Late Capitalism* (London: Verso, 1978), chap. 10.
19. Karl Kautsky, "Ultra-Imperialism," *New Left Review* 59 (1970): 41–46.
20. Schell, *Fate of the Earth*, p. 219.
21. E.P. Thompson, "Notes on Exterminism," *New Left Review* 121 (1980): 3–31.
22. Milton Fisk, "Dialectic and Determination," *Critique* 13 (1981): 79–101.
23. *The Military Balance, 1981–1982* (London: The International Institute for Strategic Studies, 1981), pp. 126–29.
24. Mandel, *Late Capitalism*, pp. 275ff.
25. Paul Baran and Paul Sweezy, *Monopoly Capital* (New York: Monthly Review Press, 1966), p. 178.
26. James O'Connor, *The Fiscal Crisis of the State* (New York: St. Martin's Press, 1973), p. 152.

AFTERWORD
THE TROUBLE WITH THE SDI

John P. Holdren

Editors' note: Due to delays in publication, the essays in this book were written more than eighteen months ago. This passage of time is most evident in the case of John Holdren's essay—the arms race, unfortunately, has not waited upon our publication schedule. We are, thus, happy to be able to include as an appendix this recent short article by Holdren on the Strategic Defense Initiative. It brings up to date his essay in that area of the arms race in which there has been the most discussion and activity in recent months. This article was adapted from Holdren's opening statement at a debate on the Strategic Defense Initiative at the National Conference of Editorial Writers, Colorado Springs, September 20, 1985.

As President Reagan sees it, the goal of the Strategic Defense Initiative is to develop the means of rendering nuclear weapons "impotent and obsolete" and, indeed, to escape the need to base our security "on the specter of retaliation, on mutual threat." This, in any case, is how he described his intentions in the March 1983 speech to the nation that launched the SDI, and he has reaffirmed this view repeatedly, most recently in his press conference of September 17, 1985.

His goal is a laudable one. I don't know anyone who is *happy* with the situation often referred to as MAD—Mutual Assured Destruction—in which the United States and the Soviet Union pin their security on threatening each other with massive devastation. Any sensible individual would prefer mutual assured survival to MAD, if mutual assured survival were available. But simply wishing for something cannot bring it about. And even spending $50 billion, $500 billion, or $1000 billion cannot do so if the goal is unattainable at any cost.

While neither scientists nor anyone else can predict the future with assurance, the overwhelming probability is that President Reagan's announced goal—a defense effective enough to make nuclear weapons obsolete—cannot be attained. The basis for this pessimistic appraisal is not that the capability to shoot down ballistic missiles in considerable numbers is beyond our reach, for that much we surely can learn to do. The real problem is this: the destructive power of nuclear weapons is so great that protection of populations requires virtual *perfection* on the part of the defense; but the diversity of means available to the attacker to spoof, counter, destroy, overwhelm, or circumvent the defense's systems puts the required degree of protection out of reach. If rendering nuclear weapons impotent is the goal, not even a few can be permitted to penetrate and explode on our cities.

This pessimism is not confined to peace marchers and the technologically uninitiated. It is the conclusion of former Defense Secretaries Robert McNamara, James Schlesinger, and Harold Brown. It is the conclusion of the most eminent, experienced, and ingenious defense scientists in the country—people such as Hans Bethe, Sidney Drell, Richard Garwin, George Rathjens, and Jack Ruina. And, more remarkably, it is also the conclusion of the overwhelming majority of the scientists and technologists who are now *working* on the SDI with the taxpayer's money.

Of the many contradictions and paradoxes that permeate the SDI, this one is perhaps the most striking. The project has been sold to the public as pursuit of a defense that will protect them—protect *people*—replacing deterrence based on fear of mutual destruction with defense that assures survival. Yet almost no one who is working on SDI is actually pursuing this goal or thinks it can be achieved. Essentially all of the work and all of the serious debate now underway on SDI in the technical community relates not to the defense of people as an escape from deterrence, but to defense of our retaliatory nuclear forces (that is, defense of weapons) as a way to *strengthen* deterrence. The aim, in other words, is not to abandon MAD, but to reinforce it by increasing the assurance that destruction would be mutual in the event we were attacked.

The more sophisticated defenders of defense have been trying to gloss over this embarrassing contradiction—between what the president proposed and what is being pursued—by means of two arguments. The first, that strengthening deterrence is after all one way to protect people, is transparent doublespeak. The president has told us repeatedly that it is his unhappiness with this form of protection that motivated him to initiate the SDI. The second argument is that pursuit of defenses capable of providing some protection to our nuclear forces, although not to our population, will strengthen deterrence in the short run at the same time as it serves as a stepping-stone toward eventual deployment of defenses good enough to make nuclear weapons—and nuclear deterrence—obsolete.

This second argument requires more careful scrutiny, but cannot survive it. The extremely low likelihood of ever attaining a defense good enough to protect people would not be a persuasive argument against pursuing it if, in fact, this pursuit would enhance deterrence in the meantime; indeed, if the pursuit were not too costly in other ways, it could even be justified if it would merely leave deterrence intact. Alas, pursuit of the SDI as presently programmed—and especially of those elements of it that have even the slightest prospect of ever being upgraded into a population defense—will undermine deterrence at its points of greatest weakness (crisis instability, irrational leaders, and accidents); it will destroy arms-race stability by ripping all restraints from the buildup of nuclear forces in every category from ICBMs to cruise missiles to manned bombers; it will stimulate an enormous and enormously expensive expansion of military competition in space; and its focus on an illusory technological panacea for a complex military and political problem will divert attention and money from less glamorous but much more realistic approaches to our security needs.

Deterrence against large-scale, out-of-the-blue nuclear attacks by rational leaders is already robust; no rational leader would contemplate such an attack, given the certainty of intolerable destruction in retaliation. This form of deterrence has not been endangered by (nor did it require) the buildups of strategic nuclear forces on both sides over the past ten years, and it does not need to be "enhanced" by SDI or anything else. If deterrence fails, it will be because a wholly irrational individual or group gains control on one side or the other; or because an escalating crisis creates incentives for desperate leaders, convinced they are about to be struck, to strike first in hope of somehow reducing the damage; or because some combination of technological glitches and human errors sets off nuclear war by mistake.

These weak points in deterrence would be made even weaker by deployment of partial defenses (the only kind we know how to deploy) along the lines envisioned in the SDI. A rational leader could not believe such defenses would actually protect his population from retaliation, but an irrational leader might. The incentives for a damage-limiting first strike in a crisis would be *increased* by partial defenses if these embody the multiple "tiers" favored by SDI enthusiasts, because such defenses would be more effective against the ragged retaliation of a wounded adversary than against the full force of a coordinated first strike. And the short reaction time and corresponding high degree of automation required in defensive systems would increase the danger that nuclear war will be initiated by false signals or some other electronic malfunction—all the more so because activation of defensive systems in time of crisis probably would be interpreted by the other side as preparation for a preemptive attack.

Even short of deployment of defensive systems, a program clearly aimed at developing them will destroy arms-race stability by providing incentives to each side to upgrade its offensive forces in ways that will ensure penetration of whatever defenses its adversary might come up with. Indeed, the phenomenon of "worst-case assessment," which has been aggravating the nuclear arms race for 40 years, doubtless would lead to offensive *over*compensation for the anticipated performance of the defense—one more way that the pursuit of defense actually would leave us even less safe than before.

It is for just this reason that the ABM Treaty of 1972 is indispensable as the centerpiece of the web of arms control agreements that have helped maintain at least a modicum of restraint in the nuclear arms competition until now. The putative violations of the ABM Treaty that each side has attributed to the other have not yet breached it in any militarily significant way. But if either side becomes convinced that the other is bent on doing so, the SALT II limits on offensive forces (unratified by the United States but still being observed by both sides) will not survive another month. In the unrestrained offense-defense competition that follows, the Partial Test Ban Treaty of 1963, the Outer Space Treaty of 1967, and even the Non-Proliferation Treaty of 1968 are likely to be early casualties.

The sole saving grace of the SDI is the possible value, as a so-called bargaining chip, of agreeing not to pursue this very dangerous program. For restricting activity on strategic defense to basic research (which is permitted by the ABM Treaty, required by prudence, and unstoppable in any case) is an essential part of an historic bargain that is now within reach. In addition to a recommitment to the ABM Treaty's proscriptions, this bargain would include a ban on further testing of antisatellite weapons and deep cuts in the offensive nuclear forces on both sides. Stopping ASAT testing is essential to stopping ABM development (and vice versa). And deep cuts in offensive forces, designed to reduce greatly the ratios of counterforce warheads to vulnerable weapons on the other side, offer the best solution to the crisis-stability concerns that the SDI is supposed to address but actually aggravates.

President Reagan, Secretary of Defense Weinberger, and ACDA Director Adelman all have insisted that the SDI can help bring about meaningful arms control. They must come to recognize that this can happen only through *giving up* the pursuit of strategic defense beyond basic research, as the cornerstone of the larger bargain just described. With respect to arms-race stability, crisis stability, and larger military and economic rationality, both sides need this bargain desperately—which is precisely what puts it within reach. But the window of opportunity may not be open for long. Propping it open—even beginning to climb through—should be the primary goal of both Mr. Reagan and Mr. Gorbachev at their November summit.

INDEX

ABOUT THE CONTRIBUTORS

AVNER COHEN is assistant professor of philosophy at Tel Aviv University. He has published articles and reviews on skepticism, medicine, and psychiatry, as well as on the history of modern philosophy.

STEVEN LEE is assistant professor of philosophy at Hobart and William Smith Colleges. In addition to writings on ethics and nuclear weapons, he has published in the areas of social philosophy, philosophy of law, and action theory.

SIDNEY AXINN is professor of philosophy at Temple University and an adjunct professor in Temple University Medical School. His publications have been on Kant, logic, and social and political philosophy, and he is currently working in the area of military ethics.

LOUIS RENÉ BERES is professor of political science and international law at Purdue University. He is the author of a number of books and articles in the area of nuclear strategy and nuclear war. His recent books are *Apocalypse: Nuclear Catastrophe in World Politics* (1980), *Mimicking Sisyphus: America's Countervailing Nuclear Strategy* (1983), and *Reason and Realpolitik: U.S. Foreign Policy and World Order* (1984).

ANNE H. EHRLICH is senior research associate in the Department of Biological Sciences at Stanford University and is on the Executive Committee of the Board of Directors of Friends of the Earth. With her husband, Paul R. Ehrlich, she has co-authored many books, including *Ecoscience* and *Extinction*.

PAUL R. EHRLICH is Bing Professor of Population Studies at Stanford University. He is the author of 150 scientific papers, a series of textbooks, several popular paperbacks (including *The Population Bomb*, *The End of Affluence*, and *The Golden Door*), and numerous articles. He is a member of the American Academy of Arts and Sciences and has received many honors, including the John Muir Award of the Sierra Club.

JEAN BETHKE ELSHTAIN is professor of political science at the University of Massachusetts, Amherst. She has published widely in the areas of feminism and political theory and is the author of *Public Man, Private Woman: Women in Social and Political Thought* (1981) and the editor of *The Family in Political Thought* (1982).

RICHARD FALK is Albert G. Milbank Professor of International Law and Practice at Princeton University and a senior fellow at the World Policy Institute. He is the author, along with Robert Jay Lifton, of *Indefensible Weapons: The Political and Psychological Case Against Nuclearism* (1982). His most recent book is *The End of World Order* (1983).

DIETRICH FISCHER is assistant professor of economics at New York University. He has worked on the global economic implications of disarmament, on the economic theory of fairness, and on alternative security systems. He is the author of *Preventing War in the Nuclear Age* (Rowman & Allanheld, 1984).

MILTON FISK is professor of philosophy at Indiana University, Bloomington. He has written on causation, the structure of physical and social individuals, historical materialism, and ethical relativity. His books include *Nature and Necessity* (1973) and *Ethics and Society* (1980), and he is presently working on a book on the philosophy of the state.

RUSSELL HARDIN is professor of political science and philosophy and chair of the Committee on Public Policy Studies at the University of Chicago. He is the editor of *Ethics* and the author of *Collective Action* (1982).

JOHN E. HARE teaches philosophy at Lehigh University. He was a staff associate with the Foreign Affairs Committee of the U.S. House of Representatives, and is co-author (with Carey B. Joynt) of *Ethics and International Affairs* (1982).

JOHN P. HOLDREN is University Professor of energy and resources at the University of California, Berkeley, and national chairman of the Federation of American Scientists. He is a regular participant in the Pugwash Conferences on Science and World Affairs and is the chairman of the U.S. Pugwash Group. He has co-authored and co-edited several books on the global human predicament. In 1981 he was awarded a five-year MacArthur Foundation Prize Fellowship.

GREGORY S. KAVKA is professor of philosophy at the University of California, Irvine. He is currently writing a book on Hobbesian moral and political theory, and has published a number of articles on moral issues concerning nuclear weapons.

DOUGLAS P. LACKEY is a professor of philosophy at Baruch College, City University of New York. He has written several articles on the morality of deterrence, and his *Moral Principles and Nuclear Weapons* is a 1984 publication of Rowman & Allanheld.

BEREL LANG is professor of philosophy and humanistic studies at the State University of New York, Albany. His recent books include *Philosophy and the Art of Writing* (1983) and *Faces, and Other Ironies* (1983). His essay in this volume is part of a work-in-progress entitled *Genocide and the Figures of Evil*.

EDWARD F. McCLENNEN is associate professor of philosophy at Washington University, St. Louis. He is co-editor of *Foundations and Applications of Decision Theory* (1978) and author of a number of articles on topics in social ethics, decision theory, and game theory. He is currently working on problems in decision theory, philosophy of economics, social welfare theory, and contract theory.

JEFFERSON McMAHAN is a research fellow in philosophy at St. John's College, Cambridge University. He is author of *British Nuclear Weapons: For and Against* (1981), as well as several articles on the rationality and morality of nuclear deterrence.

JOSEPH MARGOLIS is a professor of philosophy at Temple University, and has written widely in many areas of philosophy, including the ethical complexities of public policy issues. His most recent books are *Culture and Cultural Entities* (1983) and *Philosophy of Psychology* (1984). He is currently working on the theory of literary texts and on realism and pragmatism.

PATRICK M. MORGAN is professor of political science at Washington State University. He has written widely in the areas of arms control and international security, his works including *Deterrence, A Conceptual Analysis* (1983) and *Strategic Military Surprise*, co- authored with Klaus Knorr (1983). He is currently working on a book entitled *A Theoretical Analysis of Arms Control*.

ARNE NAESS was for 30 years a professor of philosophy, University of Oslo, Norway. He was Leader in 1948–49 of the UNESCO project on the controversies between East and West. He has published books and articles in favor of Gandhian ways of conflict resolution and in favor of skepticism.

TERRY NARDIN, associate professor of political science at the State University of New York, Buffalo, is the author of *Violence and the State* (1971), *Law, Morality, and the Relations of States* (1984), and a number of articles on the philosophy of political violence, war, and international relations.

EDMUND D. PELLEGRINO is the director of the Kennedy Institute of Ethics and John Carroll Professor of Medicine and Medical Humanities at Georgetown University. His numerous publications include *Humanism and the Physician* (1979) and *Philosophical Basis of Medical Practice* (with David Thomasma, 1981). He is the founding editor of *The Journal of Medicine and Philosophy.*

RICHARD H. POPKIN is professor of philosophy and Judaic studies at Washington University, and for the last few years has also taught at Tel Aviv University. He is the author of numerous works on the history of philosophy and Jewish intellectual history, and for many years edited the *Journal of the History of Philosophy.* He is presently working on a history of Christian Zionism.

GARY STAHL is professor of philosophy at the University of Colorado, Boulder. His research interests focus on the implications of scientific studies of evolution and development for traditional theories of human nature. His publications include work in aesthetics, and bio-medical topics.

STEPHEN TOULMIN, who studied mathematics and physics before turning to philosophy, is a professor at the University of Chicago and a member of the Committee on Social Thought. His books include *Reason in Ethics* (1949), *The Uses of Argument* (1958), and *Human Understanding* (1972). He is currently working on traditions of case reasoning in ethics.

RICHARD A. WATSON is professor of philosophy and senior research associate in earth and planetary sciences at Washington University. He is the co-author (with Patty Jo Watson) of *Man and Nature* (1969), and has written widely in many areas of philosophy, including environmental ethics. His *The Philosopher's Diet: How to Lose Weight and Change the World* will be published in 1985.